GREAT LIVES
FROM
HISTORY

GREAT LIVES FROM HISTORY

Ancient and Medieval Series

Volume 1
A-Ch'i

Edited by

FRANK N. MAGILL

SALEM PRESS

Pasadena, California   Englewood Cliffs, New Jersey

Library of Congress Cataloging-in-Publication Data
Great lives from history. Ancient and medieval
series / edited by Frank N. Magill.
   p. cm.
Includes bibliographies and index.
Summary: A five-volume set of biographical
sketches, arranged alphabetically, of 459 individ-
uals whose contributions influenced world culture
and the social development of societies flourishing
in earlier centuries.
Biography—To 500. 2. Biography—Middle
Ages, 500-1500. [1. Biography—To 500. 2. Biog-
raphy—Middle Ages, 500-1500. 3. World history.]
I. Magill, Frank Northen, 1907-
CT113.G74 1988   920'.009'01—dc19   88-18514
[B]
[920]
ISBN 0-89356-545-8 (set)
ISBN 0-89356-546-6 (volume 1)

PRINTED IN THE UNITED STATES OF AMERICA

PUBLISHER'S NOTE

Great Lives from History, Ancient and Medieval Series, is the third set in a series which, when complete, will provide readily accessible accounts of the lives and achievements of outstanding individuals from antiquity to the present. The initial set, the five-volume American Series, was published in 1987, followed the same year by five volumes covering British and Commonwealth figures. The current five volumes cover non-British figures from antiquity through the Middle Ages. A subsequent set, to be issued in 1989, will extend that coverage from the mid-fifteenth century to 1900, and the final set, to appear in 1990, will conclude with the twentieth century.

The current series includes 455 articles on 459 individuals. The articles range from approximately two thousand to three thousand words in length and follow a standard format. Each article begins with ready-reference listings, including a brief statement summarizing the individual's contribution to his or her society and later ages. The body of the article is divided into three parts. Early Life, the first section, provides facts about the individual's upbringing and the environment in which he or she was reared, setting the stage for the heart of the article, the section entitled Life's Work. This section consists of a straightforward chronological account of the period during which the individual's most significant achievements were made. The concluding section, the Summary, is not a recapitulation of what has been discussed but rather an overview of the individual's place in history. Each essay is supplemented by an annotated, evaluative bibliography, a starting point for further research; the works listed are generally available in a large number of libraries. Each essay has been written expressly for publication in this work by an academician who specializes in the area of discussion; a full list of contributors and their affiliations appears in volume 1.

The temporal and geographical scope of the Ancient and Medieval Series is necessarily broad, even excluding those British and Commonwealth figures from the same period (from Saint Bede the Venerable to John Wyclif) who are covered in the preceding series. Represented here are figures as ancient as the Egyptian king Zoser (fl. twenty-seventh century B.C.) and as late as Johann Gutenberg (d. 1468), spanning the Eastern and Western Hemispheres from China to Peru, from Africa through the Middle East to Scandinavia. Such a vast field demands careful selection from among those figures who have had a significant impact on the history of human civilization; defining those criteria must also take into account the needs of public and academic library users as well. We have therefore sought in these volumes to provide coverage that is broad in area of achievement as well as geography and chronology, while at the same time including the recognized shapers of history essential in any liberal arts curriculum: Major world leaders appear here—pharaohs, emperors, conquerors, kings and khans—as well as giants of religious faith: Buddha, Moses, Muhammad, Jesus Christ, and the priests, popes, and saints who left their imprint on our political as well as spiritual institutions. Also included in these pages are scholars, philosophers, scientists, explorers, artists, and architects—all of them architects of today's civilization. These are the individuals who brought the world to the threshold of the Renaissance.

In defining that latter term, and in distinguishing the Renaissance from the preceding Middle Ages, scholars are increasingly revising their thinking. The medieval period cannot simply be said to have "ended" any more than the Renaissance "began"; the rediscovery and propagation of classical thought and ideals made their way quite gradually into the Western world via medieval scholars such as Averroës, and can never really be said to have died altogether. Nevertheless, the "movement," if one can call it such, was well established by the mid-fifteenth century, and it is generally at that point that the coverage of these volumes ends. At the same time, earlier representatives of the Renaissance—especially in Italy, as manifested in art and architecture—will be treated in the forthcoming series covering the Renaissance through the nineteenth century.

While each set in *Great Lives from History* has its distinctive qualities, several features distinguish this series as a whole from other biographical reference works. The articles combine breadth of coverage (in contrast to the brief entries typical of many biographical dictionaries) with a format that offers the user quick access to particular information needed (in contrast to the longer, unformatted entries of encyclopedias). For convenience of reference, these volumes are indexed by area of achievement and by geographical location as well as by name.

CONTRIBUTING REVIEWERS

Linda Perry Abrams
Bob Jones University

Patrick Adcock
Henderson State University

Edward Allworth
Columbia University

J. Stewart Alverson
University of Tennessee at Chattanooga

Norman Araujo
Boston College

Martin Arbagi
Wright State University

Madeline Cirillo Archer
Duquesne University

Bryan Aubrey
Maharishi International University

Richard Badessa
University of Louisville

James R. Banker
North Carolina State University

John W. Barker
University of Wisconsin — Madison

Jeffrey G. Barlow
Lewis and Clark College

Dan Barnett
Butte College

Thomas F. Barry
University of Southern California

Iraj Bashiri
University of Minnesota, Twin Cities Campus

Michael E. Bauman
Hillsdale College

Erving E. Beauregard
University of Dayton

Albert A. Bell, Jr.
Hope College

Richard P. Benton
Trinity College, Connecticut

Carol Berg
College of Saint Benedict

Robert L. Berner
University of Wisconsin — Oshkosh

David M. Bessen
Ball State University

Terry D. Bilhartz
Sam Houston State University

Edward Bleiberg
Memphis State University

Harold Branam
University of Pennsylvania

Gerhard Brand
California State University, Los Angeles

J. R. Broadus
University of North Carolina at Chapel Hill

W. R. Brookman
North Central Bible College

David D. Buck
University of Wisconsin — Milwaukee

Jeffrey L. Buller
Loras College

Edmund M. Burke
Coe College

Robert I. Burns
University of California, Los Angeles

William H. Burnside
John Brown University

Rosemary M. Canfield-Reisman
Troy State University

Byron D. Cannon
University of Utah

Joan E. Carr
Washington University

M. G. Carter
New York University

James A. Casada
Winthrop College

James T. Chambers
Texas Christian University

Nan K. Chase
Independent Scholar

Victor W. Chen
Chabot College

Pei-kai Cheng
Pace University

Key Ray Chong
Texas Tech University

Dennis C. Chowenhill
Chabot College

John J. Contreni
Purdue University, West Lafayette

Patricia Cook
Emory University

Raymond Cormier
Wilson College

Loren W. Crabtree
Colorado State University

Owen C. Cramer
University of Chicago

Kenneth E. Cutler
*Indiana University-Purdue University at
  Indianapolis*

Ronald W. Davis
Western Michigan University

Frank Day
Clemson University

Bruce L. Edwards
Bowling Green State University

David G. Egler
Western Illinois University

Michael M. Eisman
Temple University

Robert P. Ellis
Worcester State College

Thomas L. Erskine
Salisbury State College

Clara Estow
University of Massachusetts at Boston

Gary B. Ferngren
Oregon State University

Edward Fiorelli
Saint John's University, New York

R. Leon Fitts
Dickinson College

Michael S. Fitzgerald
Purdue University, West Lafayette

Charles J. Fleener
Saint Louis University

Edwin D. Floyd
University of Pittsburgh, Pittsburgh

Robert J. Forman
Saint John's University, New York

Douglas A. Foster
David Lipscomb College

Robert J. Frail
Centenary College, New Jersey

Shirley F. Fredricks
Adams State College

Rita E. Freed
Memphis State University

Ronald H. Fritze
Lamar University, Beaumont

C. George Fry
Saint Francis College, Indiana

Richard N. Frye
Harvard University

John G. Gallaher
Southern Illinois University at Edwardsville

Keith Garebian
Independent Scholar

Daniel H. Garrison
Northwestern University

Catherine Gilbert
Independent Scholar

Paul E. Gill
Shippensburg University

Hans Goedicke
Johns Hopkins University

Karen Gould
University of Texas at Austin

Leonard J. Greenspoon
Clemson University

William S. Greenwalt
Santa Clara University

William C. Griffin
Appalachian State University

CONTRIBUTING REVIEWERS

Hassan S. Haddad
Saint Xavier College

Thomas Halton
Catholic University of America

Gavin R. G. Hambly
University of Texas at Dallas

J. S. Hamilton
Old Dominion University

David V. Harrington
Gustavus Adolphus College

Sandra Hanby Harris
Tidewater Community College—Virginia Beach

Fred van Hartesveldt
Fort Valley State College

Paul B. Harvey, Jr.
Pennsylvania State University—University Park

Carlanna L. Hendrick
Francis Marion College

Michael Hernon
University of Tennessee at Martin

Elton D. Higgs
University of Michigan—Dearborn

Richard L. Hillard
University of Arkansas at Pine Bluff

Michael Craig Hillmann
University of Texas at Austin

James Hitchcock
Saint Louis University

Charles W. Holcombe
Northeast Missouri State University

James P. Holoka
Eastern Michigan University

J. Donald Hughes
University of Denver

John J. Hunt
Saint Joseph College

Edelma Huntley
Appalachian State University

Paul Hyer
Brigham Young University

Shakuntala Jayaswal
University of New Haven

Philip Dwight Jones
Bradley University

Yoshiko Kainuma
University of California, Los Angeles

Cynthia Lee Katona
Ohlone College

Thomas O. Kay
Wheaton College

Robert B. Kebric
University of Louisville

Karen A. Kildahl
South Dakota State University

Kenneth F. Kitchell, Jr.
Lousiana State University and A&M College

Paul W. Knoll
University of Southern California

Wilbur R. Knorr
Stanford University

Z. J. Kosztolnyik
Texas A&M University

Richard J. Kubiak
Mercyhurst College

Paul E. Kuhl
Winston-Salem State University

Eugene S. Larson
Los Angeles Pierce College

John M. Lawrence
Faulkner University

Harry Lawton
University of California, Santa Barbara

Daniel B. Levine
University of Arkansas, Fayetteville

Leon Lewis
Appalachian State University

San-po Li
California State University, Long Beach

James L. Livingston
Northern Michigan University

Winston W. Lo
Florida State University

Rita E. Loos
Framingham State College

Reinhart Lutz
University of California, Santa Barbara

Peter F. Macaluso
Montclair State College

William McCabe
Columbia University

Murray C. McClellan
Emory University

C. S. McConnell
University of Calgary

C. Thomas McCullough
Centre College

Margaret McFadden
Appalachian State University

James Edward McGoldrick
Cedarville College

Kerrie L. MacPherson
University of Hong Kong

David K. McQuilkin
Bridgewater College

John D. Madden
University of Montana

Paul Madden
Hardin-Simmons University

Kenneth G. Madison
Iowa State University

Paolo Mancuso
Stanford University

Bill Manikas
Gaston College

Ralph W. Mathisen
University of South Carolina, Columbia

James M. May
Saint Olaf College

Lysle E. Meyer
Moorhead State University

David Harry Miller
University of Oklahoma

Mary-Emily Miller
Salem State College

Ian Morris
University of Chicago

Robert E. Morsberger
*California State Polytechnic University,
   Pomona*

Terence R. Murphy
American University

Gregory Nehler
Indiana University, Bloomington

Carolyn Nelson
University of Kansas

Edwin L. Neville, Jr.
Canisius College

Frances Stickney Newman
University of Illinois at Urbana-Champaign

Frank Nickell
Southeast Missouri State University

Steven M. Oberhelman
Texas A&M University

Glenn W. Olsen
University of Utah

Kathleen K. O'Mara
*State University of New York College at
   Oneonta*

Robert M. Otten
Assumption College

Lisa Paddock
Independent Scholar

Robert J. Paradowski
Rochester Institute of Technology

Joseph R. Peden
*Bernard M. Baruch College
City University of New York*

William E. Pemberton
University of Wisconsin—La Crosse

Mark Pestana
*City College of Chicago, Richard J. Daley
   College*

Susan L. Piepke
Elon College

Ernest R. Pinson
Union University

CONTRIBUTING REVIEWERS

Linda J. Piper
University of Georgia

Clifton W. Potter, Jr.
Lynchburg College

David Potter
University of Michigan, Ann Arbor

Dorothy T. Potter
Lynchburg College

David Powell
Western New Mexico University

Charles H. Pullen
Queen's University, Ontario, Canada

Thomas Rankin
Independent Scholar

Abe C. Ravitz
California State University, Dominguez Hills

John D. Raymer
Independent Scholar

Dennis Reinhartz
University of Texas at Arlington

Clark G. Reynolds
College of Charleston

Richard Rice
University of Tennessee at Chattanooga

William B. Robison
Southeastern Louisiana University

Francesca Rochberg-Halton
University of Notre Dame

Carl Rollyson
Bernard M. Baruch College
City University of New York

Joseph Rosenblum
University of North Carolina at Greensboro

Susan Rusinko
Bloomsburg University of Pennsylvania

Thomas Ryba
Michigan State University

Joyce E. Salisbury
University of Wisconsin—Green Bay

Hilel B. Salomon
University of South Carolina, Columbia

Stephen Satris
Clemson University

Daniel C. Scavone
University of Southern Indiana

Bernard Schlessinger
Texas Woman's University

June H. Schlessinger
University of North Texas

Steven P. Schultz
Loyola University of Chicago

Thomas C. Schunk
Bellevue College

Victoria Scott
Independent Scholar

John C. Sherwood
University of Oregon

H. J. Shey
University of Wisconsin—Milwaukee

T. A. Shippey
University of Texas at Austin

J. Lee Shneidman
Adelphi University

Anne W. Sienkewicz
Independent Scholar

Thomas J. Sienkewicz
Monmouth College

Andrew C. Skinner
Metropolitan State College

Ralph Smiley
Bloomsburg University of Pennsylvania

Clyde Curry Smith
University of Wisconsin—River Falls

Ronald F. Smith
Massachusetts Maritime Academy

Norman Sobiesk
Winona State University

Richard B. Spence
University of Idaho

C. Fitzhugh Spragins
Arkansas College

David L. Sterling
University of Cincinnati

David R. Stevenson
Kearney State College

Paul Stewart
Southern Connecticut State University

Jean T. Strandness
North Dakota State University

Paul Stuewe
Independent Scholar

Bruce M. Sullivan
Northern Arizona University

James Sullivan
California State University, Los Angeles

Charlene E. Suscavage
University of Southern Maine

Roy Arthur Swanson
University of Wisconsin—Milwaukee

Patricia E. Sweeney
Independent Scholar

Shelley A. Thrasher
Lamar University—Orange

Hoyt Cleveland Tillman
Arizona State University

Greg Tomko-Pavia
Independent Scholar

Antonía Tripolitis
Rutgers University, New Brunswick

Frank H. Tucker
Colorado College

Marlin Timothy Tucker
David Lipscomb College

William L. Urban
Monmouth College

Larry W. Usilton
University of North Carolina at Wilmington

Ruth van der Maas
Michigan State University

George W. Van Devender
Hardin-Simmons University

Peter L. Viscusi
Central Missouri State University

Anne R. Vizzier
University of Arkansas, Fayetteville

Heinrich von Staden
Yale University

Paul R. Waibel
Trinity College, Illinois

William T. Walker
*Philadelphia College of Pharmacy and
Science*

John Walsh
Hofstra University

Larry C. Watkins
University of Kansas

Ronald J. Weber
University of Texas at El Paso

Delno West
Northern Arizona University

Julie A. Williams
Lehigh University

Robert I. Willman
Mississippi State University

John D. Windhausen
Saint Anselm College

Johnny Wink
Ouachita Baptist University

Michael Witkoski
South Carolina House of Representatives

Frank Wu
University of Wisconsin—Madison

Vincent Yang
*Pennsylvania State University—University
Park*

Robert W. Yarbrough
Wheaton College

Clifton K. Yearley
State University of New York at Buffalo

William M. Zanella
Hawaii Loa College

Ronald Edward Zupko
Marquette University

LIST OF BIOGRAPHIES IN VOLUME ONE

LIST OF BIOGRAPHIES IN VOLUME ONE

GREAT LIVES
FROM
HISTORY

AARON

Born: c. 1395 B.C.; Egypt
Died: c. 1272 B.C.; Moserah or Mount Hor, Sinai
Area of Achievement: Religion
Contribution: The founder of the Jewish priesthood, Aaron serves as the prototype of the ideal religious leader.

Early Life

Aaron remains a figure surrounded by mystery and seeming contradiction. Even his name is questioned. Is it of Egyptian origin? Does it derive from the Hebrew word for the ark of the covenant (*arōn*) located in the Holy of Holies, that inner sanctum closed to all but the high priest? Or is it the phrase his mother, Jochebed, uttered at his birth as she lamented bearing a son: "A, harōn" (woe, alas)? (Only a few months before Aaron's birth Pharaoh had issued his decree condemning to death all male children born to the Hebrews in Egypt.)

Yet his parents seem to have made no effort to hide Aaron, as they would three years later with his brother, Moses, when he was born. Indeed, tradition maintains that Aaron's father, Amram, was one of Pharaoh's councillors and that the boy himself grew up in the palace before filling his father's post. Aaron was also emerging as a leader of his enslaved people, urging them to remain faithful to the God of Abraham and to hope for delivery from bondage. His marriage to Elisheba, daughter of Amminadab, allied Aaron with a distinguished family from the powerful tribe of Judah—his brother-in-law, Nahshon, was that tribe's leader—and so enhanced his already prominent position.

Consequently, when God instructed Moses to return from his self-imposed exile in Midian and lead the Jews out of Egypt, Moses urged that Aaron be assigned this task instead. Here, after all, was someone familiar with the Egyptian court and trusted by his own people, whereas Moses, having lived in another country for forty years, was a stranger. Moreover, Moses regarded his brother as the better orator. Although Moses finally accepted the primary responsibility, Aaron, too, would play a large role in the Exodus.

Life's Work

Just as God appeared to Moses and told him to return to Egypt, so He informed Aaron of his brother's imminent return and instructed him to meet Moses at the border of Midian. Together they appeared before the leaders of the Hebrews, Aaron speaking and performing signs to establish the legitimacy of their mission. Together also they appeared before Pharaoh to demand the release of the Jews. Once again, Aaron offered a sign of their divine ministry: He threw his rod onto the floor of the palace, and the stick turned into a snake. Pharaoh's magicians duplicated this feat, but Aaron bested them when his rod devoured theirs. Pharaoh remained unmoved, though, and the ten plagues began with Aaron's stretching his hand over the waters of Egypt, turning them to blood. Aaron would bring on the next two plagues—frogs and lice—as well, and with Moses he created the sixth, boils.

After the Exodus, the eighty-three-year-old Aaron seems to have become one of the triumvirate of leaders, sharing power with Moses and Hur. When the Amalekites attacked the Hebrews at Rephidim, Aaron stood on one side of Moses, Hur on the other, to hold up Moses' hands and so ensure the victory for Joshua and his troops. When Moses ascended Mount Sinai to receive the Ten Commandments, Aaron and Hur remained behind to govern.

The strangest episode of Aaron's life occurred about this time. Moses' lengthy absence—he would be gone forty days—persuaded the Hebrews that their leader was dead, so they demanded an idol to replace him. Hur refused to comply and was killed, as were the elders opposing this wish. Alone and unsupported, Aaron instructed the people to bring him all of their gold. Was he hoping that they would be unwilling to part with their treasure? If so, he was disappointed, for they readily complied. According to the account in certain rabbinical commentaries, he cast the gold into a furnace, apparently intending only to melt it, yet a golden calf emerged, seemingly of itself. The Hebrews responded by acclaiming the calf as the god that had led them out of Egypt. Perhaps to delay any worship of this idol, Aaron declared that the next day would be a festival for the graven image; by the time Moses returned, though, the celebration had already begun.

According to some accounts, only the intervention of Moses saved Aaron's life from divine retribution. Yet shortly afterward, Aaron was designated high priest. Was he being rewarded for his efforts to delay the idolatrous worship? Might the golden calf, in fact, have represented a deity worshipped by the Hebrews in Egypt? Was Aaron's role in its creation the cause of his elevation to the priesthood? In later Jewish worship, the temple altar had two horns, and after the division of Israel into two kingdoms, Jeroboam erected golden calves at Bethel and Dan to compete with the Temple in Jerusalem. The choice of this animal suggests lingering loyalty to a bull as deity, or at least as representative of the deity.

The consecration of Aaron to the priesthood, whatever its cause, divorced religious leadership from the secular and placed priests under the power of the latter. God was to appear only to Moses in the desert, never to the high priest, and it was Moses who dictated the laws and rituals that Aaron and his sons were to follow. This subordination would become even more pronounced as political power passed from the tribe of Levi (to which both Aaron and Moses belonged) to Benjamin and then Judah, after the conquest of Canaan and the establishment of the monarchy. That elevation to the post of high priest removed Aaron from political leadership did not escape his notice; with Miriam, his older sister, Aaron protested against Moses' emergence as sole leader. For her criticism, Miriam was afflicted with leprosy for seven days; Aaron escaped with a divine rebuke.

A more serious challenge came from Korah, a kinsman of Moses and Aaron. Organizing many of the tribal leaders, he attacked the brothers for assuming undue power, but this rebellion was quickly suppressed by an earthquake that destroyed the ringleaders and a plague that killed more than fourteen thousand others. The toll would have been higher had Aaron not taken his censer and arrested the plague by standing between the living and the dead.

To reinforce the message that Aaron was the divine choice for the priesthood, Moses instructed each tribal elder to bring his staff to the tabernacle (the tent of worship), and Aaron placed his own among them. The next morning they found that Aaron's staff had flowered and had produced almonds. The others removed their rods, while Aaron's remained in the tent as a warning against further rebellions.

Despite such challenges, it is clear that Aaron was popular—more popular, in fact, than the sometimes stern and irascible Moses. Aaron must have been an impressive figure in the camp—his flowing white beard, his priestly garments, and the breastplate of twelve precious stones commanding reverence. He was not only respected but also loved. The famous Jewish rabbi Hillel urged his students to imitate Aaron, "loving peace and pursuing peace, loving one's fellow men and bringing them nigh to the Torah."

Freed from the role of judge and lawgiver, Aaron could devote himself to teaching and making peace. Legend says that he would go from tent to tent to instruct those unfamiliar with the law. In a similar way, when he heard that two people had quarreled, he would go to one and say, "The person you argued with deeply regrets his hasty words and actions and seeks your forgiveness." Then he would go to the other party and say the same thing, thereby effecting a reconciliation. He was famous for reuniting feuding husbands and wives, who generally named their next child for him. The eighty thousand Hebrews bearing the name of Aaron attest his success as a marriage counselor.

Throughout the forty years that the Jews wandered in the desert, Aaron served as high priest, assisted by his two younger sons, Eleazar and Ithamar; his two older sons, Nadab and Avihu, had died when they offered "strange fire"—apparently some form of idolatry—in the sacred tent. Like his brother Moses and his sister Miriam, Aaron was not, however, destined to enter the Promised Land.

According to certain Jewish commentaries, it was, in fact, the death of Miriam at the beginning of the fortieth year of wandering that indirectly led to the punishment and death of both her brothers. Tradition holds that during Miriam's life a well had followed the Hebrews from camp to camp; as soon as she died, the well vanished. Lacking water at Meribah in the Wilderness of Zin, the Hebrews criticized Moses and Aaron for leading them into a wasteland. God commanded the two men to assemble the people and then speak to a rock, which would bring forth water. Distracted and angered by the threats and complaints of the people, Moses struck the rock instead, thus disobeying the divine order and diminishing the greatness of the miracle. For this failing, both men were condemned to die outside Canaan.

Aaron's death followed Miriam's by four months. Unwilling to reveal to his brother that God had decreed Aaron's death, Moses summoned Aaron and Eleazar to accompany him up Mount Hor. There they found a cave. Aaron removed his priestly garments and gave them to his son; the high priest then entered the cave, lay down on a couch, and died—as the story goes—by a kiss from the Shekinah, the Holy Spirit (c. 1272 B.C.).

The people's reaction to Aaron's disappearance again reveals his popularity. When Moses and Eleazar returned, the Hebrews suspected that they had murdered Aaron out of jealousy. Tradition maintains that to save the two from being stoned, God showed Aaron lying dead in the cave, proving that he had died naturally, not violently. For thirty days all Israel mourned Aaron's passing; when Moses died eight months later the sense of loss was not so universally shared.

Summary

As the first high priest and founder of the priestly caste, Aaron has served as the model of the religious leader. Christian theologians saw him as the prototype of Jesus Christ, differing only in the fact that Aaron sacrificed animals, whereas Christ offered himself to be killed. Though Aaron is less popular as an artistic subject than Moses, the French painter Jean Fouquet and the English painter John Everett Millais produced idealized portraits of him.

Nineteenth and twentieth century biblical scholars have been less kind, questioning his priestly role and, indeed, challenging his very existence. Whether he was the creation of some late biblical redactor or indeed Moses' brother, whom God chose to preside over the holy tabernacle, Aaron has assumed an important role in the Judeo-Christian tradition and has become inextricably associated with the early development of the Jewish religion.

Bibliography

Aberbach, Moses, and Leivy Smolar. "Aaron, Jeroboam, and the Golden Calves." *Journal of Biblical Literature* 86 (1967): 129-140. Points out the similarities between the biblical description of Aaron and that of Jeroboam and suggests that either the latter consciously imitated the former in the construction of the golden calves at Bethel and Dan or the story in Exodus was written by members of a non-Aaronite priesthood in Jerusalem to discredit the northern kingdom. Offers a careful examination of Aaron's role in the creation of the golden calf.

Ginzberg, Louis. *The Legends of the Jews.* Translated by Henrietta Szold. 7 vols. Philadelphia: Jewish Publication Society of America, 1909-1938. Draws together biblical, Talmudic, and post-Talmudic sources to create a coherent narrative of Jewish history from the Creation to the time of Esther. Aaron receives extensive coverage in volumes 2 and 3, which treat life in Egypt, the Exodus, and the wanderings in the desert.

Kaufman, Yehezekel. *The Religion of Israel.* Translated by Moshe Greenberg. Chicago: University of Chicago Press, 1960. Originally published in eight volumes in Hebrew between 1937 and 1956. The English version, condensed and translated by Greenberg, discusses the growth of Judaism and, inter alia, examines the role that Aaron and the priesthood played in the process.

Kennett, R. H. "The Origin of the Aaronite Priesthood." *The Journal of Theological Studies* 6 (January, 1905): 161-186. Seeks to reveal the character of Aaron and trace the development of his personality—and of the Jewish priesthood—through the various versions of the Pentateuch and prophetic books.

Meek, Theophile James. "Aaronites and Zadokites." *The American Journal of Semitic Languages and Literatures* 45 (April, 1920): 149-166. Maintains that two rival priestly traditions existed in early Judaism and considers the way this conflict affected the biblical portrayal of Aaron, who in places seems saintly and elsewhere idolatrous.

_____. *Hebrew Origins.* New York: Harper and Brothers, 1960. In the fourth chapter of this work, Meek discusses the rise of the Jewish priesthood. Challenging the orthodox religious view, Meek maintains that Aaron "is clearly a supernumerary who was later introduced into the [biblical] narrative as Israelite and Judean sagas became fused with the union of the two people."

Joseph Rosenblum

PIETRO D'ABANO

Born: c. 1250; Abano, near Padua, Italy
Died: 1316; Padua, Italy
Areas of Achievement: Medicine and philosophy
Contribution: Pietro founded the Paduan school of medicine, introducing elements of Arabic knowledge into Italy. While a successful professor of medicine, he worked toward a synthesis of medieval, classical, Arabic, and Jewish philosophy.

Early Life

Pietro d'Abano, also known as Peter of Abano, Petrus de Apono, and Petrus Aponensis, was born in the village of Abano near Padua in northern Italy about 1250. Not much is known concerning his family background or early years. His father was a public notary and seems to have been reasonably well-to-do, for Pietro was able to receive an unusually good education. As a youth, he went to Greece and Constantinople, where he gained a mastery of the Greek language; among his early writings are translations of works of Aristotle into Latin. The ability to read the Greek classics in the original was quite unusual in Western Europe before the invading Ottoman Turks began to force Greek scholars to flee westward from the collapsing Byzantine Empire in the mid-fifteenth century.

Upon his return from Constantinople, Pietro attended the University of Paris, perhaps the best of the few institutions of higher learning that existed in late thirteenth century Europe. He studied philosophy, mathematics, and medicine for a number of years and earned a doctorate. Pietro's fame as a scholar and teacher quickly spread, and he became known as "the great Lombard."

Life's Work

In addition to his scientific and philosophical studies, Pietro was very interested in the pseudoscience of astrology. He often included astrological considerations and prayer in his medical prescriptions. Later in his life he was responsible for the inscription of some four hundred astrological symbols on Padua's city hall. His reaching for supernatural forces was probably a reaction to the limited scientific knowledge of the fourteenth century. Pietro himself, for example, asserted firmly that it was impossible to determine the constituent parts of a compound. Thus, without outside help, the medieval scientist was so restricted as to be almost helpless. His astrological interests, however, eventually led to trouble with the Church.

Pietro was more a man of the Middle Ages than of the early Renaissance. His idea of the four elements—earth, water, air, and fire—was typical of medieval understanding of chemistry, but he went further than most medieval scholars through experimentation and critical translation of classical manuscripts. Pietro was also an eager collector of new information. He left record of an interview with Marco Polo held shortly before the latter returned to Venice in 1295. Pietro inquired about natural phenomena and drugs such as camphor, aloe, and brazil, which were imported from the Orient. He made no mention of magic or other supernatural matters.

Pietro is often called a disciple of the Arabic scholar Avicenna and even more so of Averroës, whose ideas he is supposed to have introduced into Europe. Pietro's ideas about the stages of disease—onset, increase, fullness, and decline—correspond to those of Avicenna, as does his preference for simple, natural medicines. Lynn Thorndike, however, argues quite effectively that the supposed influence of Averroës has no basis in Pietro's writings. Averroës' ideas about chemistry were more sophisticated than those of medieval Europeans such as Pietro, and Thorndike finds no reason to think that Pietro's theological ideas came from the same source. Other writers, however, suggest that Pietro's adoption of a corruption of Averroës' idea of the soul was one of the principal sources of his trouble with the Church.

In addition to numerous translations from Arabic and Greek, Pietro wrote at least ten books. The most famous is the *Conciliator differentiarum philosophorum et praecipue medicorum* (1472; conciliator of the various medical philosophies and practices), in which he attempted to reconcile the teachings of Greek, Arabic, Jewish, and Latin writers in philosophy and medicine. Although done with the usual medieval resort to authority and syllogism, this work contains much original comment and makes clear Pietro's deep commitment to astrology.

Pietro's second major work, *De venenis eorumque remediis* (1473; English translation, 1924), is a description of all important known poisons with descriptions of symptoms and antidotes or treatments. Reportedly done for a pope—possibly John XXII—it too is a mixture of astrology and superstition, but the listing of poisons and symptoms is well done.

Pietro's writings other than translations are *Expositio problematum Aristotelis* (1475; exposition of Aristotelian problems), *Hippocratis de medicorum astrologia libellus Graeco in Latinum* (1476; Hippocratus' astronomical medicine translated from Greek to Latin), *Textus Mesue emendatus Petri Apponi medici in librum* (1505; the text of Mesue amended by Dr. Pietro d'Abano), *Astrolabium planum, in tabulis ascendens, continens qualibet hora atque minuto aequationes domorum coeli, significationes* (1502; clear astronomical tables, containing the heavenly signs for any hour and minute), *Joannis Mesue additio* (1505; additions to John Mesue), *Decisiones physiognomicae* (1548; judging a person's character by physical features), *Geomantia* (1549; *Magical Elements*, 1655), and *De balneis* (1553; on baths). Many of these works were considered authoritative into the sixteenth century.

Although the details are in some dispute, Pietro's return to Padua from Paris seems to have been marked by serious trouble with the Church. Either shortly before or after his arrival in Padua, Pietro was accused of heresy and necromancy. The charges were made through the Dominican Order of friars and were based on reports of a physician named Petrus de Reggio. There are a number of reported accusations, including that he used magic to get all the money he spent returned to him; that he claimed that some biblical miracles had natural explanations; and that he adhered to the rationalistic philosophy of Averroës. Charged with several others, Pietro had to face the Inquisition. Thanks to the intervention of influential patrons—there is one report that Pietro went to Rome and won the support of Pope Boniface VIII—he was exonerated in 1306. In 1314, Pietro was offered the chair of medicine at the new University of Treviso, but he fell ill and died before he could move there. His death was fortuitous in one sense, for in 1315 the charges of heresy were renewed. Posthumously he was condemned and orders were issued for the exhumation and burning of his body. Although most authorities maintain that friends spirited the body away to a new tomb and only an effigy was burned in the public square of Padua, Thomas of Strassburg, Augustinian prior general, claims to have seen the body burned. The distinction seems academic at best.

Thorndike, who has made the most thorough study of Pietro, rejects much of the story of his troubles with the Inquisition. It was, Thorndike argues, constructed of whole cloth in the fifteenth and sixteenth centuries. Pietro may have had one brush with church authorities, but the embellishments about the body being spirited away have no basis in original sources. Thorndike is not even convinced that Pietro died on the traditionally accepted date of 1316 and suggests that he may, in fact, have taught for some years at Treviso after that date. Thorndike's arguments are well marshaled, but they have not been widely adopted by other scholars.

Summary

Pietro was a medieval scientist, but he showed some of the qualities that would mark the Renaissance as well. His critical attitude and experimental approach were signs of the future. The importance he placed on astrology and prayer as elements in medical prescriptions, however, harked back to the past.

Pietro played an important role in the development of Padua and its university into a major intellectual center. Although in the thirteenth century the University of Padua was known mostly for the study of law, by 1500 it could boast of having had many of the major scientists of the Italian Renaissance as professors or students. Pietro founded the Paduan school of medical thought, introducing both classical and Arabic sources. His willingness to question established views and to seek new information rather than depending wholly on authority was important in shaping the growing scholarly tradition of Padua.

Bibliography
Brown, Horace. "*De venenis* of Petrus Abbonus." *Annals of Medical History* 6 (1924): 25-53. A translation of Pietro's work about poisons and their symptoms and treatments, this is the only conveniently available English translation of any of Pietro's writings. It provides a good sample of the mix of superstition and science that marked his approach to medicine.
Castiglioni, Arturo. *A History of Medicine.* New York: Alfred A. Knopf, 1941. Contains a short biographical sketch of Pietro and much useful background information about late medieval medicine and the development of medical studies in Padua.
Hyde, J. K. *Padua in the Age of Dante.* New York: Barnes and Noble Books, 1966. An excellent description of late medieval Padua which provides valuable background information about the milieu in which Pietro worked.
Olschki, Leonardo. "Medical Matters in Marco Polo's Description of the World." In *Essays in the History of Medicine Presented to Professor Arturo Castiglioni on the Occasion of his Seventieth Birth Day*, edited by Henry E. Sigerist. Baltimore: Johns Hopkins University Press, 1944. Contains a discussion of Pietro's interview with Marco Polo showing the former's scientific approach to collecting new data.
Thorndike, Lynn. *A History of Magic and Experimental Science.* Vol. 2. New York: Columbia University Press, 1947. A magisterial work in eight volumes tracing the development of the techniques of modern science. Contains the most complete study of Pietro yet done.
_____. "Peter of Abano: A Medieval Scientist." *Annual Report of the American Historical Association for the Year 1919* 1 (1923): 317-326. Contains a summary of Pietro's life but is focused on historiographical sources. Attempts to show that many common beliefs about Pietro are misconceptions based on secondary sources from the fifteenth and sixteenth centuries.

Fred R. van Hartesveldt

'ABD AL-MU'MIN

Born: 1094; Tagra, Algeria
Died: May 2, 1163; Rabat, Morocco
Areas of Achievement: Warfare, government, and patronage
Contribution: Through military prowess and administrative skill, 'Abd al-Mu'min founded the Almohad empire in North Africa and the Iberian Peninsula, initiating a period of thriving commerce and artistic creativity.

Early Life

'Abd al-Mu'min ibn 'Ali ibn Makhluf ibn Yu'la ibn Marwan, born in 1094 in Tagra (now in Algeria), was the son of Ali, a humble potter and member of the Koumiya, an Arabized section of the Berber Zanata tribe. Legends arose concerning marvelous happenings in his youth: Swarms of bees were said to have alighted on him without stinging, and a holy man prophesied that the boy would conquer countries at the four cardinal points.

Ali decided that his son must have an education. Thus, 'Abd al-Mu'min studied at the school in Tagra and then at the mosque in the important Algerian city of Tlemcen. One historian wrote: "He was endowed with a lively understanding. In the time it takes a man to grasp one question, he understood ten." To further his knowledge, 'Abd al-Mu'min, accompanied by uncle Ya'lu, determined to go to the East. In 1117, that plan was scrapped at Mallala, Algeria, because of 'Abd al-Mu'min's momentous meeting with Ibn Tumart.

Ibn Tumart, a Masmuda Berber of southern Morocco, founded the Almohad movement, the name being a corruption of the Arabic *al-muwahhidun*, meaning the movement of the unitarians. Ibn Tumart placed special stress on the oneness of God and introduced into North Africa the Shi'ite notion of an infallible *mahdi* (divinely guided one). It was as he was returning from his pilgrimage to Mecca that Ibn Tumart met 'Abd al-Mu'min at Mallala. According to tradition, Ibn Tumart had prophesied their meeting.

'Abd al-Mu'min became Ibn Tumart's first disciple, accompanying him to Morocco. In 1121, Ibn Tumart established headquarters at his native village, Igliz, moving to Tinmel three years later. In 1125, Ibn Tumart proclaimed himself the *mahdi*, the imam known and infallible. 'Abd al-Mu'min served as Ibn Tumart's trusted lieutenant, spreading his doctrine, helping to organize Almohad society, and fighting against the Almoravid regime. In May, 1130, 'Abd al-Mu'min suffered wounds in the Almohad defeat by the Almoravids at the Battle of al-Buhaira. On August 13, 1130, Ibn Tumart died, having designated 'Abd al-Mu'min as the Almohad leader. For three years, Ibn Tumart's death was concealed because certain Almohads disputed 'Abd al-Mu'min's succession, arguing that he was an outsider. By 1133, however, his supporters had managed to establish his leadership.

Life's Work

   'Abd al-Mu'min determined to conquer the entire Maghrib for the Almohad cause. For several years, he prepared meticulously, gaining adherents to the Almohad message and attracting mountaineers to his army in Tinmel. Then, systematically employing guerrilla tactics against the Almoravid dynasty, he conquered the western mountain ranges of North Africa one after another: High Atlas, Middle Atlas, Rif, and the range south of Tlemcen. Emboldened, 'Abd al-Mu'min moved from the mountains. In 1144, he defeated the Almoravid ally Reverter and his Christian militia. A year later, 'Abd al-Mu'min crushed the Almoravid monarch Tashfin ibn Ali and took Oran and Tétouan. Next, after a nine-month siege, 'Abd al-Mu'min captured Fez, and, in 1147, following an eleven-month siege, Marrakech, where he executed the last Almoravid ruler. 'Abd al-Mu'min made Marrakech the Almohad capital and proceeded to massacre the Lemtuna Berbers.

   Thereupon, 'Abd al-Mu'min turned his attention to the Iberian Peninsula, where the Christians had been recovering territory because of the Almoravid decline. Because of their rigid doctrine, the Almohads encountered resistance from Iberian Muslims and Christians alike. As a result, by 1148, 'Abd al-Mu'min's authority extended to only the southwestern part of the Andalus. Regarding the Iberian Peninsula as a diversion from the task of consolidating of Almohad rule in the Maghrib, 'Abd al-Mu'min pushed no farther into Europe.

   After conquering Morocco, 'Abd al-Mu'min focused attention on the central Maghrib. Here the Hammadid kingdom existed in decline under Yahya. In 1151, by forced marches and in secrecy, 'Abd al-Mu'min and his army reached Algiers and then Bougie, the Hammadid capital, which surrendered. Next, 'Abd al-Mu'min's son took and sacked Qal'a. In 1152, the Hilalians, Arab Bedouins of the region, joined the attempt to push the Almohads to the far west. 'Abd al-Mu'min, who had been returning to Morocco, hurried back and met the enemy at Sétif, where he triumphed after a four-day battle. In this case, however, he treated the vanquished leniently.

   'Abd al-Mu'min devoted the years between 1152 and 1159 to organizing his state. He had taken the title "Caliph of Ibn Tumart," imitating Abu Bakr, the Caliph of Muhammad. He also became Amir al-Mu'minin (prince of the faithful), the first non-Arab to be so honored. Members of his family, known as sayyids, formed the elite. In 1154, 'Abd al-Mu'min proclaimed his son as successor, displacing Abu Hafs 'Umar, the first designee. 'Abd al-Mu'min sent his other sons to the principal provinces as governors. With each of them, 'Abd al-Mu'min sent a leading Almohad *shaikh* as counselor, thus joining the religious leaders to his family. 'Abd al-Mu'min used Abu Hafs 'Umar as his first vizier and then as a personal adviser; the latter's family ranked next to the sayyids. Ibn Tumart's Council of the Fifty, a consultative assembly which had representatives from the original tribes of the Almohad movement, was retained. These elements formed the aristocracy of the empire.

Using Ibn Tumart's teachings, 'Abd al-Mu'min aimed to build a unified Muslim community in the Maghrib. The bases for legislation were the Koran, the tradition of Muhammad, and the concord of Muhammad's Companions. Practical needs of justice, however, drove 'Abd al-Mu'min to tacit toleration of the Malikite system of law. To maintain and enforce Ibn Tumart's doctrine, 'Abd al-Mu'min devised special training for provincial administrators. He personally selected young men from the Masmuda tribes and trained them in Ibn Tumart's writings, archery, horsemanship, and swimming. The ruler's sons received this education as well.

As an administrator, 'Abd al-Mu'min shone in masterminding an immense geographical survey of the Maghrib. According to a Muslim historian, "From this area one-third was deducted for mountains, rivers, salt lakes, roads, and deserts. The remaining two-thirds were made subject to the land tax (*kharaj*) and the amount to be paid by each tribe in grain and money was fixed. This was the first time this was done in Barbary." 'Abd al-Mu'min used the survey to ascertain his fiscal resources. The treasury drew revenue from the taxes imposed by the Koran and from a large part of the *kharaj*. The latter applied to "unbelievers," who paid the tax as a sort of rent on their former property, its ownership having been taken by the state. The "unbelievers" comprised all non-Almohad Muslims and also those Almohads who were judged unzealous.

The pragmatic 'Abd al-Mu'min did not subject all tribes to the *kharaj*. He needed the help of nomads for manning his army in the Iberian Peninsula and for keeping order in the Maghrib. These nomads included the Hilalians who were brought to Morocco from Tunisia, the Zanata Beni 'Abd al-Wad in the area between Mina and the Moulouya, and another tribe camped in the Bougie district. Members of these tribes enforced the payment of the *kharaj* on settled tribes.

'Abd al-Mu'min encountered internal opposition to his regime. His restricting the succession to the Almohad leadership to his own family caused a rebellion in 1155. The ringleaders were Ibn Tumart's brothers, 'Abd al-'Aziz and 'Isa. They besieged Marrakech, but were defeated and executed. Along with them, 'Abd al-Mu'min executed numerous chiefs of the Hargha tribe who had been suspected of fomenting treason. Sensitive to opposition, 'Abd al-Mu'min dealt cautiously with the proud Masmuda tribes, which claimed Ibn Tumart as their own son. 'Abd al-Mu'min allowed only the Masmuda to have the honor of being called Almohads; they were also the sole group permitted to discuss and elaborate Ibn Tumart's doctrine. Furthermore, 'Abd al-Mu'min gave the Masmuda preferential treatment in taxation.

While organizing his government, 'Abd al-Mu'min gave thought also to Ifriqiya (Tunisia). Muslims there sought his help against the Norman occupation under King William I of Sicily. In two years of preparation, 'Abd al-Mu'min built seventy warships and an army of 200,000. In 1159, he led the army into Ifriqiya, his navy following along the coast. He sent one force to besiege Tunis, whose ruler was a Muslim Sanhaja chief under Norman protection. 'Abd al-Mu'min led his main army against heavily fortified Mahdiyya, the major Norman stronghold. On January 22, 1160, a seven-month siege ended, the Almohad navy having defeated a Norman relieving fleet from Sicily. 'Abd al-Mu'min and the Normans negotiated: The Normans evacuated Mahdiyya, and 'Abd al-Mu'min gave them safe passage to Sicily. Thus ended Norman rule in Africa. At this time, the Almohads captured Tunis and the interior of Ifriqiya. Now, moreover, the Muslims of Tripolitana, who had evicted the Normans in 1157, swore allegiance to 'Abd al-Mu'min.

'Abd al-Mu'min's achievements extended to still another activity: patronage of architecture. He ordered the construction of a palace and of the impressive Kutubia mosque at Marrakech, as well as the mosque at Taza. To commemorate Ibn Tumart, 'Abd al-Mu'min built a mosque at Tinmel. The design of this structure reveals influences from the surrounding area, the East, and Moorish Spain. Another of his buildings was the fortress of Ribat al-Fath.

On May 2, 1163, 'Abd al-Mu'min died at Rabat. He was buried near Ibn Tumart at Tinmel.

Summary

'Abd al-Mu'min created a new chapter in the history of North Africa. Designated by the *mahdi*, Ibn Tumart, as his successor in leading the Almohad movement, 'Abd al-Mu'min converted that spiritual body into a political regime lasting from 1130 to 1269. Throwing off his deference to Abu Hafs 'Umar, 'Abd al-Mu'min built by war an empire in North Africa and southern Spain which his family, the Mu'minid, ruled. His long military activity angered some of the original Almohads, who tried unsuccessfully to assassinate him in 1160. The conspirators also hated his magnanimous policy toward the empire's Arabs.

The reigns of 'Abd al-Mu'min, his son Abu Ya'qub Yusuf (1163-1184), and his grandson Abu Yusuf Ya'qub I (1184-1199) marked the golden age of Barbary. They brought a general revival of commerce, for the Almohads had the best fleet in the Mediterranean, and they opened the sea to Christian and Muslim traffic. Urban life continued the development begun under the previous Almoravid rule, with a new burst of creative activity stemming from Ibn Tufayl and Averroës.

Art flourished in Morocco and Spain under 'Abd al-Mu'min and his dynasty. 'Abd al-Mu'min was the founder of a new architectural style—the most original and impressive in North Africa. He gave to Andalusian artists a new spirit: an austere and simple style that resulted in a magnificent union of

Andalusian subtlety and Moroccan strength.

Nevertheless, 'Abd al-Mu'min contributed to the ultimate Almohad decline and fall. The mechanical and official nature of his piety began to loosen the Mu'minid state from the passionate and radiant zeal of Ibn Tumart, whose uncompromising stand had created the Almohad movement. Furthermore, 'Abd al-Mu'min settled some Arab Bedouin tribes in Morocco, where he wanted to train them to further his realm in Spain. Later, members of these tribes became unruly, causing anarchy in the heart of the Almohad empire.

Still, 'Abd al-Mu'min's great achievement cannot be denied: He led the Berbers in the first unification of North Africa.

Bibliography
Abun-Nasr, Jamil M. *A History of the Maghrib*. Cambridge: Cambridge University Press, 1971, 2d ed. 1975. Short, compact account of 'Abd al-Mu'min. Thought-provoking in linking his creation of a unified Muslim community to Ibn Tumart's doctrine. The relationship of the Almohad regime with previous and later dynasties is discussed. Brief bibliography, index, map.

_____. *A History of the Maghrib in the Islamic Period*. Cambridge: Cambridge University Press, 1987. Brief, excellent depiction of 'Abd al-Mu'min. More scholarly treatment than Abun-Nasr's *A History of the Maghrib*. Unannotated bibliography, index, map.

Hopkins, J. F. P. *Medieval Muslim Government in Barbary Until the Sixth Century of the Hijra*. London: Luzac and Co., 1958. One section describes the Almohad hierarchy. The entire system may have existed solely on paper. Treatment of the elaborate organization may be of interest only to scholars. One map.

Julien, Charles-André. *History of North Africa: Tunisia, Algeria, Morocco*. Translated by John Petrie; edited by C. C. Stewart and Roger Le Tourneau. London: Routledge and Kegan Paul, 1970. Very good treatment of the Almohads (forty-seven pages), placing 'Abd al-Mu'min on center stage in his varied roles. Apt quotations from sources; one map, fine bibliography.

Le Tourneau, Roger. *The Almohad Movement in North Africa in the Twelfth and Thirteenth Centuries*. Princeton, N.J.: Princeton University Press, 1969. Excellent in integrating 'Abd al-Mu'min into the Almohad movement and showing his strengths and weaknesses. Brief but good treatment of contemporary accounts and historical studies. Helpful index.

Erving E. Beauregard

'ABD AL-RAHMAN III AL-NASIR

Born: 891; Córdoba, Spain
Died: 961; Córdoba, Spain
Area of Achievement: Government
Contribution: Sound administrative, fiscal, and religious policies, military successes, astute diplomacy, and patronage of learning characterized 'Abd al-Rahman's reign, which marked the apex of Islamic power in Spain.

Early Life

The grandson of Emir 'Abd Allah and his Christian wife, great-grandson of Emir al-Mundhir and a Christian princess from Navarre, and grand-nephew of the powerful Navarrese Queen Toda, 'Abd al-Rahman spent his youth in the wealth and culture of his grandfather's palace in Córdoba. This ancestry illustrates the complex nature of Spanish society in the tenth century. Clearly the Christians and the Muslims were in conflict, but the conflict was rooted more in political and economic rivalries than in religious or cultural antagonisms. This background provided 'Abd al-Rahman with perspective and connections which he was able to exploit effectively, as his grandfather had not. When 'Abd al-Rahman inherited the throne, his authority extended only to the area around Córdoba.

During the preceding decades, Arab aristocrats and Berber military men had amassed huge landed estates which gave them a power base from which to ignore central authority. This independence was apparent particularly in certain areas of Aragon, Toledo, and Estremadura. Religious fanatics of one kind or another were in repeated revolt. Through sporadic raids and warfare, the Christian princes in the north had regained vast tracts of land that the emirate had controlled earlier. The absence of political unity and social stability had devastated the economy of Spain. While 'Abd Allah was not the strongest or wisest of emirs, he did make one outstanding decision: From among his many grandchildren, he chose 'Abd al-Rahman as his heir.

Life's Work

In 912, when 'Abd al-Rahman was twenty-three, he became the emir. He immediately undertook to rectify the political, economic, and social problems that he had inherited. His interests were many, but he gave primary attention to three major activities: the unification of his kingdom, the construction of the Madinat al-Zahra' palace, and the promotion of an economic revolution.

The first of these tasks, the unification and centralization of his kingdom, took the first twenty years of 'Abd al-Rahman's reign. He neutralized the power of the aristocracy and curbed the bellicosity of the Berber tribes by establishing a standing army, made up of slaves and foreigners from the whole of the Mediterranean world, soldiers whose first loyalty was to the caliph. This army ultimately numbered 100,000 and was supported by a third of the royal revenues.

'Abd al-Rahman defeated the religious rebels whose power centered on Bobastro and who had virtually declared their independence from the central government. He deliberately broke the independence of the governors of Saragossa, Toledo, and Badajoz, restoring their function as frontier marches whose purpose was to prevent Christian intrusion into the Córdoban kingdom. He campaigned repeatedly, though not always successfully, against the Christian kingdoms of León, Castile, Navarre, and Galicia. In the end, it was to the caliphate that the Christians went in search of physicians, musicians, architects, negotiators, tutors, and marriage alliances.

By the end of his reign, 'Abd al-Rahman had centralized his authority over Islamic Spain. He had made the Christian kingdoms tribute states but allowed them to retain governmental autonomy. By 937 he had stopped the westward expansion of the Fatimids out of Tunis, extending his sovereignty over Morocco and western Algeria. In recognition of his power, rulers of all European and eastern Islamic kingdoms commissioned emissaries to his court.

To add to his prestige and focus his authority, in 929 'Abd al-Rahman declared himself Caliph of Islamic Spain, based on his Umayyad lineage. He also took the titles "Commander of the Believers" and "Defender of the Religion of God," tacitly supporting the Malikite theological position, which was then dominant among Muslims in Spain. His assumption of these titles allowed petty chieftains in North Africa to recognize the Spanish caliph as their sovereign, rather than the schismatic and fanatical Fatimids. It also did much to focus the emerging patriotism and loyalty of his Spanish subjects.

In the economic sphere, 'Abd al-Rahman met with equal success. Production of gold, iron, silver, lead, and rubies increased. He improved and extended the canals and irrigation systems. Despite the Koranic dictates against wine drinking, the growing of grapes and the making of wine became important economic enterprises. Agriculture was diversified and expanded. Rice, peaches, oranges, apricots, sugar, cotton, pomegranates, figs, and saffron had been introduced by the Muslims into Spain; traditional crops such as wheat, other grains, and olives also continued to be cultivated.

This diversification and increased agricultural production were key elements of the prosperity of 'Abd al-Rahman's caliphate, but industry played a crucial role as well. The caliphate became known for its fine leather, superb steel, olive oil, and paper. These products were traded as far east as India for slaves, cloth, and exotic spices. 'Abd al-Rahman expanded the navy in order to protect trade routes and the merchant fleet from attacks by the Normans, Byzantines, or 'Abbasids. In the end, 'Abd al-Rahman's navy and merchant marine came to dominate the western Mediterranean.

In 936, 'Abd al-Rahman embarked upon the construction of his great palace, Madinat al-Zahra' (which means "she of the shining face"). Al-Zahra' was the caliph's favorite wife; curiously, initial funding for the palace came as a gift to the caliph from one of his concubines. The construction of the palace became a major public works project, employing ten thousand workers and three thousand animals for twenty-five years at an expense of one-third of the annual royal revenues. Materials such as ebony, gold, and ivory were imported to decorate the palace; luxurious gifts for its embellishment were received from other rulers. This sprawling palace complex, located about three miles outside Córdoba, provided a beautiful view of the city and surrounding countryside. Some have deemed it the crowning achievement of 'Abd al-Rahman's reign.

Summary

'Abd al-Rahman III al-Nasir died at the age of seventy, leaving the caliphate to al-Hakam, his son by his Basque Christian wife, al-Subh. 'Abd al-Rahman had been a determined and successful ruler. His energy was boundless, his ability undisputed, his power immense and wisely controlled. He demanded respect; he extended charity. He carefully and intelligently tended to the demands of state and religion, while conscientiously expanding the culture, refinement, and economic well-being of his realm. He had established not only the most magnificent but also the most powerful kingdom in Europe—and nowhere was this better exemplified than in his capital, Córdoba.

Half a million people populated the city, whereas London had perhaps five thousand; indeed, the population of Spain as a whole had exploded during 'Abd al-Rahman's reign. The streets of the city were paved and lighted. Resplendent with palaces, seven hundred mosques, and at least three hundred public baths, Córdoba contained seventy libraries, countless bookstores, and twenty-seven free schools.

The caliph founded the University of Córdoba in the Great Mosque and established chairs and scholarships there; it was an institution that attracted teachers and students from the whole Mediterranean world and western Asia. During the reign of his son, the royal library founded by 'Abd al-Rahman reached 400,000 volumes, a number of which serve today as the basis of the Arabic collection in the Library of the Escorial. In addition to the university, a leading center for Jewish theological studies flourished in Córdoba. Indeed, 'Abd al-Rahman's physician, Hasdai ibn Shaprut (915-970), was Jewish, a member of the Ibn Ezra family who was educated at the University of Córdoba. A man of tact and good will, he became a diplomatic, financial, and commercial adviser for the caliph. He patronized learning and gave scholarships and books to deserving students. It is said that the stature of a leader can, at least in part, be determined by the quality of the men who serve him; Hasdai, then, serves as a case in point.

Córdoba became one of the three great cultural centers of the medieval world, rivaling both Constantinople and Baghdad. Its glory, however, did not extend only to culture. The economic power of the caliphate centered in Córdoba as well. The city processed and marketed the products of the agricultural revolution of the tenth century. Great brass, glass, pottery, paper, and leather works were located there. The city housed at least thirteen thousand silk, wool, and cotton weavers. Through Córdoba and Seville (the premier port of the caliphate) flowed Spain's exports in marble, sugar, figs, cotton, olives, olive oil, wine, and saffron. Revenues from import-export duties alone financed the caliphate.

The awe and admiration inspired by this "jewel of the world" that was Córdoba was only a reflection of the stature of the caliph himself. Never again could Islamic Spain claim such a one as 'Abd al-Rahman III al-Nasir.

Bibliography
Bertrand, Louis, and Charles Petrie. *The History of Spain*. New York: Collier Books, 1971. While the information in this book is valid, the authors seem intentionally provocative. The reader is often obliged to sort through opinionated statements in an effort to uncover the facts.
Chapman, Charles E. *A History of Spain*. London: Macmillan, 1918. Now nearly a classic survey of Spanish history, this work remains a standard reference because of its objectivity, detail, and organization.
Christopher, John B. *The Islamic Tradition*. New York: Harper and Row, Publishers, 1972. This is one of the best short introductions to the history, the basic religious tenets, and the great medieval cultural synthesis of Islam, including that which occurred in Spain. Indeed, it is out of this rich medieval cultural heritage that Islam faces the modern world.
Durant, Will. *The Age of Faith*. New York: Simon and Schuster, 1950. This is the fourth volume of Durant's *Story of Civilization*, a massive synthesis. Highly readable text, a good bibliography, and helpful explanatory notes. Indexed.
Hitti, Philip K. *The Arabs: A Short History*. Chicago: Henry Regnery Co., 1962. No study of the rise of Islam, in Spain or elsewhere, is complete without reading Hitti.
——————. *Capital Cities of Arab Islam*. Minneapolis: University of Minnesota Press, 1973. Hitti describes the uniqueness of six great capitals of Islam. One of these is Córdoba, which reached its zenith of splendor, wealth, and cultural leadership under the patronage of 'Abd al-Rahman.
Jackson, Gabriel. *The Making of Medieval Spain*. New York: Harcourt Brace Jovanovich, 1972. A most insightful and evenhanded examination of medieval Spain. It stresses the rich results of the long intermingling of the Islamic, Christian, and Jewish cultures. Packed with information, this

short essay is lucid and extremely well written. Includes many excellent illustrations and a short but enlightening bibliographic essay.

Watt, W. Montgomery, and Pierre Cachia. *A History of Islamic Spain.* Edinburgh: Edinburgh University Press, 1965. This well-informed study details the influence of Islam upon the cultural development of Spain—and through Spain, all Europe. Special attention is focused on the Umayyads, of whom 'Abd al-Rahman was the greatest.

Shirley F. Fredricks

PETER ABELARD

Born: c. 1079; Le Pallet, Brittany
Died: April 21, 1142; Chalon-sur-Saône, Burgundy
Areas of Achievement: Philosophy and religion
Contribution: In philosophy Abelard developed the theory of conceptualism
to reconcile Platonic idealism with nominalism. His use of the dialectic to
explore Scripture helped shape Scholasticism, and many of his religious
views, condemned as heretical in his own lifetime, subsequently influenced
church doctrine.

Early Life

Peter Abelard was born in Le Pallet, Brittany, about 1079. His father,
Berengar, was lord of the village and a knight in the service of the Count of
Brittany; since Abelard was the oldest son, his parents expected him to succeed to these titles. Nevertheless, they did not object when he showed more
interest in intellectual than physical jousting. At fifteen Abelard left his parents, his three brothers—Raoul, Porcaire, and Dagobert—and his sister,
Denise, to study under Roscelin of Compiègne. By 1100 he had moved on to
Paris, where he attended the lectures of William of Champeaux, head of the
cathedral school and archdeacon of Notre-Dame.

At the school, Abelard demonstrated the combination of brilliance and
indiscretion that was to earn for him the title *Rhinoceros indomitus*—the
unconquerable rhinoceros. William, an extreme Platonist, maintained that
universal concepts such as "tree" exist independent of any specific examples.
Thus, there is no substantial difference between one maple tree and another,
or between an oak, a maple, or an elm. Moreover, the quality of "treeness" is
independent of any individual example. In public debate Abelard forced
William, regarded as the leading dialectician of the age, to abandon this position and accept Abelard's own view of conceptualism. Without denying
universal categories (which nominalists rejected), Abelard argued that one
knows those universals only because of individual examples; if those specimens did not exist, neither would the universal.

Life's Work

Abelard's victory won for him the respect of his fellow students and the enmity of William; both factors prompted him to leave Notre-Dame and set up
his own school, first at Melun (1102) and then at Corbeil, within five miles of
the French capital. The rivalry with Abelard may have influenced William's
decision to leave Paris as well; outside the city he established a new monastery, dedicated to Saint Victor, where he continued teaching.

William's departure left a vacancy at the cathedral school, and after Abelard recovered from an illness that had caused him to return to Brittany, he
was invited to assume the chair of his former master (c. 1108). As soon as

William learned of the appointment, he hastened back to Notre-Dame and forced Abelard to leave. Retreating first to Melun, Abelard soon was teaching at Sainte-Geneviève, at the very gates of Paris, drawing all but a handful of the students from the cathedral.

His teaching was interrupted again in 1111 when his parents decided to take Holy Orders, a common practice among the elderly in the twelfth century. Abelard had to go to Brittany to settle the family estate; then, perhaps at the urging of his mother, Lucia, he went to study theology under Anselm of Laon.

Just as William had been the most noted logician, so Anselm was the most famous religious teacher of the period. And just as Abelard had shown himself a better logician than William, so he would prove himself a better teacher of theology than Anselm. Finding the lectures at Laon dull, Abelard absented himself frequently. Students loyal to the old master challenged this lack of respect, and Abelard retorted that he himself could teach more effectively. Considering the little time that he had devoted to the subject, such a boast seemed absurd; his fellow students challenged him to make good his claim.

Abelard readily agreed, promising to lecture the next day on Ezekiel, one of the most abstruse books in the Bible. Even his opponents thought that matters had now gone too far and urged him to take time to prepare. Abelard refused; thus, when he rose to speak, he saw only a few people in the audience, all eagerly waiting for the upstart to make a fool of himself. Instead, his exegesis was so brilliant that within two days virtually all Anselm's students were attending Abelard's lectures and begging him to continue the series. Anselm thereupon forbade Abelard to teach anywhere in Laon.

By now, though, William's old post was vacant once more, and in 1112 or 1113 Abelard assumed it without opposition, inaugurating his tenure by concluding his explication of Ezekiel. Handsome, of medium height, with piercing brown eyes, he was, as even his enemies conceded, "sublime in eloquence." As *magister scholarum* of the leading school in France, if not of northern Europe, he was immensely popular. In part he owed this success to his unorthodox teaching methods. Rejecting the traditional *lectio*, in which the master read a text and then the commentaries on it, Abelard championed the *disputatio*, posing problems and resolving them through logic and careful textual analysis. Recalling those years, Héloïse wrote,

> Who among kings or philosophers could equal thee in fame? What kingdom or city or village did not burn to see thee? Who, I ask, did not hasten to gaze upon thee when thou appearedst in public, nor on thy departure with straining neck and fixed eye follow thee?

Among those impressed with Abelard's teaching was a canon of Notre-Dame named Fulbert, the uncle and guardian of Héloïse. She had been educated at the convent of Argenteuil, and by the age of fourteen, she could read Latin, Greek, and Hebrew. "La très sage Héloïs," as François Villon referred to her in 1461 in "Ballade des dames du temps jadis" ("Ballad of Dead Ladies"), may have already attended some of Abelard's lectures when in 1117 Fulbert invited Abelard to live with him on the Île de la Cité in the rue des Chantres. In return, the thirty-eight-year-old Abelard would tutor the seventeen-year-old Héloïse.

Tall, thin, with thick brown hair, gray eyes, fine features, a gracious manner, and intelligence, she might have tempted a saint left alone in her company: The sequel was not surprising. As Abelard recorded,

> More words of love than of our reading passed between us, and more kissing than teaching. My hands strayed oftener to her bosom than to the pages; love drew our eyes to look on each other more than reading kept them on our texts.

Finally, even Fulbert realized his mistake and evicted Abelard, but Héloïse was already pregnant. To protect her from her uncle's anger Abelard took her to Brittany, where their son, Astrolabe or Astrolabius, was born. To reconcile themselves to Fulbert, Abelard offered to marry Héloïse, under the condition that the marriage remain secret, and Fulbert agreed.

Héloïse strongly opposed this step, recognizing it as the worst possible solution. If the purpose of the marriage was to lessen Fulbert's shame, secrecy would not satisfy him. Any marriage would also remove Abelard's prospects for advancement in the Church, and even his reputation as a philosopher would be diminished. She argued,

> What harmony can there be between pupils and nursemaids, desks and cradles, books or tablets and distaffs, pen or stylus and spindles? Who can concentrate on thoughts of Scripture or philosophy and be able to endure babies crying, nurses soothing them with lullabies, and all the noisy coming and going of men and women about the house?

Moreover, she did not regard marriage as necessary to bind her to Abelard, to whom she was linked by a love stronger than any church vows.

Whether because of his desire to redeem Héloïse's honor, concern over Fulbert's possible vengeance, or fear that Héloïse might eventually marry another, Abelard rejected her sage advice, though to keep the marriage secret they lived apart. As Héloïse had predicted, Fulbert soon was boasting of his alliance with France's leading philosopher, and when Abelard and Héloïse denied having wed, Fulbert began to abuse his niece. Abelard thereupon removed her to the convent at Argenteuil, where she would be safe from Fulbert but close enough for him to visit.

Fulbert was now convinced that Abelard intended to force Héloïse to be-

come a nun and thereby dissolve his marriage, leaving him free for ecclesiastical advancement. The enraged canon devised a revenge that would at once
block such promotion and fittingly punish Abelard's lechery. Bribing Abelard's servant to leave the door unlocked, Fulbert, accompanied by some ruf-
fians, burst into Abelard's bedroom one night and castrated him.

Paris rallied to Abelard's support. Fulbert was stripped of his canonry and
expelled from the city. The two culprits who were apprehended—one of
them Abelard's feckless servant—were blinded and castrated. Seeing his suffering as divine retribution, Abelard gave up his post at Notre-Dame and
retired to the monastery of Saint-Denis, where he became a monk (c. 1119).
He also ordered Héloïse to assume the veil, though she had no religious vocation; indeed, he insisted that she take her vows first. Was this another sign
that he feared she might marry another? If so, he little understood her deep
love for him.

At Saint-Denis, Abelard lost little time in making new enemies by pointing
out that the monks were not adhering to the Benedictine rule. Therefore,
when Abelard asked permission to resume teaching, the abbot gladly allowed
him to establish a school at the priory, removed from the monastery. Students
again surrounded him, and for them, he prepared *Tractatus de unitate et
trinitate divina* (c. 1120), a work he would expand and revise several times
over the next sixteen years.

While the monks of Saint-Denis were delighted with Abelard's absence,
others were not pleased with his teaching. Among the disciples of Anselm
who still resented Abelard's behavior at Laon were Alberic of Rheims and
Lotulph of Novara. They maintained that a monk should not teach philosophy, that Abelard lacked the training to teach theology, and that his book,
which sought to use logic to demonstrate the existence and nature of the
Trinity, was heretical. They organized a council at Soissons in 1121 to try the
book, and they secured Abelard's condemnation. Even the presiding papal
legate regarded the decision as unjust and immediately allowed Abelard to
return to Saint-Denis.

At the monastery, Abelard embroiled himself in further controversy by
challenging the identity of the monks' supposed patron saint. So inflamed
were passions against him that he fled to Provins. The friendly Count
Theobald arranged for him to establish a hermitage near Troyes, and Abelard dedicated it to the Paraclete, or Holy Spirit. Again the orthodox ob-
jected; traditionally, hermitages were dedicated to the entire Trinity or to
Christ, never to the Paraclete.

Students cared nothing about the name, though. Leaving the comforts of
Paris they came in the thousands to till the fields and build accommodations
in order to listen again to the words of Abelard, who rewarded them with
stimulating lectures and treatises. *Sic et Non* (c. 1123) responded to criticism
that authority did not need the support of logic to establish faith. Abelard

assembled some 160 seemingly contradictory statements by the church fathers and argued that only through reason could one reconcile these. *Ethica sur liber dictus Scito te ipsum* (c. 1123; *Ethics*, 1935) postulated that sin derives from intention, not action. Performing a good deed for evil purposes is not meritorious; committing wrong unknowingly is not sinful.

These heterodox views disturbed Bernard of Clairvaux and Norbert, Archbishop of Magdeburg. In his treatise on baptism (1125), Bernard rejected Abelard's view on sin, and Abelard was so uneasy about this opposition that around 1125 he accepted the post of abbot at the monastery of Saint-Gildas-de-Rhuys (in Brittany), a place so remote that even his devoted students did not follow him there.

The buildings at the Paraclete were abandoned but soon found another use. The abbot of Saint-Denis claimed the convent of Argenteuil and expelled the nuns. Around 1128, Abelard offered his former hermitage to a group under Héloïse, and they accepted. Soon the convent was so successful that other nunneries placed themselves under Héloïse's jurisdiction, and daughter institutions had to be established to house all the members.

Abelard did not fare as well in Brittany. As at Saint-Denis, his efforts to reform the dissolute monks met with hostility. Twice they tried to poison him; when he learned of a plot to cut his throat, he fled.

Hiding and in despair, Abelard composed *Historia calamitatum* (c. 1132; *The Story of My Misfortunes*, 1922). A copy reaching Héloïse, she promptly wrote to Abelard the first of a brief but poignant series of love letters that reveal how truly she meant her statement in 1118 that she would prefer to be Abelard's mistress than Caesar Augustus' wife.

Though her love had not abated, Abelard's had. "If . . . you have need of my instruction and writings in matters pertaining to God, write to me what you want, so that I may answer as God permits me," he replied to her impassioned lines, urging her to forget their former life together. Ever obedient, preferring Abelard's religious treatises to silence, she requested and received sermons, psalms, biblical exegeses, a rule more suitable for convents than that devised by Benedict for monasteries. As she had inspired Abelard to compose love poetry during their short time together, so now she served as a religious muse.

Abelard's movements in the early 1130's are unclear, but by 1136 he was again teaching in Paris. This return to prominence aroused his enemies, chief among them Bernard of Clairvaux, who saw in Abelard's reliance on reason a challenge to faith. Whether Bernard's extensive letter-writing campaign against Abelard would have succeeded is unclear, but in 1140 Abelard's students challenged Bernard to debate their master at an assembly at Sens. Bernard at first refused, knowing that he was no match for the *Rhinoceros indomitus*. Bernard's supporters insisted that he attend, however, and he finally agreed.

Yet he had no intention of engaging Abelard in any intellectual combat. On the day before the scheduled encounter, Bernard persuaded the gathered religious leaders to condemn Abelard unheard; when Abelard entered the church of Saint-Étienne on June 3, 1140, Bernard began reading out a list of seventeen charges of heresy. Realizing that he was facing a trial, not a debate, Abelard immediately stopped the proceedings by appealing to Rome for judgment. He then left the church, intending to plead his case before the pope.

Bernard's letters moved faster than the aging Abelard, however, and Pope Innocent II owed his tiara to Bernard. At the abbey of Cluny, Abelard learned that Rome had confirmed Bernard's verdict, and the local abbot, Peter the Venerable, now urged Abelard to make peace with his old antagonist. Although Abelard consented, the rhinoceros remained unconquered. In *Dialogus inter philosophum, Judaeum et Christianum* (1141-1142; *Dialogue of a Philosopher with a Jew and a Christian*, 1979), he still maintained that unless theologians could use reason, they could not defend their faith.

Abelard composed this treatise at the monastery of Saint-Marcel, near Chalon-sur-Sâone, in Burgundy, where he had gone for his health, and there he died on April 21, 1142. He had asked to be buried at the Paraclete, and so he was. Twenty-two years later, Héloïse was laid to rest beside him. According to a chronicler, as her body was lowered into the grave, Abelard reached up to embrace his wife. Over the centuries their bodies were moved several times, but they now lie in the famous Père-Lachaise cemetery in Paris beneath the inscription, "ABELARD: HELOISE—For Ever One."

Summary

In his epitaph for Abelard, Peter the Venerable called his friend "the Socrates of the Gauls, the great Plato of the West, *our* Aristotle." Yet Abelard was neither a secular philosopher nor a religious skeptic. As he wrote in his *Apologia* (c. 1141), "I do not wish to be a philosopher by dissociating myself from Paul; I do not wish to be an Aristotle by separating myself from Christ, since there is no other name under heaven by which I can be saved."

While Bernard was wrong to view Abelard as a heretic, he was right to see Abelard as a threat to the old order. Abelard's popularity as a teacher helped create the university system, which spelled the end of the power of monastic schools. His fusion of logic and theology fostered a new scholasticism that was spread by his students, who included three future popes and the greatest classicist of the twelfth century, John of Salisbury. His manuscripts contributed to the era's intellectual renaissance.

Abelard is best remembered, however, for his association with Héloïse; over the centuries writers have found in their story an inspiration for poems, plays, and novels. A strange new twist to that famous story was introduced in the 1980's, when a computer-assisted stylistic analysis of the correspondence between Abelard and Héloïse suggested that all the letters, including those attributed to Héloïse, were in fact written by Abelard himself. Thus the possibility exists that Abelard was not only a philosopher but also, in a peculiar way, a gifted writer of fiction.

Bibliography

Abelard, Peter. *Abelard and Heloise: The Story of His Misfortunes and the Personal Letters*. Translated by Betty Radice. London: Folio Society, 1977. Abelard's account of his life and his and Héloïse's letters are available in many translations. These provide primary information about Abelard's life from his birth until around 1132.

Grane, Leif. *Peter Abelard: Philosophy and Christianity in the Middle Ages*. Translated by Frederick Crowley and Christine Crowley. New York: Harcourt, Brace and World, 1970. An excellent survey of Abelard's life set against the history, religion, and philosophy of the twelfth century. Chapter 5 neatly summarizes Abelard's views on metaphysics and religion.

Lloyd, Roger Bradshaigh. *The Stricken Lute: An Account of the Life of Peter Abelard*. London: L. Dickson, 1932. A readable biography that touches lightly on Abelard's philosophy. Stresses Abelard's modernity.

Luscombe, David Edward. *The School of Abelard: The Influence of Abelard's Thought in the Early Scholastic Period*. Cambridge: Cambridge University Press, 1969. According to the preface, "this book represents an historian's attempt to discern the ways in which Abelard's thought reached and influenced his contemporaries and successors." Drawing on a variety of sources, especially Abelard's manuscripts and the writings of his pupils, Luscombe concludes, "Abelard . . . was a major and continuing stimulus to debate and thought." A twenty-eight-page bibliography of works by and about Abelard attests the truth of this assertion.

Sikes, Jeffrey Garrett. *Peter Abelard*. Cambridge: Cambridge University Press, 1932. A scholarly and, despite its age, a most authoritative biography. Much attention is given to Abelard's views on religious and philosophical matters.

Worthington, Marjorie. *The Immortal Lovers: Heloise and Abelard*. Garden City, N.Y.: Doubleday and Co., 1960. A popular, well-written biography of the two lovers. Contains extensive quotations from *The Story of My Misfortunes* and the letters as well as novelistic re-creations of various episodes. Good on the twelfth century background.

Joseph Rosenblum

ABRAHAM

Born: c. 2050 B.C.; Ur, Chaldea
Died: c. 1950 B.C.; Macpelah, Mesopotamia
Area of Achievement: Religion
Contribution: According to Hebrew tradition and biblical record, Abraham is the ancient ancestor of the people of Israel to whom God first promised territory, nationhood, and spiritual blessing. He is therefore the key patriarch in the history of Judaism and of extreme importance as well to the development of both Christianity and Islam.

Early Life
The only historical record of the life of Abraham is found in the Pentateuch, the first five books of the Old Testament, one of the two divisions of the Bible whose composition is traditionally attributed to Moses. The full story of Abraham's life is contained in Genesis 11:27-25:11, though there are references to Abraham's life scattered throughout the rest of the Bible. The dating of Abraham's birth and early life is primarily informed guesswork, but archaeological consensus is that Abraham was born sometime around the twentieth century B.C. His father is identified as Terah in the biblical genealogy (Genesis 11:27); evidently, Terah was a wealthy man who owned property and livestock and who worshipped the pagan gods of Chaldea. Chaldea, the ancient name for Babylonia, was a center of advanced culture and commerce in antiquity, and it is quite likely that Abraham was a highly educated, cosmopolitan citizen of this society, himself no doubt wealthy. Some archaeologists contend that it is possible that Abraham left written records of his journey to the ancient Near East that were incorporated into the Pentateuch. Most modern scholars accept the substantial historicity of these narratives.

The biblical record introduces Abraham as "Abram," which means "father" in Hebrew; later in the narrative, Abram will be renamed as the better known "Abraham," which means "father of many." Abram is called by God to leave his father's house in Ur to journey to a land that God promises to him and his descendants. There is no indication in the narrative that Abram had been chosen for any particular merit or religious devotion, though later Old and New Testament writings present him as the archetypal man of faith, who serves as an example to all of the power of belief in God's sovereignty. Accompanying him on the journey are his wife, Sarah, and nephew Lot, and their families.

Most startling in this sequence of events is Abraham's willingness to abandon the pagan deities of his family to embrace a seemingly new God—and thus become a declared monotheist in a decidedly polytheistic and pagan antiquity. The next episodes reported in the life of Abram trace his growing acceptance of this unique belief and center on his journey to Canaan, the land promised to him. His path takes him and his traveling companions through Egypt and the surrounding nations. In Egypt, Abram fears that his beautiful wife will be taken from him, so he claims that she is his sister and thus attempts to deceive Pharaoh and his princes. When God reveals her true identity to the Egyptian monarch, Pharaoh orders Abram and his entourage to leave. Upon leaving Egypt, Abram and his nephew decide to go their separate ways, Lot choosing the fertile land of Sodom and Gomorrah for settlement and Abram the northern country of Hebron. These choices become fateful in the lineage of both men.

Life's Work

The life of Abraham as it unfolds in the book of Genesis encompasses the fulfillment of the promises God had announced to him before he left Ur. Important in the light of the birth of modern Israel is the fact that the land promised to Abraham is quite explicitly identified in the biblical record: God promises Abraham and his descendants possession of the whole land from the Euphrates River southwestward, an area, in fact, larger than the land area occupied by Israel since World War II.

The three most important episodes recounted in Genesis involve Abraham's attempt to secure an heir to receive the inheritance of God's promises, the institution of the covenant between God and Abraham sealed with the act of circumcision, and the judgment and destruction of the cities of Sodom and Gomorrah—Lot's new homeland—because of their rampant rebellion and decadence. It is in these episodes that the character of Abraham as a man of faith as well as of action is established and becomes the pattern for later biblical and traditional portraits of his heroism and trust.

Soon after he and Lot part company, Abram is called upon to rescue Lot; in so doing he proves himself both a good military strategist and also a devout, unselfish believer. Lot has found himself the captive of rival kings who have plundered the cities of Sodom and Gomorrah. Abram raises an army and, in saving Lot, also manages to recover all of his lost possessions and captured kinsmen. In returning from these exploits, Abram encounters the mysterious King of Salem, Melchizadek, who pronounces a blessing upon Abram for his faith and his canny defeat of the treacherous armies in the land about him. Melchizadek is also a priest of "the God Most High," or "Yahweh," the same God who has called Abraham out of Ur to a special blessing. Abram pays a tithe to Melchizadek, and, when the King of Salem praises him, Abram defers the praise to God, who had blessed him with victory.

The promises to Abraham in Genesis 12 were intended to foreshadow the tapestry of events in his life and in Genesis 15 God reiterates them as Abram continues his quest for the land. He becomes skeptical and impatient of the likelihood of their fulfillment, however, given that he is still childless because of Sarah's barrenness. Nevertheless, God renews His promise to Abram that his offspring will be as numerous as the stars in the sky and that the land and nation promised to him will indeed come to his descendants if he will only continue to trust. Thereafter, Abram is called Abraham by God, indicating the surety of His promises that he will be the father of many nations. Reluctant to wait for God's timing, Abram proceeds to father a son by Hagar, his maidservant. This son, named Ishmael, is rejected by God; Abraham is instead exhorted to await the rightful heir with patience and confidence. In Genesis 17, the covenant between God and Abraham is proclaimed once more and God asks Abraham and all the males of his household to be circumcised as a sign of their commitment to the covenant. The act of circumcision is ever after a peculiar sign of God's presence with the Hebrew people, not merely a hygienic practice but a religious symbol of dramatic proportion to every Hebrew family of God's blessing as well.

In the midst of Abraham's tribulations, he receives word that Lot's city, Sodom, will be destroyed along with Gomorrah because of its wickedness. In a famous conversation, Abraham bargains with God over the city, pleading with Him to spare the cities if He can find even ten righteous men. He cannot, and the cities are destroyed, with Lot and his family spared. On their way out of the destruction, however, Lot's wife—against the direct command of God—looks back at the fallen cities and is turned into a pillar of salt.

Because of their faith and righteousness, Abraham and Sarah are blessed with the birth of a son, Isaac—whose name meant "laughter," a reference to Sarah's incredulity at becoming pregnant at the age of one hundred. Some years later, Abraham faces the final test of faith in his life when God calls upon him to sacrifice his son. Obedient to the end, Abraham and Isaac make the long trek to an altar far from their camp where Abraham once sacrificed animals. As he prepares to offer his son, he ties Isaac down and raises his knife, about to end the boy's life. Just before the knife is plunged into Abraham's only heir, God calls upon Abraham to stop for his faith has been shown to be full and unyielding. Because of his obedient heart, God promises him once more that he will have descendants as numerous as the sand at the seashore.

Abraham eventually outlives Sarah and is blessed to see Isaac's marriage to Rebekah. Isaac and Rebekah later become the parents of Jacob and Esau, and the historical saga of Israel's development as a nation under the governance of God is initiated, a fulfillment of a divine promise to the itinerant man from Ur.

Summary

It is difficult to overestimate the impact of the life of Abraham on Hebrew culture both in the ancient and medieval world and in the modern world. His acceptance of belief in one, true God, and its implications, sets him apart in the history of religions common to his time and place. It is the name of this God (Yahweh) that Moses, the champion of Israel's flight from Egyptian captivity, invokes in confronting Pharaoh and in leading his people from bondage. Further, the promises made by the God of the Old Testament to Abraham have remained a part of the political and social history of the land of Israel even to this day and have played an essential part in the formation of modern Israel after World War II. To be a Jew is to trace one's ancestry back to Abraham and his sons, Isaac and Jacob. To adherents of Judaism, Abraham is the quintessential man of success, faith, and loyalty whose stature overshadows nearly every other ancient Hebrew notable except Moses.

Further, Abraham's character as a man of trust and perseverance has heavily influenced both Christianity and Islam to the extent that both faiths regard the biblical record of Abraham as the starting point for their own systems of doctrine. Jesus Christ, according to the New Testament, claimed to be a descendant of Abraham—basing His teaching on the authority that this heritage bestowed upon Him—while at the same time claiming that His own life, as the eternal Son of God, is in fulfillment of God's promise to Abraham that He would bless all nations through him and his descendants. Paul, the Christian convert who wrote most of the letters of the New Testament, cites Abraham as the man who exemplifies commitment and truth for Christianity, a man who was counted "righteous" not because of his works but because of his faith. Muhammad, the prophet of Islam, claimed Abraham as his forerunner as well, proclaiming that he and his message stood in the same historical and intellectual genealogy as Abraham's.

The story of Abraham's willingness to sacrifice his own son in response to the call of God has long interested artists and storytellers; in the modern age, it has come to be emblematic of the piercing moment of destiny and decision-making in an individual's life when he must make a choice that will set the pattern for the rest of his life. Abraham thus comes to represent to Jew and non-Jew alike the epitome of the "righteous man," one who takes a stand in the midst of turmoil, doubt, and confusion for the side of justice, equality, and fairness. His covenant with God and his faithfulness animate inhabitants of both Western and Eastern cultures in their quest for security and hope in a troubled world.

Bibliography
Albright, W. F. *The Archaeology of Palestine*. New York: Penguin Books, 1963. This is a standard work on the archaeology of the ancient world that remains the most comprehensive and informed overview of the historical data gleaned from the ancient world. Overall, it provides the reader with an authentic sense of the world from which Abraham came and the one to which he traveled.

Alexander, David, and Pat Alexander, eds. *Eerdmans' Handbook to the Bible*. Grand Rapids, Mich.: Wm. B. Eerdmans, 1973. This is a comprehensive handbook to biblical history and geography with helpful charts and maps that trace Abraham's journey and illuminate the specific episodes in his life drawn from the biblical text for the lay reader.

Bright, John. *A History of Israel*. Philadelphia: Westminster Press, 1975. Bright's study is probably the most thorough and compelling nontheological treatment of the history of Israel in print. Includes sections on the world of the patriarchs, ancient Chaldea, Egypt, and Israel that enlighten the story of Abraham and sustain the interest of both the common reader and the scholar with helpful "anecdotal" commentary on life in ancient times.

Harrison, R. K. *An Introduction to the Old Testament*. Grand Rapids, Mich.: Wm. B. Eerdmans, 1972. Harrison provides a complete overview of the origin, message, and impact of each book of the Old Testament which speaks directly and comprehensively to the issues of the chronology, authenticity, and influence of the life of Abraham. A comprehensive scholarly work with extensive documentation.

Kidner, Derek. *Genesis*. Downers Grove, Ill.: Inter-Varsity Press, 1968. A helpful one-volume commentary on the key biblical book containing the narratives regarding Abraham, this volume provides useful insights into what might be called the "psychology" of Abraham's call and journey to Canaan.

Kitchen, K. A. *Ancient Orient and Old Testament*. Downers Grove, Ill.: Inter-Varsity Press, 1966. An insider's look at the world of archaeology and how it functions in validating ancient records and narratives, this work is particularly helpful in its extensive tracing of the various stops in the journey of Abraham to the promised land against the backdrop of the patriarchal age.

Schultz, Samuel J. *The Old Testament Speaks*. New York: Harper and Row, Publishers, 1970. Written for the lay reader, this cogent and lucid volume presents an objective, historical analysis of the lives of the patriarchs—including a major section on Abraham—and other characters in the evolution of ancient Israel and suggests their relevance to the study of both Christianity and Islam.

Thompson, J. A. *Handbook to Life in Bible Times*. Downers Grove, Ill.: Inter-Varsity Press, 1986. A colorful, lavishly illustrated reference tool with key sections on the domestic life, travel, family customs, and cultural preoccupations of the biblical world; this work illuminates the life and times of a person living in twentieth century B.C. and thus is a helpful contextualizing volume for a study of Abraham.

Bruce L. Edwards

ABU HANIFAH

Born: c. 699; Kufa, Iraq
Died: 767; Baghdad, Iraq
Areas of Achievement: Law and religion
Contribution: Abu Hanifah, celebrated eighth century Muslim jurist and theologian, was the founder of the first of four orthodox schools of Islamic law, the Hanifite. His brilliant use of reason and his gift for systematic thought provided Muslim civilization with a coherent and applicable system of law.

Early Life

Abu Hanifah Al-Nu 'Man ibn Thabit was born in the city of Kufa, in what is now Iraq, around the year 699. Though some traditions assert that he was descended from Persian royalty, the more likely genealogy is Afghan. It seems that his grandfather, Zuta, was brought as a slave from Kabul, Afghanistan, to Kufa. Zuta came into the possession of the prominent Taym-Allah ibn Tha'laba family. For unknown reasons, Zuta was set free. He and his descendants, however, remained clients (*mawla*) of the Tha'laba family. Though born into the non-Arab or client class of Muslims in Kufa, Abu Hanifah was no stranger to wealth. His father, like the Prophet Muhammad, was a successful merchant. Abu Hanifah followed in his father's footsteps and won fame as a silk trader and cloth manufacturer. Like Muhammad, the merchant Abu Hanifah won a reputation for his honesty and generosity. Abu Hanifah endowed scholarships for needy students and shared liberally with the poor.

Economic prosperity enabled Abu Hanifah to turn from business to scholarship. That was a sound choice. With a sharp wit, a facile tongue, and a logical mind, Abu Hanifah was well fitted for the world of letters. For a while, he pursued the study of theology. His primary interest, nurtured while he was yet a merchant, was the problem of equity, establishing norms for a network of right or just relationships between human beings. As a devout Muslim, Abu Hanifah believed that ethical and legal norms were given by God through divine revelation, the Koran. On the basis of the Koran and the Hadith (a compendium of Islamic traditions), theologians, philosophers, and jurists developed rules for just living. Abu Hanifah thus turned his energies to the sacred law (Shari'a). Living, as he did, in one of the great intellectual centers of the medieval Arab world, he was able to study with a number of noted jurists, including 'Ata' (who died around 732) and Ja'far al-Sadiq (who died in 765), the founder of Shi'ite law (the minority or dissenting tradition in Islam, as opposed to the Sunni, the majority persuasion). For eighteen years, Abu Hanifah worked with one of the most brilliant of all Muslim jurists, Hammad ibn Ali Sulayman.

Abu Hanifah's students remembered their master as a tall, stately man of very impressive appearance. His demeanor was serious. Abu Hanifah had the bearing of a scholar, and an air of piety permeated his every act. He was respected as a man of firm conviction, reasoned conclusions, uncompromising integrity, and determined opinions. Because Abu Hanifah had independent means, he was not in need of royal, private, or religious patronage. His wealth gave him the freedom to exercise his native virtues of fearlessness, independence, and total disregard for the opinions and rewards of the world.

Life's Work

Upon the death of his mentor, Hammad, in 738, Abu Hanifah emerged as the leading legal thinker in Kufa and in much of the Muslim world. Because of his personal wealth, he was able to devote himself entirely to teaching and research. Under no necessity to accept either private donations or governmental appointment, Abu Hanifah had complete academic freedom. This financial security and his love of independence may explain, in part, why one of Islam's most eminent jurists never sat on the bench as a *kadi* (judge). Like the Greek philosopher Plato, who established his own Academy, Abu Hanifah attracted his own students. Relatively free of governmental pressures and of the burdens of a practicing attorney, Abu Hanifah could concentrate on the theoretical foundations of Muslim law.

In his teaching, Abu Hanifah relied heavily on dialectic, lectures, and discussions with his disciples. Like Socrates, he is said to have written little (indeed, nothing survives from his pen). His teachings, however, were copiously recorded by his students, among whom were his son Hammad and his grandson Isma'il (both of whom eventually became distinguished jurists); other disciples included such eminent thinkers as Abu Yusuf and ali-Shayhant. Abu Hanifah's principal achievement as a teacher was twofold: He was the founder of the systematic study of Islamic law, and he was also the founder of a particular school of jurisprudence, one named in his honor—the Hanifite school.

As a jurist, Abu Hanifah employed a variety of sources. He was able to draw on his own rich experience as a merchant, a man of practical affairs. Reflected in his thought are his extensive travels in the Muslim world. As one familiar with the many levels of a complex and sophisticated society, Abu Hanifah could discuss conditions of places as varied as the royal court, the slave market, and the business bazaar. In his formal legal work, Abu Hanifah, as an orthodox Muslim, accepted two primary sources for Islamic law: the divine revelation, written in the Holy Koran and given by God through the Prophet Muhammad, and the human tradition, reported in the Hadith, the sayings passed down by the Muslim community from the time of Muhammad. The relationship of Koran and Hadith was similar to that of Torah and Talmud in Judaism, for God spoke in the Koran to man's conscience and in the Hadith to human intelligence. Abu Hanifah, however, recognized the need for interpretation of these given authorities; for that reason, he was inclined to accept other authorities. Perhaps these were in a very real sense "secondary" to the primary sources, but since Muslim survival required interpretation and adaptation, the supplementary means became crucial in his thinking. Abu Hanifah allowed personal interpretation on the part of the jurist. As the one closest to the case, the judge had to trust his own intelligence and instincts, experience and evaluation. Believing all truths to be ultimately related (a corollary of the belief that God is one), Abu Hanifah also permitted argument by analogy and reasoning from the known to the unknown (by means of comparison and contrast). As a legal thinker, Abu Hanifah also permitted the notion of consensus, the consideration of the majority opinion of the Muslim world. Some dispute later arose regarding how Abu Hanifah intended such a consensus to be determined: Was it the majority opinion of the jurists, the educated classes, or the masses of Islam? Apparently, Abu Hanifah was envisioning an implicit agreement among the intellectual elite of Islam, both past and present.

The major problem that Abu Hanifah faced as a jurist was the growing complexity and confusion of Islamic law in his generation. For a century and a half, Islamic law had developed unsystematically, without clear direction or a discernment of underlying fundamental principles. Individual lawyers and judges had argued on the basis of specific situations and particular cases; the result was that conflicting verdicts were being offered in various parts of the Muslim world. Amid this cacophony of variant opinions, it was often impossible to arrive at either fundamental principles or clear lines of direction for the law in the future. Abu Hanifah's great contribution—one that was revolutionary in its implications—was to approach the law not situationally but systematically. Many jurists had looked at particulars; Abu Hanifah determined to find principles. Sifting through the vast legal writings of his time, Abu Hanifah sought universal norms and standards that would be applicable regardless of time or place. By reviewing the problems that had previously been faced by Muslim jurists, Abu Hanifah also tried to anticipate what cases might arise next and to speculate as to the proper approach to be followed.

In his work as a legal theoretician, Abu Hanifah evolved several main principles. First, the law was to be studied systematically rather than situationally, rationally rather than empirically, abstractly rather than concretely. The purpose of such a study was to locate, beneath the welter of contradictory decisions and traditions, the unifying principles of Islamic justice. Second, at all times, Abu Hanifah looked for the way of moderation or the *via media* between extreme positions; like the legal sage of ancient China, Confucius, Abu Hanifah held to the philosophy of the Golden Mean. Third, Abu Hanifah permitted the use of natural law, the findings of reason based on the physical and social sciences; this approach, as ancient as the Greek philosopher Aristotle, allowed material not covered in the Koran or the Hadith to be employed in court. God, Abu Hanifah believed, was the author of two books: nature, as the Creator, and the Koran, as the Revealer. Fourth, Abu Hanifah put a balanced emphasis on various tests of truth. One was coherence, or internal logic, another was consistency with other known truth, and a final was consequence, or the implications of an action or decision. Finally, as a rationalist, Abu Hanifah trusted the role and rule of reason in all matters not resolved by the Koran or the Hadith. In this respect, he was similar to the emperor Justinian I, the systematizer of Roman law, and to Aristotle, the father of Greek philosophy and science. For Abu Hanifah, the law was not simply a matter of external relationships between persons but also an issue of internal integrity (within the mind of the judge).

The work of Abu Hanifah within his lifetime was recognized as superior to that of his contemporaries in four respects. First, he made the law wider than had been the case in existing codes; it became not only more broadly based but also more universally applicable. Second, Abu Hanifah made the law deeper, firmly grounding it in the judge's reason and experience and the Muslim intellectual community's interpretation of Scripture, tradition, and nature. Third, Abu Hanifah made the law higher: No longer accidental and incidental, it had become intensely cerebral, theoretical, refined, and technical. Finally, the law had become narrower, for it now rested on universal moral principles, applied through a rigorous process of reasoning.

Because of his brilliant intellect, Abu Hanifah also influenced the development of Muslim theology. As a philosophical theologian, Abu Hanifah inclined toward a movement in his time that was named Murji'ism. This tendency emphasized the universal community of Islam, upholding the unity of the fellowship (*umma*) against divisive or sectarian movements. It focused on the confessional character of Islam as opposed to moralistic definitions; Islam was envisioned as the public confession of certain cardinal doctrines (God, revelation, prophecy) rather than a society composed of ethically perfect persons. Moreover, the community was seen as inclusive: If one professes the true faith, his actions, even his moral failures, cannot sever him from the Muslim nation. In these respects, Abu Hanifah was an advocate of Muslim ecumenism and inclusivism.

Apparently, Abu Hanifah tried to avoid political involvement. His century was a time of dynastic upheaval in the Muslim world. There was a growing difference of opinion as to whether the Muslim community should be led by a direct descendant of the Prophet Muhammad (the opinion of the Shi'ites, or partisans of 'Ali, Muhammad's son-in-law) or by a caliph, a successor chosen from among the majority party (the Sunnis) in Islam. Two rival caliphates came into existence, the Umayyads (after 750 exiled to Spain) and the 'Abbasids (established in Baghdad). It seems likely that Abu Hanifah had contempt for both the Umayyads and the 'Abbasids. In spite of his attempted neutrality, he was arrested and imprisoned. The circumstances surrounding his death are not clear. One account insists that the 'Abbasid caliph al-Mansur (or possibly the Umayyad governor of Kufa) asked Abu Hanifah to accept appointment as a judge; upon his refusal, the jurist was flogged and imprisoned. Another version contends that Abu Hanifah's family sympathized with the followers of 'Ali (a tradition states that " 'Ali blessed his father and his descendants"). In any case, it is known that Abu Hanifah died in Baghdad, Iraq, in 767, either while still in prison or shortly after his release. His tomb, surmounted by a lovely dome erected by admirers in 1066, is still a shrine for pilgrims.

Summary

Islamic law, along with that of the Romans and the Anglo-Saxons, is one of the great systems of human jurisprudence. The Hanifite school founded by Abu Hanifah was the earliest, and became the most widespread, of the four schools of orthodox (Sunni) Islamic law. An appealing system of justice, it has been influential in India, Pakistan, Turkey, China, Central Asia, and much of the Arab world. With a concern for equity as the chief goal of law, it has given the judge latitude to exercise private opinion (*ra'y*) and to draw on natural law. Regarded as the most liberal or tolerant of the Islamic legal systems, it stands in opposition to the position of the Hanbalite school (the more fundamentalist persuasion, represented by the Wahhabis of Saudi Arabia, who accept only the Koran and the Hadith as sources of Muslim law). It is also a more moderate system than the other two schools of Islamic law— the Malikite (prevailing in parts of North Africa) and the Shafite (influential in Egypt, Indonesia, and sections of Africa). As the pathfinder of Muslim law, Abu Hanifah ranks as one of the great jurists of Arab civilization and one of the major legal philosophers of the entire human community.

Bibliography

Boer, Tjitze J. de. *The History of Philosophy in Islam*. Translated by Edward R. Jones. 2d ed. New York: Dover Publications, 1967. This is a standard though older survey (the first edition was published in 1903); it is still useful for placing Abu Hanifah in context.

Coulson, Noel J. *A History of Islamic Law*. Edinburgh: Edinburgh University Press, 1964. Coulson has assembled a helpful survey of Muslim legal thinking as part of Edinburgh University Press's Islamic studies series. Includes a bibliography.

Fyzee, Asaf Ali Asghar. *Outlines of Muhammadan Law*. 3d ed. London: Oxford University Press, 1964. In spite of the obsolete word "Muhammadan" in its title, this volume is useful as a comprehensive study of Islamic jurisprudence.

Savory, R. M., ed. *Introduction to Islamic Civilization*. Cambridge: Cambridge University Press, 1976. A succinct overview for the beginner; this text has chapters on religion, art, history, science, and law.

Schacht, Joseph. *An Introduction to Islamic Law*. Oxford: Clarendon Press, 1964. This volume provides a critical analysis of Islamic legal concepts and precepts. Because of its approach, some devout Muslims have found it offensive.

——————. *The Origins of Muhammadan Jurisprudence*. Oxford: Clarendon Press, 1950. This is a thoughtful study by a well-respected Western scholar who has edited and translated numerous works on Islamic law. Includes a bibliography.

Watt, William Montgomery. *Islamic Philosophy and Theology: An Extended Survey*. 2d ed. Edinburgh: Edinburgh University Press, 1985. A brilliant study by one of the most celebrated of Occidental authorities, this work places Abu Hanifah within the mainstream of Muslim thought.

——————. *Islamic Political Thought: The Basic Concepts*. Edinburgh: Edinburgh University Press, 1980. In this book, the noted British scholar introduces the fundamental principles of Muslim thought in terms understandable to Western readers.

Wensinck, Arent Jan. *The Muslim Creed: Its Genesis and Historical Development*. Cambridge: Cambridge University Press, 1932. Though an older work, this text is still a useful survey of the evolution of the complex of Muslim theology-philosophy-law.

Williams, John Alden, ed. *Islam*. New York: George Braziller, 1961. This readily accessible anthology is helpful for the beginning student of Muslim thought and life. Includes a bibliography.

C. George Fry

ABUL WEFA

Born: June 10, 940; either Buzshan, Khorasan Province, or Buzadhan, Kuhistan Province, Iran
Died: July 1, 998; Baghdad
Areas of Achievement: Mathematics and astronomy
Contribution: Abul Wefa played a major role in the development of sines and cosines as they apply to the field of trigonometry. These he used to correct astronomical calculations carried forward from classical into Islamic times.

Early Life

Born in 940, during the reign of the 'Abbasid caliph al-Mutaqqi, Abul Wefa lived during a period of extraordinary cultural and intellectual productivity. His own fields of accomplishment, mathematics and astronomy, were already widely recognized as essential elements of high Islamic civilization. Very little seems to be known about Abul Wefa's early life. Apparently, his early education in mathematics occurred under the tutelage of two uncles, one of whom (Abu Amr al-Mughazili) had received formal training from the famous geometricians Abu Yahya Al-Marwazi and Abu'l Ala ibn Karnib.

Whatever the possible source of patronage for the young man's further education may have been, his decision to move to Baghdad at the age of nineteen (in 959) greatly benefited the 'Abbasid court. Baghdad at this time was politically troubled, following the seizure of *de facto* control by a military clique headed by the Persian Buyid emirs; thereafter, the Buyids dominated the house of the caliphs until their fall from power in 1055. The Buyids were inclined to favor talented Persians who were drawn toward scholarly circles in the center of the empire. It is reported, for example, that it was Abul Wefa, himself then forty years of age and well established (circa 980), who introduced the Persian scholar and philosopher Abu Hayyan al-Tawhidi into the Baghdad entourage of the vizier Ibn Sa'dan. Abu Hayyan soon became famous under the vizier's patronage, composing a major work, *al-Imta' wa'l mu'anasa* (a collection of notes drawn from philosophical and literary "salon" meetings), under a dedication to Ibn Sa'dan.

Patronage for Abul Wefa's work in courtly circles, however, must have come from a different milieu, that of the so-called Baghdad School. This scientific assembly flourished in the 'Abbasid capital in the last century before its conquest by the Seljuk Turks in 1055. According to some historians, patronage for the natural sciences in particular came precisely during the period in which Abul Wefa passed into the main stages of his scholarly career. The Buyid emir Adud al-Dawlah (978-983) had nurtured an interest in astronomy through his own studies. He passed this interest on to his son,

Saraf al-Dawlah, who built an observatory next to his palace and called scholars from all regions of the empire to glorify the reputation of his reign by carrying out scientific experiments. Abul Wefa was among this group.

Life's Work

The environment for learning in the Baghdad School, with its circle of eminent Islamic scientists, may explain how the young Persian scholar mastered so many technical fields in such a limited period of time. Beyond mere speculation regarding Abul Wefa's early personal contacts, however, one must consider the importance of translation work in the Baghdad School. Abul Wefa himself translated the work of the Greek algebraist Diophantus (fl. c. A.D. 250), who had explored the field of indeterminate algebraic equations. Abul Wefa was also known for his studies of, and commentaries on, Euclid. There are, however, no surviving texts to indicate what use he made of the work of these two forerunners from the classical pre-Islamic period.

By contrast, Abul Wefa's attention to the work of the second century Greek astronomer Ptolemy not only contributed to the preservation and transmission to the medieval West of the classical knowledge contained in Ptolemy's *Mathēmatikē suntaxis* (c. A.D. 150; *Almagest*) but also earned for him an original and lasting reputation as an Islamic mathematician. The *Almagest* examined the field of trigonometry, which proposed mathematical relationships in terms of the angles and sides of right triangles. This called for the development of sines, or systematic relationships defined in a right triangle working from one of the acute angles, symbolically represented as A. Modern trigonometry expresses this relationship as $\sin A = a/c$, or $\sin A$ is equal to the ratio of the length of the side opposite that angle (a) to the length of the hypotenuse (c).

Ptolemy, in pioneering the field of spherical trigonometry, had laid down an approximate method for calculating sines (which he described as "chords"). Abul Wefa, however, drew on his studies of Indian precedents in the field of trigonometry that were unknown to Ptolemy, as well as models provided by Abul Wefa's predecessor al-Battani (858-929), to perfect Ptolemy's chords. This was done by applying algebraic, instead of geometric, methods of systematizing the sines. In particular, Abul Wefa's development of the "half-chord" made it possible to achieve much more precise measurements that would eventually be used in surveying and navigation. The most immediate application of his tables of sines, however, was in the field of astronomy.

One of Abul Wefa's contributions which left a legacy that lasted for many centuries involved the study of evection, or irregularity, in the longitude of the moon. Later European commentators, including Louis Pierre E. A. Sédillot in the nineteenth century, looked at the Islamic astronomer's work and concluded that he, not Tycho Brahe (1546-1601), had been the first scientist to posit the theory of the "third inequality of the moon." Although this theory was later proved to be erroneous, the debate at least drew attention to the importance of Abul Wefa's originality in the field.

Abul Wefa himself compiled, in addition to his well-known tables of sines, a book of astronomical tables entitled *Zij al-wadih* (that which is clear). Like his earlier work on sines, this text is not extant in the original. Scholars tend to agree, however, that certain anonymous manuscripts preserved in European libraries, such as the *Zij al-shamil*, are taken from Abul Wefa's work.

Works that have survived and that have been at least partially translated include a book of arithmetic entitled *Kitab fi ma yahtaj ilayh al-kuttab wa l-'ummal min 'ilm al-hisab* (961-976; book on what is necessary from the science—of arithmetic for scribes and businessmen), the *Kitab fi ma yahtaj ilayh al-sani 'min al-a'mal al-handasiyha* (after 990; book on what is necessary from geometric construction for the artisan), and a book entitled *Kitab al-kamil* (translated by Carra de Vaux in the *Journal Asiatique* of 1892). It is thought that Abul Wefa may have still been in Baghdad at the time of his death in 998.

Summary

Study of the Islamic cultural milieu in which Abul Wefa lived suggests a high level of syncretic interaction between ethnic subjects of the Baghdad Caliphate—Arab, Persian, Greek, or other minorities. Abul Wefa's own career seems also to provide an example of a syncretic social hierarchy. Scientists and intellectual figures, it seems, had no reason to doubt that their accomplishments would be appreciated and supported by a ruling military elite whose social status was obviously determined by very different criteria. In this rather cosmopolitan period in Islamic history, there was room not only for scholars of diverse national origins at the caliph's court but also for representatives of different disciplines, secular and religious, to live side by side in a community that was truly representative of a world civilization. One can only understand the flourishing in Islam of such different disciplines (and the pure sciences in particular), however, if attention is given to the multiplicity of pre-Islamic sources that contributed both to the Baghdad Caliphate itself and to the highly developed cultural institutions that it supported.

Bibliography

Bell, Eric T. *The Development of Mathematics*. New York: McGraw-Hill Book Co., 1945. Begins with a historical review of the field of mathematics from the first known texts through successive stages of discoveries, ending at mid-point in the twentieth century. The chapter which is of most interest to students of Islamic science is entitled "Detour Through India, Arabia, and Spain, 400-1300." This title underscores the importance of the medieval period of Oriental history for the conservation of classical Western sources which only returned to Europe via the Islamic core zone, from eastern Iran to Spain.

Cajori, Florian. *A History of Mathematics*. New York: Macmillan, 1931. This rather dated work has several important characteristics which merit mention. It covers not only standard non-Western mathematical traditions (Hindu and Islamic) but also traditions from little-studied areas such as Mayan Central America and Japan. Cajori also manages to give detailed information on individual mathematicians' original findings while keeping information on a sufficiently comprehensible level for the layman.

Kennedy, E. S., ed. *Studies in the Islamic Exact Sciences*. Beirut, Lebanon: American University of Beirut Press, 1983. Provides a rather technical treatment of several scientific disciplines that flourished in early Islamic times, including the development, through trigonometry, of accurate astronomical calculations. A specific elaboration of Abul Wefa's work is included in this collection of essays, but the prospective reader should be aware that a substantial background in mathematics will be necessary to follow stage-by-stage explanations.

Nasr, Seyyed Hossein. *Islamic Science: An Illustrated Survey*. London: World of Islam Festival, 1976. A carefully researched photographic record of the tools of Islamic science. Textual treatment of historical figures such as Abul Wefa is more limited than in Nasr's *Science and Civilization in Islam*. The choice of illustrations, however, particularly from Islamic astronomy, is so rich that the field itself becomes a much more coherent entity.

_____. *Science and Civilization in Islam*. Cambridge, Mass.: Harvard University Press, 1968. Because this work deals with the subject of science in Islamic civilization only, it can take time to explore individual contributions at some length.

Byron D. Cannon

ADAM DE LA HALLE

Born: c. 1250; probably Arras, France
Died: c. 1285-1288; Naples, Italy, possibly after 1306, England
Areas of Achievement: Music and literature
Contribution: One of the few medieval musicians who composed both monophonic and polyphonic music, Adam de la Halle produced musical and literary works in virtually every genre of the thirteenth century.

Early Life

With almost no documentary evidence—save a few bits of information here and there in his works—any account of Adam de la Halle's life must be based on educated guesses. More than likely, he was born in the prosperous town of Arras; his name appears variously as Adam d'Arras and Adam le Boscu d'Arras. His name appears most commonly as Adam le Bossu (meaning "Adam the Hunchback"), although in *Le Roi de Secile* (written after 1285), Adam protests that while he might be called a hunchback, he is not one at all. No records reveal the origin of the name; his family may have adopted it to distinguish itself from the other Halle families in Arras. Possibly an illustrious ancestor was a hunchback, and the family retained the appellation.

In another of Adam's works—*Jeu d'Adam ou de la feuillée* (c. 1276-1277)—Adam de la Halle's father is named as a Maistre Henri de la Hale. In *Nécrologe de la Confrérie des jongleurs et de bourgeois d'Arras*, the death of Henri de la Hale's wife was recorded as 1282; the death of a Maistre Henri Bochu was recorded as eight years later, in 1290. Whether these are the composer's parents is unknown. *Nécrologe* also contains references to two women, either of whom could have been Adam's wife: Maroie li Hallee is mentioned in 1274; Maroie Hale in 1287. Given the possibilities for variation in an age when spelling had not been standardized, it would be difficult to choose between these two. Some scholars refer to *Jeu d'Adam* as evidence supporting Maroie Hale; in this work, Adam refers to his wife as still living.

Life's Work

About the rest of Adam's life, most of the clues exist in his work or in commentary about his work. There is circumstantial evidence that he studied in Paris: In *Jeu d'Adam*, he expresses his longing for his student days in Paris; furthermore, his contemporaries often described him as "maistre," indicating that he completed a more rigorous course of study than he might have received in a provincial town. Adam probably returned from Paris sometime around 1270, a date suggested by two facts: He wrote sixteen *jeux-partis* with Jehan Bretel of Arras, who died in 1272, and Bretel referred to him in the contemporaneous *Adan, a moi respondés* as well educated, suggesting that the younger *trouvère* had already undertaken a major part of his training. The *jeux-partis* on which he collaborated with other *trouvères* of Arras—he also wrote one with Jehan de Grivilier—indicate that Adam was a member of the Arras *pui*, a *trouvère* fraternity. As for his marriage, it more than likely took place in the early 1270's. In several poems, Adam speaks of having given up school and friends in order to marry his young wife, to whom he was deeply devoted.

Of Adam's fifty-four monophonic (for one voice only) works, eighteen are *jeux-partis*, on the majority of which he collaborated with other *trouvères*. The form of the *jeu-parti* involves a "questioner" who sings the first musical phrase (and therefore composes the melody) and a "respondent." Adam is the respondent in thirteen of the sixteen *jeux-partis* on which he worked with Jehan Bretel, indicating that the melodies were composed by the older man. This early collaboration was to be an important influence on Adam's musical style. Scholars have noted the strong stylistic similarities between the melody of *Adan, a moi respondés* and the melody composed by Adam for two of his *chansons*, and between other *jeux-partis* and Adam's *chanson*, *De cuer pensieu*. Adam's work shares tonality and range and phrasing with Bretel's, but Adam's melodies are more formal and sophisticated. Adam's other monophonic works, the *chansons*, for the most part remain close to the older courtly tradition of French monophonic song.

Adam de la Halle remained in Arras for only a few years after his return from Paris, and again the evidence is suggestive rather than conclusive. His *Jeu d'Adam* and his *congé*, written at about the same time (c. 1276-1277), are both farewells in which Adam declares his intention to return to Paris to continue his studies. There is some evidence that he intended to leave his adored wife in his father's care, indicating that the absence was not to be a long one; in fact, two later lyrical pieces describe his return and the joy he feels at coming back to his own land.

Jeu d'Adam is a peculiar combination of topical humor and sheer fantasy, written to amuse Adam's friends just before his departure for Paris. Lacking a fully realized plot, the rambunctious play (*jeu* means "game") involves a meeting between certain townsfolk of Arras and a group of fairies on the eve of Pentecost when, traditionally, the shrine of Notre Dame is displayed beneath a *feuillée*, or canopy of green leaves. Much of the play is devoted to humorous allusions to real persons: gluttons, alcoholics, scolding wives, uxorious husbands, a loose woman and her lovers, unethical government clerks (called "bigames") who married more than one woman for financial gain. Even Adam's own family comes in for its share of the burlesque. His father is described as a fat, stingy bigamist who loves alcohol more than anything else. Adam even pretends to be bored with his wife, thus gaining an excuse to detail her charms, which no longer excite him. Buried not too deeply in the songs and games of the play is Adam's occasionally bitter criticism of the class warfare that was destroying the social fabric of Arras.

Structurally the play consists of spoken dialogue, exchanges of songs, dances, games, jokes, and horseplay. Probably written only for the amusement of a select group of friends and acquaintances, the play may have had only one complete performance in Arras.

At some point after his second return to Arras, Adam de la Halle left his native town once more and traveled to Italy, where he entered the service of Robert II, Count of Artois, who was on a diplomatic mission for his uncle, Charles of Anjou, who was to become King Charles II of Naples. Later, Adam joined the entourage of Charles, whom he served during the wars against the Sicilians until Charles died in 1285. During his service either with Robert or with Charles, Adam wrote *Le Jeu de Robin et de Marion* (c. 1282-1283), apparently as a part of the Christmas entertainment for the amusement of expatriate northern French soldiers who were resting between battles.

In its most basic form, the plot of *Le Jeu de Robin et de Marion* describes how the shepherdess, Marion, repulses the amorous advances of a roving knight in favor of her rustic country lover, Robin. The story of a rustic maid desired by both a courtly lover and a country swain appears in dozens of pastoral lyrics popular in Adam's day. What Adam did was to dramatize a conventional story by retaining its framework (names, specific incidents, popular songs connected with the story), adding a fully realized background, and amplifying or manipulating key elements of the narrative, particularly the *bergerie*, a lyric piece describing songs, dances, and games indulged in by shepherds and their loves. The result is a highly entertaining theatrical piece.

Adam's original audience would have recognized the major characters from the courtly pastorals, but would also have been delighted with the realistic details incorporated into the traditional story. The knight takes his rebuff lightly instead of being discomfited; Robin is an amusingly awkward peasant whose affection for Marion is genuine; Marion is a simple lass who is nevertheless resourceful in her handling of the knight's advances. The games incorporated into the action are real games, popular at the time and still played today in some parts of France. Also, the dialogue is natural, even coarse at times.

In addition to his inclusion of naturalistic elements in the familiar plot, Adam added a number of popular songs, dances, and instrumental melodies. Although some of the dances would have been accompanied by singing alone, others were probably performed to the music of bagpipes, horns, and flutes. The sixteen melodies are short and rhythmic, and probably belong to a group of popular courtly melodies called *refrains*.

Among Adam's polyphonic works, the *rondeaux* have excited the most commentary for their characteristics that point ahead to the secularization of polyphonic music in the fourteenth century. Two of these *rondeaux* are typical of the thirteenth century understanding of the *rondeau* form, which at that point in the development of music encompassed virtually all songs with periodically recurring refrains; hence, these two are not true *rondeaux* in the sense that later masters would have recognized. One is a *virelai* (a medieval French song form featuring a refrain before and after each stanza); the other, a *ballade* (a medieval narrative poem, either sung or recited, containing three stanzas and an *envoi*).

Five motets have been conclusively identified as Adam's work; six others are said to be his on the basis of characteristics shared with the genuine motets. Adam's motets are basically conservative, and many include refrains quoted from his other works. The motets whose provenance is uncertain are written in a later style.

What Adam did after Charles's death is open to conjecture, although it is reasonably safe to assume that he never returned to Arras. There are only two pieces of evidence about his movements in later years, and those two are contradictory. The earlier piece is a posthumous tribute to Adam de la Halle, written in 1288 by his nephew, known variously as Jean Madot or Jehanes Mados (who may or may not be the Mados mentioned in *Jeu d'Adam*), who says that Adam left Arras to seek entertainment and company and points out that this action was foolish, since Adam was popular at home. The date of this tribute indicates that Adam died in or before 1288. The confusion comes from an English source from 1306 in which a certain "maistre Adam le Boscu" is listed among the European minstrels who have been engaged to participate in the coronation ceremonies for Edward II in 1307. "Boscu" is an unusual name, especially in conjunction with an Adam who has earned the appellation "maistre." Clearly the possibility exists that Adam did not die in Naples, although the *trouvère* who was invited to England could be a younger member of the same family, even Adam's son.

Summary

Adam de la Halle's works survive in more than two dozen manuscripts, one of which is an almost complete edition of his works classified by genre. Coming as he did between traditions, Adam wrote in a variety of genres that reflected the old (the courtly lyric, the *chanson de geste*) and the new (the decidedly bourgeois *Jeu d'Adam* and *Le Jeu de Robin et de Marion*). His position in the thirteenth century is problematic for music historians for several reasons. First, he was a master of the monophonic *chanson* and motet, both of which belonged even then to a dying tradition. Second, he composed a body of work that combined traditional texts with innovative settings, lyric poetry with the polyphony that was becoming a force to be reckoned with in music. Finally, his dramatic creations were so far ahead of his time that nothing like them was written until decades later. In fact, it is Adam's theatrical works that are his most distinctive contribution: The prose drama *Jeu d'Adam* is regarded by many to be the earliest comedy in French; the musical play *Le Jeu de Robin et de Marion* is commonly considered a precursor to comic opera with its combination of sung and spoken parts.

Bibliography
Bishop, Morris, et al. *The Horizon Book of the Middle Ages*. Boston: Houghton Mifflin Co., 1968. A well-written introduction to the world as Adam de la Halle would have known it. Specific attention is given to such topics as religious life and the Church, the Crusades, the nobility and courtly love, the growth of towns and commerce, the peasantry, literature, and art. Copiously illustrated in both color and black and white.
Caldwell, John. *Medieval Music*. Bloomington: Indiana University Press, 1978. A straightforward discussion of Western music from about 950 to 1400, with considerable attention paid to notation, which is the key to medieval musical style. An entire chapter is devoted to the period of the *ars antiqua*, during which time Adam de la Halle flourished as a well-known *trouvère*. The text is well illustrated with relevant examples (words and notation) from the works under discussion. An excellent bibliography lists not only books and articles but also the major journals in music history, as well as manuscript sources and their locations.
Evans, Joan. *Life in Medieval France*. London: Phaidon Press, 1957. A very good general introduction to France in the years before, during, and after Adam de la Halle's life. Evans discusses the nature of feudal society, life in the major cities and towns, monastic life, the Church, pilgrimages and crusades, and education. The book ends with a description of the waning of the medieval period. Color illustrations.
Frank, Grace. *The Medieval French Drama*. Oxford: Clarendon Press, 1960. A comprehensive study of both liturgical and secular plays from the five centuries or more constituting the medieval period. An entire chapter is devoted to the plays of Adam de la Halle (referred to as "Adam le Bossu" in this text) and their theatrical and social milieu. Includes a fairly comprehensive bibliography of books, periodicals, and articles, although a number of the entries are, as might be expected, in French.
Nichols, Stephen J., Jr. "The Medieval Lyric and Its Public." In *Medievalia et Humanistica*, edited by Paul Maurice Clogan. Cleveland: Press of Case Western Reserve University, 1972. A careful analysis of the nature of the audience who patronized the medieval poet-musicians. A discussion of the function of the troubadour/*trouvère* as a court poet whose work celebrated the authority and responsibilities of the aristocratic lord whom he served, as a composer and performer who responded to the tastes and needs of an elite audience from a closely circumscribed world—the kind of audience for whom Adam de la Halle wrote and performed his poems and songs.
Wilhelm, James. *Seven Troubadours: The Creators of Modern Verse*. Univer-

sity Park: Pennsylvania State University Press, 1970. Presents seven distinct lyric voices—some of them contemporaries of Adam de la Halle—of the twelfth and thirteenth centuries whose work shows the Christian-secular heritage of the High Middle Ages. The range of work discussed shows the origins, the full flowering, and the decay of a great poetic tradition which grew out of two major impulses: the Christian ethos of the eleventh century, and the instinctive urge of people to create secular songs. Although Adam is not one of the featured seven, the book is valuable for the light it sheds on his artistic and philosophical milieu.

Edelma Huntley

AESCHYLUS

Born: 525-524 B.C.; Eleusis, Greece
Died: 456-455 B.C.; Gela, Sicily
Areas of Achievement: Theater and drama
Contribution: Aeschylus' dramaturgy marks a major stage in the development of Western theater, especially tragedy.

Early Life

Knowledge of the life of Aeschylus is limited by minimal and unreliable sources. A Hellenistic biography surviving in the manuscript tradition of Aeschylus' plays is filled with ancient gossip, conjecture, and elaboration. The only extant portraits of the dramatist are probably not authentic.

Aeschylus was born about 525-524 B.C. in Eleusis, an Attic town about fourteen miles northwest of Athens. His father, Euphorion, a Eupatrid or wealthy aristocrat, had several children: at least two other sons, Cynegirus and Ameinias, and a daughter whose name is not recorded.

As a Eupatrid, Aeschylus belonged to one of the ancient and powerful landed families who had controlled Greece for generations but whose political power deteriorated in Aeschylus' own lifetime, especially in Attica. Aeschylus' birthplace was an ancient city which had retained a sense of local pride despite its incorporation into the city-state of Athens many years before. While it is uncertain whether Aeschylus was ever initiated into the famous cult of Demeter at Eleusis, he certainly grew up within its shadow. Later in life, Aeschylus is said to have been prosecuted for revealing a mystery of Demeter in one of his plays but to have been exonerated on the grounds that he had done so unwittingly.

The young Aeschylus, benefiting from the wealth and prestige of his aristocratic family, undoubtedly received a good education, founded upon the poetry of Homer. With such learning, Aeschylus developed a strong sense of a Eupatrid's civic responsibility and authority and was exposed to the traditional poetry, myths, and music upon which his tragedies were later based.

If ancient tradition can be trusted, Aeschylus began composing plays as a teenager. His early dramatic career is poorly documented. Sometime between 499 and 496, he entered the Athenian dramatic competition at the Greater Dionysia with an unknown group of plays but did not receive first prize. There is no record of how many contests he entered before his first victory in 484, again with unknown plays.

As an Athenian citizen, the young Aeschylus lived through some of the most exciting years in that city's history. In the tightly knit aristocratic society of late sixth century Athens, Aeschylus would have observed at first hand the turmoil associated with the murder of the Athenian prince Hipparchus in 514, the expulsion of his brother Hippias in 510, and the constitutional reforms of democratic Cleisthenes in 508. The progression from tyranny to democracy in Athens inevitably meant less power for the Eupatrid class. While the political position of Aeschylus and his family in this period is uncertain, these events undoubtedly encouraged the cautious conservatism which Aeschylus exhibited in later years.

The young playwright was also a soldier. In the first decade of the fifth century, the Persian Empire ruthlessly suppressed a revolt by Ionian Greek cities along the coast of modern Turkey and then invaded the mainland of Greece in retaliation for support of the Ionians. In 490, the Persian king Darius the Great was soundly defeated by united Greek forces at the battle of Marathon, where Aeschylus fought and where his brother Cynegirus died. Ten years later, during a second Persian invasion of Greece by Darius' son, Xerxes I, Aeschylus also participated in the naval battle of Salamis, at which the Athenians defeated the Persian fleet against great odds. Accounts of Aeschylus' participation in other battles, especially at Plataea in 479, must be dismissed as examples of biographical exaggeration. These victories permanently curtailed the threat of Persian domination of the Greek mainland and brought about the period of Athenian political hegemony during which Aeschylus produced all of his extant plays.

Life's Work

While the titles of at least eighty Aeschylean plays are known, only seven tragedies survive in the Aeschylean corpus. Since entries in the Greater Dionysia always consisted of three tragedies plus one satyr play, about three-quarters of Aeschylus' plays were tragedies. Plots for these plays were generally connected with the Trojan War or with the myths of Thebes and Argos. At the height of his dramatic career, Aeschylus, who acted in his own plays, was extremely successful. Of the twenty-odd productions attributed to his name, he was victorious at least thirteen times, maybe more; in addition, several of his plays were produced after his death.

Aeschylus' earliest extant work, *Persai* (467 B.C.; *The Persians*), was first performed in Athens in 472 together with the lost plays *Phineus* and *Glaucus Potnieus*. This production, which won first prize, commemorated the Athenian victory at Salamis and includes Aeschylus' own eyewitness account, placed in the mouth of a messenger. In choosing historical rather than mythical subject matter for this play, Aeschylus followed a contemporary, Phrynichus, who had earlier composed two historical plays. Aeschylus' producer for his plays of 472 was Pericles, but the playwright's association with this great Athenian statesman and champion of democracy is not necessarily an indication of Aeschylus' political inclinations, for producers were assigned by the state, not chosen by the playwright.

Shortly after 472, at the invitation of the tyrant Hieron, Aeschylus traveled to Syracuse in Sicily, where *The Persians* was reproduced. Hieron, a great patron of the arts, attracted to his court not only Aeschylus but also the philosopher Xenophanes and the poets Pindar, Bacchylides, and Simonides. During his stay in Sicily, which may have lasted several years, Aeschylus also produced another play, *Aetnae*, now lost. Since this play celebrated Hieron's founding of the city of Aetna in 476, a visit by Aeschylus to Sicily prior to 472 was once considered to have been likely, but most scholars now believe that *Aetnae* was produced sometime shortly after 472. Aeschylus' long stay in Sicily left a permanent mark on the playwright's work, which is filled with Sicilian words and expressions.

Aeschylus was certainly back in Athens by 468, for his unknown production of that year was defeated when Sophocles won his first victory at the Greater Dionysia. In the following year, Aeschylus won the competition with a group including the lost *Laius* and *Oedipus* and the extant *Hepta epi Thēbas* (*Seven Against Thebes*).

Sometime between 467 and 458, Aeschylus produced the so-called Danaid trilogy, composed of the extant *Hiketides* (463 B.C.?; *The Suppliants*, also as *Suppliant Women*) and the lost *Egyptians* and *Danaids*. For stylistic reasons, *The Suppliants* used to be considered Aeschylus' earliest extant play, until the twentieth century publication of a papyrus fragment containing part of an ancient production notice for the play. This new evidence makes it likely that Aeschylus competed in 463 with the Danaid trilogy and was victorious over Sophocles.

In 458, Aeschylus directed his last Athenian production, which included the extant *Agamemnōn* (*Agamemnon*), *Choēphoroi* (*Libation Bearers*), and *Eumenides* and the lost satyr play *Proteus*. Together, these three tragedies, known as the *Oresteia*, make up the only surviving connected trilogy. The *Eumenides* is filled with allusions to such events as the recent Athenian alliance with Argos and the reform of the ancient court of Areopagus by the democrat Ephialtes. This evidence has been interpreted to suggest both that Aeschylus supported and that he opposed the political agenda of Athens in the middle of the fifth century.

Shortly after this production, which won first prize, Aeschylus left Athens for Sicily, never to return. Ancients conjectured that the playwright left Athens because of political dissatisfaction or professional disappointment. None of the evidence is certain, however, and the reasons for Aeschylus' second journey to Sicily remain obscure.

Some scholars believe that the seventh play surviving in the Aeschylean corpus, *Prometheus desmōtēs* (*Prometheus Bound*), was composed during Aeschylus' second stay in Sicily. Others deny that the play was written by Aeschylus at all.

The playwright also wrote epigrams and elegies. Fragments of Aeschylus' elegy composed in honor of the dead at Marathon were discovered in the Athenian agora in 1933. This poem is said to have been written for a competition, at an unknown date, which Aeschylus lost to the poet Simonides.

Aeschylus died in Gela, Sicily, in 456 or 455. An ancient biography recounts the following version of Aeschylus' death: An eagle flying overhead with a tortoise in its beak mistook Aeschylus' bald head for a rock upon which to shatter the shell of its prey and thus killed the poet. The Gelans erected this inscription over the poet's tomb:

> This memorial hides the Athenian Aeschylus, Euphorion's son,
>   Who died in wheat-bearing Gela.
> The sacred battlefield of Marathon may tell of his great valor.
>   So, too, can the long-haired Mede, who knows it well.

By tradition, Aeschylus himself is said to have requested that he be remembered only as a patriotic Athenian and not as a great playwright.

Aeschylus had at least two sons, Euphorion and Euaeon, both of whom wrote plays. In 431, Euphorion defeated both Sophocles and Euripides. A few years later, Sophocles, competing with his masterpiece, *Oidipous Tyrannos* (c. 429 B.C.; *Oedipus Tyrannus*), was defeated by Aeschylus' nephew Philocles. After Aeschylus' death, a special decree was passed to permit revivals of his plays, which won several victories in subsequent years. In 405, the comic poet Aristophanes produced *Batrachoi* (*The Frogs*), in which the dead Aeschylus and Euripides debate about the quality of each other's tragedies.

Summary

Aeschylus is rightly considered the "father of Western tragedy." His works, coming at a strategic time, helped mold Greek tragedy into a great literary form. While Aristotle's statement in *De poetica* (c. 334-323 B.C.; *Poetics*) that Aeschylus "first introduced a second actor to tragedy and lessened the role of the chorus and made dialogue take the lead" cannot be proved, Aeschylus' extant plays do illustrate a skilled use of dialogue which made possible the agons, or great debates between characters so important in later Greek tragedy.

Whether Aeschylus himself introduced the second actor, he almost certainly invented the connected trilogy/tetralogy. As a rule, the group of three tragedies and one satyr play which a playwright produced at the festival were not connected thematically. It was Aeschylus who first saw the brilliant potential of linking the plays together. While his first extant play, *The Persians*, was not part of a connected group, all of his other surviving plays were. No other Greek playwright was able to make use of the trilogy form as successfully as Aeschylus did.

In *The Suppliants*, Aeschylus also experimented with the use of the chorus as dramatic protagonist. Traditionally a reflective and nondramatic element in the tragedy, the chorus became in this play the central character. Similarly, in *Eumenides* the chorus played a significant role as the prosecutor of the matricide Orestes.

Aeschylus' dramatic skills are particularly apparent in his handling of spectacular stage techniques. His plays, frequently making dramatic use of such stage trappings as altars, tombs, ghosts, and the *eccyclema*, a wheeled vehicle employed to show the interior, thus confirm Aeschylus as a master playwright who established for his successors a high standard of dramatic skill and power.

Bibliography

Herington, C. J. *Aeschylus*. New Haven, Conn: Yale University Press, 1986. An excellent introduction to Aeschylus for the general reader. One chapter is devoted to biography with a short annotated bibliography and a table of dates.

——————. "Aeschylus in Sicily." *Journal of Hellenic Studies* 87 (1967): 74-85. This discussion of the evidence for Aeschylus' trips to Sicily gives a chronology as well as a citation of the ancient evidence in Greek.

Lefkowitz, Mary. *The Lives of the Greek Poets*. London: Duckworth, 1981. A translation and analysis of the Hellenistic biography of Aeschylus, otherwise unavailable in English, can be found in this book, which also includes a bibliography.

Lesky, Albin. *Greek Tragedy*. Translated by H. A. Frankfort. New York: Barnes and Noble Books, 1965. A scholarly introduction to Aeschylus' dramaturgy, with a brief summary of his life. A bibliography is included.

——————. *A History of Greek Literature*. Translated by James Willis and Cornelis de Heer. New York: Thomas Y. Crowell, 1966. Aeschylus' place in the literature of ancient Greece can be traced in this standard history, which includes biographical information and a bibliography.

Murray, Gilbert. *Aeschylus: The Creator of Tragedy*. Oxford: Clarendon Press, 1940. Written by one of the most important scholars of Greek tragedy in the twentieth century, this book begins with a biography of the poet but does not include the revision to Aeschylus' chronology required by the papyrus find.

Podlecki, Anthony J. *The Political Background of Aeschylean Tragedy*. Ann Arbor: University of Michigan Press, 1966. This book contains an excellent life of Aeschylus in the first chapter and an interesting appendix on Aeschylus' description of the battle of Salamis.

Rosenmeyer, Thomas G. *The Art of Aeschylus*. Berkeley: University of California Press, 1982. Primarily a literary study, this work contains a short but good appendix on the life and times of Aeschylus. There is also an excellent "comparative table of dates and events" as well as a select bibliography.

Smyth, Herbert Weir. Introduction to *Aeschylus: Plays and Fragments with an English Translation*. 2 vols. New York: G. P. Putnam and Sons, 1922-1926. Rev. ed. Cambridge, Mass.: Harvard University Press, 1963. Smyth's biography of Aeschylus, found in the introduction to volume 1, is still excellent despite being published prior to the discovery of the papyrus redating *The Suppliants*.

Spatz, Lois. *Aeschylus*. Boston: Twayne Publishers, 1982. Written for the general reader, this book includes a biography and an annotated bibliography.

Thomas J. Sienkewicz

AFONSO I

Born: c. 1108; Guimarães, Portugal
Died: December 6, 1185; Coimbra, Portugal
Area of Achievement: Government
Contribution: Through astute leadership in military victories over Muslims and Christian Iberian neighbors, Afonso created the independent monarchy of Portugal and became its first king.

Early Life

In 1087, many French knights were invited by Christians of the Iberian Peninsula to help in the fight against the Muslim Almoravids. These Moroccan warriors had invaded the divided Islamic areas of Spain, and through military victories were uniting the Muslims and threatening the Christian kingdoms. One of the French nobles was Henry of Burgundy, who ingratiated himself with the Emperor of León, Alfonso VI, and married his illegitimate daughter, Princess Teresa. The county of Portugal was conferred upon Henry by his father-in-law. He was charged with the defense of the western frontier from the Muslims. Henry established his court at Guimarães, in northern present-day Portugal. It was close to Braga, which had been restored as a bishopric in 1070. One of Henry's successes was helping to achieve papal recognition of Braga's elevation to a metropolitanate.

Sometime around 1108 Teresa gave birth to a son, Afonso. The prince was reared at the court, where he was surrounded by Portuguese barons who had been appointed by Henry to be his chief officers. Henry's policy was to reward native aristocrats with estates, thus winning their loyalty and identifying his rule with the Portuguese.

Henry died in 1112, leaving Afonso, not yet five years of age, as his heir. Teresa became the regent of Portugal and used the title of queen. It was argued that this term was appropriate, as she was the daughter of an emperor. Teresa's rule was characterized by complicated intrigues. She took a lover, Fernando Peres, a Galician noble, and they produced a daughter. Teresa and Peres attempted to expand the Portugucse domain to the north, cutting into Galicia. Alfonso VII of León, Teresa's half brother, invaded Portugal in 1127, and she was forced to surrender the territory she had acquired in southern Galicia.

Young Afonso was maturing in a society that was in constant preparation for warfare. Theoretically, the enemies were the Muslims to the south, but in actuality, fellow Christians to the north in Galicia and to the east in León and Castile were a constant threat to the physical integrity of the county.

The Portuguese barons blamed Teresa and her Galician paramour for a decline in their fortunes. They began to range themselves behind someone they considered one of them: Afonso. On July 24, 1128, on the field of São

Mamede, near Guimarães, the army of Teresa and Fernando faced Afonso's barons. The young count was victorious, capturing his mother and her lover and expelling them. Afonso, Portuguese born and bred, became the ruler of the county.

Life's Work

Afonso was in his early twenties when he gained control of Portugal. No contemporary likeness of him exists, but the chronicles describe him as a man of gigantic stature with a flowing beard and enormous strength. It is also clear that he had a calculating and shrewd mind. From the beginning, he seems to have aspired to the creation of an independent Portuguese kingdom.

In the first decade of his reign (1128-1138) he was involved with various skirmishes with his Christian neighbors, and he was compelled to make token political submission to the authority of Castile. On the ecclesiastical front, Afonso was more successful in this earlier period. A resourceful and diplomatic Cluniac priest, John Peculiar, became his disciple and ally. Afonso had him installed in the episcopal office in Oporto and then saw him elevated to the archbishopric of Braga. After long and complicated intrigues, the bishop and the count achieved the jurisdictional independence of the Portuguese church from Santiago de Compostela and Toledo.

In the political arena, a new Muslim invasion of southern Iberia offered Afonso an opportunity to extend his authority southward. According to the royal chronicles, Afonso and his Portuguese army encountered the Almohad forces at a place known as Ourique. On the night before the battle, a vision of Jesus Christ inspired Afonso, so that on the next day, July 25, the Feast of Saint James, the outnumbered Portuguese were able to route the Islamic forces. The results of this encounter were impressive. Christian strongholds were established south of Coimbra, and the important Muslim city of Santarém was forced to pay tribute.

Afonso's success at Ourique may have convinced him to declare the fullness of his dominion in Portugal, which he considered to be the area north of the Tagus River. Documents of the time reveal that after 1139, instead of referring to himself as simply *infans* or *princeps*, as he had in the past, he adopted the title of *Portugalensium rex*; this was a virtual declaration of independence. By placing his kingdom under papal protection and pledging loyalty to the Holy See, he took another significant step to strengthen and secure his independence. Proclaiming himself a Knight of Blessed Peter and of the Roman Empire, he promised to pay an annual tribute of four ounces of gold in return for papal protection. A formal document setting forth these terms was published on December 13, 1143. Earlier that year, Alfonso VII met Afonso at Zamora and, evidently accepting the *fait accompli*, recognized him as King of Portugal. In the spring of 1144, Pope

Lucius II wrote to Afonso graciously accepting the proffered tribute and extending protection, but the letter was addressed simply to the *Portugalensium dux*. Not until 1179, when the independence of Portugal was firmly established, did Pope Alexander III address Afonso as king.

The mid-twelfth century was the era of the early Crusades, and Afonso actually used the Crusaders who often put into Portuguese ports on their way to Palestine. In 1140, with the help of a fleet manned by many Englishmen, he forced Muslim Lisbon to pay him tribute. By 1147, he was ready to denounce his truce with the Moors, and in that year he captured Santarém on the Tagus.

In May of the same year, a fleet of 164 ships and almost thirteen thousand men, with contingents from Germany, Flanders, Normandy, and England, set sail from Dartmouth, England. They arrived at Oporto, where they were greeted by the bishop, who invited them to aid the king in an attack on Lisbon. The bishop declared that this was a just war, worthy of their talents: "Act like good soldiers, for the sin is not in fighting war, but in fighting for the sake of booty." When the fleet reached Lisbon on June 28, Afonso outlined his proposals, and an alliance was concluded. He guaranteed to the Crusaders the plunder of Lisbon and the ransom of captives; those who wished to settle there would be given lands and would be assured the protection of their native customs and liberties. The king also exempted them and their descendants from the payment of tolls in any part of his realm. He promised to continue the siege until surrender unless he was forced to desist because of mortal illness or an attack on his kingdom from some other quarter.

The Archbishop of Braga was sent to persuade the Muslims to surrender. He charged that they had "held our cities and lands already for 358 years," and he urged them to "return to the homeland of the Moors." When this drew a negative response, the siege commenced in earnest. Catapults and towers were constructed, and the city was blockaded on all sides. The defenders appealed in vain to their fellow Muslims for relief, but at least one of their messengers was captured by the Christians, who realized their enemies' plight. When the Muslims became aware that their chances of victory were steadily lessening, they eventually asked for a truce to negotiate the terms of surrender. After a siege of seventeen weeks, the Christians made their triumphal entrance into Lisbon on October 24, 1147. Although the Muslims were permitted to leave freely, the city was sacked and many were killed. The conquest of Lisbon, which has been described by one Anglo-Norman priest, rivals the capture of Toledo (1085) and Saragossa (1118) in importance.

Afonso set to work to repopulate the newly conquered lands. Crusaders who were willing to settle received land grants near the Tagus. The Templars were given castles for the defense of the valley, and the Cistercians established monasteries to foster agricultural development. Throughout Afonso's long reign, raiding and counter-raiding persisted. He carried his frontiers beyond the Tagus Valley, annexing Beja in 1162 and Évora in 1165. Afonso's battling days came to an end when he was wounded in a skirmish with Christians at Badajoz. His leg was fractured, and he was no longer able to ride. Captured by his opponents, he was held for two months while his vassals raised ransom funds. As part of the agreement to gain his freedom, he renounced any claim to Galicia.

Afonso had renewed his connection with the House of Burgundy by marrying Mafalda, the daughter of a count of Savoy. He associated his son, Sancho I, with his power, knighting him at Coimbra in 1170. When Afonso died in 1185, his son inherited a stable and independent monarchy and his father's plans for driving the Moors out of the lands south of the Tagus.

Summary

It could be argued that were it not for Afonso I the Iberian Peninsula would be politically united today. Through his military, ecclesiastical, and political victories, he underscored the distinctiveness of the westernmost regions of Iberia. Through his successful negotiations with the Papacy and his military prowess, he achieved the recognition of Portugal as an independent kingdom, the fifth into which the Christian-dominated part of the peninsula was divided. The other kingdoms were Castile, León, Aragon, and Navarre.

In modern republican Portugal 1139 is accepted as the birth date of the State of Portugal, and Afonso I is considered the father of his nation. Similar sentiments were expressed by contemporaries of Afonso. The *Chronica Gothorum*, with a bit of exaggeration, expressed the era's view:

> He received the Kingdom and the Lord, through him, extended the frontiers of the Christians and expanded the bounds of the faithful people from the River Mondago, that flows by the walls of Coimbra, to the River Guadalquivir, that flows by the City of Seville, and from the Great Sea to the Mediterranean Sea.

Bibliography

Dos Passos, John. *The Portugal Story: Three Centuries of Exploration and Discovery*. Garden City, N.Y.: Doubleday and Co., 1969. Dos Passos, a fluent and engaging stylist, focuses on the emergence of the Portuguese empire in this volume, but his summary of Afonso's achievements is exemplary and his recounting of the siege of Lisbon is exciting.

Livermore, Harold V. *A New History of Portugal*. 2d ed. Cambridge: Cambridge University Press, 1976. The chapters on the origins of Portugal are outstanding. Clearly, but in commendable detail, the author traces Portugal's history from county to kingdom and discusses Afonso as the founder of Portugal, the conqueror of Lisbon, and an agricultural hero.

Marques, A. H. de Oliveira. *The History of Portugal: From Lusitania to Empire*. New York: Columbia University Press, 1972. One of Portugal's outstanding contemporary historians traces Afonso's career in his chapter "The Formation of Portugal." This author stresses social history and provides the reader with convincing glimpses of life in both Christian and Muslim medieval Portugal.

O'Callaghan, Joseph. *A History of Medieval Spain*. Ithaca, N.Y.: Cornell University Press, 1975. This massive survey of the history of the Iberian Peninsula from 415 to 1479 places the career of Afonso in the context of the surging Christian reconquest of the twelfth century. An excellent place to begin a bibliographic search for additional aspects of this era in Portuguese history.

Payne, Stanley G. *A History of Spain and Portugal*. Vol. 1. Madison: University of Wisconsin Press, 1973. The chapter on the emergence of Portugal provides an excellent survey of the medieval era in that region of the Iberian Peninsula. Payne's great virtue is that of placing the story of Afonso within an Iberian-wide context.

Stephens, H. Morse. *The Story of Portugal*. New York: G. P. Putnam's Sons, 1891. Reprint. New York: AMS Press, 1971. This classic survey of Portuguese history includes an extended chapter on Portugal becoming a kingdom: the reign of Afonso. Strongly influenced by nineteenth century German historiography, Stephens has gone to the original documents in order to tell his story. He calls his work "an episodical history."

Charles J. Fleener

AGESILAUS II

Born: c. 444 B.C.; Sparta
Died: c. 360 B.C.; Cyrene, Libya
Areas of Achievement: Government and warfare
Contribution: By common consent the most powerful and illustrious Greek
leader of his day, Agesilaus took Sparta to its peak of influence. Unfortunately, his policies led to a devastating defeat at Leuctra in 371, and at his
death he left an impoverished and weakened kingdom that would never
again play a dominant role in Greek affairs.

Early Life

When Eupolia, the young second wife of the aging Spartan king Archidamus II, gave birth to Agesilaus in 444, her son's prospects must have seemed
quite limited. Archidamus already had an heir apparent, Agis, by his first
wife. Worse, Agesilaus was born lame, an egregious liability in militaristic,
fitness-minded Sparta. Indeed, his very survival is remarkable, given the official inspection and possible infanticide to which the Spartan authorities subjected every infant. That he passed their scrutiny may be attributed to
Sparta's growing manpower shortage, a problem that would become acute in
Agesilaus' lifetime.

Because he was not considered an heir to the throne, from age seven to
eighteen the boy underwent the normal Spartan training—the *agoge*. Royal
heirs were normally spared this rigorous, competitive, and often-violent regimen, designed to produce the bravest, most disciplined soldiers possible.
Despite his lameness and small stature, Agesilaus excelled in the *agoge*. He
was the first to jest at his deformity and deliberately sought out the most difficult tasks to prove that his weak leg was no real hindrance. If the young
man displayed any weakness, it was excessive loyalty and favoritism to family
and friends.

At some point in his youth, Agesilaus formed a relationship that would
change the course of his life. It was customary that a Spartan youth cultivate
a special friendship with a mature man who would guide him and advance his
career. Agesilaus had the good fortune to become the special friend of
Lysander, the honored and influential general who spearheaded Sparta's victory over Athens in the Peloponnesian War. Before his extreme ambition and
egotism brought him discredit and demotion in 403, Lysander had initiated
an aggressive style of Spartan imperialism, and he would remain a powerful
advocate of Spartan expansion.

At his death in 400, after a reign of twenty-seven years, King Agis left a
son and presumptive successor, Leotychides. Nevertheless, Agesilaus asserted his own claim to the throne. His participation in the *agoge* had given
him a strong following among average Spartan citizens. There was also some

question as to the legitimacy of Leotychides, and Agesilaus made the most of it. When supporters of Leotychides recalled that an oracle had warned Spartans against the "lame kingship," Agesilaus countered that the warning was against a king of nonroyal blood. Perhaps the decisive factor in this contest was the intervention of Lysander on behalf of Agesilaus. Unable to serve as king himself, Lysander championed the claim of his friend. Leotychides lost not only the kingship but also his inheritance, and Agesilaus assumed the throne in 400, when he was about forty-four years old.

Because Sparta had a curious double monarchy with two royal houses, a Spartan king had to share his royal authority with a colleague—and potential rival. During the forty-year reign of Agesilaus, exile and premature death from disease or combat brought him five comparatively short-reigned and weak colleagues in the kingship. As a result, despite some factional disputes at home, Agesilaus had an unusually free hand to lead Sparta as he saw fit.

Life's Work

Agesilaus inherited a kingdom politically and militarily supreme in Greece, but that very fact of supremacy presented potentially dangerous temptations and challenges. Specifically, Agesilaus would have to decide whether to limit Sparta's hegemony to its traditional area of dominance, southern Greece, or extend it to include central Greece or even regions beyond. He would also have to reckon with the ambitions of a former ally in central Greece, Thebes. The Thebans wanted to unify the district of Boeotia in a federal state headed by Thebes. Agesilaus could attempt to prevent this, or he could accept it and at the same time compensate by encouraging the traditional rivalry between Thebes and its neighbor Athens.

At home, Sparta had certain long-standing internal weaknesses which needed attention, most notably the decline in the number of Spartan citizens. The gradual concentration of slave-worked land in the hands of wealthy families meant that fewer Spartans could afford to pay the dues required of all citizens. Accelerated by casualties in war and natural disasters, this trend had reduced the Spartan community to no more than three thousand male citizens at the accession of Agesilaus. His performance as king must be judged by his responses to these challenges and problems.

In his first year on the throne, Agesilaus had to deal with the revolutionary conspiracy of Cinadon, a crisis that revealed the precarious position of the dwindling Spartan citizen body. Cinadon was an "inferior," one of a sizable and growing body of Spartans who had lost their citizen status because of poverty. He based his revolutionary hopes on the fact that the Spartans were dangerously outnumbered by their subjects: the free *perioikoi*, who lived in semiautonomous villages around Sparta, and the servile Helots, who lived primarily in Messenia, west of Sparta. Cinadon boasted that his supporters— Helots, freed Helots, inferiors, and *perioikoi*—hated the Spartans so much that they would be glad to eat them raw. Because of an informant, who betrayed the plot in its early stages, Agesilaus and the other Spartan authorities were able to suppress the conspiracy, but they took no steps to correct the conditions that had engendered it.

Instead, in 396, Agesilaus undertook his first military campaign to distant Asia Minor, where he challenged the power of Persia. Agesilaus may have presented this expedition as a Panhellenic crusade on behalf of the Asiatic Greeks, but others saw it as an attempt to extend Spartan hegemony. Both Athens and Thebes refused to take part, and the Thebans further offended Agesilaus by disrupting his parting sacrifices at Aulis in Boeotia. After several victories against the Persians, Agesilaus received joint command of both land and sea forces, an honor unprecedented in Spartan history. The Asian campaign won fame for Agesilaus and much treasure for Sparta, but his victories accomplished little in the military sense. Moreover, his poor choice of an incompetent brother-in-law, Peisandros, as admiral resulted in a disastrous naval defeat in 394, which seriously weakened Sparta's position overseas. How Agesilaus might have responded to this setback is uncertain, since he had already been recalled home to help Sparta face a hostile alliance of major Greek states in the so-called Corinthian War (395-386 B.C.).

Primarily instigated by Thebes, this war challenged Sparta's domination of central Greece and had already produced the death of the reckless Lysander and the banishment of King Pausanias, Agesilaus' first comonarch. Victory in a major battle at Coronea secured Agesilaus' safe passage through Boeotia to Sparta, but it failed to reestablish Spartan preeminence in central Greece. His vengeful frontal assault on the Theban force, moreover, needlessly risked his men and produced severe casualties, including several wounds to Agesilaus himself. In subsequent engagements, Agesilaus generally got the upper hand, although one of his companies was decimated by a tactically innovative, lightly armed force near Corinth in 390. As the war became a stalemate, Agesilaus formed an alliance with his erstwhile enemy, the Persian king. By the terms of the "King's Peace" of 386, the Asiatic Greeks were abandoned to Persian domination. In return, the Persian king promised to make war on any Greek state that violated the accord and backed Sparta as overseer and arbiter of a general peace in Greece.

By a just and conciliatory administration of the King's Peace, Agesilaus might have maintained Sparta's security and hegemony indefinitely. Instead, he intervened in the affairs of other Greek states in order to install governments friendly to Sparta. Above all, he indulged his obsessive hatred of Thebes, and he condoned—if he did not instigate—the unlawful military occupation of Thebes in 382. This act more than any other outraged Greek opinion and helped the Thebans to establish an alliance with their natural rivals, the Athenians. After Thebes expelled the Spartan garrison, Agesilaus twice led invasions of Boeotia in vain attempts to recapture the city. Despite serious injuries in 377 that kept him out of military action until 370, Agesilaus continued to reject the claims of Thebes to represent all of Boeotia. He presided at a peace conference in 371, and, after a bitter exchange with the Theban leader Epaminondas, he excluded Thebes from the general peace. Then, against the advice of other Spartans, Agesilaus urged an immediate invasion of Boeotia. A momentous battle duly ensued at Leuctra, where the Spartans suffered a devastating defeat at the hands of the more tactically advanced Thebans. King Cleombrotus and four hundred of his fellow Spartans died in this conflict, the worst defeat in Spartan history.

Sparta never recovered from the setback at Leuctra. The battle itself inflicted heavy casualties on an already dangerously small Spartan citizen body and shattered the myth of Spartan invincibility. The ensuing Theban invasion of southern Greece permanently sundered Sparta's regional alliance and prompted defections among the long subordinate *perioikoi* and Helots who surrounded Sparta. In the face of the Theban advance, many Spartans panicked, while others plotted revolution. Only the energetic emergency measures of Agesilaus, who was then in his early seventies, saved the city from destruction. Worst of all in the long run, the Thebans liberated Messenia and thereby deprived Sparta of its richest agricultural district with its large number of Helot slaves.

Agesilaus refused to accept the loss of Messenia, and in the last decade of his life he pursued its recovery with a stubbornness that equaled his earlier opposition to Thebes. Unfortunately, he now ruled a weakened and impoverished Sparta with a citizen population of only one thousand. In the end, he was forced to undertake foreign mercenary service in order to finance his efforts to regain Messenia. Such was the military reputation of the aging king that rebellious Persian governors in Asia Minor and Egypt paid handsomely for his skills. In 360, after completing his final campaign in Egypt, Agesilaus set sail for home but died en route in Libya at about age eighty-four.

Summary

For more than two decades, Agesilaus II was, in effect, King of Greece. Nevertheless, his reign must be seen as a failure. A general of unquestioned talent and bravery, Agesilaus shared in the Spartans' failure to keep up with the military innovations of that time. The resulting tactical backwardness of the Spartan army helps explain the defeat at Leuctra. As a statesman, Agesilaus pursued unwise policies. The attempt to extend Sparta's hegemony was unrealistic in the light of Sparta's declining manpower, while his flagrantly aggressive administration of the King's Peace needlessly alienated other Greek states and made allies for Thebes. Above all, his relentless hatred of Thebes caused a breakdown of the common peace and led directly to the disastrous confrontation at Leuctra.

Agesilaus cannot be held responsible for the structural ills of the Spartan system, but he seems to have been blind to its most glaring problem, the decline in Spartan manpower. During his reign, the number of Spartan male citizens dropped by two-thirds to a mere one thousand. He left his son a feeble kingdom that would never again play a major role in Greek affairs.

A Spartan's Spartan, a product of the *agoge*, Agesilaus sadly exemplifies Aristotle's famous critique of the Spartans: Because their whole system was directed to securing only a part of virtue, military prowess, they did well at war but failed at the higher art of peace.

Bibliography
Cartledge, Paul. *Agesilaos and the Crisis of Sparta*. London: Duckworth, 1987. This exhaustive study from a Marxist perspective is now the starting point for serious study of Agesilaus. More than a mere biography, it places Agesilaus in the context of fourth century Greek history and provides an outstanding introduction to the whole political and social system of Sparta. Includes a very helpful chronological table.

Cawkwell, G. L. "Agesilaus and Sparta." *The Classical Quarterly* 26 (1976): 62-84. Perhaps the most favorable of the recent treatments of Agesilaus, this article argues that his aggressive policy toward Thebes was warranted. Cawkwell attributes Sparta's decline not to Agesilaus' foreign policy but to the Spartans' inability to adapt their army to the new military demands of the fourth century.

David, Ephraim. *Sparta Between Empire and Revolution (404-243 B.C.): Internal Problems and Their Impact on Contemporary Greek Consciousness*. New York: Arno Press, 1981. An excellent study of the internal problems of Sparta, this book deals with the period of Agesilaus' rule in chapters 1 through 3.

Forrest, W. G. *A History of Sparta, 950-192 B.C.* New York: W. W. Norton and Co., 1969. A brief introduction to ancient Sparta. Chapters 13 and 14 cover the period of Agesilaus' rule.

Hamilton, Charles D. "Agesilaus and the Failure of Spartan Hegemony." *The Ancient World* 5 (1982): 67-78. A balanced assessment which argues that Agesilaus' obsessive hatred of Thebes displaced his original genuine Panhellenic goals.

_____. *Sparta's Bitter Victories: Politics and Diplomacy in the Corinthian War*. Ithaca, N.Y.: Cornell University Press, 1979. An excellent detailed study of Greek international affairs in the period 405-386 B.C., this book is especially good in presenting the policies of Agesilaus and Lysander in the context of Spartan factional politics.

Plutarch. *Agesilaus*. In *Plutarch's Lives*, translated by Bernadotte Perrin, 11 vols. Cambridge, Mass.: Harvard University Press, 1959-1967. This brief biography is the most balanced ancient source for the career of Agesilaus.

Xenophon. *A History of My Times (Hellenica)*. Translated by George Cawkwell. Harmondsworth, England: Penguin Books, 1979. In this work, the Athenian soldier-historian provides a contemporary narrative of the whole period of Agesilaus' rule, the only such account to survive complete. A personal friend of Agesilaus, he participated in many of the events he describes and provides many revealing details. Unfortunately, he is biased in favor of Agesilaus and omits several very important events.

James T. Chambers

MARCUS VIPSANIUS AGRIPPA

Born: c. 63 B.C.; place unknown
Died: March, 12 B.C.; Rome
Areas of Achievement: Government and warfare
Contribution: Agrippa's military genius, on both land and sea, provided Augustus with the support he needed to establish the Roman principate. His gift for planning and building contributed to the improvement of Rome's roads, water supply, and major public buildings.

Early Life

Marcus Vipsanius Agrippa seems linked with Octavian (as Augustus was called before 27 B.C.) almost from birth. They were born into politically insignificant families in about the same year. Agrippa's equestrian (middle-class) family was obscure, and the family name (Vipsanius) was so unaristocratic that in later life he preferred not to use it at all. He and Octavian were friends from childhood and attended school together, according to the emperor's court biographer.

Nothing certain is known of Agrippa's life before 44 B.C. It seems safe to assume that he performed the military service which young men of his class were expected to undertake at that stage of their lives. At the time of Julius Caesar's assassination, Agrippa was with Octavian, Caesar's grand-nephew, in Greece, where they had been sent to study. Agrippa seems to have been chosen by Caesar as a suitable companion for Octavian, along with Gaius Maecenas and several other solid, if unspectacular, young men. When Octavian decided to return to Rome, claim his inheritance from Caesar, and become embroiled in the political and military struggle which had been ravaging the Mediterranean world for almost a century, Agrippa accompanied him.

In spite of his youth, Agrippa helped raise an army to oppose Caesar's assassins and to give Octavian leverage against Marc Antony, who had impounded Caesar's papers and money and hoped to assume the dead dictator's place. Although Antony and Octavian reached an accord in order to pursue Caesar's assassins, relations between them soon soured. In 41, with Antony in the east, his brother Lucius revolted against Octavian's authority and in opposition to his efforts to provide land for Caesar's retiring veteran soldiers. Agrippa forced Lucius to surrender early in 40, the first of his many victories on Octavian's behalf.

Life's Work

Agrippa proved how indispensable he was to Octavian by filling several important offices during the following few years. As governor of Gaul, he suppressed a revolt in the strategic southern district of Aquitania. In 37, he was Octavian's colleague in the consulship and built up the navy to oppose Sextus, who was attacking Roman shipping from bases in Sicily in a final act of opposition to the Caesarean faction's takeover of the state. This campaign brought Agrippa's engineering abilities to the fore, as he linked Lake Avernus with the Bay of Naples to create a harbor where the new fleet could be trained. His improved grappling equipment played a significant role in Sextus' defeat.

Augustus liked to boast that he had found Rome brick and left it marble, but Agrippa's buildings were as much responsible for that accomplishment as anything the emperor did. Agrippa began making his mark by repairing and upgrading the city's aqueducts during his time as an aedile in 33, a responsibility which he kept in his own hands for the rest of his life. The first of his aqueducts bore the name of the Julian family, into which Octavian had been adopted by Caesar's will. Agrippa's major building contributions were the Pantheon, one of the largest domed structures erected in antiquity, and the baths which bore his name. The Pantheon, which visitors to Rome still admire, bears Agrippa's name on the frieze, but it was rebuilt by Hadrian circa A.D. 133. How much of Agrippa's original design remains is a disputed question. Also to Agrippa's credit were a granary and a new bridge over the Tiber River. He constructed buildings and roads in the provinces as well.

If he had any political ambitions, Agrippa subordinated them to Octavian's needs. He contributed significant victories over frontier tribes in Illyria in 35 and 34 and should be credited with defeating Antony and Cleopatra VII at the Battle of Actium in 31. That victory removed Octavian's last rival and made him the undisputed ruler of Rome.

Rome had been rent by bloody civil strife since 133, because the empire had outgrown the republican constitution under which it had functioned since the overthrow of the last Etruscan king in 509. Annually elected magistrates who shared their power and could veto one another's actions could not effectively govern an empire stretching from Spain to Syria. As Julius Caesar had found, however, the Romans would not tolerate a monarch. He had taken the illegal position of dictator for life, a stopgap measure that probably crystalized the resentment against him into a fatal conspiracy.

Octavian's problem was the same as Caesar's: to find a way for one man to govern the Roman Empire while preserving the appearance of the old republic. Between 31 and 27, Octavian relied on holding the consulship, with Agrippa as his colleague in 28 and 27. While Octavian was away from Rome trying to stabilize affairs in the urbanized, Greek-speaking east (which resented its domination by the agricultural and Latin west), Agrippa directed governmental affairs in Italy and the west with the aid of Maecenas.

These two men seem to have been most influential in helping Octavian solve the dilemma of governing Rome. The historian Dio Cassius records a debate among the three of them, with speeches by Maecenas and Agrippa advocating, respectively, that Octavian become a constitutional monarch or restore the republic. The speeches summarize the two philosophical points of view, but they probably have no historical validity. The settlement which Octavian worked out with the senate in 27 appeared on the surface to gratify the Romans' desire to see their republic restored, but it actually granted to Octavian (by that time called Augustus) all the civilian and military powers necessary to make him an effective ruler.

This subtle monarchy, called the principate, had one flaw. Since it was not technically a legal magistracy or a hereditary monarchy, it could not be passed on to a successor designated by the princeps, the head of state. In 23, Augustus was taken ill and almost died. In the depths of his illness, he gave his signet ring, which served as his signature and the symbol of his power, to Agrippa, perhaps indicating his desire that his loyal friend succeed him. Upon his recovery, Augustus gave Agrippa proconsular power similar to his own.

In spite of his respect for Agrippa, Augustus soon realized that the aristocratic senate would never accept him as princeps because of his plebeian origins. Augustus hoped to groom some member of his own family to succeed him, but he had difficulty finding anyone suitable. He had only one child, a daughter Julia, so he promoted the career of his nephew Marcellus by sharing the consulship with him and marrying him to Julia.

The attention showered on Marcellus provoked the first strain between Agrippa and Augustus. It was said of Agrippa that, while he did not want to be the first man in the empire, he would be second to only one man. His departure to govern the eastern provinces, though touted as a promotion, seems to have been regarded by Agrippa as a kind of exile. He did not return to Rome until after Marcellus' untimely death in 22. In 20 and 19, Agrippa put down minor revolts in Gaul and Spain. His policy in dealing with the provinces was to defend, not expand, the borders. Soon after Agrippa's death, Augustus began listening to other advice, and Rome suffered two of its worst defeats ever in Germany.

Not all Agrippa's service to Augustus was military. In 28, he married Octavian's niece Marcella; in 21, with Augustus' approval, he divorced her to marry the widow Julia, who was then about sixteen. Augustus may have taken him as his son-in-law because Agrippa had become so powerful and so popular that he had to be taken into the imperial family or suppressed like an enemy. By Julia, Agrippa fathered two daughters and three sons, two of whom Augustus adopted and promoted as possible successors.

Augustus continued to honor Agrippa and to associate him in the imperial power. In 18, Agrippa was given tribunician power, one of the basic grants on which Augustus' position rested. The holder of this power could veto the actions of any other Roman magistrate. The grant was renewed in 13. By March of the next year, Agrippa had quieted a revolt in Pannonia (in modern

Yugoslavia) and returned to Rome ill. He died by the end of the month, and his ashes were laid in the Julian family mausoleum.

Summary

Marcus Vipsanius Agrippa was a remarkable man, willing to subordinate his military and engineering genius to the service of a friend who was less talented than himself. Writers such as Suetonius and Cornelius Tacitus, who could find some hint of scandal to besmirch any reputation, report nothing of the kind about Agrippa. In an age when treachery and shifting alliances were common in politics, Agrippa displayed unswerving loyalty to Augustus for more than thirty years. His support enabled Augustus to defeat his rivals and assume power in the first place. His buildings and public works—many of them financed out of his personal funds—contributed to the well-being and happiness of the populace of Rome. This general good feeling was an essential element in maintaining the stability of the principate. It is extremely doubtful that Augustus could have taken power in the first place or held it for long without Agrippa's assistance.

Not only did Agrippa have a profound impact on the course of events in the first century B.C. and for some time after that, but also he contributed directly as the progenitor of two later emperors. His daughter Agrippina the Elder was the mother of Caligula and the grandmother (through her daughter) of Nero. While his descendants may not have been popular leaders, Agrippa cannot be blamed for all of their flaws. Through a complex web of imperial marriages, they also carried the genes of Augustus and Marc Antony.

Agrippa would be better known if his autobiography and his geographical commentary had survived. The latter was used to make a map which was prominently displayed in Rome and was an important source for Strabo, Pliny the Elder, and other writers with geographic or ethnographic interests. The opinion of antiquity, that he was the noblest Roman of his day, has not been revised by later historians.

Bibliography

Badian, E. "Notes on the *Laudatio* of Agrippa." *Classical Journal* 76 (1981): 97-109. This article discusses a recently discovered papyrus containing a portion of Augustus' funeral oration for Agrippa.

Buchan, J. *Augustus*. Boston: Houghton Mifflin Co., 1937. This slightly romantic biography of the first Roman emperor covers in detail Agrippa's contribution to his success.

Evans, H. B. "Agrippa's Water Plan." *American Journal of Archeology* 86 (1982): 401-411. The best analysis available of Agrippa's contribution to Rome's system of aqueducts, which provided more water per person in Augustus' day than does the system of modern Rome.

Firth, J. B. *Augustus Caesar and the Organization of the Empire of Rome*. New York: G. P. Putnam's Sons, 1903. Helpful references to Agrippa throughout, and an insightful chapter on Maecenas and Agrippa.

Gray, E. W. "The Imperium of M. Agrippa: A Note on P. Colon. Inv. No. 4701." *Zeitschrift für Papyrologie und Epigraphik* 6 (1970): 227-238. This article discusses the precise dates when grants of power were given to Agrippa.

McKechnie, P. "Cassius Dio's Speech of Agrippa: A Realistic Alternative to Imperial Government?" *Greece and Rome* 28 (October, 1981): 150-155. Agrippa's speech is a set piece, not truly reflecting his views on democracy. In other passages, Dio describes Agrippa as an ardent supporter of monarchy.

Reinhold, M. *Marcus Agrippa*. Geneva, N.Y.: W. F. Humphrey Press, 1933. Despite some traces of hero worship, this volume is still the most thorough study of Agrippa available in English. It follows his career and characterizes him as a self-made man, lacking in the subtle intellect of Augustus or Maecenas but a master of practical matters of organization.

Shipley, Frederick W. *Agrippa's Building Activities in Rome*. St. Louis, Mo.: Washington University, 1933. This short book studies Agrippa's building activity by location in various districts of Rome. It also discusses the problem of determining exactly where some of the buildings were. Shipley argues that the Pantheon as Hadrian rebuilt it bears little resemblance to Agrippa's original plan.

Albert A. Bell, Jr.

AHMAD IBN HANBAL

Born: December, 780; Baghdad, Iraq
Died: July, 855; Baghdad, Iraq
Areas of Achievement: Law and theology
Contribution: Ibn Hanbal sought to conjoin jurisprudence closely with the study of texts recording the teachings and practices of the Prophet Muhammad. Ibn Hanbal's ideas and his example of steadfast resistance to political persecution inspired the formation of the fourth classical school of Islamic law.

Early Life

Ahmad ibn Muhammad, who generally became known by the surname Ibn Hanbal, handed down from his grandfather, was descended from the Arab tribe of Banu Shayban, which had played a notable part in the conquest of Khorasan. The parents of Ahmad ibn Hanbal moved from Merv, on the northeastern frontiers of Iran, to Baghdad shortly before he was born in December, 780. His father, who had pursued a military career, died when Ahmad was about three years old; a small family estate, however, provided for many of his needs during his early years. Ahmad's education centered particularly upon grammar and religious texts; he displayed a marked interest in accounts of the Prophet Muhammad and his mission. By 795, such concerns prompted him to commence a series of travels across Arabia, Yemen, and Syria; within Iraq he also visited Al-Kufa and Basra. Over a period of about eleven years, beginning at the age of twenty-three, he performed five pilgrimages to Mecca. During this time he became acquainted with a number of specialists on Islamic law and history; these contacts helped him to begin to define his own position.

Early legal theory, which had developed alongside the exegesis of Muslim traditions, was associated with schools which followed the teachings of major scholars. In addition to the Koran, many jurists accepted precedent established by custom (*sunnah*). Sayings attributed to the Prophet had been passed along from his contemporaries to their descendants and students until eventually they were transcribed; these were also regarded as authoritative. The *hadith*, or tradition, thus was also applied to the settlement of disputes at law. Some care, however, had to be taken when sources of doubtful veracity were presented. Other forms of legal reasoning were based upon the process of consensus (*ijma'*) which had evolved during the Prophet's time; some jurists accepted a wider consensus, recognizing the opinions of later scholars as well. Argument from analogy was used when a precedent for a given situation had not yet been established. Among some specialists it was held permissible for judicial authorities to formulate an opinion (*ra'y*) on matters where precedent and texts were lacking. The first school of law, founded by

Abu Hanifah (c. 699-767), allowed considerable latitude in forms of legal reasoning; this school had gained influence particularly in Iraq and Syria. During the course of his studies, Ibn Hanbal encountered proponents of Hanafi law; as his own views became more definite he rejected such teachings.

Other legal doctrines were somewhat more narrowly concerned with the reconciliation of religious writings and teachings with the requirements of judicial decision making. Malik ibn Anas (c. 715-795) had contended that, after the Koran, traditions recorded in Medina, where the Prophet's work as a statesman had commenced, should be accorded preponderant weight; similarly, the consensus of Muslim scholars should be construed in the light of the practices sanctioned in that city. The Malikite school had become important particularly in western Arabia, where local memories and interests supported such views. The teachings of Abu 'Abd Allah al-Shafi'i (767-820), whom many regarded as the founder of systematic jurisprudence (*fiqh*), established criteria by which the preeminence of original revealed authority could be upheld. In making distinctions between strong and weak traditions, he attempted to resolve problems of inconsistency which had arisen when sources of varying degrees of authenticity were cited as evidence of the Prophet's position on an issue. When further opinion was needed, Shafi'i insisted upon a consensus of the Muslim community in its entirety. His doctrines had acquired a notable following in Baghdad and Cairo, where he lived and taught. It is known that Ibn Hanbal met him in about 810, while both of them were in Iraq, and that Ibn Hanbal had access to some of Shafi'i's works. It has been claimed that at one time Shafi'i commended Ibn Hanbal for his piety and learning in the traditions. Although Ibn Hanbal's teachings in some ways resembled those of Shafi'i, in other ways they were more like those of Malik, particularly in his reliance on available traditions and unwillingness to accept other authority as legally binding.

Life's Work

Descriptions of Ahmad ibn Hanbal characterized him as having an impressive bearing and demeanor; those around him evidently were taken with his air of great learning and dignity. One biographical chronicle describes him as a man of middle height; his hair was reddish from being tinted with henna (a common practice at that time). He was married twice and, in addition to six children by a concubine, he was the father of one son by each of his wives; these two sons, Salih and 'Abd Allah, later played instrumental roles in the dissemination of their father's doctrines. In his personal habits Ahmad ibn Hanbal displayed an exemplary devotion to the principles he taught. It was said that, in the absence of traditions which would authorize him to do so, he refused to eat watermelon. He was painstakingly scrupulous in his piety; he fasted often and, following a schedule which left little time for sleep, he prayed at length during the mornings and evenings and at other set times.

Ibn Hanbal's teachings uniformly emphasized the primacy of revealed authority, and he stalwartly opposed rationalistic innovations which would permit greater scope for interpretation in questions of law and theology. He denounced conceptions which appealed to sources of judgments beyond the established law of the Koran and the traditions. In particular, his views clashed with those of the Mu'tazilites, members of a dogmatic school whose political and theological ideas reveal Hellenistic influence. The various thinkers associated with this school contended that free will rather than determinism should be accepted as a principle of man's place in the universal scheme. One of the critical questions for the Mu'tazilites was the problem of whether the Koran had been created; they maintained that it had. On a more immediate level, they posited notions of divine origins which could be used to elevate political rulers beyond the level granted them by previous doctrines. An important political implication of Mu'tazili ideas was that theological and judicial issues were subject to review on the part of the state. In 827, Caliph al-Ma'mun, anxious to shore up his government against dissension and external challenges, officially adopted tenets of the Mu'tazilah as a means of underscoring his authority on matters of faith.

Although the philosophical impulses that were at the source of Mu'tazili beliefs were of a liberal sort, in urging that reason be consulted on difficult questions of theology, the attempt to transform this position into a political creed produced an unfortunate episode known as the *mihnah* (inquisition or trial). While other thinkers bowed to the wishes of the caliph, Ibn Hanbal steadfastly refused to assert that the Koran had been created. In 833, he and another man were taken in chains and summoned before the caliph, who was then at Tarsus in southern Anatolia. Along the way it was learned that al-Ma'mun had died during a campaign against the Byzantine Empire. Ibn Hanbal was returned to Baghdad, where he was kept successively in three prisons. The new caliph, al-Mu'tasim, was unwilling to abandon the policies of his predecessor. The caliph called Ibn Hanbal before him and interrogated him on the origins of the Koran; after he would not yield on this question, Ibn Hanbal was scourged and returned to prison.

Eventually, however, he was set free. The scars which remained upon his body were taken by his followers as testimony to his willingness to suffer in the cause of his convictions. After al-Wathiq became caliph in 842, Ibn Hanbal, after a few public lectures, remained in relative seclusion; he neither took part in nor encouraged an insurrection which broke out in 844. The inquisition continued for a time, and some prominent individuals were executed or died in prison. All along, however, public opinion had opposed the state's intervention in matters of conscience, and efforts to enforce such policies increasingly had aroused consternation and disapproval. Shortly after the accession of al-Mutawakkil, in 847, the government relented; thereafter, the *mihnah* was abandoned and the caliph reaffirmed conventional Sunnism. Ibn Hanbal was officially honored by invitations to assist in the education of the young prince al-Mu'tazz, but because of his age and declining health, he excused himself from such a position.

Ibn Hanbal composed a number of works which became the basis for the school of law which bears his name. The statement that he preferred a weak tradition to a strong analogy has often been cited in connection with his teachings. For some time his renown as a traditionist surpassed his reputation as a jurist. His most extensive effort, the *Musnad*, was a collection of traditions which, with exacting care, he had traced back to their original sources. Long after it was compiled, the first printed edition of this work appeared in six volumes, containing an estimated twenty-eight or twenty-nine thousand traditions. Other writings recorded his ideas on religious and political questions; some were cast in the form of dialogues, in which he answered questions put to him by students with expositions of law according to the traditions. In short discourses he also expounded his positions on faith and prayer; a polemical work, which he evidently wrote while he was in prison, was meant to define and refute certain heresies. Some materials were also collected and edited by his sons and followers. By the time Ibn Hanbal died in Baghdad, in July of 855, he had won the admiration of many people; hundreds of thousands of people were said to have joined his funeral procession.

Summary

It has commonly been maintained that Ibn Hanbal founded not simply the fourth and last but also the most rigid and least influential among the classical schools of Islamic law. Nevertheless, his work was extremely important—sometimes in ways which belied the usual preconceptions. As a traditionist, he provided important material for the studies of leading scholars in that field, including Muhammad ibn Isma'il al-Bukhari (810-870) and Muslim ibn al-Hajjaj (c. 817-875). For centuries Hanbali doctrines were widely taught, particularly in Baghdad, but also in Damascus and to some extent in Egypt; in portions of Syria, Palestine, Iraq, and some outlying Muslim lands such ideas were received avidly. The important theorist Ibn 'Aqil (1040-1119) demonstrated the breadth and range of inquiry possible within a highly traditionalist framework. Among leading works in jurisprudence which set forth the applications of Ibn Hanbal's teachings were treatises by Muwaffaq al-Din ibn Qudamah (1146-1223) and Ahmad ibn 'Abd al-Halim ibn Taymiyah (1263-1328). During later medieval times, the Hanbali school may have declined in importance. Later, the Ottoman Empire made use of the Hanafi interpretation of Muslim law, limiting the propagation of other doctrines in central Islamic lands. In Arabia, the Wahhabi movement of the eighteenth century depended largely upon Hanbali ideas in Ibn Taymiyah's formulation for doctrinal support; later still, the kingdom of Saudi Arabia adopted this school of law in its official practice. Muslim reform movements, notably in Egypt, have been indebted to Hanbali teachings. In the twentieth century, legislation in other Arab countries on certain points has borne the imprint of Ibn Hanbal's juridical conceptions.

Bibliography
Ahmed, Ziauddin. "Ahmad b. Hanbal and the Problems of *'Iman.*" *Islamic Studies* 12 (1973): 261-270. This brief consideration of Ibn Hanbal's conception of religious faith takes particular note of the differences that arose on this count among the various Muslim schools of law.
_____. "Some Aspects of the Political Theology of Ahmad b. Hanbal." *Islamic Studies* 12 (1973): 53-66. Ibn Hanbal was willing to tolerate imprisonment and suffering partly because he rejected open rebellion against established authority; this brief study examines the bearing his views about succession to the caliphate and political legitimacy had upon his own life and thought.
Coulson, Noel J. *A History of Islamic Law*. Edinburgh: Edinburgh University Press, 1964. In this important survey of stages in the development of legal theory and practice, the author considers representative problems in jurisprudence to illustrate the uses of doctrine and sources among the various schools of law.
Khadduri, Majid. *The Islamic Conception of Justice*. Baltimore: Johns Hopkins University Press, 1984. The theory and practice of Muslim jurisprudence are considered in the light of many facets of legal and philosophical thought that have developed since early times. This study by a leading specialist discusses the applications of methods and texts to issues surrounding major movements in Islamic law.
Leiser, Gary. "Hanbalism in Egypt Before the Mamluks." *Studia Islamica* 54 (1981): 155-181. While the most celebrated proponents of Ibn Hanbal's ideas flourished in other lands, this article demonstrates that his teachings were important for legal and religious thought in Egypt long before the Mamluk seizure of power in the thirteenth century.
Makdisi, George. "The Hanbali School and Sufism." *Humaniora Islamica* 2 (1974): 61-72. Although it has commonly been maintained that the Hanbali school rejected mystical forms of thought, the author points out that at least several eminent jurists found means to reconcile concepts of religious inspiration with Ibn Hanbal's doctrines.
_____. "Hanbalite Islam." In *Studies on Islam*, translated and edited by Merlin L. Swartz. New York: Oxford University Press, 1981. This survey of the literature and polemical works that describe or disparage the Hanbali school suggests that this doctrine has not been treated as well as others. The author challenges certain adverse interpretations which have surfaced in the works of Middle Eastern writers and Western scholars.

Patton, Walter Melville. *Ahmed ibn Hanbal and the Mihna: A Biography of the Imam Including an Account of the Mohammedan Inquisition Called the Mihna, 218-234 A.H.* Leiden, Netherlands: E. J. Brill, 1897. This work, based upon some original materials, has maintained a favorable reputation as an important and detailed study even as modern scholarship has achieved advances in related areas.

Schacht, Joseph. *An Introduction to Islamic Law.* Oxford: Clarendon Press, 1964. This sound and thorough work, which has become recognized as a standard treatment of the subject, deals first with historical developments and then considers applications of law. The positions of the classical law schools are discussed in connection with patterns of influence and doctrine.

Spectorsky, Susan A. "Ahmad ibn Hanbal's *Fiqh.*" *Journal of the American Oriental Society* 102 (1982): 461-465. Ibn Hanbal's insistence that tradition was a leading source of Islamic jurisprudence was demonstrated in his unwillingness to assert that authoritative rulings could be rendered when the sources were unclear or inconsistent. This brief study presents findings from manuscript materials that confirm the general estimate of him as an adherent to the received record of early Islamic teachings.

J. R. Broadus

AKHENATON
Amenhotep IV

Born: c. 1390 B.C.; Egypt
Died: c. 1360 B.C.; Akhetaton (modern Tel el Amarna), Egypt
Areas of Achievement: Government and religion
Contribution: Akhenaton is credited with the establishment of monotheism in Egypt; he built a new capital, Akhetaton, in honor of Aton, the sun god.

Early Life

Born Amenhotep IV and also known as Amenophis IV, Akhenaton (or Ikhnaton) was the son and successor of Amenhotep III (also known as Amenophis III) of the Twenty-eighth Dynasty. Akhenaton's life and accomplishments need to be seen in the context of his family and of Egyptian history in general. Egyptian history is conventionally divided into thirty-one dynasties, which stretched from about 3100 B.C. to 332 B.C., and were succeeded by the Greek Ptolemies from 332 until 30 and the Roman emperors from 30 B.C. to A.D. 395. These dynasties are clumped together in groups under various designations, with the period of Akhenaton falling into the group of dynasties known as the New Kingdom, approximately in the middle of ancient Egyptian history.

The New Kingdom in the fifteenth century B.C. covered an area almost two thousand miles from north to south, most of it centered on the Nile River. The architects of this kingdom were Thutmose I (1525-1514), Thutmose III (1503-1450), and Amenhotep II (1453-1426). By the time of Amenhotep II, the northern city of Memphis had been in effect displaced by Thebes as the center of royal power. Three hundred miles upriver from Memphis, Thebes was the home of the royal family, and the rulers of the Twenty-eighth Dynasty began building tombs for themselves in the desolate region west of Thebes known as the Valley of the Kings. There are sixty-two tombs in the Valley, and the sixty-second one, that of the famous King Tutankhamon, was discovered in 1922 by the English Egyptologist Howard Carter.

One consequence of Thebes' rise to power was an increase in the influence of the god Amon, whose large temple was at nearby Karnak. Amon was a powerful sun god whose name is embedded in such proper names as Tutankhamon and Amenhotep. As a result of Amon's dominance at Thebes, the city became the center of religious celebrations.

Akhenaton's father, whose reign was roughly from 1416 to 1377, controlled Egypt at the peak of its power. He married, when quite young, a general's daughter named Tiy, but as was common, he had numerous concubines from Syria and other regions. Only the six children—two boys and four girls—of his marriage to Tiy, however, had royal significance. The second son, who became Amenhotep IV, was born around 1390.

Amenhotep III was an impressive man who achieved a reputation as a bold hunter and a gifted diplomat. He publicized his reign in a series of innovative scarab seals, each inscribed with a brief account of some historic event. Amenhotep III was also an ambitious builder; although early in his reign he continued to maintain a royal household in Memphis, he later moved to Thebes and spent the last ten years of his life directing construction projects in that city. At the same time, he had built the temple of Amon (in modern Luxor) near Karnak on the Nile River. The costs were enormous: The temple at Montu alone used two and one-half tons of gold and 1,250 pounds of lapis lazuli.

During these last ten years in Thebes, Amenhotep III hosted three opulent jubilees in his palace. The sybaritic life took its toll. Amenhotep III's mummy presents a fat, bald man with rotten teeth; the king died at about the age of thirty-eight and was succeeded by his second son, Amenhotep IV, or Akhenaton, as he soon came to call himself.

Life's Work

His older brother apparently having died young, Amenhotep IV ascended the throne in about 1377. One peculiarity of the new king's background is his failure to appear on his father's monuments, suggesting that for some reason his existence had deliberately been downplayed. The depictions of him show a deformed body that may have been an embarrassment to his family. His sagging belly, elongated face and neck, and feminine hips all point to a pituitary condition now known as Frölich's syndrome. Although Frölich's syndrome usually results in eunuchoidism, Amenhotep IV married Nefertiti and they had several children. Unfortunately, nothing is known about Nefertiti— she may have been Amenhotep's cousin—and it is not even certain that Amenhotep was the natural father of the children she bore.

For the first year of his reign, Amenhotep continued the building projects of his father. He then embarked on his own distinctive projects. He soon planned a spectacular jubilee, a surprising departure from the usual practice of hosting them only after a reign of thirty years; this jubilee was marked by the building of four large temples at nearby Karnak.

The historical record at this point is extremely sketchy for two reasons: When he erected his new city of Akhetaton, Amenhotep thoroughly eradicated the memorials to Amon and the other sun gods, and after his death, one of his successors, Horemheb, destroyed the four temples at Karnak, whose remains, in the form of blocks known as *talatat*, scholars have recently been painstakingly fitting together.

The reconstructed reliefs on these temple remains have produced several surprises for scholars. The *talatat* reveal, for example, that Amenhotep maintained a heavy military presence around himself at all times, a practice that implies insecurity. The *talatat* reliefs also celebrate Nefertiti in diverse depictions—especially surprising since Amenhotep himself appears nowhere in the decorations of his structures. No firm conclusions can be drawn, but it is impossible not to speculate on the possibility that Nefertiti played a much greater role in the royal planning than that evinced by the scanty evidence available before the *talatat* reconstructions.

After about five years at Thebes, Amenhotep suddenly abandoned that city and built a new capital farther north down the Nile River. This new capital was named Akhetaton, or "horizon of the Disc." At the same time, Amenhotep changed his name to Akhenaton (he who is useful to the Sun-disc). In keeping with his new name and devotion, Akhenaton declared Amon, the old sun god, anathema. He had Amon's name plastered over on all of the royal cartouches (an oblong figure enclosing a royal name or epithet) and the name Aton was then inscribed on them. Throughout the kingdom, the name Amon was also at this time desecrated wherever it appeared on such objects as walls and tombs. Akhetaton was built on what is today called Tel el Amarna, and the period of Akhetaton's dominance is designated the "Amarna Age."

Akhenaton's new city was a hastily constructed affair, probably of inferior workmanship, stretching out for seven miles along the east bank of the Nile in Middle Egypt. Akhenaton's own residence was a large village at the city's north end. An unusual walled enclosure designated *Maru-aton* dominated the southern part of the city; with its pools and gardens, it was probably a site for cult observances.

Akhenaton's mother, Queen Tiy, was part of the entourage that moved to Akhetaton, and it now appears that a second wife, known as Queen Kiya, also accompanied him to the new home, although her role and status are unclear. The military guard continued as strong around Akhenaton at Akhetaton as at Thebes, but there was a complete shuffle in the important personnel at the court. The other cities, especially Thebes and Memphis, were allowed to fend for themselves; the old elite believed that they had been snubbed by the heretic king and his parvenus in the new center of the kingdom.

In about the eleventh year of Akhenaton's rule, the royal family began dying, perhaps as a result of a plague in the region. Thus by the fourteenth year, Queen Tiy, Kiya, and four of Akhenaton's six daughters were all dead. With their passing, and the king's aging, his daughter Meretaton rose in power and esteem, and by year fifteen, she was being depicted in statuary with her husband, Smenkhkare (he whom the spirit of Re has ennobled). The epithets devoted to Smenkhkare indicate that he probably acted as the king's coregent. It is an open question whether Smenkhkare ever actually ruled by himself or whether the throne went directly to Tutankhamon upon Akhenaton's death around the year 1360.

What happened to Nefertiti during these last years of Akhenaton's reign is not known. The fact that she seems to have disappeared at about the same time that Smenkhkare came on the scene has inspired scholarly conjecture that they were the same person, but the theory is burdened by too many improbabilities to be convincing. As far as is known, she survived these final years at Akhetaton but with greatly reduced royal influence.

Tutankhamon, possibly Akhenaton's son by Kiya, moved back to Thebes after three years, and the power in the kingdom was concentrated largely in the capable hands of one of Akhenaton's top officials, Aya, who himself ruled for about four years after Tutankhamon's death. Aya's successor, Horemheb, destroyed Akhenaton's temples at Karnak, and the work and innovations of the heretic king were concluded.

Summary

Recent scholarship challenges the old romantic picture of a humanist Akhenaton, a pioneering champion of monotheism in whose steps Moses followed. The king was an insecure ruler, physically unattractive, thrust into a role that surrounded him with figures from his father's establishment whom he feared. His vacillation weakened Egypt's control of its northern provinces, and he left the administration of his kingdom to his military advisers. Donald Redford characterizes Akhenaton as a dreamy soul devoted to cultic reforms that he did not really understand. By not replacing Amon with a significant mythology, Akhenaton was actually propagating atheism. The Sun-disc, Redford says, could never be seen as "god," and Redford spells out his conception of the real focus of Akhenaton's worship:

> What it was Akhenaton tells us plainly enough: the Disc was his father, the universal king. Significant, it seems to me, is the fact that, on the eve of Amenophis III's passing, the king who sat upon Egypt's throne bore as his most popular sobriquet the title "The Dazzling Sun-disc"; on the morrow of the "revolution" the only object of veneration in the supernal realm is King Sun-disc, exalted in the heavens and ubiquitously termed by Akhenaton "my father."

Redford's contemptuous verdict on Akhenaton is that the king was an effete and slothful leader of an "aggregation of voluptuaries." Moreover, Akhenaton appears to Redford as the worst kind of totalitarian, one who demanded "universal submission" from everyone. It is a harsh verdict that Redford submits, and one that more sympathetic scholars will surely challenge as they continue to study the meager evidence of the life and accomplishments of this elusive king.

Bibliography

Aldred, Cyrill. *Akhenaten and Nefertiti*. New York: Viking Press, 1973. This catalog of an exhibition at the Brooklyn Institute of Arts and Sciences, written by one of the period's most eminent scholars, is an invaluable study of the art of Akhenaton's reign. Includes illustrations, many in color, and an extensive bibliography. Fully annotated.

_____. *The Egyptians*. Rev. ed. New York: Thames and Hudson, 1984. Aldred provides an excellent general history of the region, with many black-and-white and color illustrations. Includes a bibliography and indexes.

Baines, John, and Jaromir Málek. *Atlas of Ancient Egypt*. New York: Facts on File, 1980. Baines and Málek provide an especially full and detailed reference book, replete with excellent tables, summaries of the ancient hieroglyphic writing system, maps, and timelines.

Drury, Allen. *A God Against the Gods*. Garden City, N.Y.: Doubleday and Co., 1976. This work, along with its sequel, *Return to Thebes* (1977), provides a highly fictionalized account of the life of Akhenaton and its aftermath. Includes a bibliography, extensive notes from the editors, and illustrations.

Redford, Donald B. *Akhenaten: The Heretic King*. Princeton, N.J.: Princeton University Press, 1984. A detailed scholarly analysis of Akhenaton and his accomplishments by the man who directed the Akhenaten Temple Project. Professor Redford's account is one of the standard studies. Includes an index, bibliography, and illustrations.

Frank Day

AKIBA BEN JOSEPH

Born: c. A.D. 40; probably near Lydda (modern Lod), Palestine
Died: c. A.D. 135; Caesaria, Palestine
Areas of Achievement: Religion and politics
Contribution: The most influential rabbi in the formation of Jewish legal tradition and Mishnah, Akiba is the one scholar most often quoted in the text. He espoused the unsuccessful cause of Simeon Bar Kokhba and died a martyr. The legends about Akiba have been almost as influential as his teachings and life.

Early Life

Akiba (also transliterated Aqiba) ben Joseph was born to humble parents. His father's name was Joseph, but tradition has no other information about him. Akiba worked as an unschooled shepherd. He was part of the lower class designated as the *am-ha-aretz* (people of the land), a term of common abuse. While working for a wealthy man of Jerusalem whose name is sometimes given as Johanan ben Joshua, Akiba fell in love with his daughter, Rachel, who returned his love.

This period of Akiba's life has been variously treated in exaggerated fashion by legendary accounts. Based on the historically most reliable traditions from the Mishnah, it appears reasonably certain that Rachel, agreeing to marry him, was disinherited by her father, and the couple lived in poor circumstances. It was only after his marriage and the birth of a son (probably at about age thirty-five) that Akiba began learning how to read. After learning the basics, Akiba (probably now age forty) left both home and occupation to attend the rabbinic academy at Yavneh, in southwestern Judaea.

In the generation after the destruction of the temple (c. 80-100), the rabbinic assembly at Yavneh was presided over by Rabbi Gamaliel II (an aristocrat) as *Nasi* (Ethnarch) and Rabbi Joshua ben Hananiah (a nonaristocrat) as *Ab Bet Din* (head of the rabbinic court). It was to the latter that Akiba went for instruction, but Hananiah directed him first to Rabbi Tarfon, who was in turn his teacher, friend, and then follower. Later, Akiba studied with Rabbi Nahum of Gimzo and then Hananiah himself. Thus by birth, training, and temperament, Akiba was aligned with the more liberal antiaristocratic wing of the academy, which traced its roots back to Rabbi Hillel. Finally, Akiba studied under Rabbi Eliezer ben Hyrcanus, a leading figure of the aristocratic wing, whose tradition went back to Rabbi Shammai. Akiba's formal training came to a conclusion at Yavneh when in public debate Hananiah was defeated by Eliezer on the primacy of sacrificial duties over Sabbath rest. As the debate was being concluded, the relatively unknown Akiba entered the debate and carried the day against Eliezer. At this point, Akiba was recognized as a rabbi. He began to teach, and pupils began to seek him out.

During this thirteen-year period of study, Akiba must have spent long periods of time away from home. He was encouraged and supported by his wife. While popular legend has undoubtedly exaggerated this aspect of Akiba's life, there is an underlying truth to the material, and, more important, his love and appreciation for Rachel are reflected in his teaching.

Life's Work

In the beginning, Akiba began to teach in Yavneh and spent most of his time actively engaging in the disputes of the rabbinical assembly. These must have been vigorous, for tradition indicates that there were punishments meted out to Akiba on several occasions for his lack of respect for procedure and that at one point he left the assembly and retired to Zifron in Galilee. Akiba was later invited to return to Yavneh by Gamaliel.

Akiba was a tall man, bald, muscular from years of outdoor work. He had transformed himself into a gentle scholar who stressed the value of polite behavior and tact. This emphasis on courtesy, however, did not stop him from entering into debates and arguing passionately for his convictions. As part of his philosophy, he upheld the authority of the *Nasi*, even when he was arguing strongly against the specific ideas that the *Nasi* held.

While he was never entrusted with either of the chief offices of the assembly, he was an important member of the inner circle. When Gamaliel was removed from office because of his arrogance, it was Akiba who was chosen to inform Gamaliel. Eleazar ben Arariah was made *Nasi* in his place, but he was a figurehead, and real leadership rested with Hananiah and Akiba. Having secured dominance of the assembly, Akiba and Hananiah brought the number of the assembly members up from 32 to 72, seating younger scholars to whom Gamaliel had refused admission because of their positions, which were similar to those of Akiba. Akiba seems also to have played an important part in the restoration of Gamaliel to the position of *Nasi*. Direction of the assembly was in the hands of Gamaliel, Eleazar, Hananiah, and Akiba. At that time, he was appointed overseer for the poor. In that capacity, he traveled widely in the area, raising funds. He traveled throughout Judaea, Cappadocia, Arabia, and Egypt.

In the fall of 95, Akiba, Gamaliel, Hananiah, and Eleazar were sent as an embassy to the Emperor Domitian to calm the imperial displeasure over the fact that a member of the imperial family, Flavius Clemens, had converted to Judaism. During this visit, the rabbis probably consulted the Jewish historian and imperial freedman, Flavius Josephus, for advice on imperial protocol and influence for their petition. Before this could be done, however, Domitian died, and Nerva was appointed emperor. Although there is no written record of what was done, it would have been unthinkable for the embassy not to have given the new emperor the formal greetings of the Jewish community and to have made expressions of loyalty. Nerva was seen as opening up a new era in Jewish-Roman relations.

At this point (c. 97), Akiba was between fifty and sixty years of age. He established his own school at Bene-Berak (near modern Tel Aviv). It was during this time that Akiba's most enduring work was accomplished. In his teaching, he used a combination of demanding logic, rules of interpretation, and homely parables to put forth his ideas and ideals. He set the basic organization of what was to become the Mishnah into its six parts, and developed his ideas of interpretation of the Law based on the mystic significance of the text. In addition to a passion for social justice, he developed his unique positions on women, marriage, and other issues. None of these positions was achieved without extensive debate and discussion in Akiba's own school and in the assembly in Yavneh. There, the new leading opponent of Akiba was Rabbi Ishmael ben Elisha. Many of the teachings of these men were later arranged into opposing debates, even when it can be shown that no such discussion took place. The two men had great respect for each other and were cordial in their relations, but they were not friends.

The first generation of Akiba's disciples—Elisha ben Abuyah, Simeon ben Azzai, and Simeon ben Zoma—did not fare well. Elisha became an apostate, Simeon ben Azzai became mad, and Simeon ben Zoma lost his life. The second generation of scholars taught by Akiba, however, provided the rabbinic leadership of the next generation. Of these, Rabbi Meir and Aquila deserve special attention. Meir, who had studied with Elisha ben Abuyah and Ishmael before coming to Akiba, was responsible for continuing the arrangement of the Mishnah following the principles of Akiba. He wrote down many of the sayings of Akiba, often giving the opposing view of Ishmael. Aquila was a Greek who converted to Judaism and studied with Akiba. With Akiba's encouragement, he made a new (or made revisions to the) Greek translation of the Hebrew scriptures. For a time, Aquila seems to have been in the confidence of both the Jews and the Roman officials.

The last phase of Akiba's life is a matter of considerable debate among scholars. Relations with Rome, never good under the best of circumstances, went through a series of radical shifts. There is no clear understanding of these years since the sources (Jewish Talmudic and Roman writers) preserve the misunderstandings of the principals. What part, if any, Akiba played in the formulation of Jewish positions is not clear until the very end of the conflict. Some indicate that he used his position as overseer of the poor to travel throughout the land and ferment revolt. Others suggest that his position was essentially nonpolitical and that he did not resist until religious practices, including prayer and study, were forbidden. There is no evidence that Akiba was active in politics or any other capacity during the troubles at the end of Trajan's reign through the beginning years of Hadrian.

In about 130, to ease some of the existing tension, Hadrian sought to rebuild the temple but insisted on placing a statue of himself in it and dedicating the temple to Jupiter Capitolinus. The implications of this position for the Jews clearly was not understood by Hadrian. There is a tradition, not in itself improbable, that the rabbis selected the now-aged Akiba to lead a delegation to Hadrian to reverse this stand. It is not known whether they reached the emperor, but their efforts, for whatever reason, were unsuccessful. Open and widespread rebellion broke out, which required five years and some of Hadrian's best military talent to quell.

Of Akiba's activities during that period, only a few events are clear. The Talmudic evidence shows that Akiba was a firm supporter of living within the restrictions of 125 that forbade circumcision and severely restricted the rights of Jewish legal courts and synagogue practices. At some point in the rebellion, Akiba joined other rabbis, including Ishmael, and gave his endorsement to Simeon Bar Kokhba. Bar Kokhba (meaning son of a star), the name taken by Simeon Bar Kosiba, carried messianic implications; it was Akiba who applied the verse from Numbers 24:17, "The star rises from Jacob," to him. This stance was not without opposition. The Midrash records that "when Rabbi Akiba beheld Bar Kosiba he exclaimed, 'This is the king Messiah!' Rabbi Johanan ben Tortha retorted: 'Akiba, grass will grow in your cheeks and he will still not have come!'" (*Lamentations* 2:2). Thus, at least in the last stages, Akiba gave his support to Bar Kokhba, who claimed to be the *Nasi*, superceding the rabbinical *Nasi* at Yavneh; Akiba hailed him as Savior (Messiah).

Sometime after 130, and possibly as late as 134, Akiba was arrested and imprisoned by the consular legate, Tineius Rufus. For a while, he was allowed to have visitors and continued to teach. There is a strong element of folktale about these circumstances, and the possibility of the sources imitating the classical model of Socrates cannot be ignored. Akiba's final act of scholarship was to bring the religious calendar into order. Whether these activities were too much for the Romans to allow or whether Akiba's support of Bar Kokhba made him a symbol of resistance, Rufus brought him to trial in Caesaria and ordered his execution.

Summary

Akiba ben Joseph's most significant contributions were made to the organization of the Mishnah and the teachings in the Talmud. Akiba took the many rabbinic decisions and arranged them under these major headings: Zeraim (Seeds, on agriculture), Mo'ed (Seasons, on holidays), Nashim (Women, on marriage and divorce), Kodashim (Sanctities, on offerings), and Teharoth (Purities, on defilement and purification). These headings with their tractates (subheadings) were continued by Rabbi Meir and then codified by Rabbi Judah ha-Nasi around 200. There are more than twenty-four hundred citations of Akiba in the Talmud; he is the most frequently cited authority.

Akiba championed a special method of interpretation of the text which he learned from Rabbi Nahum of Gimzo and which he retained even though the latter abandoned it. Akiba saw hidden significance in every aspect of the received text, whether it was an unusual wording, a special grammatical form, or an aberrant spelling. He was opposed on that count by Ishmael, who declared that the Torah was written in the language of men (with its possibility of error). Akiba made his points by Ishmael's method and then would extend the argument with his method. Akiba was fond of using parable to explain ethical points.

Akiba's area of special concern was marriage, where he championed attractiveness for women as a means of holding their husbands' affections and divorce for loveless matches. He opposed polygamy, which was still permitted and practiced by the aristocrats. As an extension of this stance, he fought for and gained the acceptance of the Song of Songs (*Shir ha-Shirim*) in the biblical canon, against heavy opposition.

As important as Akiba's work was, the stories about his life have exerted an equal influence on Judaism. Many of them are gross exaggerations and many are probably apocryphal, but the points which they make are consistent with the known teachings of Akiba.

Bibliography
Aleksandrov, G. S. "The Role of Aqiba in the Bar Kochba Rebellion." In *Eliezer ben Hyrcanus*, vol. 2, by Jacob Neusner. Leiden, Netherlands: E. J. Brill, 1973. Aleksandrov refutes the position that Akiba was active in the Bar Kokhba rebellion but admits that he could have given the rebellion moral support. The volume is part of the Studies in Judaism in Late Antiquity series.

Finkelstein, Louis. *Akiba: Scholar, Saint, and Martyr*. Cleveland: World Publishing Co., 1962. The only book-length study of Akiba's life and thought in English. Finkelstein re-creates Akiba's life by taking a mildly critical look at the biographical sources and then placing the teachings of Akiba where they most easily fit into Akiba's life. Finkelstein sees Akiba representing the popular party against the aristocrats. He also sees Akiba as a pacifist to the end. Both positions are overstated and are generally not accepted by other scholars.

Ginzberg, Louis. "Akiba." In *Jewish Encyclopedia*, vol. 1. New York: Funk and Wagnalls, 1912. This brief article, although old, is extremely well-reasoned and lucidly written.

Goldin, Judah. "Toward a Profile of a *Tanna*, Aqiba ben Joseph." *Journal of the American Oriental Society* 96 (1976): 38-56. An important scholarly article which demonstrates that much of the biographical material about Akiba may be accepted as historical. Goldin's emphasis is on Akiba's marriage and his teachings regarding marriage, love, and divorce.

Neusner, Jacob. *Judaism, The Evidence of the Mishnah*. Chicago: University of Chicago Press, 1981. A distillation of Neusner's work and that of his students. He leads the critical school which rejects much of the traditional information about the rabbis' lives and questions the attribution of many teachings to specific rabbis.

_____, ed. *Studies in Judaism in Late Antiquity*. Vol. 20, *The Jews Under Roman Rule: From Pompey to Diocletian*, by E. Mary Smallwood. Leiden, Netherlands: E. J. Brill, 1976. Solid scholarly work which should be used to update Schürer. The study is concerned almost exclusively with the political aspects of the problem. Good background; understandably little on Akiba.

Schürer, Emil. *A History of the Jewish People in the Time of Jesus Christ*. Edited and abridged by Nahum N. Glatzer. New York: Schocken Books, 1961. While the bibliography of secondary sources is obsolete, that is the only unusable part of this excellent study. Schürer has an absolute command of the classical and talmudic sources and gives more detail about the Jewish problems of Trajan and Hadrian than one will find elsewhere.

Strack, Hermann L. *Introduction to the Talmud and Midrash*. Philadelphia: Jewish Publication Society of America, 1931. There are many guides to the Talmud, but this is still the best short guide.

Michael M. Eisman

SAINT ALBERTUS MAGNUS

Born: c. 1200; Lauingen, Swabia
Died: November 15, 1280; Cologne
Areas of Achievement: Education and science
Contribution: Albertus expanded scientific knowledge through experimentation and observation. As an Aristotelian, he reconciled reason with revelation.

Early Life

Albertus was born at Lauingen in Swabia, the eldest son of the Count of Bollstädt. The exact date of his birth is not known; it could have been as early as 1193 or as late as 1207. Albertus matured during the most dynamic decades in medieval history, decades marked by the rule of great medieval sovereigns such as Pope Innocent III, Philip II in France, and Ferdinand III in Castile. The Albigensian and the Fourth crusades were fought at this time, and in England, King John signed the Magna Carta. The dates, places, and content of Albertus' education are still open to speculation. Most scholars believe that he studied the liberal arts for some months in 1222 at the newly founded University of Padua.

As the University of Padua had just broken away from the University of Bologna over the issue of civil versus canon law, it would appear that Albertus' father planned for him to become a civil lawyer. That would account, too, for the strong objections of Albertus' family when, in 1223, at about the age of sixteen, he joined the Dominican Order.

As a novice, Albertus studied theology, probably at Bologna, where he was immersed in the writings of theologians ranging from Saint Augustine to Robert Grosseteste. Despite the constitutions of his order, issued in 1228, which forbade the study of books written by pagans and philosophers, Albertus knew a large number of these works, which profoundly influenced him. He read the works of Averroës, Avicenna, Pliny, Plato, and especially Aristotle. He also knew Pythagorean arithmetic, though Roger Bacon would later claim that Albertus was never a mathematician.

Life's Work

In 1228, Albertus left Bologna for Cologne, where he began his career as a teacher. In 1233, his order assigned him the lectorship in Hildesheim. Subsequently, he taught at Fribourg, Ratisbon, and Strasbourg. In 1240, he went to the University of Paris, where he earned his degree as a doctor of theology. While there, he ensured his reputation as one of the great minds of his age as a result of two diverse activities.

First, he began work on his commentaries on Aristotle, which ultimately included treatises on physics, metaphysics, logic, psychology, geography, zoology, botany, mineralogy, astrology, alchemy, chiromancy, and celestial phenomena. So well conceived and detailed were these writings that Albertus was quoted as an authority even during his lifetime. With this work, Albertus contributed significantly to the creation of Christian Aristotelianism.

Second, in 1240, as a result of polemical attacks upon the Talmud, Blanche of Castile and her son, Louis IX, called for a public debate of the merits of those attacks. Albertus was one of seven people chosen to discuss the issue. Because of this debate, Albertus' skills as a negotiator were in frequent demand.

Twice he settled disputes between the citizens of Cologne and Archbishop Conrad von Hochstein, typical examples of the struggle between feudal authority and the rising power of the middle-class townsmen. Albertus negotiated a trade agreement between Cologne and Utrecht. He settled a property dispute between Mecklenburg and the Knights of Saint John at the request of Pope Clement IV.

After receiving his doctor's degree, Albertus stayed in Paris, where he taught theology at the university from 1242 to 1248. This is the period when Thomas Aquinas and Siger de Brabant studied with him. In 1248, the Dominicans sent Albertus to Cologne to found and administer the first Dominican school in Germany. There he collaborated with Thomas and others in the formulation of a standard course of study for the schools of the order. Later, he was appointed for three years the provincial over all German Dominicans.

Albertus' administrative ability must have been equal to the quality of his teaching and negotiating, because the pope, over the objections of both Albertus and the general of the Dominicans, Humbert of Romans, appointed Albertus Bishop of Ratisbona in 1260, a position that he resigned in 1262. Almost immediately thereafter, Pope Urban IV sent him to preach the Eighth Crusade, an assignment which lasted two years. In 1264, he returned to teaching, first at Würzburg and then in Strasbourg, after which he finally returned to Cologne in 1272.

He left this oft-sought, much-desired seclusion only a few more times before his death in 1280; the first time was to attend the council at Lyons in 1274. The second occurred in 1277, when Albertus went to Paris to defend his former student Thomas (who had died in 1274) and Aristotelianism, under attack for heresy. As Albertus may have been past eighty at this time and was apparently not in good health, this action clearly indicates his dedication to Aristotelian thought and his support of Thomas.

In addition to boundless energy and practicality in everyday affairs, Albertus possessed an encyclopedic mind, unflagging curiosity, and an undaunted commitment to scholarly endeavors, as is illustrated by the subjects about which he wrote. A prolific writer, he produced at least thirty-eight volumes on interests ranging from alchemy to zoology. Albertus' scientific approach was rooted in experimentation and observation rather than in philosophical speculation and revelation. He had no patience with those who accepted dogmatic knowledge without investigation. Where experience disagreed with accepted dogma, he followed experience, preferably his own. While conceding that all things must ultimately be attributed to divine will, he argued that God worked through nature, which could be understood through reason.

More specifically, Albertus thought that there were two kinds of knowledge, that of theology, faith, and revelation and that of philosophy and natural reason. According to Albertus, there was no contradiction. Instead, he saw each activity as separate but not exclusive of the other; he harmonized the whole, using each kind of knowledge in its appropriate sphere of human inquiry. Albertus began all of his investigations with Aristotle's work and mindful of the Christian faith. Anchored in these, he allowed his empirical observations to refine, redefine, elaborate, and correct. He felt free to exercise reason on all natural phenomena.

De vegetabilibus et plantis, written around 1250, became the chief source of biological knowledge in Europe for the next three hundred years. Albertus relied almost exclusively on observation. He noted how ecological conditions, such as heat, light, and moisture, affected the way things grew. His study of plants led him close to an understanding of mutation and species modification, something he could not transfer to his investigation of animals, probably because it brought him too close to man.

De animalibus (thirteenth century) recorded Albertus' thinking on zoology. In it, his observations about German whaling and fishing were outstanding. To the standard Aristotelian catalog he added descriptions of animals that he had observed in northern Europe. Unfortunately, his understanding of animals, especially the reproductive process, fell prey to the standard misconceptions of his day; for example, he thought that the birth of monstrosities resulted from "defective female matter" which the male "vital heat" could not overcome. Nevertheless, he identified correctly the function of the umbilical cord and the placenta. Through observation, he disproved many of the traditional mystical origins and theological definitions of animals.

It was in his works *De mineralibus et rebus metallicis* (c. 1260; *Book of Minerals*, 1967) and *De causis proporietatum elementorum* (thirteenth century), however, that Albertus made his most original contributions. In them, he scientifically described various precious stones and minerals, although he often included descriptions of mystical properties. He also correctly explained why sea fossils could be found high on a mountainside. Finally, Albertus believed that the world was a sphere and held the near-heretical notion that people lived on the "underside" of that sphere; yet he still believed that Earth was the center of the universe, with all else revolving around it.

Albertus remains one of the greatest medieval theorists on physical science. Although many of his inquiries produced traditional answers, his methodology was a harbinger of modern science. He provided the framework for an understanding of the operations of the physical world, which he saw as a system of activity and constant change; this conception was contrary to the thinking of many of his contemporaries, who defined the world in static terms. He died in Cologne in 1280.

Summary

The life of Albertus Magnus, the "Christian Aristotle," spanned most of the thirteenth century. He was part of the great outburst of philosophical speculation which characterized the medieval mind. He dealt effectively with at least twelve different popes, beginning with Innocent III, popes who often challenged his methodology and thought. Albertus became the most learned man and the greatest teacher of his day; he is still the patron saint of Catholic schools.

Because of the overwhelming quantity and quality of his work and because of his excellence as a teacher, Albertus earned the titles "Magnus" and "Universal Teacher." A man of common sense, with an insatiable and healthy curiosity, he sought truth, accepted it when he found it, and conveyed it honestly to his students. Roger Bacon, who was by no means one of Albertus' supporters, conceded that Albertus was one of the greatest scholars of their day. Nevertheless, many were the pedestrian minds who accused Albertus of magic and consorting with the Devil, thinking that such breadth of knowledge could not have been gained in any other way. At times, he was considered a pantheist, although this doctrine would never have appealed to Albertus, who was a man deeply committed to God as the creator and source of all knowledge. In his belief, to understand nature was to understand God.

Although his teaching and administrative career was primarily confined to Germany, Albertus' reputation was European. While he reflected much of the temper of his age, he also helped to create it. More than anyone else, he constructed the Scholastic world system. He awakened the scientific spirit that would dominate the intellectual life of subsequent centuries. Little wonder that his contemporaries called him "Magnus."

Bibliography

Brandt, William J. *The Shape of Medieval History: Studies in Modes of Perception*. New Haven, Conn.: Yale University Press, 1966. This is an excellent study of medieval perceptions of nature, human nature, and human action, which illustrates how those perceptions defined the world for the medieval thinker. Contains extensive explanatory notes, which offset the lack of a bibliography.

Crombie, A. C. *Medieval and Early Modern Science*. Vol. 1. Garden City, N.Y.: Doubleday and Co., 1959. This is an excellent analysis of Albertus' contributions to the sciences and empirical methodology. Highly readable and contains an excellent bibliography.

Durant, Will. *The Story of Civilization*. Vol. 4, *The Age of Faith: A History of Medieval Civilization—Christian, Islamic, and Judaic—from Constantine to Dante, A.D. 325-1300*. New York: Simon and Schuster, 1950. An enjoyable work of popular history, it provides an excellent introduction to Albertus. Contains a standard bibliography and a detailed table of contents.

Gilson, Étienne. *History of Christian Philosophy in the Middle Ages*. London: Sheed and Ward, 1955. Gilson is the leading modern follower of Saint Thomas Aquinas, who thought that truth was perennial and, like Albertus, that there need not be a contradiction between reason and faith.

Haskins, Charles Homer. *The Rise of Universities*. Ithaca, N.Y.: Cornell University Press, 1923. Haskins interpretively outlines the rise of the medieval university, commenting briefly on Albertus' role. This study sparked a generation's study of medieval education.

Heer, Friedrich. *The Intellectual History of Europe*. Translated by Jonathan Steinberg. Cleveland, Ohio: World Publishing Co., 1968. An excellent analysis of the development of Western thought, with Albertus seen as a pivotal figure. This is a detailed scholarly study; the sources must be culled from copious notes.

Leff, Gordon. *Medieval Thought: St. Augustine to Ockham*. Baltimore: Penguin Books, 1958. Leff gives the reader an easily understood description of the development of the medieval mind. Describes Albertus' contributions as a synthesizer, an experimenter, an Aristotelian who reconciled reason and faith; according to Leff, he foreshadowed René Descartes and John Locke in methodology. Limited bibliography.

Thorndike, Lynn. *A History of Magic and Experimental Science*. Vols. 1 and 2, *The First Thirteen Centuries of Our Era*. New York: Columbia University Press, 1923. Thorndike remains one of the great historians of science. In this work, he describes Albertus' empirical method.

Weisheipl, James A. *The Development of Physical Theory in the Middle Ages*. Ann Arbor: University of Michigan Press, 1971. Weisheipl stresses Albertus' elaboration and extension of Aristotelian science, particularly in physics. The reader is persuaded that there was much originality in medieval scientific thought. The bibliography for this short, perceptive, and interpretive essay contains the standard works on the history of science.

Shirley F. Fredricks

ALCIBIADES

Born: c. 450 B.C.; Athens?, Greece
Died: 404 B.C.; Phrygia, Asia Minor
Areas of Achievement: Government and warfare
Contribution: Although it might be argued that Alcibiades was a demagogue, a traitor, a heretic, and morally dissolute, he was a gifted politician and military leader—and certainly one of the most romantic figures of the Peloponnesian War.

Early Life

Alcibiades was born around 450 B.C. the son of Cleinias, a wealthy aristocrat and participant in the Battle of Artemisium. His mother, Deinomache, was a member of the Alcmaeonid clan and a cousin of Pericles, in whose house the youth was reared after the death of his father in 447. Unfortunately, Alcibiades proved to be a difficult boy and failed to acquire any of his guardian's noble qualities—except, perhaps, some political ambition. Even so, according to Plutarch Alcibiades was uniquely equipped for success. He was tall, handsome, wealthy, charming, imaginative, and one of the best orators of the day; clearly, he had qualities which endeared him to the masses. At the same time, he was impious, insolent, and incurably egocentric. He could, perhaps, have become another Themistocles or Pericles were it not for the fact that he had no interest in Athenian democracy. His political affinities were probably much closer to those of Peisistratus and the other Greek tyrants.

Alcibiades' military training began at the outset of the Peloponnesian War, which forced the youth into action quickly. He served with distinction in battles at Potidaea (432 B.C.) and Delium (424 B.C.), and, as a result, Alcibiades became quite popular in Athens and elsewhere. He acquired numerous admirers—among whom was the great philosopher Socrates, who saved the youth's life in battle and then later had the favor returned. A lasting friendship was formed, although Socrates must have found his protégé's rapacious life-style intolerable at times. It was during this period that Alcibiades took a wife, a certain Hipparete of the house of Hipponius, who, after an unsuccessful attempt at divorce, closed her eyes to his infidelity and proved a dutiful wife. Together they had a son named Axiochus, who apparently acquired some of the father's less desirable traits.

Life's Work

Alcibiades began his political career in 420, when he was elected one of the ten generals of the state, a position of great importance. Unlike Pericles, who had served on the same board for more than thirty years, Alcibiades was less devoted to Athens than to himself. Realizing that war with Sparta was the quickest route to fame and fortune, he cast his lot with the radicals of the state. This political decision placed him at odds with Nicias, the leader of the conservative faction, who had effected a peace treaty with the Spartans in 421. Displeased with the lull in fighting, Alcibiades formed an alliance with Argos, Elis, and Mantinea against Sparta. He was successful and was reelected in 419 to his seat on the board of generals. Yet his moment of glory was brief. When the alliance with Argos eventually failed, Alcibiades' popularity suffered, and he lost his generalship. It was only through a brief political *amicitia* with his enemy Nicias that he narrowly averted ostracism.

His political demise did not last long. In 416, another opportunity presented itself when a delegation from the city of Egesta in Sicily appealed to Alcibiades and the radicals in Athens for assistance in war against the neighboring state of Selinus, which was supported by Syracuse. The promise of wealth and the possibility of a western empire struck a responsive chord in Alcibiades. Under his influence and over the strenuous objections of Nicias, Athens prepared to send a large amphibious force against Syracuse.

Unfortunately, the expedition was doomed from the start. Alcibiades, selected as one of the leaders, was accused by his detractors of impiety; the likelihood of his acquittal, however, prompted the opposition to postpone the trial, and Alcibiades was free, for the moment, to resume his position within the triumvirate of leadership designated for the Sicilian campaign. One of those with whom he would rule was Nicias, his former political adversary. It is not surprising that their inability to agree on strategy hindered field operations. Moreover, the siege had just begun when Athens dispatched a galley to bring Alcibiades back for his trial. Although he offered no resistance, the possibility of a death sentence in Athens led Alcibiades to escape at Thurii. From Thurii he made his way to Sparta, where he would remain for two years. While there, he earned the admiration of the Spartans with abstemious behavior. He plunged immediately into politics, urging the Spartans to assist Syracuse in its war with Athens. He also convinced the Spartans to fortify Decelea, from which they could strike into Attica. Alcibiades was determined to have his revenge.

Although Alcibiades adapted to the Spartan way and rendered valuable services, he had not abandoned all the vices of earlier years. He seduced the Spartan queen while her husband, King Agis, was away at Decelea. The queen became pregnant and gave birth to a son. By the summer of 412, it was clear that Alcibiades could no longer remain in Sparta. From there, he fled to the court of the Persian satrap of Sardis, Tissaphernes, who, like others before him, was very impressed with his peripatetic guest. Alcibiades worked hard to effect an alliance with Tissaphernes and Persia which would prove injurious to Sparta and enable him to return to power in Athens. First the democracy must be overthrown and an oligarchy established in its place, he reasoned. In the deliberations which followed, many Athenians were receptive to the plan, and in 411 an oligarchic faction took control of the government. Unfortunately, the satrap's demands were too great, and the oligarchy quickly lost faith in Alcibiades. Even so, a number of generals remained loyal to Alcibiades, who continued to control the bulk of Athens' military forces on the island of Samos.

The threat of a Spartan invasion, however, soon threw Athens into chaos; the oligarchy was toppled, and Alcibiades was recalled. Yet he did not return immediately, choosing instead to remain in the eastern Aegean Sea area, where he achieved significant victories at Cynossema and Cyzicus. In the latter engagement, all Spartan ships were either destroyed or captured, and a Spartan admiral was killed. Between 410 and 408, Alcibiades enjoyed other successes—in the Bosporus Thracius, the Hellespontus, the area neighboring the Propontis Sea, and the area north of the Aegean Sea—as he struggled to keep Athenian food supplies flowing from the Black Sea area.

By the autumn of 408, Alcibiades was supreme in the Aegean area and was now ready to return triumphant to Athens. He reached the city in the following year and was given ultimate authority over Athenian military forces. It was at this time, during the peak of his power, that he probably intended to establish a tyranny. The Spartan commander Lysander, however, turned the tide of battle in the Aegean again, with a victory at Notium over one of Alcibiades' subordinates. Even though Alcibiades was not wholly responsible for the defeat, the capricious Athenians could not forgive him. Deprived of his command, Alcibiades went into exile in Thrace. Ignored by his former countrymen and hounded by his enemies, he fled to Phrygia, where, at the insistence of Lysander, he was assassinated in 404.

Summary

When Pericles died in 429, a void was left in Athenian leadership. Into this void stepped Alcibiades. Endowed with the physical and intellectual requisites for greatness, he might have been the leader—indeed, the hero—for whom Athens was looking. Certainly Alcibiades was a great general whose judgment in military matters carried him from victory to victory and earned for him the admiration of Spartans, Athenians, and Persians. It might be argued that his superior generalship in the eastern Aegean prolonged the Peloponnesian War for the Athenians and, if the Athenian leadership had accepted his advice from exile in Thrace, Athens might not have lost the Battle of Aegospotami in 405.

Yet military victories alone are not always sufficient to attain greatness. In the opinion of most scholars, Alcibiades, although a gifted individual, was a traitor, a heretic, and an opportunist. In all arenas, he was determined to win, regardless of the cost. In the Olympic Games of 416, he entered seven four-horse teams in the chariot race and came away with all the top prizes. He was a demagogue who tempted Athens into costly schemes—such as the

Syracusan expedition of 415, which resulted in the loss of about fifty thousand men and more than two hundred triremes. He also conspired to overthrow the democracy and dreamed of the day when he might become a dictator. Alcibiades was all these things and more, yet he remains one of the most colorful and interesting figures of classical Greece.

Bibliography
Benson, E. F. *The Life of Alcibiades*. New York: D. Appleton Co., 1929. The standard biography of Alcibiades, old but still very useful. Written in large part from primary materials, especially Thucydides and Plutarch. A sympathetic study which, at times, reads like a novel. Should appeal to scholars and students alike.
Bury, J. B., and Russell Meiggs. *A History of Greece*. New York: St. Martin's Press, 1900, 4th ed. 1975. The best one-volume survey of Greek history to the time of Alexander the Great. The main events of Alcibiades' life are treated in the chapter "The Decline and Downfall of the Athenian Empire." Maps, illustrations, and copious bibliographical notes enhance the value of this volume.
Bury, J. B., S. A. Cook, and F. E. Adcock, eds. *The Cambridge Ancient History*. Vol. 5. New York: Macmillan, 1927. In four chapters covering the Peloponnesian War, from "Sparta and the Peloponnese" to "The Athenian Expedition to Sicily," W. S. Ferguson recounts the war and gives valuable insight into Alcibiades' role in it. Especially useful to the more advanced student of Greek history.
Henderson, Bernard W. *The Great War Between Athens and Sparta: A Companion to the Military History of Thucydides*. London: Macmillan, 1927. Excellent study of the Peloponnesian War. One of the better sources for the life of Alcibiades. A sympathetic survey from boyhood to death. Written in large part from primary materials. Should appeal to both scholars and students.
Meiggs, Russell. *The Athenian Empire*. Oxford: Clarendon Press, 1972, reprint 1982. Excellent political and military history of fifth century B.C. Athens. Treats the more important events in Alcibiades' career. Includes a good bibliography.
Plutarch. *The Rise and Fall of Athens: Nine Great Lives*. Translated by I. Scott-Kilvert. Baltimore: Penguin Books, 1960, reprint 1976. Plutarch was a first century A.D. Greek historian whose biographies of Greek and Roman heroes are an indispensable resource. This edition contains nine of those biographies, including that of Alcibiades. Especially useful for getting a sense of Alcibiades' character.
Starr, Chester G. *A History of the Ancient World*. Oxford: Oxford University Press, 1965, 3d ed. 1983. Good one-volume survey of ancient world from man's beginnings to fifth century A.D. Excellent bibliographical essays at

the end of each chapter. Brief survey of chief events of Alcibiades' life in a chapter entitled "End of the Golden Age."

Thucydides. *The Peloponnesian War*. Baltimore: Penguin Books, 1954, rev. ed. 1972. Written by a famous Greek historian of the fifth century B.C., this book is the most valuable source of information on the Peloponnesian War. Considered a model of objectivity and accuracy. Chronicles the main events of Alcibiades' life in scattered references, from his role in the alliance with Argos to the Athenian victory at Cynossema in 411. Most secondary accounts of Alcibiades begin with Thucydides and Plutarch.

Larry W. Usilton

ALCMAEON

Born: c. 510 B.C.; Croton, Magna Graecia (southern Italy)
Died: c. 430 B.C.; place unknown
Areas of Achievement: Medicine and philosophy
Contribution: Alcmaeon was one of the earliest Greeks known to have written on medicine and the first to have practiced scientific dissection. He held that the brain is the central organ of sensation and that health is the result of an equilibrium of qualities or forces in the body.

Early Life

Of Alcmaeon's early life almost nothing is known, except that his father's name was Peirithous and that he was a native of Croton (Greek Crotona), a coastal town inside the "toe" of Italy. Even Alcmaeon's dates are uncertain. According to Aristotle, he lived during the old age of the philosopher Pythagoras, whose life spanned much of the sixth century B.C. and who died about 490 or later. It was once assumed that, as a younger contemporary of Pythagoras, Alcmaeon probably should be placed in the sixth century. It is now widely held, however, largely from the evidence of his ideas, that he probably lived in the fifth century. The evidence at the disposal of modern scholars is not sufficient to fix the date of his lifetime more precisely.

Croton was a Greek city founded by Achaeans from mainland Greece in 710 B.C. It had a fine harbor and enjoyed extensive commerce. As a result, it became the wealthiest and most powerful city in Magna Graecia (the Greek name for southern Italy), especially after its forces defeated and completely destroyed its enemy, the neighboring city of Sybaris, in 510. It boasted the most splended temple in southern Italy, the temple of Hera Lacinia, which drew large numbers of Greeks to a great annual religious assembly. Croton was renowned for its devotion to gymnastics; one of its citizens, Milon, became the most famous athlete in Greece, having won the victory in wrestling at Olympia six times. Croton is said to have produced more Olympic victors than any other city.

Croton was also the home of a well-known school of medicine, which was perhaps the earliest in Greece and which long retained its reputation. The city enjoyed the distinction of producing the finest physicians in Greece, of whom the most prominent was Democedes, regarded as the best physician of his day (the latter half of the sixth century B.C.). His fame carried him to Aegina, Athens, and Samos, where he was employed by the tyrant Polycrates, and to Persia (as a prisoner), where he cured both King Darius the Great and his wife, Atossa, before he escaped, returning to Croton to marry the daughter of Milon.

Croton was also known as the home of the philosopher Pythagoras and his followers. Born in Samos, Pythagoras emigrated to Croton about 530, where he formed a religious brotherhood composed of about three hundred young men. Pythagoras quickly gained influence over the political affairs of the city, but growing opposition to his order led to his retirement from Croton. In the latter half of the fifth century, a democratic revolution resulted in a massacre of nearly all the members of the order. Alcmaeon is said by some ancient authors to have been a disciple of Pythagoras, but it is likely that this belief was based only on inferences from the similarities of some of his doctrines to those of the Pythagoreans. Aristotle compares his theory of opposites with that of the Pythagoreans but says that Alcmaeon either borrowed this idea from them or they took it from him. There is, in fact, no definitive evidence that associates Alcmaeon with the Pythagoreans. He lived during the period in which the Pythagorean brotherhood flourished at Croton, and he probably knew of the Pythagoreans and their beliefs. His precise relationship to them, however, is not known. Diogenes Laertius reports that Alcmaeon wrote mostly on medicine, and it has been inferred from this statement that he was a physician. Given Croton's reputation as a medical center, it is not unlikely. He wrote on physics and astronomy as well, however, and in this respect he resembles the Ionian philosophers, some of whom were interested in medicine. He was certainly a natural philosopher, interested in science and medicine; he may or may not have been a physician.

Life's Work

Alcmaeon lived in the pre-Socratic period, when the study of physiology was merely a part of philosophy. Only later did Hippocrates separate medicine from philosophy. Greek medical theory, in fact, grew out of philosophical speculation rather than the practice of medicine. Alcmaeon's contributions include both cosmological conjecture and anatomical research. He was credited in antiquity with having written the first treatise on natural philosophy. The book is no longer extant, but some idea of its contents can be gleaned from portions that were summarized by later writers. In the opening sentence of the work, Alcmaeon declared that the gods alone have certain knowledge, while for men only inference from things seen is possible. Thus, he eschewed all-encompassing, oversimplified hypotheses in favor of careful observation as the basis of understanding nature.

Nevertheless, Alcmaeon shared with the Ionian philosophers an interest in natural speculation. Thus, he posited a microcosmic-macrocosmic relationship between man and the universe. He believed that the human soul was immortal because it was continuously in motion like the heavenly bodies, which he thought divine and immortal because they moved continuously and eternally in circles. While the heavenly bodies are immortal, however, men perish because "they cannot join the beginning to the end." Alcmaeon seems to mean by this that human life is not circular but linear and thus is not eternally renewed but runs down and dies when its motion ceases.

Alcmaeon developed a theory of opposites, according to which human beings have within them pairs of opposing forces, such as black and white, bitter and sweet, good and bad, large and small. He may well have been
indebted to the Pythagoreans, who posited pairs of contrary qualities on
mathematical lines (or they may have borrowed the notion from him). Alcmaeon, however, applied his theory particularly to health and disease. He
defined health as a balance or equilibrium (*isonomia*) of opposing forces in
the body (for example, warm and cold, bitter and sweet, wet and dry). He
explained disease as the excess or predominance (*monarchia*) of one of these
qualities or pairs of opposites that upsets the balance. This predominance
could be caused by an excess or deficiency of food or by such external factors
as climate, locality, fatigue, or exertion. Alcmaeon probably based this theory on his observation of factional struggles in Greek city-states, and he may
have been influenced by the growth of democratic political ideas. Of all
Alcmaeon's theories, this concept of opposites was to be the most influential
in later Greek thought. The Hippocratic treatise *Peri archaies ietrikes* (c. 430-
400 B.C.; *Ancient Medicine*) defends and elaborates this explanation.

Alcmaeon's theoretical speculation was balanced by a notable empirical
tendency. It is this mixture of theory and observation that gives his work a
distinctive and even pioneering nature. Alcmaeon, like many pre-Socratic
philosophers, was interested in physiology, but he appears to have been the
first to test his theories by examination of the body. In a celebrated case, he
cut out the eye of an animal (whether dead or alive is uncertain). He was
apparently interested in observing the substances of which the eye was composed. Whether he dissected the eye itself is not known. He also discovered
(or inferred the existence of) the channels that connect the eye to the brain
(probably the optic nerves).

There is no evidence that Alcmaeon ever dissected human corpses, and it
is unlikely that he did so. He believed that the eye contained fire (which
could be seen when the eye was hit) and water (which dissection revealed to
have come from the brain). He concluded that there were similar passages
connecting the other sense organs to the brain, and he described the passages connecting the brain to the mouth, nose, and ears (and quite possibly
was the first to discover the Eustachian tubes). He thought that these channels were hollow and carried *pneuma* (air). Alcmaeon concluded that the
brain provided the sensations of sight, hearing, smell, and taste, for he
noticed that when a concussion occurred, the senses were affected. Similarly,
when the passages were blocked, communication between the brain and the
sense organs was cut off. Plato followed Alcmaeon in holding that the brain
is the central organ of thought and feeling, but Aristotle and many other
philosophers continued to attribute that function to the heart. Alcmaeon
also differed from most contemporary philosophers in distinguishing between sensation and thought. He observed that sensation is common to all

animals, while only man possesses intelligence.

According to Alcmaeon, whether the body was awake or asleep had to do with the amount of blood in the veins. Sleep was caused by the blood retiring to the larger blood vessels, while waking was the result of the blood being rediffused throughout the body. Alcmaeon was also interested in embryology, and he opened birds' eggs and examined the development of the embryo. He believed that the head, not the heart, was the first to develop. He resorted to speculation rather than observation in holding that human semen has its origin in the brain. He explained the sterility of mules by the theory that the seed produced by the male was too fine and cold, while the womb of the female did not open, and hence conception was prevented.

Summary

Alcmaeon is recognized as an important figure in the development of the biological sciences in ancient Greece. Although his date is uncertain and few details regarding either his career or his scientific methods are known, it is clear that he exercised considerable influence on subsequent Greek writers in the fields of medicine and biology. He introduced ideas that were later elaborated by Empedocles, Democritus, several Hippocratic writers, Plato, and Aristotle, among others. His idea that health is a balance of opposing forces in the body, although later modified, was accepted for many hundreds of years. Alcmaeon has often been called the father of embryology, anatomy, physiology, and experimental psychology. While such titles may be unwarranted, in each of these areas Alcmaeon did make significant contributions.

Regardless of whether Alcmaeon was a physician, he was one of the earliest Greeks to formulate medical theories. Many of his ideas were speculative and borrowed from earlier philosophers. Although influenced by the Pythagoreans, he avoided their mysticism, and he recognized the limitations of scientific inference. His medical theory did not grow out of medical practice but always retained a close affinity with philosophy; such theories tended to have little influence on the general practice of Greek medicine. Still, Alcmaeon's anatomical investigation (particularly his dissection of the eye) and his recognition that the senses are connected with the brain established him as a genuine pioneer in the development of Greek medical science.

Bibliography

Codellas, P. S. "Alcmaeon of Croton: His Life, Work, and Fragments." *Proceedings of the Royal Society of Medicine* 25 (1931/1932): 1041-1046. A brief but comprehensive discussion of Alcmaeon's life and contributions, published by the Royal Society of Medicine's Section on the History of Medicine.

Guthrie, W. K. C. *A History of Greek Philosophy*. Vol. 1. Cambridge: Cambridge University Press, 1962. A discussion of the evidence for Alcmaeon's dates and an examination of his medical, physiological, and cosmological theories (particularly his doctrine of the soul) by a leading expert on Greek philosophy.

Jones, W. H. S. *Philosophy and Medicine in Ancient Greece*. New York: Arno Press, 1946, reprint 1979. Provides translations of the most important sources for Alcmaeon's life and doctrines, and discusses Alcmaeon's relationship to Plato and Aristotle.

Lloyd, Geoffrey. "Alcmaeon and the Early History of Dissection." *Sudhoffs Archiv* 59 (1975): 113-147. A detailed examination of the evidence for Alcmaeon's use of dissection, which Lloyd believes Alcmaeon to have practiced in a very limited manner rather than systematically. Explores as well the history of early Greek dissection after Alcmaeon.

Sigerist, Henry E., ed. *A History of Medicine*. Vol. 2, *Early Greek, Hindu, and Persian Medicine*. New York: Oxford University Press, 1961. A general discussion of Alcmaeon and his work in the context of early Greek medicine and philosophy. Valuable for its general treatment of Greek medicine and its background.

Gary B. Ferngren

ALCUIN

Born: c. 735; probably near York, Yorkshire, England
Died: May 19, 804; Tours, France
Areas of Achievement: Education, literature, and religion
Contribution: Although an Englishman, Alcuin became court tutor and educational and religious adviser to Charlemagne, King of the Franks and Lombards. Reforms inspired by him made an indelible impression on the later traditions and practices of the Catholic church.

Early Life

Alcuin's real name was probably Alhwini. He was an Anglo-Saxon, probably from Yorkshire, England. As he began to correspond and later to work with people who knew no English and used Latin as their professional language, however, his English name must have seemed difficult to spell, if not barbarous. It was accordingly latinized to "Alcuinus" or "Albinus." The misnomer serves as a reminder that Alcuin was for much of his life an exile in a culture which, if not alien to him, was not native either.

In fact, Alcuin was a product of the first golden age of Anglo-Saxon Christianity. A hundred years before his birth, the northern area of England was still pagan; one hundred years after his death, it had once again passed under the control of pagans, this time Viking armies, a process whose beginning Alcuin lived to see. In the interval between these two heathenisms, Christian scholarship in England was developed, with Alcuin at its heart.

Alcuin was sent to the cathedral school at York Minster when only a small child. He must have been one of its first students, but it is not clear why his allegedly noble parents sent him there. It is unlikely that he was an oblate, a child literally "offered up" by its parents to the monastery, for although he ended his life as an abbot, strict monastic vows would have barred him from his life of travel and court service. Alcuin was also never ordained as a priest, signing himself always as "deacon" or as "humble deacon." Alcuin seems in fact to have functioned as a pure scholar, not aiming primarily at ecclesiastical promotion. He entered the York school in the early 740's and stayed there almost forty years. He clearly studied the seven "liberal arts," which moved from grammar, rhetoric, and dialectics to arithmetic, astronomy, music, and geometry, and participated in the buildup of books at York, which he mentions with great pride in a poem written during that time, *De pontificubus et sanctis ecclesiae Eboracensis* (*On the Bishops, Kings, and Saints of York*, translation date unknown).

Probably around 766 Alcuin became the *scholasticus*, or headmaster, of the cathedral school. On at least two occasions he went on officially sanctioned trips to the Continent. In 781, however, a new archbishop sent Alcuin to Rome to fetch the archbishop's pallium from the Pope. As he returned,

Alcuin met Charlemagne, King of the Franks and Lombards, at Parma. He was offered a post at the royal court, returned home to get permission from his king and his archbishop, and then accepted. Alcuin then traveled to France in 782, to begin the principal, if long-delayed stage of his career.

Life's Work

Many have described Alcuin as a pedant, but this characterization is unfair: He was a schoolmaster. He did with the members of the royal family—Charlemagne, his wife, and his children—what he did with the boys at York: He taught them Latin grammar above all. His treatises on grammar and spelling survive and are now universally dismissed as obvious. They were, however, at the highest level for that period, and it may have been a considerable advantage to Alcuin to be English, a native speaker of a Germanic language. The native language of much of Charlemagne's realm could be called either very early French or very late, corrupt Latin. Thus, Frankish clerics were inclined to allow their Latin to be contaminated by the popular language used all around them. To Alcuin, Latin was the language of books. He spoke it as it had been written. Accordingly, his treatises are full of elementary advice: Do not confuse *beneficus*, a doer of good, with *veneficus*, a poisoner; do not confuse *vinea*, a vine, with *venia*, permission. Just the same, the advice was certainly necessary. Alcuin acted not as a researcher, but as a preserver of knowledge.

His position at the court also gave him immense influence. It seems very likely that Charlemagne, a king of great energy who was coming into a period of success against outside enemies such as the Saxons, the Lombards, and the nomadic Avars, was concerned about the poor quality and lax discipline of his own clergy. Around 787, a few years after Alcuin had joined him, he issued a capitulary giving wide-ranging instructions to senior abbots. The abbots were, he said, to keep their rules strictly and to study grammar. The letters the king had been receiving from monasteries were well-intentioned but uncouth in language. According to the ordinance, it was doubtful whether the writers could even understand the Bible. Charlemagne urged the abbots to select qualified schoolmasters and raise the standard of education. It is clear that Alcuin the ex-*scholasticus* was behind these reforms. Later instructions insist that not only would-be monks but also all male freeborn children should be educated (an extremely ambitious project for the time).

Alcuin seems, then, to have been influential in preserving good Latin. The point about understanding the Scriptures was also a concern. Several of his own commentaries on the Bible survive, but once again he was more influential on large-scale projects. He seems to have been responsible for the massive reorganization of the Frankish liturgy—that is, the instructions for what was to be said, read, and done at all services in all Frankish churches. Many of these decisions are still being followed in modern times.

In addition, Alcuin presided over a major revision and reediting of the increasingly corrupt and badly copied texts of the Latin Bible itself. It is true that no single copy of an "Alcuinian" Bible survives—not even the copy which Alcuin presented to Charlemagne as the only suitably magnificent gift on the occasion of Charlemagne's coronation as Emperor of the Holy Roman Empire by the Pope on Christmas Day, 800. This absence is, however, a proof of success. Like much of Alcuin's work, the revised Bibles were "read to pieces." They have not survived because they were in continual use. As with grammar and liturgy, though, in editing the Bible Alcuin may have done nothing new. What he did was to reduce error and introduce a correct standard.

Alcuin had other and more public triumphs. During the 790's he confronted clerics of the Spanish church, who were promoting a new doctrine, Adoptionism, and rather unusually for the history of the Church reasoned them into retracting rather than having the king declare a crusade against them. Alcuin was also dispatched at least once to England, possibly to help smooth over dissension between Charlemagne and Offa, the powerful king of Mercia. Alcuin also enjoyed considerable literary prestige. His best-known poem is *On the Bishops, Kings, and Saints of York*, which he wrote after he left York but which is filled with pride and affection. His other poems are generally believed to be correct and skillful rather than inspiring; more than was usual at the time, they stray from religious themes to imitation of pre-Christian Latin classics. Often they appear to have been written for a court coterie of writers in whom Charlemagne took great pride. Indeed, Alcuin is said to have reproved the king for wishing for more scholars than the King of Heaven himself could provide.

A further major body of work was written, however, after Alcuin had been given permission to retire in 796, taking up the vacant appointment of abbot at the abbey of Saint Martin of Tours. These are his letters, correspondence with Charlemagne and other kings, clerics, and senior political figures of England. In one letter, he grieves with the abbot of Lindisfarne after the first, horrible, unexpected assault of the Vikings on that island monastery. In another letter, Alcuin writes a famous condemnation of secular, native song, which many scholars have seen as the oldest allusion to orally transmitted poems such as the epic *Beowulf* (first transcribed c. 1000). In other letters, he writes warningly to the King of Northumbria and encouragingly to Offa. In yet another letter, written after the deaths of both Offa and his son, he makes it clear that he thought Offa's reign was stained by judicial murder. These letters are among the clearest and most useful historical documents of the time. Their value is shown by the efforts made to preserve them.

Alcuin's influence may indeed have continued beyond his retirement, for some believe that the elevation of Charlemagne to imperial status was masterminded by his faithful adviser and deacon. Certainly, in the last decade of his life Alcuin's output remained extraordinarily high, amounting not only to hundreds of letters but also to several hagiographies and theological works. He died on May 19, 804, at Saint Martin's abbey in Tours.

Summary

Alcuin represents a particularly successful example of "cross-fertilization." In his maturity, the best scholarship in Europe was to be found in the northern part of England. Alcuin exported this scholarship to a country in sore need of it and set both religious and secular study on a sounder basis. The favor was to be returned, for as the Viking attacks on England grew stronger, both Christianity and learning fell into ignominious decline. Indeed, the great library at York, of which Alcuin was so proud, was in the end destroyed so thoroughly that not a single book from it is known to have survived. Learning was reestablished in England very largely by men from the Continent. If it had not been for Alcuin's reforms, there might have been no such men to come to the rescue.

Alcuin's effect in other areas is even harder to evaluate. No one sees him as a great literary figure, and his works are rarely translated. Yet it is quite probable that the entire daily practice of the Roman Catholic church—apart from its theory or dogma—was affected by Alcuin's decisions as to which of many conflicting forms and rituals should become standard. It has even been suggested that Church Latin is an Alcuinian "invention," Latin before that being read not as it was written but as native French or Italian speakers would naturally pronounce it. Alcuin and his colleagues brought a new rigor to the Frankish church and, indeed, to the whole of Western Christianity.

Bibliography

Duckett, Eleanor S. *Alcuin, Friend of Charlemagne: His World and His Work*. New York: Macmillan, 1951. This volume is a complete, straightforward biography. At times hagiographical in tone and reluctant to take a critical stance on politics or literary talent, Duckett has, nevertheless, written the most useful single book on Alcuin.

Ellard, Gerald. *Master Alcuin, Liturgist: A Partner of Our Piety*. Chicago: Loyola University Press, 1956. Written by a Jesuit, this extremely technical work attempts, from admittedly inadequate evidence, to determine how much of later liturgical practice can be traced back to Alcuin. It makes good use of the otherwise inaccessible Latin "Life of Alcuin."

Godman, Peter. *Poets and Emperors: Frankish Politics and Carolingian Poetry*. Oxford: Clarendon Press, 1987. Alcuin is treated here as part of an entire "court circle," and his works are set in the contexts of flattery, policy, and decision making. Included are valuable sections on Alcuin's contemporaries, such as Theodulf of Orleans and Paul the Deacon.

_____, ed. *Alcuin: The Bishops, Kings, and Saints of York*. New York: Oxford University Press, 1982. The only complete edition of a major poem by Alcuin, with full commentary and introduction. Godman argues that the poem was written after Alcuin emigrated, although the poem is valuable chiefly as a guide to Alcuin's early intellectual life.

Levison, Wilhelm. *England and the Continent in the Eighth Century*. Oxford: Clarendon Press, 1946. A clear account of the relations between England and Europe in Alcuin's century, including the missionary drive which Alcuin supported and the liturgical work. Levison points out that Alcuin himself was not always free of grammatical error.

Waddell, Helen, ed. and trans. *Medieval Latin Lyrics*. New York: Richard R. Smith, 1930. Graceful translations of several poems by Alcuin and other members of the "court circle." Particularly charming is the "Disputation Between Spring and Winter," which has been doubtfully ascribed to Alcuin yet is in a pastoral mode he employs elsewhere.

Whitelock, Dorothy, ed. and trans. *English Historical Documents*. Vol. 1, *c. 500-1042*. London: Eyre and Spottiswoode, 1955. This volume includes translations of a dozen of Alcuin's major letters. Also valuable are other items of correspondence to or from Charlemagne, referring to the political scene of Western Europe in Alcuin's lifetime.

T. A. Shippey

ALEXANDER III
Roland Bandinelli

Born: Early twelfth century; Siena, Italy
Died: August 30, 1181; Città Castellana, Italy
Area of Achievement: Religion
Contribution: Despite decades of controversy, through patience, moderation, and practicality, Alexander III established administrative and legal reforms that strengthened the papal monarchy and contributed to the development of canon law.

Early Life

Roland Bandinelli, the future Alexander III, pope from 1159 to 1181, was born early in the twelfth century in Siena, Italy. Although little is known of his early years, his family, probably descended from a French émigré of the previous century, was prominent in city affairs. The earliest substantiated fact places him as professor of theology and canon law at Bologna in the years 1139 to 1142. Since Siena's schools were not considered distinguished and the appointment was prestigious, it is thought that Bandinelli probably attended school at Bologna as well.

In 1148, he began his career at the Curia in Rome, having been deacon and canon at Pisa and probably having taught in the schools there. A series of appointments advanced his ecclesiastical career. In 1150, Bandinelli was named cardinal deacon. In 1151, he became cardinal priest and by 1153 was appointed papal chancellor, which led to his becoming one of Pope Adrian IV's closest advisers. He was entrusted with a number of diplomatic missions which enhanced his reputation among churchmen and laity. One such embassy, however, would become significant in negative ways during his own troubled papacy.

In October, 1157, Adrian IV sent a delegation of cardinals, headed by Bandinelli, to the imperial diet of the German emperor at Besançon, Burgundy. Relations between the emperor Frederick I Barbarossa and the Pope had cooled after the signing of the Concordat of Benevento in 1156. As part of the continuing struggle between spiritual and secular jurisdiction in Europe, the Pope had concluded a treaty with William I, the Norman ruler of southern Italy and Sicily. The situation in Italy was stabilized, and the treaty represented a counterbalance to the emperor's pretensions in northern Italy, where his policy was to dominate the rich cities of Lombardy. Furthermore, an important churchman traveling through Frederick's dominions had been captured, and although later freed, his captor had not been disciplined by the emperor. Papal letters had been ignored. Adrian IV considered it essential to ensure cooperation of the emperor in the future.

Admitted to an audience with the emperor and his imperial diet, Bandinelli read a letter from the Pope voicing his concerns and pointing out that the Church had accorded honor to Frederick in his coronation at Rome. The letter suggested that full cooperation with the Papacy might lead to greater benefits. The letter, written in Latin, used the word *beneficia*, which meant "benefits" in classical Latin. Rainald of Dassel, the militant German chancellor, translated it into German as *fief*, a word used to designate a landholding granted to a vassal by a lord. Angrily, he asked if the Pope meant that the emperor held his office and power as a fief from the Papacy. Tempers flared and heated discussion followed in which intemperate words were used on both sides. Frederick restrained his men but was also angered. The delegation was dismissed and sent from imperial territory. Frederick remembered the name of Roland Bandinelli.

Life's Work

When Adrian IV died on September 1, 1159, tensions between empire and papacy were still strong. Frederick sought support from the Romans and from individual cardinals by granting them gifts and honors. When the conclave met on September 4, 1159, a small but influential group nominated Cardinal Octavian, a member of a noble Roman family supportive of the emperor.

Electoral procedures were not yet clearly defined, and much confusion clouds the extant accounts. A majority of the cardinals favored the election of Bandinelli. He was a recognized scholar and jurist with a dozen years of experience in papal administration and diplomacy. He had enjoyed the confidence of Adrian IV. Of the thirty cardinals in attendance, twenty-two supported Bandinelli and seven or eight Octavian. Both men claimed the succession, Bandinelli as Alexander III and Octavian as Victor IV. The Church of Rome found itself divided for the second time in the twelfth century.

The Council of Pavia, convened by the emperor in 1160, supported the antipope Victor IV. Within six months, the kings of England and France declared for Alexander III. Other rulers from Spain to Denmark followed their lead. The greater part of western Christian Europe supported Alexander III, which enabled him to carry out ordinary papal administration and accomplish many of his goals despite exile from Rome. Aided by the regular clergy, especially the Cistercians, Alexander III was able to maintain strong lines of communication. Skillful use of legates and his own moderate position and pursuit of negotiated settlements eventually bore fruit.

The most significant accomplishment of his exile in France was convening the successful Council of Tours. On May 19, 1163, it formally opened at the Church of St. Maurice. The numbers of those in attendance (accepted by historians) include seventeen cardinals, 124 bishops, and 414 abbots as well as clerks and influential clergy and laity. The eight or nine canons resulting from the Council furthered reform of the Church by combatting both clerical abuses and "heretical" movements.

Important points included prohibitions of dividing church holdings, granting church property to lay persons, or priests hiring others to perform duties for an annual payment. Clerical usury was forbidden. No payments were to be exacted from those entering religious life. Fees were not to be levied for burial rites or assessed for anointing the faithful with chrism or oil. In short, no payment was to be demanded for any spiritual service, and all irregularities were to cease. Church property was declared immune from secular intervention. Bishops and archbishops were not to delegate their duties to priests or deacons. All those ordained to Holy Orders by Victor IV were declared to be invalid priests.

The canon on heresy was directed against the growing Catharist movement in southern France. The sect was condemned. No Catharist was to be granted land or refuge by any authority. No commercial dealings were to be conducted with them. When known, Catharists might be held in custody by local authority and their property confiscated. The death penalty was not mentioned at this point, but inquisitorial methods were discussed and are considered a prelude to the establishment of the later, infamous tribunal.

From 1164 to 1170, Alexander III was also troubled by the struggle between Archbishop of Canterbury Thomas à Becket and Henry II of England. Initiated by Becket's condemnation of the Constitutions of Clarendon (1164), which stated regalian rights as opposed to ecclesiastical, the controversy became heated. Becket insisted that the document's claims were incompatible with reformed canon law. Old legal precedents encouraged Henry II to push his claims. Challenged by continuing difficulties with Frederick, Alexander III was criticized by some contemporaries for failing to support Becket strongly and consistently. Yet many of the papal letters to the king are firm and concise, if not particularly bold. Becket's actions in numerous instances were both rash and intemperate. Undoubtedly Alexander III proceeded cautiously both because of his own problems and his position of moderation. Following the brutal murder of Becket in December, 1170, a long period of shock and indignation resulted in Becket's early canonization. It took several more years for the legates to reopen the see of Canterbury and complete the penitential duties of the crown.

In 1165, Alexander III returned to Rome. Victor IV had died in 1164, but a new antipope, Paschal III, succeeded him. Frederick's invasion of Rome in 1167, despite heroic resistance on the Pope's behalf, sent Alexander III in flight to the southern part of the papal states. Again, Alexander III was able to continue his diplomatic and administrative activities, sometimes enjoying cordial relations with other states after complicated negotiations. Hungary, the Crusader states of the Levant, and other Christian communities became strong allies. Correspondence with the Byzantine emperor began a cautious exploration of possible reunion.

The long schism came to an end with a series of misfortunes suffered by Frederick. The decimation of his army by plague shortly after his capture of Rome, the loss of Rainald of Dassel, the growth of power in northern Italy represented by the Lombard League, which inflicted a defeat on imperial forces at Legnano in 1176, and the guiding of his own conscience led to reconciliation with Alexander III in Venice in 1177. It would be difficult to assess the victory of either participant. Theoretical statements were avoided and individual compromises were made. Each could believe that he had not done badly in the settlement.

Although the situation in Rome continued to be tumultuous and difficult, Alexander III returned to the area, often residing outside the city itself. In 1179, he convened the third Lateran Council, to his great satisfaction. Considered to be one of four Lateran councils best studied as a whole, Alexander presented a wide array of subjects for discussion. If he did not resolve them, he enhanced the chances for possible later solutions.

In 1181, still troubled by his problems with the fickle Romans, he died at Città Castellana, Italy, bringing to a close one of the longest and most troubled papal reigns of the Middle Ages.

Summary

The difficulty in evaluating Alexander III's role in the development of papal monarchy from Gregory VII to the pinnacle of its power in the pontificate of Innocent III lies in the complexity of the changes occurring in the twelfth century. It is necessary to understand Alexander III's place in the twelfth century world. He was a product of a great renaissance of learning and a contemporary of Gratian, the great expositor of Roman law, whose *Decretum* (c. 1140) was the basis for the flowering of canon law. Scholars have proved that Alexander III depended heavily upon Gratian's work. He was a contemporary, too, of Peter Abelard, the brilliant logician, theologian, and teacher, whose new dialectics created a debate that divided the Church to the days of Saint Thomas Aquinas. That Abelard influenced Alexander III is equally clear. Abelard's insistence on the role of reason, even to illuminate revealed faith, found in Alexander III a strong advocate. This pope was a man of learning and a lawyer. If his interests were not as wide as those of his fellow scholars, they were equally deep. Not given to broad theocratic principles or statements, Alexander III worked more successfully to solve specific problems dealing with the role of the church in the affairs of the world. His work for clarity and consistency in law had great influence. One area of his life not yet sufficiently studied is his interest and work in marriage law, where he insisted that mutual consent was the basis for the legality of the contract.

Alexander III was also a religious man. Even the most bitter of opponents acknowledged his moral stature. He admired the austere life and believed that to judge fairly, preach fervently, and give worthwhile penances made a good pope as well as a good priest. He was committed to missionary work, particularly in Scandinavia. His interest in crusading activity in the East was strong.

If Alexander III proved contradictory in his actions, or inconsistent in his support of individuals or causes, it would seem to have been dictated by the struggles of the moment. He produced much given the constant threats of exile and schism and the very real danger he frequently faced. As his funeral cortege approached Rome, an angry mob threw mud and dirt upon his bier. Alexander III's problems were not solved even by his death.

Bibliography

Baldwin, Marshall. *Alexander III and the Twelfth Century*. New York: Newman Press, 1968. First-rate discussion of the role of the Pope and his place in twelfth century history. Contains useful introductory material; individual chapters cover major problems of the Pontificate. Conclusion, notes, and bibliography are useful.

Knowles, David. *Thomas Becket*. Stanford, Calif.: Stanford University Press, 1971. A succinct account of the issues between king and archbishop written by an acknowledged scholar in the field. Knowles, a member of the Benedictine Order, adds intimate knowledge of ecclesiastical history to his command of English history. Balanced, but sympathetic to Alexander.

Mann, Horace K. *The Lives of the Popes in the Early Middle Ages*. 19 vols. London: K. Paul, Trench, Trubner, 1923-1932. An old but still valuable study of the lives of the popes to 1305. A good starting point for the student. Continuing scholarship has superseded this work on numerous specific points.

Munz, Peter. *Boso's Life of Alexander III*. Translated by G. M. Ellis. Totowa, N.J.: Rowman and Littlefield, 1973. A splendid translation and edition of an original source by a contemporary and associate of Alexander. The introduction by the editor is extremely useful, incorporating the best scholarship to date. Understandably pro-Alexander.

_____, ed. *Frederick Barbarossa: A Study in Medieval Politics*. Ithaca, N.Y.: Cornell University Press, 1969. Probably essential for an understanding of imperial policy. Well written but lengthy. Individual subjects, however, are easily found through index. Especially useful as a balance to the overly sympathetic accounts from the papal point of view. Excellent example of the use of biography as a means of focusing on complex historical problems.

Somerville, Robert. *Pope Alexander III and the Council of Tours: A Study of Ecclesiastical Politics and Institutions in the Twelfth Century*. Berkeley: University of California Press, 1977. The reader is advised that this is a specialized book, not a monographic study easily read. Contains lists of canons, titles, and names relating to the Council. Sections on preparation for convening the Council and its formalities help understanding of such sessions. Demonstrates how historians use primary material.

Anne R. Vizzier

ALEXANDER THE GREAT

Born: 356 B.C.; Pella, Macedonia
Died: June 13, 323 B.C.; Babylon
Areas of Achievement: Government and conquest
Contribution: By military genius, political acumen, and cultural vision, Alexander unified and Hellenized most of the civilized ancient world and in so doing became a legendary figure in subsequent ages.

Early Life

Born into royalty of King Philip II of Macedonia and Olympias, daughter of King Neoptolemus of Epirus, Alexander was educated during his early teenage years by the Greek philosopher Aristotle. Although tutor and pupil later differed on political matters such as Alexander's decision to downgrade the importance of the city-state, Aristotle performed his assigned task of preparing his young charge for undertaking campaigns against the Persian Empire as well as inculcating in him a love of learning so vital to Hellenic (that is, Greek) culture.

In 340, at age sixteen, Alexander's formal training ended with his appointment to administer Macedonia while Philip was absent on a campaign. Young Alexander won his first battle against a force of Thracians and in 338 distinguished himself as commander of the left wing during Philip's crushing victory over the combined Greek army at Chaeronea. A break with his father over the latter's divorce and remarriage led Alexander to flee with his mother to Epirus. Although father and son reaffirmed their ties, Alexander feared for his status as successor. Philip's assassination in 336, along with the army's support of Alexander, eliminated all doubt of his kingship, and he had the assassins and all of his apparent enemies executed.

Life's Work

At the age of twenty, Alexander proceeded to fulfill Philip's planned attack on Persia and thereby to free Greeks living under Persian rule in Asia Minor (Turkey). Soon, however, he determined to place himself on the throne of Persia. Anxious to represent all Greece at the head of a Panhellenic union, he first received the approval and military support of the Greek League at Corinth and the endorsement of the oracle at Delphi as invincible. (The Romans later called him "the Great.")

In order to consolidate his rear guard in Europe before crossing into Asia, he spent the year 335 subduing restive peoples north and west of Macedonia and crushing an Athenian-endorsed revolt of Thebes by taking and razing the city of Thebes, killing six thousand and selling the rest as slaves. His harsh policy had the desired effect of discouraging further attempts by the

Greeks to undermine his authority. Alexander therefore had no need to punish Athens, center of Hellenic culture, source of the largest navy available to him, and vital to the financial administration of the territories he would conquer. Nevertheless, he remained sufficiently suspicious of the Athenians to decline employing their fleet against Persia. The only Greek city-state openly disloyal to Alexander was Sparta, but it was isolated and later brought into line by Alexander's governor of Greece.

Alexander crossed the Hellespont (Dardanelles) into Asia Minor with his army of thirty-five thousand Macedonians and Greeks in the spring of 334 intent on humbling the Persian army and gaining spoils adequate to restore the strained Macedonian treasury. The army was a superbly balanced force of all arms, based on the highly disciplined maneuvers of the Macedonian phalanx and cavalry. With its offensive wing on the right, the infantry phalanxes would advance steadily, using their longer spears and supported by light-armed archers and javelin throwers. That was in reality a holding force, however, for while it moved forward, the cavalry attacked the enemy's flank and rear. If that did not succeed, then the infantry would institute a skillful fighting withdrawal to open a gap in the enemy's line and to gain the higher ground. This difficult maneuver thus created a flank, upon which Alexander's men would then rush. The key to success was timing, and Alexander's great ability was knowing where and when to strike decisively. Then he pursued the retreating enemy, who could not regroup. Alexander's tactical skills triumphed almost immediately when he met and crushed a Persian army at the river Granicus, largely as a result of his realization that victory was possible only after an interceding river was crossed.

No less a genius as a strategist, Alexander neutralized the Persian fleet by marching down the coasts of the Eastern Mediterranean, taking the enemy's seaports by land. To establish himself as a liberator, he dealt harshly only with those cities which opposed his advance, and he installed Greek-style democracies in those which yielded without a fight. Indeed, he retained local governors, customs, and taxes, insisting only upon loyalty to himself instead of to King Darius III of Persia. This political policy had the additional logistical benefit of making available supplies crucial to keeping his army in the field. To provide balanced governments of occupation, however, as at Sardis, he appointed a Macedonian governor with troops, a local militia officer as fortress commander, and an Athenian overseer of monies. Also, the fact that the army was accompanied by scientists, engineers, and historians is evidence that he planned a long campaign to conquer all Persia and to gather new knowledge as inspired by Aristotle.

The conquest of Asia Minor was completed in the autumn of 333 when Alexander crushed Darius' army at Issus on the Syrian frontier, then advanced down the coast, receiving the submission of all the Phoenician cities except Tyre. Enraged by its defiance, he besieged Tyre for seven months, building a long mole (causeway) with siege towers and finally assaulting the city in July, 332. Tyre suffered the same fate as Thebes, and the rest of the coast lay open to Alexander, save for a two-month standoff at Gaza. Then Egypt welcomed him as a deliverer, whereupon he established the port city of Alexandria there. Returning to Syria, he advanced into Mesopotamia, where he routed the Grand Army of Darius at Arbela (or Gaugamela) in mid-331. One year later, Darius was killed by a rival as Alexander advanced eastward, the same year that Alexander burned down the Persian royal palace at Persepolis.

Alexander's vision of empire changed from 331 to 330 to that of a union of Macedonians and Persians under his kingship. He began to wear Persian dress, married the first of two Persian princesses after conquering the eastern provinces in 328, and later prevailed upon the Macedonian troops to do the same. As his men increasingly resisted such alien practices, Alexander ordered the execution of some of the most vocal critics, notably his second in command, Parmenio, his late father's intimate counselor, who was the spokesman for the older opponents of assimilation. In spite of such excesses, the army remained loyal and followed Alexander into India to his last great victory—one over local rulers at the Hydaspes River in June, 326, using native troops and methods, as well as elephants. Now his Macedonian troops, however, tired and homesick, refused to go on, and he had no choice but to end his offensive. His engineers thereupon built a fleet of more than eight hundred vessels which ferried and accompanied the army downriver to the Indus, then to the Indian Ocean and west again to Persia. Heavy fighting, severe desert terrain, and unfavorable weather inflicted much suffering and heavy losses on his forces.

By the time he reached Susa, administrative capital of the Persian Empire, in 324, Alexander had indeed fashioned a sprawling empire. He had established numerous cities bearing his name and had infused Asia with the dynamic Hellenic culture which would influence the region for centuries to come. In addition, he now attempted greater racial intermixing, which led to another near-complete break with his fellow Macedonians. Alexander, ever more megalomaniacal, pronounced himself a god and had more of his subordinates put to death, usually during drunken sprees. These were so frequent in his last seven years that there is every reason to believe he had become a chronic alcoholic. As a result of one binge at Babylon in 323, he became ill and died ten days later; he was thirty-three years old. His empire was quickly divided among his successor generals, who eliminated his wives and two children.

Summary

Inculcated by Aristotle with the superiority of high Greek culture, Alexander the Great undertook the political unification of the Greek world along

Panhellenic lines, followed by its extension over the vast but internally weak Persian Empire. His tools were the superb Macedonian army inherited from his father and his own genius at command. As one success followed another, however, his horizons became broader. He identified himself with the religion and deities of each land he conquered, especially Egypt, and ultimately seems to have concluded that it was his destiny to merge most of the known world under common rule. That vision possibly included Carthage and the Western Mediterranean, though death denied him further territorial acquisitions.

Alexander's shrewd administrative skills enabled him to succeed in the five major facets of statehood. In religion, he began with the Greek pantheon but then recognized all faiths, with himself as the common godhead. Hellenic culture was also the intellectual power which drove his social ambitions and which prevailed in spite of his attempts to amalgamate it with Persian ways, leaving a predominantly Hellenistic world in his wake. In the economic sphere, he followed the Greek practices of silver-based coinage, which with Persian gold brought about common commercial practices and general prosperity. As one of the greatest generals in history, Alexander obtained victory with skillful tactics, flexibility, a keen sense of logistics, and superior leadership, followed by an effective system of garrisons with divided commands. His charismatic personality and vision combined all these elements into the final one—firm, dynamic, political rule. Once Alexander passed from the scene, however, the system could not be sustained. Nevertheless, his example of continental empire contributed to the eventual rise of the Roman Empire and the expansion of Christianity.

Bibliography

Arrianus, Flavius. *The Life of Alexander the Great*. Translated by Aubrey de Sélincourt. Baltimore: Penguin Books, 1958. The best and most reliable of the ancient works on Alexander, actually entitled the *Anabasis*, though preoccupied with the military aspects. For the most part, it takes the form of straight narrative.

Badian, Ernst. "Alexander the Great and the Unity of Mankind." *Historia* 7 (1958): 425-444. A rejection of other scholars' attempts to idealize the man, viewing him instead as merely pragmatic and thus reflecting the ongoing debate about Alexander's true motives.

Burn, A. R. *Alexander the Great and the Hellenistic Empire*. London: Hodder and Stoughton, 1947. An almost complete rejection of Alexander as a heroic figure, denying the impact ascribed to him by most other writers.

Engels, Donald W. *Alexander the Great and the Logistics of the Macedonian Army*. Berkeley: University of California Press, 1978. A masterful use of mathematics to ascertain the four-day carrying load of Alexander's soldiers and the means by which these considerations influenced his strategy and movements.

Fox, Robin Lane. *Alexander the Great*. New York: Dial Press, 1974. A direct, no-nonsense use of the sources to fashion a serious examination of Alexander, scholarly in every way except exhaustive citations and virtually ignoring Tarn's thesis, which Fox rejects.

Fuller, J. F. C. *The Generalship of Alexander the Great*. New Brunswick, N.J.: Rutgers University Press, 1960. The best work on Alexander's military achievements, complete with campaign maps and battle diagrams; by a retired British general and leading military pundit of the twentieth century.

Green, Peter. *Alexander the Great*. London: Weidenfeld and Nicolson, 1970. A judicious biography, replete with illustrations of the territory that Alexander traversed, which rejects the "brotherhood of man" ascribed to Alexander's motives by others and includes many surviving legends.

Hammond, N. G. L. *Alexander the Great: King, Commander, and Statesman*. Park Ridge, N.J.: Noyes Press, 1980. A good overview with an appendix on the question of Alexander's drinking and possible alcoholism.

M'Crindle, J. W. *The Invasion of India by Alexander the Great as Described by Arrian, Q. Curtius, Diodorus, Plutarch, and Justin*. Westminster: Archibald Constable and Co., 1893. Reprint. New York: Barnes and Noble Books, 1969. A specialized treatment of Alexander's Indian foray, reprinted from the original 1893 edition, which includes the verbatim accounts of the ancient authorities Arrian, Quintus Curtius Rufus, Plutarch, Diodoros Siculus, and Justin (useful for comparisons) and an informative biographical appendix.

Savill, Agnes. *Alexander the Great and His Time*. New York: Citadel Press, 1966. A sound volume for the general reader which draws on most ancient and modern scholarship.

Tarn, W. W. *Alexander the Great*. 2 vols. Cambridge: Cambridge University Press, 1948. A complete and sympathetic biography—the most influential one in English, by a leading Hellenistic historian who views Alexander as having sought the brotherhood of man; especially useful for its in-depth review of all the ancient authorities.

Wilcken, Ulrich. *Alexander the Great*. Translated by G. C. Richards. Reprint. New York: W. W. Norton and Co., 1967. An excellent, balanced treatment of Alexander's life and achievements, introduced by lengthy discussions of the Greek world in the fourth century B.C. and of his father, Philip II. This translated reprint of the 1931 work includes a useful historiographical overview by Eugene N. Borza.

Clark G. Reynolds

ALEXANDER NEVSKY

Born: c. 1220; Northern Pereiaslavl, Vladimir-Suzdal
Died: November 14, 1263; Gorodets, Vladimir-Suzdal
Areas of Achievement: Government and conquest
Contribution: Alexander strengthened the Republic of Novgorod by defeating Swedish, Livonian, and German invaders. By skillful diplomacy and appeasement policies, he also secured limited autonomy for the entire Grand Duchy of Vladimir-Suzdal from the Tatars of the Golden Horde.

Early Life

Alexander Nevsky, nephew of Grand Prince Yury Vsevolodovich (1189-1238), was born to Prince Yaroslav Vsevolodovich of Northern Pereiaslavl, a principality located in Suzdal. Alexander, who had seven paternal uncles and seven brothers, spent his youth in Northern Pereiaslavl and then in Novgorod. Yaroslav was hired as a Novgorodian service prince in 1222, mainly to defend the merchant-dominated society from foreign attackers. In 1236, Yaroslav left to assume the princely throne at Kiev, compelling the Novgorodians to accept his sixteen-year-old son, Alexander, as successor in the republic. Yaroslav held Kiev but a short time before he was ousted by Mikhail of Chernigov. Meanwhile, young Alexander attempted to build a stronger government and a wider territorial base for Novgorod.

Life's Work

Alexander's rule in Novgorod began in 1236. Three years later he married Alexandra, Princess of Polotsk, a principality between Smolensk and Lithuania. In the 1250's, Lithuania began its absorption of the old lands of Kievan Russia, including part of Polotsk, held in special regard for Nevsky because of his wife's family there. Eventually all the lands of Polotsk would become part of Lithuania. Nevertheless, Alexander was able to repel Lithuanian attempts to seize Novgorod and its tributary principality of Pskov. In response to Lithuanian raids on Smolensk and Kamno in 1239, he erected a number of defensive forts in the south along the Shelon River. Conflict erupted with Lithuania in 1245, when troops invaded areas to the north and south of Novgorod. Alexander's armies from Novgorod, Tver, Pskov, and Dmitrov stopped the invasions, causing the deaths of eight Lithuanian princes and Russian recapture of booty and lands. Three years later another Lithuanian invasion near Smolensk was stopped, but one of Alexander's brothers was killed in the warfare.

Alexander's leadership in the defense of Novgorod and the other Russian lands from incursions of Swedes and Germans is equally well-known. Some sources portray him as a hero, the savior of Orthodoxy. Twice Alexander was engaged in defense against Swedes; one of these battles took place along the

Neva River on July 15, 1240, and explains the sobriquet "Nevsky." Alexander's mounted brigade surprised the encamped Swedes, while infantry attacked Swedish ships in dock to prevent arrival of reinforcements. These battles (or skirmishes, as one authority avers) were part of the continuing struggle between Russians and Scandinavians for control of the Finnish lands and not, as some early sources attest, part of a papal plan of Germans, Danes, and Swedes to absorb Novgorod at a time when it was weakened by Tatar rule.

Describing the defense against German Teutonic Knights (the Order of Swordbearers of Livonia) is more complicated because of German support both in Pskov and in Novgorod itself. The nature of such support and the reasons for it are unclear, but the Prince of Pskov and the mayor allowed Germans entry to the city. The German party in Novgorod influenced Nevsky to leave the city with his family for northern Pereiaslavl after returning from the encounters with the Swedes. German invasions, however, prompted the assembly to recall Alexander on his own terms. Upon his return, several German partisans in the city were executed. Alexander's military forces then drove the Germans from the north of the city and retook Pskov, punishing those who had aided the knights. The stage was set for the celebrated "battle on the ice" against German and Estonian forces near Lake Peipus.

Alexander's tactic was to lure the German forces toward the shoreline by feigning a flight, enabling the cavalry detachments to descend from the flanks upon the forces in disarray; it is said that five hundred Germans died in the battle. The victory on April 5, 1242, was followed by a march of fifty German and Estonian knights as prisoners through the streets of Pskov, after which the order signed a treaty ceding all of its conquered lands. Stories of Nevsky's battles assume epic, even biblical, proportions in the romantic accounts of contemporaries. The difference between the numbers killed and taken prisoner in Russian and Estonian accounts is immense, and some modern authorities are convinced that the battles involved far fewer combatants than the Russian chroniclers attest.

Family rivalries played a major part of Alexander's mature life. When Yaroslav died in 1246, Alexander's uncle Sviatoslav Vsevolodovich became grand prince and confirmed the patrimonies which Yaroslav had assigned to his sons. Within a year, Alexander's brother Andrew overthrew his uncle and seized the grand princely throne, which required the approval of the Tatars. Andrew and Alexander went to Saray to debate the issue, but Batu Khan dispatched them to distant Karakorum for a final decision. Andrew, though younger than Alexander, was awarded the title, and Alexander was given the rule of Kiev and the lands of southern Russia. They returned to Russia in 1249, and Andrew remained the grand prince for three more years.

When troubles arose between Andrew and the Golden Horde, a Tatar army drove Andrew from his capital, Vladimir, on the Kliazma River. Andrew and his brother Yaroslav defended the region as best they could but in the end were forced to flee: Andrew to Sweden and Yaroslav to Pskov. Andrew and his father-in-law, Daniel of Galicia-Volhynia, had conspired against the Tatars who discovered the plot. The Tatars conferred with Alexander and then attacked, before Andrew and Daniel could coordinate their plans. Thus, Alexander became grand prince. The brothers later made peace; Andrew was given Nizhni Novgorod and Suzdal in 1255, and Yaroslav was later provided with Tver.

The grand princely rule of Alexander (1252-1263) was marked by continued accommodation to the Golden Horde, strong support for Russian Orthodoxy vis-à-vis the Roman church, and a firm policy against opposition within his realm. His chief support came from Metropolitan Kirill, who crowned him in Vladimir, later buried him with full honors, and probably commissioned the biography of Alexander. Kirill encouraged his conciliation of the Tatars and established an Orthodox bishopric in Saray itself. Kirill gained much for the Orthodox church from the Golden Horde: no taxation, no conscription, and no inclusion in the census. He persuaded Alexander to reject the blandishments from the Roman pope and strengthened the historical image of Alexander as the savior of the Orthodox church from the West.

Throughout his reign, Alexander continued to defend the frontiers against incursions of Germans, Lithuanians, and Swedes. In 1253, Russian forces under Alexander's son Dmitry seized Tartu from the Teutonic Knights. When Swedes built a fortress on the Narva River in 1256, Alexander himself led a Novgorodian army that frightened them away, after which there were no more Swedish incursions for nearly twenty-five years. In 1262, the King of Lithuania switched allegiances from Rome and the Teutonic Knights to Suzdal, whereupon a combined Russian-Lithuanian-Polotskian army attacked the German post at Tartu. The murder of the Lithuanian king later that year ended the promising alliance.

Relations with the Mongol or Tatar Southeast were different. Rejecting Andrew's idea of uniting all against the Golden Horde, Alexander chose to submit for the sake of limited independence. Novgorod was the trouble spot in this pro-Tatar policy, since antagonism to the Golden Horde was keen there. When Alexander sent his twelve-year-old son Vasily (1240-1271) to rule for him, Novgorodians replaced him with his uncle Yaroslav. Alexander marched on the city, forcing his brother to flee and threatening to punish the lesser boyars, the merchants, and the mayor. Only the intercession of the archbishop prevented violence.

New troubles arose in 1257, when the Tatars sent census takers and tax collectors to the city. Young Vasily supported the resistance, and when the Tatars and Alexander arrived, he fled to Pskov, only to be captured and imprisoned by his father. Vasily's supporters were either executed or mutilated. The angry Tatars then summoned Alexander and his two brothers

Yaroslav and Andrew to Saray. Alexander, his troops, and Tatar officials went to Novgorod in 1260 in order to enforce the census and tax. Again, the city divided between the greater boyars who supported the grand prince and the lesser citizens who chose resistance. The grand prince's troops easily overcame the rebels, and Alexander, with Tatars by his side, rode through the streets of the city. Novgorod had submitted.

The famed rising of 1262 against Tatar rule came not in Novgorod, however, but in Rostov, Vladimir, Suzdal, and Yaroslavl, occasioned by Tatar demands for slaves and conscripts for the Persian War. The princely class did not support the rebels, and the movement took on the character of a general popular uprising. Alexander was again summoned to Saray to explain the behavior of his subjects. Did he save Russians from reprisals or simply explain his inability to control his subjects? The sources are unclear, but Berke Khan kept him there for the winter of 1262-1263, when he became ill. Alexander left in the spring, but instead of going to Vladimir, he went north to Gorodets, in Andrew's patrimony. There, he took monastic vows and died about six months later, on November 14, 1263. His body was taken for burial in Vladimir eleven days later.

The timing of Alexander's death has led to speculation that he was poisoned by the Golden Horde, since his father and younger brother Yaroslav also died after leaving the Tatar capital. In any case, his last mission was at least successful, since the Tatars launched no punitive expedition northward and ceased the demands for conscripts.

Summary

Alexander Nevsky remains an intriguing figure in Russian medieval history. Ironically regarded as a hero even by the Soviet state, he had openly submitted to the mighty Golden Horde. For somewhat similar reasons, medieval churchmen and modern statesmen magnify Nevsky's role in withstanding the challenges of the West. Yet some analysts discount the danger of a major Western invasion, noting that Alexander's defense of the borders was little more than what previous princes had done. The Orthodox church, ever conscious of its rivalry with Rome, saw security in the conciliatory policies of Alexander, but Tatar policies were always tolerant of foreign religions. Was Alexander's delicate treatment of Saray responsible for the paucity of Tatar reprisals against Russians, or were the Tatars simply too busy with the military threats from Persia? Clearly, Alexander's defeat of his brothers signaled the end of effective Russian resistance to the Golden Horde for more than a century. Also, Andrew's policy of resistance can be seen as unrealistic when one recalls that Daniel died without the Western Crusade that he and Andrew had expected.

Alexander's accession to the grand princely throne in 1252 may mark the real beginnings of the "Tatar Yoke," since there was no further resistance to this Oriental administration for nearly 125 years. Furthermore, the accession of Alexander to the principality of Kiev a few years earlier discontinued the political links between northern and southern Russia, since the prince never went to Kiev; its lands were absorbed by the expansionist state of Lithuania.

After Alexander's death, his sons were either too weak (Vasily) or too young (Dmitry, Andrew, and Daniel) to succeed him. News of Alexander's death prompted Novgorodians to replace his son Dmitry with Yaroslav of Tver. Berke Khan chose Yaroslav over the older Andrew to be grand prince. Although Alexander had failed to change the method of lateral succession, his son Daniel became the first permanent ruler of Moscow, founding a junior princely line that would produce the first czar, Ivan IV Vasilyevich, also known as Ivan the Terrible, who presided over the canonization of Alexander in 1547; later, Peter I (Peter the Great) moved Alexander's body to St. Petersburg to rest in a monastery dedicated to him at the end of Nevsky Prospekt.

No paintings of Alexander have survived, but his helmet is prominently displayed in the Moscow Armory. Residing in the Leningrad Hermitage is an enormous silver tomb for Nevsky constructed by master craftsmen in 1750-1753 in Petersburg. A cathedral in Sofia, Bulgaria, was named after Alexander in honor of Russian support during the nineteenth century. Sergei Eisenstein's film about Alexander Nevsky was released in 1938, and during World War II Joseph Stalin established the Order of Alexander Nevsky to honor Red Army soldiers.

Bibliography

Fennell, John. *The Crisis of Medieval Russia, 1200-1304*. London: Longman, 1983. A recent and most critical account of this medieval hero and his betrayal of his brothers Andrew and Yaroslav.

Halperin, Charles J. *Russia and the Golden Horde: The Mongol Impact on Medieval Russian History*. Bloomington: Indiana University Press, 1985. In contrast to Fennell, the author is sympathetic to Alexander's policy of appeasement and its results. He also minimizes the magnitude of Novgorod's resistance to the Tatar tax colletors.

Michell, Robert, and Nevill Forbes, trans. *The Chronicle of Novgorod, 1016-1471*. New York: AMS Press, 1970. An indispensable source for the study of Alexander's role in Novgorod—but written from the tendentious outlook of medieval churchmen. The author is unknown.

Paszkiewicz, Henryk. *The Rise of Moscow's Power*. Translated by P. S. Falla. New York: Columbia University Press, 1983. In a full account, the author argues that Alexander was poisoned by the Tatars because he had outlived his usefulness and was, in any case, too popular.

Presniakov, A. E. *The Formation of the Great Russian State: A Study of Russian History in the Thirteenth and Fourteenth Centuries*. Translated by A. E.

Moorhouse. Chicago: Quadrangle Books, 1970. First published in Russian in 1918, this seminal work analyzes the disintegration of Russian political affairs. The author stresses Alexander's family relationships and the centrifugal trends, inevitable despite the presence of charismatic leadership.

Vernadsky, George. *The Mongols and Russia*. New Haven, Conn.: Yale University Press, 1953. The classic account by the late dean of American scholars of medieval Russia. It should be read in conjunction with the revisionist version by Fennell.

Zenkovsky, Serge A., ed. "Tale of the Life and Courage of the Pious and Great Prince Alexander." In *Medieval Russia's Epics, Chronicles, and Tales*. New York: E. P. Dutton, 1974. The basic account which depicts Alexander as the savior of the land from the West. Its omissions are as revealing as the hagiography.

John D. Windhausen

ALFONSO X

Born: November 23, 1221; probably Burgos, Castile
Died: April 4, 1284; Seville, Andalusia
Areas of Achievement: Government, literature, law, and historiography
Contribution: Alfonso's wide-ranging interests earned for him the title "el
Sabio," or "the Wise." In literature, law, historiography, and science, this
King of Castile and León sponsored numerous advances of lasting con-
sequence for Spanish culture.

Early Life

Alfonso X was born the eldest of fourteen children. His father was the revered Ferdinand III, who took advantage of rapidly moving events and
expanded his double kingdom of Castile and León into the rich and densely
populated regions of southern Spain. Alfonso's grandfather Alfonso VIII
had won a most decisive battle in the centuries-long war between Christians
and Moors for control of the Iberian Peninsula. This victory by Christians at
Las Navas de Tolosa in 1212 made it possible for Ferdinand III to capture the
major cities of Córdoba (1236), Jaén (1246), and Seville (1248). Thus, the
heart of Islamic al-Andalus (Andalusia) was incorporated into the kingdom
of Castile and León.

Prince Alfonso spent his early childhood in Galicia, under the care of sur-
rogate parents. His education was of a high order, and his military training
was not neglected. While his first thirty years were spent in the shadow of his
father, Alfonso did demonstrate military prowess in the field as well as political initiative. When barely twenty years of age, Alfonso negotiated and
applied military pressure to force the Muslim kingdom of Murcia to pay tribute to Castile, thus giving the central power a window on the Mediterranean.
In 1248, Alfonso was involved in the successful siege of Seville.

Alfonso was betrothed to Violante of Aragon in 1242; their family eventually numbered five sons and five daughters. Unfaithful after the fashion of
powerful men of his era, Alfonso sired at least one illegitimate child, Beatriz,
who eventually became Queen of Portugal.

Life's Work

From the moment Alfonso crowned himself in 1252, he entertained grandiose ambitions of becoming emperor of all Spain. His father had died while
planning to invade Africa to ensure the safety of his conquests on the peninsula. These schemes to take the war to the infidels' homeland, however, were
not successful. On another international front, Alfonso sought to become
Holy Roman emperor through claims that he had inherited through his German mother. After paying enormous bribes, he was indeed elected in 1257.
The next fifteen years, however, were marked by obsessive but fruitless ef-

forts to validate his title from afar. His competitor, Richard of Cornwall, was able to go to Germany and press his claim in person. After Richard died in 1272, Alfonso was finally able to travel over the Pyrenees Mountains to appeal to Pope Gregory X, who persuaded him to renounce his claim.

Throughout his reign, Alfonso was beset by revolts; in 1252, there was a Muslim uprising, and a group of Christian nobles followed suit in 1254. In 1264, Moroccan forces crossed the Mediterranean to support Granada and Murcia in a revolt against Christian Andalusia. Alfonso was able to put down this threat and annex Murcia to his kingdom. Granada was thus left as the only Muslim state on the peninsula; it paid tribute to Alfonso from 1266 onward.

In 1275, North African armies again invaded Christian Spain. Alfonso's eldest son, Ferdinand (Fernando de la Cerda), was killed in the fighting, and his second son, Sancho, became a hero by defeating the invaders. This seeming success laid the foundation for Alfonso's final and greatest political debacle.

Son Sancho, the hero, proceeded to claim the position of heir apparent. According to Alfonso's recently proclaimed laws, however, the slain Ferdinand's son was next in line. The issue of succession was complicated by the fact that Ferdinand's male children were also nephews of the King of France. Alfonso vacillated; in 1281, he seemed to bend to French demands. Taking advantage of accumulated grievances against his father, Sancho then declared himself regent and led a rebellion of nobles against Alfonso. Sancho gained the backing of the Valladolid Cortes (the parliament of Castile) as well as that of Aragon, Portugal, and Islamic Granada. Alfonso was forced to flee to his beloved Seville, where he died.

It is clear, then, that Alfonso did not earn the title "El Sabio" on the strength of his political acumen. A review of his economic policies reveals a similarly mixed legacy. On the positive side, Alfonso promoted the establishment of town fairs to enhance trade in his domains. He ordered the incorporation of the Mesta, the guild of the sheep and wool industry, which was to become a vital element in central Castile's economy during the late Middle Ages. On the other hand, Alfonso spent prodigiously on his many political and cultural projects; his pursuit of the Holy Roman emperorship, for example, was extremely expensive. The results of this extravagance were increased taxation, the consequent alienation of his subjects, and inflation, which led to the devaluation of Castile's currency.

It is on the cultural front that Alfonso's achievements are most laudable. His patronage of—and personal involvement in—scholarship and the arts resulted in an outpouring of creative works from his court. Alfonso's name is associated with major translations, law codes, works of fiction and poetry, astronomy, advances in education, chronicles, and even games.

A year before his coronation, he oversaw the publication of *Calila e Digna*

(1251), a translation of the Arabic tales of the *Kalila wa-Dimna*. The Alfonsine astronomical tables, with their suggested astrological impact, were published during the first decade of his reign. His compilation of Roman law, the *Espéculo* (speculum), appeared in 1260. A most original and impressive work, and the project that most clearly reveals his direct involvement, is the *Cántigas de Santa María* (c. 1279; songs to Saint Mary). This complex masterpiece, twenty-five years in the making, represented a fusion of poetry, music, and dance. The *Cántigas de Santa María* appeared in Galician, the language then considered proper for lyric poetry. Alfonso is well-known, however, for his use and promotion of Castilian, which became the foundation of modern Spanish. Indeed, some have called him the father of Castilian prose.

Most scholars probably would point to Alfonso's monumental law code, Las Siete Partidas, as his most important single work. Based on Roman law, it contained discourses on manners and morals and developed a theory of the king and his people as a corporation. It moved beyond feudal conceptions of monarchy in representing the monarch as the agent not only of God but also of his subjects. In 1348, long after Alfonso's death, Las Siete Partidas was proclaimed the law of all Castile and León. It continues to influence jurisprudence in Spain and abroad to the present. In fact, in the month of the seventh centennial of Alfonso's death, April, 1984, the Supreme Court of the United States cited Las Siete Partidas in a decision concerning lands in California.

Alfonso can be said to have founded Spanish historiography. He was responsible for the *Crónica general*, a history of Spain that was completed by his son Sancho, as well as for a more general history that began with an account of the Creation. Here, as in his other works, Alfonso's desire to synthesize knowledge from diverse sources—classical, Hebrew, Christian, and Islamic—is evident.

One of Alfonso's most popular works, and yet another demonstration of his wide-ranging interests and accessibility to readers throughout the ages, is his celebrated book on chess. It appeared in 1283, not long before his tragic death.

Summary

After reviewing the career of Alfonso X, one might conclude that it is more appropriate to translate his sobriquet, "el Sabio," as "the Learned" or "the Erudite" rather than "the Wise." The sixteenth century Jesuit historian Juan de Mariana summarized Alfonso's reign by suggesting that he turned his back on practical political life in order to pursue scholarship and that thus, "meditating on the stars, he lost the earth."

Of incalculable importance was Alfonso's decision that almost all of his publications and royal decrees should be issued in Castilian rather than medieval Europe's usual Latin. In this way Alfonso, almost single-handedly, elevated Castilian into a flexible, sophisticated vernacular tongue. Eventually, his language of choice came to dominate most of the Iberian Peninsula, and he may be considered the father of the language now called Spanish and spoken by many millions of persons.

While Alfonso's end was tragic, his achievements on all levels were impressive. He was directly involved, as prince and king, in some of the most spectacular triumphs of the Spanish Reconquest. He restructured the administration of his expanded realms, promoted a legal and cultural renaissance, and supported commercial and technological breakthroughs. Additionally, Alfonso presided over a period of wide-ranging cultural exchanges among Christian, Islamic, and Jewish cultures, a cross-fertilization that affected the evolution of Western civilization on many levels. More than seven hundred years after his death, Alfonso el Sabio is considered by historically conscious Spaniards to be one of their nation's greatest monarchs.

Bibliography
Alfonso X. *Las Siete Partidas*. Translated by S. P. Scott. New York: American Bar Association, 1931. An excellent translation, accompanied by insightful comments and information on this seminal legal code from Alfonso the Learned, lawgiver.
Burns, Robert I., ed. *The Worlds of Alfonso the Learned and James the Conqueror: Intellect and Force in the Middle Ages*. Princeton, N.J.: Princeton University Press, 1985. Seven scholars present papers on the theme of "intellect and force in the Middle Ages" of Spain. Editor Burns's introduction and epilogue contain excellent summaries of the achievements of Alfonso.
Hillgarth, J. N. *The Spanish Kingdoms, 1250-1516*. 2 vols. New York: Oxford University Press, 1976-1978. This synthesis of the late medieval era begins with the reigns of Ferdinand III and Alfonso X. The latter, through the chronicles he sponsored, is a primary source for the historian of his age. The bibliography in this volume is a good place to start a search for Alfonso's creative works, many of which have been translated into English.
O'Callaghan, Joseph. *A History of Medieval Spain*. Ithaca, N.Y.: Cornell University Press, 1975. This massive survey of the history of the Iberian Peninsula from 415 to 1479 places the career of Alfonso within the context of the Reconquest and the Spanish medieval renaissance.
Payne, Stanley G. *A History of Spain and Portugal*. Vol. 1. Madison: University of Wisconsin Press, 1973. The chapter on Castile-León in the era of the Reconquest provides an excellent survey of the exploits of Alfonso VIII, Ferdinand III, and Alfonso X. Payne's great virtue is that of placing his story within an Iberian-wide context.
Thought: A Review of Culture and Ideas 60 (December, 1985). In this special

issue devoted to an examination of "the emperor of culture," eight scholars focus on the polymath's cultural achievements. The essays are scholarly papers that develop aspects of Alfonso's successes.

Charles J. Fleener

ALHAZEN

Born: 965; Basra, Iraq
Died: 1039; Cairo, Egypt
Areas of Achievement: Physics, astronomy, mathematics, and medicine
Contribution: Alhazen, Islam's greatest scientist, devoted his life to physics, astronomy, mathematics, and medicine. His treatise *Optics*, in which he deftly used experiments and advanced mathematics to understand the action of light, exerted a profound influence on many European natural philosophers.

Early Life

Abu 'Ali al-Ḥasan ibn al-Haytham (commonly known as Alhazen, the Latinized form of his first name, al-Ḥasan) was born in Basra in 965. He was given a traditional Muslim education, but at an early age he became perplexed by the variety of religious beliefs and sects, because he was convinced of the unity of truth. When he was older, he concluded that truth could be attained only in doctrines whose matter was sensible and whose form was rational. He found such doctrines in the writings of Aristotle and in natural philosophy and mathematics.

By devoting himself completely to learning, Alhazen achieved fame as a scholar and was given a political post at Basra. In an attempt to obtain a better position, he claimed that he could construct a machine to regulate the flooding of the Nile. The Fatimid caliph al-Hakim, wishing to use this sage's expertise, persuaded him to move to Cairo. Alhazen, to fulfill his boast, was trapped into heading an engineering mission to Egypt's southern border. On his way to Aswan, he began to have doubts about his plan, for he observed excellently designed and perfectly constructed buildings along the Nile, and he realized that his scheme, if it were possible, would have already been carried out by the creators of these impressive structures. His misgivings were confirmed when he discovered that the cataracts south of Aswan made flood control impossible. Convinced of the impracticability of his plan, and fearing the wrath of the eccentric and volatile caliph, Alhazen pretended to be mentally deranged; upon his return to Cairo, he was confined to his house until al-Hakim's death in 1021.

Alhazen then took up residence in a small domed shrine near the Azhar Mosque. Having been given back his previously sequestered property, he resumed his activities as a writer and teacher. He may have earned his living by copying mathematical works, including Euclid's *Stoicheia* (c. fourth century B.C.; *Elements*) and Ptolemy's *Mathēmatikē suntaxis* (c. A.D. 150; *Almagest*), and may also have traveled and had contact with other scholars.

Life's Work

The scope of Alhazen's work is impressive. He wrote studies on mathematics, physics, astronomy, and medicine, as well as commentaries on the writings of Aristotle and Galen. He was an exact observer, a skilled experimenter, and an insightful theoretician, and he put these abilities to excellent use in the field of optics. He has been called the most important figure in optics between antiquity and the seventeenth century. Within optics itself, the range of his interests was wide: He discussed theories of light and vision, the anatomy and diseases of the eye, reflection and refraction, the rainbow, lenses, spherical and parabolic mirrors, and the pinhole camera (camera obscura).

Alhazen's most important work was *Kitāb al-Manāzir*, commonly known as *Optics*. Not published until 1572, and only appearing in the West in the Latin translation *Opticae thesaurus Alhazeni libri vii*, it attempted to clarify the subject by inquiring into its principles. He rejected Euclid's and Ptolemy's doctrine of visual rays (the extramission theory, which regarded vision as analogous to the sense of touch). For example, Ptolemy attributed sight to the action of visual rays issuing conically from the observer's eye and being reflected from various objects. Alhazen also disagreed with past versions of the intromission theory, which treated the visible object as a source from which forms (simulacra) issued. The atomists, for example, held that objects shed sets of atoms as a snake sheds its skin; when this set enters the eye, vision occurs. In another version of the intromission theory, Aristotle treated the visible object as a modifier of the medium between the object and the eye. Alhazen found the atomistic theory unconvincing because it could not explain how the image of a large mountain could enter the small pupil of the eye. He did not like the Aristotelian theory because it could not explain how the eye could distinguish individual parts of the seen world, since objects altered the entire intervening medium. Alhazen, in his version of the intromission theory, treated the visible object as a collection of small areas, each of which sends forth its own ray. He believed that vision takes place through light rays reflected from every point on an object's surface converging toward an apex in the eye.

According to Alhazen, light is an essential form in self-luminous bodies, such as the sun, and an accidental form in bodies that derive their luminosity from outside sources. Accidental light, such as the moon, is weaker than essential light, but both forms are emitted by their respective sources in exactly the same way: noninstantaneously, from every point on the source, in all directions, and along straight lines. To establish rectilinear propagation for essential, accidental, reflected, and refracted radiation, Alhazen performed many experiments with dark chambers, pinhole cameras, sighting tubes, and strings.

In the first book of *Optics*, Alhazen describes the anatomy of the eye. His description is not original, being based largely on the work of Galen, but he modifies traditional ocular geometry to suit his own explanation of vision.

For example, he claims that sight occurs in the eye by means of the glacial humor (what would be called the crystalline lens), because when this humor is injured, vision is destroyed. He also uses such observations as eye pain while gazing on intense light and afterimages from strongly illuminated objects to argue against the visual-ray theory, because these observations show that light is coming to the eye from the object. With this picture of intromission established, Alhazen faces the problem of explaining how replicas as big as a mountain can pass through the tiny pupil into the eye.

He begins the solution of this problem by recognizing that every point in the eye receives a ray from every point in the visual field. The difficulty with this punctiform analysis is that, if each point on the object sends light and color in every direction to each point of the eye, then all this radiation would arrive at the eye in total confusion; for example, colors would arrive mixed. Simply put, the problem is a superfluity of rays. To explain vision, each point of the surface of the glacial humor needs to receive a ray from only one point in the visual field. In short, it is necessary to establish a one-to-one correspondence between points in the visual field and points in the eye.

To fulfill this goal, Alhazen notices that only one ray from each point in the visual field falls perpendicularly on the convex surface of the eye. He then proposes that all other rays, those falling at oblique angles to the eye's surface, are refracted and so weakened that they are incapable of affecting visual power. Alhazen even performed an experiment to show that perpendicular rays are strong and oblique rays weak: He shot a metal sphere against a dish both perpendicularly and obliquely. The perpendicular shot fractured the plate, whereas the oblique shot bounced off harmlessly. Thus, in his theory, the cone of perpendicular rays coming into the eye accounts for the perception of the visible object's shape and the laws of perspective.

Book 2 of *Optics* contains Alhazen's theory of cognition based on visual perception, and book 3 deals with binocular vision and visual errors. Catoptrics (the theory of reflected light) is the subject of book 4. Alhazen here formulates the laws of reflection: Incident and reflected rays are in the same plane, and incident and reflected angles are equal. The equality of the angles of incidence and reflection allows Alhazen to explain the formation of an image in a plane mirror. As throughout *Optics*, Alhazen here uses experiments to help establish his contentions. For example, by throwing an iron sphere against a metal mirror at an oblique angle, he found that the incident and reflected movements of the sphere were symmetrical. The reflected movement of the iron sphere, because of its heaviness, did not continue in a straight line, as the light ray does, but Alhazen did not contend that the iron sphere is an exact duplicate of the light ray.

Alhazen's investigation of reflection continues in books 5 and 6 of *Optics*. Book 5 contains the famous "Problem of Alhazen": For any two points opposite a spherical reflecting surface, either convex or concave, find the point or points on the surface at which the light from one of the two points will be reflected to the other. Today it is known that the algebraic solution of this problem leads to an equation of the fourth degree, but Alhazen solved it geometrically by the intersection of a circle and a hyperbola.

Book 7, which concludes *Optics*, is devoted to dioptrics (the theory of refraction). Although Alhazen did not discover the mathematical relationship between the angles of incidence and refraction, his treatment of the phenomenon was the most extensive and enlightening before that of René Descartes. As with reflection, Alhazen explores refraction through a mechanical analogy. Light, he says, moves with great speed in a transparent medium such as air and with slower speed in a dense body such as glass or water. The slower speed of the light ray in the denser medium is the result of the greater resistance it encounters, but this resistance is not strong enough to hinder its movement completely. Since the refracted light ray is not strong enough to maintain its original direction in the denser medium, it moves in another direction along which its passage will be easier (that is, it turns toward the normal). This idea of the easier and quicker path was the basis of Alhazen's explanation of refraction, and it is a forerunner of the principle of least time associated with the name of Pierre de Fermat.

Optics was Alhazen's most significant work and by far his best known, but he also wrote more modest treatises in which he discussed the rainbow, shadows, camera obscura, and Ptolemy's optics as well as spheroidal and paraboloidal burning mirrors. The ancient Greeks had a good understanding of plane mirrors, but Alhazen developed an exhaustive geometrical analysis of the more difficult problem of the formation of images in spheroidal and paraboloidal mirrors.

Although Alhazen's achievements in astronomy do not equal those in optics, his extant works reveal his mastery of the techniques of Ptolemaic astronomy. These works are mostly short tracts on minor problems, for example, sundials, moonlight, eclipses, parallax, and determining the *gibla* (the direction to be faced in prayer). In another treatise, he was able to explain the apparent increase in size of heavenly bodies near the horizon, and he also estimated the thickness of the atmosphere.

His best astronomical work, and the only one known to the medieval West, was *Hay'at al-'alan* (tenth or eleventh century; on the configuration of the world). This treatise grew out of Alhazen's desire that the astronomical system should correspond to the true movements of actual heavenly bodies. He therefore attacked Ptolemy's system, in which the motions of heavenly bodies were explained in terms of imaginary points moving on imaginary circles. In his work, Alhazen tried to discover the physical reality underlying Ptolemy's abstract astronomical system. He accomplished this task by viewing the heavens as a series of concentric spherical shells whose rotations were interconnected. Alhazen's system accounted for the apparent motions of the heavenly bodies in a clear and untechnical way, which accounts for the book's popularity in the Middle Ages.

Alhazen's fame as a mathematician has largely depended on his geometrical solutions of various optical problems, but more than twenty strictly mathematical treatises have survived. Some of these deal with geometrical problems arising from his studies of Euclid's *Elements*, whereas others deal with quadrature problems, that is, constructing squares equal in area to various plane figures. He also wrote a work on lunes (figures contained between the arcs of two circles) and on the properties of conic sections. Although he was not successful with every problem, his performance, which exhibited his masterful command of higher mathematics, has rightly won for him the admiration of later mathematicians.

Summary

Alhazen was undoubtedly the greatest Muslim scientist, and *Optics* was the most important work in the field from Ptolemy's time to Johannes Kepler's. He extricated himself from the limitations of such earlier theories as the atomistic, Aristotelian, and Ptolemaic and integrated what he knew about medicine, physics, and mathematics into a single comprehensive theory of light and vision. Although his theory contained ideas from older theories, he combined these ideas with his new insights into a fresh creation, which became the source of a new optical tradition.

His optical theories had some influence on Islamic scientists, but their main impact was on the West. *Optics* was translated from Arabic into Latin at the end of the twelfth century. It was widely studied, and in the thirteenth century, Witelo (also known as Vitellio) made liberal use of Alhazen's text in writing his comprehensive book on optics. Roger Bacon, John Peckham, and Giambattista della Porta are only some of the many thinkers who were influenced by Alhazen's work. Indeed, it was not until Kepler, six centuries later, that work on optics progressed beyond the point to which Alhazen had brought it. Even Kepler, however, used some of Alhazen's ideas, for example, the one-to-one correspondence between points on the object and points in the eye. It would not be going too far to say that Alhazen's optical theories defined the scope and goals of the field from his day to ours.

Bibliography

Grant, Edward, ed. *A Source Book in Medieval Science*. Cambridge, Mass.: Harvard University Press, 1974. A compilation of readings from medieval natural philosophers, including several selections in English translation from the works of Alhazen.

Hayes, John Richard, ed. *The Genius of Arab Civilization: Source of Renaissance*. Cambridge, Mass.: MIT Press, 1978. In this beautifully illustrated book, several international authorities discuss the achievements of

Islamic culture. Abdelhamid I. Sabra's chapter on the exact sciences contains an account of Alhazen's work in the context of Islamic intellectual history. Includes indexes and a bibliography.

Lindberg, David C. *Theories of Vision from al-Kindi to Kepler*. Chicago: University of Chicago Press, 1976. Lindberg surveys visual theory against the background of ancient accomplishments. His chapter on Alhazen's intromission theory is excellent.

_____, ed. *Science in the Middle Ages*. Chicago: University of Chicago Press, 1978. Through the expertise of several historians of medieval science, this book examines in depth all major aspects of natural philosophy in the Middle Ages. The approach is not encyclopedic but interpretative. Lindberg is the author of the chapter on optics, in which Alhazen's work is clearly explained.

Nasr, Seyyed Hossein. *Islamic Science: An Illustrated Study*. Westerham, England: World of Islam Festival Publishing Co., 1976. The first illustrated study ever undertaken of the whole of Islamic science. Using traditional Islamic concepts, Nasr discusses various branches of science, including optics.

_____. *Science and Civilization in Islam*. Cambridge, Mass.: Harvard University Press, 1968. This book is the first one-volume work in English to deal with Islamic science from the Muslim rather than the Western viewpoint. Its approach is encyclopedic rather than analytic, but it does contain a discussion of Alhazen's work in its Muslim context.

Sabra, Abdelhamid I. *Theories of Light from Descartes to Newton*. London: Oldbourne Book Co., 1967. Though this book is mainly centered on seventeenth century theories of light, Sabra discusses in detail the impact of Alhazen's ideas on the optical discoveries of such men as Descartes and Christiaan Huygens.

Robert J. Paradowski

ALP ARSLAN

Born: c. 1030; Central Asia
Died: 1072; near Tirmidh (modern Termez, U.S.S.R.)
Areas of Achievement: Government and warfare
Contribution: The second sultan of the Seljuk dynasty, Alp Arslan consolidated and extended the conquests of his predecessor, Toghrïl Beg; his reign, together with that of his son Malik-Shah, constituted the zenith of the empire of the Great Seljuks.

Early Life

Alp Arslan, the second and most famous of the sultans of the Seljuk dynasty, was born around 1030 to Chaghrï Beg, brother of the Turkish warlord Toghrïl Beg. During the 1040's, Toghrïl invaded Iran with his Türkmen followers, became the protector of the 'Abbasid caliph in Baghdad and thereby the champion of Sunni (orthodox) Islam, and founded an empire which extended over much of the Middle East. Alp Arslan's Turkish name (his Arabic names and titles were Adud al-Dawla Abu Shuja Muhammad ibn Daud Chaghrï Beg) was a combination of the words *alp*, meaning warrior or hero, and *arslan*, meaning lion, apt sobriquets for so renowned a military leader.

His great-grandfather, Seljuk, the eponymous ancestor of the Seljuk dynasty, had been a clan leader among the tribes that composed the confederacy of the Oguz Turks, who in the tenth century occupied the steppes between the Aral Sea and the Volga River. Seljuk himself had thrown off his allegiance to the *yabghu*, as the supreme ruler of the Oguz was known, and led his clansmen and a growing body of Türkmen followers as soldiers of fortune in the service of the rulers of Khwarizm and Transoxiana. His base of operations was in the neighborhood of Jand, on the north bank of the Syr Darya River, where eventually he was buried. One source states that he went to the aid of one of the last rulers of the Samanid dynasty of Bukhara, under attack from the Qarakhanid Turks, advancing from what is now Chinese Central Asia. By then, he had become a Muslim. His sons, Arslan Israil, Mikhail, and Musa, followed their father's example in taking advantage of the anarchy in Central Asia which accompanied the fall of the Samanids and the rise of the Qarakhanids. The unusual personal names of these three have led scholars to wonder whether they are indicative of Nestorian Christian or Jewish Khazar influence.

Mikhail's sons, Toghrïl Beg and Chaghrï Beg, were the founders of Seljuk rule in the Middle East. Even before their defeat of the Ghaznavid sultan (until then, ruler of much of the Iranian Plateau as well as Afghanistan) at Dendenkan, between Merv and Sarakhs, in 1040, Toghrïl Beg had entered Neyshabur, the principal city of Khorasan, and proclaimed himself sultan.

After Dendenkan, Chaghrï Beg turned east to occupy Balkh and Tukharistan in northern Afghanistan. Toghrïl Beg then proceeded with the systematic conquest of central and western Iran and of Iraq. He occupied Baghdad in 1055 and again in 1058, where he assumed the role of protector of the caliph. In 1062, in a reluctant break with past precedent, the latter agreed to Toghrïl Beg's marriage to his daughter.

While Toghrïl Beg was pursuing his triumphant course in the west, Chaghrï Beg was acting as the quasi-independent ruler of Khorasan and part of the Amu Darya River valley, with his headquarters at Merv. His eldest son, Qavurt, had embarked upon the conquest of Kerman and southeastern Iran (where his descendants were to rule until 1186), while his other sons (among them Alp Arslan) accompanied Toghrïl Beg on his campaigns in Iraq and western Iran. During his last years, Chaghrï Beg chose, perhaps as a result of poor health, to make use of Alp Arslan in the government of Khorasan, thereby providing him with administrative experience which would stand him in good stead for the future. It was during this period, under his father's tutelage, that he came into contact with the man who would eventually become his chief minister and adviser, Nizam al-Mulk, whom Chaghrï Beg on his deathbed urged Alp Arslan to appoint as his vizier. Undoubtedly, a significant factor in the success of Alp Arslan's reign was his appreciation of the talents of Nizam al-Mulk as an administrator and the consequent partnership of sultan and vizier in the government of the empire. At Chaghrï Beg's death (c. 1060), Toghrïl Beg confirmed Alp Arslan as the new ruler of his father's vast appanage in the northeast.

No likeness of Alp Arslan survives, but he was said to have been a tall and imposing figure of exceptional strength, his great height enhanced by his preference for an unusually high headdress. A quaint tradition records that before he drew his bow, a servant had to tie back his immense mustache, which would otherwise have become entangled in his bowstring.

Life's Work

Like other ruling groups from Central Asia, the early Seljuks viewed sovereignty as being invested in the family as a whole, rather than in a single individual, an attitude which Toghrïl Beg had done little to discourage. At his death in 1063, therefore, there was a predictable familial struggle over the succession. Childless himself, Toghrïl Beg had designated as his successor another of Chaghrï Beg's sons, Sulaiman, the favorite candidate of the late sultan's powerful vizier, al-Kunduri. Perhaps because Sulaiman's accession would have confirmed the already dominant position enjoyed by al-Kunduri, some of Toghrïl Beg's former Mamluk (slave) commanders favored Alp Arslan, who had already established a formidable reputation as ruler of Khorasan. In the contest which followed, Sulaiman was easily outmaneuvered, and al-Kunduri was executed at the instigation of Nizam al-Mulk.

A more formidable threat was posed by Alp Arslan's kinsman Qutlumush ibn Arslan Israil, the able and energetic son of Alp Arslan's granduncle. Qutlumush's power base lay in the northwest, in the direction of the Caucasus, and he commanded the loyalty of formidable numbers of Türkmen warriors who were dismayed at the centralizing processes which marked the transformation of Seljuk rule from predatory raiding to empire building. Qutlumush pressed his own claim to the throne with an appeal to the traditions of the steppes: "By right, the sultanate should come to me, because my father was the senior and leading member of the tribe." His forces advanced to the vicinity of Rayy (near modern Tehran) but were defeated by troops loyal to Alp Arslan. Qutlumush himself died shortly afterward, apparently killed by a fall from his horse. His followers were not so easily dealt with, and it was largely on their account that Alp Arslan was eventually drawn into direct confrontation with the Byzantines.

There were other challenges to Alp Arslan's authority. Toghrïl Beg had married a daughter of the ruler of Khwarizm who had a son by a previous marriage, and although this son was not a Seljuk, he attracted some support among the disaffected. More serious was the revolt in Kerman of Alp Arslan's older brother, Qavurt, whose delayed resentment at the elevation of his younger sibling surfaced in 1067. Alp Arslan was forced to invade Kerman and also Fars, which Qavurt had previously seized from a local dynasty, but the two brothers were eventually reconciled.

Alp Arslan must have been familiar with the course of Toghrïl Beg's difficult negotiations with the 'Abbasid caliph, and it seems that he himself was determined to avoid situations in which disputes might develop as to the respective powers and prerogatives of caliph and sultan. On his accession, he obtained formal recognition from the long-reigning caliph al-Qaim, with whom his uncle had dealt, but he declined to visit Baghdad in person or to become involved in the intrigues of the caliphal court. While keeping his distance, he did, however, keep a close watch on affairs in Baghdad. Alp Arslan's prime concern was to prevent any augmentation of the influence of the Fatimid caliphs in Cairo, Shi'ites whose secret emissaries worked assiduously for the Fatimid cause in a region (Iraq) where a number of the Arab emirs were themselves Shi'ites. To that extent, at least, he and the 'Abbasid caliph had common ground for cooperation. Hence, he was careful to ensure that his military representative (*shahna*) in Iraq was personally acceptable to the caliph, while Nizam al-Mulk endeavored to work closely with the caliph's successive viziers. The policy of avoiding Baghdad while treating the caliph with a blend of courtesy and firmness undoubtedly paid off: In 1066, when Alp Arslan designated his son, Malik-Shah, as *valiahd* (heir apparent) and had his name read in the *khutba* together with his own, he was able to secure caliphal recognition for him, and in 1071-1072, one of Alp Arslan's daughters was married to al-Qaim's heir, al-Muqtadi.

Although Alp Arslan's reputation as one of the greatest medieval Muslim rulers arose in part from his spectacular success against the Byzantines at Manzikert in 1071, it is unlikely that he cherished the ambition to be a *ghazi* (warrior for the faith). On the other hand, he cannot have been unhappy to see the restless Türkmens devote their energies to *jihad* (holy warfare) on the Byzantine marches, an undertaking which deflected their attention from the heartlands of the Seljuk empire. The danger was that the Türkmens, who included many former followers of Qutlumush, as they pressed forward, would wholly emancipate themselves from Seljuk control and perhaps even set up an independent state. Thus, Alp Arslan was compelled early in his reign to turn his attention to the northwest. Several major dynasties based upon the Iranian Plateau (for example, the Sassanids, the Il-Khans, and the Safavids) found it necessary to seek control of the strategic region between the Black Sea and the Caspian, bounded on the north by the Caucasus and on the south by the Araks River; to this rule Alp Arslan was no exception. In 1064, therefore, within a year of his accession and the overthrow of Qutlumush, he invaded Byzantine Armenia, capturing its administrative capital, Ani, and obtaining the submission of the great fortress of Kars. He then advanced into Georgia, where he married a niece of the Georgian king. Three year later, in 1067, he marched into Arran (the country between the Araks and Kura rivers), where he received the formal submission of its ruler, Fadh II ibn Shavur of the Shaddadid dynasty. Shortly afterward, the ruler of Shirvan also submitted, with the result that Seljuk suzerainty was extended along the western shores of the Caspian as far north as Darband. Then, in 1068, a further invasion of Georgia, this time led by the Shaddadid ruler of Arran, reaffirmed Alp Arslan's overlordship over that now-isolated Christian kingdom (Armenia had finally come under Muslim rule and the Byzantine frontier had contracted in a westerly direction).

Initially, the Seljuks, as they advanced into the Middle East, had appeared to have as their goal the occupation of the Iranian Plateau. That achievement, however, had inevitably led to the conquest of Iraq, partly because of the need to put down the prevailing anarchy there and partly to counter long-standing Fatimid ambitions in that area. Toghrïl Beg's occupation of Baghdad had forced the Seljuk sultanate and the 'Abbasid caliphate into a symbiotic relationship, which committed the sultan to restoring Sunni orthodoxy and combating Shi'ite heterodoxy in the Fertile Crescent. In consequence, a principal concern of Alp Arslan from the time of his accession was the question of the military frontier with the Fatimids in northern Syria. By 1070, the matter of relations with the Fatimids was coming to a head: That year, the sharif of Mecca informed Alp Arslan that the *khutba* in Mecca was no longer being said in the name of the Fatimid caliph in Cairo but in that of the 'Abbasid caliph and the Seljuk sultan, a circumstance which the sultan sought to turn to his advantage. Furthermore, a delegation of rebellious

Egyptian emirs was seeking his assistance in overthrowing Fatimid rule. Alp Arslan therefore began to plan the invasion of Fatimid Syria and perhaps to contemplate a subsequent invasion of Palestine and Egypt.

Meanwhile, however, the virtually independent Türkmens were raiding deep into Byzantine Anatolia, plundering throughout the countryside and, wherever possible, breaking into the cities, including those two later centers of Seljuk rule, Konya and Kayseri. The Byzantines, predictably, reacted to protect the line of communication with their most easterly outposts: Malatya, Diyarbakir, Antioch, and Edessa. In 1070, therefore, the Byzantine emperor, Romanus IV Diogenes, sent an expedition to reinforce these cities. While much obscurity surrounds Seljuk-Byzantine relations of this period, it appears that Alp Arslan, preoccupied with his plan to attack the Fatimid strongholds in Syria, agreed to sign a truce with the emperor. While the two imperial powers sought to stabilize the border zones between them, however, the sultan was in no position to control the Türkmens in eastern Anatolia, and it was their ongoing predatory raids which finally provoked the emperor into mounting a major military expedition against them. Assembling a huge force at his base in Erzurum, he proceeded to lead his troops into the Armenian districts north of Lakc Van.

Alp Arslan, regarding this move as a breach of the recent truce, abandoned his siege of a Fatimid client in Aleppo and hastened to bar the emperor's further advance. The two armies met at Manzikert (modern Malazgirt) and fought the great battle of August 26, 1071, which resulted in the utter destruction of the Byzantines and the capture of the emperor himself. Alp Arslan treated his captive honorably, releasing him in exchange for a ransom, promises of tribute and a marriage alliance, and probably cession of territory, but these arrangements were voided by the emperor's deposition and blinding upon his return to Constantinople that same year. Hence, the issues at stake between the two empires were left unresolved. Following Manzikert, Alp Arslan had only a year to live, but during the reign of his son Malik-Shah (1073-1092), Sulaiman ibn Qutlumush, the son of Alp Arslan's old rival, penetrated Anatolia as far west as the Aegean Sea, capturing Nicaea (modern Iznik) around 1077.

The Battle of Manzikert has been correctly viewed as one of history's decisive battles, for it marked the formal beginning of the process whereby the Byzantines eventually suffered the permanent loss of provinces which were major sources of revenue and recruits; the Turks became the conquerors of, and eventually the dominant ethnic group in, Anatolia; and Christian and Hellenistic Asia Minor became Muslim Turkey. Indirectly, Manzikert led to the appeal by a later Byzantine emperor (Alexis I Comnenus) for military assistance from Latin Christendom and hence to Pope Urban II's famous sermon at Clermont in 1095, which unleashed two centuries of crusading zeal in the Middle East and the eastern Mediterranean. In this light, the account of

Manzikert which reached the Latin West through the writings of the historian of the First Crusade, William of Tyre, who heard that the battle "was fiercely contested by almost equal forces," bears examination. William was completely mistaken as to Alp Arslan's treatment of Romanus Diogenes, but his account, the stuff of legend, conformed to Christian preconceptions of their Islamic adversaries:

> The foe, magnificent but infidel, elated by his great success and rendered still more arrogant by victory, commanded that the emperor be brought before him. Seated upon his royal throne, he ordered Romanus to be thrown beneath his feet, and, to show his contempt for the Christian name and faith, in the presence of the attendant princes, he used the emperor's body as a footstool, mounting and dismounting upon it.

Although throughout his reign Alp Arslan's main concern (like Toghrïl Beg's) seems to have centered upon western Iran and the Fertile Crescent, he could not altogether ignore his eastern borders with his Ghaznavid and Qarakhanid neighbors. As far as the Ghaznavids were concerned, the treaty which had followed the 1040 Seljuk victory at Dendenkan continued in force. With the Qarakhanids, now masters of Transoxiana (Bukhara, Samarkand, and western Farghana), there remained residual tension, for they were longstanding antagonists of the Seljuks and now their possessions included territory formerly ruled by Alp Arslan's father, Chaghrï Beg. Early in Alp Arslan's reign, the sultan had campaigned in the western Qarakhanid Khanate, which was then ruled by the pious and respected Tamghach Khan Ibrahim ibn Nasr. As the years passed, however, the two rulers gradually had developed a kind of modus vivendi exemplified by a series of marriage alliances, including the marriage of a daughter of Alp Arslan to Ibrahim's successor, Shams al-Mulk Nasr, and the marriage of Alp Arslan's heir, Malik-Shah, to a Qarakhanid princess. War broke out between Alp Arslan and Shams al-Mulk Nasr, however, in 1072. One version of the story asserts that Shams al-Mulk Nasr had caused the death of the sultan's daughter, suspecting her of having urged the Seljuks to invade his territory; Alp Arslan thereupon led a large army across the Amu Darya. Soon after the crossing, he ordered the execution of a Mamluk who had disobeyed him. The condemned man, enraged at what he regarded as an act of injustice, broke loose from his escort and stabbed the sultan to death.

Summary

Building upon the foundations laid by Toghrïl Beg, Alp Arslan consolidated and extended his predecessor's conquests to create an empire extending almost from the Mediterranean to the Pamirs. Under the aegis of his brilliant minister, Nizam al-Mulk, that empire acquired the character of a traditional Irano-Islamic monarchy, with the Seljuks cast in the role of renovators of a hitherto decrepit political order. Inevitably, war and administrative tasks left Alp Arslan little opportunity to establish a reputation as a great patron, and the achievements of the Seljuks in literature, architecture, and the decorative arts belong to a later age.

At Manzikert, Alp Arslan changed the course of Middle Eastern history, for his victory foreshadowed the end of Byzantine Christian dominance in Asia Minor and its ultimate Turkification and Islamization, while also contributing to the call for a crusade in Latin Christendom. Alp Arslan figures in the Muslim historiographical tradition as a brave soldier, a pious Muslim, a champion of the faith, and a just and, for the most part, magnanimous ruler.

Bibliography
Bartold, Vasilii V. *Turkestan down to the Mongol Invasion*. Translated by T. Minorsky. Edited by C. E. Bosworth. 3d ed. London: Gibb Memorial Series, 1968. This authoritative study of those areas of Central Asia ruled by the Russian czars in the nineteenth century is the work of one of the greatest of Russian Islamicists. Although the English translation first appeared in 1928, there is no immediate likelihood of its being superseded. Covering the Islamic period down to the first quarter of the thirteenth century, it is especially good on the Seljuks and their contemporaries.
Bosworth, C. E. "The Political and Dynastic History of the Iranian World (A.D. 1000-1217)." In *The Cambridge History of Iran*, vol. 5, edited by J. A. Boyle. Cambridge: Cambridge University Press, 1968. This chapter provides a masterly and very detailed review of the Seljuk period. The reign of Alp Arslan and the vizierate of Nizam al-Mulk are both discussed.
Cahen, Claude. "Alp Arslan." In *The Encyclopaedia of Islam*, vol. 1. 2d ed. Leiden, Netherlands: E. J. Brill, 1960. This is the best short account of the career of Alp Arslan.
——————. *Pre-Ottoman Turkey*. New York: Taplinger Publishing Co., 1968. This definitive study of the Seljuk period of Turkish history gives a straightforward, scholarly account of the rise of the Seljuks and their involvement in Anatolia prior to 1071.
Friendly, Alfred. *The Dreadful Day: The Battle of Manzikert, 1071*. London: Hutchinson, 1981. A highly readable but also very detailed account of Manzikert and the events leading up to it. Written for the nonspecialist.
Lambton, Ann K. S. "The Internal Structure of the Saljuq Empire." In *The Cambridge History of Iran*, vol. 5, edited by J. A. Boyle. Cambridge: Cambridge University Press, 1968. This is the best account, by a leading authority, of the political and administrative institutions of the Seljuk empire; it can be usefully supplemented by the same author's *Continuity and Change in Medieval Persia* (Albany: State University of New York Press, 1988).

Luther, K. A. "Alp Arslān." In *Encyclopaedia Iranica*, vol. 1. London: Routledge and Kegan Paul, 1985. Somewhat longer than Cahen's article for *The Encyclopaedia of Islam* (see above), Luther's contribution is particularly valuable for its listing of the sources available for the study of Alp Arslan's reign.

Müneccimbasi, Ahmet ibn Lutfullah. *A History of Sharvan and Darband in the Tenth-Eleventh Centuries*. Translated and edited by V. Minorsky. Cambridge: W. Heffer, 1958. This translation and abridgment of an eleventh century work dealing with the minor Islamic dynasties of the Seljuk period in the area north of the Araks River and south of the Caucasus Mountains is essential reading for understanding the circumstances which drew Alp Arslan into this region. See also Minorsky's *Studies in Caucasian History* (London: Taylor's Foreign Press, 1953).

Rice, Tamara Talbot. *The Seljuks in Asia Minor*. London: Thames and Hudson, 1961. A popular account of the Seljuks, their culture and arts, in the series Ancient Peoples and Places. Attractively illustrated, it is particularly useful as a guide to the better known Seljuk monuments in Turkey.

Vryonis, Speros. *The Decline of Medieval Hellenism in Asia Minor and the Process of Islamization from the Eleventh Through the Fifteenth Century*. Berkeley: University of California Press, 1971. This fine study of the complex interaction of political, social, and cultural developments as Byzantine rule gave way to that of the Turks in Anatolia sheds much light upon the circumstances under which the Türkmens penetrated the Byzantine frontier both before and after the Battle of Manzikert.

Gavin R. G. Hambly

SAINT AMBROSE

Born: 339; Augusta Treverorum, Gaul
Died: April 4, 397; Milan, Italy
Areas of Achievement: Religion and government
Contribution: By the practical application of Roman virtue and Christian ethics Ambrose established the Nicene Creed as the orthodox doctrine of Christianity and asserted the spiritual authority of the church over the state.

Early Life

Ambrose is a good example of why Christianity replaced traditional paganism as the official religion of the Roman Empire. The son of one of the highest civilian officials in the Roman hierarchy, he was educated in the best Roman tradition and reared in a devout Christian family. When Ambrose was born, his father, Aurelius Ambrosius, was Praetorian Prefect of Gaul and could offer Ambrose every advantage of Roman life. Ambrosius died when Ambrose was still an infant, and thus it was left to his mother, whose name is unknown, to rear the young Ambrose, his sister Marcellina, and his brother Satyrus. Almost immediately the family returned to Rome. Little is known about this time in Rome except that Ambrose and his brother attended the usual Roman schools, where they learned grammar and composition by reading and reciting the works of the Roman masters. Ambrose stated that he most enjoyed Cicero, Vergil, and Sallust. Later both brothers studied rhetoric and prepared for careers in the civil service.

Christianity seems to have been established within the family well before Ambrose's birth. The family boasted of a holy ancestor, a great-aunt Soteris, who had suffered martyrdom in 304 during the persecutions propagated by Diocletian. The depth of this belief first appeared on the feast of the Epiphany in 353, when Marcellina, in the presence of Pope Liberius, dedicated her virginity to God and committed herself to the practice of an ascetic life. Afterward, Marcellina continued to live in her mother's house and with her mother formed the core for one of the first groups of patrician women who renounced the world and gave themselves up to Christian study, prayer, and good works.

The effects of a Christian life were not immediately obvious in Ambrose's own life. In 365, Emperor Valentinian I appointed him and Satyrus legal advocates in Sirmium at the tribunal of the Praetorian Prefect of Italy, Africa, and Illyria. Both men impressed successive prefects with their eloquence and intelligence and advanced quickly. As a result, in 370 both received provincial governorships. Ambrose became governor of Aemilia-Liguria in northern Italy. Since the capital of the province was at Milan, then the principal seat of the Imperial Government in the West, Ambrose became known to the most important people of the time. An anecdote in the biography written after his death by his secretary Paulinus indicates how popular a governor he was. In 373, when Bishop Auxentius died, governor Ambrose, in an effort to keep the peace, addressed the bickering factions of orthodox and Arian Christians. From the crowd a child's voice was heard to call "Bishop Ambrose." It was enough to start a public outcry for his consecration as the next Bishop of Milan.

Life's Work

Ambrose's whole career as Bishop of Milan was directed toward defending what he called the "cause of God," which included the advocacy of an orthodox Christian doctrine, the defining of Church authority, and the disestablishment of pagan state religion. From the time of his consecration, Bishop Ambrose had made known his opposition to the Arian heresy, but he was unable to influence the Emperor Valentinian I. To maintain public order, Valentinian followed a policy of neutrality toward the different religions of the empire, even though he himself was a Christian. Ambrose's first successes were in shaping the attitudes and programs of the Emperor Gratian. His strongly worded statement against Arianism, *De fide* (380), used extensive scriptural quotations to present the argument that orthodoxy provided a physical protection for the empire. Ambrose pointed out that the Goths had devastated the Arian provinces of the Balkan Peninsula but that the provinces defended by the orthodox Gratian were spared. Convinced by the argument, Gratian enlisted Ambrose as an adviser and teacher. It was probably Ambrose who inspired Gratian's firm stands against heresy and his decree for the removal of the Altar of Victory from the Senate House in 382. The Altar of Victory to the people of the time was a symbol of the ancient association of paganism and the Roman government.

Ambrose's relationship with Gratian proved his powers of persuasion, but it established no real authority for the Church. Since the time of Constantine the Great, emperors had freely interfered in Church affairs as a legitimate function of their office. After Gratian's death in 383, Justina and her son Valentinian II represented the imperial family in Milan. They favored Arian doctrine. At the beginning of 385 Justina ordered Ambrose to assign a church for Arian worship. Ambrose refused, saying that sacred things were not subject to the power of the emperor. He was unwilling to allow the gains made against heresy to be lost as the result of changes in the religious preference of the civil authorities. For more than a year, Ambrose resisted the queen mother's demands and the pressures of the emperor. At times he physically obstructed troops trying to occupy Christian churches. In the end he was successful for several reasons. First, Ambrose's popularity ensured broad public support for his stand. Second, while excavating for the construction of the new basilica, workmen discovered the skeletal remains of two large men. Ambrose interpreted the finds as the remains of the martyred saints Gervasius and Protasius, a sign from Heaven on the correctness of his position. The emperor found it difficult to combat a sign from God. Third, in 387 the usurper Magnus Maximus moved his armies toward Milan, and Valentinian and Justina fled. Circumstances left Ambrose in control in Milan.

The prestige which Ambrose achieved as the result of his successful resistance to Justina and Valentinian was the basis for future success in asserting Church authority over the authority of the soldier emperor Theodosius the Great. In late 388, at the instigation of the local bishop, a mob looted and burned a Jewish synagogue at Callinicum in Syria. The news of the event reached Milan in a report that also told of monks destroying a chapel of a Gnostic sect. In the interest of public order, Theodosius ordered reparations. In particular he ordered the bishop to rebuild the synagogue at his own expense and to see to the restoration of the stolen articles. The offending monks were to be punished. Ambrose was appalled. In a letter written to Theodosius, he took the position that if the bishop rebuilt the place of worship for the enemies of Christ he would be guilty of apostasy. It would be better for the bishop to refuse and become a martyr for not obeying the emperor. Ambrose's position was that the maintenance of civil law is secondary to religious interests. Even Theodosius' amended order that the state rebuild the synagogue would not satisfy Ambrose. A bold sermon, delivered while Theodosius was in the congregation, demanded that there be no reparation of any kind. In the past, Ambrose stated, gross breaches of public order by pagans and Jews against Christians had gone unpunished. He had in mind the violence that had occurred during the reign of the Emperor Julian. It was perverse reasoning, but it was effective. Theodosius yielded, not because he accepted Ambrose's argument but because politically he could not afford to alienate the popular bishop. In the dispute with Justina, Ambrose had proved his ability to arouse public sentiment. Unfortunately, Ambrose's stance provided a justification for anti-Semitism throughout the Middle Ages.

This public humiliation of the emperor had a chilling effect upon Ambrose's relationship with the imperial court, and for a time Theodosius preferred the advice of others. One result was Theodosius' cruel response to a violent outburst by the citizens of the Greek city of Thessalonica. During the summer of 390, the Thessalonians became upset over the quartering of barbarian troops within the city. When Botheric, the barbarian commandant, ordered the imprisonment of a popular charioteer and refused to allow him to participate in the upcoming public games, riots erupted. An angry mob savagely attacked Botheric, killed him, and dragged his body through the streets. Theodosius was furious and yielded to counsel that he punish the city. He soon repented his anger, but too late to stop a general massacre. Enticed to attend a gala exhibition in the circus, the citizens filled the arena. At a signal the gates were shut and armed soldiers rushed in, attacking and killing indiscriminately anyone they found. For three hours, no distinctions were made between citizens and visitors, guilty and not guilty, young and old. In all, at least seven thousand people died.

Ambrose's response, after a judicious delay, was to excommunicate the emperor. Tradition has it that the proclamation was made publicly and that the emperor was ordered to undergo public penance, which would have increased Theodosius' humiliation before Ambrose. Yet the letter in which Ambrose refused the Sacraments to the emperor is a model of tact and restraint. Ambrose acts the part of the concerned confessor and moral guardian. His position is the sanctity of divine law over a man who has sinned grievously against God and humanity. Thus, while Theodosius again had to yield to the bishop's authority, he submitted to spiritual and not secular authority. In effect, Theodosius recognized the Church's right to preserve the fundamental principles of religion and morality over princes and people alike. The affair actually brought Ambrose and Theodosius closer together. Thereafter, Ambrose was Theodosius' chief spiritual adviser and confidant. They were truly partners in establishing the Nicene ideals in the Western church. Together, they defined the Nicene Creed as the orthodox religion. Ambrose outlived Theodosius by only three years. He died on the Vigil of Easter.

Summary

Ambrose is best known for asserting the dominance of Church authority over the Emperor Theodosius. Through his example, future ministers of the Gospel confidently claimed the right to judge, condemn, punish, and pardon princes. Ambrose was not motivated by any personal desire to demonstrate priestly power over the sovereign. Even in the episode of Callinicum, which was so little to his credit, he acted according to what he saw as the interests of the Church. In his mind, church and state were dominant in two separate but mutually dependent spheres. It was the function of the church to pray for the state and to act as its spiritual leader, while the state was the secular arm of society, which facilitated the spiritual purpose of the church. His confrontations with Theodosius and other secular leaders arose from the conviction that they had crossed the line separating church and state and were interfering in spiritual affairs. These became the principles which guided both civil and papal law in the Middle Ages.

This approach was a direct result of Ambrose's Roman, Stoic upbringing. In a very practical way, he was able to use what was best of Roman values as the foundation of everyday Christian virtue. Ambrose was convinced that because of the tremendous gulf between God and humankind, the day-to-day adherence to faith was the issue of greatest importance. He was not an original thinker, preferring to use his tremendous gift for oratory as a tool for education. Concern with the details of Scripture as they applied to life situations prompted him to rely on allegory, especially in his discussions of the Old Testament. The result was a dynamic body of doctrine and a devout core of converts, the most famous of whom was Saint Augustine. Typically, as one practical way to increase the involvement of women and children in church services, Ambrose advocated a greater use of music in religious services. Although not the first to use music in the liturgy, he is considered the father of liturgical music.

Bibliography

Campenhausen, Hans von. *Men Who Shaped the Western Church*. Translated by Manfred Hoffmann. New York: Harper and Row, Publishers, 1964. A collection of short analytical biographies for seven of the best-known men in Latin Christianity, the aim of this book is to depict how personality contributed to the differences between the Greek and Latin churches. The biography of Ambrose highlights his contribution to the practical legalism of Western Christianity.

Deferrari, Roy J., ed. *The Fathers of the Church*. Vols. 26, 42, 44, 65. New York: Fathers of the Church, 1954-1972. A collection of significant pieces of Ambrose's writings. Volume 26 contains ninety-one of his letters and is the most useful biographical source.

Dudden, F. Homes. *The Life and Times of St. Ambrose*. 2 vols. Oxford: Clarendon Press, 1935. The standard, most thorough treatment of Ambrose's life. It combines biographical detail with insightful analysis and source criticism and corrects many of the mistaken ideas about Ambrose. Contains an extensive bibliography.

Gilliard, Frank D. "Senatorial Bishops in the Fourth Century." *Harvard Theological Review* 77, no. 2 (1984): 153-175. In an examination of the class origins of prominent fourth century bishops, Gilliard seeks to determine if social class aided those who attained high church office, and whether that affected the conversion of the Roman aristocracy.

King, N. Q. *The Emperor Theodosius and the Establishment of Christianity*. Philadelphia: Westminster Press, 1961. A useful account of the secular leadership in the fight for Christian orthodoxy. It addresses the obstacles of conscience and civil disorder which concerned Theodosius in his support of Ambrose. The view is through the eyes of Theodosius, Christian and emperor.

Paredi, Angelo. *Saint Ambrose: His Life and Times*. Translated by Joseph Costelloe. Notre Dame, Ind.: University of Notre Dame Press, 1964. A history of the period in which Ambrose lived, not a biography. Religious in its outlook, it is more accepting of the legends and less critical of the sources than are most scholarly treatments.

Paulinus. *Life of St. Ambrose by Paulinus*. Translated by John A. Lacy. New

York: Fathers of the Church, 1952. Paulinus' biography is the basic source for information about the life of Ambrose. Paulinus was enamored of Ambrose and considered him a saint. He retells fantastic events as truth.

Ronald J. Weber

ANAXAGORAS

Born: c. 500 B.C.; Clazomenae, Anatolia
Died: c. 428 B.C.; Lampsacus
Areas of Achievement: Philosophy, natural history, and science
Contribution: By devising a philosophical system to explain the origins and
  nature of the physical universe which overcame the paradoxes and inconsistencies of earlier systems, Anaxagoras provided an indispensable
  bridge between the pre-Socratic philosophers of the archaic period of
  Greek history and the full flowering of philosophy during the Golden Age
  of Greece.

Early Life
  Virtually nothing is known of Anaxagoras' parents, his childhood, his
adolescence, or his education. Born into a wealthy family in an Ionian Greek
city, he almost certainly was exposed to the attempts by Ionian philosophers,
especially Parmenides, to explain the physical universe by postulating that
everything is made from a single primordial substance. Anaxagoras apparently realized even before he was twenty years of age that such an assumption could not explain the phenomena of movement and change, and he
began to devise a more satisfactory system.
  He grew to adulthood during the turbulent years of the wars of the Greek
city-states against the Persian Empire. His own city, Clazomenae, forced to
acknowledge the suzerainty of Darius the Great in 514, joined the Athenian-
aided Ionian revolt against Persia in 498. That revolt was ultimately suppressed in 493. Anaxagoras' childhood was spent during a time when the
echoes of Athens' great victory over Darius at Marathon in 490 were rever-
berating throughout the Hellenic world.
  According to tradition, Anaxagoras became a resident of Athens in 480.
That a young scholar should be attracted to the intellectual and artistic center of Greek civilization is not surprising, but it is doubtful that this change of
residence took place in 480. Xerxes I chose that year to attempt to realize
Darius' dream of conquering the Greek polis. His plans were frustrated and
his great host scattered at the battles of Salamis and Plataea during that same
year. The next year, the Ionian cities of Asia Minor again rose in rebellion
against Persia, and in 477, joined with Athens in the Delian League. The
League succeeded in expelling the Persians from the Greek states of Asia
Minor. It seems more likely that the young Anaxagoras came to Athens after
the alliance between the Ionian cities and the Athenians.
  While in Athens, Anaxagoras became friends with the young Pericles and
apparently influenced him considerably. Several classical scholars have concluded that Anaxagoras' later trial was engineered by Pericles' political rivals, in order to deprive Pericles of a trusted friend. Convicted of impiety

after admitting that he thought the sun was a huge mass of "hot rock," Anaxagoras went into exile at Lampsacus, where many young Greeks came to study with him before his death, probably in 428.

Life's Work

Sometime in or shortly after 467, Anaxagoras published his only written work, apparently entitled *Nature*. Of this work, only seventeen fragments totaling around twelve hundred words have survived, all recorded as quotations in the works of later generations of philosophers. That so few words could have inspired the more than fifty books and articles written about him in the twentieth century alone is ample testimony to Anaxagoras' importance in the evolution of Greek philosophy and natural science.

Anaxagoras' book was an ambitious attempt to explain the origins and nature of the universe without recourse (or so it seemed to many of his contemporaries) to any supernatural agents. Other Ionian philosophers, notably Parmenides, had preceded Anaxagoras in this endeavor, but their systems were logically unable to explain the multiplicity of "things" in the universe or to explain physical and biological change in those things because they had postulated that all things are made from the same basic "stuff." Anaxagoras overcame the logical inconsistencies of this argument by postulating an infinite variety of substances that make up the whole of the universe. Anaxagoras argued that there is something of everything in everything. By this he meant that, for example, water contains a part of every other thing in the universe, from blood to rock to air. The reason that it is perceived to be water is that most of its parts are water. A hair also contains parts of every other thing, but most of its parts are hair.

In the beginning, according to the first fragment of Anaxagoras' book, infinitely small parts of everything in equal proportions were together in a sort of primal soup. In fragment 3, he proposes a primitive version of the law of the conservation of energy, by saying that anything, no matter how small, can be divided infinitely, because it is not possible for something to become nonexistent through dividing. This idea of infinite divisibility is unique to the Anaxagorean system; no philosopher before or since has proposed it.

This universal mixture of all things acquired form and substance, according to fragment 12, through the actions of *nous*, or "Mind." Mind, Anaxagoras argues, is not part of everything (though it is a part of some things), nor is a part of everything found in Mind (though parts of some things are found in Mind). Mind set the primal soup into rotation and the different things began to "separate off," thus forming the universe. The rotation of the primal mixture not only separated everything according to its kind (but not perfectly, since everything still contains parts of every other thing) but also supplied heat, through friction. Among other things, friction ignited the sun and the stars. Considerable disagreement over the exact meaning Anaxagoras was trying to convey with the term "Mind" has colored scholarly works on his book since Aristotle and continues to be a controversial issue.

Anaxagoras' system not only enabled him and his students to describe all existing objects, but it also permitted the explanation of physical and biological change. It was the introduction of the idea of Mind and its action as a formative agent in the creation of the universe for which Anaxagoras became famous and which rejuvenated Socrates' interest and faith in philosophy.

Sometime after 467, Anaxagoras was accused of and tried for impiety (denying the gods) and "medism" (sympathizing with the Persians). The actual date of his trial and subsequent banishment from Athens is still hotly debated among classical scholars. The traditional date accepted by most historians is 450, but this seems unlikely for several reasons. By 450, the charge of medism could hardly have been a serious one, since the Persian wars were long since over. Also, had he been in Athens in 450, the young Socrates would almost certainly have met him personally, but Socrates' own words indicate that he knew Anaxagoras only through his book. Finally, Anaxagoras' friend Pericles would have been fully able to protect his mentor from political opponents in 450. An earlier date for his exile from Athens seems likely. Some scholars have attempted to solve this problem by postulating that Anaxagoras visited Athens one or more times after being exiled shortly after the publication of his book. This seems the most reasonable explanation to reconcile the dispute, especially since several ancient sources place him in Athens as late as 437.

One of Anaxagoras' most notable achievements during his stay in Athens was to postulate the correct explanation for a solar eclipse. Anaxagoras was apparently the first to argue that an eclipse occurs when the moon (which he said was a large mass of cold rocks) passes between the Earth and the sun (which he said was a larger mass of hot rocks). He may have reached this conclusion after the fall of a large meteorite near Aegypotomi in 467, which excited wide discussion throughout the Hellenic world.

After leaving Athens, Anaxagoras spent his remaining years as the head of a flourishing school at Lampsacus. How his philosophical system may have changed over the years between the publication of his book and the end of his life is unknown. He died at Lampsacus, probably in 428.

Summary

The thesis that Anaxagoras greatly influenced Socrates and Aristotle is easily proved by their elaborate discussions of his system in their own words. Through those two most influential of all Greek thinkers, he has had a profound impact on all subsequent generations of philosophers and natural scientists in the Western world. Some of Anaxagoras' critics, both ancient and modern, accuse him of merely substituting the word "Mind" for "God," or "the gods." Thus in their estimation his philosophy becomes merely a humanistic religion. Other critics have dismissed Anaxagoras' teachings as simplistic and unworthy of serious consideration. His supporters, from Aristotle to the present, have defended him as a pioneering thinker who provided much of the inspiration for the flowering of post-Socratic philosophy during the Golden Age of Greece and the Hellenistic world.

Early critics and supporters alike may have missed an important point in the Anaxagoras fragments. Late twentieth century work on Anaxagoras points out that his concept of Mind giving form to the universe is not far removed from the position of some modern physicists who argue that our perception of the universe is determined by our own senses, which provide an imperfect understanding at best. Anaxagoras may well have been trying to express this same concept (that without cognitive perception there is no form or substance to the universe) without possessing the technical language to do so.

Bibliography
Davison, J. A."Protagoras, Democritus, and Anaxagoras." *Classical Quarterly*, N.s. 3 (1953): 33-45. Establishes Anaxagoras' position vis-à-vis other Greek philosophers and shows his influence on the "atomist" school that succeeded him. Also contains some information on his early life not available elsewhere in English and argues for an early date for his exile from Athens.
Gershenson, Daniel E., and Daniel A. Greenberg. *Anaxagoras and the Birth of Physics*. New York: Blaisdell Publishing Co., 1964. This controversial work suggests that the Anaxagoras fragments are not really the words of Anaxagoras, but rather his words as interpreted by later philosophers, notably Simplicius, who succeeded him. Contains a good, if somewhat theoretical, explanation of Anaxagoras' system.
Guthrie, W. K. C. *A History of Greek Philosophy*. Vol. 2. Cambridge: Cambridge University Press, 1965. Contains the most complete account available of Anaxagoras' life. Puts his life and teachings in the context of his times.
Kirk, G. S., and J. E. Raven. *The Presocratic Philosophers: A Critical History with a Selection of Texts*. Cambridge: Cambridge University Press, 1957. A very readable account of Anaxagoras' life and works and of his place in the history of philosophy.
Mansfield, J. "The Chronology of Anaxagoras' Athenian Period and the Date of His Trial." *Mnemosyne* 33 (1980): 17-95. Offers the most convincing arguments concerning Anaxagoras' arrival in Athens, his trial, and his banishment. Also contains references to Anaxagoras' relationship with Pericles and the political motives behind the former's exile.
Schofield, Malcolm. *An Essay on Anaxagoras*. Cambridge: Cambridge University Press, 1980. A clear, witty exposition of the philosophy of Anaxag-

oras and his importance in the history of philosophy. Perhaps the best work on Anaxagoras' system and its meaning available in English.

Taylor, A. E. "On the Date of the Trial of Anaxagoras." *Classical Quarterly* 11 (1917): 81-87. A good discussion of the backdrop against which Anaxagoras' sojourn in Athens was played and the political and intellectual milieu during which his book was written.

Teodorsson, Sven-Tage. *Anaxagoras' Theory of Matter*. Göteborg, Sweden: Acta Universitatis Gothoburgensis, 1982. Although this book is too difficult for the average reader (its author includes quotations throughout the text in six different languages), it is valuable because it contains the best English translation of the Anaxagoras fragments.

Paul Madden

ANAXIMANDER

Born: c. 610 B.C.; Miletus, Greek Asia Minor
Died: c. 547 B.C.; probably Miletus
Areas of Achievement: Natural history, astronomy, and geography
Contribution: Anaximander realized that no ordinary physical element could
    be the source of the world's diversity; instead, he saw that the fundamental
    stuff must be an eternal, unlimited reservoir of qualities and change.

Early Life

Anaximander was a fellow citizen and student of Thales, the Milesian usually credited with having inaugurated Western philosophy. Thales, some forty
years older than his protégé, put none of his philosophical thought in writing
and maintained no formal pedagogical associations with pupils. Yet Thales'
cosmological views (as reconstructed by historians) doubtless inspired Anaximander, and Anaximander finally expanded on Thales' ideas with innovative
leaps in conceptual abstraction.

Anaximander was known in his day for his practical achievements and his
astronomical discoveries. Anaximander is said to have been chosen by the
Milesians as the leader for a new colony in Apollonia on the Black Sea. He
traveled widely and was the first Greek to publish a "geographical tablet," a
map of the world. The map was circular, and it was centered on the city of
Delphi, since Delphi was the location of the *omphalos*, or "navel" stone, that
was thought to be the center of Earth. Anaximander is also said to have
designed a celestial map and to have specified the proportions of stellar
orbits. In addition to the celestial map, he built a spherical model of the stars
and planets, with Earth located at the center and represented as a disk or
cylinder whose height was one third its diameter. The heavenly bodies were
rings of hollow pipe of different sizes that were placed on circling wheels in
ratios of three to six to nine, in proportion to the magnitude of Earth. This
model was dynamic; the wheels could be moved at different speeds, making
it possible to visualize patterns of planetary motion. Anaximander is also
credited with inventing the sundial, or gnomon, and with having discovered
the zodiac.

All these eclectic interests and discoveries illustrate, with elegance, Anaximander's particular genius, namely, his rational view of the world. This way
of thinking was quite an innovation at a time when both scientific and proto-
philosophical thought took their content from the mythical and literary traditions, and thus were marked by vagueness and mystery. Anaximander viewed
the world as steadily legible; he had the expectation of its rational intelligibility. His map of the world and his model of the heavens show his anticipation
of symmetry and order. Earth, he argued, remained at rest in the center of
the cosmos by reason of its equidistance at all points to the celestial circum-

ference; it had no reason to be pulled in one direction in preference to any other. He projected the celestial orbits in perfect and pleasing proportions, and he anticipated regular motions.

Anaximander's mapping and modeling techniques themselves were products of his rationalistic thinking. Models and maps relocate some set of unified phenomena into a new level of abstraction. Implicit in map and model design is the assumption that the abstractions will preserve the intelligible relationships present in the world that they reproduce. Thus Anaximander's introduction of models and maps represents a tremendous and utterly original conceptual leap from the world "seen" to the world's operations understood and faithfully reproduced by the abstracting human mind.

Life's Work

Anaximander's rational view of the world received its fullest and most innovative expression in his philosophy of nature. Here one finds the first unified and all-encompassing picture of the world of human experience in history that is based on rational deduction and explanation of all phenomena.

In order to understand Anaximander properly, his terminology must be put into its historical context. What Anaximander (and Thales as well) understood by "nature" is not quite the same as its modern sense. In Ionian Greece, *physis* denoted the process of growth and emergence. It also denoted something's origin, or source, that from which the thing is constantly renewed. Nature, in the Ionian sense of *physis*, had nothing to do with matter; even Aristotle was mistaken in thinking that it did. In fact, no word for matter even existed in Anaximander's day. It is also important to note that Anaximander's thought is reconstructed entirely from ancient secondary sources. The one extant fragment of Anaximander's own words is the quotation of an ancient historian. Thus, any explication of Anaximander's thought is to some extent conjectural and interpretive.

Anaximander's philosophy of nature arose in part as a response to Thales' ideas on nature. Thales held that Water was the nature of everything. This meant, in the light of the ancient idea of *physis*, that Water was the origin of everything, that everything was sustained by, and constantly renewed from, Water. This notion does not have any allegorical or mythical connotations in Thales' formulation. Water is the ordinary physical stuff in the world, not some engendering god such as the Oceanus of Thales' predecessors. That is the reason Thales is the first philosopher: He had a theory about the origin of things that competed with ancient creation myths.

Anaximander agreed with Thales that the origin of the things of the world was some common stuff, but he thought that the stuff could not be some ordinary element. He rejected Thales' conception on purely logical grounds, and his reasoning was quite interesting. How could any manifestly singular stuff ever give rise to qualities that pertained to things differently constituted, such as earth and fire? What is more, if Water were the source of things, would not drying destroy them? Thus, reasoned Anaximander, the thing with which the world begins cannot be identical with any of the ordinary stuff with which humans are acquainted, but it must be capable of giving rise to the wide multiplicity of things and their pairs of contrary qualities. What therefore distinguishes the source from the world is that the source itself is "unbounded": It can have no definite shape or quality of its own but must be a reservoir from which every sort or characteristic in the world may be spawned. So Anaximander called the source of things this very name: *apeiron*, Boundlessness, or the Boundless. Anaximander designated the Boundless an *arche*, a beginning, but he did not mean a temporal beginning. The Boundless can have no beginning, nor can it pass away, for it can have no bounds, including temporal ones.

Thus the eternal source, the Boundless, functions as a storehouse of the world's qualities, such that the qualities that constitute some present state of the world have been separated out of the stock, and when their contrary qualities become manifest, they will, in turn, be reabsorbed into the reservoir. When Earth is hot, heat will come forth from the Boundless; when Earth cools, cold will come forth and heat will go back. For Anaximander, this process continued in never-ending cycles.

The cause of the alternating manifestations of contrary qualities is the subject of the single existing fragment of Anaximander's own words, the only remains of the first philosophy ever written. Out of the Boundless, Anaximander explains, the worlds arise, but

> from whatever things is the genesis of the things that are, into these they must pass away according to necessity; for they must pay the penalty and make atonement to one another for their injustice according to the ordering of Time.

History has produced no consensus of interpretation for this passage and its picturesque philosophical metaphor for the rationale of the world. Anaximander was probably thinking of a courtroom image. Each existing thing is in a state of "having-too-much," so that during the time it exists it "commits injustice" against its opposite by preventing it from existing. In retribution, the existing thing must cede its overt existence for its opposite to enjoy and pay the penalty of returning to the submerged place in the great Boundless reservoir. This cycling, he added, is how Time is ordered or measured. Time is the change, the alternating manifestation of opposites.

Here is the apotheosis of Anaximander's rational worldview. The world's workings are not simply visible and perspicuous, but neither are they whimsical and mysterious. The hidden workings of things may be revealed in the abstractions of the human mind. The world works, and is the way that it is, according to an eternal and intelligible principle. What is more, this world and its workings are unified, indeed form a cosmos. The cosmos, in turn, can be understood and explained by analogy with the human world; the justice sought in the city's courts is the same justice that sustains everything that human perception finds in the universe.

Summary

Classical antiquity credited Thales with having pioneered philosophy. Anaximander, with his scientific curiosity and his genius for abstract insight, poised philosophical inquiry for new vistas of exploration; his new philosophical approach inaugurated penetrating, objective analysis. His principle of the eternal Boundless as the source of the world's multifarious qualities and change forms the conceptual backdrop against which twenty-five centuries of science and natural philosophy have developed.

Two particular innovations of Anaximander have never been abandoned. First, his extension of the concept of law from human society to the physical world continues to dictate the scientific worldview. The received view in Anaximander's time—that nature was capricious and anarchic—has never again taken hold. Second, Anaximander's invention of the use of models and maps revolutionized science and navigation and continues to be indispensable, even in people's daily lives. All scientific experiments are models of a sort: They are laboratory-scale contrivances of events or circumstances in the world at large. Purely visual three-dimensional models continue to be crucial in scientific discoveries: the so-called Bohr model of the atom played a crucial role in physics; the double-helical model was important to the discovery of the structure and function of DNA. Maps are taken for granted now, but if human beings had relied on verbal descriptions of spatial localities, civilization would not have proceeded very far.

Thus, Anaximander's innovations and influence persist. Indeed, it is difficult to imagine a world without his contributions. Anaximander himself could hardly have seen all the implications of his discoveries, for even now one can only guess at the future direction of abstract thought.

Bibliography
Brumbaugh, Robert S. *The Philosophers of Greece*. New York: Thomas Y. Crowell, 1964. This volume contains a short, digested chapter on Anaximander's life and accomplishments. Emphasizes cartography and engineering. Includes a reproduction of the first map designed by Anaximander.
Burnet, John. *Early Greek Philosophy*. 4th ed. New York: Barnes and Noble Books, 1945. A detailed scholarly analysis of Anaximander's thought in the context of comparisons with, and influences on, other pre-Socratic philosophers.
Guthrie, W. K. C. *A History of Greek Philosophy*. Vol. 1, *The Earlier Presocratics and the Pythagoreans*. Cambridge: Cambridge University

Press, 1962. Contains a chapter on Anaximander's cosmology. Focuses in a very close analysis on the concepts of *apeiron* and *apeiron* as *arche*.

Kahn, Charles H. *Anaximander and the Origins of Greek Cosmology*. New York: Columbia University Press, 1960. Surveys the documentary evidence for Anaximander's views, reconstructs a detailed cosmology from documentary texts, and devotes an entire chapter to analysis and interpretation of Anaximander's fragment.

Kirk, Geoffrey S., and John E. Raven. *The Presocratic Philosophers*. Cambridge: Cambridge University Press, 1957. Contains a chapter on Anaximander and a close formal analysis of textual testimony on Anaximander's thought.

Seligman, Paul. *The "Apeiron" of Anaximander*. London: Athlone Press, 1962. A detailed analysis of the *apeiron* as a linguistic concept and as a metaphysical entity.

Wheelwright, Philip, ed. *The Presocratics*. New York: Macmillan, 1966. A primary source. Contains the Anaximander fragment in translation. Also contains testimonies from Aristotle and other Greek and Latin sources who read and commented on Anaximander's treatise.

Patricia Cook

ANAXIMENES OF MILETUS

Born: Early sixth century B.C.; probably Miletus
Died: Second half of the sixth century B.C.; place unknown
Areas of Achievement: Philosophy and science
Contribution: Anaximenes was the last of the great early pre-Socratic thinkers from Miletus and the first, apparently, to attribute the nature of matter
entirely to physical rather than moral laws. Thus, his ideas provided a necessary step from the generalized ideas of Thales to the specific physical
ideas of the Atomists of the fifth century.

Early Life

The writings of Anaximenes of Miletus no longer exist. Thus, knowledge
of Anaximenes is based on a few statements made by Aristotle and later
writers on the history of Greek philosophy, some of whom quote earlier writers whose work is now lost. A few of these earlier writers show that they had
access to Anaximenes' writings, but it is difficult to determine the veracity of
any of their statements. Thus, scholars have almost no reliable information
about Anaximenes' life; not even his dates can be accurately ascertained, and
only the most general of assumptions can be made. These biographical assumptions are usually applied to Thales and Anaximander as well as Anaximenes. These men were the most famous thinkers from Miletus, then the
largest and most prosperous Greek city on the west coast of Asia Minor.

While they are known only for their philosophical work, it is believed that
all three were financially secure and that philosophical thought was for them
an avocation. Apparently, Anaximenes was the youngest of the three. Some
sources suggest that Anaximenes was the pupil of Anaximander, while others
suggest that he was a fellow student and friend. Most scholars place the work
of Anaximenes after the fall of Sardis to Cyrus the Great (c. 545 B.C.) and
before the fall of Miletus (494 B.C.).

Life's Work

Anaximenes' work must be viewed against the background of sixth century
Miletus and the work of his predecessors. Miletus in the sixth century was a
flourishing center between the eastern kingdoms and the mainland of
Greece. The city was ruled by a ruthless tyrant, Thrasybulus, whose methods
of control were to do away with anyone who looked threatening.

It has been suggested that the emergence of tyranny in Miletus was the
crucial factor in the emergence of philosophy, that the need to overthrow the
existing myth-centered system of values was behind philosophical speculation. It has also been said that the emergence of philosophy coincides with
the emergence of participatory forms of government, the development of
written codes of law, and the expansion of the role of nonaristocrats in gov-

ernment through oratory, which encouraged logical argument and objective reasoning. As attractive as these theories may be, they overlook the fact that Miletus itself was under the rule of a tyrant who discouraged participatory democracy absolutely.

It seems more logical to conclude that philosophy became a means of escaping the brutality of the immediate, political world. Travel brought Milesians in contact with Egypt and Phoenicia—and eventually Mesopotamia. Milesians developed an independence of thought that led them to use their knowledge of the pragmatic world gained through observation to see the contradictions in the mythologies of different peoples and to make the leap to a nonmythologaical explanation of causation and the nature of matter.

The work of Anaximenes was summarized in a single book whose title is unknown. In the fourth century, Theophrastus, Aristotle's successor, is said to have noted its "simple and economical Ionic style." One supposes that this comment refers to the shift from writing in poetry to writing in prose. Clearly, Anaximenes was more concerned with content than with the conventions of poetical expression.

Anaximenes wrote that "air" was the original substance of matter. Scholars of ancient history agree, however, that the exact meaning of this statement is unclear. To take the position that all other matter was derived from air, Anaximenes must have believed that air was a changeable substance which, by rarefaction and condensation, was able to take other forms. When rarefied, it became fire; when condensed, it became wind, clouds, water, earth, and finally stones. Thus, Anaximenes had modified Thales' idea that water was the original substance and contradicted Anaximander's thesis of unchanging infinity while still staying within the Milesian monist tradition.

Having determined the nature of air and its properties, Anaximenes apparently developed other ideas by extension. Topics which he addressed include the nature of hot and cold as expressions of rarefaction and condensation, the divine nature of air, the motion of air, cosmogony, and cosmological problems. Under the latter heading he seems to have commented on the nature of Earth, which he saw as flat and riding on a cushion of air, and the nature of heavenly bodies. In his consideration of meteorological phenomena, Anaximenes seems to have followed Anaximander rather closely. Anaximenes' description of air also resembles Hesiod's description of Chaos. Both Chaos and air surround Earth, persist within the developed world, and can be characterized by darkness, internal motion, divinity, immense size, and probable homogeneity.

Anaximenes, like his two predecessors, challenged the mythological world of Homer and Hesiod by introducing free and rational speculation. Anaximenes also presented a challenge by writing in prose. Prior to this, poetry had been the perferred form for serious expression—not only in literature but also in politics. By writing in prose, the early philosophers moved, in part, from the world of the aristocrat to that of the new man of Greece: the hoplite, the merchant, the small, free farmer. While this new method of thought was not accepted by the average Greek (nor even, one suspects, the average Milesian), it did gain respect and placed philosophical speculation on an elevated footing.

For Anaximenes, unlike his predecessors, however, the differences that could be observed in matter were not qualitative but quantitative. Thus it is that he was the first to suggest a consistent picture of the world as a mechanism.

Summary

Any account of Anaximenes' life and ideas must by virtue of scant evidence be unsatisfactory. Yet in spite of a lack of information about him and his ideas, his place in and contribution to intellectual development are clear. Anaximenes' methods were far more influential than his specific theories on matter. Together with Thales and Anaximander, he was the first to free speculative thought from mythology and mythological terms. The methods of these three thinkers are the foundation for all modern scientific and philosophical thought. They began with intellectual curiosity about the nature of matter and combined this curiosity with keen observation of the world around them—with little regard to prior religious explanations.

At first glance, Anaximenes' ideas about air seem regressive. When, however, the idea is seen as a more general concept—as the first theory to explain a single substance capable of changing its form—its sophistication can be appreciated. Most ancient thinkers agreed that Anaximenes provided a better explanation of natural phenomena.

It is a small step from Anaximenes' ideas of rarefaction and condensation to Empedocles' definition of matter and the atomic theories of Heraclitus of Ephesus and Democritus. Clearly, no one in the modern world would take these ideas at face value, but with a small shift in the translation of Anaximeneian terms, one approaches the modern concepts of states of matter and the relationship between energy and matter. Thus, Anaximenes is an important figure in the development of Western philosophical and scientific thought.

Bibliography

Barnes, Jonathan. *The Presocratic Philosophers*. London: Routledge and Kegan Paul, 1979, rev. ed. 1982. Contains a section on Anaximenes as well as scattered comments on his ideas. Barnes is most at home with philosophical discourse and relates ancient philosophical concepts to more modern thinkers. With bibliography and concordances of ancient sources.
Burnet, John. *Early Greek Philosophy*. 4th ed. London: Adam and Charles

Black, 1930. The major ancient texts are translated and the ideas of Anaximenes discussed in this excellent work.

Guthrie, W. K. C. *A History of Greek Philosophy*. Vol. 1, *The Earlier Presocratics and the Pythagoreans*. Cambridge: Cambridge University Press, 1962. Contains an extended section on Anaximenes which is judicial and well-balanced. Guthrie's account is used as the standard by historians. With good bibliographies and concordances of ancient sources.

Hurwit, Jeffrey M. *The Art and Culture of Early Greece, 1100-480 B.C.* Ithaca, N.Y.: Cornell University Press, 1985. An exciting analysis of Greek life that integrates studies of literature, philosophy, and art.

Kirk, G. S., and J. E. Raven. *The Presocratic Philosophers*. Cambridge: Cambridge University Press, 1957. The most extensive attempt to reconstruct Anaximenes by examining all of the relevant ancient references with detailed discussions of each text. The relevant Greek and Latin texts are given, with translations provided in the notes. Includes interpretation based on the texts but little or no reference to other modern scholarly ideas. Contains concordances of ancient texts.

Stokes, M. C. *The One and Many in Presocratic Philosophy*. Washington, D.C.: Center for Hellenic Studies with Oxford University Press, 1972. While this book is not about Anaximenes, he looms large in the investigation, and Stokes's ideas about him are important. Stokes investigates the relationship between Anaximander's and Anaximenes' ideas, as well as the relationship of Anaximenes to ancient Near Eastern thought and Hesiod.

Sweeney, Leo. *Infinity in the Presocratics: A Bibliographical and Philosophical Study*. The Hague: Martinus Nijhoff, 1972. Each of the pre-Socratics is discussed in terms of his contribution to this specific topic. Important discussions on the usability of each ancient source for Anaximenes are included.

Michael M. Eisman

SAINT ANTHONY OF EGYPT

Born: c. 251; Coma, near Memphis, Egypt
Died: Probably January 17, 356; Mount Kolzim, near the Red Sea
Areas of Achievement: Religion and monasticism
Contribution: A Christian hermit renowned for his ascetic labors and Gospel teachings, Anthony became celebrated within Christendom as the founder of the eremitic movement and the father of monasticism.

Early Life

Saint Anthony of Egypt was born about the year 251 in the village of Coma (the modern Queman el Aroune) in Upper Egypt. The only son of wealthy Coptic Christian parents, Anthony spent his childhood along the Nile working on the family farm and attending the village church with his pious sister and parents. Because his father feared the worldly learning of Greek academies, Anthony never attended school and did not learn to read or write. His religious training, therefore, was limited to the instructions he received from his parents and from the local priest, who read from the Coptic Bible. While not interested in questions of theology, Anthony was deeply sensitive to spiritual matters. Even as a child he preferred spending time alone in prayer and meditation to playing games with his friends.

At about age twenty, Anthony suffered the death of both his father and mother. Though a young man of considerable inherited wealth, Anthony became depressed and overburdened with the responsibilities of administrating his 130-acre estate and caring for his young sister. In church, Anthony heard the priest read the Gospel story of a rich young man who asked Jesus what he must do to inherit eternal life. Jesus' reply, "If thou wilt be perfect, go, sell that thou hast and give to the poor, and thou shalt have treasure in heaven; and come, follow me" (Matthew 19:21), haunted Anthony, for he (like the protagonist in the story) was rich, had from birth followed all the commandments of the law, and yet still lacked spiritual maturity. That day Anthony decided to respond literally to the Gospel command. He gave his personal possessions to the inhabitants of Coma, sold his estate, and gave the proceeds to the poor, reserving only a small sum for the benefit of his sister.

Soon after that event, upon hearing the reading of another scriptural command, "Take therefore no thought for the morrow: for the morrow shall take thought for the things of itself" (Matthew 6:34), Anthony determined to make a complete break with his former life. Taking his sister to a convent to be educated for a religious life, Anthony moved to a hut at the edge of the village and sought direction from a hermit on how to live a holy life. Clothed only in a camel's hair garment, Anthony studied how to resist worldly temptations by prayer, fasting, mortification, and manual labor.

Life's Work

Anthony, for all of his asceticism, did not achieve sanctification without a struggle. Despite his renunciation of all earthly pleasures, memories of his former life and possessions as well as erotic visions disrupted his quest for spiritual fullness. According to his biographer Saint Athanasius, the Devil "raised up in [Anthony's] mind a great dust-cloud of arguments, intending to make him abandon his set purpose." Anthony persevered and gradually learned to overcome the temptations of his thoughts.

After years of self-conquest on the borders of the village, Anthony was ready to attack the Devil in his own territory. Anthony left his arbor hut and moved farther into the desert, into the mortuary chamber of an Egyptian tomb. Permitting the visits of only one friend, who brought him bread and water at infrequent intervals, Anthony challenged the forces of Satan by entering the dark burial cell which Egyptians believed was haunted by demons. In closing the door behind him, Anthony symbolically severed himself from the world of the living.

The modern mind can only interpret the accounts of Anthony's struggles with the Devil in the tomb as fantasies conjured by his excessive fasting. For contemporaries of Anthony, however, his confrontation with Satan—which included battling demons disguised as bulls, serpents, scorpions, and wolves—was perceived as physical and real. When he emerged after sixteen years in the subterranean tomb, Anthony was widely renowned as a warrior of God who had fought and conquered the powers of darkness.

Anthony's thirst for solitude, which first prompted him to withdraw to the outskirts of the village and then to the burial chamber on the fringe of the desert, finally drove him into the depths of the desert. He withdrew to Mount Pispir, near the Nile.

Anthony at first lived in total seclusion—praying, fasting, and weaving mats from palm leaves. Disciples brought him supplies of bread occasionally, but he fasted for days at a time. As news of Anthony's disappearance into desert isolation spread, a train of visitors followed him into the wilderness. Some went simply out of curiosity; others sought spiritual guidance. Although at first Anthony attempted to avoid the visitors, in time he acquiesced and assumed pastoral responsibilities: praying for the sick, driving out demons, offering instructions for holy living, and training seekers in the path of asceticism.

Pispir became a monastery, and in or near 313, Anthony moved still farther away, settling in a cave on Mount Kolzim near the Red Sea. He remained in this remote setting, receiving some visitors, for the rest of his life.

Anthony's teachings generally emphasized one's interior development. Unimpressed with mere human knowledge, Anthony reminded his followers that the mind created letters, not letters the mind, and that therefore "one whose mind is sound has no need of letters." Rather than coveting worldly wisdom, Anthony urged his disciples to live every day as if it were their last, always remembering that "the whole of earth is a very little thing compared with the whole of heaven." He warned them against taking pride in their own accomplishments or in thinking that in giving up worldly pleasures they were making great sacrifices. He urged his followers constantly to inspect their spiritual progress, not worrying about things that do not last, but gathering those "that we can take with us: prudence, justice, temperance, fortitude, understanding, charity, love of the poor, faith in Christ, graciousness, hospitality." For Anthony, asceticism was not an end in itself, but a necessary means to spiritual maturity.

On one occasion, probably in the year 311, Anthony visited the city of Alexandria, where he offered encouragement to Christians being persecuted under the edict of the emperor Maximinus Daia. A short time later, after Constantine emerged as head of Rome, Anthony received a letter from the newly converted Christian emperor seeking spiritual guidance. Although unable either to read the message or to pen a response, Anthony dictated for the Roman emperor the following reply: "Practice humility and contempt of the world, and remember that on the day of judgment you will have to account for all your deeds." In 338, Anthony again left his retreat for Alexandria, allegedly to help the orthodox bishop Athanasius in his theological struggle with the Arian Christians, who denied that Christ was equal in essence with the Father. As Saint Athanasius, this church leader would write the biography of Anthony. Such contact with the outside world—with people of power—was rare. Anthony much preferred the simplicity of desert life, which did not distract him from concentrating on spiritual matters.

Saint Jerome told a story about a visit in 341 between Anthony and the 113-year-old Saint Paul of Thebes, a hermit who allegedly had not seen either man or woman for more than ninety years. While this story is no doubt apocryphal, the legend was celebrated by Christians for centuries and served as an inspiration for numerous artists, including the master of Dutch Renaissance art, Lucas van Leyden.

In the year 356, Anthony—knowing that he was about to die—invited his closest followers to come to his desert hermitage in order to give them a parting farewell. To his surprise, thousands responded to the invitation. Anthony walked among this throng of pilgrims, blessed them, and asked them to persevere in their devotion to God. According to tradition, Anthony died on January 17, 356, at the age of 105.

Summary

It is ironic that Saint Anthony of Egypt—an unassuming, deeply private, illiterate man, who refused to pander to crowds and who renounced the efforts of the establishment to reconcile Christianity with culture—became the celebrated founder of the eremitic movement and the father of monasticism. As a result of his ascetic example and teachings, during his lifetime and for a hundred years following his death, hermitages sprang up and the deserts of Egypt became cluttered with the cells of anchorites. Stories of his desert retreat, circulated by Saint Athanasius' *The Life of Saint Anthony the Hermit*, spread across the empire to Rome, Palestine, Gaul, and Spain. Constantine and his sons wrote to him. Saint John Chrysostom in his homilies designated Anthony as the greatest man Egypt had produced since the time of the Apostles. During the third and fourth centuries, thousands of pilgrims followed Anthony's example and flocked to the desert. The exodus was so great that a traveler through Egypt and Palestine about 394 reported that the dwellers in the desert equaled the population living in the towns.

For fifteen hundred years, the temptations of Anthony have captured the imagination of artists, who have delighted especially in picturing the more dramatic episodes of devils in hideous and alluring disguises tempting, frightening, and beating the desert saint. From Saint Athanasius to Gustave Flaubert and Anatole France, Anthony has been portrayed as the prototype of a man who suffers temptation and through the power of renunciation, overcomes it.

In an age filled with Christological problems and theological hairsplitting, Anthony and the desert fathers proclaimed a message of righteous living and simplicity of life. His teaching—"No one of us is judged by what he does not know, and no one is called blessed because of what he has learned and knows; no, the judgment that awaits each asks this: whether he has kept the faith and faithfully observed the commandments"—offered a corrective to the tendency at the time to define Christianity in purely philosophical or religious terms. Anthony's ascetic labors and simple teachings introduced themes that would run throughout the history of the monastic movement.

Bibliography

Athanasius, Saint. *The Life of Saint Anthony the Hermit*. Translated and annotated by Robert T. Meyer. Westminster, Md.: Newman Press, 1950. Saint Athanasius' biography is the single most important primary source on the life of Anthony.

Chadwick, Henry. *The Early Church*. London: Penguin Books, 1968, reprint 1974. The best single-volume introduction to the history of the Christian church during the first through fourth centuries.

Fülöp-Miller, René. *The Saints That Moved the World: Anthony, Augustine, Francis, Ignatius, Theresa*. Translated by Alexander Gode and Erika Fülöp-Miller. New York: Thomas Y. Crowell, 1945. Contains an eighty-page chapter on Anthony, bibliography, and index.

Nigg, Walter. *Warriors of God: The Great Religious Orders and Their Founders*. Translated and edited by Mary Ilford. New York: Alfred A.

Knopf, 1959. The opening chapter provides a scholarly treatment of Anthony and his impact upon the monastic movement.

Queffelec, Henri. *Saint Anthony of the Desert*. Translated by James Whitall. New York: E. P. Dutton, 1954. An entertaining biography based on Saint Athanasius' account.

Waddell, Helen. *The Desert Fathers*. New York: Henry Holt, 1936. A translation from the Latin of the writings of the desert fathers. Includes many of the sayings attributed to Anthony.

Ward, Maisie. *Saints Who Made History: The First Five Centuries*. New York: Sheed and Ward, 1959. A lively, nonscholarly account of the lives of early saints of the Church. Includes a fourteen-page treatment on Anthony.

Terry D. Bilhartz

SAINT ANTHONY OF PADUA

Born: August 15, 1195; Lisbon, Portugal
Died: June 13, 1231; Arcella, near Padua, Italy
Areas of Achievement: Religion and education
Contribution: Anthony of Padua was one of the most eloquent Franciscan preachers and the first teacher of the Franciscan School of Theology. He is credited with introducing the theology of Saint Augustine into the order and was named a Doctor of the Church.

Early Life

Anthony of Padua was born in Lisbon on August 15, 1195, and received the name Fernando (Ferdinand) at baptism. It is asserted that his father was Martin de Boullion, descendant of the renowned Godfrey de Boullion, commander of the First Crusade, and that his mother, Theresa Travejra, was a descendant of Froila I, fourth King of Asturias.

After he had completed the course at the Cathedral School of Saint Mary, Ferdinand, at the age of fifteen, joined the Canons Regular of Saint Augustine in the convent of Saint Vincent outside the city walls in September, 1210. Two years later, he went to the Monastery of the Holy Cross in Coimbra, where he remained for eight years. In Coimbra, he became an expert in biblical studies. It is believed that he was ordained a priest in 1218.

In 1220, he saw the bodies of the first five martyrs of the Franciscan Order (Saints Berard, Peter, Otho, Aiuto, and Accursio) being returned from Morocco, where on January 16, 1220, they had been killed for their faith. Ferdinand was so moved by the desire for martyrdom that he set his heart on becoming a Friar Minor. That same year, 1220, he received the Franciscan habit from the friars of the Convent of the Holy Cross at Olivares (near Coimbra), who were accustomed to beg alms from the canons. He took the name Anthony, a name that was later assumed by the convent at Olivares itself.

Life's Work

At his own request, Anthony was sent as a missionary to Morocco in December, 1220. There, however, he was stricken with a severe illness which affected him the entire winter, and he was compelled to return to Portugal the following spring. Driven off course by a violent storm, his ship landed in Sicily.

Anthony was informed by the Franciscans in Messina that a general chapter of the order was to be held at Assisi on May 30, 1221. He arrived in time to take part in the famous Chapter of the Mats, in which three thousand friars participated. It was here that he met Saint Francis and was assigned to Bologna, in the Province of Romagna.

For a time, Anthony resided in solitude and penance in the hermitage of Monte Paolo near Forlì. It was at Forlì that his talents as a preacher became known. Because of the absence of the regularly appointed preacher for the ordination of some Dominicans and Franciscans at Forlì, in 1222, Anthony was asked to preach the sermon. His eloquence and the depth of his knowledge astonished the audience.

Francis wrote to Friar Anthony in 1223 and appointed him the first professor of theology for the Franciscan Order. He commanded him to teach in such a manner as to perpetuate the spirit of prayer and piety advocated in the rule. Anthony is credited with introducing the theology of Saint Augustine to the Franciscan Order—a union which was to become the characteristic mark of Franciscan theology.

Anthony spent some time in Vercelli between 1222 and 1225, where he discussed mystical theology with Thomas of Saint Victor, known as Thomas Gallus (d. 1246), the founder and abbot of the monastery of Saint Andrew. They became personal friends. Thomas was well-known for his translation, commentary, and synthesis of the pseudo-Dionysian works. Thomas had a strong influence on early Franciscans such as Alexander of Hales, Saint Bonaventure, and Adam of Marisco. He was so impressed by Anthony's knowledge that he asserted that "aided by divine grace, he drew most abundantly from the mystical theology of the Sacred Scripture."

Anthony taught successively at Bologna, Toulouse, and Montpellier. In 1223, he started a school of theology for the friars, who called him "Pater Scientiae" and "Doctor Veritatis." This school eventually developed into the school of theology of the University of Bologna. At Arles, Toulouse, and Montpellier, he taught in the order schools, not in the city universities. Toulouse had no public faculty of theology before 1229; Montpellier's was founded after 1240 and Bologna's after 1300. During this period, five Franciscan houses were founded—at Nice, Bordeaux, La Réole, Saint-Jean-d'Angély, and Le Puy-en-Velay.

Because he was such an inspiring preacher, Anthony was commissioned to preach against the heretics in northern Italy (from 1222 to 1224) and against the Albigensians in southern France in 1224. Between 1227 and 1230, his preaching mission brought him back to Italy. During Lent in 1231, he preached daily in Padua.

Anthony's sermons attracted enormous crowds. People would begin to gather in the middle of the night to obtain good seats, shops would close, and Anthony had to be protected from souvenir hunters and the press of the crowd. He avoided preaching during harvesttime so as not to interfere with this important farm work.

Only two series of Anthony's sermons have survived, one for saints' feast days and one for Sunday. He is the only early Franciscan preacher whose actual words have been preserved. The printed sermons are in Latin, and they are very long and argumentative. The sermons can be described as moral and penitential in tone; it is known, however, that the later ones became more dogmatic. Anthony underscored his points by frequent reference to Scripture. Though the Franciscans were not the first to introduce biblical examples into sermons, their development of this practice revolutionized the art of preaching.

After the death of Francis of Assisi on October 3, 1226, Anthony returned to Italy, where he was elected Provincial of Romagna-Emilia. After his election as guardian of the convent at Le Puy-en-Velay, he became the leader of the more rigorous party in the Franciscan Order, who were opposed to the modifications introduced by Elias of Cortona, general of the order.

During the year 1228, Anthony preached in the Venetian province and gave the Advent sermons in Florence; he preached a Lenten series in Florence the following year. At the end of 1229, he took up his last permanent residence at Padua, at a convent which he himself had founded in 1227. At the General Chapter on May 30, 1230, he resigned his provincial office, but in June he was sent as a member of a special commission to Rome to confer with Pope Gregory IX concerning the interpretation of the rule. (Gregory was the same pope who had invited Anthony to preach in Rome in 1227.) During the winter of 1230-1231, he worked on a revision of his sermons. In 1231, he preached his last course of Lenten sermons.

Anthony's audience at times numbered as high as thirty thousand people. Since church buildings could not accommodate his listeners, he was obliged to speak in the open air. He preached to the public perched in an oak tree at Camposanpiero in 1231.

Two weeks before his death, Anthony stood on the summit of a hill which overlooked Padua and blessed the city—as the dying Francis had once blessed his beloved Assisi—saying, "Blessed be thou, O Padua! Beautiful is thy site, rich thy fields, but Heaven is about to crown thee with a glory still richer and more beautiful."

Before he could return to Padua, Anthony died in Arcella on June 13, 1231, at the age of thirty-five. At the first news of his death, children ran about the streets crying out, "The saint is dead!" At his canonization on May 30, 1232, Gregory IX declared him to be a "teacher of the Church," and Pius XII made him a Doctor of the Church with the title "Doctor Evangelicus" on January 16, 1946.

Summary

Besides being a scholar and teacher, Anthony was a preacher of great force and persuasiveness. In mystical theology, he prepared the way for Saint Bonaventure, Saint Teresa of Avila, and Saint John of the Cross. With other members of the Franciscan school, in infused contemplation he attributed the primary force to the will. He was a forerunner of John of the Cross in teaching the classical doctrines of the passive, sensitive, and intellectual activities of the soul. Anthony's mysticism was, however, not as austere as Saint John's, for he says that the devout individual may request the spiritual consolations that increase his love for God.

In 1263, when the relics of Saint Anthony were being transferred to a new chapel erected in his honor at Padua, it is said that Bonaventure found the saint's tongue preserved whole amid Anthony's ashes. Picking it up, Bonaventure said: "O blessed tongue, which always blessed the Lord and caused others to bless Him, now it is revealed how great was thy merit before God." Because of the many miracles recorded at Anthony's tomb, he is chiefly remembered as a wonder-worker, and he continues to be widely venerated in the Roman Catholic church.

Bibliography

Beahn, John E. *A Rich Young Man*. Milwaukee, Wis.: Bruce Publishing Co., 1953. A realistic story about Saint Anthony that is based on history and traditions. This 250-page work is partly fictional, but it is well-written and captures the spirit of the age and of the Franciscan Order which Anthony embraced. It is less useful on analysis and interpretation and has no illustrations or index.

Clausen, Sophronius. *St. Anthony: Doctor of the Gospel*. Translated by Ignatius Brady. Chicago: Franciscan Herald Press, 1973. A good short life of Anthony, translated from the German. The 140-page work has thirty-two pages of pictures and many quotations from Anthony's sermons. This work is useful because it attempts to present an authentic life of Anthony and omits legends or tales that cannot be verified. There is no bibliography.

Dent, Francis. *Saint Anthony of Padua and the Twentieth Century*. New York: P. J. Kennedy and Sons, 1899. This study is an old but useful examination of Anthony's life. The author's last four chapters describe how the devotion to Saint Anthony grew and gives detailed accounts of the particular favors attributed to his intercession. Though it makes references to other writers who have examined the life of Anthony, it does not provide a bibliography or index.

Franciscans of the U.S.A. *St. Anthony, Doctor of the Church Universal: Souvenir of the Commemorative Ceremonies*. Washington, D.C.: Catholic University of America Press, 1946. A collection of five essays dealing with Anthony as a preacher and theologian and with his relationship with the people. These essays contain analysis and interpretation not found in other works. A good summary of Anthony's contributions.

Huber, Raphael. *St. Anthony of Padua, Doctor of the Church Universal: A Critical Study of the Historical Sources of the Life, Sanctity, Learning, and Miracles of the Saint of Padua and Lisbon*. Milwaukee, Wis.: Bruce Publishing Co., 1947. This critical study is an indispensable and comprehensive source for the life and work of Anthony of Padua. There are well-organized chapters that examine his life, his preaching and teaching career, and the authentic as well as the spurious writings. Well documented, with an extensive annotated bibliography. Included is a literary evaluation of the works on Anthony from a historical perspective. Includes texts of three sermons.

Moorman, John. *A History of the Franciscan Order from Its Origins to the Year 1517*. Oxford: Clarendon Press, 1968. A scholarly study of the Franciscan Order that is filled with references and a large bibliography. It is an indispensable source for Anthony and his age, for it contains numerous references to primary materials arranged chronologically.

O'Brien, Isidore. *Enter Saint Anthony*. Chicago: Daughters of St. Paul, 1976. An inspiring life of St. Anthony that touches upon all important aspects of his life and work. The author provides accurate and stimulating information on the career and work of Anthony and the temper of the age. The work does not, however, contain a bibliography or index.

Stoddard, Charles W. *St. Anthony, the Wonder Worker of Padua*. 2d ed. Rockford, Ill.: TAN Book Publishers, 1971. Written for the general reader, this book does justice to the life and career of Anthony of Padua. It is a well-rounded account in 127 pages, but it is without bibliography or index.

Zawart, A. "The History of Franciscan Preaching and of Franciscan Preachers 1209-1927." *Franciscan Educational Conference*, vol. 9. St. Bonaventure, N.Y.: St. Bonaventure University Press, 1927. A detailed study of the character of Franciscan preaching as a new development in medieval religious practice. A valuable analysis of the character of religious life in Anthony's time.

Peter F. Macaluso

ANTIGONUS I MONOPHTHALMOS

Born: 382 B.C.; probably Macedonia
Died: 301 B.C.; Ipsus, Phrygia, Asia Minor
Areas of Achievement: Government and warfare
Contribution: Though Antigonus failed to unify Macedonian conquests after Alexander the Great's death in 323 B.C., he did establish an eponymous dynasty (Antigonid), which was to rule Macedonia and exert a great influence on Greek affairs elsewhere until the Roman victory at the Battle of Pydna in 168 B.C.

Early Life

Antigonus' father was an aristocrat named Philip. Beyond this fact, nothing of significance is known about Antigonus' life before his service in Alexander's army and his appointment to the governorship of Phrygia in 333 B.C. at the age of forty-nine.

Antigonus is known to have been a tall man; his appellation, Monophthalmos (One-Eyed), or Cyclops, referred to his having lost an eye. It is not known whether this blinding occurred in battle or by some other means. To conceal the handicap, Apelles, the famous artist at the Macedonian court, departed from custom and painted a portrait of Antigonus in profile.

Life's Work

Before attention is turned to the course of Antigonus' life and work, it is helpful to survey the situation immediately following the death of Alexander the Great in 323 B.C. Alexander left no arrangement for succession. The assembly of the Macedonian army determined that rule be given to Alexander's half brother, Philip III, and his unborn son, Alexander IV, but the real control of Alexander's empire lay in the hands of Antipater, in Greece, and Perdiccas, in Asia. In the struggle for power which ensued (in the year 321), Antigonus sided with Antipater against Perdiccas. After Perdiccas was assassinated, Antigonus was given command of Antipater's army in Asia and continued the war against Perdiccas' brother, Alcetas, and Eumenes, Satrap of Cappadocia. Antipater died in 319. Antigonus continued fighting against Eumenes until 316, when, through intrigues and deceit, he managed to have him executed. Eumenes' remains were cremated, placed in a vessel, and returned to his wife and children. Among Alexander's successors, Antigonus was now in the strongest position to reunite the lands conquered by Alexander.

Antigonus was unquestionably desirous of sole rule, and his ambition was immediately recognized by his regal adversaries, Ptolemy, Lysimachus, Cassander, and Seleucus, all of whom allied themselves against Antigonus in a war lasting from 315 to 311. The war had no clear resolution; its temporary end came after Antigonus' son, Demetrius Poliorcetes, was defeated by Seleucus and Ptolemy at the Battle of Gaza in 312. Peace was made between Antigonus and all of his adversaries except Seleucus. Still, the ambitions of all involved could not be suppressed, and war broke out again one year later and lasted until Antigonus' death in 301.

In the first war, most of the fighting had taken place in Asia Minor; in the war of 310-301, the final resolution would be reached in Asia Minor at the Battle of Ipsus in Phrygia, but mainland Greece was the scene of many of the most important battles. Antigonus came to recognize, perhaps a bit too late, the importance of support from the Greek cities on the mainland. In 307, Antigonus' son, Demetrius Poliorcetes, took control of Athens from Cassander's representative, Demetrius of Phaleron, and a democratic constitution was reestablished in Athens. As an expression of gratitude, the Athenians granted divine honors to Antigonus and Demetrius. Antigonus' intervention on behalf of the Athenian democracy impressed many other Greek city-states, and by 302 most of mainland Greece had rallied in his support. Highlights of the war on mainland Greece are vividly recounted by Plutarch in his "Life of Demetrius," written in the early second century A.D. In spite of some major military and naval successes in Asia Minor, the war on that front was, for Antigonus, indecisive. It was his successes against Cassander on mainland Greece, more than anything, that forced his opponents to realize that their positions would be secure only with the elderly Antigonus out of the way. Attacks on Antigonus' positions in Asia came from all sides, and the situation became so serious that he recalled Demetrius, together with his army, from mainland Greece to stand with him. The decisive battle was fought at Ipsus in 301, and Antigonus, now about eighty years of age, died in this battle. Thus, at the time of his death this great general was pursuing the same course that he had pursued throughout his life: a military resolution to a political problem.

Summary

Antigonus fell between two worlds. Born and educated amid the fragmented politics of competing Greek city-states, he could have had no idea, even as a mature man, of the profound changes Alexander was to bring about. In this new world, the only exemplar of success available was Alexander's, and that was primarily military and not political. Alexander's early death prevented him from demonstrating whether his political leadership was as adept as his military.

Antigonus was not alone in following Alexander's lead; all the *diadochoi* (successors to Alexander) were as quick as Antigonus to rely on the sword as the means of obtaining the power that they sought. It was Antigonus, however, who had the means to consolidate Macedonian conquests, for he was the most successful of Alexander's successors militarily. His ultimate failure to unite Alexander's conquests through force, in spite of his most advantageous situation, should have shown the futility of such an approach in the face of a coalition of equally determined, although individually less powerful, dynasts. This lesson was not learned, and the result was almost constant warfare among Hellenistic monarchs who continued to present themselves as Alexander's rightful successor until Rome's final victory in the Greek East at the Battle of Actium in 31 B.C. Thus, it was the ambitions and methods of Antigonus, almost as much as those of Alexander, that served for some two hundred years as an example for those who sought to control the Greek world.

Bibliography

Austin, M. M. *The Hellenistic World from Alexander to the Roman Conquest: A Selection of Ancient Sources in Translation*. Cambridge: Cambridge University Press, 1981. Offers translations of and introductions to many important documentary sources, primarily epigraphical, which are not generally available. This collection of primary source material contains a number of documents which bear directly on Antigonus' attempts to unify Alexander's conquests.

Bar-Kochva, B. *The Seleucid Army*. Cambridge: Cambridge University Press, 1976. Describes and interprets the changes in the strategy and tactics of land warfare that led to Antigonus' military successes and the continuing domination of the Macedonians over the art of warfare until Rome's victory at Pydna in 168 B.C.

De Ste. Croix, G. E. M. *The Class Struggle in the Ancient Greek World: From the Archaic Age to the Arab Conquests*. Ithaca, N.Y.: Cornell University Press, 1982. Presents a Marxist view of the decline of Greek democracies. This volume is the masterpiece of a very distinguished ancient historian; it is particularly valuable for its focus on the role of political factions in Antigonus' struggle for the support of city-states on mainland Greece and Asia.

Gardner, Jane F. *Leadership and the Cult of Personality*. London: Samuel Stevens, 1974. Emphasizes the importance of controlling armies and populations through the projection of a royal personality. It discusses both leadership theory and the concrete ways in which Alexander and those who followed him manipulated regal propaganda.

Gruen, Erich S. *The Hellenistic World and the Coming of Rome*. 2 vols. Berkeley: University of California Press, 1984. A revisionist interpretation of the course of Roman expansion in the Greek East. Gruen presents a view of Roman imperialism that is more sympathetic to the Roman position than the position taken by most scholars. This volume contains a good review of the battle among Alexander's successors. Includes a helpful bibliography.

Simpson, R. H. "Antigonus the One-Eyed and the Greeks." *Historia* 8 (1959): 385-409. This article presents a detailed account of the relations between Antigonus and the city-states on the Greek mainland, alliances that played a decisive role in convincing Antigonus' opponents to unify against him.

Smith, R. R. R. *Hellenistic Royal Portraits*. Oxford: Oxford University Press, 1988. An account of the visual image of kingship which Hellenistic dynasts chose to present. This study is lavishly illustrated. Includes reproductions of portraits in varied media (including coins and marble). A valuable archaeological complement to the literary and documentary evidence.

Tarn, W. W. *Hellenistic Civilization*. 3d ed. London: Edward Arnold, 1952. A standard, but somewhat dated, survey of the Hellenistic world. Includes chapters on the social, economic, and cultural history of the period.

Walbank, R. W. *The Hellenistic World*. Cambridge, Mass.: Harvard University Press, 1981. The best general account of the period, by a scholar who devoted his life to its study. It combines a narrative account of military and political events with sections on the rich and varied cultural life of the Hellenistic world.

John Walsh

ANTIOCHUS THE GREAT

Born: 242 B.C.; possibly Antioch
Died: 187 B.C.; Elymais, near Susa
Areas of Achievement: Warfare and conquest
Contribution: Antiochus went the furthest of any of the successors of Alexander the Great toward reuniting what had once been the vast Alexandrian empire.

Early Life

Antiochus, who was probably born in Antioch, the capital city of the Seleucid empire, was the younger son of Seleucus II and Laodice II. Nothing is known about his early life. When his father died in 226, his older brother, Seleucus III, fell heir to the empire and all of its problems, not the least of which was Asia Minor, formerly held by the Seleucids but now controlled by Attalus of Pergamum. One unsuccessful attempt had already been made to regain this territory. During the second, in 223, Seleucus was assassinated by two of his own generals. Since he had no heirs, his younger brother Antiochus succeeded him.

Antiochus was eighteen years old at his brother's death and living in Babylon—possibly as regent of the east since that was the usual Seleucid practice—but many thought him too young for the throne. His cousin Achaeus, who had punished Seleucus' murderers, was popular with the army, but he remained loyal to the ruling house. Finally, Antiochus was recognized as successor under the tutelage of Seleucus' former adviser, Hermias, Achaeus was given control of military affairs in Asia Minor, and two brothers, Molon and Alexander, were sent as governors (satraps) to Media and Persia respectively. Trouble began almost immediately: Although Achaeus remained loyal for some time and even regained much of Asia Minor from Attalus, Hermias became excessively arrogant, and, in 221, the brothers in the east rebelled against Seleucid authority. These actions marked the beginning of an almost constant state of war which would continue throughout the reign of Antiochus.

In 221, with Achaeus operating successfully in Asia Minor, the first priority for the Seleucid government was the rebellion of Molon. Hermias, who was still in control, appointed Xenon and Theodotus as commanders against Molon, while convincing the king to make war against Ptolemy IV of Egypt for possession of Coele-Syria, but when Molon easily defeated his opponents and Antiochus' southern campaign proved futile, the king turned to the recovery of his eastern territories. In early spring of 220, Antiochus held a council to plan his campaign. There were two important results of this meeting: Antiochus proved himself able to choose the best strategy—the immediate crossing of the Tigris River—and in crossing the river he, for the first time, split his army in three parts, initiating what would become his standard policy for advancing his forces. The majority of Molon's army, refusing to fight a Seleucid king, surrendered to Antiochus at the first opportunity. The two rebel brothers committed suicide; Antiochus was now in full command in the east.

Three problems remained: Hermias; Achaeus, now the self-proclaimed king of Asia Minor; and the subjection of Coele-Syria. Antiochus ordered the assassination of Hermias, ignored Achaeus, whose men also refused to fight a Seleucid ruler, and marched his army south, where he was at first successful. His youthful inexperience, however, led him to delay battle against a Ptolemaic army until his opponent had the advantage, and in 217 he suffered a humiliating defeat at Raphia. Ptolemy fortunately agreed to a peace treaty, thus ending the war.

Life's Work

Antiochus gained the title of "the Great" because through successful military strategy and shrewd diplomacy he managed to reunite most of the territory which had been assigned to Seleucus I after the death of Alexander the Great. His prestige had suffered a blow at Raphia, but he redeemed himself by defeating Achaeus and regaining Seleucid Asia Minor. After a long siege, the capital city of Sardis fell in 214, and the citadel was betrayed a year later. Achaeus was first mutilated and then beheaded. Some sort of understanding with Attalus of Pergamum, his other rival in Asia Minor, seems to have been reached, since by 212 Antiochus had turned his back on the west in order to attempt the restoration of his eastern dominions. The Greek historian Polybius (c. 200-118) gives a fairly comprehensive account of Antiochus' movements up to this time, although most of the war against Achaeus is missing. Now, unfortunately, the detailed history of Antiochus ends, just as he begins his eastern campaigns.

By 212, Antiochus was in Armenia, where he settled affairs by arranging the marriage of his sister Antiochis to King Xerxes. Two years later, he had arrived at the Euphrates River and in the next year reached the limits of the Seleucid empire in Media. He could have stopped there, but Parthia and Bactria, once part of the empire, had seceded in 250, and his plan was to regain all the lost territories, a very expensive endeavor. It was in Ecbatana, the old summer capital of the Persian kings, that Antiochus for the first time robbed a temple treasury, an act that was to become a policy for both him and his successors.

Although the Parthians put up a stiff resistance, by 209 they had been defeated and had agreed to an alliance. Bactria was invaded in the next year; peace came two years later with another alliance. Antiochus then continued on to India to renew Seleucid relations with the new border king, from whom he received 150 elephants. He had thought of invading Arabia, but after sailing down the Arabian coast, he abandoned the idea. He was back in Syria by 204, with a reputation second only to that of Alexander. From this time on, he would be called Antiochus the Great.

Now that the king had experience and maturity, he made his final attempt to gain Coele-Syria, this time backed by an alliance with Philip V of Macedonia. Appian (c. 160 A.D.) gives the terms of the agreement, but the sources are uniformly silent on this war, the Fifth Syrian War. Ptolemy V was still a child, but his general, Scopas, moved an army across the Sinai Peninsula. The two forces met at Panion in 200 in a battle in which Antiochus' elephants played an important role in gaining for him a decisive victory. After winning the complete submission of Palestine, including Jerusalem, Antiochus decided against an invasion of Egypt and returned to Asia Minor. Ptolemy had agreed to a treaty in which he ceded Coele-Syria to the Seleucid empire. The war finally ended in 195, when Ptolemy promised to marry Antiochus' daughter Cleopatra.

Meanwhile, Philip V had been courting disaster in the north. Rhodes and Pergamum had allied against him and called on Rome for help. The Romans declared war on Philip in 200, but also sent an embassy to Antiochus warning him that Egypt was under Roman protection, a threat he could hardly take seriously. The embassy arrived shortly after his success at Panion. By the spring of 197, the Seleucid army was in Asia Minor, along with a navy of three hundred ships just off the southern coast. The navy was stopped for a while by a Rhodian ultimatum, but after news of Philip's defeat by the Romans in 196 arrived, the Rhodians withdrew, leaving Antiochus free to take the western coast of Asia Minor to the Troas, his original plan. The city of Lampsacus appealed to Rome, but the Seleucid army was in Thrace before the Roman ambassadors caught up with it. Antiochus' answer to Roman charges of aggression was that he did not meddle in Italian affairs and Rome had no business in Asia. Shortly after that, the king lost almost his entire fleet in a storm off the coast of Syria.

Antiochus was now at the height of his power; unfortunately, he did not know when to stop. The Aetolians, unhappy over Rome's settlement with Philip, convinced Antiochus to join an anti-Rome coalition which never materialized. In the latter part of 192, a small Seleucid army arrived, the forerunner of a much larger contingent, at Demetrias. The Aetolians, who had promised the king their full support, were distressed by the size of his force, and both Philip and the Achaen League to the south had decided to ally with Rome. In 191 a joint Roman-Macedonian army faced the Seleucid forces at Thermopylae. Antiochus' reinforcements had not arrived and the promised Aetolian aid proved illusory. When it became evident that he could not win, Antiochus fled, losing most of his army in what was more a skirmish than a battle.

Antiochus' loss was the result not so much of Aetolian deceit as of the failure of his officers back in Asia to send him the necessary reinforcements. Even then, as was proved by Philip's earlier losses, the clumsy phalanx was no match for the Roman legion. Antiochus discovered that for himself when the Romans invaded Asia Minor. The Roman historian Livy (c. 59 B.C.- A.D. 17) claims that the king, once he had escaped from Greece, believed that he had nothing more to fear from the Romans, that they would not follow him to Asia. If so, he had badly misjudged Roman determination to end the Seleucid threat forever. The Romans were also well aware that Antiochus had welcomed Hannibal, their most feared enemy, to his court. A Roman fleet first cleared the Aegean sea of Seleucid ships, and by either late 190 or early 189 (historians do not agree on the date) Antiochus fought his last major battle in the field outside Magnesia and lost. He could do nothing more than ask for and accept whatever terms the Romans offered.

Even before Antiochus' final defeat, his eastern dominions had begun to break away. After Magnesia, the Seleucid army was no longer a threat and the empire dissolved. As soon as the peace was signed, Antiochus appointed his son Seleucus as joint king to rule Syria, which was all the Romans had left him, while he turned again to the east. A year later, Antiochus was dead, killed while attempting to loot a temple in the Elymaean hills. His son succeeded as Seleucus IV.

Summary

With the defeat of Antiochus by the Romans, the Eastern world was lost to Western culture. The Seleucid empire crumbled, and Rome could hold only the areas bordering the Mediterranean Sea. These were so systematically exploited by Roman policy that they almost gladly welcomed the Muslim armies of the seventh century A.D.

Antiochus was perhaps not a great king or a great general. He made the same mistake of pressing too hard with his right wing at Magnesia that he had made at Raphia, and he was very unwise in antagonizing the Romans by invading Greece. He had been reared on stories of Alexander, however, and he came closer than anyone else in his attempt to restore the empire to its original size. He could be cruel when necessary, as he was with Achaeus, but his eastern campaigns were marked by leniency and diplomacy, and he refused to hand over Hannibal when the Romans demanded it. There is no record of any domestic rebellion during his long reign. The worst charge against him is the one that led to his death. Ancient temples were also treasuries, and Antiochus was constantly in need of money. It is a sad commentary on his priorities that his last act was one of sacrilege.

Bibliography

Bar-Kochva, B. *The Seleucid Army: Organization and Tactics in the Great Campaigns*. Cambridge: Cambridge University Press, 1976. This work contains several chapters giving the details from ancient sources on the major battles fought by Antiochus. Includes maps of the battlefields and interesting analyses of strategy.

Bevan, Edwyn Robert. *The House of Seleucus*. 2 vols. London: Edward Arnolds, 1902. Still the only comprehensive work on the Seleucids in English. Gives a full, although dated, account of the reign of Antiochus.

Cook, S. A., F. E. Adcock, and M. P. Charlesworth, eds. *The Cambridge Ancient History*. Vols. 7 and 8. New York: Macmillan, 1928, 1930. Includes a scholarly analysis of motives behind Antiochus' actions not contained in new edition of *The Cambridge Ancient History*. Indexes, maps, and chronological tables.

Kincaid, C. A. *Successors of Alexander*. London: Pasmore and Co., 1930. Kincaid presents brief sketches of four successors, concluding with Antiochus. A good summary of the campaigns and policies, but excuses the weaknesses of the king.

Livy. *Rome and the Mediterranean*. Translated by H. Bettenson. Harmondsworth, England: Penguin Books, 1976. An excellent translation of the part of Livy's history concerning Rome's move toward the East. A Roman interpretation of Antiochus' actions. Includes an introduction by A. H. McDonald.

Rawlings, Hunter R. "Antiochus the Great and Rhodes, 197-191 B.C." *American Journal of Ancient History* 1 (1976): 2-28. An analysis of Rhodes's inconsistent policy concerning Antiochus and the Aegean Sea. Rawlings claims that Rhodes cooperated with Antiochus after Rome defeated Philip but deserted him after his naval defeat in 191.

Linda J. Piper

MARC ANTONY

Born: c. 82 B.C.; place unknown
Died: 30 B.C.; Alexandria, Egypt
Areas of Achievement: Politics, warfare, and government
Contribution: The military and political defeat of Antony by Octavian (later known as Augustus) resulted in the demise of the republican form of government in Rome and the creation of the Roman Empire, which would rule much of the known world for some five hundred years.

Early Life

Marcus Antonius (called Marc Antony in English) was born into a distinguished Roman family around 82 B.C. His grandfather, also named Marcus Antonius, had attained the highest offices of Roman public life. Antony's father, Marcus Antonius Creticus (died c. 72 B.C.), however, did not equal his father's distinction. More important for Antony's future, on his mother's side he was related to Julius Caesar. Until he was about twenty-five, Antony, not unlike many of his contemporaries, was a profligate: His moral failings and excesses were detailed by Cicero, his enemy, in a series of attacks known as *Philippicae* (44-43 B.C.; *Philippics*, 1926), and his energy was no doubt wasted, as Plutarch stated, "in drinking bouts, love-affairs, and excessive spending." He studied rhetoric in Athens and from there turned his attention to a military career and public life. By that time, many of the characteristics (both good and bad) which constituted Antony's personality had developed: his bawdy and often self-deprecating sense of humor, his familiarity with the men under his command, his liberality, and his attraction to the Greek way of life. Antony's family claimed descent from the Greek hero Hercules, and his Roman nose and other features encouraged positive comparisons between Antony and images of Hercules. Antony also cultivated a forceful and powerful appearance in figure, dress, and demeanor at public functions.

Life's Work

It is true that in the end Antony lost the struggle against Octavian for control of the Roman world, but this should not negate the accomplishments of a truly remarkable Roman who had a long and successful military and political career. Antony's failure was the result not of his character or tactics, as some of his critics believe, but of his opposition to Octavian, the most successful of all Roman politicians and one of the most astute and imposing political figures of all time. Antony's early political career was bound closely to that of Julius Caesar. In 51, he served as a junior officer under Caesar's command, and under Caesar's patronage he rose very quickly to a position only second in importance in the Caesarean forces. After this, there is some evidence of a rift between Caesar and Antony, who seems not to have participated in Caesar's final victories over Pompey the Great. Nevertheless, Caesar and Antony were sufficiently close politically that Antony was a colleague in the consulship of 44, the year of Caesar's assassination. Antony's intentions after Caesar's death are impossible to determine. His inflammatory and dramatic reading of Caesar's will may be seen as an attempt to seize control of Rome. On the other hand, such funerary demonstrations were well within the traditionally accepted bounds of political and familial behavior in the Roman Republic. Antony's attitude toward Caesar's assassins was at first ambivalent and conciliatory, but ultimately tensions between Antony and Marcus Junius Brutus, one of Caesar's assassins, led to hostilities.

At this point, Octavian, Caesar's adopted son, entered the political and military scene; he defeated Antony at Mutina in 43. This defeat did not destroy Antony's position—his support was too strong. The Second Triumvirate, an arrangement lasting five years, was created; the three members, Marcus Aemilius Lepidus, Antony, and Octavian, were assigned with the task of "establishing the form of republican government." The Roman world was split among the triumvirs, while at Rome a reign of terror resulted, and thousands of Romans perished as the triumvirs persecuted their enemies. The most notable casualty of this reign of terror was Antony's particular adversary and critic, Cicero. Having accomplished his goals in Rome, Antony turned his attention to the East. For all of their significant differences, Antony and Octavian shared a common purpose. It was to the advantage of both to move against the republican forces led by Caesar's assassins; after the victory at the Battle of Philippi (42 B.C.), the only opposition to the triumvirate left was Pompey the Younger, the son of Pompey the Great.

After Philippi, Antony remained in the East to restore order to the provinces. His first step was to set up Herod and his brother, Phasael, over Judaea. Antony then met with Cleopatra VII at Tarsus in 41. (Cleopatra's spectacular arrival in her golden barge was recorded by Plutarch and later portrayed by William Shakespeare in *Antony and Cleopatra*, c. 1606-1607.) The political significance of this meeting was underscored by the establishment of a personal relationship which would capture the imagination of subsequent generations. Antony visited Cleopatra in the winter of 41-40, and twins were born after his departure. The relationship continued until Antony's death, and his connection with Cleopatra was in large measure responsible for his ultimate defeat.

Antony was separated from Cleopatra from 40 to 37 as a result of a serious threat from an old Roman enemy from the east, the Parthians. In 53, a Roman army under Marcus Licinius Crassus had been defeated at Carrhae, and revenge was never far from the Romans' minds. In 40, the Parthians moved as far west as Syria and Antony was determined to repulse this attack. A crisis in the west intervened, and Antony was forced to return to Italy to mediate a struggle between Octavian and Antony's wife and brother. Hostilities

were averted when Octavian and Antony reached an agreement at Brundisium in 40. In the meantime, Antony's wife, Fulvia, had died; Antony
strengthened his ties to Octavian through the time-honored Roman tradition
of an arranged marriage with Octavian's sister, Octavia. Antony returned to
Athens with Octavia, and a daughter, Antonia, was born to them. Soon after, Antony was again forced to return to Italy and his arrangement with
Octavian was formally renewed at Brundisium for another five years. During
all of this, Octavia proved a loyal and helpful wife and on occasion supported
Antony against her brother.

Antony and Octavia returned to Athens, but not long after the birth of a
second daughter, Octavia was sent back to Italy. Once matters at Rome were
settled, Antony once again turned his attention to the campaign against the
Parthians. After initial Roman victories, he decided to launch a full-scale expedition into the Parthian homeland. In preparation for this very risky enterprise, Antony sought support from the rulers of Roman client-states in the
Near East. Among these rulers was Cleopatra. Their personal relationship
resumed and a son, Ptolemy Philadelphus, was born in 36. There was now no
retreating from their personal and political alliance: Politics and love became
one. Antony's first full campaign in 36 against the Parthians was a disaster; it
was only with great difficulty that the remaining members of the Roman
force were able to escape complete destruction. A second campaign in 33
was more successful, but it fell short of complete victory. Nevertheless,
Antony felt confident enough to assign dominion over much territory under
Roman influence to Cleopatra and her children in a settlement known as the
"Alexandrian Donations." Thus, on three fronts Antony lost whatever support he may have had at Rome: military failure against the Parthians, individualistic settlement of territories under Roman influence, and rejection
of Octavian's sister as his Roman wife.

Antony's independent actions in the East, together with Octavian's aggressive behavior at Rome, led to a final confrontation. Octavian sensed the
weakness of Antony's position at Rome, and he made public the supposed
conditions of Antony's will. Its exact text remains unknown, but the effect of
its publication is certain. War followed, and Antony and Cleopatra were
defeated by Octavian in a naval battle at Actium in September of 31. They
fled to Egypt, where, about a year later, Antony, under the mistaken impression that Cleopatra had already killed herself, committed suicide and died in
her arms. Some time after this, Cleopatra did the same; according to tradition, she used the poison of an asp.

Summary

Literary sources present a very negative picture of Marc Antony's personality and achievements, probably because Octavian won, and much of history has been written under the direct influence of winners. Antony's youth-

ful excesses made it easy for critics to claim that his failure was the result of a life devoted to pleasure and self-gratification; although there is some truth to this, it nevertheless offers a one-sided view. He was an excellent general whose soldiers responded with devotion and loyalty. His administration of the Greek East was efficient and without many of the failings of his predecessors. Antony was politically astute, but he failed to appreciate sufficiently the impact of his image at Rome as a Hellenistic potentate. His enduring relationship with Cleopatra did great harm to his standing, and some even began to believe that Antony's devotion to her led to his considering moving the seat of imperial power from Rome to Alexandria. Octavian, a master propagandist, took advantage of this situation by contrasting his traditional Roman values with Antony's Eastern way of life.

Antony's person and career highlight the tensions present in Roman society during the last century of the Republic between conservative Roman values and the more attractive Hellenistic way of life. As Augustus, Octavian based his rule on a return to the old Roman values, but most of the autocrats who succeeded him followed Antony's style more closely. Indeed, the division of the Roman Empire between East and West, which Antony may have seen as inevitable, eventually became reality. The history of the Roman Empire has shown that Antony's vision and style would become the rule rather than the exception.

Bibliography

Charlesworth, M. P., and W. W. Tarn. *Octavian, Antony, and Cleopatra*. Cambridge: Cambridge University Press, 1965. This is an abridged, but detailed and valuable, account of the relations among these three in the years between 44 and 30 B.C. Originally published in volumes 9 and 10 of *The Cambridge Ancient History* (1934).

Cicero, Marcus Tullius. *Philippics*. Translated by Walter C. A. Ker. Cambridge, Mass.: Harvard University Press, 1951. These orations, composed in 44 or 43 B.C., provide graphically detailed and scathingly personal attacks on Antony's moral character. Their tone is so hostile, however, that they cannot be taken at face value.

Huzar, Eleanor G. *Mark Antony: A Biography*. New York: Methuen and Co., 1986. A readable account of Antony's life. Well documented, it attempts to provide a more balanced view of Antony's career by separating negative propaganda from fact.

Kent, J. P. C. *Roman Coins*. Rev. ed. New York: Harry N. Abrams, 1978. A lavishly illustrated collection of numismatic evidence; contains material important for understanding the ways in which Antony wished to present his image to the public.

Plutarchus. *Life of Antony*. New York: P. F. Collier and Son, 1909. Written early in the second century A.D., this biography provides the most complete and engaging narrative account of Antony's life. Much of it is overtly hostile to Antony, and Plutarch chose to emphasize his subject's vices. The account of the love affair which led to Antony's and Cleopatra's suicides is among the most stirring stories of antiquity and formed the basis for Shakespeare's *Antony and Cleopatra*.

Syme, R. *The Roman Revolution*. Oxford: Oxford University Press, 1939. An eminent historian's masterful interpretive account of the reasons for the collapse of the Republic. Syme uses prosopographical analysis to explain the ways in which relations among aristocratic Romans led to Octavian's victory.

Toynbee, Jocelyn Mary Catherine. *Roman Historical Portraits*. London: Thames and Hudson, 1978. This study effectively combines visual and literary evidence in an exploration of the historical tradition in which the portraits of Antony and Octavian must be understood.

John Walsh

APOLLONIUS OF PERGA

Born: c. 240 B.C.; Perga, Asia Minor
Died: c. 170 B.C.; Alexandria, Egypt
Areas of Achievement: Mathematics and astronomy
Contribution: One of the ablest geometers in antiquity, Apollonius systematized the theory of conic sections in a treatise that remained the definitive
introduction to this field until modern times. His study of circular motion
established the foundation for Greek geometric astronomy.

Early Life

Information on Apollonius' life is meager. Born at Perga after the middle
of the third century B.C., he studied mathematics with the successors of
Euclid at Alexandria. His activity falls near the time of Archimedes (287-
212 B.C.), but links between their work are indirect. In his surviving work,
Apollonius once mentions the Alexandria-based geometer Conon of Samos,
but his principal correspondents and colleagues (Eudemus, Philonides, Dio-
nysodorus, Attalus I) were active at Pergamum and other centers in Asia
Minor. It appears that this circle benefited from the cultural ambitions of the
new Attalid dynasty during the late third and the second centuries B.C.

Life's Work

Apollonius' main achievement lies in his study of the conic sections. Two
properties of these curves can be distinguished as basic for their conception:
First, they are specified as the locus of points whose distances x, y from given
lines satisfy certain second-order relations: When $x^2 = ay$ (for a constant line
segment a) the curve of the locus is a parabola, when $x^2 = ay - ay^2/b$ the
curve is an ellipse (it becomes a circle when $b = a$), and when $x^2 = ay +
ay^2/b$ it is a hyperbola. The same curves can be produced when a plane inter-
sects the surface of a cone: When the plane is parallel to the side of the cone,
there results a parabola (a single open, or infinitely extending, curve); when
the plane is not parallel to the side of the cone, but cuts through only one of
its two sheets, there results an ellipse (a single closed curve); and when it cuts
through both sheets of the cone, there results a hyperbola (a curve consisting
of two separate branches, each extending indefinitely).

The curves were already known in the fourth century B.C., for the
geometer Menaechmus introduced the locus forms of two parabolas and a
hyperbola in order to solve the problem of doubling the cube. By the time of
Euclid (c. 300 B.C.), the formation of the curves as solid sections was well
understood. Euclid himself produced a major treatise on the conics, as had a
geometer named Aristaeus somewhat earlier. Since Archimedes often assumes theorems on conics, one supposes that his basic reference source
(which he sometimes cites as the "Conic Elements") was the Euclidean or

Aristaean textbook. Also in the third century, Eratosthenes of Cyrene and Conon pursued studies in the conics (these works no longer survive), as did Diocles in his writing on burning mirrors (extant in an Arabic translation).

Apollonius thus drew from more than a century of research on conics. In the eight books of his treatise, *Cōnica* (*Treatise on Conic Sections*, 1896; best known as *Conics*), he systematized the elements of this field and contributed many new findings of his own. Only the first four books survive in Greek, in the edition prepared by Eutocius of Ascalon (active at Alexandria in the early sixth century A.D.), but all of its books except for the eighth exist in an Arabic translation from the ninth century.

Among the topics that Apollonius covers are these: book I, the principal constructions and properties of the three types of conics, their tangents, conjugate diameters, and transformation of axes; book II, properties of hyperbolas, such as their relation to their asymptotes (the straight lines they indefinitely approach, but never meet); book III, properties of intersecting chords and secants drawn to conics; book IV, how conics intersect one another; book V, on the drawing of normal lines to conics (lines defined as the minimal distance between a curve and given points); book VI, on similar conics; book VII, properties of the conjugate diameters and principal axes of conics; book VIII (lost), problems solved via the theorems of book VII.

As Apollonius states in the prefaces to the books of his treatise, the chief application of conics is to geometric problems—that is, propositions seeking the construction of a figure satisfying specified conditions. Apollonius includes only a few examples in the *Conics*: for example, to find a cone whose section produces a conic curve of specified parameters (I 52-56), or to draw tangents and normals to given conics (II 49-53 and V 55-63). Much of the content of the *Conics*, however, deals not with problems but with theorems auxiliary to problems. This is the case with book III, for example, which Apollonius says is especially useful for problem solving, but which actually contains no problems. In his preface, he explicitly mentions the problem of the "locus relative to three (or four) lines," all cases of which, Apollonius proudly asserts, can be worked out by means of his book III, whereas Euclid's earlier effort was incomplete.

The significance of problem solving for the Greek geometric tradition is evident in works such as Euclid's *Stoicheia* (*Elements*) and *Ta dedomena* (*Data*). In more advanced fields such as conic theory, however, the surviving evidence is only barely representative of the richness of this ancient activity. A notable exception is the *Synagōgē* (*Collection*), a massive anthology of geometry by Pappus of Alexandria (fourth century A.D.), which preserves many examples of problems. Indeed, the whole of its book VII amounts to an extended commentary on the problem solving tradition—what Pappus calls the "analytic corpus" (*topos analyomenos*), a group of twelve treatises by Euclid, Apollonius, and others. Of the works taken from Apollonius, two are extant—*Conics* and *Logou apotomē* (*On Cutting Off a Ratio*, 1987)—while another five are lost—*Chōriou apotomē* (cutting off an area), *Diōrismenē tomē* (determinate section), *Epaphai* (tangencies), *Neyseis* (vergings), and *Topoi epipedoi* (plane loci). Pappus' summaries and technical notes preserve the best evidence available regarding the content of these lost works. Thus it is known that in *Epaphai*, for example, Apollonius covered all possible ways of constructing a circle so as to touch any combination of three given elements (points, lines, or circles); in *Neyseis* he sought the position of a line verging toward a given point and such that a marked segment of it lies exactly between given lines or circles; in *Topoi epipedoi* circles were produced as loci satisfying stated conditions, several of these being equivalent to expressions now familiar in analytic geometry.

It is significant that these last three works were restricted to planar constructions—that is, ones requiring only circles and straight lines. Pappus classifies problems in three categories: In addition to the planar, he names the solid (solvable by conics) and the linear (solvable by special curves, such as certain curves of third order, or others, such as spirals, now termed "transcendental," composed of coordinated circular and rectilinear motions). For Pappus, this scheme is normative; a planar solution, if known, is preferable to a solid one, and, similarly, a solid solution to a linear. For example, the problems of circle quadrature, cube duplication, and angle trisection can be solved by linear curves, but the last two can also be solved by conics and so are classed as solid. Historians often misinterpret this classification as a restriction on solutions, as if the ancients accepted only the planar constructions. To the contrary, geometers throughout antiquity so fully explored all forms of construction as to belie any such restriction. Presumably, in his three books on planar constructions, Apollonius sought to specify as completely as possible the domain of such constructions rather than to eliminate those of the solid or linear type. In any event, from works before Apollonius there is no evidence at all of a normative conception of problem-solving methods.

There survive isolated reports of Apollonian studies bearing on the regular solids, the cylindrical spiral, irrationals, circle measurement, the arithmetic of large numbers, and other topics. For the most part, little is known of these efforts, and their significance was slight in comparison with his treatises on geometric constructions.

Ptolemy reports in *Mathēmatikē suntaxis* (c. A.D. 150; *Almagest*) that Apollonius made a significant contribution to astronomical theory by establishing the geometric condition for a planet to appear stationary relative to the fixed stars. Since, according to Ptolemy, he proved this condition for both the epicyclic and the eccentric models of planetary motion, Apollonius seems to have had some major responsibility for the introduction of these basic models. Apollonius studied only the geometric properties of these models, however, for the project of adapting them to actual planetary data became a concern only for astronomers such as Hipparchus a few decades later in the second century B.C.

Summary

If Apollonius of Perga did indeed institute the eccentric and epicyclic models for planetary motion, as seems likely, he merits the appellation assigned to him by historian Otto Neugebauer: "the founder of Greek mathematical astronomy." These geometric devices, when adjusted to observational data and made suitable for numerical computation, became the basis of the sophisticated Greek system of astronomy. Through its codification by Ptolemy in the *Almagest*, this system flourished among Arabic and Hindu astronomers in the Middle Ages and Latin astronomers in the West through the sixteenth century. Although Nicolaus Copernicus (1473-1543) made the significant change of replacing Ptolemy's geocentric arrangement with a heliocentric one, even he retained the basic geometric methods of the older system. Only with Johannes Kepler (1571-1630), who was first to substitute elliptical orbits for the configurations of circles in the Ptolemaic-Copernican scheme, can one speak of a clear break with the mathematical methods of ancient astronomy.

Apollonius' work in geometry fared quite differently. The fields of conics and advanced geometric constructions he so fully explored came to a virtual dead end soon after his time. The complexity of this subject, proliferating in special cases and lacking convenient notations (such as the algebraic forms, for example, of modern analytic geometry that first appeared only with François Viète, René Descartes, and Pierre de Fermat in the late sixteenth and the seventeenth centuries), must have discouraged further research among geometers in the second century B.C.

In later antiquity, interest in Apollonius' work revived: Pappus and Hypatia of Alexandria (fourth to early fifth century A.D.) and Eutocius (sixth century) produced commentaries on the *Conics*. Their work did not extend the field in any significant way beyond what Apollonius had done, but it proved critical for the later history of conic theory, by ensuring the survival of Apollonius' writing. When the *Conics* was translated into Arabic in the ninth century, Arabic geometers entered this field; they approached the study of Apollonius with considerable inventiveness, often devising new forms of proofs, or contributing new results where the texts at their disposal were incomplete. Alhazen (early eleventh century), for example, attempted a restoration of Apollonius' lost book VIII.

In the early modern period, after the publication of the translations of Apollonius and Pappus by Federigo Commandino in 1588-1589, the study of advanced geometry received new impetus in the West. Several distinguished mathematicians in this period (François Viète, Willebrord Snel, Pierre de Fermat, Edmond Halley, and others) tried their hand at restoring lost analytic works of Apollonius. The entirely new field of projective geometry emerged from the conic researches of Gérard Desargues and Blaise Pascal in the seventeenth century. Thus, the creation of the modern field of geometry owes much to the stimulus of the *Conics* and the associated treatises of Apollonius.

Bibliography

Apollonius. *On Cutting Off a Ratio*. Translated by Edward Macierowski. Fairfield, Conn.: Golden Hind Press, 1987. This translation is literal and provisional; a full critical edition is being prepared by Macierowski.

_____. *Treatise on Conic Sections*. Translated and edited by Thomas Little Heath. Cambridge: Cambridge University Press, 1896. Translation in modern notation, with extensive commentary. Heath surveys the older history of conics, including efforts by Euclid and Archimedes, and then summarizes the characteristic terminology and methods used by Apollonius. A synopsis appears in Heath's *History of Greek Mathematics* (Oxford: Clarendon Press, 1921), together with ample discussions of the lost Apollonian treatises described by Pappus.

Hogemdijk, J. P. *Ibn al-Haytham's Completion of the "Conics."* New York: Springer-Verlag, 1984. This edition of the Arabic text of Alhazen's restoration of the lost book VIII of the *Conics* is accompanied by a literal English translation, a mathematical summary in modern notation, and discussions of the Greek and Arabic traditions of Apollonius' work. See also Hogemdijk's "Arabic Traces of Lost Works of Apollonius" in *Archive for History of Exact Sciences* 35 (1986): 187-253, which represents an edition, with English translation, of medieval Arabic documents revealing knowledge of certain works of Apollonius.

Knorr, W. R. *Ancient Tradition of Geometric Problems*. Cambridge, Mass.: Birkhauser Boston, 1986. A survey of Greek geometric methods from the pre-Euclidean period to late antiquity. Chapter 7 is devoted to the work of Apollonius, including his *Conics* and lost analytic writings.

Neugebauer, Otto. *A History of Ancient Mathematical Astronomy*. New York: Springer-Verlag, 1975. The section on Apollonius in this work provides a detailed technical account of his contributions to ancient astronomy.

Pappus of Alexandria. *Book 7 of the "Collection."* Translated by A. Jones. New York: Springer-Verlag, 1986. A critical edition of Pappus' Greek text (collated with the former edition of F. Hultsch in volume 2 of *Pappi Collectionis Quae Supersunt*, 1877), with English translation and commentary. Pappus' book preserves highly valuable information on Apollonius' lost works on geometric construction. Jones surveys in detail Pappus' evidence of the lost works and modern efforts to reconstruct them.

Toomer, G. J. "Apollonius of Perga." In *Dictionary of Scientific Biography*, vol. 1. New York: Charles Scribner's Sons, 1970. What is known of Apollonius' life and work is here summarized, with an extensive bibliography. For a discussion of the earlier field of conics, see also Toomer's translation of Diocles' *Peri pyreiōn*: *Diocles on Burning Mirrors* (New York: Springer-Verlag, 1976).

Waerden, Bartel Leendert van der. *Science Awakening*. Translated by Arnold Dresden. Groningen, Netherlands: Noordhoff, 1954. In this highly readable survey of ancient mathematics, Waerden includes a useful synopsis of the geometric work of Apollonius.

Zeuthen, H. G. *Die Lehre von den Kegelschnitten im Altertum*. Copenhagen: Höst and Sohn, 1886. The definitive modern study of Apollonius' work in the conics, with detailed discussions also of the earlier history of the conics and of Apollonius' lost works. Zeuthen's principal theses are discussed by Heath, Toomer, Jones, and Knorr (see above).

Wilbur R. Knorr

ARCHIMEDES

Born: 287 B.C.; Syracuse, Sicily
Died: 212 B.C.; Syracuse, Sicily
Areas of Achievement: Science, mathematics, and engineering
Contribution: The greatest mathematician of antiquity, Archimedes did his
best work in geometry and also founded the disciplines of statics and
hydrostatics.

Early Life

Few details are certain about the life of Archimedes. His birth in 287 B.C.
was established from a report, about fourteen hundred years after the fact,
that he was seventy-five years old at his death in 212 B.C. Ancient writers
agree in calling him a Syracusan by birth, and he himself provides the information that his father was the astronomer Pheidias, the author of a treatise on the diameters of the sun and moon. His father's profession suggests
an explanation for the son's early interest in astronomy and mathematics.
Some scholars have characterized Archimedes as an aristocrat who actively
participated in the Syracusan court and who may have been related to King
Hieron II, the ruler of Syracuse. He certainly was friendly with Hieron and
Hieron's son Gelon, to whom he dedicated one of his works. (Original titles
of Archimedes' works are not known, but most of his books were first translated into English in 1897 in the volume *Works.*)

Archimedes traveled to Egypt to study in Alexandria, then the center of
the scientific world. Some of his teachers had, in their youth, been students
of Euclid. He made two close friends in Alexandria: Conon of Samos, a
gifted mathematician, and Eratosthenes of Cyrene, also a good mathematician. From the prefaces to his works, it is clear that Archimedes maintained
friendly relations with several Alexandrian scholars, and he played an active
role in developing the mathematical traditions of this intellectual center. It is
possible that he visited Spain before returning to Syracuse, and a return trip
to Egypt is also a possibility. This second visit would have been the occasion
for his construction of dikes and bridges reported in some Arabian sources.

In Syracuse, Archimedes spent his time working on mathematical and
mechanical problems. Although he was a remarkably ingenious inventor, his
inventions were, according to Plutarch, merely diversions, the work of a
geometer at play. He possessed such a lofty intellect that he considered these
inventions of much less worth than his mathematical creations. Plutarch may
have exaggerated Archimedes' distaste for engineering, because there is evidence that he was fascinated by mechanical problems from a practical as well
as theoretical point of view.

In the stories that multiplied about him, Archimedes became a symbol of
the learned man—absentminded and unconcerned with food, clothing, and

the other necessities of life. In images created long after his death, he is depicted as the quintessential sage, with a heavily bearded face, massive forehead, and contemplative mien. He had a good sense of humor. For example, he often sent his theorems to Alexandria, but to play a trick on some conceited mathematicians there, he once slipped in a few false propositions, so that these individuals, who pretended to have discovered everything by themselves, would fall into the trap of proposing theorems that were impossible.

Life's Work

The range of Archimedes' interest was wide, encompassing statics, hydrostatics, optics, astronomy, and engineering, in addition to geometry and arithmetic. It is natural that stories should tell more about his engineering inventiveness than his mathematical ability, for clever machines appealed to the average mind more than abstract mathematical theorems. Unfortunately, many of these stories are doubtful. For example, Archimedes is supposed to have invented a hollow, helical cylinder that, when rotated, could serve as a water pump, but this device, now called the Archimedean screw, antedates its supposed inventor.

In another well-known story, Archimedes boasted to King Hieron that, if he had a place on which to stand, he could move the earth. Hieron urged him to make good this boast by hauling ashore a fully loaded three-masted merchantman of the royal fleet. Using a compound pulley, Archimedes, with modest effort, pulled the ship out of the harbor and onto the shore. The compound pulley may have been Archimedes' invention, but the story, told by Plutarch, is probably a legend.

The most famous story about Archimedes is attributed to Vitruvius, a Roman architect under Emperor Augustus. King Hieron, grateful for the success of one of his ventures, wanted to thank the gods by consecrating a golden wreath. Upon delivery, the wreath had the weight of the gold supplied for it, but Hieron suspected that it had been adulterated with silver. Unable to make the goldsmith confess, Hieron asked Archimedes to devise some way of testing the wreath. Since it was a consecrated object, Archimedes could not subject it to chemical analysis. He pondered the problem without success until one day, when he entered a full bath, he noticed that the deeper he descended into the tub, the more water flowed over the edge. This suggested to him that the amount of overflowed water was equal in volume to the portion of his body submerged in the bath. This observation gave him a way of solving the problem, and he was so overjoyed that he leapt out of the tub and ran home naked through the streets, shouting: "Eureka! Eureka!" Vitruvius then goes on to explain how Archimedes made use of his newly gained insight. By putting the wreath into water, he could tell by the rise in water level the volume of the wreath. He also dipped into water lumps of gold and silver, each having the same weight as the wreath. He found that the wreath caused more water to overflow than the gold and less than the silver. From this experiment, he determined the amount of silver admixed with the gold in the wreath.

As amusing and instructive as these legends are, much more reliable and interesting to modern historians of science are Archimedes' mathematical works. These treatises can be divided into three groups: studies of figures bounded by curved lines and surfaces, works on the geometrical analysis of statical and hydrostatical problems, and arithmetical works. The form in which these treatises have survived is not the form in which they left Archimedes' hand: They have all undergone transformations and emendations. Nevertheless, one still finds the spirit of Archimedes in the intricacy of the questions and the lucidity of the explanations.

In finding the areas of plane figures bounded by curved lines and the volumes of solid figures bounded by curved surfaces, Archimedes used a method originated by Eudoxus of Cnidus, unhappily called the "method of exhaustion." This indirect proof involves inscribing and circumscribing polygons to approach a length, area, or volume. The name "exhaustion" is based on the idea that, for example, a circle would finally be exhausted by inscribed polygons with a growing number of sides. In *On the Sphere and Cylinder*, Archimedes compares perimeters of inscribed and circumscribed polygons to prove that the volume of a sphere is two-thirds the volume of its circumscribed cylinder. He also proves that the surface of any sphere is four times the area of its greatest circle.

Having successfully applied this method to the sphere and cylinder, Archimedes went on to use the technique for many other figures, including spheroids, spirals, and parabolas. *On Conoids and Spheroids* treats the figures of revolution generated by conics. His spheroids are what are now called oblate and prolate spheroids, which are figures of revolution generated by ellipses. Archimedes' object in this work was the determination of volumes of segments cut off by planes from these conoidal and spheroidal solids. In *On Spirals*, Archimedes studies the area enclosed between successive whorls of a spiral. He also defines a figure, now called Archimedes' spiral: If a ray from a central point rotates uniformly about this point, like the hand of a clock, and if another point moves uniformly along this line (marked by the clock hand), starting at the central point, then this linearly moving and rotating point will trace Archimedes' spiral.

Quadrature of the Parabola is not Archimedes' original title for the treatise, since "parabola" was not used in the sense of a conic section in the third century B.C. On the other hand, quadrature is an ancient term: It denotes the process of constructing a square equal in area to a given surface, in this case a parabolic segment. Archimedes, in this treatise, proves the theorem that the area of a parabolic segment is four-thirds the area of its greatest inscribed triangle. He is so fond of this theorem that he gives different proofs for it. One proof uses a method of exhaustion in which the parabolic segment is "exhausted" by a series of triangles. The other consists of establishing the quadrature of the parabola by mechanically balancing elements of the unknown area against elements of a known area. This latter method gives an insight into how Archimedes discovered theorems to be proved. His most recently discovered work, *Method of Mechanical Theorems* (translated in 1912), provides other examples of how Archimedes mathematically balanced geometrical figures as if they were on a weighing balance. He did not consider that this mechanical method constituted a demonstration, but it allowed him to find interesting theorems, which he then proved by more rigorous geometrical methods.

Archimedes also applied geometry to statics and hydrostatics successfully. In his *The Equilibrium of Planes*, he proves the law of the lever geometrically and then puts it to use in finding the centers of gravity of several thin sheets of different shapes. By center of gravity, Archimedes meant the point at which the object can be supported so as to be in equilibrium under the pull of gravity. Earlier Greek mathematicians had made use of the principle of the lever in showing that a small weight at a large distance from a fulcrum would balance a large weight near the fulcrum, but Archimedes worked this principle out in mathematical detail. In his proof, the weights become geometrical magnitudes acting perpendicularly to the balance beam, which itself is conceived as a weightless geometrical line. In this way, he reduced statics to a rigorous discipline comparable to what Euclid had done for geometry.

Archimedes once more emphasizes geometrical analysis in *On Floating Bodies*. The cool logic of this treatise contrasts with his emotional discovery of the buoyancy principle. In this work, he proves that solids lighter than a fluid will, when placed in the fluid, sink to the depth where the weight of the solid will be equal to the weight of the fluid displaced. Solids heavier than the fluid will, when placed in the fluid, sink to the bottom, and they will be lighter by the weight of the displaced fluid.

Although Archimedes' investigations were primarily in geometry and mechanics, he did perform some interesting studies in numerical calculation. For example, in *Measurement of the Circle* he calculated, based on mathematical principles rather than direct measurement, a value for the ratio of the circumference of a circle to its diameter (this ratio was not called pi until much later). By inscribing and circumscribing regular polygons of more and more sides within and around a circle, Archimedes found that the ratio was between $223/71$ and $220/70$, the best value for π (pi) ever obtained in the classical world.

In *The Sand-Reckoner*, Archimedes devises a notation suitable for writing very large numbers. To put this new notation to a test, he sets down a number equal to the number of grains of sand it would take to fill the entire universe. Large numbers are also involved in his treatise concerned with the famous "Cattle Problem." White, black, yellow, and dappled cows and bulls are grazing on the island of Sicily. The numbers of these cows and bulls have to satisfy several conditions. The problem is to find the number of bulls and cows of each of the four colors. It is unlikely that Archimedes ever completely solved this problem in indeterminate analysis.

Toward the end of his life, Archimedes became part of a worsening political situation. His friend Hieron II had a treaty of alliance with Rome and remained faithful to it, even after the Second Punic War began. After his death, however, his grandson Hieronymus, who became king, was so impressed by Hannibal's victories in Italy that he switched sides to Carthage. Hieronymus was then assassinated, but Sicily remained allied with Carthage. Consequently, the Romans sent a fleet under the command of Marcellus to capture Syracuse. According to traditional stories, Archimedes invented devices for warding off the Roman enemy. He is supposed to have constructed large lenses to set the fleet on fire and mechanical cranes to turn ships upside down. He devised so many ingenious war machines that the Romans would flee if so much as a piece of rope appeared above a wall. These stories are grossly exaggerated if not totally fabricated, but Archimedes may have helped in the defense of his city, and he certainly provided the Romans with a face-saving explanation for their frustratingly long siege of Syracuse.

Because of treachery by a cabal of nobles, among other things, Syracuse eventually fell. Marcellus ordered that the city be sacked, but he made it clear that his soldiers were to spare the house and person of Archimedes. Amid the confusion of the sack, however, Archimedes, while puzzling over a geometrical diagram drawn on sand in a tray, was killed by a Roman soldier. During his lifetime he had expressed the wish that upon his tomb should be placed a cylinder circumscribing a sphere, together with an inscription giving the ratio between the volumes of these two bodies, a discovery of which he was especially proud. Marcellus, who was distressed by the great mathematician's death, had Archimedes' wish carried out. More than a century later, when Cicero was in Sicily, he found this tomb, overgrown with brush but with the figure of the sphere and cylinder still visible.

Summary

Some scholars rank Archimedes with Sir Isaac Newton and Carl Friedrich Gauss as one of the three greatest mathematicians who ever lived, and historians of mathematics agree that the theorems Archimedes discovered raised Greek mathematics to a new level of understanding. He tackled very difficult and original problems and solved them through boldness and vision. His skill in using mechanical ideas in mathematics was paralleled by his ingenious use of mathematics in mechanics.

The Latin West received its knowledge of Archimedes from two sources:

Byzantium and Islam. His works were translated from the Greek and Arabic into Latin in the twelfth century and played an important role in stimulating the work of medieval natural philosophers. Knowledge of Archimedes' ideas multiplied during the Renaissance, and by the seventeenth century his insights had been almost completely absorbed into European thought and had deeply influenced the birth of modern science. For example, Galileo was inspired by Archimedes and tried to do for dynamics what Archimedes had done for statics. More than any other ancient scientist, Archimedes observed the world in a way that modern scientists from Galileo to Albert Einstein admired and sought to emulate.

Bibliography
Aaboe, Asger. *Episodes from the Early History of Mathematics*. New York: Random House, 1964. After a brief account of Archimedes' life and a survey of his works, the third chapter of this book presents three samples of Archimedean mathematics: the trisection of an angle, the construction of a regular heptagon, and the determination of a sphere's volume and surface area.
Bell, E. T. *Men of Mathematics*. New York: Simon and Schuster, 1937. A widely available popular collection of biographical essays on the world's greatest mathematicians. Bell discusses Archimedes, along with Zeno of Elea and Eudoxus, in an early chapter on "Modern Minds in Ancient Bodies."
Clagett, Marshall. "Archimedes." In *Dictionary of Scientific Biography*, edited by Charles Couston Gillispie, vol. 1. New York: Charles Scribner's Sons, 1970. Clagett is an eminent scholar of Archimedes, and in his five-volume work, *Archimedes in the Middle Ages* (1964-1984), he has traced the medieval Latin tradition of Archimedes' works. This article makes his major insights on Archimedes available to the general reader.
Dijksterhuis, E. J. *Archimedes*. Princeton, N.J.: Princeton University Press, 1987. This edition of the best survey in English of Archimedes' life and work also contains a valuable bibliographical essay by Wilbur R. Knorr.
Finley, Moses I. *A History of Sicily*. Vol. 1, *Ancient Sicily*. New York: Viking Press, 1968. Finley's account of the history of Sicily from antiquity to the Arab conquest has a section explaining how the politics of the Second Punic War led to Archimedes' death.
Heath, T. L. *A History of Greek Mathematics*. 2 vols. Oxford: Clarendon Press, 1921. A good general survey of ancient Greek mathematics that contains, in volume 2, a detailed account of the works of Archimedes. This book and the author's *Works of Archimedes* (1897, with supplement 1912) unfortunately use modern notation, which risks misrepresenting the thrust of Archimedes' proofs.
Kline, Morris. *Mathematical Thought from Ancient to Modern Times*. New

York: Oxford University Press, 1972. Kline's aim is to present the chief ideas that have shaped the history of mathematics rather than the people involved. Consequently, his treatment of Archimedes emphasizes the themes of his work rather than the events of his life.

Lloyd, G. E. R. *Greek Science After Aristotle*. New York: W. W. Norton and Co., 1973. Lloyd's book, intended for the general reader, centers on the interaction of Hellenistic science and mathematics with religion, philosophy, and technology. It contains a brief but good account of the life and work of Archimedes in this larger intellectual context.

Van der Waerden, B. L. *Science Awakening*. New York: John Wiley and Sons, 1963. A survey of ancient Egyptian, Babylonian, and Greek mathematics. The chapter on the Alexandrian era (330-220 B.C.) contains a detailed account of Archimedes' life, legends, and mathematical accomplishments.

Robert J. Paradowski

ARETAEUS OF CAPPADOCIA

Born: Probably second century A.D.; Cappadocia, Roman Empire
Died: Date unknown; place unknown
Area of Achievement: Medicine
Contribution: Considered by many the greatest ancient physician after
   Hippocrates, Aretaeus wrote the best and most accurate descriptions of
   many diseases and made landmark studies of diabetes and neurological
   and mental disorders.

Early Life

Not even the exact century of Aretaeus of Cappadocia's birth is known;
most scholars agree on the second century A.D., although a few offer the first
or third century. Aretaeus' epithet is "Cappadocian," implying that he was
born in that most eastern of Roman provinces. No other information about
his life is certain. Scholars conjecture, however, that he studied in Egypt at
Alexandria, founded in 331 B.C. as the major center for medical study,
research, and teaching. Aretaeus mentions Egypt in his works and describes
its geography and some diseases and therapeutics unique to that country.
Some scholars also believe that Aretaeus practiced medicine in Rome; he
prescribed wines known to second century Rome—namely, Falernian, Fun-
dian, Sequine, and Surrentine.

Aretaeus was an Eclectic by practice and a Pneumatist by training. After
Hippocrates in the fifth century B.C. there was little advance in the knowledge of disease and its treatment, although there were significant gains at Alexandria in the area of anatomy because of the dissections of human bodies.
Instead, post-Hippocratic physicians tended to theorize about medicine as a
philosophy and to develop various schools of medicine. Dogmatism and
Empiricism were the first schools. The Dogmatists employed theoretical
principles; they believed that reason and systematic studies of anatomy and
physiology were necessary for the physician. The Empiricists, on the other
hand, rejected theory and anatomy; they stressed experience and observation. The "tripod" of the Empiricists' knowledge was personal observation,
researched historical observation, and use of analogy in analyzing unknown
cases.

Two schools developed in reaction to the Dogmatists and Empiricists.
Methodism, founded in the late first century B.C., rejected the theory of the
humors so prevalent in Hippocratic medicine and advocated an atomic
stance. The Methodists considered disease an interference of the normal
position and motion of the atoms in the human body; treatments were prescribed to restore the proper order of the atoms—relaxants to counteract
excessive tension, astringents to counteract excessive looseness.

The Pneumatic school, established around A.D. 50 by Athenaeus of Attaleia, stressed *pneuma*, meaning "vital air" or "breath." The beliefs of the Pneumatists were a combination of the Stoic philosophy, with its emphasis on primordial matter, the *pneuma*, from which all life comes, and Hippocratic pathology. Disease occurs when an imbalance of the four humors (blood, phlegm, black bile, and yellow bile) disturbs the *pneuma* in the human body.

Each of these various schools had both strengths and glaring weaknesses in their theories and practices. The knowledge of these weaknesses, coupled with Roman common sense, which rejected the Greek love of theory, led most Roman physicians, beginning with Archigenes (who flourished around A.D. 100), to pick and choose among the various doctrines and ideas of the four schools. Such physicians were called Eclectics. That Aretaeus was an Eclectic is obvious from his work: For example, although he followed Pneumatism in its concept of the vital breath and its relation to the four humors, Aretaeus pursued anatomy and physiology avidly, as the Dogmatists did, yet he also relied heavily on observation and experience in the manner of an Empiricist; his emphasis on simple regimens and treatments recalls the Methodist school as well as Hippocrates.

Life's Work

Aretaeus refused to be dogmatic and speculative. He attempted to describe diseases in clear, scientific, and rational terms, and his writings bear the marks of careful thought and extensive clinical experience. Aretaeus wrote seven works, two of which survive: *Peri aition kai semeion oxeon kai chronion pathon* (*On the Causes and Symptoms of Acute and Chronic Diseases*, 1856) and *Oxeon kai chronion nouson therapeutikon biblion* (*Book on the Treatment of Acute and Chronic Diseases*, 1856). The lost works discussed fevers, surgery, pharmacology, gynecology, and prophylaxis. Aretaeus wrote in Ionic Greek, a dialect which had not been in use for centuries; he chose the Ionic style to imitate Hippocrates, who also wrote in that dialect.

Aretaeus followed the Methodist classification of diseases into chronic and acute; the distinction was made on the course of the disease, that is, whether the disease lasted over a long period of time or was of a short duration and reached a "crisis" (the point in the progress of the disease when the patient recovered or died). Chronic diseases include paralysis, migraine headaches, and insanity, while examples of acute diseases are pneumonia, pleurisy, tetanus, and diphtheria. Aretaeus' descriptions of these and other diseases show him to be an accurate observer who was concerned more for the patient than for theory itself. His accounts, so important in the history of medicine, may be summarized in the following categories: anatomy and physiology, symptomatology (physical description of diseases such as diabetes, leprosy, and ulcers), neurology and psychiatry, surgery, and therapeutics.

Aretaeus devoted more attention to anatomy and physiology than most ancient physicians. As stated earlier, Aretaeus followed the Pneumatist doctrine: He believed that the body is composed of the four humors and of spirit (*pneuma*), and the proper mixture and interplay of these elements constitutes health. Blood is formed in the liver from food; phlegm is secreted by the brain into the other organs; yellow bile comes from the liver, black bile from the spleen. The most important organ is the heart, since the heart is the site of heat and *pneuma*. The heart draws the *pneuma* from the lungs, which are stimulated by it. Respiration itself depends upon the movement of the thorax and diaphragm and also upon the lungs' contraction and expansion. Regarding the nervous system, nerves originate in the brain; this idea was based on the perception that the spinal cord was a prolongation of the brain. All nerves cross between their origin in the brain and their final termination in the body; Aretaeus based this belief on his startling observation that a cerebral lesion caused paralysis on the opposite side of the body.

Aretaeus knew much about circulation. The aorta, he stated, comes from the heart and is located to the left of the vena cava; the aorta carries the *pneuma* to the other organs. The veins, which originate in the liver, bring the blood to all the body. Aretaeus asserted that the content of the arteries was light-colored, that of the veins dark. The liver itself is composed mostly of blood and produces blood and bile; if it becomes inflamed, jaundice results. Aretaeus wrote remarkable accounts of the kidneys and the bile ducts. He thought of the kidneys as cavities which acted like sieves for collecting urine and were connected to the bladder by two tubes, one from each kidney. Digestion of food occurs not only in the stomach but also in the intestines. The portal vein takes the food after digestion to the liver, where it is taken out as blood by the vena cava to the heart. This scheme shows that Aretaeus was aware of nearly all circulatory processes and the direction of blood flow in the veins.

One of Aretaeus' greatest accomplishments was his practice of physical diagnosis. He used anatomical inspection, distinguishing the appearances of ulcers in the small and large bowels, for example. Also, before he discussed a disease, Aretaeus prefixed an anatomical and physiological introduction concerning the part(s) of the body afflicted by the disease (this is the method used in many modern medical textbooks). In his physical examinations, Aretaeus employed auscultation of the heart, palpitation of the body (to check for enlargement of the liver and spleen), and percussion of the abdomen. Aretaeus always noted carefully the patient's symptoms: temperature, breathing, pulse, secretions, color of skin, and condition of the pupils. In the tradition of Hippocrates, Aretaeus related diseases to foods eaten by the patient and to climate, time of year, and environment.

Aretaeus' symptomatology is considered excellent by medical historians and, in some instances, not improved upon even by contemporary medicine. Especially praiseworthy are Aretaeus' accounts of hematemesis, jaundice, dropsy, tuberculosis, tetanus, epilepsy, and cardiac syncope. Aretaeus distinguished between pneumonia and pleurisy and is credited with the initial descriptions of diphtheria and asthma. He was the first European to write a symptomatic account of diabetes, and he gave the disease its name. Aretaeus correctly thought of diabetes as a progressive form of dropsy with polyuria and excessive thirst that results in emaciation of flesh. Finally, Aretaeus' accounts of leprosy are invaluable. He offered useful distinctions between the types of leprosy: elephantiasis (the tuberous form of leprosy) and the maculo-anesthetic form, which involves mutilation of the body; he also provided the first recorded instance of isolating lepers and distinguished between conveyance of disease by actual contact (contagion) and transmission of disease at a distance (infection).

Aretaeus' discussions of neurological and mental diseases are important. He divided such illnesses into acute and chronic classes. The acute diseases, as he described them, are phrenitis (a febrile delirium or, at times, meningitis); lethargy (a comatose state, or encephalitis); marasmus (atrophy); apoplexy (an acute form of paralysis); tetanus; and epileptic paroxysm. Chronic diseases include cephalaea (migraine headache), vertigo (chronic paralysis), and all forms of insanity. Especially important are Aretaeus' astute distinctions between apoplexy, paraplegia, paresis, and paralysis; the basis of division was the extent of loss of movement and sensation. Aretaeus was the first to distinguish between spinal and cerebral paralysis: When the paralysis is spinal, it occurs on the same side as the lesion; when cerebral, the paralysis occurs on the opposite side (crossed paralysis).

Aretaeus' clear and full discussion of the different kinds of insanity has remained unsurpassed. He noted the stages by which intermittent insanity (manic depression) can become a senile melancholia that does not remit. While the former may be treated by phlebotomy, wormwood, and black hellebore (a plant that produces violent shocks to the nervous system similar to those in modern electric shock treatment), senile melancholia is incurable.

Aretaeus' book on surgery has been lost; he did, however, refer to surgery throughout his extant writings. Aretaeus recommended craniotomy (trepanning) for epilepsy and for cephalalgia and cephalaea (acute and chronic headache, respectively). He used catheters for urological diseases and mentioned surgery to remove kidney stones. It should be noted that surgery was not commonly practiced in antiquity, but when it was deemed necessary, the practicing physician usually performed it.

Aretaeus' treatments of disease are conservative. As in his discussions of the causes and forms of diseases, Aretaeus relied on experience and common sense, not abstract theory. He rejected tracheotomy and pleaded for extreme caution in the application of phlebotomy, venesection, cupping, and leeches: Aretaeus argued that only in severe cases should much blood be removed. Instead, he used purgatives, emetics, suppositories, laxatives, ointments, and poultices. Aretaeus also stressed exercise, massages, baths, temperate lifestyles, and a healthy diet including milk, fruits, vegetables, and foods without starch and fat. It is interesting that Aretaeus also prescribed opium for people afflicted with feverish delirium.

Summary

No ancient medical writer, except perhaps Hippocrates, surpassed Aretaeus of Cappadocia for vividness and clarity in the description of diseases. Aretaeus' descriptions of diabetes, tetanus, diphtheria, leprosy, asthma, and mental and neurological disorders are especially valuable and are landmarks in medical history. Aretaeus tried his best to put his symptomatology on a sound anatomical basis; for every disease, he supplied splendid accounts of anatomy. He gave therapeutics and cures for every disease, acute and chronic; his treatments are simple and rational. In his writings, Aretaeus was perhaps the most unbiased physician in antiquity, rejecting dogmatic thought, theory, and superstition. Finally, Aretaeus was unique in refusing to abandon the patient who was incurable; while even Hippocrates recommended turning away hopeless cases, Aretaeus ordered all measures to be taken, and, when those failed, he offered support and sympathy.

Bibliography
Allbutt, Sir Thomas. *Greek Medicine in Rome*. New York: Macmillan, 1921. Still one of the best textbooks on the medical schools and the practice of medicine in the Roman Empire. Chapter 11 ("Some Pneumatist and Eclectic Physicians") discusses Aretaeus and is superb in providing background information to the Eclectic and his writings.
Aretaeus of Cappadocia. *The Extant Works of Aretaeus the Cappadocian*. Edited and translated by Francis Adams. London: Sydenham Society, 1856. Reprint. Boston: Milford House, 1972. The only available translation of Aretaeus' work. The introduction to Aretaeus, his background, and his work is somewhat difficult for the nonspecialist, and the antiquated English of the translation is forbidding.
Cordell, E. F. "Aretaeus of Cappadocia." *Bulletin of The Johns Hopkins Hospital* 20 (1909): 371-377. This volume provides a very useful discussion of the physiology, symptomatology, and therapy in Arctacus' works. Intended for a knowledgeable but general audience.
Leopold, Eugene. "Aretaeus the Cappadocian: His Contribution to Diabetes Mellitus." *Annals of Medical History* 2 (1930): 424-435. An excellent, straightforward account of Aretaeus' life and writings. Especially good is the discussion of Aretaeus' place in the history of medicine and diabetes. Very readable.
Mettler, Cecilia. *History of Medicine*. Philadelphia: Blakiston Co., 1947. Mettler offers an exhaustive survey of Aretaeus' discussions and treatments of diseases. One must use the index, however, as the accounts are

scattered throughout the text according to typology of disease.

Neuburger, Max. *History of Medicine*. Translated by Ernest Playfair. London: Oxford Medical Publications, 1910. This classic text has useful chapters on the Pneumatists and Eclectics and Aretaeus, in particular. With invaluable discussions of the various medical schools of Aretaeus' time.

Robinson, Victor. *Pathfinders in Medicine*. New York: Medical Life Press, 1929. This volume includes an essay on Aretaeus designed for lay readers. It is excellent as a general introduction to Aretaeus, although it lacks references and notes.

Stannard, J. "Materia Medica and Philosophic Theory in Aretaeus." *Sudhoffs Archiv für Geschichte der Medizin und der Naturwissenschaften* 48 (March, 1964): 27-53. Contains extensive discussion of the therapeutics, especially dietetics, of Aretaeus. Invaluable for information on Aretaeus and his relation to Pneumatism.

Steven M. Oberhelman

ARISTOPHANES

Born: c. 450 B.C.; Athens, Greece
Died: c. 385 B.C.; Athens, Greece
Areas of Achievement: Theater and drama
Contribution: Aristophanes' highly entertaining plays provide the only extant examples of Old Comedy, and his last works anticipate the shift to the New Comedy of Menander, Terence, and Plautus. His writings reveal much about not only dramaturgy in late fifth century B.C. Athens but also the social, political, and economic conditions of the time.

Early Life

The son of Philippos, who may have been a landowner in Aegina, Greece, Aristophanes was born in Athens about 450 B.C. Though little is known about his early life, he was clearly well-educated, for his plays quote or allude to many sources. These works also suggest a deep interest in public affairs, and Aristophanes was to serve as representative of his district on the Athenian Council.

His literary ability became apparent quite early: When he was between seventeen and twenty-three years old he began participating in Athens' annual dramatic competitions. The Lenaian Dionysia, or Lenaia, held in Gamelion (January-February), was devoted largely to comedies, whereas the Great, or City, Dionysia, established in 536 B.C. and celebrated in Elaphebalion (March), presented tragedies but also offered three comic plays. Both festivals were religious as well as literary, honoring Dionysus, the god of wine, and associated with agriculture in general.

The comedies derived both their name and purpose from the ancient komos, or procession of rejoicing in the vital forces of nature, which supposedly drove away evil spirits and guaranteed continued fertility of the land and its inhabitants. Bawdy jokes and costumes that include large phalluses constitute part of the ritual, as does the gamos, or sexual union, that frequently concludes the plays. Similarly, the mockery of prominent political or cultural figures serves as a liberating force that temporarily allows free rein to irrational and suppressed urges; such antics are connected with the madness of intoxication.

To these satiric and sexual elements, Aristophanes added a lyricism rivaling that of any other Hellenic poet. An excellent example appears in the parabasis (choral interlude) of *Ornithes* (c. 414; *The Birds*), which begins with a summoning of the nightingale:

> Musician of the Birds
> Come and sing
> honey-throated one!

> Come, O love,
>   flutist of the Spring,
>   accompany our song.

The Chorus then presents a myth of the creation of the world through the power of Love, all told in lyrical anapests.

Only a fragment survives of Aristophanes' first play, *Daitalēis* (banqueters), which won second prize at the Lenaia of 427, yet the remains suggest that the dramatist already was treating an issue which would become important in his more mature writing. Though still a young man himself, he attacks Athenian youth and their new ways, especially modern modes of education. An old man sends one son to the city, while the other remains in the country. The former learns only to eat, drink, and sing bawdy songs; his body is no better trained than his mind. When he returns home he is too weak to work and no longer cares whether he does.

Babylōnioi (Babylonians), another lost play, was produced at the Great Dionysia of 426 and won first prize. Cleon, the Athenian demogogue then in power, had undertaken a policy of mass terror to force Athens' allies to support its military efforts against Sparta in the Peloponnesian War. As a believer in peace and pan-Hellenism, Aristophanes attacked Cleon's measures. Cleon responded by taking Aristophanes to court. Despite the playwright's claim in his next comedy that during the proceedings he almost "gave up the ghost," he does not seem to have been punished severely, if at all. As is evident from his next plays, he was undeterred from speaking out against war and against Cleon.

Life's Work

Acharnēs (*The Acharnians*), which in 425 won first prize at the Lenaia (a major dramatic competition devoted largely to comedies), continues to attack Cleon's war policy. When the demigod Amphitheus raises the question of peace in the Athenian assembly, he is ejected. Dikaiopolis (which means Honest Citizen or Just City), a refugee farmer whose land has been ravaged by war, supports this pacific plea and sends Amphitheus to Sparta to negotiate a separate peace for himself. When the demigod returns with a thirty-year treaty, the Acharnians attack him. These old men, represented by the Chorus, have suffered in the war, but they want revenge, not peace. Dikaiopolis must defend his views while he rests his head on a chopping block, so that if he fails to persuade the Chorus that his policy is best, they can kill him at once. His speech divides the old men, who resolve to summon Lamachos, a general, to argue the matter further. The agon, or debate, ensues, allowing Aristophanes to present further arguments against the war. The Chorus finally sides with Dikaiopolis, but Lamachos leaves vowing eternal resistance.

The farmer now sets up a market. While the play shows him prospering through peace, it also reveals the hardships of war. For example, a Megarian has become so impoverished that he is willing to sell his daughters for a pittance. The final scenes highlight the contrast between the policies of Cleon and Aristophanes: Lamachos returns from war wounded just as Dikaiopolis, victorious in a drinking bout, appears with two young women to celebrate wine and fertility, the gifts of Dionysus and peace.

In *Hippēs* (424; *The Knights*), which took first prize at the Lenaia, Aristophanes again attacks Cleon. A lost play, *Holkades*, presented at the next Lenaia, is still another attack on Cleon. Then, at the Great Dionysia, Aristophanes turned his attention to a different subject in *Nephelai* (423; *The Clouds*). Strepsiades (Twisterson) has fallen deeply in debt because of the extravagance of his wife and the gambling of his horse-loving son, Pheidippides. To cheat his creditors, Strepsiades resolves to send the youth to the Phrontisterion (Thinkery), the local academy run by Socrates, who can make the weaker side appear the stronger. When Pheidippides refuses to attend, his father enrolls instead. Despite his best efforts, the father cannot grasp the new learning, and at length his son agrees to enter the academy.

Now Pheidippides must choose a mentor; Dikaios Logos (Just Cause) and Adikos Logos (Unjust Cause) offer themselves, and to help Pheidippides choose they engage in a debate, or agon. Dikaios Logos speaks for the old morality and simple life, but when Adikos Logos advocates skepticism and amorality, even Dikaios Logos is converted. Pheidippides becomes certified as an adept at the new philosophy and even teaches his father enough to allow Strepsiades to outwit two of his creditors.

The old man's triumph is, however, short-lived. When Strepsiades reproves his son for singing an obscene song by Euripides, Pheidippides beats him. The father appeals to the Clouds, those symbols of obscurity and form without substance that are the deities and patrons of Socrates' school. They, however, side with the son, who has used his new skill to argue that, because Strepsiades, when he was stronger, would beat Pheidippides, Pheidippides may now beat his father. Enraged, Strepsiades heeds the advice of Hermes and burns down the Phrontisterion.

In 399, *The Clouds* was used as evidence against Socrates, yet Aristophanes' attitude toward the philosopher may be more sympathetic than the play suggests. During its performance, Socrates is supposed to have stood up in the stadium to point out how closely the actor's mask resembled him, and Plato later included Aristophanes in the *Symposium*, where he is treated kindly. Perhaps, in fact, Socrates was among the few who actually enjoyed the piece, for it received only the third prize at the festival; Aristophanes blamed its failure on its being too intellectual for the masses.

Sphēkes (*The Wasps*), which won second prize at the Lenaia of 422, returns to political issues, as Aristophanes once more criticizes Cleon as well as the litigious nature of the Athenians. In the autumn of 422, Cleon died, and ten days after the Great Dionysia of 421 Athens concluded a peace treaty with Sparta. Aristophanes' *Eirēnē* (*Peace*), which won second prize that year, celebrates the end of the fighting, as Trygaios rides to heaven on a giant dung-beetle to rescue Eirēnē from the clutches of Polemos (War). He also saves Opora (Harvest) and Theoria (Ceremony), the private and public benefits of peace. The former becomes his wife; the latter he gives to the Athenian Council. As the play ends, Trygaios regains his youth and is guaranteed perpetual fertility through his union with the goddess.

None of Aristophanes' plays from the next several years has survived, though he apparently returned to the theme of regeneration in *Geras* (c. 421) and *Amphiaraus* (c. 414). His next extant piece, *The Birds*, dates from the Great Dionysia of 414, at which it won second prize. Pisthetairos (Trusty) and Euelpides (Son of Good Hope) have tired of the corruption, fast-paced life, and litigious habits of their fellow Athenians and so resolve to find a pastoral retreat among the birds. Aristophanes demonstrates that though one can leave Athens, one cannot suppress the Athenian *polupragmosunē*, that energy, daring, curiosity, restlessness, and desire for ever-expanding empire.

Instead of basking in rural retirement, Pisthetairos and Euelpides create Nephelokokkugia (Cloudcuckooland), which chooses Athena as its patroness, builds a wall like that surrounding the Acropolis, and undertakes a blockade to keep the smoke of burnt offerings from reaching the gods. In short, these refugees from Athens create a city very much like the one they have fled, except that they are now rulers instead of subjects. Nephelokokkugia does differ from its earthly counterpart in some respects, though, for Pisthetairos expels informers, oracle-mongers, and lawyers, while he treats poets well. In other words, he eliminates those elements whom Aristophanes regarded as preying on their fellow Athenians. In the final scenes, the blockade of the gods succeeds: The Olympians surrender to the birds, Pisthetairos becomes a deity, and he marries the divine Basileia.

The success of the blockade marks another difference between Nephelokokkugia and Athens. As spectators watched *The Birds*, the Athenian fleet was sailing toward disaster in Sicily. In 413, the Peloponnesian War resumed, and, as a result, so did Aristophanes' criticism of the fighting. In the Lenaia of 411, he offered his solution to end the conflict. Women in Athens were virtually powerless, but in *Lysistratē* (*Lysistrata*), they become the architects of peace by refusing to sleep with their husbands until the fighting ends. In a display of pan-Hellenism, they also recruit women from all of Greece to join the sexual embargo.

The results of this effort are soon apparent in the enlarged phalluses of the husbands. Naturally, this tumidity is comical, and the large phallus is ritualistic as well. In another sense, though, it represents all the thwarted desires of Greece: the yearning for peace, prosperity, normalcy. It also links Spartan and Athenian by showing their common humanity, a point Aristophanes emphasizes further by showing that Greeks have cooperated before and can again. The Dionysian power of sex achieves peace between the warring parties as the play ends in a reconciliatory gamos.

Thesmophoriazousai (411; *Thesmophoriazusae*) dates from about the same time as *Lysistrata* and was performed either at the Great Dionsia of 411 or during the Lenaia of the following year. The piece has little political significance; instead, it satirizes several tragedies by Euripides, who had already been a comic target of Aristophanes in several of his earlier pieces. Yet, as *The Clouds* does not imply that the dramatist disliked Socrates, so *Thesmophoriazusae* should not be read as a true condemnation of Euripides.

In fact, *Batrachoi* (405; *The Frogs*), Aristophanes' next surviving comedy and the last surviving work of Old Comedy, suggests that Aristophanes admired his fellow playwright. As the piece opens, Dionysus is preparing to go to Hades to resurrect Euripides, who had died in 406 (as had Sophocles). The god arrives just in time to judge a debate between Aeschylus and Euripides, each of whom claims to be the better writer. The succeeding agon reveals Aristophanes' keen critical sense. Euripides points out that he used common language so that the audience would understand him; Aeschylus replies that his own language is dignified and elevated to encourage spectators to aspire to lofty ideals. Euripides explains that his characters are drawn from real life; Aeschylus maintains that heroic figures are more appropriate for tragedy because ordinary people cannot serve as good examples.

Although Dionysus admires both writers, he finally decides to resurrect Aeschylus, for the older dramatist represents the values Aristophanes himself admired. Aeschylus had fought in the Battle of Marathon (490) and revered the customs and gods of Athens, whereas Euripides was modern and skeptical, embracing values Aristophanes had repeatedly attacked.

Thirteen years separate *The Frogs* and Aristophanes' next play, *Ekklesiazousai* (c. 392; *Ecclesiazusae*). As in *Lysistrata*, women here seize control of events to create a Utopian society. Peace is no longer an issue, because in 404 Sparta defeated Athens and tore down the vanquished city's walls. The new philosophy is no concern, either; in 399, Socrates had been executed. Although Athens was beginning to recover from a decade of economic, political, and social turmoil—in 395, it rebuilt its walls, for example—the play reflects a new mood and new conditions. Both here and in *Ploutos* (388; *Plutus*) the role of the chorus is greatly diminished, perhaps because the city could not afford to pay for one. Gone, too, is the sharp personal satire, as is criticism of contemporary events. Instead, the plays are escapist fantasies, one promising a communistic paradise, the other a society in which all receive their just desserts.

Aristophanes died shortly after the performance of *Plutus* but left two plays that his son Araros produced. *Aiolosikōn* was presumably a parody of one of Euripides' plays which is not extant, and *Kōkalos* seems to be based on the myth of a Sicilian king, who is the hero of one of Sophocles' lost plays. *Kōkalos*, which, like *Aiolosikōn*, was produced about 385, introduces a love story involving Daedalus and one of the king's daughters, and it presents a recognition scene of some sort; both features were to become standard in New Comedy.

Summary

Aristophanes, the advocate of the old order, helped to create a new kind of play. Crafty servants such as Cario in *Plutus*, lovers thwarted by their elders such as those in *Ecclesiazusae*, intrigue, disguise, and recognition scenes such as the ones believed to be in *Kōkalos* became hallmarks of New Comedy. By the first century A.D., Plutarch in his *Moralia* (c. 75; *The Philosophie, Commonly Called the Morals*) would condemn the coarseness of Old Comedy, characterizing Aristophanes' plays as resembling "a harlot who has passed her prime."

Aristophanes' plays remain historically important. Not only do they provide the only surviving record of the form and content of Old Comedy, but also they reveal much about daily life in late fifth century Athens. "Great, charming, and eloquent," Quintilian called Aristophanes' works, and the 150 extant manuscripts of *Plutus* alone attest his enduring popularity in antiquity. Modern productions, unencumbered by prudery, have demonstrated the vitality and beauty of his comedies, which, though written for a particular time and place, continue to speak to people everywhere.

Bibliography

Croiset, Maurice. *Aristophanes and the Political Parties at Athens.* Translated by James Loeb. London: Macmillan, 1909. As the title suggests, Croiset focuses on the political implications of Aristophanes' plays. He offers a good discussion of the military, political, social, and economic milieu of Aristophanes' Athens.

David, Ephraim. *Aristophanes and Athenian Society of the Early Fourth Century B.C.* Leiden, Netherlands: Brill, 1984. Seeks to fill a gap in studies of Aristophanes, which concentrate on his contributions to Old Comedy and his comments on Athens during the Peloponnesian War. David instead examines the two extant plays dating from the 300's, giving special attention to the economic situation they address.

Murray, Gilbert. *Aristophanes: A Study.* Oxford: Oxford University Press, 1933. Although Murray claims in the preface that the book contains little research, it reflects decades of study. Murray had published a chapter on Aristophanes almost forty years earlier and in the interim had taught and translated the comedies. He concentrates on analyzing the plays and their revelation of Aristophanes' attitudes, but he also gives useful information about dramatic conventions and historical events that influence the plays.

Reckford, Kenneth J. *Aristophanes' Old-and-New Comedy: Six Essays in Perspective*. Chapel Hill: University of North Carolina Press, 1987. Aimed at nonspecialists who want to gain more familiarity with Aristophanes, as well as students and teachers of the playwright. Examines Aristophanes and his world from six perspectives: religious, psychological, theatrical, poetic, political, and literary-historical.

Spatz, Lois. *Aristophanes*. Boston: Twayne Publishers, 1978. After an introductory chapter on the nature of Old Comedy, Spatz presents a roughly chronological discussion of Aristophanes' contributions to this genre, focusing especially on the lesser-known works. Includes a helpful annotated bibliography.

Ussher, Robert Glenn. *Aristophanes*. Oxford: Clarendon Press, 1979. Part of the New Surveys in the Classics series, this work offers an excellent brief introduction to the poet and his plays. Includes a chronology of the surviving comedies and discusses them in terms of structure, theme, character, language, staging, and performance. Contains a good bibliography of primary and secondary sources.

Joseph Rosenblum

ARISTOTLE

Born: 384 B.C.; Stagirus, Chalcidice, Greece
Died: 322 B.C.; Chalcis, Euboea, Greece
Areas of Achievement: Philosophy, ethics, natural history, and science
Contribution: Building on Plato's dialogical approach, Aristotle developed
what is known as the scientific method. In addition, he founded the
Lyceum, the second university-type institution (after Plato's Academy),
which, with its vast collections of biological specimens and manuscripts of
verse and prose, housed the first research library.

Early Life

Aristotle was born in the town of Stagirus, located on the northeast coast
of the Chalcidice Peninsula in Greece, most likely in 384 B.C. His father,
Nicomachus, was a physician and a member of the clan, or guild, of the
Asclepiadae, as had been his ancestors; the family probably had migrated
from Messenia in the eighth or seventh century B.C. Aristotle's mother was
from Chalcis, the place where he sought refuge during the last year of his
life. Both parents died while Aristotle was very young.

Aristotle was adopted and reared by Proxenus, court physician to Amyn-
tas II of Macedonia (an occasional source suggests that Nicomachus also held
this position, but others disagree); it is likely, therefore, that young Aristotle
lived part of his youth at Pella, the royal seat. He may even have learned and
practiced surgery during this time.

Aristotle's early environmental influences helped determine his outlook:
his detached, objective way of looking at a subject, his interest in biological
science, and his universality. In his early life, Aristotle was surrounded by
physicians and princes, not philosophers. When he was eighteen, he was sent
to Athens for training in the best school available, Plato's Academy, where
he would spend the next twenty years. Thus ended the first of the four
phases of Aristotle's life.

Life's Work

Aristotle's career divides itself naturally into three periods: the twenty
(some say nineteen) years at Plato's Academy, from 368 to 348; the thirteen
years of travel, from 348 to 335; and the return to Athens, or the years in the
Lyceum, from 335 to 323.

When young Aristotle arrived at the Academy, Plato was away on a second
journey to Syracuse. When the master returned the following year, however,
Aristotle became his prize student and ardent friend. Although most of
Aristotle's earlier works have been preserved only in fragments, usually in
quotations within works by later scholars of the Peripatetic School, several
are attributed to this period and the one that followed.

As Plato's method was dialogue, Aristotle, like other students at the Academy, began writing in dialogue. Aristotle was influenced by Plato about the time the master altered his own form, moving toward dialogues other than those with Socrates as questioner and main speaker. Aristotle, in turn, made himself the main speaker in his own dialogues.

Some scholars consider *De anima* the best of Aristotle's works from this period. Translated as *On the Soul*, this work treats the soul and immortality, and is imitative of Plato's *Phaedo*, which was written circa 388-366 B.C. (Critic Werner Jaeger believes that each of Aristotle's early dialogues was influenced by a particular Platonic dialogue, that the student was still dependent on the master as far as metaphysics was concerned but independent in the areas of methodology and logic.) Aristotle's *Protrepticus* (*Protreptics*) is named for a term designating a letter written in defense of philosophy; the method employed in this work (questions and answers by teacher and student) is from Plato, but the protreptic form is borrowed from the philosopher Isocrates, who was also at Athens during this time. In the year 348 (or 347), two events influenced Aristotle's future: the death of Plato (and possibly the choice of a new leader of the Academy), which caused Aristotle to leave Athens, and Philip II's destruction of Stagirus, which caused the philosopher to look elsewhere for a new home.

With a fellow Academic, Xenocrates, Aristotle left Athens for Mysia (modern Turkey), accepting the invitation of Hermeias, a former fellow student at the Academy who had risen from slavery to become ruler of Atarneus and Assos. Aristotle presided over his host's small Platonic circle, making of it a school modeled after the Academy. He married Pythias, niece and adopted daughter of Hermeias, after the ruler's death; they had a daughter, also named Pythias. His wife lived until late in Aristotle's so-called second Athenian period. After three years came another move, this time to Mytilene on the nearby island of Lesbos; it is possible that Theophrastus found him a suitable place of residence there. Having begun research in marine biology at Assos, Aristotle continued this work at Mytilene. During these years, he probably wrote *De philosophia* (*On Philosophy*), *Ethica Eudemia* (*Eudemian Ethics*), and early portions of *Physica* (*Physics*), *Metaphysica* (*Metaphysics*), and *Politica* (*Politics*).

In 343, Aristotle accepted Philip's invitation to move to Pella and become tutor to his thirteen-year-old, Alexander (the Great). The tutoring lasted until Alexander became regent in 340. It is uncertain whether Aristotle remained in Pella or moved to Stagira, which had been rebuilt by Philip in honor of Aristotle. With the assassination of Philip in 335 and the resultant accession of Alexander, Aristotle returned to Athens.

This time Aristotle's purpose was not to attend the Academy but to found its greatest competitor. The Lyceum was situated on rented property just outside the city, since an outsider could not own Athenian land. In addition to the marine specimens Aristotle himself had collected, the school housed many more. It is said that Alexander became his old teacher's benefactor, donating eight hundred talents and instructing all under his command throughout the world to preserve for Aristotle any unusual biological specimens. The site was probably to the northeast of the city, where lay a grave sacred to Apollo Lyceius and the Muses, a place where Socrates had enjoyed walking.

In addition to specimens, the Lyceum housed hundreds of manuscripts and numerous maps. The objects in the museum were used to illustrate Aristotle's lectures and discussions. In the mornings, he utilized the peripatetic (walking) method by strolling through the trees, discussing with more advanced students difficult (esoteric) subjects; in the evenings, he would lecture to larger groups on popular (exoteric) subjects. Logic, physics, and metaphysics were discussed; lectures included rhetoric, sophistic, and politics. In turn, Aristotle seems to have prepared and made available two types of notes: preliminary ones, from which he lectured, and more polished treatises, based on the discussions. Many of these have survived as his later, published works. They are in the form of treatises rather than dialogues.

With the death of Alexander and the rise of feelings in Athens against Macedonians, especially those who had been close to Alexander, Aristotle left Athens for his mother's birthplace of Chalcis, where he died a year later of a disease that had afflicted him for some time.

In his later years at Athens, Aristotle is described as well-dressed, enjoying the easy life of self-indulgence; he was bald and thin-legged with small eyes; he spoke with a lisp and had a mocking disposition and a ready wit. After the death of his wife, he lived with a mistress, Herpyllis, in a permanent but nonlegal relationship. Together, they had a son, whom Aristotle named Nicomachus, after his father.

Summary

Aristotle developed through the earliest stage for about seventeen or eighteen years, moving in circles with doctors and princes. He then spent the next twenty years at the Academy with Plato, both imitating and growing away from his great master. Aristotle learned the method of dialogue while he moved toward his own method; he respected and loved Plato but questioned some Platonic thought, such as the theory of forms (dualistic being). During the next thirteen or fourteen years in Asia Minor, he established a smaller academy and did biological research, continuing the writing of dialogues as he had done at Athens but developing his own method of writing treatises. For three years he was tutor to Alexander, becoming lifelong friends with the future conqueror and ruler of the Mediterranean world but failing to impart his own political views to his student.

When Aristotle returned to Athens to found and preside over the Lyceum, he perfected his scientific method of examining specimens and establishing logical systems of substantiation before arriving at tentative conclusions, a method that has continued to modern times. Through his teaching, he influenced a few advanced students and the large public groups who heard his lectures. Through the Peripatetic School, his work continued for centuries and many of his writings were preserved to influence even later centuries. He learned from and utilized the thought of Greek philosophers from Thales to Plato, extending their ideas and synthesizing them. He perfected the method of Socrates (who had intended such an extension himself) by reaching conclusions rather than probing endlessly. Plato and Aristotle have been more influential than all other Western philosophers, advancing Greek philosophy to its greatest height.

Bibliography
Ackrill, J. L. *Aristotle the Philosopher*. New York: Oxford University Press, 1981. According to this interesting guidebook, "What really characterizes Aristotle as a philosopher is not the number and weight of his conclusions (his 'doctrines'), but the number and power and subtlety of his arguments and ideas and analyses."
Aristotle. *The Works of Aristotle Translated into English Under the Editorship of W. D. Ross*. 12 vols. Oxford: Clarendon Press, 1908-1952. This multivolume text of Aristotle's works, translated over many years, is the recommended version for English-reading students.
Brumbaugh, Robert S. *The Philosophers of Greece*. Albany: State University of New York Press, 1981. This introductory volume traces Greek philosophy from Thales to Socrates, Plato, and Aristotle. Focusing on three important regions—Ionia, southern Italy/Sicily, and Athens—Brumbaugh reviews three questions asked by the Greeks: What is being (what is real)? What am I? and Is there one world or many?
Cantor, Norman F., and Peter L. Klein, eds. *Ancient Thought: Plato and Aristotle*. Vol. 1, *Monuments of Western Thought*. Waltham, Mass.: Blaisdell Publishing Co., 1969. In this volume, contrasts between the two great philosophers are noted.
Ferguson, John. *Aristotle*. Boston: Twayne Publishers, 1972. Assisting the general reader in the study of Aristotle's works, this book presents chapters such as "Life and Times," "The Lost Dialogues," "Philosophy of Nature," "Psychology," and "The Legacy of Aristotle." Part of Twayne's World Authors series.
Fuller, B. A. G. *History of Greek Philosophy: Aristotle*. New York: Henry Holt, 1931. Reprint. New York: Greenwood Press, 1968. Chapter 1 tells of Aristotle's life, while chapters 2 through 11 treat the various phases of his philosophical thought from metaphysics to form and matter, including Aristotelian physics, concern for the unmoved mover, logic, ethics, politi-

cal thought, rhetoric, and poetics. The final chapter provides a useful review.

Jaeger, Werner. *Aristotle: Fundamentals of the History of His Development*. Translated by Richard Robinson. Oxford: Clarendon Press, 1934, 1948. A translation from the German, this volume attempts to show that Aristotle's views were not static. Jaeger traces Aristotle's development through three life stages—"The Academy," "Travels," and "Maturity"—and treats both biographical data and the works. Here, Aristotle is approached according to the Aristotelian developmental method. A highly recommended source.

Kiernan, Thomas P., ed. *Aristotle Dictionary: With an Introduction by Theodore E. James*. New York: Philosophical Library, 1962. This useful dictionary of Aristotelian terms is preceded by a 157-page introduction outlining the philosopher's life and works. Well-organized and readable.

McKeon, Richard. *Introduction to Aristotle*. New York: Modern Library, 1947. The general introduction is divided into treatments, including the life and times, scientific method in the philosophy, theoretical and practical sciences, and influence. Works and their respective introductions are treated in sections entitled "Logic," "Physics," "Psychology and Biology," "Ethics," "Politics," and "Rhetoric and Poetics."

Ross, Sir David. *Aristotle*. Rev. ed. New York: Barnes and Noble Books, 1949. Following a very detailed overview of the life and works, this source treats the works under the same headings as does McKeon. Much attention is given to whether a work is authentic, Ross often ruling that it is not. This approach contrasts with that of Jaeger, who tends to regard many works as authentic. Includes detailed data regarding Aristotle's successors, citers, and commentators in the main text and in a chronology at the end.

Wilbur, James B., and Harold J. Allen. *The Worlds of Plato and Aristotle*. American Book Co., 1962. This volume treats the philosophies of the two men "as whole perspectives of life and the world by utilizing the actual writings." Plato is the subject of the first half, Aristotle the second. The general introduction to the latter discusses the two men, then Aristotle's method. Numerous selections from the works are discussed and cited under six topics and many subtopics.

George W. Van Devender

ARISTOXENUS

Born: 375-360 B.C.; Tarentum
Died: Date unknown; probably Athens
Area of Achievement: Music
Contribution: The theoretical writings on music by Aristoxenus established a foundation upon which modern theory is based.

Early Life

Aristoxenus, born in Tarentum, was a Greek philosopher and music theorist who flourished during the fourth century B.C. He received his earliest musical training at the hands of his father, Spintharus, who enjoyed some reputation as a musician. He later studied with Lamprus of Erythrae, of whom little is known. In time Aristoxenus moved to Athens, where he studied with the Pythagorean Xenophilus—important in view of the position he was to take in his theoretical treatises. He also studied at the Lyceum with Aristotle. Because Aristoxenus later competed, although unsuccessfully, with Theophrastus, a colleague, for headship of the Lyceum around 322, it may be assumed that Aristoxenus was a superior student and respected in scholarly circles.

Life's Work

Aristoxenus was apparently a prolific writer, with one source attributing more than 450 works to him, although only a few Aristoxenus fragments have survived. The writings, which cover a variety of topics, including works on music, biography, history, and philosophy, reflect the diversity of his studies. All the fragments are of interest, but the most important of the extant fragments pertain to music: Aristoxenus made his truly original contribution as he challenged the way that theorists, past and contemporary with him, had studied and written about music. So great was his influence that theorists and philosophers on music who followed him were compelled to address his arguments.

Numbering among the music fragments that survive are parts of three books entitled *Harmonika stoicheia* (*The Harmonics*, 1902), the contents of which are believed to have been derived from Aristoxenus' earlier writings on the subject. Much of what is known about ancient Greek theory comes from his writings and the writings of later men, such as Plutarch, Cleonides, and Aristides, who expounded upon Aristoxenus' principles.

In addition to *The Harmonics*, there is a fragment on rhythm, consisting of approximately 250 lines, which was treated by Aristides several centuries later. While Aristoxenus' work reveals a man who could be rather pompous and contentious, his writings are clearly the product of a first-rate mind.

Aristoxenian theory was about melody and articulated a system that addressed the issues of pitch, intervals, genera, systems, modes, and modulation as they applied to melody. The smallest consonant interval recognized in his system was a perfect fourth, which also formed the fixed outer boundary of a four-note unit called a tetrachord. The tetrachord was a kind of building block which, in combination with other tetrachords, formed larger structures. The tetrachord could belong to one of three types, or genera: diatonic, enharmonic, or chromatic. This system was determined according to the placement of the two inner notes that fell within the boundary of the fixed interval of the fourth, which was formed by the two outer notes of the tetrachord. The varied placements of the two inner notes of the tetrachord were known as shadings, or colors. Aristoxenus recognized two alternative positions of the inner notes in the diatonic genus and three in the chromatic, although he accepted that the variety of shadings was theoretically infinite.

The tetrachords could be combined, either sharing a common note and called conjunct or, if a whole step separated the two tetrachords, called disjunct. The combining of the tetrachords produced three important larger theoretical structures known as the Greater Perfect System, the Lesser Perfect System, and the Immutable System. The Greater Perfect System consisted of two pairs of conjunct tetrachords with an added note, or, in modern terminology, it can be seen in its diatonic form as a two-octave scale ranging from A to a′ as seen on the piano keyboard. The range most used for the writing of Greek melodies, however, appears to have been the octave e′ to e, and the Greater Perfect System was probably regarded as a central octave from e′ to e lying within the A to a′ range previously noted and with a conjunct tetrachord on either end and an added note on the bottom. The Greater Perfect System produced seven different species of the octave, since a different intervallic sequence would occur for the octave scale built on each of the seven different pitches represented in the system as it is brought within the central octave of e′ to e.

The Lesser Perfect System consisted of three conjunct tetrachords with an added note that, using the piano keyboard for purposes of illustration, had the range of A to d′. The Lesser Perfect System is believed to have assisted in the function of change, or modulation, from one species to another.

The Immutable System was a combination of the Lesser Perfect and Greater Perfect systems and could be performed at various pitch levels. Such a structure was called a *tonos*. Aristoxenus identified thirteen different *tonoi*. The term is not without ambiguity, and scholars are not exactly sure what the term meant to Aristoxenus. It is, however, generally believed that the octave species and the *tonos* were one and the same during the time of Aristoxenus.

Aristoxenus' approach to the theory of music, conceived around 320, was unique for his time. A superior student of Aristotelian logic who was familiar with the "new math," geometry, Aristoxenus turned both logic and geometry to his advantage as he defined the way subsequent theorists were to look at the discipline of music. His treatise was not simply an exercise in abstract logic. He elevated the musician's "ear" to a level equal with the intellect. By doing so, he recognized the value and importance of the commonsense judgment of the practicing musician.

Aristoxenus' writings clearly challenged both the teachings of Pythagoras, who flourished around 530 B.C. and whose reputation and writings were legendary by the time of Aristoxenus, and those of a group known as the Harmonists.

The supporters of Pythagoras' theories about music were scientists and mathematicians who were not interested in explanations or observations about the interplay of musical elements or about the science of music itself. They believed that understanding numbers was central to understanding the universe, and, therefore, it was quite logical to express musical intervals, of key importance to the Pythagoreans, in terms of mathematical ratios.

The Harmonists, criticized by Aristoxenus for failing to establish a rigorous system, were interested in the practical and empirical aspects of music theory but fell short of articulating an acceptable system. They were preoccupied with the identification and measurement of microintervals, which emphasized the study of certain scales to the exclusion of others.

A key factor in Aristoxenus' approach was his description of sound as a continuum, or line, along which the pitch could come to rest at any point, permitting him the freedom to create intervals of varying sizes without regard to whether the interval could be expressed using rational numbers. While abstract mathematical expression of a musical interval had become most important to the Pythagoreans and the Harmonists, Aristoxenus focused instead on the development of a system which would afford him the freedom and flexibility to identify subtleties of scalar structure. He based his system on judgments made by the ear and then represented it through geometric application.

Summary

Aristoxenus was the earliest writer on music theory known to address practical musical concerns. When he took the unique position that the ear along with the intellect should be used in the study of music, he established a precedent that ultimately altered the course of music theory. In effect, he redefined what music theory was, taking it out of the hands of the scientists and mathematicians and creating a new discipline which focused only on the interrelationship of musical elements. His arguments, which owed much to Aristotelian influence and methodology, enabled him to produce a clearly defined and organized system of music theory.

Bibliography

Aristoxenus. *"The Harmonics" of Aristoxenus*. Translated by Henry Macran. Oxford: Clarendon Press, 1902. The only English translation of Aristoxenus' main work, it also contains some commentary and some biographical material. Invaluable for the reader who is restricted to English.

Barker, Andrew. "*Hoi Kaloumenoi harmonikoi*: The Predecessors of Aristoxenus." *Proceedings of the Cambridge Philological Society* 24 (1978): 1-21. Discusses the issues of Aristoxenian theory as perceived by Aristoxenus with respect to his predecessors. Compares the different positions.

——————. "Music and Perception: A Study in Aristoxenus." *Journal of Hellenic Studies* 98 (1978): 9-16. Examines Aristoxenus' approach to music theory through an attempt to clarify the exact role the ear plays in relation to the intellect and also with respect to mathematics.

Crocker, Richard. "Aristoxenus and Greek Mathematics." In *Aspects of Medieval and Renaissance Music*, edited by Jan LaRue. New York: W. W. Norton and Co., 1966. An excellent article that discusses the key aspects of Aristoxenus' theories on music. Compares and explains Pythagorean arithmetic with Aristoxenus' use of geometric principles to illustrate and explain his new theories on music.

Henderson, Isobel. "Ancient Greek Music." In *The New Oxford History of Music*. Vol. 1, *Ancient and Oriental Music*, edited by Egon Wellesz. London: Oxford University Press, 1957. An excellent study of ancient Greek music with considerable treatment of Aristoxenus. There is a brief discussion of the Harmonists and the Pythagoreans. The history, issues, and elements of Greek music are all discussed.

Levin, Flora. "Synesis in Aristoxenian Theory." *American Philological Transactions* 103 (1972): 211-234. Asserts that Aristoxenus established a new science that used only materials that belonged to music. Makes the case that Aristoxenus' system goes beyond cold facts and dry rules in an attempt to identify what is music.

Lippman, Edward. *Musical Thought in Ancient Greece*. New York: Columbia University Press, 1964. It is not necessary to be a practicing musician or theorist to appreciate or understand this book. There is an excellent treatment of Greek ethics, philosophy, and aesthetics of music.

Rowell, Lewis. "Aristoxenus on Rhythm." *Journal of Music Theory* 23 (Spring, 1979): 63-79. Provides a translation of Aristoxenus' fragment on rhythm. Rowell identifies the fragment as being in an Aristotelian format and discusses Aristoxenus' concept of rhythm.

Winnington-Ingram, R. P. "Aristoxenus." In *New Grove Dictionary of Music and Musicians*, edited by Stanley Sadie, vol. 1. 6th ed. New York: Macmillan, 1980. The article contains important biographical material. The author discusses the philosophical differences between Aristoxenus and the Pythagoreans. He also provides a summary of Aristoxenus' contribution to theory. There is a short but important bibliography at the end of the article.

Michael Hernon

ARNOLD OF VILLANOVA

Born: c. 1239; Valencia, Spain? or Provence region, France?
Died: 1311; Genoa, Italy
Areas of Achievement: Medicine and religion
Contribution: The first great figure of European medicine, physician to kings and popes, Arnold joined Arabic theory to European empiricism. His more than seventy scientific works and translations made him an influential medical theorist down past the sixteenth century, just as his radical theology and stormy life made him lastingly controversial.

Early Life

France, Italy, and Spain have claimed Arnold as a native son. "Villanova" may derive from Villeneuve-les-Vence, or else Villeneuve-Loubet, in Provence, where he had relatives. By one theory, his family were Jews who, on converting to Christianity, moved to Catalonia and then Valencia. Arnold himself said that he was "born of the soil, lowly and obscure" and called himself "an unlearned country-fellow." Contemporaries called him a Catalan, which he accepted, and his early editors used that as an alternate surname. The only language in which he wrote, besides Latin, was Catalan. The kingdom of Valencia, just conquered from the Muslims by Catalonia-Aragon, always claimed Arnold for its own. The great fourteenth century Valencian writer Francesc Eiximenis took it as common knowledge, within a lifetime of Arnold's death, that the latter was a native of Valencia. The settlers in Valencia, and even those in Murcia to its south, were called "true Catalans" by the contemporary memoirist Ramón Muntaner; famous medieval Valencians such as Vicent Ferrer and the Borgia popes, as well as the Majorcan Anselm Turmeda, were also called Catalans. Thus, Arnold was probably born in Valencia, after the fall of its capital in 1238. Arnold had properties in Valencia and, more significant, was ordained as a cleric in minor orders in the Valencian diocese; his daughter Maria became a nun at Valencia city in 1291.

In 1982, John Benton published a note from a medieval manuscript archived in Pasadena, California, indicating that Arnold was born at Villanueva de Jilóca near Huesca in Aragon and that some of his relatives still lived there in the mid-fourteenth century. Benton suggested that Arnold learned his Arabic from the conquered Muslims there and was an Aragonese by early training. There is no evidence, however, that Arnold knew any Aragonese, while he is a major figure in Catalan literature. Moreover, it is unlikely that Aragon's acculturated Muslim farming communities, with their Arabic dialect, were the source of his classical Arabic and his knowledge of its literature. Valencia was an advanced Islamic society, barely come under colonial rule, with its Muslim aristocracy, savants, and schools intact during the long decades of Arnold's education. As a Valencian, Arnold's environment would have been multiethnic, among affluent Muslim and Jewish communities in a land of international ports, lush farmlands, and dangerous revolts on the part of the Muslim majority—a far cry from the bleak and rocky uplands of Aragon.

Life's Work

Arnold of Villanova (Arnau de Vilanova in his native Catalan) was graduated around 1260 from the celebrated medical university in Montpellier, then part of the wider realms of Aragon-Catalonia. He may have done postdoctoral work at Naples under the physician Giovanni de Casamicciola. Presumably during his Montpellier sojourn, he married Agnès Blasi of that city, herself of a lineage of physicians. In the early 1280's, he studied Hebrew and the Talmud under the Arabist-Hebraist Ramón Martí at the Dominican school in Barcelona. Famous by 1281, Arnold became the main physician to King Peter III of Aragon-Catalonia, receiving the huge stipend of two thousand Barcelonan sous on condition of living in Barcelona near the court (another indication that his home was not Catalonia but Valencia). Other gifts included the castle of Ollers. Arnold continued to enjoy royal support under Peter's successors, Alfonso III (reigned 1285-1291) and James II (reigned 1291-1327), and he was released to reside in Valencia, which he did from 1286 to 1289.

Called to teach at Montpellier for a decade, Arnold began to publish apocalyptic religious works, prophesying the coming of Antichrist in 1345 (later revised to 1368) and demanding moral reform. When James II sent the respected doctor on a diplomatic mission to Philip IV of France, Arnold spread his radical theology so passionately that the theologians of the University of Paris had him tried and condemned in 1299. Pope Boniface VIII and King Philip secured his release. Grateful for Arnold's cure of his renal affliction, the pope lent him the castle of Scorcola near Anagni as a retreat in which to study and write. Arnold returned to his post with the royal family in 1302. He soon became embroiled in a theological battle with the Dominicans of Gerona and Castellón de Ampurias, and he disputed before the archbishop at Lérida and the king at Barcelona. At Valencia, his polemics prompted the Inquisition to excommunicate him. His patient and protector Boniface VIII died in 1303, but the new pope (Benedict XI, whom Arnold treated for gallstones) shielded him. Further religious polemic got Arnold imprisoned briefly at Perugia in Italy. Under the protection of Frederick III of Sicily, however, he continued his religious writings at Messina.

In 1305, Arnold returned to Barcelona to exhort James II to crusade against Islamic Almería. Continuing to write on medical and religious topics, and by now the European leader of the visionary evangelical movement called the Spirituals, Arnold went to Narbonne and Marseilles; in 1308, he was in Messina, where he interpreted an obsessive dream for King Frederick. In 1309, he was at the court of his friend and patient Pope Clement V in Avignon; in 1310, he was back with Frederick III briefly and in the siege of Almería and then at Messina again. Journeying by sea to Avignon, he died near Genoa and was buried there in 1311. During all these travels, he had enthusiastically propagated the astrological, alchemical, and occult themes then popular in Islam. His method of exegesis by symbolic letters, borrowed from the Jewish Cabalists, disturbed some contemporaries. Suspected of converting to Judaism, he was in reality an anti-Judaic proselytizer. In 1316, the Inquisition at Tarragona condemned a number of his religious approaches. At the same time, he was hailed internationally as a great physician.

In later medieval Mediterranean Europe (as distinguished from the inland and northern regions), a physician was a prestigious personage, expected to be a general savant, a repository of philosophical and even theological ancient knowledge, and also a man active in public affairs. He was a welcome decoration in the courts of the powerful. This model echoes the Islamic *hakim*, extending to the Jews with Arabist training who functioned at the court of the kings of Aragon-Catalonia. Training of physicians in Europe, though often still accomplished through private apprenticeship, had become a university function, so that the university title "doctor" and the renown of the universities themselves were reflecting more glory on the profession. Seen in this light, Arnold's almost comic embroilment in the Spirituals' cause makes more sense; it was then the premier public polemic in Europe. Arnold's diplomatic projects are also thus explained. He never lost sight, however, of his own priorities: He was a physician, in an era of revolutionary advances in surgery, anatomy, and the professionalization of medical work.

Arnold's medical theory has been summed up as "Galen Arabicized." He not only translated Arabic medical works into Latin, including those of the Valencian Abu Salt, but also revered the classic Muslim physicians and integrated their findings with Western medical knowledge and practice. His *Aphorismi de gradibus* (aphorisms on the degrees), done in the late 1290's, revolutionized the study of pharmacology with its theory of compound medicines and its application of mathematics. It organized traditional knowledge into one unified field, while rejecting previous forms of classification. Arnold composed some seventy medical books and treatises in Latin, over a wide range of topics. His work on preventive medicine and hygiene, *Regimen sanitatis* (1307; management of health), enjoyed great popular success; the Queen of Aragon ordered a version translated into Romance for wider diffusion, and a Hebrew version appeared. In all, Arnold wrote eleven such books. He also wrote a book titled *De conservatione juventutis et retardatione senectutis* (1290; *The Conservation of Youth and Defense of Age*, 1544). Other works specialized in bleeding, fevers, poisons, sexual intercourse, conception, sterility, dreams, food for the sick, eye troubles, epilepsy, wines, waters, antidotes, leprosy and contagious diseases, the heart, meat-eating, and medical theory. He discoursed on the value of bathing, kinds of baths, and their effects. He also took up questions on surgery, an art being revolutionized by the treatise of Abulcassis (al-Zahrawi) that he had translated and by pioneering theories on disease as anatomically focused.

The historian of Spanish medieval medicine Luis García Ballester sees Arnold as a frontier phenomenon, a fusion of Arabic, Jewish, and European medical traditions which flowered until supplanted by the Scholastic model of the Italians. Arnold was an academician, and his talent was for joining practice to theory. A catalog of his library survives, affording insights into his intellectual tastes. He was not interested, for example, in Islamic theology. He collected not only Arabic books but also works in Greek, a language he learned only late in life.

Summary

Arnold was the greatest physician in the West since ancient Rome. Physician and spiritual adviser to four kings, physician to three popes, and for a decade the most celebrated teacher at Europe's greatest medical university, Montpellier, Arnold was a tireless author and translator of medical works. More than any medieval figure, he represents the juncture of Arabic with European medicine, theory with practice. At the same time, he was a major figure in public affairs, from diplomatic missions to crusade propaganda; he became the leader of the apocalyptic Spirituals movement then agitating Europe. His writings show his contribution to the evolution of the Catalan language and literature. He had close associations with the Jewish community in southern France, partly to borrow cabalistic knowledge and partly with proselytizing intent. His incessant travel, and the explosive energies visible both in his production of books and in the disputations which made him leader of the Spirituals (and landed him in prison several times), made him one of the best-known public men of his age.

Bibliography

Arnold of Villanova. *Arnaldi de Villanova: Opera Medica Omnia*. Vols. 2 and 16. Edited with introductions by Michael R. McVaugh. Granada, Spain: Seminarium Historiae Medicae Granatensis, 1975. Despite the work's Latin title and edited text, and its Spanish printer, the introductions to these volumes are in English, by the major authority on Arnold. The second volume, *Aphorismi de gradibus*, has 143 pages in English on Arnold's contribution to medieval pharmacology.

Benton, John F. "The Birthplace of Arnau de Vilanova: A Case for Villanueva de Jilóca near Daroca." In *Viator: Medieval and Renaissance Studies*, vol. 13. Berkeley: University of California Press, 1982. The most exciting contribution to the study of Arnold's early years, though controversial in its interpretation. Contains additional information on his career and a bibliography in notes.

Burns, Robert I. "The Medieval Crossbow as Surgical Instrument: An Illustrated Case History." *Bulletin of the New York Academy of Medicine* 48 (September, 1972): 983-989. Reprinted as chapter 7 of Burns's *Moors and Crusaders in Mediterranean Spain* (London: Variorum, 1978). Six thirteenth century panels illustrate a surgical procedure, including the preparation of the patient beforehand by assistants and the formal dress of physicians. The case is explained from contemporary surgical manuals, with relevant bibliography. The site was Elche in the Kingdom of Valencia; the time was Arnold's young manhood.

McVaugh, Michael R. "Quantified Medical Theory and Practice at Fourteenth-Century Montpellier." *Bulletin of the History of Medicine* 43 (September/October, 1969): 397-413. An early presentation of themes expanded by McVaugh in his later introduction to Arnold's works (see above) on mathematical formulas applied to compound medicines.

Siraisi, Nancy G. *Taddeo Alderotti and His Pupils: Two Generations of Italian Medical Learning*. Princeton, N.J.: Princeton University Press, 1981. Though it does not deal with Arnold, this work gives the best introduction in English to the new medicine of the thirteenth century, a panoramic and profound examination of a Mediterranean region then vying with Arnold's Montpellier and Catalonia. Its extensive bibliography includes all the important background books and articles.

Robert I. Burns

ARNOLFO DI CAMBIO

Born: c. 1245; Colle di Val d'Elsa, Italy
Died: Between 1302 and 1310; Florence, Italy
Areas of Achievement: Art and architecture
Contribution: As chief architect of Florence during the end of the thirteenth century, Arnolfo directed the construction of some of Florence's principal monuments and brought the Italian classical tradition together with elements of the French Gothic.

Early Life

Little is known of Arnolfo di Cambio's early years. From 1266 to 1268, Arnolfo worked as chief assistant to Nicola Pisano, Italy's first great sculptor; together they created the pulpit in the cathedral in Siena, Italy. Arnolfo may also have worked with Pisano at about the same time on the tomb of Saint Dominic in the Church of San Domenico in Bologna. Around 1272, Arnolfo constructed the monument to Cardinal Annibaldi in the Church of San Giovanni Laterano of Rome. This work may have been commissioned by Emperor Charles I of Anjou, who became Arnolfo's patron in 1271, when the sculptor went to Florence after leaving Pisano's shop. The monument to Annibaldi reflects the characteristics of Arnolfo's early work, with graceful yet stiff drapery and simple treatment of the facial features—expressing the restraint of classical Roman sculpture, which was Arnolfo's model.

Arnolfo continued to distinguish himself as a sculptor of funerary monuments during this first stage of his artistic career. Two of Arnolfo's notable works of this period are the monument to Cardinal Guillaume de Braye in San Domenico in Orvieto (1282) and the ciborium (an ornamental altar canopy) in San Paolo Fuori le Mura in Rome (1285). The monument to Cardinal de Braye combines the energetic Gothic figures of Saint Peter and Saint Dominic with a restrained, classical rendering of the Virgin as an empress holding her son. The strong horizontal lines, maintained by the ornamentation of the pedestal and sarcophagus, temper the vertical quality of the Gothic design. Similar effects are found in the ciborium in San Paolo Fuori le Mura. The figures of the saints reflect the restrained, sober classicism of early Christian work. Moreover, the Gothic design is consistently controlled: The trilobed arches are gently rounded, conveying spaciousness rather than strong upward movement; the pediment gables and pinnacles are countered with strong horizontal lines accented by the decorative use of nearly black marble. These two characteristics of Arnolfo's sculptures—the serene, controlled spirit of sculptured portraits and the de-emphasis of vertical movement—are also trademarks of Arnolfo's architectural work.

Life's Work

Arnolfo's classicism, distinctive in his sculptures in Rome, is most evident in the Tuscan capital of Florence, where he served as the city's *capomaestro*, or chief architect, probably beginning in 1284. In many respects, Tuscany was based on classical precedent, and Florence, of all Tuscan cities, took this precedent most seriously, modeling its own republican government after the Roman Republic. Giovanni Villani, in 1338, referred to Florence as "the daughter and creature of Rome." As *capomaestro* of Florence, Arnolfo was charged with extensive city planning, culminating in the reconstruction for which Florence has been famous ever since. Pressured by the city's growth (its population had surpassed fifty thousand by the end of the thirteenth century) and strengthened by the success of the city's banking and wool industry, the guilds and prominent families of Florence were eager to have the city stabilized through comprehensive city planning. Arnolfo directed a building campaign for a new set of city walls (it would be the third set, the last having been built in 1170). These walls would draw into the city's circumference the enclaves, at opposite edges of the city, of the two powerful brotherhoods, the Dominicans and the Franciscans, as well as the neighborhoods along the banks of the south side of the Arno River. The building campaign also called for a new cathedral and a new town hall, the Palazzo Vecchio. In addition, the communal granary, also a monument to the city's guilds, was slated for renovation.

These three focal points of the new city—cathedral, town hall, and guild hall—were to be united by the widening of the straight thoroughfare, Via Calzaioli. Thus public monuments would dominate over private ones, and the republic of Florence would become a more vivid expression of classical ideals, including Aristotle's notion that city walls add strength and beauty and the Roman contention that wide, straight streets (*pulchrae, amplae, et rectae*) contribute health, convenience, and beauty to a city. Arnolfo was designer and director of all these projects, although none was completed during his lifetime. In addition to these public works, Arnolfo started restorations of the Franciscan abbey church known as the Badia and designed the Franciscan Church of Santa Croce, one of the most famous monuments of Florence. Arnolfo was probably also responsible for refacing the baptistry, situated a few yards west of the new cathedral.

By the time Arnolfo began the work of enlarging Florence and constructing its major religious and secular buildings, the city had already established an architectural tone that was consistent with Arnolfo's own tastes. Italian Gothic was a combination of classical and French Gothic influences, with the classical dominating. This classical influence is most dramatically represented in the Italian Romanesque style found in the Benedictine Abbey Church of San Miniato al Monte, located on a hill across the Arno from the site of Santa Croce. San Miniato al Monte's round arches supported by columns and its triangular pediment are imitative of classical architecture. The stark contrast between the white and dark green marble used as paneling for the church's façade is pure Romanesque, having no parallel in antiquity, but the classical proportions emphasized by the façade's geometric patterns are strong echoes of classical forms, whose gentle curves and strong horizontal lines are the antithesis of the Gothic style. The Church of San Miniato al Monte was begun in 1013, but the Florentines of the thirteenth century regarded it as far older than it was, a survival from Roman antiquity. For an architect of Arnolfo's time, influenced by the attraction to classical forms that was to become a trademark of the Renaissance, this accessible "ancient" model could not be ignored.

The Church of Santa Maria Novella, begun a generation before Arnolfo became *capomaestro* of Florence, offered a precedent of compromises between these Italian classical ideals and the French Gothic tradition so popular throughout the Middle Ages. The ceiling of the church is a stone vault instead of the open timbered roof of other Tuscan churches, such as San Miniato al Monte. The usual effect of this vaulting is a feeling of vertical thrust, but in this Tuscan rendering the vertical thrust is minimized by many elements. The spacing of the interior columns along the nave of the church creates square nave bays and proportionally longer aisle bays than are found in Gothic churches. The heights of the arcade and clerestory are nearly equal, creating the illusion that the roof is shorter than it is. In addition, the vaults and arches are made from *pietra serena*, a dark gray stone of Tuscany, and stand outlined against the plaster walls. The effect of these features is an interior that feels spacious, light, and broad, unlike a narrow and vertical Gothic interior. In these respects, the Church of Santa Maria Novella is the structural predecessor to Arnolfo's two great churches, Santa Croce and Florence's cathedral, Santa Maria del Fiore.

Arnolfo designed Santa Croce closely after Romanesque models. The ceiling of Santa Croce takes after San Miniato al Monte rather than Santa Maria Novella; the church has an open-trussed, wooden roof rather than stone vaulting. The lighter weight ceiling allows for lighter supporting columns, which give the church's nave its Tuscan openness. Gothic influence, however softened, is evident not only in its pointed arches but also in its long, rather narrow aisle bays and nave bays wider than they are long.

The Cathedral of Santa Maria del Fiore is perhaps Arnolfo's chief achievement. The most striking monument of Florence, it brings together the dominant elements of Tuscan art. Santa Maria del Fiore is the architectural culmination of an age, integrating native Tuscan qualities with the Italian Romanesque and the French Gothic. In order to appreciate Arnolfo's design, however, one must ignore the alterations that were made by later designers who finished the cathedral complex. Giotto (c. 1266-1337), who succeeded Arnolfo as *capomaestro*, did not attempt working on the church proper but designed and began construction of the bell tower. Francesco Talenti, a subsequent *capomaestro*, altered the church's façade and enlarged the floor space, extending the nave and broadening the transepts and chancel. Although they violated the original scale of the building, Talenti's changes otherwise respected Arnolfo's design. Arnolfo's original plan survives in manuscript, and his design for the façade is depicted in a thirteenth century painting by Bernardino Poccetti.

The Tuscan tradition is evident in Santa Maria del Fiore's interior, which is similar to the interior of Santa Croce and Santa Maria Novella in its openness and classical pilasters. Like Santa Croce, it has horizontal lines coursing the interior perimeter above the aisle arches. The cathedral's Gothic vaulted ceiling, like that of Santa Maria Novella, is lightened through the use of *pietra serena* and plaster. The colored marble outlining geometric patterns on the exterior is an Italian Romanesque feature. In the interior, the octagonal opening at the crossing mirrors the octagonal form of the baptistry. It is this octagon that is the most distinguishing feature of the cathedral, giving shape to the open center of the interior. The dome above it, spanning the complete width of the nave, creates a spaciousness unmatched by other Italian churches of the period. Arnolfo, no doubt responding to pressure from Florentine patrons to outdo rivaling cathedrals in Pisa and Siena, was intent on the octagonal form, but such a design required very sophisticated engineering. This problem would not be solved until more than one hundred years later, when Filippo Brunelleschi (1377-1446) came up with a plan that enabled the dome to be built. With its completion, Arnolfo's intention was realized: The French Gothic style that was so influential in the late Middle Ages informs and gives grace to this cathedral, which nevertheless leaves as its dominant impression a light spaciousness, the quality that was native to the architecture of Arnolfo's Italian heritage.

Summary

In his time, Arnolfo di Cambio's talents were well-recognized. The Florentines, in 1300, declared him officially exempt from tax obligations because he was the best known and most highly respected architect of church buildings. As sculptor, architect, and city planner, he can also be appreciated for his range of talents, a sort of precursor of the ideal of the Renaissance man.

Arnolfo's legacy as a sculptor is his creation of a blend of classical and contemporary Italian forms. His subdued, classical draperies and his warmly human, yet austere, portraits look forward to the human figures painted by Giotto (many of which appear as frescoes in Arnolfo's Church of Santa Croce). Arnolfo's funerary monuments, particularly the monuments to Cardinal Annibaldi in Rome and to Cardinal de Braye in Orvieto, became the principal models of Gothic funerary art.

Arnolfo's distinctive architecture, however, became his most wide-ranging contribution. The architecture of Italy's Renaissance, which had Florence as its capital, generally carries forward the synthesis of styles that Arnolfo realized. Evidence of this is seen most notably in Brunelleschi's Florentine churches, Santo Spirito and San Lorenzo. Though Brunelleschi, as a Renaissance architect, was concerned with consistent mathematic proportions in his buildings to an extent not realized in Arnolfo's age, he nevertheless maintains the same uniquely Italian balance of the Romanesque, Tuscan, and Gothic styles that Arnolfo first mastered. Even Brunelleschi's balanced proportions can be seen foreshadowed in the evenly radiating aisles of the broad central octagon at the center of Florence's cathedral.

Creator of a native art, like Dante writing in the vernacular and Giotto expressing biblical themes in classically influenced Italian portraits, Arnolfo strengthened and gave longevity to the Italian style in art.

Bibliography

Kostoff, Spiro. *A History of Architecture: Settings and Rituals*. New York: Oxford University Press, 1985. An extremely accurate and thorough source of information about the architectural precedents to Arnolfo and Arnolfo's achievement. Two chapters contain the information on Arnolfo: "The Urbanization of Europe: 1100-1300" and "Edges of Medievalism." Useful photographs, drawings, and maps pertaining to Arnolfo's buildings in Florence. Scholarly, but readable. Contains a glossary and an index. An unannotated bibliography is included at the end of every chapter.

Murray, Peter. *The Architecture of the Italian Renaissance*. New York: Schocken Books, 1986. Includes an excellent, clear account of Romanesque and Gothic influences in Tuscany before and during Arnolfo's time. Discusses Arnolfo's achievement, with more accurate information than is available in older accounts. Also includes drawings and photographs of Arnolfo's architectural work, a carefully annotated bibliography, and an index.

Ruggiers, Paul G. *Florence in the Age of Dante*. Norman: University of Oklahoma Press, 1964. The product of a Fulbright, this work includes a wealth of background information about medieval Italy, including many references to Arnolfo's activities. Concerned with history rather than art criticism, Ruggiers places Arnolfo in context. Extremely readable. Scholarship on Arnolfo's work and life has changed significantly since the publication of this book, making this study somewhat outdated. Indexed, with an unannotated bibliography organized by topic.

Vasari, Giorgio. *Lives of Painters, Sculptors, and Architects*. London: Everyman, 1980. A classic biography of Italian artists by a Renaissance Italian painter, written more than two hundred years after Arnolfo's death. Though riddled with inaccuracies (Vasari indiscriminately mixed legend with history), it is still valuable as an appreciation of the genius of Arnolfo from an artist's point of view. Treats Arnolfo as Arnolfo di Lapo, a composite figure that includes Arnolfo di Cambio. If not a consistently reliable account, it nevertheless shows how Arnolfo was viewed until the twentieth century.

Dennis C. Chowenhill

ARYABHATA

Born: A.D. 475 or 476; Kusumapura, India
Died: c. A.D. 550; place unknown
Areas of Achievement: Mathematics and astronomy
Contribution: Aryabhata, the first great Hindu mathematician-astronomer,
in 499 wrote *The Aryabhatiya*, which describes the axial rotation of Earth
and presents many innovative rules of arithmetic and planar and spherical
trigonometry, and solutions to quadratic equations.

Early Life

Aryabhata was born in 475 or 476 at Kusumapura, also known as the City
of Flowers, a small town on the Jumna River near its confluence with the
Ganges River. Aryabhata's hometown was not far from Pataliputra (now
called Patna). Parts of Pataliputra, including Aśoka the Great's ancient royal
palace, had been falling into ruins since Candra Gupta II moved the imperial
seat from there some seventy-five years before. Pataliputra, a major center
of astrology, mythology, and religion, presented a special problem for the scientist. Buddha, tradition held, crossed the Ganges there and prophesied the
future greatness of the city, which supposedly had been founded by Putraka,
knight of the magic cup, staff, and slippers, and his princess, Patali. In developing his scientific theories, Aryabhata had to contend with these mythological beliefs and popularly held ideas that Earth was flat and that certain heavenly bodies, called *asuras*, were nonluminous, invisible, and demoniac.
Although Aryabhata rejected these ideas, astrologers stubbornly clung to
them for centuries after his death. It is ironic that Aryabhata lived in
Pataliputra and not six hundred miles away in Ujjain in Central India, where
science and astronomy, and not religion and astrology, prevailed: Aryabhata's achievements outshone those of any of the scientists at Ujjain at that
time and he would later receive recognition as the first of the great Hindu
mathematician-astronomers.

Aryabhata, despite the geographic distance from the scientists at Ujjain,
was clearly influenced by their style of writing. He, like they, wrote in verse
and often presented a mathematical problem in the form of a story, suitable for reading at social occasions. Indeed, at the time, intellectuals would
publicly challenge one another to create and solve difficult mathematical
problems. Aryabhata also followed the common practice of writing in two
different scientific realms. Like many other important Hindu scientists, including the later Brahmagupta (c. 598-c. 660) and Bhāskara (1115-1185), Aryabhata explored both mathematics and astronomy; they all considered
themselves primarily astronomers and believed that mathematics was useful
only in solving astronomical questions. Also like the other Hindu writers,
Aryabhata carefully studied the works of his predecessors, borrowing and

building on their ideas in his writings. Aryabhata was particularly interested in the work of the Greek arithmetician Diophantus on indeterminate equations and the ancient Hindu astronomer Parasara's studies of comets and planetary motion.

Life's Work

The culmination of Aryabhata's studies and struggles against myth was his masterwork, the *Aryabhathiya* (*The Aryabhatiya*, 1927), which he wrote, according to his own account, in 499. Three-quarters of *The Aryabhatiya* deals with astronomy and spherical trigonometry. The remainder is composed of thirty-three rules in arithmetic, algebra, and plane trigonometry, including quadratic equations, the sums of powers of the first n natural numbers, and a table of sines. This work represented what was then currently known, combined with his own theories.

Aryabhata's work in astronomy was very advanced for his time. He was the first Hindu known to have described Earth as a sphere, calculating the diameter at 1,050 *yojana*, or, at 7.6 miles per *yojana*, equal to 7,980 miles. This idea greatly troubled the Hindu priests, who stubbornly held to the traditional views of Earth presented in the Vedas and the Puranas. Earth, according to the Vedas, was flat and circular, with the heavens above, through which the moon, sun, and stars moved, with a middle air containing clouds, birds, and demigods between. The Puranas compared Earth's shape to that of the back of a turtle: round on the top and flat on the bottom, with the rounded part projecting above a surrounding body of water.

Aryabhata, with his naked eye, no doubt, carefully observed and diligently recorded the motion of the planets and stars, describing their orbits as circular or elliptical epicycles, noting the apsides and nodes. Predating Nicolaus Copernicus by a millennium, Aryabhata theorized that the apparent movement of these heavenly bodies was caused by the daily rotation of Earth about its axis and Earth's rotation around the sun. He understood how the tilt of Earth as it orbited the sun caused equinoxes and solstices.

Aryabhata explained that Earth was spun by a surrounding spherical sac of "aerial fluid" with a circumference of 25,790 miles. These were theories that would be greatly studied, and mostly rejected, by later Hindu astronomers, particularly Brahmagupta, who questioned the theory of an aerial fluid and wondered why lofty objects did not fall, if Aryabhata was indeed correct.

Aryabhata established a sect of astronomy that based its observations on the theory that the astronomical day began at sunrise at Lanka (Ceylon), through which passed both the Hindu meridian and the equator. Other sects established the beginning of the astronomical day at noon or midnight at Lanka and arrived at different results.

Although Aryabhata used mathematics as only a tool to understand astronomy, some of his mathematical theories are of interest and importance.

The first Hindu known to have studied algebra, Aryabhata gives the sum of the first, second, and third powers of the first n natural numbers, the solution integers of certain indeterminate equations of the first degree, and the general solution of a quadratic equation.

In *The Aryabhatiya*, Aryabhata presents a table of sines of angles for use in astronomy. In order to do so, Aryabhata had to make considerable advances over the trigonometry of Hipparchus and Ptolemy. These two scholars, for example, in studying an angle of 60° formed by two rays emanating from the center of a circle, had studied the chord and arc subtended by the angle. One of Aryabhata's major advances was to consider instead half of the length of the chord, associated with half of the angle, in this case 30°. Thus, he built the right triangle that forms the basis of all modern trigonometric functions. Aryabhata found that the half-chord (which he called by the Hindu word *jiva*) of 30° was 1710'. Aryabhata calculated a number of *jiva*, which are really sines, for different angles in the first quadrant, at intervals of 3.75°; his results appear in a table in *The Aryabhatiya*. To calculate his values, Aryabhata used a formula probably equivalent to:

$$\sin(n + 1)a - \sin na = \sin na - \sin(n - 1)a - \sin na/\sin a$$

a formula, correct except for the last term, which he may have taken from the *Surya Siddhanta* (400), an anonymous Hindu work on astronomy from the fifth century.

Aryabhata also presented ideas that contributed to the solving of indeterminate equations such as an equation presented by Diophantus, $ax \pm by = c$, where a, b, and c are constant integers. This work was later built on by Brahmagupta. Aryabhata also solved the divisor problem of $x = q_1 t_1 = q_2 t_2 + r_2$, using the continued fraction method. He was interested in the latter equation for its usefulness, among other things, in studying the Hindu calendar year, which he calculated to be equal to 365 days.

Aryabhata also put forth the basic but extremely useful tool of inversion. Stated simply, inversion meant finding the solution by converting addition to subtraction and multiplication to division, as extraction of the square root becomes squaring, and vice versa. In one famous problem he asks (in the typical style of the time) a beautiful maiden with "beaming eyes" to calculate according to the method of inversion the number which, when multiplied by 3, increased by ¾ of the product, divided by 7, diminished by ⅓ of the quotient, multiplied by itself, diminished by 52, then, following the extraction of its square root, increased by 8, and finally divided by 10, gives the number 2. The method of inversion calls for starting with the number 2 and working backward, inverting each operation, to reach the answer, 28.

Aryabhata also devised formulas for extracting square roots and cube roots. His formulas—$(a + b)^2 = a^2 + 2ab + b^2$ and $(a + b)^3 = a^3 + 3a^2 b$

$+ 3ab^2 + b^3$—involved first dividing a number into periods of two and three digits, indicating that Aryabhata probably knew of the principle of number positions and may have known about zero. The ideas of number position and zero, perhaps for the first time in Hindu mathematics, were explicitly presented in the improved number system of Bhāskara I, one of the pupils whom Aryabhata taught following the completion of *The Aryabhatiya*. (Bhāskara I must be differentiated from later scholars of the same name.)

Aside from teaching, Aryabhata continued to write on mathematics after completing his masterwork, *The Aryabhatiya*. He completed a treatise in which he expounded the *arddharatrika* system, but the work has been lost. Around 530, Aryabhata calculated an extremely accurate value for π (62,832/20,000 or 3.1416), which he may have discovered through examination of a regular polygon of 384 sides. Although this approximation for π was more accurate than any figure previously given by the Babylonians, the Egyptians, or Archimedes (207-212 B.C.), neither Aryabhata nor any other Hindu mathematician before the twelfth century used it. They preferred to use the traditional but less accurate values of $22/7$, $\sqrt{10}$, $16/9$, or simply 3.

Summary

Aryabhata's work is an odd mixture of the correct and mistaken. He correctly calculated the formula for the area of an isosceles triangle, which is one half of the base multiplied by the height. Yet, he badly botched the formula for the volume of a sphere. His formula, $\pi^{3/2}r^3$, would make π equal to 16/9, or 1.78, a far less accurate figure than the 3.1416 which he had elsewhere calculated. This error was possibly derived from the $(16/9)^2$ or 3.16 given by Ahmes (c. 1550 B.C.). Aryabhata also erred with the formula for the volume of a pyramid, stating that it was equal to half of the product of the base and the altitude.

Aryabhata correctly stated that the moon and the primary planets did not shine their own light but rather reflected that of the sun. He used this knowledge to determine what caused eclipses. He incorrectly thought, however, that the stars also reflected the light of the sun. He understood that Earth rotated, yet he believed that the stars, despite their complex orbits, were in fixed places in the heavens. Any unbiased consideration of the sum of his work must consider his mistakes along with his achievements.

Despite the importance of Aryabhata's achievements, his work did not readily reach the scientific center of Ujjain. When it finally did reach Ujjain, it greatly interested Brahmagupta, Bhaskara, and other scholars, who in particular studied Aryabhata's work on indeterminate equations and the structure of the solar system. One indication of the high regard in which *The Aryabhatiya* was held by the Hindus is that at least twelve commentators wrote on it. Aryabhata's work also reached the Arabs, and it was translated around 800 under the title *Zij al-Arjabhar*, Arjabhar being the Arabic translation of Aryabhata. This translation appeared two or three decades after Brahmagupta's masterwork, the *Brahma sphuṭa siddhānta* (c. 628), had been translated into Arabic. Together, these two books, by the first two great Hindu astronomer-mathematicians, greatly influenced the development of nascent Arabian mathematics.

Bibliography

Cajori, Florian. *A History of Mathematics*. London: Macmillan, 1919, 2d ed. 1924. A comprehensive history of mathematics, with a particular emphasis on the formulas used by various mathematicians. Cajori gives information on Aryabhata's work on inversion, extraction of square and cube roots, indeterminate equations, and π.

Dube, Bechan. *Geographical Concepts in Ancient India*. Varanasi, India: National Geographic Society of India, 1967. This work expounds ideas of Hindu scientists ranging from the layout of houses and the shape of Earth to the structure of the universe. It also includes information on Aryabhata's concept of the calendar.

Eves, Howard. *An Introduction to the History of Mathematics*. New York: Holt, Rinehart and Winston, 1964, 3d ed. 1969. Textbook that covers the history of mathematics up to the beginning of calculus. This book was one of the first to include mathematical problems at the end of each chapter. It includes information on Aryabhata's work on inversion, formulas for the volumes of spheres and pyramids, and several terms for half-chords.

Hooper, Alfred. *Makers of Mathematics*. New York: Random House, 1948. Explains Aryabhata's place in the history of the development of sines.

Menon, C. P. S. *Early Astronomy and Cosmology*. London: George Allen and Unwin, 1932. A good overview of Hindu, Chinese, and Babylonian astronomy, with data on Aryabhata's contribution to Meru cosmology.

Smith, David E. *History of Mathematics*. 2 vols. New York: Dover Publications, 1958. A well-documented textbook covering everything from prehistoric math to calculus, with particular attention to the geographic and racial considerations as well as a chronological sequence. Volume 1 presents a formula Aryabhata used for summing an arithmetic series after the pth term and some interesting information on Pataliputra. Volume 2 gives a portion of Aryabhata's table of sines, compared to modern values, and the formula he may have used to calculate them.

Waerden, B. L. van der. *Science Awakening*. Translated by Arnold Dresden with additions by the author. Groningen, Netherlands: P. Noordhoff, 1954. An unusually well-illustrated history of mathematics, the volume contains many useful diagrams and photographs of texts. It also includes an explanation of a system of numerical notation used by Aryabhata and some information on his pupil Bhāskara I.

Frank Wu

ASCLEPIADES OF BITHYNIA

Born: 124 B.C.; Prusa (Cios), Bithynia
Died: c. 44 B.C.; Rome
Area of Achievement: Medicine
Contribution: Asclepiades was the first physician to establish Greek medicine in Rome.

Early Life

Asclepiades, whose father was probably Andreas, a noted physiologist of the time, was born in Prusa, also called Cios, in Bithynia, Asia Minor. A widely read man, he seems to have had a liberal education in his youth. Apparently, there was enough money for him to be able to travel and study.

After studying rhetoric and medicine in Athens and Alexandria, he practiced medicine, first in Parion, a town on the Hellespont (Dardanelles), and later in Athens. After extensive traveling, in the year 91 he settled in Rome, where he may have become a Roman citizen. A man of amiable manners, good fortune, and worldly prosperity, Asclepiades formed friendships with such prominent individuals as Cicero and Marc Antony.

Preferring the freedom of a solitary life in a suburban villa, Asclepiades refused the invitation of King Mithradates of Pontus to join his court. Though he did not participate in public debates, he was not afraid to disagree with others. He condemned all those who thought that anatomy and physiology were the foundation of medicine. He was responsible for introducing Democritus' atomistic philosophy to Rome.

His daily routine included three basic activities: visiting and treating the sick throughout the city, giving written advice, and writing books. Although he was a voluminous author, little remains of the twenty or more treatises he prepared. Specific dates of his works are not known; the fragments that remain have been assigned English titles according to their subject matter. He wrote one book of definitions, one commentary on some of the short and obscure works of Hippocrates; one treatise on fevers, and three on febrile, inflammatory, and acute diseases. He also wrote *Concerning Common Aids*, a precursor of modern guides to healthy living; *Enemata*, which was frequently quoted by Aulus Cornelius Celsus in *De medicina* (c. A.D. 30; English translation, 1830); and *Method of Giving Wine in Sickness*.

Asclepiades also offered public lectures on medicine and had a large number of students. Applying many of his principles, these students, led by Themison of Laodicea, later founded the Methodist school, which emphasized diet and exercise in the treatment of illness.

By the age of thirty, Asclepiades was already famous. Some of that fame had grown from a story about him which circulated in Rome. According to this story, one day Asclepiades encountered a funeral procession. Just as the corpse was placed upon the pyre and the fire was about to be lit, he ordered the ceremony stopped, had the body taken down and delivered to his home, administered restoratives, and soon revived the man.

A statue excavated in Rome in 1700 was assumed to be a correct likeness of Asclepiades. From this it would appear that he was a man of slender stature who possessed a rather tranquil countenance.

Life's Work

Asclepiades was one of the foremost physicians of his century, exhibiting rich practical and philosophical attainments, versatility of mind, and an ability to make rapid diagnoses. Opposing the Hippocratic idea that morbid conditions resulted from a disturbance of the humors of the body, he held that nothing happened without a cause and that the causes of events were always mechanical—that is, dependent upon matter and motion.

The medical practice that Asclepiades founded was based on a modification of the atomic, or corpuscular, theory of Democritus, the Greek philosopher, according to which disease resulted from an irregular or inharmonious motion of the corpuscles of the body. Asclepiades believed that these masses were in continual motion, splitting into fragments of different shapes and sizes which then re-formed to create perceptible bodies. These particles were separated by invisible gaps, or pores. Friction between the particles created normal body heat; jamming the pores, or obstruction, was the cause of fever and inflammatory disorders. Fainting, lethargy, weakness, and similar complaints were attributed to an abnormal relaxation of the pores. Since disease was attributed to either constricted or relaxed conditions of the body's solid particles, Asclepiades founded his therapy on the efficacy of systematic interference as opposed to the healing power of nature. The regimens that he prescribed incorporated such therapies as fresh air, light, appropriate diet, hydrotherapy, massage, clysters or enemas, local applications, and, occasionally, very small amounts of medication.

For those complaints which he believed to be caused by obstruction, he proposed various kinds of exercise to relax the pores; in this way, the free transmission of the interrupted atoms or molecules would be facilitated. For pain, localized venesection might be cautiously practiced, but only for instant relief, because bleeding tended to draw off the finer, more vital atoms first and leave the coarser atoms behind. Rigor, or rigidity of the body, might result.

He believed that dropsy, an excessive accumulation of fluid in the tissues, resulted from an infinite number of small holes in the flesh that converted all the food received into water. How such a conversion might occur, however, he did not explain. To illustrate that the brain was the seat of the finest atoms, he performed decapitation experiments on animals such as eels, tortoises, and goats.

Asclepiades condemned purgatives, emetics, and drugs. Instead, he relied greatly on changes in diet, accompanied by friction, bathing, and exercise. He paid special attention to the patient's pulse. His remedies were directed to the restoration of harmony, based on the fundamental principle that treatments should be given promptly, safely, and pleasantly. For relaxants, he used wine and massage; to stimulate patients, he used wine, cold water, vinegar, and narcotics. He taught that patients tolerated diseases differently. Exercise, in his view, was unnecessary for healthy people. In cases of dropsy, he recommended making small cuts near the ankles to release the fluid. He advised that, when tapping was done to remove fluid, the opening be made as small as possible.

Asclepiades was particularly interested in psychiatric cases. He placed these patients in brightly lit, well-ventilated rooms, used occupational therapy, prescribed exercises for improving the memory and increasing attention, soothed them with music, and used wine to induce sleep.

According to Pliny the Elder, the Roman naturalist and writer, Asclepiades had three principal modes of cure. The early stages of illness often called for "gestation," which consisted of being transported in some way such as a boat or litter to exhaust the patient's strength and cause fever. Asclepiades also used suspended beds that could be rocked, as well as hanging baths and other forms of hydrotherapy. He firmly believed and taught that one fever was to be cured by another. The second mode was friction or massage. The third mode was wine, which he gave to febrile patients and used as a stimulant in cases of lethargy. He believed that it was necessary to force a patient to endure thirst. All patients were required to fast during the first three days of illness. In later stages, wine and moderate amounts of food were allowed.

Asclepiades showed great accuracy in distinguishing between various diseases, describing and dividing them into acute and chronic classes. For example, he gave a correct description of malaria; he also observed the psychic complications that occurred in cases of pneumonia and pleurisy. His special attention was devoted to chronic diseases, conditions which had been somewhat neglected by Hippocrates.

Asclepiades wagered that he would never die of disease; indeed, he is not known to have ever fallen ill. His death, at an advanced age, was the result of an accidental fall down a flight of stairs.

Summary

Asclepiades of Bithynia may be ranked as the first physician to introduce Greek medicine to Rome. A full assessment of his merits cannot be made because most of his writings have been lost. The fragments of them which have surfaced in later literature deal with subjects such as the pulse, respiration, heart disease, ulcers, climate, drugs, and the preparation of remedies.

By the fourth century, Asclepiades was almost forgotten. His critics had characterized him as a man of natural talents acquainted with human nature and possessed of considerable shrewdness but little scientific or professional skill. Galen strongly opposed him because Asclepiades had been the first to attack and repudiate the humoral teachings of Hippocrates. Pliny also disliked him and regarded him as a charlatan.

On the other hand, Celsus, the first compiler of medical history and procedures, admitted that he learned much from Asclepiades. Galen grudgingly credited Asclepiades as having pioneered two surgical procedures, laryngectomy and tracheotomy. As has been noted, his ideas were influential in the development of the Methodist school, with its emphasis on diet and exercise. Furthermore, Asclepiades was a pioneer in the humane treatment of mental patients.

Bibliography

Allbutt, Sir Thomas C. *Greek Medicine in Rome: The Fitzpatrick Lectures on the History of Medicine Delivered at the Royal College of Physicians of London in 1909-10*. London: Macmillan, 1921. This series of lectures addressed to interested physicians and others with a strong medical background may be too abstract for the general reader. It is a complete medical history of the period with extensive commentary on all major figures, but only one brief chapter on Asclepiades. Excellent illustrations, bibliography, and additional chronology.

Cumston, Charles Greene. *An Introduction to the History of Medicine: From the Time of the Pharaohs to the End of the Nineteenth Century*. New York: Alfred A. Knopf, 1926. This volume, which contains only one brief chapter on Asclepiades, is a compilation of numerous essential contributions to the general subject of a history of medicine. Written for the general reader and as an introduction for students of medicine, it is a lengthy work containing many illustrations but limited bibliographical material.

Gordon, Benjamin Lee. *Medicine Throughout Antiquity*. Philadelphia: F. A. Davis Co., 1949. Gordon's book contains only a very brief section on Asclepiades, along with scattered page references. The author makes mention of a wide-ranging array of facts that are not ordinarily accessible to a busy practitioner or to lay people interested in medical history. There are brief reference notes and a few illustrations but no chronology or bibliography.

Green, Robert M., ed. and trans. *Asclepiades, His Life and Writings: A Translation of Cocchi's "Life of Asclepiades" and Gumpert's "Fragments of Asclepiades."* New Haven, Conn.: Elizabeth Licht, 1955. Green has prepared a complete translation of *Discorso primo di Antonio Cocchi sopra Asclepiade* (c. 1740) and of selections from Christian Gumpert's *Fragmenta* (1794), a compilation of extant writings of Asclepiades. This volume contains the most detailed information available in English for the general reader, although it lacks reference notes and a bibliography.

Major, Ralph. "Medicine in the Roman Empire." In *A History of Medicine*. Springfield, Ill.: Charles C Thomas, 1954. This chapter includes a brief section on Asclepiades. There is no presumption of background knowledge about medical history. Very limited information is presented and few illustrations are given. There is no chronology and only a limited bibliography.

Rawson, Elizabeth. "The Life and Death of Asclepiades of Bithynia." *Classical Quarterly* 32, no. 2 (1982): 358-370. Rawson presents a critical analysis of the information known about Asclepiades. A scholarly approach utilizing much research in Latin and Greek sources, but no translations of the numerous quotes are given. It presumes extensive background knowledge concerning Asclepiades as well as the period in which he lived.

Rita E. Loos

AL-ASH'ARI

Born: 873 or 874; Basra, southern Mesopotamia
Died: 935 or 936; Baghdad, Iraq
Areas of Achievement: Religion and philosophy
Contribution: Al-Ash'ari initiated a theological movement which gave human reason only a limited role in demonstrating religious truths: Dialectical argument was acceptable if it remained subordinate to revealed facts.

Early Life

Al-Ash'ari (full name, Abu al-Hasan 'Ali ibn Isma'il al-Ash'ari) was born in Basra in southern Mesopotamia (modern Iraq) in 873 or 874. He may have been a descendant of the famous Abu Musa al-Ash'ari (died 662 or 663), a Companion of the Prophet Muhammad. Nothing is known about al-Ash'ari's early life, though it is evident from his subsequent activities that he received the usual education of his time: studies in grammar, the Koran, Traditions of the Prophet Muhammad, canon law, and Scholastic theology. It can also be assumed that he was deeply influenced by the intellectual turmoil of an age of violent ideological conflict, during which renewed interest in Greek philosophy intensified the clash between the ultrarationalist Mu'tazilites and the fundamentalist theologians. He became a pupil of the leading Basran Mu'tazilite, Abu 'Ali Muhammad ibn 'Abd al-Wahhab al-Jubba'i (died 915 or 916), and flourished as an aggressive debater in law and dogmatics.

At about the age of forty, in 912 or 913, al-Ash'ari underwent a radical conversion away from the extreme rationalism of his master al-Jubba'i, and made a declaration of repentance in the mosque, announcing his return to strictest orthodoxy and rejecting outright the subordination of religious beliefs to rational principles. About this abrupt change of direction two different stories are told, which, although they are later embellishments to al-Ash'ari's biography, are significant because they reflect his role in the development of Islamic theology.

The first story tells of three dreams; in two of them the Prophet orders al-Ash'ari to return to traditional orthodoxy, but in the third he commands him not to abandon dialectical theology either. In the best-known version of the second story, al-Ash'ari silences al-Jubba'i with an unanswerable riddle of three brothers, one dying as a baby (hence too young for Paradise or Hell), one rewarded with Heaven for his virtuous life, and one sent to Hell for his sins. The infant challenges God on his fate: Why was he not allowed to live and earn salvation? Al-Jubba'i replies that God would say that He knew that the child would grow up to be a sinner, and out of divine justice He brought his life to an early end. On hearing this, the third brother now cries out from Hell: Why did He not kill me too, before I had a chance to sin? Al-Jubba'i, naturally, is incapable of resolving the dilemma. It was this demonstration of the incapacity of human reason which was said to have turned al-Ash'ari away from the Mu'tazilite movement, one of whose central beliefs was that God could not be anything but absolutely just.

Life's Work

There are two ways to approach al-Ash'ari: evaluating him either by his reputation or by his writings. He is credited with a large number of works (106 titles are known), but not all of the few that have survived are accepted as genuine. Furthermore, their character varies according to whether they were composed before or after his conversion.

Four works may be considered representative of al-Ash'ari's output. His *Maqalat al-Islamiyin wa-ikhtilaf al-musallin* (*Discourses of the Muslims*, 1930) is noteworthy as one of the first treatises on the Islamic sects and was an important source for later historians of religion. It is divided into two parts, one dealing with the Muslim sects and the other with the views of the Scholastic theologians (*mutakallimun*). There may also have been a third part examining the opinions of the philosophers. *Al-Ibanah 'an usul al-diyanah* (*The Elucidation of Islam's Foundation*, 1940) is an outline of the principles of Islam, perhaps written soon after his conversion to strict orthodoxy and therefore extremely hostile to the unbridled use of human reason in theological argument. A third work, *Risalat isthsan al-khawd fi 'ilm al-kalam* (best known as *al-Hathth 'ala al-bahth*; *Incitement to Investigation*, 1953), strongly defends the use of reason and is critical of those same orthodox thinkers whose ranks al-Ash'ari had so dramatically rejoined. To their claim that rational speculation is heretical, al-Ash'ari replies that to prohibit the use of reason in the absence of all Koranic and extra-Koranic support is itself a heresy. Finally, the *Kitab al-luma'* (*Book of Highlights*, 1953) should be mentioned. It is a late work, similar to *Incitement to Investigation* in its rigorous defense of Islam by the use of dialectic, and it was probably al-Ash'ari's most popular treatise, to judge by the commentaries and refutations it provoked.

Far more significant than al-Ash'ari's writings is the body of ideas attributed to him and constituting the theological system named for him. Ash'arism's general aim was to achieve a true synthesis of purely logical argument and the transcendental elements of revealed religion. A non-Muslim is likely to be unimpressed by the apparent contradictions this method produces, but it would be a gross error to devalue the absolute importance of all the issues involved by relegating them to the status of mere Scholastic quibbles.

Ash'ari's method typically combines rational argument with an appeal to Koranic authority, so that each reinforces the other. Thus, to refute the Mu'tazilite preference for mechanical causality (which threatened to make God subject to natural laws), al-Ash'ari attacks on two fronts. Rationally, it is self-evident that man is not in control of the universe and cannot create himself; his continued existence therefore must be attributable to a higher cause. Hereupon, al-Ash'ari invokes Koranic verses to confirm by revelation what he has just established by reason. God's unity is similarly demonstrated by pointing out the logical absurdity of predicating omnipotence of more than one deity, and again the case is supported by Koranic quotations.

By this type of argument, Ash'arism constructed a theology which re-solved—or at least acceptably accounted for—all the major points of doc-trinal dispute. The rather numerous individual topics may be conveniently subsumed under two broad categories: dogma relating to God and dogma in which man is the main focus.

The Koran and the subsequent tradition are very explicit regarding God's qualities. Logic is equally insistent that the oneness of God is incompatible with the medieval scientific principle of substance and accident, that is, that all beings are complex insofar as their attributes are additional to their sub-stance. There are two extreme solutions to this dilemma: One is to prohibit inquiry into the question altogether, which was approximately the position of the fundamentalists, and the other is to affirm the unity of God by denying that He has any attributes at all, which was essentially the view of the Mu'tazilites. Either way, the theological consequences were disturbing: The fundamentalists were obliged to accept things which they could not under-stand (God's location, for example; the Koran describes Him as sitting on a throne), while the Mu'tazilites reduced God to a construct of the mind ruled by the laws of thought (the faithful will not see Him in the afterlife, because it is inconceivable that He should be anywhere to be seen). Al-Ash'ari and his followers arrived at a reconciliation of this type of contradiction by com-bining belief in revealed truth with acceptance of logical arguments designed to show that God's attributes were of a different nature from man's, thus nei-ther depriving Him of attributes nor negating His oneness. It is important to stress here that al-Ash'ari was seeking not a compromise between the two opposing views but a total victory for fundamentalist theology, expressed in terms which would silence both sides. The weaknesses of the two extremes are clear, but the intention of al-Ash'ari's reasoning was to make the fun-damentalist position logically unassailable.

Man's theological status was equally problematical, especially in the matter of free will. The fundamentalists naturally adhered to the Koranic assertions of God's unqualified omnipotence, while the Mu'tazilites had to argue that there could be no responsibility (hence no reward for virtue or punishment for sin) without free will, thereby restricting God's powers. Al-Ash'ari's solu-tion is simply brilliant. Man's actions are indeed all created by God, including even the accountability for those actions which man "acquires" as he per-forms them. This "acquisition" (*kasb*) is one of al-Ash'ari's most inspired theological insights: Drawing on a commercial metaphor in the Koran ("every man must stand surety for what he has acquired"—that is, he will be judged accordingly), he elaborated a perfectly coherent doctrine of individual responsibility. Man "buys" his actions, which is to say, he accepts them exactly as a purchaser does under Muslim law, with eyes open and with full satisfaction (*rida*). The concept is ethically watertight: Man acts as he is predestined to act, but he always knows what God has determined to be right or wrong, and it is the acceptance (*kasb*) of that knowledge which will send him eventually to Heaven or Hell.

Summary

A brief description of Ash'arism cannot give an adequate impression of the subtlety and breadth of al-Ash'ari's ideas, which ranged from the most abstruse questions of metaphysics to practical matters of worldly ethics. What must be stressed, however, is that his solutions were found acceptable by numerous Muslims of undoubted intellectual superiority, of whom the greatest is al-Ghazzali (1058-1111), the single most influential Muslim thinker. Ash'arism clearly answered Islam's need to harmonize the intellectual's insistence on systematic coherence with the fundamentalist's refusal to question matters of revelation. Even Sufi mystics are among his followers, and the foundation of the Nizamiyya College in Baghdad in 1070 represents the elevation of Ash'arism to an officially sponsored state doctrine. Ironically, this reconciliation of faith and reason is exactly what al-Ash'ari's bitterest opponents, the Mu'tazilites, strove for and failed to accomplish.

Although al-Ash'ari's position in the history of Islamic theology is clearly defined in the Muslim tradition, there is still much uncertainty about him in Western scholarship. Disagreement among non-Muslims springs from the difficulty of accepting Islamic religious premises and an understandable inclination to regard Islamic theological speculation as sterile and abstract. Al-Ash'ari is thus a somewhat contradictory figure to non-Muslims; indeed, he has been called a "man with two faces" for his apparent vacillation between the extremes of blind fundamentalism and radical enlightenment. To see al-Ash'ari in this polarized way, however, is to deny the very synthesis he created. In theological terms, he was never anything but ultraconservative, yet he also managed to remove from Islam (or at least to make it possible through his champion al-Ghazzali) that fear of intellectualism which had made the Mu'tazilites so unpopular despite their pious intentions. In fact, al-Ash'ari's hostility toward the unthinking kind of Muslim who believes by mere "imitation" (*taqlid*) was far stronger than his opposition to the inquisitive Mu'tazilites.

How much of Ash'arism is al-Ash'ari's personal achievement and how much is attributable to natural adjustments within Islam as it progressed toward doctrinal maturity may not be very important to determine. Ideological movements in Islam usually spring from the teachings of a major figure and then take on a life of their own, so that the question of originality retreats into the background. None of al-Ash'ari's ideas is totally without precedent; the use of reasoned theological argument (*kalam*) to analyze and defend religious doctrine, the tone of uncompromising orthodoxy, and concepts such as "acquisition" (*kasb*) can all be observed in or traced to earlier sources. In the end, therefore, al-Ash'ari should perhaps be judged in terms of the tradition that bears his name, which gives a full and satisfying role to the powers of man's intellect in working with a set of revealed Islamic beliefs.

Bibliography

Abdul Hye, M. "Ash'arism." In *A History of Muslim Philosophy*, edited by M. M. Sharif, vol. 1. Wiesbaden, West Germany: Harrassowitz, 1963. Chapter 9 contains a sober, detailed, and informative account of al-Ash'ari and his ideas from the Muslim perspective. Particularly helpful in its clear and concise summaries of the doctrinal issues, setting al-Ash'ari in the wider context of Islamic theology.

Ash'ari, 'Ali ibn Isma'il al-. *Abu 'l-Ḥasan 'Alī ibn Ismā'īl al-Aš'arī's Al-Ibānah 'an uṣūl ad-diyānah (The Elucidation of Islām's Foundation)*. Edited and translated by Walter Conrad Klein. New Haven, Conn.: American Oriental Society, 1940. Reprint. New York: Kraus Reprint Corp., 1967. Translation (somewhat shaky) of a major work, with a convenient introduction giving a brief outline of al-Ash'ari's life and doctrines.

——————. *The Theology of al-Ash'arī*. Translated by Richard J. McCarthy. Beirut, Lebanon: Imprimerie Catholique, 1953. Accurate and well-annotated translation of two of al-Ash'ari's most important works, the *Kitab al-luma'* and the *al-Hathth 'ala al-bahth*, with the original Arabic text and useful biographical and bibliographical material. A reliable rendering of the key ideas and issues.

Frank, Richard M. "Elements in the Development of the Teaching of al-Ash'arī." *Muséon* 101 (1988). Thorough analysis of al-Ash'ari's views on the rational approach to theology, the attributes of God, and the nature of the Koran. Emphasizes the consistency of al-Ash'ari's thinking in spite of his apparent changes of allegiance. Other studies by Richard M. Frank should also be consulted.

Goldziher, Ignaz. *Introduction to Islamic Theology and Law*. Translated by Andras and Ruth Hamori. Princeton: Princeton University Press, 1981. The classic treatment of the topic, this work, first published in 1910, is still widely accepted. This edition contains an updated bibliography and notes. Chapter 3, "The Growth and Development of Dogmatic Theology," gives a great deal of space to al-Ash'ari. A certain skepticism permeates Goldziher's presentation.

Gwynne, Rosalind W. "Al-Jubbā'ī, al-Ash'arī, and the Three Brothers: The Uses of Fiction." *The Muslim World* 75 (1985): 132-161. Detailed literary study of the anecdote, showing how it was incorporated only later into al-

Ash'ari's biography. An illuminating discussion of the way doctrinal developments can become personalized retrospectively.

Hourani, George E. *Reason and Tradition in Islamic Ethics*. Cambridge: Cambridge University Press, 1985. Chapter 9, "Ash'arī," is a short, lucid account, supplemented by many other references in the rest of the book which help to locate al-Ash'ari and his school in the general context of Islamic theology.

Makdisi, G. "Ash'arī and the Ash'arites in Islamic Religious History." *Studia Islamica* 17/18 (1962/1963): 37-80, 19-39. A radical (and not universally accepted) reassessment of al-Ash'ari which rejects the authenticity of the *Incitement to Investigation* and argues that al-Ash'ari's real opponents were not the Mu'tazilites or Hanbalis but the Shafi'i school of law.

Watt, W. Montgomery. *Free Will and Predestination in Early Islam*. London: Luzac, 1948. Chapter 6 describes al-Ash'ari's solution to the problem of free will and offers some valuable corrections to common misconceptions regarding al-Ash'ari's true position in the debate between fundamentalists and rationalists.

_____. *Islamic Philosophy and Theology*. Chicago: Aldine Publishing Co., 1962. The best starting point: concise and readable summaries with guidance for further reading, placing al-Ash'ari in the wider theological context. An enlarged version of this work was published in 1985.

Wensinck, A. J. *The Muslim Creed: Its Genesis and Historical Development*. London: Frank Cass, 1932, reprint 1965. Not an easy book to read, but filled with authoritative information. Sets the theological issues in their historical context; especially useful in showing how Islamic issues relate to Christian doctrinal developments.

M. G. Carter

ASHIKAGA TAKAUJI

Born: 1305; Japan
Died: 1358; Kyoto, Japan
Areas of Achievement: Government and military affairs
Contribution: Through dogged military prowess and ruthless political decisiveness, Takauji prevented Japan from swinging back to an outdated Chinese-style imperial government and placed power fully in the hands of rising new military clans. The Ashikaga shogunate which he founded hastened innovations in politics, culture, and economics that launched Japan's High Middle Ages.

Early Life

Ashikaga Takauji was born in 1305, the son of Ashikaga Sadauji of the Seiwa Genji branch of the Minamoto clan, which had founded the first shogunate, or military government, at Kamakura in 1185. His mother was of the Hojo family, which had dominated the latter years of the Kamakura shogunate. The only portrait reputed to be of Takauji shows him mounted in a heroic pose, brandishing his curved sword in full armor. He is bullnecked with a black mustache and goatee. It is typical of the battle portraits of the day. In fact, Takauji was thoroughly typical of a time in which, paradoxically, family loyalties and spartan courage were revered but betrayal and intrigue played a major part in politics.

The Kamakura shogunate under which Takauji was reared exemplified the Japanese genius for maintaining the fiction of an emperor while allowing administration by the military powers. The charade of an emperor "appointing" a shogun to oversee the details of politics served to protect the imperial court, rendering the emperor a mere figurehead. Courtiers and warriors alike drew their incomes from agricultural estates called *shoen*, which were overseen by stewards appointed by the shogun. Provincial military governors, like the Ashikaga, were also appointed by and owed their loyalties to the Kamakura shogunate.

Stable as the system had been for more than a century, unrest was growing by the beginning of the fourteenth century. Dwindling returns from the *shoen* led everyone to seek a larger share. In 1318, Go Daigo, heir to one of the two family lines which systematically alternated in the imperial reign, legally acceded to the throne and began a movement to take back into the emperor's hands all administrative power. In 1333, the shogunate, determined to exterminate this movement, dispatched an army under the command of Takauji.

Life's Work

There was widespread resentment in Japan against the Kamakura shogunate, which, having grown stale and overly complex at the top, was unable to distribute satisfactory rewards. Sensing this, Takauji suddenly declared for the emperor and promptly seized the shogunate's offices in Kyoto, while another army attacked and captured the shogunate's main headquarters at Kamakura. Victory over the Hojo gave Go Daigo his chance to assert direct personal imperial rule. Known as the Kemmu Restoration, from 1333 to 1336, it was a naïve and unrealistic program to bring the institutions of military rule under long-superseded organs of pre-1185 imperial government. Takauji, who aspired to be shogun, was bypassed in favor of Go Daigo's son, Prince Morinaga. By 1335, Takauji had turned against Go Daigo, whom he drove out of Kyoto, and proceeded to set up the emperor Komyo of the rival alternate line in his place. Go Daigo thereupon fled to the town of Yoshino, south of Kyoto, where he and his successors maintained their claim as rightful rulers. From 1336 to 1392, therefore, two emperors contested the throne. The period, known as the Northern and Southern Dynasties, is one of extensive fighting during which, until his death, Takauji strove to maintain his vision of a new order.

Takauji received the title of shogun from the emperor of the Northern Court at Kyoto in 1338 and thus became the first in a line of Ashikaga shoguns who ruled Japan as military dictators for the next 235 years. During most of his time as shogun, Takauji had to deal simultaneously with the civil war against the supporters of the Southern Court and with the infighting among his own supporters. The internal strife centered on the antagonism between Takauji's brother, Ashikaga Tadayoshi, and the vassal chieftains Ko no Moronao and his brother Moroyasu. Tadayoshi had closely supported his brother in his defeat of the Kamakura shogunate and then in his turnabout against Go Daigo. Takauji's shogunate, in fact, divided responsibilities between Takauji, who handled military affairs, and Tadayoshi, who oversaw many of the judicial and administrative matters. An able administrator, Tadayoshi at first worked harmoniously with his brother.

Moronao, a loyal vassal with high ambitions, was charged with military recruitment among the small clans in the Kyoto area. In this capacity, he sought to dispossess court nobles of their *shoen* in order to offer further rewards to the military. Tadayoshi, fundamentally more conservative than either Moronao or Takauji, opposed this plan and plotted to have Moronao assassinated. The plot was discovered, and Tadayoshi was ordered, as punishment, to become a monk in 1349. In 1350, he offered his services to the Southern Court and then attacked his own brother in 1351, killing Moronao in battle. In turn, he was defeated and taken prisoner. Takauji evidently had him poisoned in 1352. Fratricide was not uncommon in medieval Japan, but the disarray it caused among Takauji's allies kept the Southern Court's fortunes alive longer than might have been expected. Nevertheless, by the time of his death in 1358, Takauji managed to bequeath to his son, Ashikaga

Yoshiakira, a fairly stable regime that had at last overcome its internal strife and eliminated the offensive power of the Southern Court.

The atmosphere in which two imperial courts battled for legitimacy had produced more than its share of dissidents, rebels, double-crossers, and malcontents. That meant that Takauji and his successors had to be both able generals and fast-footed administrators. Takauji had to innovate for his political survival by establishing a government significantly different from Kamakura predecessors while still retaining whatever shreds of tradition would lend legitimacy to his rule. The basic Ashikaga code, the Kemmu Formulary of 1336, was declared to be an addendum to the Kamakura code established in 1232. Also, Takauji appointed many Kamakura bureaucrats in a bid for legitimacy based on continuity. Yet he also eliminated many encrusted and outdated layers of bureaucracy inhabited by imperial aristocrats and recruited new social elements, including merchants, whose talents answered the needs of a society and an economy that was changing and expanding. He and his successors, moreover, were willing to promote mercantile wealth and, eventually, to license foreign trade, which speeded diversification away from self-centered agrarianism.

Takauji chose to place his shogunate in Kyoto, the old imperial capital, partly to distance himself from the failed Kamakura shogunate but principally to take advantage of the prestige of being at the seat of the imperial government. Militarily, Kyoto was a more strategically central location. The surrounding region was the most agriculturally productive area in Japan. Because of its long association with imperial government, it was one of the few truly urban areas of Japan at that time, with a comparatively large market. The interaction between this market and the growing production was to produce the core of a sophisticated money economy, with a large free laboring class working for wages, an advanced credit and banking system, and an active craft manufacturing establishment.

Takauji took care not to ignore the outlying areas. The eastern provinces, which were the heartland of many in the Ashikaga camp, were particularly volatile. Takauji shifted trusted officials back and forth between Kyoto and the eastern administrative center of Kamakura. Takauji himself ruled from Kamakura during his struggle with Tadayoshi and left his son Yoshiakira there for a time. In the process, Kamakura took on a status of "deputy shogunate." In the southern island of Kyushu, where the Ashikaga had no real vassal ties, Takauji established a permanent shogunate representative.

The finances of the Kamakura shogunate had been based on fixed shares of the incomes of supervisory estate stewards and of the provincial governors, all of which were appointed by the shogun from among those with vassal ties to the shogun's family. Thus, they relied for their revenues on loyalties that were almost familial. Takauji presided over a much more complex and potentially unstable structure, so he sought to immunize himself from dependence on vassal ties for taxation by supporting his government directly from the Ashikaga estates, some sixty *shoen* scattered throughout the country. He continued the practice of appointing military governors to provinces and his main authority was exerted through these governors, but his government income was personal. Ashikaga Takauji died of cancer in 1358.

Summary

When his regime was first founded, Takauji asked his legal experts for advice on the shaping of his government. They responded, "Does one follow the path of an overturned wagon?" The meaning he evidently derived from this response was that, while precedent must not be utterly violated, one must be willing to carve new paths in a brutal and uncertain world. Takauji and his successors, in fact, introduced the bulk of Japan's major political innovations for the next three centuries. Yet the meaning of most of what he had set in motion by his victories and by his political arrangements was not apparent at the time he died.

It was his grandson, the third shogun Yoshimitsu, who reaped the economic benefits of foreign trade and enhanced mercantile activity. The later Ashikaga shoguns also witnessed the extraordinary cultural flowering of arts and religion which is the main contribution of feudal Japan to modern Japan. It was during the Ashikaga age that the unique Zen culture permeated art, philosophy, and drama. Takauji was exceptionally pious, a diligent Zen practitioner and talented poet, but it was his successors who saw Zen combine with aristocratic culture to tame the rude samurai into poets, artists, connoisseurs, and meditators.

Bibliography

Grossberg, Kenneth Alan. *Japan's Renaissance: The Politics of the Muromachi Bakufu*. Cambridge, Mass.: Harvard University Press, 1981. This volume is a highly literate and knowledgeable account of the economy, bureaucracy, and military of the Ashikaga shoguns. Focusing mainly on Takauji's successors, Grossberg argues that the Ashikaga shoguns, often dismissed in general histories as presiding over a loose and uncoordinated polity, can be compared favorably to European Renaissance rulers.

Hall, John Whitney. *Government and Local Power in Japan, 500-1700: A Study Based on Bizen Province*. Princeton, N.J.: Princeton University Press, 1966. This study grew out of field investigations conducted in the 1950's in Okayama Prefecture. Despite the title, the book frequently departs from strictly local events to fill in developments in Japan as a whole. Hall's analysis of land administration and the transformation of provincial governors into leaders of independent principalities has become the point of departure for a whole generation of American scholars.

Kitabatake, Chikafusa. *A Chronicle of Gods and Sovereigns: "Jinno shotoki" of Kitabatuke Chikafusa*. Translated by H. Paul Varley. New York: Columbia University Press, 1980. A translation of the *Jinno shotoki*, written in 1339 and revised in 1343 by Kitabatake, a prominent Southern Court loyalist and the major combatant against Takauji. Kitabatake asserts forcefully the unbroken descent of Japanese emperors from the gods who created Japan, and his chronicle is a polemic for a return to the type of imperial rule Japan had before the shoguns, whose exercise of a monopoly of power he regarded as a perversion.

McCullough, Helen Craig, trans. *The Taiheiki: A Chronicle of Medieval Japan*. New York: Columbia University Press, 1959. A straightforward translation of one of the most famous of Japanese war tales, ironically entitled "The Great Peace." Largely favorable to the Ashikaga family, it was written sometime between the 1330's and 1370's by an unknown compiler and is the record of the battles and, to some extent, the intrigues of the period during which Takauji was rising to power. Contains an introduction and notes.

Sansom, George Bailey. *A History of Japan, 1334-1615*. Vol. 2. Stanford, Calif.: Stanford University Press, 1961. This is the second volume of a three-volume history of Japan which is arguably the most complete general history of premodern Japan available. This well-illustrated work, based entirely on Japanese sources, is indispensable for anyone writing on medieval Japan. Includes a wealth of detail on the political changes wrought by military defeats and victories, on changing alignments, and on matters of religion and art.

David G. Egler

ASHURBANIPAL

Born: c. 685 B.C.; Nineveh, Assyria
Died: 627 B.C.; Nineveh, Assyria
Areas of Achievement: Government, architecture, art, and literature
Contribution: The last great king of ancient Assyria, Ashurbanipal lived within a generation of its total annihilation. Inside his exquisitely decorated palace complex at Nineveh, he brought together a magnificent library of cuneiform writing upon clay tablets, which included materials from twenty-five hundred years of achievement by Sumerians, Akkadians, Babylonians, and Assyrians.

Early Life

Ashurbanipal was born toward the end of a fifteen-hundred-year period of Assyrian ascendancy. His name in Assyrian is Ashur-bani-apli (the god Ashur has made a[nother] son), affirming that he was not intended to stand in the line of royal accession.

His father, Esarhaddon, youngest son of Sennacherib, had become heir when the crown prince, Ashur-nadin-shumi, was deposed by rebels from his position as vassal for Babylon. Esarhaddon was not the son of Sennacherib's queen, Tashmetum-sharrat, but of the West Semitic "palace woman" Zakutu, known by her native name Naqi'a. The only queen known for Esarhaddon was Ashur-hamat, who died in 672.

Ashurbanipal grew up in the small palace called *bit reduti* (house of succession), built by Sennacherib when he was crown prince in the northern quadrant of Nineveh. In 694, Sennacherib had completed the "Palace Without Rival" at the southwest corner of the acropolis, obliterating most of the older structures. The "House of Succession" had become the palace of Esarhaddon, the crown prince. In this house, Ashurbanipal's grandfather was assassinated by uncles identified only from the biblical account as Adrammelek and Sharezer. From this conspiracy, Esarhaddon emerged as king in 681. He proceeded to rebuild as his residence the *bit musharti* (weapons house, or arsenal). The "House of Succession" was left to his mother and the younger children, including Ashurbanipal.

The names of five brothers and one sister are known. Sin-iddin-apli, the intended crown prince, died prior to 672. Not having been expected to become heir to the throne, Ashurbanipal was trained in scholarly pursuits as well as the usual horsemanship, hunting, chariotry, soldierliness, craftsmanship, and royal decorum. In a unique autobiographical statement, Ashurbanipal specified his youthful scholarly pursuits as having included oil divination, mathematics, and reading and writing. Ashurbanipal was the only Assyrian king who learned how to read and write.

In 672, upon the death of his queen, Esarhaddon reorganized the line of succession at the instigation of his mother. He used the submission of Median chieftains to draft a treaty. The chieftains swore that if Esarhaddon died while his sons were still minors, they and their descendants would guarantee the succession of Ashurbanipal as king of Assyria and Shamash-shum-ukin as king of Babylon. A monumental stela set up two years later in a northwestern province portrays Esarhaddon in high relief upon its face and each of the sons on a side. These portraits, the earliest dated for Ashurbanipal and his brother, show both with the full beard of maturity.

The princes pursued diverse educations thereafter. Extant letters from Shamash-shum-ukin offer his father reports of the situation in Babylon; Ashurbanipal at home received letters as crown prince. The situation came to an immediate crisis in 669, when Esarhaddon, on campaign to Egypt, died suddenly. Ashurbanipal did not accede to the kingship of Assyria until late in the year. His grandmother required all to support his sole claim to the throne. The official ceremonies of coronation came in the second month of the new year, and within the same year (668), Ashurbanipal installed his brother as king of Babylon. The transition took place smoothly, and the dual monarchy of the youthful brothers began. Texts describe their relationship as if they were twins. It was clear, however, that Ashurbanipal, as king of Assyria, like his fathers before him, was also "king of the universe."

Life's Work

One of the first challenges that Ashurbanipal had to face was a rebellion in a region of Egypt over which Esarhaddon had established Assyrian sovereignty. In 667, the ousted king Taharqa came as far north as Memphis, which he recaptured. The Assyrian army rushed south to defeat him, but he again fled. Ashurbanipal enlisted new troops from Syria and followed, capturing Thebes. Three vassals were found guilty of plotting against Assyria, and they were sent to Nineveh. One of them, Necho, convinced Ashurbanipal of his personal loyalty and was returned to his position in Sais in the Delta.

After Taharqa's death, Tanutamon tried to drive out the Assyrians. He captured Memphis and drove the Assyrian vassals into the Delta. With the return of Ashurbanipal and the Assyrian army, Tanutamon fled back to Thebes, which again fell to the Assyrians. In the course of this war, Necho had fallen, and his son Psammetichus I was installed as vassal at Sais; he became king of all Egypt upon the death of Tanutamon.

These events in Egypt, and Ashurbanipal's success in maintaining his position, made a considerable impression on the contemporary world. The Phoenician states, such as Sidon, quieted down. In Anatolia, Gyges, King of Lydia, sought Ashurbanipal's help against the Cimmerians, offering to acknowledge Assyrian suzerainty. There was a similar gesture from the Urartian king. Ashurbanipal did not, however, succumb to the temptation to get entangled in an impossible war with the mountainous Cimmerians.

Rather, he turned against the Elamites. In the campaign against their capital at Susa, the Elamite army was routed and their king, Tept-Humban (Teumman), was killed. This event was portrayed afterward in a chamber of Sennacherib's "Palace Without Rival," which had become Ashurbanipal's residence upon accession. In Teumman's place, a prince, Ummannish, who had earlier fled to the Assyrian court, became king.

The Assyrian empire stretched from Egypt to Urartu, from Lydia to Susa, along the full extent of both the Tigris and the Euphrates. Shamash-shum-ukin could not help feeling overshadowed by his brother, who, though technically his equal, treated him as another vassal. Messengers went out secretly from Babylon to other discontented states; in 651, Shamash-shum-ukin initiated full revolt, together with Gyges of Lydia, Ummanigash of Elam, Arabians, and others. Ashurbanipal implored the gods to save him. The chronicle of his inscriptions reflects the new situation created by the revolt; the one who had been called his "full brother" became the "faithless, hostile brother."

The army from Arabia was delayed, so that Shamash-shum-ukin had to face the entire Assyrian army alone. He withdrew into the fortified cities in Babylonia. The Assyrians proceeded to lay siege to one after another. In 648, realizing that all was lost, Shamash-shum-ukin threw himself into the fire which consumed his palace at Babylon. For the remainder of Ashurbanipal's reign, Babylon was held directly by Assyria. The official in charge, according to all subsequent Babylonian sources, was named Kandalanu; he is impossible to identify further, unless the name is a Babylonian throne name for Ashurbanipal. Kandalanu disappeared in the same year in which Ashurbanipal died.

Ashurbanipal undertook several more campaigns between 648 and 642, including at least two against Elam. He penetrated to Susa and sacked it thoroughly. There was one final campaign against the Arabs, fought as a running battle between his cavalry and the Arabs' mounted camel corps. Ashurbanipal returned from these forays with ample spoils to finance the construction of his grand new palace on the site of the old "House of Succession."

In decorating the walls of this palace, Ashurbanipal repeated the artistic narration of the earlier defeat of Teumman, giving thereby a second version to that in Sennacherib's palace. The most intriguing detail is the final celebration of the victory, in which Ashurbanipal with his queen are served a repast outdoors under some grapevines within which hangs the severed head of the disobedient vassal. Fully illustrated are the victories over Shamash-shum-ukin in 648, the Elamites in 642, and the Arabians. More noteworthy are the extensive scenes of a rather boyish Ashurbanipal hunting—none more exquisitely rendered than the one in which he single-handedly slaughters a pride of lions. Visitors to his palace got a clear impression that this king of Assyria was not merely a great king, but indeed "king of the universe."

From any later perspective, the destructive events of the 640's may be judged as contributory to the final end of Assyria. Yet the last fifteen years of reign appear so quiescent that Ashurbanipal went to his grave assured of the permanence of the land of Ashur that had been his inheritance.

Summary

Ashurbanipal left behind an impressive legacy in architecture, in artistic decoration, and in the collection of the literary treasures of the past, which he greatly enjoyed personally. This is borne out not merely by inscriptional claim, but also by lengthy colophons which he personally added to a wide variety of texts, gathered for the library at Nineveh from all parts of Mesopotamia and from all periods of time, going beyond the Babylonia of Hammurabi to what Ashurbanipal called the "obscure Akkadian and even more difficult Sumerian" on tablets he thought to have come "from before the Flood."

The letters he wrote to request manuscripts indicate that he knew where older collections existed and what they contained: the scholarly apparatus for reading and writing the cuneiform script, including multilingual dictionaries; collections of omens, essential for prognostication of every element of the royal life; and cycles of conjurations, incantations, and prayers, often with interlinear translation of the original Sumerian. To these essentials were added epics of gods or heroes, including previous kings; collections of fables, proverbial wisdom, and unusual tales, some humorous; and a miscellany reflecting the operations of the scribal school and its scholarship, especially in law.

Ashur-etil-ilani and Sin-shar-ishkun, two of his sons, succeeded him, but immediately faced increasing pressure from many opponents. The last Assyrian ruler was an army general, Ashur-uballit II, who held off as long as he could the final destruction of the Assyrian state by retreating to Harran, after the capitals fell to the combined strength of the Medes and Babylonians.

The biblical tradition recalled Ashurbanipal as "the great and noble Asnappar" who had "deported and settled, in the cities of Samaria and in the rest of the province called 'Beyond-the-River,'" various conquered peoples from Babylonia and Elam. The Greek tradition conflated Ashurbanipal with his brother Shamash-shum-ukin into a cowardly, effeminate "Sardanapalus" who presided over Assyria's destruction and committed suicide. Sardanapalus became well-known through George Gordon, Lord Byron's verse drama of 1821 and Eugène Delacroix's 1827 painting. Neither of these is characterized by historical veracity, since they were both products of the Romantic era, which immediately preceded the archaeological rediscovery of the real Ashurbanipal.

Bibliography

Barnett, R. D. *Sculptures from the North Palace of Ashurbanipal at Nineveh (668-627)*. London: British Museum, 1976. The history of the excavations and of the reconstruction of the plans of the palace is covered, with an explanation of the location within the chambers of all known sculpted slabs. Photographs and drawings are laid out to illustrate the slabs in their discovered configuration in this massive folio.

Grayson, A. K. "The Chronology of the Reign of Ashurbanipal." *Zeitschrift für Assyriologie* 70 (1980): 227-245. This study serves as a guide to the texts, historiographically evaluated, and to the correlation of detail within the various text editions to the actual events and their dates. It does not address the problems of the conclusion of the reign.

Luckenbill, Daniel David, trans. *Ancient Records of Assyria and Babylonia*. Vol. 2, *From Sargon to the End*. Chicago: University of Chicago Press, 1927. An English translation of the inscriptions of the kings of Assyria. This volume covers Ashurbanipal and his three predecessors, Sargon II, Sennacherib, and Esarhaddon.

Oates, J. "Assyrian Chronology, 631-612 b.c." *Iraq* 27 (1965): 135-159. This effort to identify the sources and define the issues related to the conclusion of Ashurbanipal's reign judiciously sifts the conflict of opinion which has dominated Assyriology. Extensive bibliographical notes and internal catalogs of data guide the reader.

Olmstead, A. T. *History of Assyria*. New York: Charles Scribner's Sons, 1923, reprint 1960. Written in the immediate wake of World War I, this comprehensive history was selected for reprinting for its mastery of Assyrian materials and their critical evaluation. Ashurbanipal and his capital receive extensive treatment in chapters 30-47.

Reade, J. E. "Assyrian Architectural Decoration." *Baghdader Milleilungen* 10/11 (1979/1980): 17-110, 71-87. This series of articles provides a comprehensive and comparative study of the four major Assyrian palaces excavated since the mid-nineteenth century, with reference to techniques and subject matter, narrative composition, the immense scale of the art, and the architectural context.

Smith, C. C. "Some Observations on the Assyrians and History." *Encounter* 30 (1969): 340-353. This methodological essay on the nature of source materials coming from ancient Assyria and its kings indicates what they knew, how, and why, as well as the significance of that information to them. The Assyrian Royal Tradition is given focus, while the bibliographical notes provide an introduction to the subject. (Readers, please note: This *Encounter* is published by the Christian Theological Seminary in Indianapolis; it is not to be confused with the British journal of the same name.)

Clyde Curry Smith

ASHURNASIRPAL II

Born: c. 915 B.C.; Ashur, Assyria

Died: 859 B.C.; Kalhu, Assyria

Areas of Achievement: Warfare, government, architecture, and art

Contribution: Ashurnasirpal II created the Neo-Assyrian empire, expanding its boundaries to the Mediterranean coast and into the mountainous regions north and west of the Tigris homeland. At Kalhu, he built an enormous fortress capped by his magnificent palace, which featured the first extensive use of decorated bas-relief.

Early Life

The royal name Ashur-nasir-apli means "the god Ashur protects the son (as heir)." On each decorative slab in his palace, Ashurnasirpal II noted the names of his father, Tukulti-Ninurta II, and his grandfather, Adad-nirari II, along with a summary of his military and architectural achievements. He knew that his great-grandfather Ashur-dan II had "freed cities and founded temples," setting in motion the process of reorganizing and expanding the Assyrian empire which had been reduced to the capital area.

Adad-nirari II had made the first Assyrian attack to the east, into the Tigris' tributary basin. South of the Diyala River, he had defeated the Babylonian king, precipitating a revolution in Babylon and ensuring the perpetuation of the peace treaty by intermarriage. By treaty renewal during a period of eighty years, from the reign of Tukulti-Ninurta II through that of Ashurnasirpal's grandson, Shamshi-Adad V, parity was maintained by Assyria and Babylonia, which secured Assyria's southern front.

Adad-nirari II told of making new plows throughout Ashur-land, heaping up grain, and increasing the breed and quantity of horses. Tukulti-Ninurta II had continued this economic development, which served as a base for serious expansion.

The Nairi states to the north were fragmented remains of the Hurrian kingdom, which had been demolished by royal Assyrian predecessors five centuries earlier. These states were related to the territory known as Hanigalbat and to the important Urartian mountain kingdom around Lake Van. To the northwest were Aramaean tribal states, related to peoples beyond the Euphrates. It was against these states that Tukulti-Ninurta had begun campaigning when his reign prematurely ended.

Life's Work

Ashurnasirpal II came relatively young to the throne, but continued the expansion begun by his grandfather and father with unparalleled energy. The army was reorganized, with cavalry units introduced for the first time to supplement infantry, which were accompanied by chariotry. The latter afforded mobility during long treks. The bas-relief art of Ashurnasirpal portrays improved vehicles of six-spoked wheels pulled by four horses, with three men standing upon the armored platform. Ashurnasirpal fired bow and arrow from such a chariot, and the increased firepower was a significant development for his military strategy and tactics. The army was furnished with battering rams and other siege machines. The former appear as a kind of pointed-nosed tank with four wheels, propelled against city gates by the strength of the many men who could be sheltered under its armored top and sides. It was during Ashurnasirpal's reign that elephants were first employed by a king on campaign.

With Ashurnasirpal came an advanced art of beleaguering cities, and few were prepared to withstand his attack. Sculptures show these sieges, the prodigious amounts of tribute garnered, and a propagandistic expression of the requisite levels of brutality. In his inscriptions, Ashurnasirpal claimed to have employed this brutality so that conquered domains would not again rebel by withholding tribute. Minor princes saw the better part of valor in paying the requisite tribute before the siege and annually thereafter.

Ashurnasirpal's army employed its innovative tactics in continuous campaigns throughout his reign, although specific details are fully documented only for his initial years, from 883 to 878. Some scattered, undated events of the following decade and a half can be identified, but during this later period, the main energy of the king was given over to architectural construction and artistic enterprises recording the events of the first years.

Of the surrounding lands, only Babylonia in the south was not invaded during Ashurnasirpal's reign. The most significant results of Ashurnasirpal's campaigns were in the north and northwest. The land of Nairi (later Armenia) and the Habur region were secured. He forced the ruler of Bit-Adini on the Euphrates to pay tribute and thus secured a bridgehead across that river, allowing not merely his army but also his merchant envoys to pass without duty. Later campaigns took him as far as the Mediterranean, where in a traditional gesture he dipped his weapon into the sea to symbolize its incorporation within his empire.

The methods of drawing conquered peoples into the Assyrian empire were redefined. Adopting the words of an ancient predecessor Tukulti-apal-Esharra I (also called Tiglath-pileser), Ashurnasirpal affirmed, "To Ashur's land I added land, to Ashur's people I added people." His annexation proceeded in three ways. First, peripheral states were assumed to owe lavish tribute, which was collected whenever the Assyrian army was at their borders. Second, interim states submitting directly to Assyria paid yearly, nonruinous tribute and retained native rulers and almost complete self-government. The Assyrian official who remained to see that tribute was sent regularly to the capital could call on the army to enforce compliance. Third, conquered neighboring states became direct provinces, receiving an appointed governor supported by a military garrison. These states were under the same administrative system as Assyria itself and were required to pay the same taxes in goods or in conscripted labor and military service.

To control an empire conceived in these new ways with enlarged levels of displayed military power required not only a new capital city but also a revised conception of its fortresslike structure. The new capital at Kalhu was laid out by Ashurnasirpal on the east bank of the Tigris, nineteen miles north of its junction with the Greater Zab; its walls enclosed an irregular rectangle some seven thousand feet east to west by fifty-five hundred feet north to south, an area of 884 acres.

Two citadels formed the southeast and southwest corners within the walls which Ashurnasirpal completed. The *ekal masharti*, or arsenal, occupied the somewhat lower southeast citadel, but it was not fully completed until the days of his son Shalmaneser III (named for Shalmaneser I, whom Ashurnasirpal knew to have begun the original fortifications on the site of Kalhu).

On a height some sixty-five feet above the plain, the original acropolis of the southwest citadel formed an irregular rectangle because of the abutment of its western edge along the original bed of the Tigris. In the northwest corner, the remains of the ziqqurat rose to a conical peak one hundred feet high; at its base Ashurnasirpal built the temple for the war god Ninurta.

To the south of the ziqqurat and accompanying temple, a huge palace complex occupied six and a half acres; upon its rediscovery in the mid-nineteenth century it was dubbed the "Northwest Palace of Ashurnasirpal II." At its northern end was the administrative wing, with a variety of bureaucratic chambers, including a records repository, surrounding a great open court area which was used for ceremonial and reception functions. At the southern end were the domestic suites, including harem quarters. In neither of these wings were the walls decorated with bas-relief slabs.

Beginning from the south side of the great open court of the northern administrative wing, stretching southward to the southern domestic wing, was a central ceremonial block, which opened impressively off the southern side of the great courtyard through two massive, magnificently decorated gateways leading to the largest room of the palace, the throne room. With the exception of one built by Sennacherib at Ninua (Nineveh), the room is the largest within any Assyrian palace, measuring 154 feet by 33 feet. Tribute bearers from all parts of the empire were led into this room, as the bas-relief slabs of the entrance document, with details such as the type of tribute borne and the garments worn by the divergent ethnic representatives.

On the south side of the throne room lay an inner courtyard. Beyond, through a series of gateways, was a further maze of chambers, many of them decorated, like the throne room, with huge bas-relief slabs standing at least seven feet high from floor level. Only the throne room walls portray the fury of the king as hunter of lions and destroyer of cities. Another nine rooms have slabs with a single large relief, cut across the middle by a band of inscription right over the figures. Each room shows minor variations in lines of text or exact detail of royal campaigns during the first six years, reflecting the sequence in the construction process. In one corridor leading to the throne room, an inscribed stela of 864, with a relief portraying the king, records a celebration of the completion of the great palace and an exotic arboretum—a banquet at which 69,574 people from the extent of the empire, including the sixteen thousand inhabitants of Kalhu and fifteen hundred palace officials, were in attendance. The menu was varied and prodigious, and the feast lasted ten days.

When Ashurnasirpal died, in 859, his body was laid to rest in a gigantic sarcophagus made from a single block of diorite weighing eighteen tons, at the old capital of Ashur, the source of the Assyrian royal tradition. His inscribed memorial stela was placed in the row with his predecessors'.

Summary

Numerous portraits of the king came from the sculptured rooms. Sections of this bas-relief have been excavated and sent to many parts of the world, making Ashurnasirpal's face the best-known of all Assyrian kings'. A variety of quasi-human, quasi-divine creatures are shown accompanying the king in the performance of ritual duties. The inner core of the ceremonial midsection of the palace was the setting for a peculiar mix of propagandistically displayed belligerence, formally arranged processionals, and mysterious rites of purification. The effect was that the farther the king and his advisers penetrated into the inner chambers, the more they perceived the need for exorcism. Fearful things of humans and gods surrounded Ashurnasirpal II. Empire was an awesome matter, even for its creator.

He was succeeded by his son Shalmaneser III, grandson Shamshi-Adad V, and great-grandson Adad-nirari III, who attempted to match the achievements of their distinguished predecessor. At a later date, Sargon II remodeled a section of the great palace for his own use, leaving inscriptional tribute to his ancestor. Esarhaddon rebuilt the *ekal masharti* and the canal which provided water from the Zab, but was at his death in the process of dismantling the "Northwest Palace" so that he might use the reverse of its wall slabs in the decoration of a palace which he had only begun to construct. Ashurbanipal reconstructed the Ehulhul Temple at Harran, which Ashurnasirpal II had founded, and honored the earlier king's work. Then began that silence from which his memory was not disinterred until A. H. Layard began excavations at Kalhu on November 9, 1845, and brought to light the remarkable bas-reliefs, the inscriptions, and the monumental buildings of Ashurnasirpal II.

Bibliography

Brinkman, J. A. *A Political History of Post-Kassite Babylonia, 1158-722 B.C.* Rome: Pontificium Institutum Biblicum, 1968. This standard of historiographic excellence mines all material pertinent to the period with enormous bibliographic detail in its extensive notes.

Grayson, A. K. *Assyrian Royal Inscriptions.* Vol. 2, *From Tiglath-pileser I to Ashur-nasir-apli II.* Wiesbaden, West Germany: Otto Harrassowitz, 1976. A complete reediting in English translation of all source materials is the intention of this series. A consideration of Ashurnasirpal II occupies about half of this volume.

Mallowan, M. E. L. *Nimrud and Its Remains.* 3 vols. London: Collins, 1966. Sir Max Mallowan reexcavated the principal features of Kalhu between 1949 and 1962. These volumes, the third of which contains maps and plans, detail the history of the site, the previous excavations, and the materials found in the remains of Ashurnasirpal's "Northwest Palace."

Paley, S. M. *King of the World: Ashur-nasir-pal II of Assyria 883-859 B.C.* Brooklyn, N.Y.: Brooklyn Museum, 1976. Many museums around the world received examples of the bas-relief slabs from the "Northwest Palace." The Brooklyn Museum used the occasion of publishing its own holdings to reconstruct the plan of the palace and identify the original location of all known examples.

Reade, J. E. "Assyrian Architectural Decoration." *Baghdader Mitteilungen* 10/11 (1979/1980): 17-110, 71-87. This series of articles provides a comprehensive comparative study of the four major Assyrian palaces excavated since the mid-nineteenth century, with reference to techniques and subject matter, narrative composition, the immense scale of the art, and the architectural context.

Stearns, J. B. *Reliefs from the Palace of Ashurnasirpal II.* Graz, Austria: Ernst F. Weidner, 1961. John Barker Stearns began the effort to identify all surviving examples of Ashurnasirpal palace relief slabs held in museum collections around the world and to classify their types and functions.

Clyde Curry Smith

AŚOKA THE GREAT

Born: c. 302 B.C.; probably near Pataliputra, Magadha, India
Died: c. 232 B.C.; place unknown
Areas of Achievement: Government and religion
Contribution: Through energetic and enlightened administration of his kingdom, Aśoka spread the Buddhist faith in all directions and, by means of his Rock, Pillar, and Cave edicts, provided India, the districts surrounding India, and, ultimately, the entire world with an example of regal compassion that is as admirable as it is rare.

Early Life

What can be known of the life of Aśoka derives from two primary sources: First, the legends that sprang up during and after his death (and which are often suspected of helping to grind certain zealous religious axes); second, Aśoka's own "sermons in stone," the thirty-five edicts which he began issuing in 260 and which were inscribed on rocks, pillars hewn from sandstone, and the walls of caves in the Barabar Hills of ancient Magadha. Therefore, only a very fragmentary early life can be pieced together. There is much to be left to conjecture and little to be known with certainty.

Aśoka was the son of Bindusara and the grandson of Chandragupta Maurya, the founder of the Mauryan dynasty and consolidator of a great empire that included all northern India as far west as the Hindu Kush. A charming legend is told of the naming of Aśoka. His mother, who may have been named Subhadrangi, was supposedly kept away from the king's bed by party politics; finally gaining access to the bed, she bore the king a son and said thereafter, "I am without sorrow," which is to say, in Sanskrit, "Aśoka."

Aśoka is reputed to have been ungainly in appearance and, perhaps, to have been disliked by his father. In his early manhood, however, he was called upon by Bindusara to put down a revolt in Taxila and from there to proceed to Ujjain to act as a viceroy. Aśoka appears to have had numerous brothers and sisters, and, if certain Ceylonese legends are accepted, he was most cruel to his brothers in the process of jockeying for the succession to the throne, murdering ninety-nine of them before becoming king. Such an account, however, may well be part of the tradition of Chandasoka (Black Aśoka), the epithet intended to indicate that, before his conversion to Buddhism, he was a man whose ruthlessness and cruelty knew no bounds. That there was a struggle for the throne is supported by the fact that Aśoka's accession to it (c. 274) occurred four years before his coronation. That blood might have been shed in the process of Aśoka's becoming king seems not unlikely. Hsuan Tsang, a Chinese Buddhist pilgrim who traveled in India in the seventh century A.D., reports having seen a high pillar which commemorated the site of what had been called "Aśoka's Hell," a prison which housed a series of elaborate torture chambers. According to one of the legends, Aśoka's enlightenment came about when he beheld a Buddhist holy man whose imperviousness to torture moved him to become aware in a painful way of his cruelty, destroy the prison, and relax the laws against criminals. Solider evidence, however, indicates that Aśoka's conversion may well have been the consequence of his beholding, not the indestructibility of a holy man, but rather the extreme destructibility of the Kaliṅga people in southeastern India. In 262, Aśoka fought and won a war against the Kaliṅgas; in Rock Edict 13, referring to himself as "Priyadarsi, Beloved of the Gods," he chronicled his conversion, noting that 150,000 persons were captured, 100,000 were slain, and many times that number had died from the general effects of the war. The havoc that the war had wreaked had caused Aśoka to become intensely devoted to the study, love, and inculcation of *dharma*. This intense devotion, coupled with his sorrow and regret, had led him to desire "security, self-control, impartiality, and cheerfulness for all living creatures." He went on in the edict to announce a radical new program for his empire: He would abandon military conquest and would try to effect moral conquest in and among people.

Life's Work

In 260, Aśoka issued the first of the Rock Edicts and made his first "pious tour." Both edict and tour were part of his plan to endow his people with *dharma*. The concept of *dharma* is a complex one generally, and it becomes no simpler in Aśoka's use of it. For him, it had to do both with his Buddhist underpinnings and with morality and righteousness in general. *Dharma* was something he did out of Buddhist piety; it was also a complex of responses to life available to non-Buddhists. It was a kind of ecosystem, a recognition that one's well-being was closely and eternally connected with the well-being of everyone else. Aśoka's attempt to promulgate this understanding represents a tremendous evolution in the moral development of mankind.

Aśoka had the edict written in the languages of the districts where they were to be placed. Monumental Prakrit, a kind of lingua franca for India at the time, was the primary language of the edicts, but on the western frontier of the kingdom, edicts written in Greek and Aramaic have been found. Noting that in past times rulers had made great pleasure trips through the land, Aśoka determined to embark upon another series of tours, during which he would talk to people about *dharma*, visit the aged, and give gifts and money to those in need.

In 257, Aśoka appointed the first *dharma-mahamatras*, the officers of an institution charged with traveling about the kingdom and helping to spread *dharma*. Interestingly, these men were responsible for spreading the Aśokan notion of *dharma* through all sects; they were not supposed to attempt sectarian conversions but were rather to supervise the distribution of various gifts and to help promote conformity to the ideals of compassion, liberality, truthfulness, purity, gentleness, and goodness. Aśoka worried about the almost reflexive tendency of people dedicated to a particular religion to quarrel over dogma, and some of his sternest statements in the edicts address this problem; in one inscription, he baldly proclaims that dissident nuns and monks must be expelled from their order. Aśoka recognized two ways in which people could advance in *dharma*: moral prescription and meditation. The teachers of any religious sect, be it Buddhist, Christian, Islamic, or any other, are always ready to provide moral prescription. So, in fact, was Aśoka, and he did so in the edicts. In Pillar Edict 7, however, he acknowledged that people make greater progress in *dharma* through practicing meditation than through heeding moral prescription.

There has been considerable argument concerning the precise nature of Aśoka's religion. The edicts have little to say of doctrinaire Buddhism. Aśoka's tolerance of other religions is declared clearly and eloquently in the inscriptions. He often spoke of *svarga* (Heaven) and the possibility of obtaining it through *dharma*. He had nothing to say on stone or pillar of *nirvana*, a veritable plank in the Buddhist platform. Some scholars have been led by these facts to suggest that Aśoka was—as Akbar was to be almost two thousand years later—a practitioner of some sort of universal religion. In many other ways, however, Aśoka strongly supported and promoted *dharma* as revealed in and through Buddhism, and his religion's spread through western Asia during his reign was certainly in part a result of those tremendous administrative energies that helped further his humanitarian purposes.

Throughout the 250's, Aśoka made moral tours, erected Buddhist shrines, and commissioned edicts. In 258-257, he issued in one body the fourteen Major Rock Edicts and granted cave dwellings to the Ajivikas, an order of Buddhist monks. In 250, he made a pilgrimage to Lumbinī Garden, the birthplace of the Buddha, and erected there a commemorative pillar. In 243-242, he issued the Pillar Edicts.

According to one account of Aśoka's last days, by 232 he had lost his power to the high officials of the court. In his old age, Aśoka supposedly nominated as his successor Samprati, one of his grandsons. Under the influence of the usurping officers, Samprati proceeded to abuse his grandfather, reducing Aśoka's allowances so drastically that, finally, for dinner the aging king would be sent only half an amalaka fruit on an earthen plate. How or where Aśoka died remains a matter of conjecture, but that he died in straitened circumstances seems likely.

Summary

That might makes right is an idea that has been taken for granted by such historical leaders as Alexander the Great, Julius Caesar, and Genghis Khan. What made Aśoka great was his grasping another truth and giving it life in third century India. In Rock Edict 13, he asserted that "the chiefest conquest is the conquest of Right and not of Might," and he went on to make his deeds commensurate with his rock-inscribed words. He abolished war within his empire immediately after he had subdued the Kaliṅgas. He never fought another one. That he desired to civilize both his people and neighboring peoples is made clear by the testimony of the edicts; the usual formula, however, the one that equates civilization of a people with subjugation, did not apply. Aśoka did not give up entirely the idea that chastisement may on occasion be necessary, though, for he reminded the forest people who had come under his sway that they must grow in *dharma*, and he reserved the right to exercise punishment, despite having repented of his violent ways, in order to make them cease their criminal behavior. The edicts of Aśoka reveal a fascinating blend of the practical and the ideal, the proud and the humble; they record the workings of a complex mind.

Writing of Aśoka in *The Outline of History* (1921), H. G. Wells judged:

> Amidst the tens of thousands of names of monarchs that crowd the columns of history, their majesties and graciousnesses and serenities and royal highnesses and the like, the name of Asoka shines, and shines almost alone, a star. From the Volga to Japan his name is still honoured. China, Tibet, and even India, though it has left his doctrine, preserve the tradition of his greatness. More living men cherish his memory to-day than have ever heard the names of Constantine or Charlemagne.

The high-flown rhetoric of this passage ought not to bias one against the beauty of its vision. If most people do not today cherish the memory of Aśoka above the memories of Constantine the Great and Charlemagne, that fact is perhaps a measure of the twentieth century's bad taste in heroes.

Bibliography

Bhandarkar, D. R. *Aśoka*. Calcutta, India: Calcutta University Press, 1925. A spirited and at times combative rehearsal of Aśoka's life and works, dealing especially well with the Aśokan concept of *dharma* and according Aśoka a high place in history. Contains translations of the Rock and Pillar Edicts accompanied by detailed notes.

Campbell, Joseph. *The Masks of God: Oriental Mythology*. New York: Viking Press, 1964. This volume contains a brief, but luminous, discussion of Aśoka, comparing the destiny of Buddhism under Aśoka to that of Christianity under Constantine the Great and noting the absence from the Rock Edicts of certain fundamental Buddhist doctrines.

Durant, Will. *Our Oriental Heritage*. New York: Simon and Schuster, 1935. Durant presents a respectful but slightly skeptical account of the life of Aśoka, seeing the seeds of the downfall of the Mauryas in the very piety of Aśoka that is so admired. Provides an especially vivid description, by way of Hsuan Tsang, of "Aśoka's Hell."

Mookerji, Radhakumud. *Aśoka*. London: Macmillan and Co., 1928. A scholarly biography which, like Bhandarkar's book, accords Aśoka a high place in the moral annals of humankind. It contains copiously annotated translations of the Rock and Pillar Edicts and three cave inscriptions as well as appendices concerning the chronology of the edicts and the scripts, dialects, and grammar of the texts.

Nikam, N. A., and Richard McKeon. *The Edicts of Aśoka*. Chicago: University of Chicago Press, 1959. This handy translation of all the edicts except for the Queen's Edict and some variants of the minor edicts also features a brief introduction that makes interesting comparisons between Aśoka and other great world figures such as Hammurabi, Charlemagne, Akbar, and Marcus Aurelius.

Thapar, Romila. *Aśoka and the Decline of the Mauryas*. New York: Oxford University Press, 1961. A thoroughgoing study of the life and times of Aśoka featuring an account of the disrepair into which his empire fell after his death. Includes numerous valuable appendices concerning the historical record of Aśoka's period based on pottery and coins, the geographical locations of the edicts, and the titles of Aśoka. A translation of the edicts is also provided.

Wells, H. G. *The Outline of History*. New York: Macmillan, 1921. A vivid and highly laudatory account of Aśoka, allotting him a more significant place in history than that of Alexander the Great and arguing that the epithet "great" is more properly applied to Aśoka.

Johnny Wink

SAINT ATHANASIUS

Born: c. 293; Alexandria, Egypt
Died: May 2, 373; Alexandria, Egypt
Areas of Achievement: Religion and historiography
Contribution: For half a century, Athanasius helped to maintain Christian orthodoxy in the Eastern church from his position as Bishop of Alexandria. His defense of the doctrine of the Trinity was influential in the formulation of the Nicene Creed.

Early Life

Athanasius was born about A.D. 293 in Alexandria, one of the leading cities of Egypt. Since its founding in 332 B.C. by Alexander the Great, Alexandria had been a focal point of the Greco-Roman world. Its beautiful harbor served as a center for extensive trade with all parts of the Mediterranean. The native flax of Egypt was woven into linen which was shipped as far away as Britain, and Alexandria enjoyed a world monopoly on the papyrus plant and its products—not only writing materials but also sails, mats, and sandals.

With a population of a million or more in Athanasius' time, Alexandria was not only a commercial and administrative center but also one of the greatest centers of learning in the ancient world. The Alexandrian library preserved documents from all parts of the ancient Near East and accommodated scholars from the entire Mediterranean area. It was here that the Greek Old Testament, the Septuagint, had been translated from the original Hebrew by Jewish scholars. Alexandria was a cosmopolitan city with large populations of Egyptians, Jews, Greeks, and Romans. Its array of palaces and public buildings, gardens and groves, pagan temples and Christian churches, made Alexandria one of the wonders of the Roman Empire.

Athanasius' parents, who were moderately wealthy, provided him with a liberal education, typical of the Greek culture in which he lived. He learned Greek, Latin, Egyptian antiquities, philosophy, and religion, but it was the Holy Scriptures that impressed him most. Alexandria was a focal point of intense persecution of Christians during the reign of Diocletian and Galerius, and several of Athanasius' teachers, along with many church leaders, suffered martyrdom. Athanasius well understood the seriousness of converting to the Christian faith.

Athanasius was an earnest and diligent young man who early came to the attention of Alexander, the Bishop of Alexandria from 312 to 328. The bishop helped in the boy's education, and eventually Athanasius became his secretary and a presbyter under his supervision.

Athanasius was very small of stature, rather stooped, and somewhat emaciated in appearance. He had a forceful personality and sharpness of intellect. Though he was gentle and meek of spirit, he was driven by a determination to keep the orthodox Christian faith no matter what the cost, no matter how many opposed him. His inner intensity made him quick of movement and constantly active. He was known for his deep faith in God, and he manifested an ability to inspire steadfast loyalty in the congregations he served, despite persecution, exile, and denunciations.

Life's Work

The fierce persecution of the Church abruptly changed when Constantine became emperor and began to favor Christianity throughout the Empire. Such a sudden change must have been difficult for Athanasius and his fellow Christians to comprehend. The amazement and incredulity that they experienced is reflected in Eusebius of Ceasarea's description of a church council:

> No bishop was absent from the table of the emperor. Bodyguards and soldiers stood guard, with sharp swords drawn, around the outer court of the palace, but among them the men of God could walk fearlessly and enter the deepest parts of the palace. At dinner [they ate with the emperor.] Easily one could imagine this to be the kingdom of Christ or regard it as a dream rather than reality.

Some of those who enjoyed Constantine's favor bore scars from the Diocletian era, such as Bishop Paphnutius from Egypt, who had lost an eye in that persecution, and Paul of Caesarea, who had been tortured with a red-hot iron under Licinius and was crippled in both hands. A disadvantage of Constantine's patronage of the Church, however, was that the power of the state would be used to enforce church discipline, as Athanasius learned later when he was exiled by Constantine to the Rhineland region of Germany.

The Roman emperor called the first ecumenical council of the Church, which met at Nicaea, in Asia Minor, in 325. ("Ecumenical" literally means "of the empire.") Constantine himself presided over the beginning sessions of this great assembly of the leadership of the Church and in so doing set an important precedent of involvement between church and state that lasted throughout the European Middle Ages and into modern times: Decisions of church councils were to be enforced by political authorities. For many years there had been local and regional synods or councils, but the idea of bringing together the entire Church, East and West, was new.

The Nicene Council met only twenty miles from the imperial palace of Nicomedia, easily accessible by sea and land from all parts of the Roman Empire. Some three hundred bishops and more than a thousand presbyters and laymen assembled in an effort to bring unity to the Church. Most of these people were from the Eastern church; only seven came from Europe. At least one, a Persian bishop, was from outside the Roman Empire. The council met from mid-June to the end of July, discussing theology and matters ecclesiastical in Latin and translating speeches into Greek.

Athanasius, a young archdeacon at the time, accompanied his bishop, Alexander, and spoke often at the council, demonstrating a brilliant intellect and impressive eloquence. Though only twenty-seven at the time, Athanasius set forth an influential defense of the orthodox position that Christ was God from all eternity, uncreated and equal to God the Father. The result was the Nicene Creed, recited by millions of Christians worldwide in their liturgy:

> We believe in One God, the Father Almighty,
> Maker of all things visible and invisible,
> and in one Lord Jesus Christ, the Son of God, . . .
> begotten not made, One in essence with the Father,
> by Whom all things were made, both things in Heaven
> and things in Earth. . . .

The Nicene Creed is acknowledged by Eastern Orthodox, Roman Catholic, and Protestant churches alike. The Greek Orthodox Church annually observes (on the Sunday before Pentecost) a special feast in memory of the Council of Nicaea.

In 328, Athanasius succeeded Alexander as Bishop of Alexandria and remained in that position, except for five exiles, for forty-six years. As a defender of the orthodox faith, he was popular in the Alexandrian church where he ministered. He was, however, opposed by the Arians, those who thought of Christ as a great teacher, but less than God Himself. The Emperor Constantine, more interested in unity than in truth, thought the matter merely one of theological semantics. Hoping to have more uniformity and less discord in the Church, he removed Athanasius from his office and banished him from Alexandria.

When Constantine died in 337, Athanasius returned, but soon he was exiled a second time for seven years, which he spent in Rome, where the orthodox position was strongly affirmed. The sons of Constantine, acting on the suggestion of Julius, Bishop of Rome, convened another church council at Sardica in 343. There Athanasius was reinstated as bishop.

Before long it became apparent that the differences between the Arian bishops and the orthodox leaders were more than doctrinal. The Arians gained support from the Roman Emperor Constantius because of their belief that the Church should submit to the emperor in doctrinal as well as administrative matters. Arguing from Scripture, Athanasius insisted on the independence of the Church in doctrine. As a result, Athanasius in 356 was again sent into exile, this time for six years in the Egyptian desert, where he became a close acquaintance of the famed Anthony, who helped begin the Western system of monasteries.

In 361, the pagan Emperor Julian recalled banished bishops on both sides of the controversy. By diligent and wise administration, Athanasius restored harmony to his diocese, but Julian exiled him for a fourth time and sent two hired assassins to kill him on board an imperial ship. Athanasius, however, managed to escape from the ship while it was sailing up the Nile River.

Athanasius returned to Alexandria after Julian's death, but endured yet a fifth and final brief exile under the Emperor Valens. He spent the last seven years of his life mostly undisturbed in his diocese. He continued writing, content to see the vindication of the orthodox position in the Church. He died in 373; his epitaph, "Athanasius contra mundum" (Athanasius against the world), reflected the steadfastness with which he had stood his ground against all opposition.

Throughout his tumultuous life, Athanasius was a prolific writer. He was noted for his theological depth, intellectual precision, and clarity of style; he wrote to make his meaning plain, not to embellish or entertain. He incisively demolished his opponents' arguments and methodically built a logical structure for his own position. Most of his works were written in response to some pressing matter or in defense of an action or position. Though he wrote in Greek, his works are now known solely by their Latin titles.

Athanasius' writings fall into several categories. For example, he produced apologetical works in defense of Christianity, such as *De incarnatione Verbi Dei* (before 325; *On the Incarnation of the Word of God*). Many of his theological works were written to defend the orthodox Nicene faith. For example, he wrote a letter in this regard to the bishops of Egypt and Libya (356) and a commentary on the decrees of the Council of Nicaea (352), *Contra Arianos* (350; *An Apology Against the Arians*) and *Apologia ad Constantinum* (356; *An Apology to Constantius*). Athanasius also wrote exegetical works interpreting Scripture; in his commentary on the Psalms, he followed the allegorizing style of the Alexandrian school in identifying in these Hebrew worship songs many types of Christ and the Church. Also in this category is his synopsis of the Bible. Of his devotional works, his *Epistolae festales* (*The Festal Epistles*) are most interesting. During the Easter season, these letters were read in the churches to edify and exhort the congregations.

Summary

Athanasius was not a historian, but many of his writings provide important primary source materials for historians. His *Historia Arianorum* (*History of the Arians*) is a good example, as is *An Apology Against the Arians*. Athanasius is noted for his great accuracy and his practice of documenting his assertions. Thus, later generations were indebted to him not only for his histories but also for the compilation of many documents of the fourth century.

Athanasius' biography of Saint Anthony helped to extend the monastic system into Europe. Anthony, a native of Upper Egypt, lived a completely solitary life for a time in the Egyptian desert. Others who followed his example became known as monks, from the Greek word *monachoi* (people who live alone). Athanasius was impressed by Anthony's deep spirituality, and it was through Athanasius that Anthony began to realize that he needed to take more interest in the welfare of the Church. When Athanasius visited Rome in 340, during his second exile, he explained to the Roman Christians the life-style of the Egyptian monks and thus introduced monasticism into the Western church.

Because of the early period in which he lived, Athanasius' listing of the canon of Scripture has been of great interest to later theologians. His thirty-ninth Festal Epistle of Easter, 367, made mention of all the books now included in the New Testament, but in the older order of the Gospels, Acts, the General Epistles, Paul's Epistles (including Hebrews), and the Apocalypse. His Old Testament canon comprised twenty-two books, as in the Alexandrian Jewish system, not the older Talmudic listing of twenty-four. The Apocrypha, accepted by the later Roman Catholic church, was not included in Athanasius' list.

Throughout his long life, Athanasius demonstrated a remarkable lack of self-interest and ambition. Though he held one of the great bishoprics of the Eastern church, he never compromised what he was convinced to be the truth. His manner was humble and conciliatory, but for him, truth was not subject to political compromise. His contemporaries were strengthened by his stability, consistency, and courage in the midst of tribulation, and the later Church is indebted to him for the clarity of his theology.

Bibliography

Athanasius. *The Life of Saint Antony.* New York: Newman Press, 1978. Translated with notes by Robert T. Meyer. This brief volume brings insight into the thinking of a man who had a great influence upon Athanasius: the Egyptian monk Saint Anthony.

Bruce, F. F. *The Spreading Flame: The Rise and Progress of Christianity from Its First Beginnings to the Conversion of the English.* Grand Rapids, Mich.: Wm. B. Eerdmans Publishing Co., 1958. An excellent detailed history of the early Church. There are many references to Athanasius, but the principal value of this book is in providing the historical context in which Athanasius lived. The author is an outstanding expert in his field.

Frend, W. H. C. *The Rise of Christianity.* Philadelphia, Pa.: Fortress Press, 1984. A useful introduction to church history. Includes a seventy-five-page chart which gives a synopsis of events in three categories from 63 B.C. to A.D. 615. Also includes five unusual maps which shed light on the text. Frend makes many references to Athanasius.

Latourette, Kenneth Scott. *A History of Christianity.* New York: Harper and Row, Publishers, 1953. The first three hundred pages of this classic fifteen-hundred-page history of Christianity are useful in interpreting Athanasius' role in the early Church and later Roman Empire.

Schaff, Philip. *History of the Christian Church*. Vol. 3, *Nicene and Post-Nicene Christianity*, A.D. *311-600*. New York: Charles Scribner's Sons, 1884. The most exhaustive church history available in the English language. The section on Athanasius, Constantine, and the Nicene Council are absolutely indispensable for an understanding of the life and influence of Athanasius. Schaff is noted for the thoroughness of his history and the detailed precision of his narrative.

A Select Library of Nicene and Post-Nicene Fathers of the Christian Church. Vol. 4., *Athanasius: Select Works and Letters*. Grand Rapids, Mich.: Wm. B. Eerdmans Publishing Co., 1891, reprint 1978. This six-hundred-page book is indispensable for understanding Athanasius. It contains a detailed account of his extant writings, with helpful editorial notes. Contains index, tables, and appendix.

Shelley, Bruce. *Church History in Plain Language*. Waco, Tex.: Word Books, 1982. Though this volume is rather sparse on Athanasius, it is valuable for its accessibility. Recommended for those with little background in church history. Makes clear what the conversion of Constantine meant to the Church.

William H. Burnside

ATTILA

Born: 406?; Pannonia?
Died: 453; probably Jazberin
Areas of Achievement: Government and conquest
Contribution: By uniting all the Hunnic tribes from the northern Caucasus to the upper Danube River, rendering the Romans a tributary state, Attila fashioned the most powerful empire of the West in the fifth century.

Early Life

The movement of the Huns from Asia westward through the steppes in the fourth century caused the Great Migration of Germans and Alans into Europe. By 420, the Huns had found a home in Pannonia, the seat of the main body of the nation, which was divided into three ulus, each ruled by a khan. Here was a strategic base for later operations in Italy and the Balkans. The Huns' superior cavalry tactics were well publicized, and the Romans of the East and West soon realized the need to appease them.

When Khan Roila died in 433 or 434, two of his nephews, Attila and his brother Bleda, were elected as joint rulers. Nothing is known of the early life of Attila or of his grandparents and mother. He was the son of Mundjuk, brother of Roila and Oktar. Mundjuk may have been a co-khan with Roila, but the evidence is unclear. What is certain is that Mundjuk and Oktar died before Roila did and that Attila became the chief khan, subordinating his older brother from the start.

The Roman statesman and writer Cassiodorus described Attila as Asian in appearance, beardless, flat-nosed, and swarthy. His body was short and square, with broad shoulders. He was adept at terrorizing enemies with the use of his deep-set eyes. Edward Gibbon, in *History of the Decline and Fall of the Roman Empire*, says that he was feared as much for his magic as for his militarism.

Life's Work

The death of Roila brought relief to Constantinople since the late king of the Huns was planning an invasion of Eastern Rome. Bishops attributed his death to the intervention of God. Attila quickly exhibited a genius for leadership and statesmanship. His first task was to settle the disputes with the Romans at Constantinople, demanding an end to the use of Huns in their service. Attila and Bleda met Roman envoys from both empires at the River Morava to sign a treaty in 434. Negotiating from horseback, as was the Hunnic custom, they secured from Emperor Theodosius II the promise to end the use of Hunnish warriors, the return of those in his service, free access to border towns for Hunnish merchants, and the doubling of the annual tribute of gold from 350 to 700 pounds. Two of the fugitives handed back to the Huns were young boys, Mama and Atakam, relatives of the khans who summarily were crucified. The Roman Flavius Aetius continued to use Huns and Alans against Germans in the West.

After this treaty of Margus with Theodosius, Attila and Bleda devoted their efforts to consolidating the eastern possessions. Striving to unite all the ulus under their rule, the khans forged an empire from the northern Caucasus to central Europe. Within five years this objective was reached, and the brothers divided their administration into two sections.

Meanwhile Persians attacked Roman Armenia in 438 in a war that lasted fifteen years, and the Romans were hoping to recover Carthage in North Africa from the Vandals, who posed a danger to Roman shipping. Partly because of other problems, the Roman emperor neglected payments to the Hun and was preparing new operations against the Vandal Gaiseric and the Sassanian shah in Persia, allies of Attila. With the opportunity at hand, Attila launched an invasion of the Eastern Roman Empire in 441. Gibbon says that this move was prompted by Gaiseric. In any case, Attila's forces moved rapidly across the Morava, seizing Margus, Constantia, Singidunum (Belgrade), and Sirmium, the key to the defense of the Danube. A puzzling one-year truce followed, enabling the Romans to prepare for defense. An angry Attila launched a new offensive in 443, destroying Ratiaria and Naissus, birthplace of Constantine, and Sardica (Sophia), thus opening the highway to the capital. Roman armies led by Aspar, an Alan, contested the Huns but were no match for the swiftly moving forces of Attila. Although Constantinople was well defended by troops and terrain, Theodosius decided to sue for peace and so paid six thousand pounds of gold to Attila to make up for his arrears of tribute. The treaty of Anatolius was signed on August 27, 443.

Within two years, Bleda was officially removed from power and soon after was killed by Attila himself. No details exist about the power struggle between the brothers. Attila was master of the entire Hunnic world empire and would have no more rivals.

The location of Attila's court is only educated conjecture. Hungarians argue that it was located about thirty-six miles west of Buda, at Jazberin. Others suggest that the location was at Tokay or Agria, all in the plains of upper Hungary. This court included a wooden palace on a hill, as well as another for his chief wife, Queen Cerca, houses for his adjutants, storehouses, service buildings, and even a stone bathhouse. All were enclosed by a wooden wall. At table, Attila ate only meat, used wooden utensils, and never tasted bread. Inside the spacious palace were servants of many nationalities: Alans, Greeks, Germans, Romans, and Slavs.

The same international character prevailed within the Hunnish borders, as Attila's policy of no taxation attracted many settlers. Taxation was unnecessary, owing to the large tribute from Constantinople and annual collections of booty from warfare. Even the army comprised other nationalities. Persian engineers from the shah and deserters from the Romans helped Attila's forces prepare for siege warfare against stone walls. Slavs, taught the methods of warfare by the Huns, formed special detachments in the khan's armies, evidenced by references to the troops drinking kvas.

The Huns invaded Rome again in 447, but there are no sources indicating the motive—perhaps Attila needed more plunder. The Eastern Romans were besieged by famine and plagues and not likely to provoke the Huns. Nevertheless, Attila invaded with armies of subject peoples augmenting his Huns. In the midst of the campaign, a fierce earthquake struck the Eastern Roman world, destroying sections of the walls around Constantinople. The people summoned the determination to rebuild the fortifications hastily and even constructed another, outer wall to ward off the Huns. West of the capital a pitched battle took place at Utus. Although the Huns won the battle, it was fought so energetically by the Romans that the Huns suffered serious losses. Choosing to bypass the capital, Attila contented himself with enormous plunder in the Balkans. This would be his last victory over Roman forces.

That same year, the khan received news of a renegade Hunnic nation in Scythia. The Acatziri were corresponding with the emperor at Constantinople, posing a danger to Attila's rearguard position. Consequently, Attila's forces crushed the rebels, and Ellac, Attila's son, was sent to rule over them. There followed the second peace of Anatolius, in 448.

Attila found it necessary to construct an intelligence network to combat Roman espionage. At one point his German agent, Edecon, was drawn into a scheme to assassinate Attila in 448. Sent to Constantinople on business, he was "bribed" by a Roman official of the emperor, the eunuch Chrysaphius, to join the plot. Loyal to Attila, Edecon feigned acceptance and exposed the affair to the khan, who then exploited the matter to obtain more tribute from Constantinople.

Attila next considered a plan to marry Honoria, the sister of Emperor Valentinian III. The Roman princess herself initiated the idea, perhaps in bitterness after having been placed in confinement by her mother for many years following a teenage pregnancy, or to avoid marrying an old Roman courtier and friend of her brother. The khan saw an opportunity to demand one-half of the imperial lands as dowry for the marriage. When the emperor's expected refusal arrived, Attila prepared for war. Honoria was sent to Ravenna, Italy, by Valentinian, who called upon Aetius to defend the imperial borders. Both sides sought allies as Aetius gained the support of Visigoths, Burgundians, and most of the Franks; Attila won the support of the younger of the two Frankish brother-rulers, as well as the Ostrogoths, Vandals, and Alans.

The Alans of Gaul were compelled to accede to Aetius, and the great battle of the nations occurred at Châlons in June, 451. The Huns were disheartened for failure to capture the city of Orléans and then weakened by guerrilla tactics as they made their way to plains more suited to their cavalry. Attila delivered an inspiring address to his soldiers on the eve of battle, but the opposing armies were strong. The coalitions fought a bloody encounter but the result was indecisive. Attila led his forces back to the Danube and the Visigoths retreated to Toulouse. His plan to take the Western Empire failed, so Attila prepared to invade Italy. Aetius found it more difficult to defend this region, since he feared the consequences of bringing Visigoths to Italy. In 452, Attila invaded across the Alps, coming to Milan, where he met Pope Leo (the Great) and two Roman senators, who convinced him to turn back. It was unlikely that idealism was the issue; rather, the epidemic of dysentery among his troops and the imminent arrival of Aetius' forces via Ravenna more likely encouraged the retreat. It is also probable that Leo gave ransom for the release of prominent prisoners. Nevertheless, the Huns devastated the plains of Lombardy, forcing many to flee to the lagoons of the Adriatic Sea, where the Venetian republic arose. Returning home, Attila wished instead to strike at Byzantium.

Once back in the Danubian country, however, the khan, who had numerous wives, married again, this time to a German named Ildico. After the usual wedding party, Attila lay down to rest and was later found dead in his bed (453). Despite rumors that he was stabbed or poisoned by Ildico (who was found at his bedside), it is more likely that he simply choked to death on vomit or blood from a hemorrhage. Hunnic warriors immediately cut off part of their own hair and disfigured their own faces with deep wounds, as was their mourning custom.

The khanate was divided among Attila's three sons: Dengizik, Ernack, and Ellac. The latter was killed the next year, when a rebellion occurred; the other two brothers took their ulus to Dacia and Bessarabia for a time. Other bands of Huns penetrated the right bank of the Danube, settling in the Roman world as allies. Most of the Alans supported the Byzantines when the forces of Dengizik were crushed in a war of 468-469. The Great Bulgarian nation of the Huns disintegrated in the East as well, as some joined Slavs to find their way to the southern Balkans to a land that bears their Hunnic name. Other Bulgar descendants of the Huns settled for a while on the upper Volga River until they were absorbed into the nomad empire of the Khazars.

Summary

Attila was never a divine-right monarch in the sense of a Persian shah or even the Macedonian Alexander the Great. He never posed as a god before his people but, rather, wore simple clothing without jewelry, mixing with his people—often without bodyguards. Attila did not create a permanent administrative structure for the Hunnic nation; his influence, while truly awesome, was temporary for the Huns. He seemed to profit little from cultural contacts with the Romans of the East or West; most artistic objects traced to Hunnish origins have been discovered in the Ukraine or Volga River regions, not from the Danubian plains. Nor did Attila's Huns adopt the Roman proclivity for the plow, as some eastern Huns did.

Attila's empire helped to hasten the fall of the Roman Empire in the West. Although his forces did not destroy the Roman imperial structure, they weakened the mystique of Rome by their continuous exactions of tribute. In the steppelands of the East, they destroyed the German and Iranian control of the Russian world, preparing the way for the next nomad empire, that of the Khazars, and even teaching the hitherto peaceful Slavs how to defend themselves from future invaders.

Ironically, by 451 the Roman tribute had ceased and the aura of Attila's invincibility had vanished. His armies had failed at Châlons, he could no longer intimidate subject nations, and his resources were quickly disappearing. Then, when the Italian campaign was cut short, his allies grew restive without the gold and booty of former days. Perhaps his timely death preserved his historical reputation.

Bibliography
Gibbon, Edward. *History of the Decline and Fall of the Roman Empire*. Reprint. New York: Modern Library, 1932. A vivid picture of Attila's personality and his court is presented by this master eighteenth century historian, who has culled a wealth of detail from limited sources.
Gordon, G. D. *The Age of Attila: Fifth Century Byzantium and the Barbarians*. Ann Arbor: University of Michigan Press, 1966. This valuable work cleverly arranges selections of primary sources to relate the history of Attila's age.
Jones, A. H. M. *The Decline of the Ancient World*. New York: Holt, Rinehart and Winston, 1966. Jones's work includes a short but useful presentation of the relationships among Attila, Aetius, and Theodosius.
Macartney, C. A. "The End of the Huns." *Journal of Hellenic Studies* 10 (1934): 106-114. This article attempts to locate the various branches of the Huns following the death of Attila.
Mänchen-Helfen, Otto J. *The World of the Huns: Studies in Their History and Culture*. Edited by Max Knight. Berkeley: University of California Press, 1973. The most scholarly treatment of the subject, by a recognized authority who died before completing the manuscript. It is replete with excellent linguistic analysis of the sources.
Thompson, E. A. *A History of Attila and the Huns*. London: Oxford University Press, 1948, reprint 1975. Still the most readable and clear presentation of the life of Attila. Its scholarly treatment holds up well under later academic scrutiny.

Vernadsky, George. *Ancient Russia*. New Haven, Conn.: Yale University Press, 1943. The chapter on the Huns is a short but remarkably complete story that is not limited to the settlements in Southern Russia. The author was the leading authority on Russian history in America for many years.

John D. Windhausen

SAINT AUGUSTINE

Born: November 13, 354; Tagaste, Numidia
Died: August 28, 430; Hippo Regius, Numidia
Areas of Achievement: Religion and philosophy
Contribution: Renowned for his original interpretations of Scripture and extensive writings—in particular, his *Confessions*—Augustine was the greatest Christian theologian of the ancient world.

Early Life

Aurelius Augustinus was born of middle-class parents, Patricius and Monica, in the Roman province of Numidia (now Algeria). His pious mother imbued him with a reverence for Christ, but as he excelled in school he found the Church's teachings and practices unsatisfactory. As he studied at nearby Madauros and then Carthage, he was swayed by various philosophies. From 370 to 383, with the exception of one year in Tagaste, he taught rhetoric in Carthage. Part of these early years were wasted (he later regretted) on womanizing, but this experience created in him a lifelong sensitivity to overcoming the desires of the flesh. Upon the birth of an illegitimate son, Adeodatus, in 373, Augustine identified himself with the prophet Mani, who had preached a belief in the spiritual forces of light and darkness which also included Christ as the Redeemer. Hoping to explore the tension in this dualism, Augustine was disappointed by the shallow intellect of the Manichaean bishop Faustus and became disillusioned with that faith.

Desirous of a fresh outlook and a better teaching position, Augustine sailed to Rome in 383 and the next year began teaching rhetoric in Milan. There he was awakened to the potential of Christian theology by the sermons of Saint Ambrose and, in particular, the Neoplatonism of Plotinus. In this philosophy—the beliefs of Plato adapted to Christianity by Plotinus—the individual can only know true existence and the one God by searching within to attain unity with God's love. Only spiritual faith, and not reason or physical appearances, could provide the ultimate answers. At first a skeptic, Augustine began his inner search and in 386 had a mystical experience in which he believed he had discovered God. Resigning his teaching position, Augustine converted completely to Christianity and was baptized by Ambrose at Milan in the spring of 387.

Life's Work

Augustine plunged into the cause of discovering and articulating God's will as a Christian philosopher. He did so with such zeal that a steady stream of treatises flowed from his pen. He returned to Numidia in 389 and established a monastery at Hippo, intending to live there quietly and write. He was ordained as a priest in 391, and he became Bishop of Hippo in 396. Thus, instead of developing his theological ideas systematically, Augustine revealed them in sermons, letters in reply to queries for guidance, tracts against separatists, and books. In addition, he wrote a lengthy autobiography of his early life, *Confessiones* (397-400; *Confessions*).

God, in Augustine's view, is at the center of all events and explanations. Such a theocentric philosophy depends on Holy Scripture; for Augustine, the Psalms, Genesis, and the First Letter of John were especially important. His commentaries on the first two sources are famous treatises, along with *De Trinitate* (c. 419; *On the Trinity*) and *De civitate Dei* (413-427; *The City of God*).

God, as "the author of all existences" and "the illuminator of all truth," is Wisdom itself and therefore the highest level of reality. The second level is the human soul, which includes memory, understanding, and will. By looking to God, the individual discovers the true knowledge that God has already bestowed upon him. All things emanate from that ultimate authority; through faith, one gains truth, the use of reason being only secondary. The third and lowest level of reality is the human body, whose greatest ethical happiness can only be realized by aspiring to God's love. Human beings are endowed with the free choice to do good or evil, but God by divine grace may bestow the greater freedom of enabling a person to escape an attraction to evil. Similarly, revelation frees the mind from skepticism. By grappling with the elusive problem of evil, Augustine managed to bring better focus to an issue of universal concern to all religions.

Also a practical thinker, Augustine was an acute observer of the natural universe. By focusing on God in nature, however, and believing that true knowledge came only through spiritual introspection, he came to regard physical things as least important and science as having little utility. Faith rather than reason provides the ultimate truth. By the same token, Augustine viewed history optimistically; humankind was saved by Christ's sacrifice on the Cross, the premier event of the past.

The collapse of Roman hegemony to barbarian invasions, even as Augustine preached his sermons on faith, caused many doubters to blame Christianity for Rome's decline. Augustine refuted this accusation in *The City of God*. He envisioned two cities, the heavenly City of God and the other one an earthly entity, patterned respectively after the biblical examples of Jerusalem—which means "Vision of Peace"—and Babylon, permeated with evil. Whereas perfection is the hallmark of the City of God, Augustine offered important guidelines for the conduct of human cities. Earthly "peace" he defined as harmonious order, a condition whereby a person, a community, or a state operates by the ideals of felicity (good intentions) and virtue (good acts) without suffering under or imposing dominion. No pacifist, Augustine believed that a nation might go to war, but only on the authority of God and then to achieve a "peace of the just." "Good men undertake wars," he wrote to Faustus the Manichaean in 398, to oppose evil enemies: "The real evils in war are love of violence, revengeful cruelty, fierce and implacable enmity, wild resistance, and the lust of power."

The greatest challenge to Augustine's teachings centered on the issue of how the individual might escape the evils of the flesh—whether by one's own choice or by the initiative of God through divine grace. Augustine insisted on the latter and regarded the Pelagians as heretics for arguing the former view. As Saint Paul taught, each person is guilty of Original Sin, must admit it, and can only accept salvation from God's grace through the Holy Spirit. Indeed, Augustine concluded early in his episcopate that God decides which elected souls will receive divine grace—a clear belief in the predestination of each individual. The barbarian army of the Vandals was at the gates of Hippo when Augustine died.

Summary

Saint Augustine was, by any measure, a genius of Christian philosophy and has been so venerated since his death. That all subsequent Christian thinkers owe him an immense debt is evident from the continuous outpouring of reprints of his vast works and discussions concerning his ideas. He brought focus to the major issues which continue to challenge the Church to the present day, and he motivated key figures to adopt aspects of his thinking outright. In the early Middle Ages, Charlemagne founded the Holy Roman Empire in the mistaken belief that Augustine's *The City of God* had been written as a blueprint for a divine kingdom on earth. Saint Thomas Aquinas accepted Augustine's notions of predestination for the later Middle Ages, as did John Calvin during the Protestant Reformation. The power of Augustine's theology has remained undiminished through the ages.

Bibliography

Ancient Christian Writers: The Works of the Fathers in Translation. Westminster, Md.: Newman Press, 1946-   . A major English-language multivolume collection of the early theological thinkers. Eight volumes have been published on Augustine.

Bourke, Vernon J. *The Essential Augustine*. New York: Mentor-Omega, 1964. An excellent collection of excerpts from Augustine's principal writings, introduced topically by this Thomist writer. Includes a bibliography. Still useful as an introduction is Bourke's *Augustine's Quest of Wisdom* (Milwaukee: Bruce, 1945), augmented by Bourke's anthology of his own essays, *Wisdom from St. Augustine* (Houston: Center for Thomistic Studies, 1984).

Brown, Peter. *Augustine of Hippo*. Berkeley: University of California Press, 1967. One of the best biographical accounts of Augustine, which uses the chronological approach to show Augustine's writings as they evolved during his lifetime. Heavily annotated. Complemented by Brown's volume which places Augustine in context: *Religion and Society in the Age of St. Augustine* (New York: Harper and Row, Publishers, 1972).

Chadwick, Henry. *Augustine*. New York: Oxford University Press, 1986. This volume in the Past Masters series provides a concise introduction to Augustine's thought.

Deane, Herbert A. *The Political and Social Philosophy of St. Augustine*. New York: Columbia University Press, 1963. A treatment of the theology and psychology behind Augustine's notion of "Fallen Man." Focuses on morality and justice, the state and order, war and relations among states, the church, state, heresy, and Augustine's view of history.

Gilson, Etienne. *The Christian Philosophy of St. Augustine*. Translated by L. E. M. Lynch. Rev. ed. New York: Random House, 1960. Perhaps the best and most scholarly work on Augustine's philosophy. A translation of the 1943 version in French, more than half of which is annotations. Gilson regards Augustinianism as the discovery of humility, built upon charity.

Lawless, George P. *Augustine of Hippo and His Monastic Rule*. Oxford: Clarendon Press, 1987. An excellent summary of the lifetime work of the late Luc Verbraken, tracing the monastic orientation of Augustine's life and showing how his love of friends in a community setting established the monastic tradition in the Christian West.

Markus, R. A., ed. *Augustine: A Collection of Critical Essays*. Garden City, N.Y.: Anchor, 1972. An anthology of in-depth essays by prominent interpreters of Augustine, extensive in its coverage of his various interests.

Meer, F. G. L. van der. *Augustine the Bishop*. New York: Sheed and Ward, 1960. Reviews Augustine's adult life after becoming Bishop of Hippo. Augmented by archaeological information from North African digs.

Nash, Ronald H. *The Light of the Mind: St. Augustine's Theory of Knowledge*. Lexington: University Press of Kentucky, 1969. Contests Augustine's illumination of knowledge as interpreted by Bourke, Gilson, and other Thomist writers.

Oates, Whitney J., ed. *Basic Writings of St. Augustine*. 2 vols. New York: Random House, 1948. Volume 1 includes the *Confessions*, volume 2 *The City of God* and *On the Trinity*, with introductions by Oates. Random House's Modern Library published the *Confessions* in 1949, translated by Edward B. Pusey with an introduction by Fulton J. Sheen, and *The City of God* in 1950, translated by Marcus Dods with an introduction by Thomas Merton.

O'Daly, Gerard. *Augustine's Philosophy of the Mind*. Berkeley: University of California Press, 1987. The first monograph in more than a century to analyze Augustine's arguments about the mind.

Clark G. Reynolds

AUGUSTUS
Gaius Octavius

Born: September 23, 63 B.C.; Rome
Died: August 19, A.D. 14; Nola
Area of Achievement: Government
Contribution: Through his political skill and intelligence, Augustus transformed the chaos that followed the assassination of Julius Caesar into the long-lasting Roman Empire.

Early Life

The first emperor of Rome was born Gaius Octavius, and during his youth he was known to history as Octavian. His family was an old and wealthy one from the small town of Velitrae (Velletri), about twenty miles southeast of Rome. The Octavii were not, however, a noble family; they were of the equestrian order, which meant that they did not sit in the Roman senate and thus could not hold the higher offices of the state. Octavian's father, a supporter of Julius Caesar, was the first of the family to achieve those distinctions; he died when Octavian was four.

Octavian's great-uncle was that same Julius Caesar whom he so admired, and Caesar discerned in the young man possibilities of future greatness. At sixteen, Octavian planned to accompany Caesar to Spain in his campaign against the forces of Pompey the Great, Caesar's enemy in the civil wars. Delayed by illness, Octavian followed Caesar, risking considerable hardship along the way, including a shipwreck from which he narrowly escaped. Although he arrived after the hostilities had ended, his daring and initiative greatly impressed Caesar.

In 44 B.C., while Caesar was preparing his campaign against the Parthian empire in the east, Octavian went on ahead, intending to join the army en route. He was in Apollonia, in the Adriatic coast, when he learned that Caesar had been assassinated in Rome on the ides of March (March 15). Along with this shocking news, he soon learned that in his will Caesar had named him heir to the bulk of the dictator's vast estate and, much more significantly, had adopted him. Although it was impossible to transmit political office or power through inheritance, Caesar had clearly signaled his choice of successor. Octavian, in turn, indicated his determination to claim his rights by an immediate return to Italy and by taking the name Gaius Julius Caesar. At eighteen he was prepared to contest control of the Roman world.

Portrait busts, statues, and the writings of historians have left a clear picture of the first emperor. He was of average height and wore lifts in his sandals to appear taller. His hair was blondish, and his teeth were small and widely spaced. The ancient historian Suetonius describes Octavian as handsome, and other writers have remarked on his calm, quiet expression. He had clear, bright eyes and liked to believe that a certain divine radiance could be seen in them. Throughout his life he was bothered by a number of illnesses, some of them quite serious; perhaps because of his poor health he was temperate in his habits, drinking little and eating lightly. Although a conscientious administrator, he hated to rise early, and his chief pastime was gambling with his friends. More than anything else, his actions and achievements clearly indicate that he was a man of great ambition and clear intelligence with a profound perception of the qualities of others.

Life's Work

When Octavian returned to Italy, he had two immediate goals: to claim his inheritance from Caesar and to avenge his adoptive father's death. He first tried to establish an alliance with Marc Antony, a close associate and colleague of Caesar, but Antony took a harsh attitude toward the much younger man and even blocked the implementation of Caesar's will. As a result, Octavian went over to the side of the senate, which was attempting to regain control of the state. With the help of Octavian and an army raised largely from Caesar's veterans, the senatorial forces defeated Antony at Mutina (Modena, northern Italy) in 43 B.C. Octavian quickly realized, however, that the senate planned to use him to remove Antony as a threat and then discard him. The orator Cicero summed up their plan for Octavian: "The young man is to be praised, honored, and exalted." In Latin the last word can be understood as a pun for "removed."

Sensing this design, Octavian arranged a meeting with Antony and Marcus Aemilius Lepidus, another associate of Caesar. The three formed the Second Triumvirate, patterned on the earlier alliance of Caesar, Marcus Licinius Crassus, and Pompey. Both triumvirates became the effective power of the Roman world, largely because of their command of military forces. The Second Triumvirate was sealed by marriage: Octavian wed the daughter of Antony's wife; later, Antony would marry Octavian's sister.

The triumvirs quickly had themselves voted unlimited powers and began to eradicate their opposition, especially those associated with the murder of Caesar. A proscription was proclaimed, and hundreds of Romans, including Cicero, were put to death. Octavian and Antony then confronted the army of Marcus Junius Brutus and Gaius Cassius Longinus, the leaders of the conspiracy against Caesar. In the Battles of Philippi in Greece (October 23 and November 14, 42 B.C.), the last forces capable of restoring the republic were smashed.

Octavian and Antony divided the Roman world between them, Octavian taking the west, Antony the east. Lepidus was shunted aside and sank into obscurity, eventually ending his life under house arrest. Relations between the two major partners steadily deteriorated. The alliance was patched up by marriage, and in 36 B.C. the two cooperated in the defeat of Sextus Pompeius (son of Pompey the Great) in Sicily. Developments after that, however, led to inevitable conflict.

While in the east, Antony formed a close liaison with Cleopatra, Queen of Egypt and former lover of Caesar. Antony granted her territories once held by Egypt but now subject to Rome, and he displayed signs of establishing an independent monarchy in Asia. Octavian skillfully exploited the antiforeign sentiments that these actions aroused, and in 32 B.C. Rome declared war on Antony and Cleopatra.

Octavian gathered a fleet and an army and moved east. Under his friend Marcus Vipsanius Agrippa, the Roman forces defeated those of Antony and Cleopatra at the naval battle of Actium, off the Greek coast, on September 2, 31 B.C. The two lovers escaped to Egypt, but when surrounded by Octavian's forces, they committed suicide. Octavian annexed Egypt as a Roman province; he was now sole ruler of the Roman state.

His position was still precarious, however, and for the rest of his life he had to balance the reality of his power carefully with the appearance of a restored republic. Although briefly considering a true return to the republic, Octavian realized that it was impossible, since it would lead to bloody civil war. Instead of claiming or accepting offices of overt power—such as the dictatorship— which had brought about the death of Caesar, Octavian was content to serve in more traditional ways, such as consul (thirteen times in all) or tribune. His most frequently used title was an innovation: *princeps* (short for *princeps civitatis*, "first citizen"); this appellation was vague enough not to offend, yet sufficient to preserve his authority.

In 27 B.C., Octavian was granted the title Augustus by the senate, indicating the religious aspect of his position; throughout his reign, Augustus artfully underscored the moral need for a strong ruler to end centuries of internecine bloodshed. It is as Augustus that he is best known to history.

As ruler, Augustus' major concerns were internal reform and external defense. In Rome, he revised the senate roll, striking off many who were unfit to serve. He vigorously enforced laws against immorality, even sending his own daughter into exile for her numerous and blatant adulteries. His own life was less circumscribed. He stole his wife, Livia, from her first husband and was married to her while she was pregnant; he was known later for his many affairs, showing a particular preference for young virgins.

Nevertheless, he was careful in his observance of ancient Roman religious rituals and in A.D. 12 was elected *pontifex maximus*, or head priest. Whenever possible, he revived old customs and mores, attempting to strengthen patriotism and social order. His many building projects, especially in Rome, repaired years of neglect and greatly improved life in the city.

Along the borders, Augustus was content to maintain existing boundaries for most of the empire. In Germany, he made an effort to extend the limits of Roman rule to the Elbe. These attempts were abruptly ended in A.D. 6, when

German tribes ambushed and massacred three legions under the command of Publius Quintilius Varus. The disaster caused Augustus to fix the boundaries at the Rhine; for a long time after he could be heard crying out in his palace, "Varus, give me back my legions!"

As he grew older, Augustus attempted to fix the succession of power, realizing that he must provide for an orderly transition lest his accomplishments be destroyed in another round of civil war. When his three grandsons either died or proved unfit, he was forced to turn to Tiberius, Livia's son by her first husband. Tiberius had long served Augustus in civil and military posts and had been advanced as heir on several occasions, only to be set aside for a candidate more suitable to Augustus' needs. At last, however, he was adopted by Augustus and served as his colleague and virtual coemperor until Augustus' death.

Augustus died in A.D. 14 and the fact that Tiberius succeeded him without a renewal of internal strife and disastrous civil war is perhaps the best indication of Augustus' success in creating a new and lasting political order—the Roman Empire.

Summary

One of the sayings attributed to Augustus is that he found Rome a city of brick and left it one of marble. This is literally true: His extensive renovation and construction transformed Rome from top to bottom—from its temples to its sewer system. A similar transformation was wrought by Augustus in the whole of the Roman world.

He found a state that was wracked by internal unrest, one that was seemingly incapable of ruling itself without resorting to self-destructive civil war. Through patience, tact, and, when necessary, force, he translated the ruins of the republic into the edifice of the empire. So difficult a task, to refound the Roman state, was made all the harder by the need to disguise its true nature. Throughout his reign, Augustus carefully retained the forms and procedures of a republic, deferring to the senate, refusing extravagant titles, and being careful to allow others a measure of honor and prestige—although never enough to threaten his preeminent position.

Augustus' major accomplishments were to establish the Roman Empire and to become its first emperor, almost without public notice. While all knew that power had shifted into the hands of one man, the shift had been accomplished in such a gradual, subtle fashion, and with such positive results, that few openly complained. Most Romans probably approved of the changes made by Augustus. There was security, increasing prosperity, and, above all, peace. The arts flourished, and the golden age of Roman literature under Augustus produced such lasting writers as Horace, Ovid, Livy, and Vergil.

Augustus restored peace to a society that badly needed it. Conflicts continued on the borders, but internal warfare came to an end. In one of his most significant acts, Augustus closed the gates to the temple of Janus, an act done only when Rome was formally at peace. Before his time, the gates had been shut only twice in Rome's long history. More than anything else it was this peace, this Pax Romana and the blessings it brought, that caused a grateful senate to accord Augustus the title *pater patriae*—father of his country.

Bibliography
Buchan, John. *Augustus*. Boston: Houghton Mifflin Co., 1937. A popular history by a well-known novelist who uses his skills to present a briskly moving but informative narrative. While Buchan's work has been dated in some respects by more recent scholarly studies and findings, it remains a good starting point for the student.
Grant, Michael. *The Roman Emperors: A Biographical Guide to the Rulers of Rome, 31 B.C.-A.D. 476*. New York: Charles Scribner's Sons, 1985. A lucid, compressed review of the life and times of Augustus, placing him within the context of his society. Once again, Grant demonstrates his ability as a historian to unearth new and interesting insights from well-known material.
_____. *The Twelve Caesars*. New York: Charles Scribner's Sons, 1983. This volume takes the ancient biographer Suetonius as its starting point but goes far beyond him in its exploration and explanation of the difficulties and accomplishments of Augustus. Grant is especially good in delineating the agonizingly careful line Augustus had to trace in establishing an empire on the ruins of a fallen, but still potent, republic.
Jones, A. H. *Augustus*. Edited by M. I. Finley. New York: W. W. Norton and Co., 1971. A well-researched and well-presented overview of Augustus' life and career, giving equal attention to both. Jones is particularly good in considering the various aspects of the new empire both in chronological terms and in separate, in-depth considerations, offering the reader either a broad or concentrated treatment depending on his needs.
Massie, Allan. *The Caesars*. New York: Franklin Watts, 1984. A popular biography of Rome's imperial rulers, and a good place to start a study of Augustus. The section on the first emperor is well done and provides several interesting views of his task in setting up the imperial system.
Suetonius, Gaius Tranquillus. *Lives of the Twelve Caesars*. Edited by Joseph Gavorse. New York: Modern Library, 1959. Suetonius is long on incident and short on evaluation, but his lively portrait of Augustus has never been surpassed. While other, later authors have given more facts about the founder of the empire, Suetonius presents him as a human being. This work certainly deserves its reputation as a classic.

Michael Witkoski

AVERROËS
Ibn Rushd

Born: 1126; Córdoba, Spain
Died: 1198; Marrakech, Morocco
Areas of Achievement: Scholarship and philosophy
Contribution: Jurist, physician, and philosopher, Ibn Rushd was one of the
last of a line of medieval Muslim scholars who sought to reconcile the
truths of revealed religion and dialectical reasoning. Known to the medieval Christian Schoolmen by the name of Averroës, he exercised an overwhelming influence upon Latin thought through his commentaries on
Aristotle.

Early Life

Abu al-Walid Muhammad ibn Ahmad ibn Muhammad ibn Rushd, generally known as Ibn Rushd, and to the medieval Christian West as Averroës,
was born in 1126 into a distinguished Spanish-Arab family of jurists in Córdoba, the former capital of the Umayyad Caliphate in Spain. His grandfather, who died in the year of his birth, had been a distinguished Malikite
jurisconsult, who had held the office of chief *qadi* (Muslim judge) of the city,
as well as *imam* (prayer leader) of its great mosque, still one of the most celebrated monuments of early Islamic architecture. Ibn Rushd's father was also
a *qadi*, and in the course of time he too would follow the family calling. His
biographers state that he was given an excellent education in all the branches
of traditional Islamic learning, including medicine, in which he was the pupil
of a celebrated teacher, Abu Jafar Harun al-Tajali (of Trujillo), who may
also have initiated him into a lifelong passion for philosophy. The young
scholar was also influenced by the writings of one of the most famous thinkers of the previous generation, Ibn Bajja of Saragossa (died 1138), known to
the Latin Schoolmen as Avempace.

By 1157, Ibn Rushd, now thirty years old, had made his way to Marrakech
in Morocco, at that time the capital of the North African and Spanish empire
of the Almohads, where he was perhaps employed as a teacher. Ibn Rushd
lived during a very distinctive period in the history of Islam in Spain and the
Maghrib. A century before his birth, the disintegration of the Caliphate of
Córdoba had led to the fragmentation of Muslim Spain among the so-called
Party Kings (Arabic *muluk al-tawaif*), who in turn had been overthrown by
the Berber tribal confederacy of the Almoravids (Arabic *al-murabitun*,
"those dwelling in frontier fortresses"). These fanatical warriors from the
western Sahara had quickly succumbed to the hedonistic environment of
Spanish Islam, only to be replaced by another wave of Berber fundamentalists, the Almohads (Arabic *al-muwahhidun*, "those who affirm God's
unity"). Under 'Abd al-Mu'min (reigned 1130-1163), who assumed the title

of caliph, the Almohads conquered all southern and central Spain as well as the North African littoral as far east as modern Libya.

Within the context of the cultural and intellectual history of the Muslim West, the Almohads played a highly ambiguous role. The spearhead of a puritanical movement sworn to the cleansing of Islam of latter-day accretions and to a return to the pristine mores of the days of the Prophet and the "Rightly-Guided Caliphs" (Arabic *al-Khulafa al-Rashidun*), they were also the heirs, through their conquests, to the intellectually precocious and culturally sophisticated traditions of Muslim Spain. The ruling elite seems to have dealt with this paradox by developing a deliberate "double standard": Within the walls of the caliph's palace and of the mansions of the great, the brilliant civilization of an earlier age continued to flourish, while outside, in street and marketplace, obedience to the Shari'a, the law of Islam, was strictly enforced at the behest of the clerical classes, the *ulama* (persons learned in the Islamic "sciences") and the *fuqaha* (those learned in jurisprudence). The life of Ibn Rushd himself points to a similar dichotomy. Outwardly, he was a *qadi* and a *faqih*, a judge and a jurisprudent; inwardly, he was a *faylasuf*, a philosopher with an insatiable urge to pursue speculative inquiry by rational argument, and to delve deep into the infidel wisdom of the ancients.

In 1163, 'Abd al-Mu'min was succeeded by his son, Abu Ya'qub Yusuf, who throughout his reign (1163-1184) was to be a generous patron and friend to Ibn Rushd. Apparently, it was a contemporary scholar, Ibn Tufayl (c. 1105-1184), known to the Latins as Abubacer, who first presented Ibn Rushd to Abu Ya'qub Yusuf, probably around 1169. Tradition relates that, at their first meeting, the caliph began by asking Ibn Rushd (who may already have been working on a commentary on Aristotle's *De caelo*) about the origin and nature of the sky. While the latter hesitated, uncertain as to how to reply to questions which raised dangerous issues of orthodoxy, the caliph turned to converse with Ibn Tufayl, and in so doing revealed his own extensive learning. Reassured, Ibn Rushd embarked upon a discourse which so displayed the depth and range of his scholarship that the delighted caliph thereafter became his ardent disciple. It was on this occasion, too, that Abu Ya'qub Yusuf complained that the existing translations of the works of Aristotle were too obscure for comprehension and that there was need for further commentaries and exegeses. Ibn Tufayl remarked that he himself was too old to assume such an undertaking, at which Ibn Rushd agreed to assume the task that was to become his life's work.

Life's Work

The name of Ibn Rushd is inextricably linked with that of Aristotle, and it is for his commentaries on the works of the latter that, under the name of Averroës, he became so famous in the Christian West. Since the end of antiquity, no one had studied the writings of Aristotle, or what passed for his writings, so carefully as Ibn Rushd, and in his numerous commentaries, many of which are now lost or are known only through Hebrew or Latin translations, he set out to remove the exegetical accretions of earlier ages. The Great Commentator, as the Latin Schoolmen liked to call him, did not perhaps have a very original mind, but he did have a highly analytical one, capable of great critical penetration.

Ibn Rushd understood Aristotle better than his predecessors had done because his powers of analysis enabled him, almost alone in the Arabo-Aristotelian philosophical tradition, to circumvent the glosses superimposed upon Aristotle by a spurious tradition which had for so long concealed the real Aristotle, consisting of such works as the *Theologia Aristotelis* derived from Plotinus, the *Liber de causis* of Proclus, and the commentary on Aristotle of Alexander of Aphrodisias. This "contamination of Aristotle," as David Knowles, in *The Evolution of Medieval Thought* (1962), has described it, laid upon medieval Arab and Jewish scholars alike the temptation to undertake "a synthesis in the systems of Plato and Aristotle," but this was a false trail which, for the most part, Ibn Rushd avoided following, largely on account of his intellectual acuity. On the other hand, he was a man of his times. Preoccupied as he was with political thought and its relationship to personal conduct, he nevertheless did not have access to Aristotle's *Politics*. He was therefore forced to rely upon Plato's *Republic* and *Laws* and Aristotle's *Nichomachean Ethics*, and was heavily dependent upon his predecessor al-Farabi. Ibn Rushd had no knowledge of Greek. Therefore, he was compelled to study both Aristotle and Aristotle's Greek commentators in Arabic translations made from Syriac or, more rarely, from the original Greek. This fact alone makes his achievement the more remarkable. It helped him that, from the outset of his career as a scholar, his unabashed admiration for Aristotle as a thinker drove him to try to uncover the authentic mind beneath the palimpsests of later generations, the mind of the man who, in his words, "was created and given to us by divine providence that we might know all there is to be known. Let us praise God, who set this man apart from all others in perfection, and made him approach very near to the highest dignity humanity can attain" (quoted by Knowles).

Although Ibn Rushd has come to be known first and foremost as a philosopher, to his contemporaries he was probably regarded primarily as a jurist and a physician. In 1169, the year which saw the beginning of his long and fruitful intellectual friendship with Abu Ya'qub Yusuf, he was appointed *qadi* of Seville, where, always preoccupied with his writing, he complained of being cut off from access to his library in Córdoba. He returned to the latter city as *qadi* in 1171, but it seems that throughout the 1170's he traveled extensively within the caliph's dominions, perhaps undertaking roving judicial commissions for the government. In 1182, he was summoned to Marrakech to succeed Ibn Tufayl as the caliph's physician. He had already written extensively on medical subjects, for in addition to the celebrated *Kitab al-kulliyat* (c. 1162-1169; a seven-part encyclopedia of medical knowledge, later translated into Latin as *Colliget*), he had written several commentaries on Galen. It is not certain how long he served as Abu Ya'qub Yusuf's physician, for not long afterward he was appointed chief *qadi* of Córdoba, the post that his grandfather had formerly held. Since Abu Ya'qub Yusuf was killed in battle at Santarém (Portugal) in 1184, it is possible that the prestigious appointment was made by Abu Ya'qub Yusuf's son and successor, Abu Yusuf Ya'qub (reigned 1184-1199), nicknamed al-Mansur, "The Victorious." For most of his reign, Abu Yusuf Ya'qub showed himself as well disposed toward Ibn Rushd as his father had been, but during 1195 the philosopher experienced a brief period of disgrace and danger.

The Christian powers of the north were now mustering their forces, and Abu Yusuf Ya'qub needed to rally his subjects for the approaching struggle. For that, he needed the unqualified support of the *ulama* and *fuqaha*, which in turn involved his unequivocal commitment to orthodoxy. The *fuqaha* insisted that Ibn Rushd be silenced for spreading doctrines that were subversive of faith, such as the Aristotelian theory of the eternity of the world, which denied God's act of creation, and for his rejection of the divine knowledge of particulars, which called into question God's omniscience. Ibn Rushd was compelled to appear before some kind of hostile gathering in Córdoba, his books were publicly burned, and his enemies bombarded him with false accusations and scurrilous libels. His actual punishment, however, was quite mild—temporary exile to the town of Lucena, south of Córdoba—and it cannot have done much to assuage the wrath of his foes. Shortly afterward, the caliph won a great victory over the Christians at Allarcos, midway between Córdoba and Toledo (July 19, 1195), the last triumph of Muslim arms in the peninsula. In consequence, he apparently felt less dependent upon the goodwill of the *fuqaha*, and upon returning to his capital of Marrakech he summoned Ibn Rushd to join him. The old man (for he was now in his seventies) did not have long to enjoy his restoration to favor. He died in 1198 in Marrakech, where his tomb still stands, although he was subsequently reinterred in Córdoba. Abu Yusuf Ya'qub died within months of the passing of his most celebrated subject.

As a thinker, Ibn Rushd was in the mainstream of Muslim Scholasticism, as well as being one of its last significant practitioners. Like his great predecessors in the Muslim East, he sought to establish an honored place for philosophy within the broader context of Muslim thought and learning. Contrary to the later and quite erroneous Christian notion of him as a champion of rationalism who denied the truths of revealed religion, Ibn Rushd was a devout Muslim who never set philosophy on a pedestal in order to challenge religious belief. Throughout his life, he stoutly denied that there was any inherent contradiction between philosophical truth, as established by the speculative thinker, and the certainties of faith embodied in the Koran and the Shari'a, the religious law which provided the social bounds within which the Muslim community and the individual Muslim lived their lives—and which, as a *qadi*, it was his duty to uphold. In his celebrated *Tahafut al-tahafut* (c. 1174-1180; *The Incoherence of the Incoherence*, 1954)—a defense of philosophy against the attacks made upon it by the eleventh century theologian and mystic al-Ghazzali in his *Tahafut al-falasifa* (1095; *The Incoherence of the Philosophers*, 1958)—he takes it as axiomatic that the philosopher will subscribe to the teachings of the highest form of revealed religion of the age in which he lives (by which he meant Islam). In *Kitab fasl al-maqal* (c. 1174-1180; *On the Harmony of Religion and Philosophy*, 1961), he assumes the compatibility of philosophical truth and revelation: Where there appears to be a conflict, that is the result of human misunderstanding, as in the case of diverse interpretations of scripture. The Muslims, he writes, "are unanimous in holding that it is not obligatory either to take all the expressions of Scripture in their apparent meaning or to extend them all from their apparent meaning to allegorical interpretation. . . . The reason why we have received a Scripture with both an apparent and an inner meaning lies in the diversity of people's natural capacities and the difference of their innate dispositions with regard to assent." In other words, people can believe only what their natural abilities allow them to comprehend, and this affects, among much else, the relationship between religion and philosophy, and the philosopher's place in society.

Summary

Ibn Rushd was one of the most formidable thinkers in the entire intellectual history of Islam, but he was also, in a very real sense, the end of a line. In the Muslim East, of which he lacked direct experience, the heritage of speculative philosophy had long since withered away in the face of Ash'arite orthodoxy and a growing preoccupation with transcendent mysticism. In the Muslim West, which was his home, the end came more rapidly and more completely. It was an accident of history that during the late twelfth century the caliphs of the puritanical Almohads had tolerated such men as Ibn Tufayl and Ibn Rushd. Fourteen years after Ibn Rushd's death, the Almohads went down in defeat in one of history's truly decisive battles, Las Navas de Tolosa (1212), which heralded the end of Muslim rule in Spain and, with it, Arabo-Hispanic civilization. Thereafter, the Maghrib turned in upon itself, and the intellectual life of the Muslim West, to which Ibn Rushd had contributed so much, slowly drew to its close. Its last representative, the Tunisian, Ibn Khaldun (1332-1406), ended his days in Cairo.

Yet Ibn Rushd, whom the Muslim world soon forgot, enjoyed a posthumous and enduring fame in lands which he had never visited and in a civilization which, had he known it, he would probably have despised. A principal component of the twelfth century European renaissance was the work of the translators of Toledo (reconquered by Alfonso VI of Castile from the Muslims in 1085), who made available in Latin the riches of Arabic, Hebrew, and Greek thought. When the pace of translation intensified during the thirteenth century, attention centered upon the works of Aristotle and upon the Aristotelian commentaries of Ibn Rushd. Among Christian translators, Michael Scott (1180-1235) made available Ibn Rushd's commentaries on *De caelo* and *De anima*, among others; Hermann the German translated the middle commentaries on the *Nichomachean Ethics*, *Rhetoric*, and *Poetics*; and the Italian, William of Lunis, the commentaries on Aristotelian logic. No less prominent were the Jewish translators. Jacob Anatoli made available Ibn Rushd's middle commentaries on the *Categories*, *De interpretatione*, *Analytica priora*, and *Analytica posteriora*; Solomon ben Joseph ibn Ayyub, the middle commentary on *De caelo;* Shem-Tob ben Isaac ibn Shaprut, the middle commentary on *De anima*; and Moses ben Samuel ibn Tibbon, a record output of commentaries. As a result of this activity, Ibn Rushd became, along with Aristotle, one of the most explosive elements in the development of medieval Christian thought.

Misread and misunderstood, Ibn Rushd—or Averroës, as the Latins called him—became the personification of the human reason, unaided by divine illumination, arrogantly pitting itself against Providence. Almost from the first appearance of Latin translations of his works, there was an odor of brimstone about him. In 1277, the Bishop of Paris censured 219 errors held by Aristotle or Averroës, by which time his alleged disciples, the Latin Averroists, headed by Siger of Brabant, were drawing upon themselves the magisterial denunciations of Thomas Aquinas, whose schematic endeavor to reconcile faith and reason nevertheless derived from the labors of Ibn Rushd a century earlier. Dante, encountering him in Limbo, was correct in his emphasis when he wrote, "Averroës, che'l gran comento feo" ("Averroës, who made the Great Commentary"), but even he could not have imagined the extent of Ibn Rushd's influence on the intellectual history of late medieval Europe.

Bibliography
Arnaldez, R. "Ibn Rushd." In *The Encyclopaedia of Islam*, 2d ed. Vol. 3. Leiden, Netherlands: E. J. Brill, 1971. This is a succinct but also detailed article on Ibn Rushd's life and thought, to which is added an excellent bibliography with which to follow up issues raised within the article itself. Strongly recommended.
Averroës. *Averroës' Middle Commentaries on Aristotle's Categories and "De interpretatione."* Translated by Charles E. Butterworth. Princeton, N.J.: Princeton University Press, 1983. This is the first volume in a projected

series of translations of Ibn Rushd's middle commentaries, based upon the new critical edition of the Arabic texts, now in course of publication in Cairo under the auspices of the American Research Center in Egypt.

_____ . *Averroës on Plato's "Republic."* Translated by Ralph Lerner. Ithaca, N.Y.: Cornell University Press, 1974. The translator maintains that his version is "an improvement in accuracy and intelligibility" over its predecessor, E. I. J. Rosenthal's *Commentary on Plato's "Republic"* (Cambridge: Cambridge University Press, 1956). The Arabic original is missing, and this translation is based upon a Hebrew translation of the early fourteenth century by Samuel Ben Judah. This work provides an excellent example of Ibn Rushd's methods as a commentator.

_____ . *On the Harmony of Religion and Philosophy.* Translated by George F. Hourani. London: Luzac, 1961. In addition to a translation of the *Kitab fasl al-maqal*, in which Ibn Rushd argues that the apparent contradictions between faith and reason are reconcilable, Hourani includes a translation of its short appendix and an extract from another treatise.

_____ . *Tahafut al-tahafut (The Incoherence of the Incoherence).* Translated by Simon van den Bergh. London: Luzac, 1954. This is an excellent translation of Ibn Rushd's spirited rejoinder to the assault made upon philosophy by al-Ghazzali in *The Incoherence of the Philosophers*.

Hitti, Philip K. *Makers of Arab History.* New York: St. Martin's Press, 1968. The chapter on Ibn Rushd in this collection of popular biographies provides a lively introductory account of the man and his thought, and a useful starting point for further study. The book also contains biographies of al-Ghazzali, al-Kindi, and Avicenna.

Peters, F. E. *Aristotle and the Arabs: The Aristotelian Tradition in Islam.* New York: New York University Press, 1969. A scholarly as well as lively and stimulating account of the place of Aristotelian thought within the Islamic intellectual tradition. This book is essential reading for anyone seriously interested in the background to Ibn Rushd's life and work, written by one of the leading Western scholars in the field.

Rosenthal, E. I. J. *Political Thought in Medieval Islam: An Introductory Outline.* Cambridge: Cambridge University Press, 1958. Pages 175-209 provide an excellent discussion of Ibn Rushd's political and social thought, based upon his knowledge of such Platonic and Aristotelian texts as were available to him, as well as the writings of al-Farabi, but stressing Ibn Rushd's undoubtedly original contribution. Includes an interesting account of the ideas of al-Bajja.

Watt, W. Montgomery. *Islamic Philosophy and Theology.* Edinburgh: Edinburgh University Press, 1962. This is one of the best (and shorter) general accounts of Islamic philosophy, written by a leading scholar in the field.

Gavin R. G. Hambly

AVICENNA
Abu 'Ali al-Husain ibn 'Abd-Allah ibn Sina

Born: August or September, 980; Afshena, Transoxiana Province of Bukhara, Persian Empire
Died: 1037; Hamadhan, Iran
Areas of Achievement: Philosophy, medicine, law, astronomy, and philology
Contribution: Avicenna was the first Islamic thinker to synthesize the philosophy of Aristotle and Plato with Islamic traditions. His writings on medicine were studied in Europe as late as the seventeenth century.

Early Life

Abu 'Ali al-Husain ibn 'Abd-Allah ibn Sina was born in 980 to Abd-Allah of Balkh (now in Afghanistan), the well-to-do governor of an outlying province under Samanid ruler Nuh II ibn Mansur. Avicenna may have descended from a Turkish family on his father's side, but his mother, Sitara, was clearly Iranian.

After his brother, Mahmud, was born five years later, the family moved to Bukhara, one of the principal cities of Transoxiana and capital of the Samanid emirs from 819 to 1005. Exhibiting an early interest in learning, young Avicenna had read the entire Koran by age ten. His father was attracted to Isma'ili Shi'ite doctrines, preached locally by Egyptian missionaries, but Avicenna resisted his father's influence. There was much discussion in his home regarding geometry, philosophy, theology, and even accounting methods. Avicenna was sent to study with an Indian vegetable seller who was also a surveyor. It was from him that Avicenna became acquainted with the Indian system of calculation, making use of the zero in computations.

A well-known philosopher came to live with the family for a few years and had an extraordinary influence on the young scholar. Abu 'Abd Allah al-Natili stimulated Avicenna's love of theoretical disputation, and the youth's earlier readings in jurisprudence enabled him to tax al-Natili's powers of logic daily. The tutor convinced Abd-Allah that Avicenna's career should be only in learning. Avicenna was studying Aristotelian logic and Euclidean geometry when the teacher decided to move to a different home. Soon Avicenna had mastered texts in natural sciences and metaphysics, then medicine, which he did not consider very difficult. He taught physicians, even practicing medicine for a short time. At the age of sixteen, he was also engaging in disputations on Muslim law.

For the next year and a half, Avicenna returned to the study of logic and all aspects of philosophy, keeping files of syllogisms and praying daily at the mosque for guidance in his work. So obsessed did he become with philosophical problems and so anxious to know all that he hardly took time for sleep. Aristotle's *Metaphysica* (*Metaphysics*) became an intellectual stumbling block until his reading of a work by Abu Nasr al-Farabi clarified many ideas for him. Soon all of Aristotle became understandable, and Avicenna gave alms to the poor in gratitude.

When Sultan Nuh ibn Mansur of Bukhara became ill, he sent for Avicenna, upon the advice of his team of physicians. Because of his help in curing the ruler, Avicenna gained access to the palace library, thus acquainting himself with many new books. When not studying, Avicenna was given to drinking wine and satisfying a large sexual appetite which he retained to the end of his life. Avicenna claimed that after the age of eighteen he learned nothing new, only gained greater wisdom. When the palace library was destroyed in a fire, critics blamed Avicenna, who, they said, wished to remove the sources of his ideas. There is no proof of that charge.

Life's Work

Avicenna's writing career began in earnest at the age of twenty-one with *al-Majmu* (1001; compilation), a comprehensive book on learning for Abu al-Hasan, a prosodist. Then he wrote *al-Hasil wa al-mahsul* (c. 1002; the sun and substance), a twenty-volume commentary on jurisprudence, the Koran, and asceticism. There soon followed a work on ethics called *al-Birr wa al-ithm* (c. 1002; good works and evil). The sponsors made no copies of them, a matter of some concern to the author.

His father died in 1002, and Avicenna was forced to take government service. He reluctantly left Bukhara for Gurganj, the capital of Khwarazm, where he met Emir Ali ibn Ma'mun. From Gurganj, he moved to Fasa, Baward, Tus, Samanqan, and thence to Jajarm on the extreme end of Khurasan. He served Emir Qabus ibn Wushmagir until a military coup forced Avicenna to leave for Dihistan, where he became ill. After recovering, he moved to Jurjan.

In Jurjan, Avicenna met his pupil and biographer, Abu 'Ubaid al-Juzjani, who stayed with him throughout much of the remainder of his life. Juzjani thought him exceptionally handsome and wrote that when Avicenna went to the mosque on Friday to pray, people would gather to observe at first hand "his perfection and beauty." While in Jurjan, Avicenna wrote *al-Mukhtasar al-awsat* (the middle summary on logic), *al-Mabda' wa al-ma'ad* (the origin and the return), and *al-Arsad al-kulliya* (comprehensive observations). There also Avicenna wrote the first part of *al-Qanun fi al-tibb* (*Canon of Medicine*), *Mukhtasar al-Majisti* (summary of the *Almagest*), and yet other treatises. One modern scholar lists one hundred books attributed to him. Another says that the list of Avicenna's works includes several hundred in Arabic and twenty-three in Persian.

From Jurjan, Avicenna next moved to al-Rayy, joining the service of al-Saiyyida and her son, Majd al-Dawlah. Civil strife forced him to flee to Qazwin; from there he moved to Hamadhan, where he managed the affairs of Kadhabanuyah. He was called to the court of Emir Shams al-Dawlah to treat the ruler for colic, after which Avicenna was made the vizier of his emirate. Because of a mutiny in the army, however, the emir was forced to discharge him. After matters calmed down, Avicenna was called back and reinstated as vizier. During this period, public affairs occupied his daytime hours, and he spent evenings teaching and writing. When the emir died, Avicenna went into hiding, finishing work on his *Kitab al-shifa* (book of healing). He was arrested for corresponding with a rival ruler, but when Emir 'Ala' al-Dawlah attacked Hamadhan four months later, Avicenna was set free.

Avicenna left Hamadhan for Isfahan with his brother, two slaves, and al-Juzjani to serve Emir 'Ala' al-Dawlah. The emir designated every Friday evening for learned discussions with many other masters. Not present was a famous scholar and rival of Avicenna, Abu al-Rayhan al-Biruni, with whom he carried on a rather bitter correspondence. They had been clients at many of the same courts, but never at the same time. At Isfahan, Avicenna completed many of his writings on arithmetic and music. He was made an official member of the court and accompanied the emir on a military expedition to Hamadhan.

When he was rebuked by the emir's cousin, Abu Mansur, for feigning expertise in philology, Avicenna was so stung by the criticism that he studied this subject frantically, compiling his discoveries in a book entitled *Lisan al-'Arab* (the Arabic language). During these years, he also continued other experiments in medicine and astronomy. He introduced the use of medicinal herbs and devised an instrument to repair injured vertebrae. He understood that some illnesses arose from psychosomatic causes, and he wrote extensively on the pulse, preventive medicine, and the effects of climate on health. On May 24, 1032, he observed the rare phenomenon of Venus passing through the solar disk.

When he became ill in Isfahan, one of his slaves filled his meal with opium, hoping for his death and an opportunity to steal his money. Yet Avicenna managed to recover under self-treatment. Soon, however, he had a relapse; he died in 1037. Most authorities say that he died and was buried in Hamadhan.

Summary

The *Canon of Medicine* remained a principal source for medical research for six centuries, perhaps second only to the Christian Bible in the number of copies produced. Between 1470 and 1500, it went through thirty editions in Latin and one in Hebrew; a celebrated edition was published on a Gutenberg press in Rome in 1593. Avicenna's principal literary contribution was the invention of the Rubaiyat form, quatrains in iambic pentameter, later made famous by Omar Khayyam. Most important of all, Avicenna's philosophical system helped to stimulate a genuine intellectual renaissance in Islam that had enormous influence not only in his own culture but in Western Europe as well. Thomas Aquinas, Averroës, John Duns Scotus, Albertus Magnus, and Roger Bacon learned much from Avicenna, even though they disagreed on some particulars.

Most intriguing to the medieval Scholastics were Avicenna's insistence upon essences in everything, the distinction between essence and existence (a notion derived from al-Farabi), the absence of essence in God (whose existence is unique), and the immortality of the soul (which animates the body but is independent of it).

According to some scholars, Avicenna's insistence upon observation and experimentation helped to turn Western thought in the direction of the modern scientific revolution. His theories on the sources of infectious diseases, his explanation of sight, his invention of longitude, and his other scientific conclusions have a truly remarkable congruence with modern explanations. The application of geometrical forms in Islamic art, his use of the astrolabe in astronomical experiments, and his disputations on the immortality of the soul demonstrate Avicenna's universal genius.

Bibliography

Afnan, Soheil M. *Avicenna: His Life and Works*. London: George Allen and Unwin, 1958. The author stresses the impact of Avicenna's philosophy upon the thinkers of the Arabic-speaking world.

Arberry, Arthur J. *Avicenna on Theology*. London: John Murray, 1951. This important brief work contains Avicenna's own autobiography and its continuation by his disciple and companion, Abu 'Ubaid al-Juzjani, as well as Arberry's discussion of Avicenna's defense of monotheism and the immortality of the soul.

Avicenna. *The Life of Ibn Sina: A Critical Edition*. Translated by William E. Gohlman. Albany: State University of New York Press, 1974. Contains an annotated edition of Avicenna's autobiography, the contemporary account of his life by Juzjani, and a critical examination of the bibliography about Avicenna.

Brown, H. V. B. "Avicenna and the Christian Philosophers in Baghdad." In *Islamic Philosophy and the Classical Tradition: Essays to Richard Walzer*, edited by S. M. Stern, Albert Hourani, and Vivian Brown. Columbia: University of South Carolina Press, 1973. A clear presentation of Avicenna's philosophical differences with both Aristotle and the Peripatetic thinkers of the Baghdad school, despite his fundamental adherence to the rationalism of Aristotelian traditions. The Greek master's ambivalence on the purposiveness of nature led Avicenna to reject any rational choice in nature, in contrast to the approach of the Baghdad scholars.

Copleston, Frederick. *A History of Philosophy*. Vol. 2. Westminster, Md.:

Newman Press, 1955. Copleston clarifies not only the contributions of Arab philosophy to European medieval thought but also the diversity within this Islamic renaissance. Particular attention is focused upon Avicenna and Averroës.

Goichon, Amélie M. *The Philosophy of Avicenna and Its Influence on Medieval Europe*. Translated by M. S. Khan. Delhi: Motil al Banarsidass, 1969. Three lectures, originally in French, make up the three chapters of this fine work on the main theses of Avicenna's philosophy, the adaptation of the Arabic language to Hellenic thought, and the influence of Avicenna's ideas on European intellectual developments in the Middle Ages. Not addressed are Avicenna's contributions to medicine and the natural sciences.

Hitti, Phillip K. *Makers of Arab History*. New York: St. Martin's Press, 1968. This eminent historian of the Arab world discusses Avicenna and twelve other outstanding figures, from Muhammad to Ibn Khaldun. A valuable feature of this work is its incorporation of eight historical maps.

Maurer, Armand A. *Medieval Philosophy*. New York: Random House, 1962. Reprint. Toronto: Pontifical Institute of Mediaeval Studies, 1982. Maurer presents a summary of Avicenna's arguments on being, necessity, and essence; on proofs for the existence of God; on the doctrine of creation; and on man's intuitive knowledge of his soul. Although an Aristotelian, Avicenna, according to Maurer, also had links with the Neoplatonists and the later followers of Saint Augustine.

Morain, Lloyd L. "Avicenna: Asian Humanist Forerunner." *The Humanist* 41 (March/April, 1981): 27-34. A valuable article containing numerous reproductions of artifacts and sketches of Avicenna. Anatomical drawings used in Avicenna's writings and other depictions of his medical treatments appear in this article as well as portraits, a commemorative stamp, and a photograph of his mausoleum.

Peters, F. E. *Aristotle and the Arabs*. New York: New York University Press, 1968. *Falsafah*, the term used to describe the tenth century reception of classical Greek science and philosophy, was in fact a blend of Hellenic learning with Islamic ideas. This is the subject of Peters' book, but the synthesis of which he writes is not only that of Islam and Hellenism but that of scholarship on this subject since the nineteenth century.

John D. Windhausen

BASIL THE MACEDONIAN

Born: 812 or 813; Charioupolis, in Macedonia, Byzantine Empire
Died: August 29, 886; Constantinople, Byzantine Empire
Areas of Achievement: Government and law
Contribution: Through his strength, intelligence, and excellent administration, Basil established the 189-year Macedonian dynasty, which brought Byzantium to great heights. He imparted such vitality to an ancient imperial tradition that it has been emulated by modern nations.

Early Life

Basil was born in Macedonia, the eldest son of a couple commonly called Constantine and Pancalo. The father of Constantine appears to have been an Armenian, Hmayeak, known sometimes by his name in Greek form, Maiactes. The mother of Constantine may have been a daughter of Leo V, the ruler of Byzantium from 813 to 820, also of Armenian descent. Cyril Toumanoff has traced Hmayeak's ancestry through the Armenian Mamikonian princes and the Arsacid rulers to the Achaemenid monarchs of Persia. The presence of the Armenians in Macedonia was not unusual, as Byzantium often moved groups of its minorities to areas which it wished to strengthen and develop. Macedonia was under attack by the Bulgars during Basil's childhood, and there are unconfirmed reports that he and his family were taken captive by them for a time.

Basil did not learn to read and write until late in life, but he credited his father with being his principal instructor in the wisdom of life. A large, handsome man, he became a skilled rider and breaker of horses and developed impressive strength and athletic ability. These traits helped open his path to greatness when, as a young man, he moved to Constantinople. Also helpful were well-placed fellow Armenians, one of whom engaged Basil as his stable master. This man was a courtier with access to the Emperor Michael III, who ruled from 842 to 867. When a wrestler was needed at the palace to defeat a Bulgarian challenger, Basil was taken there and won easily. On a royal hunting trip, Basil was present when the emperor's horse ran away. Vaulting into the saddle with great skill, he brought the steed back safely. The tall and personable Basil became a favorite of Michael III.

Life's Work

Basil divorced his first wife, Maria, the mother of his son Constantine, in 865 and married Eudocia, Michael III's concubine. In 866, Michael had Basil crowned as a co-emperor, but in 867, Michael had a new favorite, so Basil, with the help of several relatives and friends, murdered Michael, becoming sole emperor of the eastern empire in 867. With Eudocia, Basil had three sons: Leo, born in 866; Alexander, born in 870; and Stephen, born in 871.

The favorite son, Constantine, was crowned co-emperor in 869, as was Leo in 870, these steps being taken to provide for an orderly succession to the throne.

Basil had great plans for his beloved Constantine. In 868, he tried to arrange his marriage to the daughter of Louis II, Roman emperor in the West. Since Louis had no sons, such a marriage could have reunited the two halves of the Roman Empire. Basil's extension of Byzantine control in southern Italy annoyed Louis, however, and the perennial quarrel about papal claims to authority over the Christians of the eastern empire also divided them. The marriage project failed, and the death of Constantine in 879 came as a bitter blow to the emperor. There are scholars who claim that the next heir, Leo, was actually the son of Michael III, but an analysis of the funeral oration delivered by Leo VI when Basil died shows him to be Basil's son, as does the fact that Basil could have eliminated Leo and arranged for the succession of one of his younger sons.

Under Basil I, the Byzantine navy became a dominant power in the eastern Mediterranean. When the Arab fleet attacked along the eastern shore of the Adriatic Sea, laying siege to Dubrovnik in 867, a strong Byzantine naval force compelled them to abandon the siege and retire to the southwest. Byzantine missionary efforts led to the Christianization of the Serbians and the Slavic groups on the southeastern shore of the Adriatic, and progress was made with conversions in Bulgaria and Macedonia. There and in Russia the use of Slavic languages in Slavic letters—an alphabet devised by missionaries of Greek origin—aided the spread of the faith. The drawing of the Slavic peoples of the Balkans and Russia into the Byzantine cultural, religious, and political orbit was a major achievement. Although Syracuse in Sicily was lost to the Muslims, the Byzantine position in the mainland of southern Italy was improved, against both Muslims and the adherents of the Roman Empire in the West.

Conditions were exceptionally favorable for Byzantium at this time because of Muslim divisiveness. Egypt established its own rulers in 868, and there were civil wars among the Arabs of North Africa. In the eastern part of the Islamic world, the rising power of the Turks was causing disunity. The Byzantine forces were able to advance their frontiers into what is southeastern Turkey today. The Armenians and their neighbors were thus shielded somewhat from Muslim pressures, and Armenia's relations with the empire were generally positive.

The Byzantine occupation of Tephrice, capital of the Paulicians—a deviant Christian sect—also moved the border eastward. That victory came in 872, and in the next year Basil's army moved forward in the region of the Euphrates River, taking Zapetra and Samosata. Basil was a ruthless and cruel leader, but he knew how to select highly effective commanders for his forces on land and sea. He motivated them thoroughly, supervising and coordinating them well. The concept of the Christian Empire, which had often been weakened by the divisive influence of the iconoclasts—those who opposed the use of holy images in the Church—exercised an inspirational and unifying role. Basil began the forging of real nationalism, or, to use Romilly Jenkins' term, "uniculturalism."

Basil was more a military leader than an intellectual, but his dynastic and family arrangements made it possible for his successors, some of whom tended to be more intellectual or even ineffectual, to blend their rulership's legitimacy with leadership from the armed forces. This was sometimes done by the marriage of legitimate heirs to successful generals or by regency and co-emperorship between such partners. Basil also bequeathed an intricately organized civil service, administrative continuity, and a foundation of much-improved law codes.

Basil desired to revive and update the legal system of the empire by preparing an overarching code of Greco-Roman legislative acts. Emperor Justinian I, who ruled from 527 to 565, had codified the laws of ancient Rome, collecting and publishing all the valid imperial edicts. He had also published the collected writings of the classical Roman jurists, thus bringing the vast and frequently conflicting rulings of those jurists into one orderly system. Basil saw that the updating of such a system would provide an underlying unity for a regime which rested on an uneasy partnership of rough soldiers and cultivated bureaucrats, bridging their mutual suspicion and dislike. Not only would government and individual affairs be properly regulated but also a better framework would underlie the expanding commerce of the empire. Byzantium was the center of flourishing trade between Europe and Russia on the one hand and the commercial routes eastward into Asia on the other. The traders who moved goods through Mesopotamia and Persia, as far as India and China, contributed significantly to the economic well-being of the realm.

Basil wished to adapt the legal system to changed conditions, adding the many laws which were issued after Justinian's time. Not only was a house-cleaning of the old material needed, but Basil also planned to accompany the code with explanations of the Latin words and phrases in Greek. The Greek language would be used for the code, but the old Latin references need not remain obscure.

The new compilations prepared under Basil's administration included a manual of legal science to explain the law and its penalties. Basil realized that the full code might not be issued in his time, and, as it turned out, most of the material was published in the reign of his son, Leo VI. Basil did publish *Procheiron* and *Epanagoge* during his lifetime. The voluminous codes, in two sets of forty and sixty volumes, were drafted under Basil and published by his successor as the *Basilics*. The influence of these ambitious works was felt not only during the ensuing six centuries of Byzantine history but also in

Russia, where the works from Basil's reign were quoted in seventeenth century documents of the government and courts.

Especially interesting in Basil's legal material is the general theory set forth on the rights and duties of the various components of the government and the church authorities, under the emperor and the patriarch of the Church. These two supreme heads had parallel functions, the first to serve the material needs of the people, the second to see to their spiritual condition. The two were to cooperate for the benefit of all humankind.

In August of 886, Basil was mortally injured during a hunt. Taken back to Constantinople, he died nine days later, on August 29, 886. To his son, now Leo VI, he left a stable, well-organized nation, extending from southern Italy east to the Caucasus and from the banks of the Danube River on the north to Syria in the south.

Summary

The firm foundation laid by Basil the Macedonian, through strong government and a homogenized culture, unified a multiracial empire which could have been dissolved by its diversity. The Armenian and Slavic minorities were two groups which took a major part in leading the empire's forces, running its government, and enriching its commerce. He also resolved several potential religious schisms during his reign.

Basil's dynasty spread Byzantine influence throughout Europe. His great-great-granddaughter, Theophano, married the Western Roman emperor Otto II and became a forebear of Edward I of England and most later European dynasties. Her sister Anna married Vladimir of Kiev, the Christianizer of Russia. Vladimir's granddaughter, Anna, was the wife of King Henry I of France; her son was the first of many kings in the West to be named Philip. She was mindful, in selecting the name, of her supposed descent from Philip II, King of Macedon, the father of Alexander the Great. The uses of these two names by the much later rulers of expansionist Spain and Russia, respectively, demonstrate the vitality even into modern times of the dynamic Byzantine imperial concept.

The heirs of Basil I were well-advised to emulate his governmental acumen, but with respect to aggressive empire-building, this emulation has been a tragic force in history. For centuries, Russia saw itself as the "Third Rome," Constantinople having been the second. Many modern imperialists have dignified their tyrannies as continuations of the ancient empires, appropriating such symbols as the fasces, eagles, and the titles czar and kaiser, derived from the earlier term, caesar.

Bibliography

Charanis, Peter. "The Armenians in the Byzantine Empire." *Byzantinoslavica* 22 (1961): 226-240. A detailed account of this minority in Byzantium, with special attention to the time of Basil I and his dynasty.

Diehl, Charles. *Byzantine Portraits*. Translated by Harold Bell. New York: Alfred A. Knopf, 1927. Lively sketches of important figures of the empire, including a section on Basil I.

_____. *Byzantium: Greatness and Decline*. Translated by Naomi Walford. New Brunswick, N.J.: Rutgers University Press, 1957. A well-organized work in four sections: "Evolution of Byzantine History," "Elements of Power," "Elements of Weakness," and "Byzantium's Contribution to the World." Includes a bibliography.

Diener, Bertha. *Imperial Byzantium*. Translated by Eden and Cedar Paul. Boston: Little, Brown and Co., 1938. Generally a very useful survey, but the dynastic tables contain errors.

Ostrogorski, George. *History of the Byzantine State*. Translated by Joan Hussey. Oxford: Basil Blackwell, 1956. An excellent, thorough history. Contains an especially good explanation of the sources on the subject, such as original contemporary materials.

Sherrard, Philip. *Byzantium*. New York: Time-Life Books, 1966. Notable for being composed in considerable part of pictures drawn from very early chronicles, showing events in Byzantium. Much attention to Basil I.

Vasiliev, A. A. *History of the Byzantine Empire*. Translated by Mrs. S. Ragozin. 2 vols. Madison: University of Wisconsin Press, 1928-1929. A standard authority, but especially recommended for its chapter on "The Study of Byzantine History."

Vryonis, Speros. *Byzantium and Europe*. New York: Harcourt, Brace and World, 1967. Good source on this key aspect of Basil's role in history and ideology.

Wagner, Anthony. *Pedigree and Progress*. London: Phillimore and Co., 1975. Contains a detailed account of the Asian antecedents of Basil I, his dynasty, its marriages and relationships with the European nations. Provides relevant portions of Cyril Toumanoff's book. *Manuel de Généalogie et de Chronologie pour l'Histoire de la Caucasie Chrétienne* (Rome: Edizioni Aquila, 1976, not otherwise available in English).

Frank H. Tucker

AL-BATTANI

Born: 858; near Haran, north-central Syria
Died: 929; Kasr al Djiss, region of Samarra, Iraq
Area of Achievement: Astronomy
Contribution: Al-Battani examined and corrected, through application of trigonometry, astronomical theories first put forward by the second century Alexandrian Ptolemy.

Early Life

Born near Haran in north-central Syria in 858, the young Abu 'Abd Allah Muhammad ibn Jabir ibn Sinan al-Battani al-Harrani al-Sabi' moved with his and several other families to Rakka on the Euphrates River midway on the caravan route between Aleppo and the Upper Mesopotamian city of Mosul. This migration may be explained in part by the *nisba*, or nickname, retained by the future Islamic astronomer. "Al-Sabi'" may refer to his family's earlier adherence to the so-called Sabian sect, which was reputed to follow a mixture of Christian and Islamic principles. Whatever the family's original religious orientation, Abu 'Abd Allah's later fame was won under the banner of Islam, the faith he ultimately followed. After his move to Rakka as a youth, al-Battani spent the remainder of his life in the same geographical and cultural environment.

No specific information is available on al-Battani's formal education. It is not known, for example, whether his original training was obtained in a fully secular "scientific" or in a religious setting. It was as a youth in Rakka, however, that al-Battani decided to devote himself to careful study of ancient texts, especially those of Ptolemy, which provided him with the knowledge needed to carry out the series of astronomical observations which would make him famous, not only in the Islamic world but in the medieval European West as well.

Life's Work

Al-Battani, known to the West as Albatenius, contributed greatly to advances in the field of trigonometry. To carry out key calculations, he relied on algebraic rather than geometric methods. Like his somewhat lesser known later follower Abul Wefa (940-998), al-Battani focused much of his attention on the theories of the second century Alexandrian astronomer Ptolemy. Several Islamic scholars before him had been intrigued by Ptolemy's approach to the phenomenon of the oscillatory motion of the equinoxes. Al-Battani's contemporary Thabit ibn Qurrah tried to account for this by supplementing Ptolemy's theory, merely adding a ninth sphere to the Greek scientist's assumption of eight spheres; al-Battani, however, remained doubtful. He was convinced that trigonometry should be developed more effectively for the purpose of achieving greater precision in already known methods of making these and other astronomical calculations. This goal led him to explore and expand the relevance of sines. His use of the Indian sines, or half chords, enabled him to criticize Ptolemy's conclusions in several areas.

For example, Ptolemy had insisted that the solar apogee was a fully immobile phenomenon. Al-Battani, however, was able to observe that in the seven centuries since Ptolemy's time there had been a notable increase in the sun's apogee. His further observations suggested that the apogee was affected by the precession of the equinoxes. To explore this theory required a substantial revision of methods of proposing equations to represent the passage of time in accurate astronomical terms; room had to be made for accommodating slow secular variations. As part of this process, al-Battani set out to correct Ptolemy's theory of the precession of the equinoxes.

The phenomenon of eclipses was also a field incompletely pioneered by Ptolemy. Interest in this subject motivated al-Battani to make a variety of studies that aided subsequent astronomers in their calculations to determine the time of the visibility of the new moon. His treatment of the phenomena of lunar and solar eclipses provided the basic information that would be used by European astronomers as late as the eighteenth century. Most notably, Richard Dunthorne used al-Battani's work in his 1749 study of the apparent acceleration of the motion of the moon. In addition, mention of solutions al-Battani proposed for the field of spherical trigonometry appears in many earlier European works, including those of Regiomontanus (1436-1476).

In a somewhat more practical vein easily appreciated by the layman, al-Battani's observations allowed him to determine the length of the tropic year and, significantly, the precise duration of the four seasons of the year.

One of the most original areas of al-Battani's work involved the use of horizontal and vertical sundials. Through their use, he was able to denote the characteristics of a so-called "horizontal shadow" (*umbra extensa*). These he used to reveal cotangents, for which he prepared the first known systematic tables. Similarly, his study of "vertical shadows" (*umbra versa*) provided pioneer data for calculating tangents.

Most of al-Battani's important findings in the field of astronomy were contained in his major work, *Kitab al-zij* (c. 900-901; best known as *De scientia stellarum* or *De motu stellarum*). As the Latin titles suggest, this magnum opus was first circulated widely among scholars of the early period of the European Renaissance. The work was translated originally by Robertus Retinensis in Spain in the twelfth century. In the thirteenth century, King Alfonso of Spain had a direct Arabic-to-Spanish translation prepared. *De scientia stellarum* later gained added attention from modern scholars such as the Italian C. A. Nallino, who edited and translated the Latin text, providing essential commentaries that enhance contemporary understanding of the Islamic scholar's original contributions.

Unfortunately, modern scholars' familiarity with other important writings by al-Battani is limited to what can be gleaned from references to them in other Islamic authors' works. A "Book of the Science of Ascensions of the Signs of the Zodiac," a commentary on Ptolemy's *Apotelesmatika tetrabiblos*, and a third work on trigonometry, for example, are all lost in their original versions.

Summary

The scholarly career of al-Battani provides an example of the diversity of pre-Islamic sources that contributed to the rise of Islamic science. It also illustrates the importance of such scientists' work in saving traces of pre-Islamic contributions to knowledge during the Dark Ages of European history, when much of the classical heritage of Western civilization was lost. To speak of al-Battani's role as that of an interim transmitter of knowledge, however, would be to miss the essential importance of scientific endeavors in his era. It is clear, for example, that al-Battani was dissatisfied with interpretations offered by his classical and Indian forerunners. By the time his work of reinterpretation was translated for transmission to the European world, it reflected numerous original contributions. Thus, in regard to the reemergence of Western science during the classical revival period of the Renaissance, it can be said that many of the principles upon which it was based came from Islamic sources.

The fact that such advances in several fields of "pure" science were actively sponsored by the early Islamic caliphs—themselves assumed to be primary guardians of the religious interests of their realm—is of major significance. In al-Battani's age, knowledge was still recognized as something necessarily derived from syncretic sources. Tolerance for the exploration of different secular scientific traditions did not, however, survive too many successive generations. Narrowness of views in the eastern Islamic world a mere century and a half after al-Battani's contributions would make the role of Western translators of Arabic scientific works just as vital to the conservation of cumulative knowledge in world culture as the work of Islamic translators and commentators had been after the end of the classical era. Outstanding figures such as al-Battani, therefore, definitely span world civilizations and reflect values that are universal. These are easily recognized as such beyond the borders of their chronological time or geographic zone.

Bibliography

Anawati, G. "Science." In *The Cambridge History of Islam*, edited by P. M. Holt, Ann K. S. Lambton, and Bernard Lewis, vol. 2. Cambridge: Cambridge University Press, 1970. This chapter first places the general field of science within the overall framework of Islamic civilization. It explores interrelationships between religious and scientific attitudes toward knowledge and how each of the two domains was affected by developments in the other. The body of the chapter consists of a field-by-field review of the most important Islamic accomplishments, including advances in arithmetic, algebra, geometry, trigonometry, optics, mechanics, astronomy and astrology, and medicine (including chemistry).

Bell, E. T. *The Development of Mathematics*. New York: McGraw-Hill Book Co., 1940. This comprehensive work on mathematics begins with a historical review of the field from the first known texts through each successive stage of discoveries, ending at the mid-point of the twentieth century. The chapter which is of most interest for students of Islamic science and culture is entitled "Detour Through India, Arabia, and Spain, A.D. 400-1300." Other sections of the book mention the specific contributions of Islamic scholars such as al-Battani to topical subsections of the field of mathematics, including geometry, invariance, and others. Index, but no bibliography.

Cajori, Florian. *A History of Mathematics*. 2d ed. New York: Macmillan, 1931. Although this book is rather old, it has several important advantages over other general histories. First, there is coverage not only of "standard" non-Western mathematical traditions (such as the Hindu and Islamic) but also of traditions that rarely receive attention (such as the Mayan and Japanese). Another positive attribute is Cajori's rather detailed discussion of contributions by individual mathematicians. Some technical explanations are offered, but at a level which is comprehensible to the layman.

Nasr, Seyyed Hossein. *Islamic Science: An Illustrated Study*. London: World of Islam Festival Publishing Co., 1976. Somewhat less academic than the same author's 1968 publication (see below), this book contains an attractive collection of illustrations that bring to life the world of Islamic science. These include not only intricate miniatures depicting flora and fauna but also cosmic charts and photographs of astronomical instruments and remains of observatories similar to the ones that would have been used in al-Battani's time. Glossary and bibliography.

_____. *Science and Civilization in Islam*. Cambridge, Mass.: Harvard University Press, 1968. This survey text deals only with scientific endeavors in Islamic civilization, which allows it to examine individual contributions with thoroughness. Includes chapters on the "sciences of man," including both philosophy and theology. Extensive bibliography.

Byron D. Cannon

BAYBARS I

Born: c. 1223; northern shore of the Black Sea
Died: July 1, 1277; Damascus
Area of Achievement: Government
Contribution: Through military prowess, administrative skill, courage, and practical good sense, Baybars rose from slavery to become the virtual founder and most eminent representative of the Mamluk (slave) Dynasty in medieval Egypt.

Early Life

Baybars I, al-Malik al-Zahir Rukn al-Din Baybars al-Salihi, was born around the year 1223 in what is now southern Russia. A member of the tribe of Kipchak Turks living on the north shores of the Black Sea, Baybars was a victim of the Mongol invasion of his native region in the late 1230's. By the time he was fourteen, Baybars had become a prisoner of war; he was sold in the slave market in Sivas, Anatolia. Syrian merchants took him deep into the Arab world, where Baybars eventually became the property of al-Malik al-Salih Najm al-Din Ayyub, sultan of the Ayyubid Dynasty in Egypt.

This was a time of political fragmentation in the Arab world, following the breakup of the 'Abbasid empire (750-1258) and the fall of Baghdad to the Mongols. Various local regimes, or principalities, had arisen in the void created by the collapse of the 'Abbasid state. The Ayyubids in Egypt, like other territorial princes, began to rely heavily on imported Turkish slave troops for their defense. It was for this purpose that Baybars was either sold or given to the sultan.

Sultan al-Salih sent Baybars off to an island in the Nile for military training. The adolescent Turk did well and, following graduation from a military academy and emancipation, was enrolled in the Sultan's prestigious Bahriyya regiment. Baybars had found his place in life, and the events had been set in motion that would make him "the Napoleon of medieval Egypt."

A double danger faced the Ayyubids in Egypt in the mid-thirteenth century. One threat was from the West, the other from the East. Both perils were military in nature. By sea, across the Mediterranean, came the French Crusaders. By land, across the steppes of Asia, came the Mongols. Both intruders had to be repelled if Muslim Egypt was to develop in security. As Napoleon Bonaparte later made his reputation by defending the Revolution, so Baybars secured his fame by protecting Egypt from these two dangers.

Baybars' initial assignment was to repel a French invasion of Egypt. Since 1096, Crusaders from Western Europe had attempted to regain control of the Holy Land. While many European nations participated in the Crusades, the French kingdom often took the leadership. This was the case with the last of the two "traditional" Crusades, the Sixth and the Seventh. Both were undertaken by Louis IX of France, a Catholic celebrated for his piety; they were occasioned by the loss of the Crusader Kingdom of Jerusalem to the Mongols in 1244. Louis was persuaded that the best way to liberate Jerusalem was not by means of a direct or frontal attack but by diversionary measures in Arab North Africa. These would distract Muslim attention from Jerusalem. Louis, as a matter of fact, would die in the second of these invasions of North Africa (at Tunis in 1270). His initial adventure in Arab Africa was almost equally fatal. Louis invaded the Ayyubid Sultanate, taking Dumyat (Damietta) in the Nile Delta. At this juncture, the sultan turned to Baybars for help. The elite forces of the Ayyubid army, the Bahriyya, led by Baybars, defeated the French at al-Mansurah in February, 1250. Louis was captured and was held by the Ayyubids for ransom. As a result, the reputation of Baybars was established, and the Ayyubid Dynasty was relieved of the danger of invasion.

Before Baybars could direct his attention toward the other danger, the Mongols, there was an internal crisis within the Ayyubid regime. Conscious of their own power, the Mamluk, or Turkish slave soldiers, with Baybars' cooperation, rose in revolt against the new Ayyubid sultan, Turan Shah. Turan Shah was murdered, and a period of confusion followed which was resolved when the first Mamluk (slave) sultan, Aybak, came to power. For reasons that are not entirely clear, Baybars offended the first Mamluk sultan and, like the Old Testament soldier David who offended his commander-king, Saul, he had to go into exile in 1254. For six years, Baybars was a "soldier of fortune" in Syria.

Baybars, however, was much too valuable a person for the Mamluks not to employ. A new sultan, al-Muzaffar Sayf al-Din Qutuz, invited him to return to Egypt in 1260. Baybars was restored to his rank in the Mamluk army and was given a suitable income. Now he was assigned to the task of delivering Egypt from the Mongol threat. Baybars took his forces to the Holy Land, where he defeated a Mongol army near Nabulus in 1260. Apparently, Baybars was disappointed when, following this victory, he was denied a suitable reward (it is thought that he wanted the city of Aleppo). During a quarrel that may have been occasioned by a Mongol slave girl, Baybars joined other officers in a palace coup; Qutuz was assassinated. Thus for the second time, Baybars had been involved in the murder of his master. The ambitious officer now became Baybars I, the fourth Mamluk sultan. For all practical purposes, Baybars was the true founder of the *Dawlat al-atrak* (the dynasty of the Turks). Perhaps he had set a dangerous precedent in obtaining power by assassination. Other Turkish tribes, such as the Ottomans, however, used a similar procedure, the "law of strangulation," whereby the most powerful of the sultan's sons ascended the throne after murdering his brothers. Baybars, however, proved able to maintain himself on the throne of Egypt.

Baybars ruled effectively because of his outstanding personal qualities. Known as a strict Muslim, Baybars, like the Prophet, was a man given to victory in battle and generosity in peace. Celebrated for his athletic ability, Baybars enjoyed hunting, polo, jousting, and archery. A man of courage, he inspired enormous loyalty among his followers and was capable of commanding great sacrifice from his soldiers. Though he came to power by assassination, Baybars ruled securely and retained the respect and obedience of his subordinates. Baybars came to be celebrated in the popular imagination as a "fair and able ruler." He came to be known as the subject of a body of folk literature, the *Sirat Baybars*. Thus, not only was Baybars a legend in his own lifetime but he also became an archetypal symbol of the just king for later generations.

Life's Work

Baybars was to be the greatest of the Mamluk sultans. For seventeen years (1260-1277), he devoted himself to carrying out three great roles: warrior, ruler, and reformer.

Baybars' reign was dominated by war. One of the great military commanders of the Middle Ages, Baybars conducted thirty-eight campaigns in Syria, fought nine battles with the Mongols, and was involved in five major engagements with the Armenians. It is reported that Baybars took personal command of the army in fifteen battles. Because of the military requirements of his reign, Baybars was outside his capital city, Cairo, for almost half the time he was sultan. On twenty-six occasions, Baybars left Cairo, traveling more than sixty-six thousand miles.

The assignment Baybars faced as sultan was the same that he had received as a staff officer: to secure the safety of Egypt from both the Crusaders and the Mongols. He began by taking up the campaign against the Crusaders. From 1265 to 1271, Baybars conducted a war against the Crusaders in Palestine. As a result, Baybars forced the Knights Hospitallers to surrender Arsuf in 1265, and within a year Safad, which had been in the control of the Knights Templars, fell. Jaffa and Antioch were occupied by May, 1268, and within another three years the ultimate doom of the Crusaders was sealed. Their eventual expulsion from the Middle East had been assured.

Having secured his realm from French invasion, Baybars turned his attention eastward. While the Mongols were his main enemy, there were also other threats in Asia. From their bases in Iran, the Mongols had felt free to invade Syria. Baybars prevented this by refortifying Syria, attacking the Armenians (who had been allies of the Mongols), and waging unrelenting war on the Mongols. As a result, Syria was pacified, secured, and united to Egypt. Baybars also destroyed the power of a militantly anarchist Muslim sect, the Assassins of Syria, and was able to invade Anatolia, taking the city of Caesarea (now Kayseri) from the Seljuk Turks in 1276. Concurrently, campaigns were undertaken in Africa to guarantee the safety of Egypt. Expeditions southward to Nubia and westward into Libya both proved successful.

Many scholars have tried to explain the military success of Baybars. Eight factors are usually offered as reasons for his brilliance as a warrior. First, he had a very fine model: Baybars consciously chose to imitate Saladin. The founder of the Ayyubid Dynasty in Egypt, Saladin (1138-1193) is regarded by many as the greatest Muslim military hero of all time. Baybars attempted to live up to the high standards of courage, courtesy, and character embodied by this great warrior. Second, Baybars had outstanding personal qualities and mental attitudes; he was an energetic man "who dominated events with an imperturbable optimism." Third, he was committed to careful planning. Attention to detail meant that he left nothing to chance. To the extent that preparation made it possible, Baybars was in control of the situation. Fourth, under his leadership Egypt was remilitarized and turned into an adequate base of operations. Fortifications were rebuilt; arsenals, warships, and merchant vessels were constructed. Fifth, Baybars' foresight, his sense of a world perspective, and his understanding of regional military realities enabled him to capitalize on Egypt's geographic location at the crossroads of the Middle East. Sixth, Baybars relied on an excellent communications system. News came to him from all parts of his empire at least twice a week; more urgent matters were brought to the sultan's attention by means of carrier pigeons. Seventh, Baybars established a brilliant espionage system so that he was able to know in advance of his enemies' moves. Eighth, perhaps the keystone in this entire arch of military brilliance was Baybars' many talents as a field commander. He was able to make quick decisions, to command the unflinching loyalty of his troops, to furnish an example of personal courage and vitality, and to evoke love and respect from his supporters at home.

As a ruler, Baybars was known for achievement in several major areas. He maintained the strength of the military, for he realized that his power was based on the army. It was his decision to continue the already established pattern of recruiting Turkish slaves. An alliance with the Mongols of the Golden Horde in southern Russia made this possible.

Moreover, Baybars expanded the influence of Egypt. The annexation of Syria was one expression of this goal; the establishing of diplomatic relations with the various Mediterranean powers was another. Baybars' envoys were favorably received by Emperor Michael VIII Palaeologus in Byzantium, securing the grain trade and once more opening the Bosporus and the Black Sea to Egyptian navigation. Ambassadors were also sent to various courts, including those of Manfred of Sicily, Charles of Anjou (later King of Naples and Sicily), James I of Aragon, and Alfonso X of León and Castile. Such an aggressive foreign policy, coupled with Baybars' military brilliance, reestablished Egypt as the key state in the Arab world.

Baybars was clearly successful in legitimizing his regime. Here again, a comparison with Napoleon Bonaparte is helpful. As Napoleon invited the pope, the representative of a world faith, to attend his coronation, so

Baybars won the endorsement of the caliphate for his government. In 1261, Baybars invited the exiled heir of the 'Abbasid Caliphate to take up residence in Cairo. While the caliph lacked political power, he had enormous popular prestige and spiritual influence. Offering sanctuary to the spiritual leader of Islam was an act of absolute brilliance. It cost Baybars nothing, but it gained respectability for his government throughout the orthodox (Sunni) Muslim world. This prestige would endure until Egypt's defeat by the Ottoman Turks in 1515 and the concomitant removal of the caliphate from Cairo to Istanbul.

Baybars was a reformer. As a devout Muslim, he was persuaded that the very center of a society must be religious faith. Accordingly, the restoration of religion was a major aim of his regime. Among his many building projects was a great mosque complex in Cairo that was named in his honor. Baybars recognized all four schools of orthodox Islamic law—Hanifite, Hanbalite, Shafite, and Malikite—and appointed judges from each of these traditions to serve in his courts. A strict moralist, he prohibited the sale and consumption of alcohol, commanded the giving of alms, facilitated the pilgrimage to Mecca, enforced the fast, and richly endowed Muslim schools and mosques. Baybars could not reform the principles of his religion, for he regarded them as ultimate and eternal, but he could promote the ardent practice of the faith. It is in that sense that Baybars was a genuine reformer.

One can only speculate as to the further extent of his accomplishments had Baybars not died prematurely on July 1, 1277, in Damascus; a poisoned cup intended for another had come to his hand. His body was buried at the al-Zahiriyah in Damascus, but his spirit lived on in the imagination of the Arab people.

Summary

In a time of fragmention and confusion throughout the Muslim world, Baybars I was able to create a strong Arab state at the very heart of the Middle East. The real founder of the Mamluk Dynasty, which survived not only his death but also the Turkish conquest in 1515, perishing finally with the arrival of Napoleon in Egypt in 1798, he brought stability and order to Egypt. A military genius, Baybars defended the Mideast against major adversaries from both the West and the East: the Crusaders and the Mongols. Had he not come to power, Egypt might have been carved up into Crusader kingdoms, as had been the case along the Levantine coast, or, worse still, the Mongols might have devastated not only Palestine and Syria but also the North African coast. It can be said, then, that Baybars was not simply the Napoleon of the Arab Middle Ages and the real founder of the Mamluk Dynasty but a genuine savior of Egypt as a nation and as a culture.

Bibliography

Ayalon, David. *Studies on the Mamluks of Egypt, 1250-1517.* London: Variorum Reprints, 1977. This is a useful introduction to the Slave Dynasty in medieval Egypt. The volume comprises addresses, essays, and lectures by the author. Includes bibliographical references and an index.

Hitti, Philip K. *History of the Arabs from the Earliest Times to the Present.* London: Macmillan, 1937. 10th ed. New York: St. Martin's Press, 1970. This is a standard text for the entire spectrum of Arab history. Includes illustrations, genealogical tables, maps, and bibliographical references.

Hodgson, Marshall G. S. *The Venture of Islam: Conscience and History in a World Civilization.* 3 vols. Chicago: University of Chicago Press, 1974. A masterful history of the Muslim centuries, this work skillfully combines narrative and interpretation. Hodgson's study begins with Islam's classical age and ends with modern times. Indexed.

Holt, Peter Malcolm, Ann K. S. Lambton, and Bernard Lewis, eds. *The Cambridge History of Islam.* 2 vols. Cambridge: Cambridge University Press, 1970. This valuable survey of the entire adventure of Islam places the time of Baybars I in context. Includes illustrations, maps, and bibliographies.

Lane-Poole, Stanley. *A History of Egypt in the Middle Ages.* London: Methuen and Co., 1901, 4th ed. 1925. This vintage work remains a comprehensive and valuable study. Includes a map and other illustrations. Part of The History of Egypt series, edited by W. M. F. Petrie.

Muir, William. *The Mameluke: Or, Slave Dynasty of Egypt.* New York: AMS Press, 1973. With the work of Lane-Poole (see above), this book remains the standard survey of the Mamluk era. Originally published in London in 1896. Includes illustrations.

Runciman, Steven. *A History of the Crusades.* 4 vols. Cambridge: Cambridge University Press, 1951-1958. The definitive study of the Crusades by a sophisticated British scholar. Illustrations, maps, and a genealogical table.

Von Grunebaum, Gustav Edmund. *Classical Islam: A History, 600-1258.* Translated by Katherine Watson. Chicago: Aldine Publishing Co., 1970. This excellent survey provides useful background on the Umayyad and 'Abbasid caliphates that set the stage for the "age of principalities," in which Baybars I was crucial.

_____. *Medieval Islam: A Study in Cultural Orientation.* Chicago: University of Chicago Press, 1946, 2d ed. 1953. A fine companion volume to *Classical Islam,* by the same author (see above). Part of the University of Chicago's Oriental Institute series. Contains maps and bibliographical footnotes.

C. George Fry

SAINT BENEDICT OF NURSIA

Born: c. 480; Nursia, Umbria, Italy
Died: c. 547; Monte Cassino, Campania, Italy
Areas of Achievement: Monasticism and religion
Contribution: Over fifty years of his life, Benedict took the Greek pattern for the monastic life and adapted it for systematic use in the Latin church; the resulting *Rule of St. Benedict* became the model for all subsequent monastic movements.

Early Life

Although the dates of his life are in doubt, it appears that Saint Benedict of Nursia was born about 480, while Simplicius was Bishop of Rome and Odoacer was King of Italy. Benedict's parents, according to ancient tradition, were Euproprius and Abundantia, people of rather high social standing. It is possible that Benedict's father was a town councilman or a magistrate.

The only primary source for the study of Benedict's life is the *Dialogues of Saint Gregory the Great*, Pope from 590 to 604. This source relates practically nothing about Benedict's parents, but it does contain something about his sister Scholastica and his nurse. Tradition says that Benedict and his sister were twins. Gregory reported that the two loved each other dearly and that both, from an early age, wanted to serve God. The nurse's name may have been Cyrilla, for that is what early biographers of Benedict called her. There is, unfortunately, no reliable information about the home life of these two future saints, but Gregory indicates that Benedict and Scholastica had no interest in worldly pursuits.

Benedict received what Gregory called a liberal education in Rome. This indicates that he attended a Latin grammar school, where he was offended by the evil conduct of other students. He finally decided to discontinue his education and to adopt an ascetic life as the way to God. At about age seventeen he forsook family, school, and possessions to become a monk. The exact circumstances surrounding this decision are not known, but he left Rome in search of a way to practice piety.

Life's Work

By renouncing worldly pleasures, Benedict committed himself to a monastic life that was to last about fifty years. He joined monks at Enfide, east of Rome, but he remained there for only a short time. For the next three years he lived secluded in a cave near Subiaco, about forty miles from Rome, a barren place where Emperor Nero had once maintained a villa.

Life in the hermitage was difficult—just as Benedict wished, for he sought to win God's favor by rigorous self-denial. He suffered severe temptations at times, despite the isolation of his residence, and at one point he became so inflamed with lust that he almost abandoned asceticism. The monk, however, defeated the temptation by leaping into a thicket of thorn bushes, from which he emerged bruised, cut, and bleeding—but rid of his lust. He later reported that this experience had given him final victory over sexual desires.

When Benedict arrived at Subiaco, Romanus, a monk from the nearby house at Vicovaro, met him and led him to the cave which became his home for three years. Romanus and his associates eventually asked Benedict to become their abbot, and after much hesitation, he agreed. Although he disliked leaving his solitude, he saw an opportunity to lead a community of ascetics that was greatly in need of reform. Benedict sought to eliminate laxity and to restore faithful adherence to the principle of self-denial. His efforts aroused animosity from some monks, and they conspired to remove him. After some dissidents tried to poison him, the abbot left the community and resumed the life of a hermit.

His solitude did not, however, last long. Benedict was concerned for the souls who came to him for counsel, and he eventually organized them into twelve houses, which were united under his authority in an association of monasteries—the first Benedictine institutions in history. The monks' reputation for piety soon attracted adherents from Rome, who joined a movement which corresponded closely to the monastic pattern common in the Church of the East.

Benedict might have remained at Subiaco for the rest of his life had not a vicious plot destroyed his tranquillity. The saint's enemy was Florentius, a local priest of ungodly character who was embarrassed by the devout lives of Benedict and his monks. The cleric feigned friendship by sending the abbot a gift of food, which he had poisoned. When that effort failed, Florentius employed seven lewd women to dance in the monastery garden to entice the monks. Benedict believed that the priest's hatred for him was the motive behind his machinations, so the abbot determined to leave Subiaco in order to protect his disciples from further attacks on their virtue. He explained to his brethren that God, by a direct revelation, had commanded him to depart, so his decision was irrevocable. Florentius did not, however, enjoy his triumph very long. As the hate-filled priest stood on a balcony watching Benedict leave Subiaco, the porch collapsed under him, and he was killed, which Gregory concluded was divine retribution.

With a small band of disciples, Benedict terminated his thirty-year ministry at Subiaco and traveled to Monte Cassino, about eighty miles south of Rome. This area had once been the site of altars and sacred groves for the worship of Apollo and other pagan gods. Some of the local peasants were still members of heathen cults when the monks arrived. Benedict demolished at least one altar in current use and cut down a sacred grove. He replaced the implements of paganism with chapels in honor of Saint Martin of Tours and Saint John the Baptist.

Although Benedict went to Monte Cassino to found a monastery for the practice of the ascetic life, he soon accepted an obligation to seek the conversion of pagans in the neighborhood, an endeavor which succeeded well. The most enduring feature of Benedict's work at Monte Cassino is, however, the monastic rule which ever since has borne his name. This is the only writing from the saint's own hand to survive.

The Benedictine Rule gradually became the standard for monastic practice throughout the Western church. It was not, however, entirely original with Saint Benedict. Later research has shown that it was preceded by the *Regula magistri*, whose author is anonymous. It is evident that Benedict borrowed heavily from this document. The Rule of Saint Benedict quotes from the Bible and the church fathers, especially Augustine, Jerome, Cyprian, and Leo. It reveals the author's familiarity with Eastern fathers such as Pachomius and Basil, who wrote rules for monks of Greek Christendom. Benedict's reliance on the *Regula magistri* and other sources shows that he did not consider himself an innovator or the founder of a new religious movement. He instead accepted the concepts of his predecessors and adapted them to his own needs and those of his disciples. The synthetic character of the Benedictine Rule was actually part of its strength, which may account for the broad acceptance it achieved.

It is rather interesting that, in composing his Rule, Benedict drew extensively from the writings of two earlier monastic leaders who held contradictory doctrines of salvation. Saint Augustine of Hippo (354-430) had produced a rule for monks of his diocese in North Africa, and John Cassian (died c. 435) had done the same for those in southern Gaul. Augustine was the champion of salvation by grace alone, while Cassian contended that grace enabled man to perform works of righteousness which, if sufficiently meritorious, God would reward with salvation. Cassian's view, commonly called Semi-Pelagianism, became very popular in southern Gaul, but the Catholic church condemned it as heresy at the Synod of Orange in 529. Condemnation did not, however, lead to the demise of Semi-Pelagianism, as the Rule of Saint Benedict shows clearly. In the prologue to his Rule, the abbot wrote:

> Let us encompass ourselves with faith and . . . good works, and guided by the Gospel, tread the path He [Christ] has cleared for us. Thus may we deserve to see Him who has called us into His Kingdom. . . . If we wish to be sheltered in this Kingdom, it can be reached only through our good conduct.

Although Benedict affirmed that Divine Grace enables one to perform good works, it is evident that he regarded such works as meritorious toward salvation. In fact, Cassian and those who espoused his teaching saw clearly that the Augustinian belief that salvation is a free gift of grace undermines the entire philosophy of monasticism, something which the great Bishop of

Hippo had failed to perceive.

The Benedictine Rule then prescribes a style of life intended to win salvation by self-denial. Benedict ordered that monks subscribe to vows of poverty, chastity, and obedience. He wanted his disciples to forsake individualism and to perform spiritual and physical good works in the community. He wanted monasteries to be self-sufficient so that monks would "not need to wander about outside, for this is not good for their souls." He made the abbot master of the community, to whom the monks owed unqualified obedience. The Rule is not all-inclusive but allows the abbot considerable latitude. It is more a compendium of principles than a code of precise precepts. The Frankish emperor Charlemagne (ruled 768-814) promoted ecclesiastical reforms which featured observance of Benedict's Rule, and the emperor's son Louis the Pious (ruled 814-840) made it the standard for monastic houses in Germany and France. Although Benedict did not presume that his Rule would gain universal acceptance in the Catholic church, all later monastic charters have been chiefly modifications of his original work.

Benedict of Nursia died about 547 at Monte Cassino, forty-six days after his sister Scholastica. Although he had shown no signs of illness, six days before he died he told his followers to open his grave so that he could see the remains of Scholastica, with whom he was to be buried.

Pope Gregory believed that Benedict worked miracles and that he possessed the gift of prophecy. In the *Dialogues*, therefore, miracle tales abound. Among them are wonders which correspond to events in the Bible, such as bringing water out of rocks, causing an iron blade to rise from the bottom of a lake, and enabling a disciple to walk on water. There is one account of the abbot restoring a dead person to life.

Summary

The significance of Saint Benedict of Nursia for the development of Latin Christendom can scarcely be exaggerated, even if one discounts the miracles that Gregory the Great attributed to him. Benedict's monks soon established a daughter house at Terracina, the first of many extensions—eventually thirty-seven thousand others dotted the landscape of Christendom. Although he did not produce syllabi for scholarly activities, his order became famous for the learned writings of medieval authors such as Bede and Alcuin. When, by the tenth century, monasticism in general had declined, the Cluniacs and Cistercians arose to restore adherence to the Benedictine Rule.

In 1964, Pope Paul VI made Benedict patron saint of Europe. Although he was not the first Latin monk, he was surely the most influential, and the prevalence of the Semi-Pelagian doctrine of salvation in modern Catholicism bears witness to the pervasiveness of the ascetic world-and-life view which monks have, since his time, promoted. Benedict's motto was *Ora—Labora*, Praise and Work.

Bibliography

Benedict, Saint. *Rule of St. Benedict*. Translated with introduction and notes by Anthony C. Meisel and M. L. del Mastro. Garden City, N.Y.: Doubleday and Co., 1975. A highly readable translation, with useful notes and a bibliography. Excellent for the general reader.

—————————. *Rule of St. Benedict in Latin and English with Notes*. Edited by Timothy Fry and Imogen Baker. Collegeville, Minn.: Liturgical Press, 1981. Critically prepared text with very helpful biographical sketch of author.

Chadwick, Owen, ed. *Western Asceticism*. Philadelphia: Westminster Press, 1958. Contains writings of John Cassian as well as Benedict.

Chapman, Dom John. *Saint Benedict and the Sixth Century*. Reprint. Westport, Conn.: Greenwood Press, 1971. A technical study regarding historical transmission of the Rule. Includes some useful background data.

Doyle, Francis Cuthbert. *The Teaching of St. Benedict*. New York: Catholic Publication Society, 1887. A short life, with extensive commentary on Benedict's Rule.

Duckett, Eleanor Shipley. *The Gateway to the Middle Ages: Monasticism*. Reprint. Ann Arbor: University of Michigan Press, 1961. Extensive coverage of Gregory and Benedict by a great medievalist.

Dudden, F. Homes. *Gregory the Great, His Place in History and Thought*. 2 vols. New York: Russell and Russell, 1967. Despite its age, this is still the major work on the subject; valuable for Gregory's view of Benedict.

Gregory the Great. *Dialogues*. Translated by Odo John Zimmerman. New York: Fathers of the Church, 1959. The only surviving primary source on Benedict, in a readable translation.

Maynard, Theodore. *Saint Benedict and His Monks*. New York: Sheed and Ward, 1954. A semipopular treatment by a prolific Catholic author.

Payne, Robert. *Fathers of the Western Church*. New York: Viking Press, 1951. Interesting sketches of leading churchmen of ancient and medieval periods by a skillful professional writer. The articles on Gregory and Benedict are especially good.

Tosti, Luigi. *Saint Benedict: An Historical Discourse on His Life*. London: Kegan Paul, Trench, Trübner and Co., 1896. Though based on competent research, this book was written to excite devotion to the saint; it is chiefly hagiography with uncritical narrations of miracle tales.

James Edward McGoldrick

BENJAMIN OF TUDELA

Born: Twelfth century; Tudela, Navarre
Died: 1173; Castile
Area of Achievement: Geography
Contribution: Benjamin's account of his travels presents the best record available of the number, the leaders, and the social, religious, and economic conditions of the Jews in southern Europe and the Middle East during the twelfth century. At the same time, he provides the best documentation of trade and commerce in these areas in the period between the Second and Third Crusades.

Early Life

All that can be learned of the life of Rabbi Benjamin ben Jonah of Tudela is found in his only surviving literary work, *Massa'ot* (c. 1173; *The Itinerary of Benjamin of Tudela*, 1840), and its Hebrew preface, written by a contemporary of Benjamin. This preface refers to Benjamin as "a wise and understanding man, learned in the Law and the Halacha [Book of Practices]," and observes further that "wherever we have tested his statements we have found them accurate, true to fact and consistent; for he is a trustworthy man." Unfortunately, Benjamin stood outside his narrative, revealing little about himself as he chronicled what he had seen and heard during his travels.

The Hebrew preface speaks of Benjamin as a rabbi, and in his observations Benjamin demonstrated a familiarity with the rabbinical literature of his time as well as a thorough knowledge of the Hebrew Bible. He wrote in a formal medieval Hebrew sometimes called Rabbinic Hebrew. He seems to have known Arabic, for his account is filled with phrases from that language. In fact, in that his native city, Tudela, was located in al-Andalus, or Muslim Spain, Arabic may well have been his mother tongue. Benjamin no doubt grew to maturity in two cultural worlds: one of Arabic science and culture and another of Jewish culture based on the Bible and the classical works of the rabbis such as the Talmud. His careful description of commercial activities indicates that he was probably a merchant by profession.

Benjamin did not explain his reasons for making his journey. He may have gone as a pilgrim to worship before the relics of the Hebrew past, many of which he described in the course of his travels, or his object may have been trade and mercantile operations, since he spent so much time describing those that he saw among the people he visited. He may also have been motivated by a concern for his fellow Jews. The period of the Crusades had already witnessed the extermination by Christian Crusaders of whole communities of Jews in Germany and along the routes to Palestine, and even in Benjamin's Spain his Jewish brethren were caught between the Christian soldiers of the Reconquista and the occupying Muslims of al-Andalus. Perhaps he hoped to find places of asylum for his fellow Jews in the lands he visited. This would account for his careful descriptions of independent communities of Jews which had rulers of their own and owed no allegiance to outsiders. Indeed, Benjamin may have been motivated by all of these considerations.

Life's Work

The only claim to importance of Benjamin of Tudela is *The Itinerary of Benjamin of Tudela*, his record of a journey which he took from his birthplace in northern Spain to Baghdad and perhaps beyond, and his return by way of Egypt and Sicily. He left Tudela in 1159 or 1160 and was back in Spain by 1173, the year in which he died.

Most scholars make a distinction between what Benjamin saw and what he heard. His descriptions of communities in Spain, southern France, Italy, the Byzantine Empire, Palestine, and Iran are detailed and accurate, so that there is little doubt that he visited them. Of areas to the east of Baghdad, however, his descriptions are brief, sketchy, and filled with fabulous stories, so that most who have studied Benjamin's work agree that his accounts of places beyond the Persian Gulf are based on what he heard from merchants and other travelers whom he met in Baghdad, where he spent considerable time. On his return route, Benjamin visited Aden, Yemen, Egypt, and Sicily. He makes reference to Germany, Bohemia, Russia, and northern France at the end of his account, but there is little reason to believe that he actually visited them. Of the nearly three hundred locations mentioned by Benjamin, those communities given the most coverage are Rome, Constantinople, Nablus, Jerusalem, Damascus, Baghdad, Cairo, and Alexandria.

The importance of *The Itinerary of Benjamin of Tudela* is that it is the earliest, the best, and in some cases, the only source of information for many facets of the history of the regions through which he traveled at the time of the Crusades. Without question, Benjamin's account is the fullest and most accurate record of the condition and numbers of the Jews in the twelfth century. For most of the Jewish communities that Benjamin actually visited, he provides the reader with the names of the leaders and the sizes of the congregations; in many cases, he lists the occupations of the people—silk and purple cloth makers in Thebes, dyers in Jerusalem, silk cloth makers and merchants in Constantinople, glassmakers in Tyre. Indeed, until the discovery in the nineteenth century of merchant letters stored in the attic of the synagogue in Cairo, Benjamin's account was the sole source of information for the vast and diverse trade on the Mediterranean Sea and the Indian Ocean during the period in which he wrote. While the letters augment Benjamin's account, they do not challenge its basic accuracy.

On numerous other matters, Benjamin was the first European commentator. He was the first from the West to describe with accuracy the sect of the

Assassins in Syria and Iran, the first to point to the island of Kish (or Kis) in the Persian Gulf as the chief emporium in the Middle East for the goods of India, and the first to refer to China by its modern name.

Benjamin's account is also valuable for showing the diversity of religious beliefs and practices among the people he met or of whom he heard, whether they were Jews, Christians, Muslims, or pagans. He described strange worship patterns, burial customs, diets, and other deviations from what he considered to be normal practice. For example, he described the Jews of Nablus, whose alphabet lacked three letters. While they knew the law of Moses, their alphabetical deficiency, according to Benjamin, deprived them of dignity, kindness, and humility. Benjamin was also aware of the issues that separated the Roman Christians from those of Byzantium, as well as the struggle between the "Protector of the Faithful" in Cairo and the "Protector of the Faithful" in Baghdad, which disrupted the unity of the Muslim community.

Two of the most extensive and useful descriptions in Benjamin's account are those of the cities of Constantinople and Baghdad, two cities that in his estimation had no peer. Constantinople was visited by merchants from every country, and its storehouses of silk, purple, and gold were without equal. He estimated that the city received twenty thousand gold pieces every year as tribute from merchants who entered by sea and land, and from the rents of shops and markets. According to Benjamin, the Greek inhabitants were very rich: "They go clothed in garments of silk with gold embroidery, and they ride horses, and look like princes." To protect themselves, the Greeks hired mercenaries, for they were "not warlike, but . . . as women who have no strength to fight." No Jews were permitted in the city, except one who was the emperor's physician, and through him the oppression of the Jews who lived outside the city was somewhat alleviated.

Baghdad is clearly the city that made the greatest impression on Benjamin. He noted that there were twenty-eight synagogues, ten rabbinical academies, and forty thousand Jews there, all dwelling "in security, prosperity and honour under the great Caliph." While devoting much space to the wonders of the city and the character of the caliph—a ruler who supported himself by the work of his own hands and gave generously to the poor but kept members of his family bound by iron chains and under perpetual guard for fear of rebellion—Benjamin was most eloquent when he described the exalted role held by the exilarch, whom the Jews called "Our Lord, the Head of the Captivity of All Israel." This man, according to Benjamin, had been given authority by the caliph over all the Jews in the Muslim Empire. Every subject of the caliph, Jew and Muslim alike, was required to rise up before the exilarch and salute him. Each Thursday a triumphal parade through the streets of Baghdad preceded the exilarch's meeting with the caliph at the royal palace. The exilarch, possessed of great property, bestowed charity and benevolence upon his people.

Aside from the more serious aspects of his account, readers may find much of interest in Benjamin's retellings of fanciful stories that he heard. He tells, for example, of the pillar of salt into which Lot's wife was turned, observing that "the sheep lick it continually, but afterwards it regains its original shape." Stranger still is his fable of the sun-worshippers of Khulam (Quilon), who embalmed their dead with spices and then placed them in their homes "so that every man can recognize his parents, and the members of his family for many years."

Summary

While Benjamin's account undoubtedly reflects his interests as a pilgrim, a merchant, and a Jew who may have been seeking places of asylum for his co-religionists, it is the good fortune of his readers that his other interests were diverse. Though he was at his best in describing the conditions of the Jews in the communities which he visited, as well as the economic endeavors in which they and other peoples engaged, Benjamin was also skillful in discussing architectural wonders, religious relics, social customs, religious beliefs and practices, and forms of government. His analysis of the power of the caliph of Baghdad and the exilarch has been noted; he also offers useful discussions of the power exercised by the "Old Man of the Assassins," the leaders of the Turkish tribes, and the priests of Ceylon, who controlled their people through trickery and witchcraft.

The ultimate significance of Benjamin's narrative can be judged by the numerous editions and translations through which it has passed. Cited by various writers in the Middle Ages, when it circulated in manuscript, it was first printed in 1543. Since then it has gone through many printings, both in the original Hebrew and in modern languages. No scholarly work on the Middle East in the twelfth century can be complete without drawing directly or indirectly upon this work. While recent research has cast additional light on many of the topics covered by Benjamin's work, regarding those things which he claims to have seen himself few significant errors have been exposed. In large part, *The Itinerary of Benjamin of Tudela* has stood the test of time.

Bibliography

Baron, Salo W. *A Social and Religious History of the Jews*. 8 vols. New York: Columbia University Press, 1952. Volumes 3, 4, 5, 6, and 7 contain numerous citations of Benjamin, in which his data are compared and contrasted with information from other sources for the same period.

Beazley, C. Raymond. *The Dawn of Modern Geography: A History of Exploration and Geographical Science*. 2 vols. London: J. Murray, 1897-1906. Reprint. New York: Peter Smith, 1949. Volume 2 of this work focuses on the period from 900 to 1260, including a fifty-page analysis of Benjamin's writings. Where errors in Benjamin's account are noted, the appropriate corrections are made.

Benjamin of Tudela. *The Itinerary of Benjamin of Tudela*. Translated with an introduction and notes by Marcus Nathan Adler. London: H. Frowde, 1907. Contains an improved translation of the text, a useful introductory essay, notes, an English index to the text, and a map showing the route taken by Benjamin.

_____. *The Itinerary of Rabbi Benjamin of Tudela*. Translated with an introduction and notes by A. Asher. 2 vols. London: A. Asher and Co., 1840. Volume 1 contains the earliest English translation of the text, an informative introductory essay, and a bibliography. Volume 2 contains extensive notes on the text and two expository essays.

Signer, Michael A. Introduction to *The Itinerary of Benjamin of Tudela*. New York: Joseph Simon, 1983. This volume includes a reprint of the Adler translation along with Adler's and Asher's introductory essays. The excellent introduction by Signer gives fresh insights into Benjamin's motives for making the journey and writing his account. Maps included.

Paul E. Gill

SAINT BERNARD OF CLAIRVAUX

Born: 1090; Fontaines-les-Dijon, Burgundy
Died: August 20, 1153; Clairvaux, Champagne
Areas of Achievement: Religion and church reform
Contribution: In the first half of the twelfth century, Bernard epitomized the
   monastic ideal and served as adviser and critic to kings, popes, bishops,
   abbots, and other leading figures in Western Europe.

Early Life

Bernard was born in 1090 in Fontaines-les-Dijon, the son of Tescelin le Sor, a rich and valiant Burgundian knight. Aleth, his mother, was a dutiful wife; her saintly behavior had a considerable impact on her son. At an early age, Bernard was enrolled in a church school at Châtillon-sur-Seine, where he impressed everyone with his love of learning. He mastered the trivium and became somewhat familiar with the quadrivium. After his mother's death, he was left with the difficult choice of a vocation in the secular world, perhaps that of a knight like his father, or in the Church, which had been his mother's preference. Bernard was tall and attractive with a noble countenance, but he was too delicate and sensitive to become a warrior. Thus, he was destined from before birth, according to one account, to become a monk.

There followed a period of preparation. In a short time, Bernard's charismatic personality influenced many others to eschew the secular world. Around 1113, Bernard and about thirty companions were admitted to the Cistercian monastery of Cîteaux, which was renowned for its austerities. Not only was this an important step in Bernard's life, but it was also a significant event in the history of the fledgling Cistercian Order.

Life's Work

During his novitiate, Bernard earned the admiration and wonder of all with his ascetic behavior. In the meantime, Cîteaux had grown so rapidly that it became necessary to found new colonies. In 1115, although only twenty-four years old, Bernard was selected to lead one of these expeditions. He and twelve companions took up residence in the Valley of Wormwood and began construction of the monastery known as Clairvaux. Cîteaux's newest daughter prospered under Bernard's guidance, but the rigors of office, coupled with an inclination toward extreme asceticism, ruined his health and brought him close to death. At the behest of Guillaume de Champeaux, Bishop of Châlons-sur-Marne, Bernard was relieved of his abbatial duties for a year to regain his strength.

At the end of the year, Bernard returned to his monastic office, but he never fully recovered. At times he had such difficulty digesting his food that he had to vomit into a pit dug for the purpose near his seat in choir. Pale and emaciated, his appearance was at once forbidding and ethereal. Bernard's happiest moments were spent in his cell praying, fasting, studying, and writing. During infrequent intervals of leisure, Bernard wrote a prodigious number of sermons and letters. The sermons were written on spiritual subjects such as humility, pride, the love of God, the Virgin Mary, and church reform, while the letters were addressed to kings, popes, bishops, monks, and others on a multitude of subjects.

Bernard became the most famous monk of his day, preaching a doctrine which called on ecclesiastics and laymen alike to repent of their sins, embrace Christ, and live a monastic life. Many were won to monasticism, the Cistercian Order in particular. Even the famous, such as the brother of the French king, sought the peace of the cloister. So eloquent was Bernard that mothers hid their children lest they be led away by the monastic Pied Piper. As the order grew in numbers, new houses were founded in France, Germany, Italy, Spain, England, and Scandinavia. In 1135 Clairvaux found it necessary to relocate closer to the Aube River to permit additional growth.

Bernard would have been quite happy to restrict himself to the management of Clairvaux and its daughter houses. Yet the great abbot lived in close proximity to a violent and chaotic world whose repercussions sometimes reached Clairvaux. Never a shrinking violet, Bernard became involved in nearly all the important political and ecclesiastical issues of Western Europe during a period of thirty years. Sometimes he advised kings. On other occasions, he took issue with their policies, especially those which threatened the freedom of the Church. Louis VI of France was reproved for intervening in the affairs of the Bishop of Paris and for appointing a prelate as seneschal, while his son, Louis VII, was censured many times for inappropriate behavior.

Nor was the Church spared Bernard's whip. Among other issues, Bernard was determined to carry forward the ecclesiastical reform movement begun in the eleventh century by Pope Gregory the Great. Convinced that Cistercian monasticism was superior to all other forms, Bernard never ceased to castigate others, especially the Cluniacs, who, he believed, had lost their religious zeal and become spiritually decadent. In 1137, he prevented a Cluniac from becoming Bishop of Langres, gaining the office for one of his own Cistercian monks. In such matters, Bernard was often intransigent and self-righteous, but he was also capable of great warmth. Although Bernard and Peter the Venerable, the Abbot of Cluny, had their differences, they became good friends.

Bernard was also concerned about those who had become enamored of the world and its pleasures. Suger, the Abbot of Saint-Denis and adviser to both Louis VI and Louis VII, was scolded for his great wealth and earthly concerns. Bernard found the secular clergy and even the peasantry guilty of similar offenses. Even the pope did not escape Bernard. In *De consideratione* (*Treatise on Consideration*, 1641), composed late in his life and addressed to

Eugenius III, a former disciple, Bernard reminded the pontiff of his Christian responsibilities and exhorted him to reform a corrupt Curia.

When he was not lecturing popes and kings, Bernard lashed out at those individuals and groups who threatened the orthodoxy and unity of the Church. One particularly difficult issue which occupied much of his time was the schism of 1130. In that year, on the death of Honorius II, two popes were elected by disputing factions within the College of Cardinals. Innocent II was eventually compelled to flee Italy when his adversary, Anacletus II, became violent. At the Council of Étampes, convened by Louis VII, Bernard threw his support to Innocent, who, he believed, had been properly elected and was the more worthy of the two. Over the next seven years, Bernard worked to win recognition of Innocent, traveling throughout Europe, crossing the Alps three times in one winter, meeting and corresponding with the most important political and ecclesiastical figures in Europe. With the death of Anacletus in 1137, Bernard's choice was finally enthroned, and the schism was ended.

Nevertheless, there was little rest for the weary monk. In 1139 Bernard's close friend, William of Saint-Thierry, informed him that Peter Abelard, one of the most brilliant intellectuals of the age, was teaching a dangerous theology which substituted reason for revelation. Abelard also espoused heretical ideas about the Trinity; among other things, he said that the Holy Spirit was not coequal with the Father and the Son. It was with great reluctance and possibly some trepidation that Bernard left Clairvaux to confront Abelard at the Council of Sens in 1140. Bernard refused to debate the issues, preferring instead a stratagem which condemned Abelard's entire approach. Humiliated, Abelard withdrew from the encounter, fell ill, and died several years later at Cluny. Bernard won, but he has been severely criticized through the ages for his narrow-minded approach to the debate.

Although Bernard successfully quashed Abelard's heresy, there was much work to be done. In 1145 Europe received the shocking news that Edessa had fallen to the Muslims. The event was of special interest to Bernard. In his youth, the First Crusade had captured Jerusalem. Later, in 1128, at the Council of Troyes, Bernard drew up a charter for the Knights Templars, a military-monastic group whose chief concern was the defense of Palestine. Thus Bernard emerged from the cloister to prepare for what would be his last major battle. In 1146 he preached the Second Crusade at Vézeley and then spent considerable time and energy promoting the venture in France and Germany. As a result, both Louis VII of France and Conrad III of the Holy Roman Empire took up the cross. The Crusade eventually failed, and Bernard's popularity suffered greatly. Nevertheless, in spite of failing health, Bernard remained very active in his last years, and he even dreamed of leading another expedition to liberate the Holy Land. He died at Clairvaux on August 20, 1153.

Summary

For more than thirty years, Bernard of Clairvaux was the spokesman for Western Christendom. Although his first love was the contemplative life of the monastery, he was frequently summoned by the outside world. He was a friend and adviser to kings, popes, bishops, and abbots. Nothing which might impact adversely on the Church escaped his notice. Many times he left his monastery to reprove those who threatened the Church—truculent feudal magnates, wealthy prelates, heretics, and the infidels who threatened Palestine.

His impact on the Cistercian Order, monasticism, the Church, indeed, Western Europe, is inestimable. When he and his monks settled at Clairvaux, there were only five Cistercian houses. By the time of his death in 1153, there were 343 abbeys, sixty-eight of which had been founded directly from Clairvaux. Without a doubt, Bernard's charismatic personality was the single most important factor in the rapid growth of the order. Moreover, his humility, ascetic life-style, and devotion to God earned for him the admiration of both ecclesiastics and laymen. He was, in many ways, a miracle worker, and in 1174, less than twenty-five years after his death, he was canonized.

Bibliography

Balzani, Count Ugo. "Italy, 1125-1152." In *The Cambridge Medieval History*, vol. 5. Cambridge: Cambridge University Press, 1948. In a chapter from one of the most comprehensive multivolume surveys of the Middle Ages, Balzani provides information on Bernard's role in the schism of 1130 and the Second Crusade. Designed for the knowledgeable reader.

Daniel-Rops, Henri. *Bernard of Clairvaux*. New York: Hawthorn Books, 1964. Approximately half the book is devoted to Bernard's life. The balance treats the history of the Cistercian Order from his death to the present. An excellent introductory work.

Evans, G. R. *The Mind of St. Bernard of Clairvaux*. Oxford: Clarendon Press, 1983. A more advanced study of Bernard's intellectual life. Focuses primarily on his education, preaching, sermons, and theology. The author provides a good chronology of Bernard's life.

Hoyt, Robert S., and Stanley Chodorow. *Europe in the Middle Ages*. New York: Harcourt Brace Jovanovich, 1957, 3d ed. 1976. A good general history of the Middle Ages. Included is a brief sketch of Bernard's life which considers his influence on literature, art, and thought.

Knowles, David. *Christian Monasticism*. New York: McGraw-Hill Book Co., 1969, reprint 1977. An excellent introduction to the subject of monasticism, ranging from the earliest Christian monks to the modern world. Bernard's impact on the Cistercian movement is discussed briefly in a chapter on monastic expansion.

Lawrence, C. H. *Medieval Monasticism: Forms of Religious Life in Western*

Europe in the Middle Ages. New York: Longman, 1984. A brief history of the monastic movement from the desert hermits to the friars. The author includes a valuable chapter on Bernard and the Cistercian Order.

Morison, James Cotter. *The Life and Times of Saint Bernard, Abbot of Clairvaux*. London: Macmillan and Co., 1868. An old work, but still useful. Provides a sympathetic view of the saint's life using material from primary sources and frequent, interesting digressions.

Painter, Sidney, and Brian Tierney. *Western Europe in the Middle Ages, 300-1475*. New York: Alfred A. Knopf, 1970, 4th ed. 1983. An excellent general history of Western Europe, with scattered references to Bernard. A brief overview of his career with reference to his impact on the Cistercian Order.

Strayer, Joseph R. *Western Europe in the Middle Ages*. Englewood Cliffs, N.J.: Prentice-Hall, 1955, 2d ed. 1974. A brief survey of medieval civilization with a number of references to Bernard, including a short biography. A good springboard to more advanced studies.

Thompson, Alexander Hamilton. "The Monastic Orders." In *The Cambridge Medieval History*, vol. 5. Cambridge: Cambridge University Press, 1948. A good discussion of the various monastic orders, beginning with the Benedictines. Included is valuable information on Bernard and the Cistercians.

Larry W. Usilton

AL-BIRUNI

Born: 973; Khiva, Khwarizm (modern Soviet Uzbekistan)
Died: c. 1050; probably Ghazna, Afghanistan
Areas of Achievement: Historiography and science
Contribution: One of the greatest scholars of medieval Islam, al-Biruni was both a singular compiler of the knowledge and scientific traditions of ancient cultures and a leading innovator in Islamic science.

Early Life

Abu al-Rayhan Muhammad ibn Ahmad al-Biruni was of Iranian descent and spent most of his childhood and young adult years in his homeland of Khwarizm, south of the Aral Sea. (His sobriquet derives from *birun*—"suburb"—in reference to his birth in an outlying neighborhood of Khiva.) Little is known of al-Biruni's childhood except for the important matter of his education, which was directed by the best local mathematicians and other scholars; his exceptional intellectual powers must have become apparent very early. Al-Biruni's religious background was Shi'ite, although in later years he professed agnostic leanings. A precocious youth, while still a student in Khwarizm al-Biruni entered into correspondence with Avicenna (Ibn Sina), one of the leading lights of Islamic medicine. Some of Avicenna's replies are preserved in the British Museum.

Although he published some material as a young student, the scope of al-Biruni's intellectual powers only became apparent when he left Khwarizm to travel and learn further. In al-Biruni's age, the key to scholarly success lay in attaching oneself to a powerful and influential court society and obtaining noble patronage. He found the first of many such benefactors in the Samanid sultan Mansur II, after whose demise he took up residence in the important intellectual center of Jurjan, southeast of the Caspian Sea. From here, al-Biruni was able to travel throughout northeastern Iran.

Life's Work

While at Jurjan, al-Biruni produced his first major work, *al-Athar al-baqiyah 'an al-qurun al-khaliyah* (*The Chronology of Ancient Nations*, 1879). This work is an imposing compilation of calendars and eras from many cultures; it also deals with numerous issues in mathematics, astronomy, geography, and meteorology. The work is in Arabic—the major scientific and cultural language of the time—as are nearly all al-Biruni's later writings, although he was a native speaker of an Iranian dialect. As would have been common among Muslim scholars of his time, al-Biruni also was fluent in Hebrew and Syriac, the major cultural and administrative languages in the Semitic world prior to the Arab conquest.

Around 1008, al-Biruni returned to his homeland of Khwarizm at the invitation of the local shah, who subsequently entrusted him with several important diplomatic missions. In 1017, however, his tranquil life as a scholar-diplomat took a rude turn. The shah lost his life in a military uprising, and shortly thereafter forces of the powerful Ghaznavid dynasty of neighboring Afghanistan invaded Khwarizm. Together with many other scholars—as part of the booty of war—al-Biruni found himself led away to Ghazna, which was to become his home base for the remainder of his life.

Ironically, this deportation afforded al-Biruni his greatest intellectual opportunity. The Ghaznavids appreciated scholarly talent, and the sultan, Mahmud, attached al-Biruni to his court as official astronomer/astrologer. Mahmud was in the process of expanding his frontiers in every direction. The most coveted lands were in India, and during the sultan's campaigns there al-Biruni was able to steep himself in the world of Hindu learning. In India, he taught eager scholars his store of Greek, Persian, and Islamic knowledge. In return, he acquired fluency in Sanskrit, the doorway to what was, for al-Biruni, essentially a whole new intellectual universe.

In 1030, al-Biruni completed his marvelous *Tar'ikh al-Hind* (translated by Edward Sachau as *Al-Beruni's India*, 1888). This masterpiece remains, in the eyes of many scholars, the most important treatise on Indian history and culture produced by anyone prior to the twentieth century. The degree of scholarly detachment and objectivity displayed in *Al-Beruni's India* is almost without parallel for the time, and the work consequently is still of enormous value to contemporary scholars.

Almost at the same time, al-Biruni produced another work dedicated to the sultan Mas'ud ibn Mahmud, heir to the Ghaznavid throne. *Kitab al-qanun al-Mas'udi fi 'l-hay'a wa 'l-nujum* (c. 1030; *Canon Masudicus*, 1954-1956) is the largest and most important of al-Biruni's mathematical and geographical studies.

During his long and productive life, al-Biruni authored many other treatises of varying length—he himself claimed to have produced more than one hundred—in addition to those mentioned above. They include essays on arithmetic, geometry, astronomy, and astrology, a pioneering effort in mineralogical classification, and, toward the end of his career, material on the medical sciences. His compendia of Indian and Chinese minerals, drugs, potions, and other concoctions, still not systematically studied, may be of immense value to pharmacology. Some of these works have been lost; they are known only through references by other scholars. Many survive but await translation into European languages.

Summary

In the golden age of medieval Islam, a small number of incredibly versatile and creative intellects stood at the interface of Semitic, Hellenistic, Persian, and Hindu culture and learning. Their syntheses and insights often brought about quantum leaps in scientific and historical thought in Islam—so vast, in fact, that in some cases their achievements were fully appreciated only by later ages better prepared to comprehend them. Al-Biruni was one of these intellects, to some historians the most important of all. *The Chronology of Ancient Nations*, for example, constitutes an unprecedented attempt to periodize the history of the known world by comparing and cross-referencing large numbers of chronologies and calendrical systems. His work provides a basis for chronological studies which has yet to be fully exploited.

Al-Biruni's immense store of astronomical and geographical knowledge led him to the verge of modern scientific ideas about the earth and the universe. He was familiar with the concept that Earth rotates on its axis to produce the apparent movement of celestial bodies, rather than those bodies revolving around Earth (although he did not necessarily endorse the idea). His insights with respect to geography were profound. On the basis of reports of various flotsam found in the seas, al-Biruni reasoned that the continent of Africa must be surrounded by water, thus taking exception with the Ptolemaic cosmography popular in Christendom, which held that Africa extended indefinitely to the south. Upon examining the Indus Valley in what is now Pakistan, al-Biruni correctly guessed that it had once been a shallow sea filled in through the centuries by alluvial deposits from the river. Al-Biruni also explained the operation of artesian springs and wells essentially in terms of modern hydrostatic principles. He devised a system of geographical coordinates which is still a marvel to cartographers.

In medieval Islam, the significance of scholarship may often be determined by how frequently a scholar's materials were copied by later generations of researchers (a practice for which modern scholars are grateful, since much otherwise would now be lost). The thirteenth century geographer Yaqut, for example, cited al-Biruni extensively in his own work. Yaqut's material on oceanography and general cosmography is drawn almost verbatim from his illustrious predecessor.

Like many scholars in Islam's golden age, al-Biruni was a polymath, a Renaissance man before there was a Renaissance. Some modern scholars have criticized him for writing extensively on astrology, usually at the behest of his noble patrons. Astrology, however, was in a certain sense a means of popularizing the science of the time, and al-Biruni most likely used it to reach a lay audience, just as contemporary popular science writers often simplify and make use of analogy. He seems to have regarded astrology as a gesture to simple people who wanted immediate, practical results from science.

Al-Biruni's astounding versatility has prompted some to place him in a league with Leonardo da Vinci as one of the greatest geniuses of all time. The most appropriate description, however, comes from his students, patrons, and other contemporaries. To them, al-Biruni was simply "The Master."

Bibliography

Al-Biruni Commemorative Volume. Calcutta: Iran Society, 1951. A collection of essays in observance of the millenary of al-Biruni's birth (according to the Islamic calendar). These essays cover every major aspect of al-Biruni's learning and thought, including, for example, his knowledge of Sanskrit literature, his contributions to comparative religion, his analysis of trigonometry, his views on alchemy and astrology, and his general philosophical system. Another commemorative volume, published for the Christian millenary (Karachi, 1979), contains a similar variety of studies.

Chelkowski, Peter J., ed. *The Scholar and the Saint: Studies in Commemoration of Abu'l-Rayhan al-Biruni and Jalal al-Din al-Rumi*. New York: New York University Press, 1975. These essays from a 1974 conference cover such topics as al-Biruni's concepts of India, his use of Hindu historical material, Sanskrit astronomical texts, Muslim times of prayer and their relation to seasonal changes in daylight, and other topics.

Davidian, M. L. "Al-Biruni on the Time of Day from Shadow Lengths." *Journal of the American Oriental Society* 80 (1960): 330-335. Davidian discusses al-Biruni's two methods of determining time from shadow, one using simple arithmetic and the other more precise trigonometric methods. His sources show heavy reliance on Persian and Hindu mathematics, thus offering an example of how al-Biruni's works reveal relationships among early astronomical traditions.

Kazmi, Hasan Askari. "Al-Biruni's Longitudes and Their Conversion into Modern Values." *Islamic Culture* 49 (1975): 165-176. Here is an attempt to convert al-Biruni's calculations to modern longitudinal values, as others have done for Ptolemy, and to judge the accuracy of al-Biruni's reckoning. Lists comparative values and shows that he was often accurate to within less than three degrees.

Kennedy, E. S., ed. and trans. *The Exhaustive Treatise on Shadows*. Vol. 2. Aleppo, Syria: Institute for the History of Arabic Science, University of Aleppo, 1976. This volume presents a commentary on al-Biruni's treatise on shadows; a consideration of his overall influence on the history of science is also included.

Memon, M. M. "Al-Beruni and His Contribution to Medieval Muslim Geography." *Islamic Culture* 13 (1939): 213-218. Useful in delineating al-Biruni's sources for Eastern Asia and the Indian Ocean and his notes on Siberian localities, this article presents translated quotes on the notion of a South Pole; dimensions and shape of the earth; physical forces such as water erosion, soil types, nature of the moon, and tides; and map projections.

Pines, S. "The Semantic Distinction Between the Terms 'Astronomy' and 'Astrology' According to al-Biruni." *Isis* 55 (1964): 343-349. Pines argues that al-Biruni, although a practicing astrologer, regarded it as a pseudoscience, a protective device to give the public practical results and allow astronomers to pursue serious interests unhindered by religious or political authorities.

Yasin, Mohammed. "Al-Biruni in India." *Islamic Culture* 49 (1975): 207-213. This summary of al-Biruni's views of India show him to have been basically detached and descriptive on matters such as manners, dress, and customs, even on religion, refusing to assist Muslim missionary efforts. Whenever he criticizes Indian ways, he always reminds readers of what life was like for the Arabs before Islam.

Ziauddin, Ahmad. "Al-Biruni." *Islamic Culture* 5/6 (1931/1932): 343-351, 363-369. Ziauddin reports on a 1928 interview with Edward Sachau, chief translator of the works, who called al-Biruni "the greatest intellect that ever lived on this earth." The discussion contains speculation on how much al-Biruni was influenced by the heterodox Shi'ite sect of Islam.

Ronald W. Davis

GIOVANNI BOCCACCIO

Born: June or July, 1313; Florence or Certaldo, Italy
Died: December 21, 1375; Certaldo, Italy
Areas of Achievement: Literature and scholarship
Contribution: Boccaccio was the father of Italian and European narrative.
He was also a pioneer of Latin and Greek scholarship in the late Middle
Ages and, along with Petrarch, a precursor to the Renaissance Humanists.

Early Life
Giovanni Boccaccio was the illegitimate son of a merchant of Certaldo,
identified as Boccaccio di Chellino, and was probably born in Florence in
June or July, 1313. Some scholars believe that Boccaccio was the product of a
relationship between his father and an unknown Parisienne. That, however,
is unlikely. Although his father did travel to Paris for extensive periods and
the identity of his mother is not known, Boccaccio was absolutely Tuscan in
blood and spirit. His father legitimized him about 1320 and gave him a
decent education, sending him to the school of a famous educator, Mazzuoli
da Strada, whose son, Zanobi, later to achieve some fame as a poet,
remained a lifelong friend and correspondent of Boccaccio.

In 1327, Boccaccio's father was sent to Naples to head the branch of the
Bardi banking company there. He took his son with him, having clearly
planned for him a life in commerce. The King of Naples, Robert of Anjou,
was eager to establish lines of credit with the major Florentine banking
houses. Under the Angevins, Naples was a commercial hub and, since King
Robert had a taste for culture, a major center of learning. Boccaccio's
formative years were spent in this vibrant southern capital. While in theory
he was learning the business of banking (for which had little inclination), his
attention was drawn to the dynamic life of the port and the tales of merchants who arrived from all corners of the Mediterranean. Through the royal
court and library, he came into contact with some of the most distinguished
intellectuals of his day. Among them was Cino da Pistoia, a contemporary of
Dante and surviving member of the *dolce stil nuovo* (sweet new style) school
of poets, who introduced Boccaccio to vernacular love poetry in the Tuscan
tradition. Paolo da Perugia, the royal librarian, probably inspired Boccaccio's
later, encyclopedic works, while the scholar Dionigi da Borgo san Sepolcro
introduced him to the genius of Petrarch and an encounter with Barlaam da
Calabria began Boccaccio's lifelong fascination with Greek.

Naples was also a city of beautiful women, who both stimulated the young
man's senses and inspired his first literary efforts: romances in prose and
verse which were close to the tradition of French love poetry (the height of
fashion in Angevin Naples). Like Dante's Beatrice and Petrarch's Laura,
Boccaccio's Fiammetta served as a Muse, inspiring the works of the first half

of his career. She has frequently been identified as Maria of Aquino, the illegitimate daughter of King Robert. Yet, like the notion of Boccaccio's Parisian mother, this idea must be dismissed as myth, in part encouraged by Boccaccio himself, who sought to romanticize his life into a story overshadowed by the cloud of illegitimacy.

An important friend of Boccaccio during this period was the Florentine Niccolò Acciaiuoli, who was to exercise considerable influence over the life of the writer. Acciaiuoli had embarked on a political career that was to make him a major figure in the history of the Angevin dynasty, both before and after the death of King Robert in 1343; yet he was also to prove an unreliable friend to the scholarly Boccaccio, who tended to be dazzled by his countryman's charisma.

Before leaving Naples, Boccaccio had composed *La Caccia di Diana* (c. 1334; Diana's hunt), a bucolic narrative in *terza rima* (a verse form first used by Dante), and the lengthy *Il filostrato* (c. 1335; *The Filostrato*, 1873), a version of the tale of Troilus and Cressida in octave form. He had completed the prose romance *Il filocolo* (c. 1336; *Labor of Love*, 1566) and had certainly begun the *Teseida* (1340-1341; *The Book of Theseus*, 1974), the story of Palamon and Arcite. *The Filostrato* and *The Book of Theseus* are of particular interest, since they are respectively the sources of Geoffrey Chaucer's *Troilus and Criseyde* (1382) and "The Knight's Tale" from *The Canterbury Tales* (1387-1400).

Life's Work

When Boccaccio returned to Florence at the end of 1340, he found a city in crisis. His father had preceded him in 1338, following the closing of the Bardi office in Naples. An upheaval in the banking world had brought many major Florentine companies close to bankruptcy, and the Black Death had devastated the city in early 1340. Boccaccio's father, having weathered severe financial setbacks, had been married again, to a woman for whom the son expressed little sympathy. Naples must have seemed far away, and Florence a dreary alternative.

During the next decade, however, Boccaccio established himself as the leading storyteller of his generation. *Il ninfale d'Ameto*, also known as *Commedia delle ninfe* (1341-1342; comedy of the nymphs), is modeled after Dante's *La vita nuova* (c. 1292; *Vita Nuova*, 1861; better known as *The New Life*, 1867). *L'amorosa visione* (1342-1343; English translation, 1986) is a lengthy disquisition on love in *terza rima* and is a direct predecessor of Petrarch's *Trionfi* (1470; *Tryumphs*, 1565; also known as *Triumphs*, 1962). The *Elegia di Madonna Fiammetta* (1343-1344; *Amorous Fiammetta*, 1587) is a psychological novel, entirely in prose, which tells of Fiammetta lamenting the departure from Naples of a young Florentine merchant. All the above works show Boccaccio closely bound to the medieval tradition of moral reflection on, and allegorization of, love. In particular, Boccaccio was faithful to the *dolce stil nuovo*, which derived from contemporaries of Dante who celebrated the themes of sacred and profane love.

While the Black Death of 1348 was profoundly disastrous, it actually furthered Boccaccio's career by providing the starting point for his masterpiece, *Decameron: O, Prencipe Galeotto* (1349-1351; *The Decameron*, 1620). This collection of one hundred stories, carefully grouped around three central themes (Fortune, Love, and Wit), established Boccaccio as one of the founders of European narrative and served as a sourcebook for future storytellers (including Chaucer and William Shakespeare). It is a wonderful literary synthesis, weaving the idealized loves of the medieval tradition into the lies of merchants and adventurers. Set against the backgrounds of cities such as Florence, Naples, and Milan, the stories emphasize intelligence and individual initiative. They move beyond the Middle Ages, pointing the way toward the Renaissance. The plague killed Boccaccio's father and stepmother, making him the head of the family and the arbiter of its affairs. The fact that the book grew out of this period of despair indicates the author's desire for the restoration of order out of chaos and his respect for human law in the midst of social dislocation.

Crucial to Boccaccio's spiritual and artistic development in these years was his friendship with Petrarch, whom he had admired from a distance but finally met in Florence in September, 1350. The devotee of Laura was en route to Rome when he was entertained at Boccaccio's house and introduced to a distinguished circle of admirers. In the spring of 1351, Boccaccio led a delegation to Padua, where Petrarch was residing, bringing with him the official restoration of citizenship to the poet (Petrarch's father having been exiled, along with Dante, in the political crisis of 1300). Boccaccio also offered Petrarch a professorship at the newly established University of Florence—which he declined. In a garden in the shadow of the city cathedral, these two masters of Italian letters spent weeks in intimate conversations (faithfully transcribed by Boccaccio, who always regarded himself as the "disciple") on questions of literature, such as the nobility of Latin authors, the strengths of the vernacular, and the moral function of poetry. They also discussed political matters, expressing their devotion to the ideals of freedom in the Florentine republic and the hatred of tyranny as embodied by the Visconti of Milan.

Two years later (July, 1353) Boccaccio was offended to learn that his noble friend had accepted a stipend from that same dynasty he had condemned in writing and conversation and had settled in the despised Milan. There was in Petrarch's character both a conservatism and a cultivation of self-interest that set him apart from his more consistent and idealistic admirer. Boccaccio—a true Florentine—could not contain himself and gave vent to his indignation in an angry epistle to which Petrarch did not reply. In time, however, the two friends were reconciled, and their correspondence on literary and moral matters continued unabated until Petrarch's death in 1374. There would be further encounters: one in the hated Milan (1359), a visit marked by the planting of an olive tree in Petrarch's garden, and another (March, 1363) in Venice, which afforded Boccaccio great consolation, since it followed a most dispiriting visit to Naples in search of preferment from his old acquaintance and nemesis, Acciaiuoli, who appears to have treated the author of *The Decameron* with cavalier indifference. Furthermore, when Boccaccio experienced a religious crisis in 1362, Petrarch persuaded his dear friend not to abandon the vocation of literature and not to burn (for whatever symbolic reasons) the manuscript of *The Decameron*.

In all these years Boccaccio was also at the service of the republic when required and actively engaged in diplomatic activities. He twice led delegations to the papal court in Avignon (in 1354 and 1365). The intention was to assure the Pope of Florence's devotion to the papacy, as well as to encourage Urban V to restore the pontificate to Rome. In spite of his age and growing corpulence, as well as the dangers from bandits, both journeys were diplomatically successful and rich in pleasant memory, including visits to Petrarch's old estate in idyllic Vaucluse.

By early 1361, Boccaccio had retired to Certaldo, following a reported conspiracy against the current Guelph faction then governing Florence in which several of the writer's most influential friends were said to be implicated. It seemed a politic moment to remove himself to the country. Certaldo thereafter remained his home and refuge. In this final chapter of his life, three themes persisted: fidelity to relatives and friends (notably Petrarch), prompt service to the republic, and tireless devotion to literature.

Summary

Clearly reflecting the influence of Petrarch, Giovanni Boccaccio's work reveals a man with scholastic and classical interests and a wish for partial withdrawal from the world. *De casibus virorum illustrium* dates from the period between 1355 and 1374 (translated as *The Fall of Princes*, 1431-1438), and *De mulieribus claris* (c. 1361-1375; *Concerning Famous Women*, 1943) was clearly written as its companion volume. The most ambitious of these scholarly works, the *Genealogia deorum gentilium* (genealogies of the Gentile gods), was written and revised during the last twenty years of his life, but a first draft was complete by about 1360. To these major compilations, one must add Boccaccio's devotion to Greek studies and his invitation to the great Greek scholar Leontius Pilatus to live with him in Florence in 1360. Boccaccio not only worked with Pilatus on a translation of Homer but also had him appointed professor of Greek at the university in Florence.

These Latin works emphasize his contribution to the burgeoning climate of Humanism (meaning, on one level, a devotion to classical learning), which was the central feature of intellectual life in the Renaissance. Boccaccio's works in Latin are quite different from those of Petrarch in that they are compendia and intended as reference works for future scholars. Largely forgotten by modern scholars, they earned for Boccaccio enduring fame throughout the Renaissance and into the nineteenth century. For later story-tellers, they offer a rich source of material for fiction and fable.

Boccaccio's religious crisis of 1362 helps to explain the strong thread of moral reflection on the vagaries of human fortune in these works, which all told illustrate a conscious redirection of energies toward religious contemplation. Connected with these themes are the fourteenth and fifteenth books of the *Genealogia deorum gentilium*, which amount to a defense of poetry as a force for moral improvement and religious regeneration. A similar impulse lies behind Boccaccio's *Trattatello in laude di Dante* (1351, 1360, 1373; *Life of Dante*, 1898) and the public lectures he gave on Dante (from to 1373-1374). *Life of Dante* was begun in the 1350's and continued to be revised into the last years of his life. It represents Boccaccio's modest devotion to the poet who, although ill-treated by his countrymen, was still upheld as one of the great glories of the republic. Those public lectures on Dante and the news of the death of Petrarch in July, 1374, link the three founders of Italian literature, who established the standards of achievement in the epic, the lyric poem, and the short story for succeeding generations.

Bibliography

Bergin, Thomas G. *Boccaccio*. New York: Viking Press, 1981. Essentially a study of the works. Includes useful, if prosaic, summaries of the later Latin writings. The longest chapter is that on *The Decameron*, and the most interesting chapters cover Boccaccio's life and depend largely on Branca's *Profilo biografico*.

Boccaccio, Giovanni. *The Decameron*. Translated by G. H. McWilliam. Harmondsworth, England: Penguin Books, 1972. The best modern English translation available of Boccaccio's masterpiece. Includes a lively introduction, along with some interesting observations on the history of the various English translations.

Branca, Vittore. *Boccaccio: The Man and His Works*. Translated by Richard Monges. New York: New York University Press, 1976. This work is the indispensable biography of Boccaccio, on which all students of the writer depend. It is a careful reconstruction of the major events in the life, with reference to the literary works, correspondence, and contemporary documents. A comprehensive portrait of the author emerges, while popular myths (too long in circulation) are demolished. Includes the English translation of *Profilo biografico*, a biography by Branca.

_____. *Boccaccio Medievale*. Florence, Italy: Sansoni, 1970. A polemical assessment of Boccaccio's work from the most authoritative commentator on this author. Focusing on *The Decameron*, this volume presents Boccaccio essentially as a product of medieval culture and is intended to counteract the prevailing view that the writer from Certaldo was essentially a Renaissance personality.

Chubb, Thomas Caldecot. *The Life of Giovanni Boccaccio*. London: Cassell, 1930. This old fashioned biography illustrates too vividly the vices of nineteenth century scholarship: the tendency to write Boccaccio's life as if it were a novella and to accept certain myths encouraged by Boccaccio himself.

Cottino-Jones, Marga. *Order from Chaos*. Lanham, Md.: University Press of America, 1982. An academic study of Boccaccio's attempt to reestablish order through art: the aesthetic reflection of the human attempt to re-create social harmony out of the dislocation of the plague. Not for first-time readers of Boccaccio.

MacManus, Francis. *Boccaccio*. London: Sheed and Ward, 1947. Written just after World War II, with the intention of restoring to Italy, by way of praise of one of her great writers, some of the dignity the country had lost during the years of Fascism. The style is lively, but the author spends too much time coloring his narrative and lends too much credence to some of Boccaccio's literary fancies.

Serafini-Sauli, Judith Powers. *Giovanni Boccaccio*. Boston: Twayne Publishers, 1982. A very useful introduction to Boccaccio's works. Introductory chapters deal with the writer's background and the early years in Naples. Each section is preceded by biographical information as a preface to the commentary. Contains a good bibliography, with details of the works in Italian, Latin, and English translations.

Harry Lawton

BOETHIUS

Born: c. 480; Rome, Italy
Died: 524; Pavia, Italy
Areas of Achievement: Philosophy, theology, and literature
Contribution: Adding knowledge of Greek thought to his Christian Roman
   background, Boethius became one of the most important mediators be-
   tween the ancient and medieval worlds.

Early Life

Anicius Manlius Severinus Boethius was born into the patrician Roman
family of the Anicii, whose members figure prominently in Roman history as
far back as the Third Macedonian War in the second century B.C. The
Manlius and Severinus families also could boast of eminent forebears. Boethius' own father held several important offices under Odovacar, the first
Germanic ruler of the Italian peninsula. In 480, the supposed year of Boethius' birth, the old Roman families were adjusting and contributing to the
reign of a "barbarian" king. When Boethius' father died, perhaps in the early
490's, another distinguished Roman, Quintus Aurelius Memmius Symmachus, became the boy's guardian.

An old tradition that Boethius was sent to Athens to study Greek has no
basis in fact; he might as well have been sent to Alexandria, which by the late
fifth century had replaced Athens as a center of Greek studies. Wherever he
studied, it is clear that Boethius mastered Greek at a time when it was
becoming a lost skill in Rome, and in the process he developed a strong
interest in the great Greek philosophers on whom Roman thinkers had
depended heavily for centuries. It is likely that Plato's *Republic* convinced
him of the advisability of philosophers entering public life, and he combined
an ambitious program of study and writing with public service. As a young
man, he married Rusticiana, his guardian's daughter, with whom he had two
sons. Boethius may have met the Ostrogothic king Theodoric, who had displaced Odovacar, in 500 when the ruler, who maintained his headquarters at
Ravenna, visited Rome. At any rate, many of the traditional Roman offices
persisted, and Boethius rose to the consulship in 510, when he was about
thirty.

Life's Work

Boethius' earlier writings cannot be dated with any confidence. Of his five
theological tractates, *De Trinitate* (*On the Trinity*), dedicated to his father-in-
law, Symmachus, shows his determination to use reason in support of a doctrine which he recognized as standing firmly on a foundation of Christian
faith. His interest in harmonizing revealed religion with the discoveries of
pre-Christian thinkers foreshadows the work of the medieval Scholastic

philosophers many centuries later. *On the Trinity* represents his attempt to reconcile for intellectual Christians the seemingly contradictory doctrines that God was one but consisted of three persons.

In addition to the tractates, Boethius wrote on all four subjects of the ancient quadrivium: arithmetic, music, geometry, and astronomy, although his works on the last two subjects have not survived. His most voluminous extant works, however, deal with one of the subjects of the trivium: logic. He translated treatises by Aristotle and Porphyry, wrote commentaries on these works as well as on Cicero's *Topica*, and produced original monographs on such subjects as categorical syllogisms and systems of logical classification. His overriding ambition, to harmonize the philosophies of Plato and Aristotle, probably bogged down amid the pressures of his public career.

After serving as consul, he became a Roman senator according to ancient tradition, and in 520 or 522 he obtained an important post with authority over most other government positions, the *magister officiorum*, or Master of Offices. This appointment would have involved moving to Theodoric's court at Ravenna and leaving behind the library at Rome that had sustained his scholarly endeavors. Also in 522, his sons were both appointed as consuls, although Boethius himself at this time could not have been much more than forty years of age.

With family prestige at this high point, Boethius was drawn into the struggle between Italy's Ostrogothic king and the Roman senate. Theodoric, who had been educated in Constantinople and who owed his kingship to the Eastern Roman emperor Zeno, brought with him a substantial retinue of his Germanic brethren, many of them subscribers to the Arian heresy, which held that Jesus was not coeternal with God the Father. Despite the potential for ethnic and religious conflict, Theodoric established a reputation for tolerance, impartiality, and devotion to the goals of peace and prosperity. Yet it was Theodoric who imprisoned, tortured, and eventually executed the renowned scholar and previously trusted official, Boethius.

Like philosophically minded civil servants before and after his time, Boethius found much to distress him in government, including rampant corruption. "Private pillage and public tributes," as he put it, depleted the treasury, and when he interceded to protect principled officials from the clutches of greedy courtiers, he made influential enemies. His troubles mounted when he rose to the defense of a fellow ex-consul and senator named Albinus, who was suspected of treason. It appears that Boethius was motivated primarily by a desire to defend the reputation of the senate as a whole from suspicions of complicity in the alleged treachery. Boethius apparently admitted to the suppression of evidence which he considered damaging to the integrity of the senate, a course of action inevitably leading to charges against him. Accused of plotting against Theodoric in favor of Justin I, the reigning Eastern emperor, Boethius was conveyed to Pavia in 522 and imprisoned there. Under the strain of a conviction he considered entirely unjustified, he produced his masterpiece, *De consolatione philosophiae* (*The Consolation of Philosophy*). If his previous writings and his government service had made him a notable man, this work commanded the attention of the West for more than a thousand years thereafter.

Although conceived as a tribute to philosophy and exhibiting features of his plan to synthesize the best in Greek philosophy, *The Consolation of Philosophy* endures as a human record of doubt, discouragement, and suffering transformed by a rethinking of basic philosophical tenets into a triumph of the spirit. Even more than his Christian faith, philosophy sustained Boethius in his two years of confinement. This work consists of five main divisions or "books," each formed of alternating verse and prose sections. The prose parts develop the situation and introduce the thoughts which it generates; the verses concentrate lyric bursts of emotion and meditations on his plight.

To dramatize the conflicts within him, Boethius resolves his mental and emotional state into two components represented by the discouraged prisoner and an awesome visitor to his cell, Lady Philosophy. She listens to his complaints and gradually brings him around to the reaffirmation and fuller understanding of conviction which his ordeal has undermined. In some poems is heard the prisoner's voice, in some the sage counselor's. In this way, Boethius externalizes and gives artistic shape to the inner dialogue which he must have conducted in his cell to forestall despair. First, Philosophy must convince him that Fortune, while not a source of happiness, is not truly the prisoner's enemy either. Her presumed benefits—worldly prosperity, honors, and other pleasures which the historical Boethius had enjoyed—have no intrinsic value. The source of all goodness is God, who permits evil and an apparently random distribution of adversity and prosperity. Boethius' questions lead Philosophy to the relationships of fate, chance, God's omniscience, Providence, and free will. With the prisoner now able to view the mind as free to surmount all human confinement, book 5 plumbs the deeper problem of human freedom in general. Philosophy upholds the paradoxical freedom of the will in the sight of an omniscient and providential God. At length she convinces Boethius that no human or divine necessity stands in the way of the most valid exercise of the will: the pursuit of virtue.

Though presumably reconciled to his unjust sentence, Boethius reached no reconciliation with his accusers, and he died in prison in 524, either from the effects of torture or by explicit order. Almost immediately his friends and admirers began to regard him as a martyr for his faith; his local followers in Pavia acclaimed him as a saint. The existing evidence suggests that he suffered and died not for specifically religious convictions but for moral and political ones. Even after his other works ceased to be generally read, *The Consolation of Philosophy* continued to attract readers and translators. He would have been pleased to know that two of England's greatest monarchs, Alfred the Great in the ninth century and Queen Elizabeth I seven centuries later, became philosopher-kings enough to make their own translations. Like his beloved Plato, Boethius had found a form for his philosophy that earned for it the status of a literary classic.

Summary

Although Boethius possessed both literary ability and the discipline of a professional writer, it took imprisonment to make him a philosophical poet. His earliest admirers valued not only his thought but also the integrity and courage that shine through both metrical and prose sections of *The Consolation of Philosophy*. These readers, members of an increasingly Latinate culture, could hardly have appreciated fully his efforts to keep the West in touch with Greek antiquity. At the same time, the rise of vernacular tongues and the Church's adaptation of Latin to its own purposes meant that the classical Latin verse forms which Boethius could still practice proficiently became a lost art. In this sense, he can be considered the last of the classical Latin poets as well as one of the last representatives of Greco-Roman culture generally.

Boethius also became that quintessentially medieval scholar, the Catholic theologian, and although little of the theologian shows through in his last work, there is not the slightest reason to believe that he ever abjured Christianity. On the contrary, he was believed to have been put to death for trying to protect the Church from persecution by heretics. None of his medieval enthusiasts saw anything remarkable in his exclusion of specifically Christian doctrine from *The Consolation of Philosophy*. He was simply operating as a philosopher and thus keeping theology and philosophy distinct.

In time, Boethius' versatility was bound to recommend him to scholars, among them the recoverers of the Greek heritage that had slipped almost completely from sight in the centuries between the breakup of the Roman Empire and its comeback through Arabic sources beginning in the eleventh century. Successive waves of intellectuals, from the Scholastics of the twelfth and thirteenth centuries to the scientists of the sixteenth and seventeenth centuries, were in a better position than were early medieval people to understand the import of Boethius' pursuit of Greek learning. By modern times, Boethius could be seen as a pivot between the ancient and medieval worlds generally, between classical and Christian Latinity, and between pre-Christian Hellenism and Renaissance Humanism.

Had he lived longer and found more extensive opportunities to translate Greek texts and synthesize Greek thought, Boethius might well have forestalled the loss of the Greek intellectual heritage, but his work was sufficient to demonstrate that "pagan" philosophy could animate the life of a practicing Christian and even provide spiritual sustenance in adversity. It is hardly surprising, then, that *The Consolation of Philosophy* held its grip on posterity for so long. Revered by the two greatest Catholic medieval poets—Dante and Geoffrey Chaucer—translated by Renaissance Protestants such as Queen Elizabeth I and Henry Vaughan, and admired by later skeptical historians such as Edward Gibbon and Arnold Toynbee, Boethius achieved a universal appeal. Because there are greater and more representative philosophers, theologians, and poets in his tradition, Boethius is far less generally known than Plato or Saint Thomas Aquinas or Dante, but it is difficult to think of another figure of Western civilization who combined so competently all of these activities. This competence is particularly astonishing given the nature of the early sixth century, the beginning of the period long designated the "Dark Ages."

Bibliography
Bark, William. "Theodoric vs. Boethius: Vindication and Apology." *American Historical Review* 49 (1944): 410-426. In this and other articles, Bark examines with a critical eye the legends that have encrusted Boethius' life over the centuries. He focuses on the political events and theological controversies against which the relationship between the Ostrogothic king and his Roman subordinate must be read.
Barrett, Helen M. *Boethius: Some Aspects of His Times and Work*. Cambridge: Cambridge University Press, 1940. Reprint. New York: Russell and Russell, 1965. One of the older books on Boethius, Barrett's remains a good introduction. It provides an introductory historical survey, sets Boethius firmly in this context, and interprets the scanty details of his life in a balanced and sensible way. Subsequent scholarship has supplemented but rarely contradicted the picture of Boethius given here.
Boethius. *The Consolation of Philosophy and the Theological Tractates*. Translated by H. F. Stewart and E. K. Rand. Cambridge, Mass.: Harvard University Press, 1953. The question of the value of Boethius' own account of his ordeal is controversial. Although a work of fiction, *The Consolation of Philosophy* uses its fictional elements primarily to dramatize the conflicts within a popular and successful man whose career has ended in rejection and imprisonment. No reader is likely to confuse the imaginative and factual portions of his story.
Chadwick, Henry. *Boethius: The Consolations of Music, Logic, Theology, and Philosophy*. Oxford: Clarendon Press, 1981. Unlike other writers, who have tended to concentrate on the Christian, the poet, the philosopher, or the educational theorist, Chadwick aims to show Boethius' career as a unified whole. He has succeeded in writing the most comprehensive book about his life and work.
Coster, C. H. "Procopius and Boethius." *Speculum* 23 (1948): 284-287. While not trying to revive Boethius' long-standing reputation as a Christian mar-

tyr, Coster argues that he was so understood for centuries and that protection of the Church against heresy may have been among his motives in opposing Theodoric.

Gibson, Margaret, ed. *Boethius: His Life, Thought, and Influence*. Oxford: Basil Blackwell, 1981. This book contains a variety of Boethian material, including two valuable biographical essays. John Matthews studies Boethius as a thoroughgoing Roman affirming ancient traditions and offices against the Ostrogothic king. Helen Kirkby stresses Boethius' determination to continue the Roman habit of enriching Latin culture with Greek philosophical and educational thought.

Procopius. *Procopius, with an English Translation by H. B. Dewing*. London: W. Heinemann, 1914-1940. Volumes 3 and 4 of this set include Procopius' *The Gothic War* and incorporate for the first time details of Boethius' life in the record of political struggle in the Italian peninsula. Procopius was a Byzantine historian whose life overlapped that of Boethius.

Reiss, Edmund. *Boethius*. Boston: Twayne Publishers, 1982. Reiss argues the case against accepting too literally the autobiographical details in what he regards as a highly polished work of fictional art. He tends to reject the assumption that the quotations and other specific knowledge demonstrated in *The Consolation of Philosophy* constitute a feat of memory by a prisoner without access to a library.

Robert P. Ellis

BOHEMOND I

Born: c. 1052; southern Italy
Died: March 7, 1111; Apulia, southern Italy
Area of Achievement: Warfare
Contribution: Bohemond was one of the leaders of Europe's most successful
  Crusade to the Holy Land and the founder and first prince of Antioch.

Early Life

Bohemond I was the firstborn son of Robert Guiscard, the most successful of that small band of eleventh century Norman adventurers who reclaimed southern Italy and Sicily from Byzantine, Italian, and Muslim forces. By the time of his death in 1085, Guiscard had become Duke of Apulia and Calabria, overlord of Sicily (then being subdued by his younger brother Roger), and vassal, ally, and protector of the Pope.

Guiscard's first wife, a Norman woman named Alberada, gave birth to their son Bohemond in the early 1050's, perhaps 1052. While Bohemond was still a small boy, Guiscard had his marriage to Alberada annulled so that he could make a more advantageous union with Sigelgaita, sister of the Prince of Salerno. Little else is known about Bohemond's early years, except that he probably learned to read and write Latin and that he certainly learned the art of war as his father's apprentice. Bohemond grew to be a very tall, broad-shouldered, muscular man with a slightly stooped carriage. He had fair skin, yellow hair, and blue-gray eyes.

In 1081, Guiscard and Bohemond attempted the conquest of the Byzantine Empire, which then dominated the southern Balkans and Greece. On the eve of the invasion, Bohemond's stepmother deprived him of his inheritance as firstborn by persuading Guiscard to name the eldest of their three sons, Bohemond's half brother Roger, heir to the duchy. Had the conquest of the Byzantine Empire succeeded, Bohemond's inheritance probably would have come out of the spoils.

The invasion began well. Bohemond, who was then about twenty and already skilled enough to be second-in-command, secured a beachhead by conquering Avlona, participated in the successful sieges of Corfu and Durazzo, and defeated Byzantine armies in the field. The Byzantine emperor, Alexius I, meanwhile, encouraged his German allies to invade Italy and Guiscard's ever-restive barons in southern Italy to rebel. Because the Normans had insufficient monies and troops to handle all the conflicts simultaneously, they withdrew to Italy in late 1083.

In October, 1084, the Normans invaded again. Their initial successes were followed by an outbreak of disease in their camp. Bohemond became ill and returned to Italy to recuperate. Before he could return to the war in the summer of 1085, his father died, and his half brother Roger, the new duke, called off the invasion and brought the troops home.

Bohemond declared war on Duke Roger in order to win from him a share of the patrimony from which he had been excluded. By 1090, Bohemond had seized most of Apulia (the heel of Italy), including important towns such as Taranto and Bari. What chiefly prevented him from conquering more was intervention by his uncle, Count Roger of Sicily, whose own advantage lay in keeping southern Italy divided between his nephews.

Thwarted by his uncle and half brother, Bohemond found an outlet for his acquisitiveness and bellicose energy when Pope Urban II preached the Crusade in 1095. Then vast new opportunities opened for him.

Life's Work

With protestations of goodwill toward his former enemy Alexius, Bohemond led a large contingent of Norman warriors and kinsmen to Constantinople late in 1096 in order to take part in the Crusade to liberate the Holy Land from Turkish Muslims. By the following spring, a number of small armies led by other European warlords had also arrived at Constantinople. Those forces constituted the First Crusade.

The Crusaders were united in their overall objective but in little else. The greed, pride, and jealousy of their leaders resulted in a lack of unified command and in dangerous rivalries among them, especially between Bohemond and Count Raymond IV of Toulouse. The Crusaders also disagreed about the extent of obligation and alliance to their host, Alexius. Bohemond became his vassal, a status which later caused trouble, as it gave Alexius a claim to what Bohemond acquired.

A joint Crusader-Byzantine army invaded Asia Minor in the spring of 1097 but cooperated only long enough to besiege and liberate the city of Nicaea. Thereafter, while Alexius stayed behind to secure western Asia Minor, the Crusaders struck out toward the Holy Land. Near Dorylaeum on July 1, Turkish cavalry attacked. In the battle which ensued, Bohemond commanded one of the Crusader contingents. The Turks were defeated so decisively that the Crusade could pass through the remainder of Asia Minor without incident.

The Crusade emerged onto the plains of northern Syria in the autumn of 1097 and there began what proved the most difficult, and for Bohemond the most important, operation of the campaign—the siege of ancient, rich, and well-fortified Antioch. Bohemond and Raymond both coveted the city as spoil. For Bohemond, the challenge was to work with Raymond to capture Antioch at the same time he worked against him to secure it as his own.

The siege of Antioch took eight months (from October, 1097, to June, 1098). Famine, disease, desertions, and occasional attacks by Turkish relief columns slowed progress. A breakthrough finally came when a disgruntled defender of one of Antioch's towers offered secretly to betray the city to

Bohemond. Bohemond negotiated the price of this treachery and then approached his fellow captains with the proposal that whoever first breached the defenses would be named governor. Raymond would not agree, but once the other captains did, Bohemond led his troops to the tower commanded by the traitor and began the predictably successful final assault. Antioch fell on June 3. Raymond's forces seized the Bridge Gate Tower and the former governor's palace to prevent Bohemond's control of the city, but before Bohemond could combat them, a greater threat appeared outside the walls.

A Turkish army under Kerboga of Mosul appeared at Antioch a few days after the Crusaders captured the city and began a siege. The Crusaders then had to defend the city, which was low on provisions as a result of their own recent siege. The miraculous discovery of what was alleged to be the Holy Lance which pierced the side of Jesus boosted the morale of the Crusaders, but it was Bohemond who finally saved them. He persuaded them that the best defense was to attack, and then, on June 28, 1098, he led the attack which defeated and drove off Kerboga's army. Antioch was secure, yet its ownership was not determined until the following spring, when, in the absence of his colleagues who had gone to liberate Jerusalem, Bohemond forcefully ejected Raymond's garrisons from their positions in the city.

Bohemond's tenure as Prince of Antioch lasted five years (from 1099 to 1104). Most of that time he spent at war or in prison. He fought to defend his principality from Alexius, who demanded that Antioch be surrendered to him; he fought to defend it from Raymond, who still wanted it; and he fought to enlarge it at the expense of his Muslim neighbors. While fighting Muslims in the summer of 1100, Bohemond was captured. He spent the following three years in a Turkish prison, until ransomed for 100,000 gold pieces. Meanwhile, his nephew Tancred had served as regent in Antioch. Bohemond resumed control of the principality briefly upon his release in 1103. The following year, however, he reinstalled Tancred as regent so that he could return to Europe, ostensibly to raise money for the debts incurred by his wars and his ransom but actually to raise an army with which to relieve pressure on Antioch by attacking Alexius' empire from the west.

Bohemond's reputation as a great warrior guaranteed for him a favorable reception by the Pope and the great men of Italy and France, whom he visited during the years from 1105 to 1107. He regaled his hosts with tales of the Crusade and of Byzantine treachery and extorted from them financial and military backing for a crusade against Alexius. Philip of France also gave him the hand in marriage of his daughter Constance.

In October, 1107, approximately thirty-four thousand Italian and French Crusaders under Bohemond invaded the Byzantine Empire, using the same strategy that Bohemond and Guiscard had used in the 1080's. They took Avlona but were resisted while besieging Durazzo. The defenders thwarted all of their efforts to breach, to mine, and to surmount Durazzo's walls, while

Alexius' land and naval forces denied them access to the interior and easy communications with Italy. Those obstacles, plus disease, hunger, and desertion, sapped the strength of the invaders and forced Bohemond to negotiate withdrawal to Italy. By September, 1108, the Crusade was over. Bohemond returned to Apulia in disgrace.

The humiliation of the failed Crusade wore off in time. By the spring of 1111, Bohemond was again collecting an army, probably to take to Antioch. Before completing his preparations, he became ill and died. He was then approximately fifty-nine years of age.

Bohemond and Constance had had two sons during their five-year marriage; the first died in infancy, and the second, named Bohemond, succeeded his father in Apulia and eventually also in Antioch.

Summary

Bohemond I was a conspicuously successful example of the bellicose, acquisitive warlord of medieval Europe. From landless warrior in 1085, he rose to become, by 1106, the leader of Apulia and Antioch and the son-in-law of the King of France. Self-interest seems to have motivated him more than high principle; he participated in the Crusade for what he might win more than for the pious intent of the enterprise. Indeed, he only visited Jerusalem once, briefly, after it had been liberated.

What was his goal? Were his accomplishments part of a larger unrealized plan? Here scholars are left to speculate, for Bohemond kept his own counsel. It could be that his acquisition of Antioch was simply successful opportunism. It could also be that taking Antioch was part of a larger plan to link in profitable commerce the ports of Apulia with a major Levantine trading center. More ambitious still, it could be that Antioch was part of a plan to conquer the Byzantine Empire—his father's unrequited ambition. There was contemporary precedent for such grandiose schemes in William, Duke of Normandy's conquest of England. If Bohemond made such plans, it was lack of resources more than lack of skill which prevented their realization.

Indeed, in military skills, Bohemond was among the most adept of that age, the failed Crusade of 1107 notwithstanding. At Dorylaeum and at Antioch he displayed his competence in the major facets of contemporary war: pitched battle and siege craft. Had it not been for his skills, the First Crusade might have failed at Antioch, and the two hundred years of crusades which helped broaden European horizons during the Middle Ages might not have followed.

Bohemond's administrative skills might also have been considerable. Antioch proved to be one of the most durable of the Crusader states, but how much of Antioch's government was designed by Bohemond during his brief tenure as its prince remains uncertain. Contemporary accounts by both his friends and enemies concentrate mostly on his career as a warrior.

Bibliography

Comnena, Anna. *The Alexiad*. Translated by E. R. A. Sewter. New York: Penguin Books, 1969. Anna was the daughter of Bohemond's nemesis, the Byzantine emperor Alexius. This history of her father's reign has problems of bias and of imprecise chronology and geography but is nevertheless and eyewitness account by one who saw and described Bohemond.

Hill, John H., and Laurita L. Hill. *Raymond IV, Count of Toulouse*. Syracuse, N.Y.: Syracuse University Press, 1962. This biography concentrates on Raymond as a crusader and relies on the history of the Crusade by Raymond's admiring chaplain, Raymond of Aguilers. The account is predictably critical of Bohemond.

Hill, Rosalind, ed. *The Deeds of the Franks and the Other Pilgrims to Jerusalem*. New York: T. Nelson and Sons, 1962. The anonymous author of this work was one of Bohemond's vassals. His account covers the Crusade to 1099 and was published almost immediately thereafter. Bohemond took this work with him to Europe in 1005 and disseminated it. Virtually every other twelfth century account of the First Crusade was borrowed from this one.

Krey, August C. *The First Crusade*. Princeton, N.J.: Princeton University Press, 1958. Excerpts from all the major chronicles, including those cited elsewhere in this bibliography, and from some letters are here combined to describe the Crusade with a vividness only participants could provide.

Nicholson, Robert L. *Tancred: A Study of His Career and Work in Their Relation to the First Crusade and the Establishment of the Latin States in Syria and Palestine*. Chicago: University of Chicago Press, 1940. This published doctoral dissertation illuminates not only the military exploits of Tancred but also his complex and largely cooperative relationship with Bohemond.

Runciman, Steven. *A History of the Crusades*. Vol. 1, *The First Crusade and the Foundation of the Kingdom of Jerusalem*. Cambridge: Cambridge University Press, 1951. The first volume of this multivolume work provides a detailed history of the First Crusade through Christmas, 1100. There is a discussion of primary sources in an appendix and a more up-to-date bibliography than that in the source by Ralph B. Yewdale listed below. A highly regarded work.

Yewdale, Ralph B. *Bohemond I, Prince of Antioch*. Princeton, N.J.: Princeton University Press, 1924. An uncompleted Princeton dissertation published after Yewdale's death by a teacher who thought it a significant contribution to the field. Yewdale is sympathetic to Bohemond but not uncritical. Excellent bibliography of primary sources and lengthy, if now dated, list of secondary sources.

Kenneth E. Cutler

SAINT BONAVENTURE
Giovanni di Fidanza

Born: 1217 or 1221; Bagnoregio, Italy
Died: July 15, 1274; Lyons
Area of Achievement: Religion
Contribution: Bonaventure combined an early commitment to the ideals of Saint Francis of Assisi with great preaching and teaching abilities; he wrote several works on spiritual life and recodified the constitution of the Franciscans. Noted for his ability to reconcile differing groups and individuals, Bonaventure proved himself a defender of both human and divine truth and an outstanding witness for mystic and Christian wisdom.

Early Life

Bonaventure was born either in 1217 or 1221 in Bagnoregio—in the Viterbo Province, Papal States. Not much is known of his family. His father was a medical doctor, Giovanni di Fidanza. (Fidanza was not a family name, but the name of a grandfather.) His mother was called Maria di Ritello, or simply Ritella. He was very ill as a boy and was said to have been saved from death by the intercession of Saint Francis of Assisi. Bonaventure recorded his cure in his life of Saint Francis. It is recorded that the young Bonaventure received his early schooling at the Franciscan friary in Bagnoregio. He showed scholastic ability and was sent to be a student at the University of Paris in 1235 or 1236.

It was in Paris that Bonaventure met many of the Franciscan friars and entered the Franciscan Order (in either 1238 or 1243). Called Giovanni since birth, he received the name Bonaventure soon after entering the order. In accordance with the Franciscan regulations of the time, he was considered a member of the Roman province of his birth. After receiving a master of arts degree from the University of Paris in 1243, he studied theology at the Franciscan school in Paris for the next five years, under Alexander of Hales and John of La Rochelle until their deaths in 1245. He probably continued with the masters Eudes Rigauld and William of Meliton; later, he was influenced by the Dominican Guerric of Saint-Quentin and the secular master Guiard of León.

During these years Bonaventure began teaching the brothers in the local Franciscan friary. In 1248, he became a teacher of Scripture, lecturing on the Gospel of Luke and other portions of the Bible. From 1250/1251 to 1253, he lectured on the *Sententiarum libri IV* (1148-1151; *Sentences*) at the University of Paris. This work was a medieval theology textbook written by Peter Lombard, a twelfth century Italian theologian. Bonaventure's commentaries on Scripture and the *Sentences* enabled him to receive the licentiate and doctorate from the chancellor of the University of Paris. The chancellor acted in the name of the Church; therefore, this licentiate allowed Bonaventure to teach anywhere in the Christian world at the end of the 1252/1253 academic year. He was placed in charge of the Franciscan school in Paris, where he taught until 1257.

Paris at that time was a hotbed for theological study. Thomas Aquinas had arrived to study in 1252; he and Bonaventure became good friends. Yet the secular masters opposed the Mendicants, and although Bonaventure presented at least three series of disputed questions in Paris between 1253 and 1257, some authors claim that he was not accepted into the guild, or corporation, of the masters of the university until October 23, 1257.

Life's Work

The years between 1248 and 1257 proved to be a productive time for Bonaventure. He produced many works: not only commentaries on the Bible (not all of which have survived) and the *Sentences* but also the *Breviloquium*, which provided a summary of his theology, showing his deep understanding of Scripture, early church fathers (especially Saint Augustine), and philosophers (particularly Aristotle). He adapted the older Scholastic traditions, perfecting and organizing a fresh synthesis. Bonaventure urged that the theologian be allowed to draw on logic and all the profane sciences. He thought of truth as the way to the love of God. In 1256, he and the Dominican Thomas Aquinas defended the Mendicants (Franciscans and Dominicans) from an attack by William of Saint-Amour, a university teacher who accused the Mendicants of defaming the Gospel by their practice of poverty and wished to prevent them from attaining any teaching position.

The Franciscan Order itself was experiencing an internal struggle, between those who wanted a more rigorous poverty and those who wanted to relax the strict views of poverty established by Saint Francis. Pope Alexander IV commanded the minister general of the Franciscans, John of Parma, to resign his office. A chapter gathering was called at Rome late in January, 1257. Because of his defense of the Franciscans and the fact that he was an exemplary person patterning himself after Saint Francis, Bonaventure was elected minister general on February 2, 1257. He was to hold that post for seventeen years.

By placating the Spirituals (who opted for a more rigorous poverty) and reproving the Relaxati, Bonaventure reformed the order in the spirit of Saint Francis. The restoration of peace and reconciliation of opponents, a special talent of Bonaventure, was accomplished through extensive visits to all the provinces of the order and through his own practice of the Franciscan way of life. It was during these travels, despite health problems, that his reputation as a preacher was earned. His election to office had ended his teaching career, but it created preaching opportunities. Throughout Europe, his eloquence, knowledge, and simplicity caught the attention of high dignitaries and the laity. He also administered the order, presiding over the general chapters and guiding the continued growth of the Franciscans.

Bonaventure's new tasks did not prevent him from continuing his writing. In his visits to the provinces in October, 1259, he stopped at La Verna. There he wrote *Itinerarium mentis in Deum* (*The Journey of the Mind to God*, or, as George Boas translated it, *The Mind's Road to God*). At this time, without ceasing to be a Scholastic, Bonaventure became a mystic, aligning himself more clearly with the inner life of Saint Francis. He merged Augustine's intellectual contemplation of truth with the Dionysian notion of truth as the ecstatic knowledge of God. He used as his model Saint Francis, whose vision of the seraphim at La Verna had shown how the heights of contemplation could be reached. Bonaventure also had the example of Brother Giles of Assisi, although to a lesser degree than Saint Francis. He wrote other works in this period, including *De triplici via* (English translation retains the original title) and *De perfectione vitae ad sorores* (*Holiness of Life*).

In 1260, Bonaventure was in France preparing for the Pentecost Chapter at Narbonne, which was to codify the Franciscan ordinances into a new set of constitutions. It was this chapter which charged him with writing a new biography of Saint Francis. To gather material, Bonaventure visited all the places that had been significant to Francis and interviewed those of the early friars who were still alive. While working on this project, he presented himself to the new pope, Urban IV, elected in August, 1261. Late in that year or in the following year, Bonaventure was forced to submit the previous minister general, John of Parma, to a trial because of John's continued adherence to Joachism. On April 8, 1263, Bonaventure was in Padua for the transferral of the relics of Saint Anthony, and on May 20 he was in Pisa for a general chapter where some forty liturgical statutes and rubrics were introduced, ending about fifty years of work in the Franciscan Order. Bonaventure gave each of the thirty-four provincials present a copy of his new *Legenda major et legenda minor* (*The Life of Saint Francis of Assisi*). That year he also wrote *De sex alis seraphim* (*The Virtues of a Religious Superior*).

In 1264, he spent some time at the papal court, and in the spring he gave a sermon on the Body of Christ at a consistory of Urban IV. In March, 1265, he was at Perugia to present himself to the new pope, Clement IV. In November the new pope nominated Bonaventure to be Archbishop of York, but he refused the post. At the general chapter at Paris, May 16, 1266, Bonaventure continued to correct abuses in the order, especially those regarding matters of poverty. The chapter also ordered that all other biographies of Francis be destroyed, since Bonaventure had provided a new one.

Until as late as mid-1268, Bonaventure lived at a small friary in Mantessur-Seine, France, where he continued his ascetical writings and preached at the university. His Lenten conferences of 1267 (on the Ten Commandments) and 1268 (on the gifts of the Holy Spirit) attacked current trends. On July 8,

1268, he was in Rome receiving the Archconfraternity of the Gonfalonieri into spiritual communion with the Franciscans, staying in Italy through the chapter of Assisi in May. When he returned to Paris, he found that Gerard of Abbeville, a teacher of theology, had renewed the charge of William of Saint-Amour against the Mendicants. Bonaventure responded by upholding the Christian faith while denouncing unorthodox views in a work that was not only a refutation of heretical opinions but also the presentation of a positive theology of religious life in imitation of Christ. It showed that Bonaventure was less interested in external regulations than building up an inner spirit of prayer and devotion and creating right attitudes using the examples of Christ and Francis. Here one can see Bonaventure's doctrine of illumination, discussed in *The Journey of the Mind to God*, in operation: the cooperation given the soul when it acts as the image of God.

In June, 1272, Bonaventure was in Lyons for the Pentecostal General Chapter. The following spring, 1273, he was in Paris for the last time; there, he began work on *Hexaëmeron* (*Collations on the Six Days*), his theological testament to refute those who exaggerated the rationalism of Aristotle in opposition to the inspiration of the Scriptures. In this same year, Pope Gregory X named him the Cardinal Bishop of Albano, Italy. He proceeded with the pope to Lyons for the Second Council of Lyons and was consecrated as bishop November 11 or 12, 1273. In the capacity of legate, Bonaventure helped the pope prepare for the Council of Lyons, which opened on May 7, 1274. To continue his work at the council, he resigned as minister general of the Franciscans. Bonaventure continued to lead in the reform of the church, reconciling the secular (parish) clergy with the Mendicants. He preached at least twice at the council and effected a brief reunion of the Greek church with Rome.

Bonaventure died unexpectedly on the night of July 14/15, 1274, leaving his last work unfinished. He was buried on July 15 in the Franciscan church in Lyons, with the pope attending. At the fifth session of the council, July 16, all priests of the world were ordered to celebrate a mass for his soul.

The impression Bonaventure made on contemporaries is summarized in the notes of the Council of Lyons, which indicate sorrow at his death. He was canonized on April 14, 1482, by Pope Sixtus IV, who also enrolled him with the mass and office of a confessor bishop. On March 14, 1588, another Franciscan pope, Sixtus V, gave Bonaventure the designation Doctor of the Church. In 1434, his body was transferred to the church dedicated to Saint Francis in Lyons, with an arm taken to his native Bagnoregio. During the Huguenot uprising in France, his body, except the head, was destroyed by fire. His head was destroyed by fire during the French Revolution.

Summary
Saint Bonaventure is properly considered the second father of the Francis-

cans and a prince of mystics. He personified the ideals of Saint Francis of Assisi in teaching, in preaching, in writing, and in living his life. He had an immediate and a lasting influence on the Scholastics of the thirteenth century. He was an influential guide and teacher of spiritual life, particularly in Germany and the Netherlands. His influence has been maintained through the Roman College of St. Bonaventure, founded by Pope Sixtus V in 1587. He was depicted in medieval art, and modern scholars consider him one of the foremost men of his age, a true contemporary of Saint Thomas Aquinas.

Bibliography

Analecta Franciscans, sive chronica aliaque varia documents ad historium fratrum minorum spectantia. 10 vols. Florence: Quaracchi, 1885-1941. An excellent source for original documents on the Franciscans. For Bonaventure, see especially volume 3, pages 323-355, which contain a review of his early life and more details on the years 1257 to 1274. A knowledge of Latin is necessary, particularly where there are corrections of some errors in Luke Wadding's scholarship.

Bonaventure, Saint. *A Franciscan View of the Spiritual and Religious Life, Being Three Treatises from the Writings of Saint Bonaventure Done in English by Dominic Devas.* London: T. Baker, 1922. Contains biographical notes. One of the works translated is *De sex alis seraphim.*

_____ . *The Life of Saint Francis.* Translated by E. Gurney Salter. London: J. M. Dent and Co., 1904. There are other translations of this work in numerous languages. It was this work which became the official biography in 1266. Not only does this work aid in an understanding of Francis, but it also contributes to a deeper understanding of Bonaventure.

_____ . *The Mind's Road to God.* Translated by George Boas. New York: Liberal Arts Press, 1953. An English translation of what is considered one of the masterpieces of medieval philosophy. This volume is addressed to undergraduate students of the history of philosophy.

_____ . *The Works of Bonaventure: Cardinal, Seraphic Doctor, and Saint.* Translated by José de Vinck. 5 vols. Paterson, N.J.: St. Anthony Guild Press, 1960-1970. Includes the *Breviloquium* and *Collations on the Six Days.*

Bougerol, J. Guy. *Introduction to the Works of Saint Bonaventure.* Paterson, N.J.: St. Anthony Guild Press, 1964. This is a study of Bonaventure's doctrine and life. The year 1217 is used as the birth date in the chronology of his life. There is also a useful bibliography. As the title suggests, this volume is an introduction. It is hoped that the reader will go on to original Bonaventure writings.

Wadding, Luke, ed. *Annales Minorum seu Trium Ordinum.* 25 vols. Rome: St. Francisco Institutorum, 1731-1886. An indispensable reference for the history of the Franciscans, though later scholarship has pointed to some errors in Wadding, mostly concerning dates. A knowledge of Latin is necessary for an understanding of the annotations and general comments.

Mary-Emily Miller

SAINT BONIFACE
Wynfrith

Born: c. 675; Crediton, Devonshire, England
Died: June 5, 754; Dokkum, the Netherlands
Areas of Achievement: Religion and church government
Contribution: Boniface left England to assist in the conversion of pagan Germany. He brought Christianity to many areas and in others set the Church on a new and sounder basis, earning the title "the Apostle of Germany."

Early Life

The original name of Saint Boniface was Wynfrith or Wynfrid. He was born around 675 and was sent to the monastery at Exeter to be reared as a monk. In later years, he would claim to be of humble birth, but it seems likely that this claim was only a conventional profession of humility. Several of his relatives appear to have had noble rank. There is a tradition that he was born at Crediton, and though it cannot be traced further back than the fourteenth century, Crediton is near enough to Exeter for the story to be plausible.

Exeter does not seem to have satisfied Wynfrith, and perhaps in the 690's he transferred to the monastery at Nursling, near Southampton, also a Benedictine house and also in the kingdom of Wessex, but possibly with better scholarly endowments. Wynfrith gained a reputation for his learning and piety (though in the unchristianized England of that time there may have been few competitors). He compiled England's first Latin grammar; it is interesting to note, though, that according to *The Life of Saint Boniface*, written by the priest Willibald, when Wynfrith was first introduced to Pope Gregory II in 719, he begged to make his profession of faith in writing, as his spoken Latin did not meet Vatican standards.

Wynfrith's English colleagues thought well of him. In 712, a synod of Wessex priests and bishops chose him as their emissary to the Archbishop of Canterbury. After he had made a first, brief visit to the Christian mission in Frisia in 716, the monastery of Nursling tried to hold this valuable man by making him abbot. They were, however, too late. Wynfrith had decided to leave England and work with the already established Christian missions in Germany. In 718, he left England, never to return.

Life's Work

The problems facing Wynfrith were complex. From the time of their own conversion, the Anglo-Saxons had felt a strong urge, even a responsibility, to spread the Gospel to their Germanic cousins who had remained on the Continent. The kinship, it seems, was recognized on both sides. Later, in a letter of 738 asking for the prayers of the English, Boniface (as he would come to be known) says that even the pagans declare, "We are of one and the same blood and bone." Yet, however welcome a friendly mission from the Anglo-Saxons might be, the next neighbor of many of the Germanic tribes, especially of the Saxons and the Frisians, was the aggressive Christian kingdom— later Empire—of the Franks. The pagans, as a result, were very likely to see behind the missionary the Frankish imperialist, and to react in very hostile fashion. In addition, relations between the English missionaries and the Frankish church were rarely good. The former thought the latter corrupt, immoral, and self-interested; the latter thought the former were moving in on their territory.

Wynfrith, accordingly, did not plunge straight into missionary work, but went to Rome. In 719, he introduced himself to Pope Gregory II, and on May 15, he received a mandate from him, letters of support and introduction, and, in recognition of his new status, the new name of Bonifatius, or Boniface. Boniface in this way received protection from Frankish interference. Gregory and his successors, in turn, would have new provinces added to the Church, whose example in the end affected even the disorganized and unreliable Franks.

Boniface returned to the mission in Frisia established by his famous countryman Saint Willibrord (658-739) and worked there for three years. Like the monks of Nursling, Willibrord tried to retain him by offering him a bishopric, but Boniface refused. It was not that there was no work to do, for the Frisians (though situated handily close to England on the North Sea coast running up from the Netherlands through Germany to Denmark) remained among the most obdurate pagans of all. Boniface may have believed that there were less stubborn souls to win elsewhere, or he may have preferred independence. In any event, he returned to Rome, was consecrated a bishop there on November 30, 722, gave a personal oath of loyalty to the Pope, and returned not to Frisia but to central Germany. He took with him a letter of recommendation from the Pope to Charles Martel, the powerful ruler of the Franks. Boniface's success would depend in no small part on this combination of papal support and government protection.

Boniface worked in Germany for some sixteen years, mostly in the provinces of Hesse and Thuringia. The most famous story about him comes from Willibald's account, written by an otherwise unknown English monk not long after Boniface's death, though it seems that Willibald had not known Boniface personally. He relates that Boniface had decided to challenge the pagans by felling the sacred oak at Geismar in Hesse, which was dedicated to Donar, the god of thunder (the German equivalent of the Norse god Thor). In the presence of many angry pagans, Boniface lifted his ax to it. At the first strike, the oak fell into four parts, as if blown down from Heaven. If the story has any truth, it may show that Boniface believed in a policy of confrontation—which was, in the end, to cause his death.

Assisted by many Anglo-Saxon volunteers, Boniface established churches and monasteries, converting and baptizing large numbers. He was made an archbishop in 732 by Pope Gregory II, but had no bishops under him for several years. Possibly as a result of this odd status, Boniface made a third trip to Rome in 738 to confer with the Pope, and then turned to a new phase of large-scale organization.

Moving to the relatively Christianized south of Germany, he set up a new Bavarian "province" of the Church, with four bishoprics in it. He also established bishoprics in Hesse, Thuringia, and Franconia, ending with eight bishops subordinate to him. This looks rather like an exercise in "empire-building," but Boniface seems to have succeeded in it, first because the new bishops were often Boniface's Anglo-Saxon assistants, who had no doubt volunteered to join him because of his own personal prestige, and second because he was careful always to clear himself with successive popes. The exercise was in any case necessary and had many good effects. With eight bishops, and the support of Carloman I and Pepin III, the heirs of Charles Martel, Boniface was able to call a series of synods between 740 and 747 to reform the Frankish church. The Frankish church was shamed into reluctant imitation and cooperation. One final problem was solved when Boniface—until then an archbishop without a seat—was given Cologne for his base. His base was later changed to Mainz, as a result of Frankish objections.

With these successes behind him, Boniface, by this time in his late seventies, decided to return to the scene of his first mission in Frisia, in 753. There, however, resistance to the Franks and the Christians was still strong, exacerbated by decades of war. When Boniface tried to hold a mass baptism on June 5, 754, near the town of Dokkum, armed pagans attacked him. Boniface forbade resistance and was killed, by tradition holding up a Gospel book. Many of his followers were killed with him. Willibald's *The Life of Saint Boniface* rather gloatingly reports that the Christian Frisians, unencumbered by Boniface's scruples about nonviolence, armed themselves and successfully counterattacked the pagans. Even if this story is true, it made no difference to the overall situation in Frisia. Boniface's body was recovered and taken for burial to the abbey at Fulda in Hesse, which he had founded.

Summary

A considerable part of Saint Boniface's correspondence has survived. It makes, for the most part, rather uninspiring reading. With the exception of the general "Letter to the English" of 738, which makes a straightforward appeal to love and piety, Boniface's letters are those of a busy administrator. He worries about recurring problems, often related to being short of assistants: What is he to do about priests unworthy of their cloth? Can he still use them, or must they be discarded? Is the Pope supporting him, or are people going behind his back to reverse his decisions? More technical queries include the degrees of kinship prohibiting marriage; pagan and Christian definitions of incest often differed. Can food offered to idols be used after it has been blessed in Christian fashion? What are the rules about re-baptism? Often, it would appear to a modern reader, Boniface fusses needlessly over details—for example, ordering re-baptism in cases where a priest, through ignorance, has made a mistake in his Latin. The deed and intent were not enough for him; the words had to be right, too.

On the other side, those writing to Boniface must often (one senses) have driven him close to despair. The Bishop of Winchester, who had probably never met a hostile pagan, sent Boniface advice on how to convert people. One of the several popes Boniface served so loyally asked him to be sure that bishops' sees were established in proper cities, not mere townships. Where Boniface was to find these cities, in the forests of central Germany, the Pope did not say. Meanwhile, though the King of Mercia appears not to have replied to the strong letter of reproof that Boniface sent to him in 746/747 regarding his sins, the King of Kent did write in the most cheerful fashion, in or near 750, saying how delighted he was that Boniface was praying for him, and could Boniface send him a pair of good German falcons, preferably big enough to attack crows? Letters such as these both attest Boniface's international prestige and offer insight into the unexpectedly mundane problems of missionary life.

Boniface's main achievement, perhaps, was to live so long and remain so undiscouraged. Sparks of Christianity often fell on the pagan North. Usually they were snuffed out after a few years. Boniface was one of the few who survived hostility from the pagans, jealousy or indifference from the Christians, and the discouragement and death of his supporters. He built missionary fervor into a structure which, perhaps most important, would no longer need fervor to sustain it. When he died, the Church in Germany was too strongly rooted to need great individuals for survival. Boniface made scattered missions into an organized Church, and, by his example to the Franks, brought the whole of northwest Europe into a better relationship with Rome. Later kings, popes, and emperors were to build on this stable foundation.

Bibliography

Albertson, Clinton, ed. and trans. *Anglo-Saxon Saints and Heroes*. Bronx, N.Y.: Fordham University Press, 1967. Contains seven lives of Anglo-Saxon saints, the last being Willibald's *The Life of Saint Boniface*. The annotation given is fuller than in Talbot, and there may be interest also in comparing the early account of Boniface with similar accounts of his predecessors.

Duckett, Eleanor S. *Anglo-Saxon Saints and Scholars*. New York: Macmillan, 1947. Includes a major chapter on the life of Boniface. While written in a subjective and novelistic style, it is backed by solid research. Includes anecdotes about the period which are sometimes revealing.

Emerton, Ephraim, ed. and trans. *The Letters of Saint Boniface*. New York: Columbia University Press, 1940. The best complete English version of the more than one hundred letters. While they are sometimes frustratingly bureaucratic, they offer a picture of an eighth century personality almost unrivaled in detail.

Levison, Wilhelm. *England and the Continent in the Eighth Century*. Oxford: Clarendon Press, 1946. The fourth chapter is devoted to Boniface. The work is especially valuable in setting him in the context of earlier missions and of general European politics. An appendix gives a full account of the manuscripts of the letters.

Stenton, Frank M. *Anglo-Saxon England*. 3d ed. Oxford: Clarendon Press, 1971. Though Boniface cannot be treated extensively in this general history, Stenton's account includes a useful map and has valuable observations on the letters, on political realism, and on events after Boniface's death.

Talbot, C. H., ed. and trans. *The Anglo-Saxon Missionaries in Germany*. New York: Sheed and Ward, 1956. Gives a well-chosen selection from Boniface's correspondence, together with a translation of Willibald's biography and lives of four other early missionaries. Includes a short introduction and a good bibliography (largely of foreign-language material).

Whitelock, Dorothy, ed. and trans. *English Historical Documents: Volume 1, c. 500-1042*. London: Eyre and Spottiswoode, 1955. In addition to some fourteen letters to, from, or about Boniface and two extracts from Willibald, this volume contains large selections of similar letters and lives, as well as of chronicles and narrative sources, which help to put Boniface in the context of his times.

T. A. Shippey

BONIFACE VIII
Benedict Caetani

Born: c. 1235; probably Anagni, Italy
Died: October 12, 1303; Rome, Italy
Areas of Achievement: Religion and government
Contribution: Though pope for only nine years, Boniface represents both the
zenith and nadir of papal power and papal monarchy. In his clash with the
secular rulers of Western Europe, Boniface insisted upon the ultimate
earthly authority of the Papacy.

Early Life

Boniface VIII, probably born in Anagni in 1235 and christened Benedict
Caetani, was one of the younger sons of Roffred Caetani and his wife,
Emilia, the niece of Pope Alexander IV. His family seems to have been moderately wealthy, owning some land, and well-connected to the Church. Very
little is known of Benedict's life before 1275. In the 1250's and 1260's, however, he apparently joined his uncle Peter, who had been made Bishop of
Todi in 1252, and studied civil law there with Master Bartolus, traveling on
occasion to Spoleto to study with other masters. In 1263 or 1264, he probably
studied law for a short time at the great law school in Bologna. At about the
same time, Benedict embarked on his career in the Church, first working as
a secretary of Cardinal Simon of Brie and, from 1265 to 1268, accompanying Cardinal Ottoboni Fieschi on a diplomatic mission to England. When
Ottoboni became Pope Adrian V in 1276, Benedict was appointed to supervise the collection of certain papal taxes in France. Achieving this post marks
the beginning of Benedict's rapid ascent through the ranks of the growing papal bureaucracy. From tax supervisor to papal notary to inquisitor's assistant,
Benedict learned not only the complex workings of the Church's government,
but also the intricacies of canon law. When his old master Simon of Brie
became Pope Martin IV in 1281, the new pope rewarded his former secretary
by making him a cardinal—the cardinal-deacon of St. Nicholas in Carcere
Tulliano.

A cardinal in the late thirteenth century could wield much power within
the Church's bureaucracy, especially by managing the incomes of numerous
benefices and overseeing delicate diplomatic negotiations. Medieval popes
perceived themselves to be the peacemakers of Christendom, individuals
who could nurture truces or settle disputes between warring secular powers
or churchmen. They relied upon their industrious cardinals or legates to aid
in the maintenance of peace. To support the great business of the cardinals,
the pope granted numerous benefices—churches, canonries, and deaconries,
each producing an annual income—to his trusted officers. In addition, cardinals, such as Benedict, often received gifts and gold from kings, princes,

bishops, and noblemen who sought the cardinals' favors or political support. Throughout the 1280's and the early 1290's, Cardinal Benedict served as a legate for Popes Martin IV, Honorius IV, and Nicholas IV, traveling to France and throughout Italy to aid in keeping the peace between often quarrelsome monarchs. Having gained much experience in the service of the Papacy, Benedict achieved even greater prominence in 1285 when Honorius IV appointed him chief examiner of bishops, an office which offered much prestige and permitted Benedict to establish political liaisons with many of the bishops appointed to dioceses across Europe.

Life's Work

When Pope Nicholas IV died in 1292, political rivalries between two great Italian families kept the papal election process from a speedy conclusion. After wrangling for twenty-seven months, the cardinals, including Cardinal Benedict Caetani, selected a hermit, Peter of Morrone, to be the new Pope Celestine V. The politically convenient solution of choosing a nonentity to be pope proved disastrous. Although the cardinals who had supported the rival factions in the College thought that a hermit pope would permit them to continue to jockey for power, Celestine turned out to be semi-literate, untrained in religious and doctrinal matters, and partial to rustic rather than courtly life. During the nearly four months that Celestine ruled, it became painfully obvious that he did not wish to be pope and that his performance of papal duties was unsatisfactory and irregular. On December 13, 1294, Celestine took the unprecedented step of announcing his abdication. Ten days later, the College of Cardinals reassembled to choose a successor and, on Christmas Eve, 1294, Benedict Caetani was elected pope, adopting the name Boniface VIII. In later years, suspicion was cast upon this election because Cardinal Benedict had been one of the legal experts who provided advice on Celestine's resignation. Some were to argue that this advice had been self-serving.

Boniface's nine-year reign was one of the most controversial pontificates of the Middle Ages. As pope, he not only directly confronted the royal power of the English and French monarchs but also raised questions about his own faith (he believed in the power of amulets and magic) and the propriety of his defense of the Church.

Boniface's relationship with the secular monarchs of Europe focused on the question of precisely what powers a monarch could exercise over clergymen who lived within his or her kingdom. In the final years of the thirteenth century, the kingdoms of England and France once again found themselves engaged in conflict, and the monarchs of both kingdoms desperately needed funds to support their costly war efforts. The monarchs claimed the power to collect taxes not only from their lay subjects but also from their clerical ones, since all subjects, regardless of their status, received the benefits of royal protection within the kingdom. Boniface opposed the clerical payment of royal taxes, primarily because he himself desired to collect taxes from clergymen in order to finance his own struggles against the Colonna family in Italy and the Ghibellines, who advocated a strong, antipapal, imperial presence in papally dominated Italy. Furthermore, Boniface felt that by allowing monarchs to tax clergymen, the Church would be compromising its hard-won supremacy, fought for and defended for two centuries. In response to the taxation measures of Edward I of England and Philip IV of France, Boniface issued the bull *Clericis laicos* in 1296, in which he declared that, according to canon law, the clergy was composed of individuals who had special personal and property privileges not accorded to others. Because of this special quality, clergymen could only be taxed after the pope had given his authorization. Failure to obtain this authorization could result in the excommunication of anyone who collected tax revenues from the clergy.

Neither Philip nor Edward was intimidated by Boniface's declaration. Philip ordered an end to the export of money from France—effectively ending the collection of taxes by the papacy in France—and Edward declared all clergymen who refused to pay taxes to be outlaws, thereby removing them from royal protection and subjecting them to banditry. In the face of this opposition, Boniface backed down in 1297, saying that in times of emergencies—determined by the secular rulers—clergymen could make voluntary "gifts" to monarchs, in lieu of tax payments. The pope's retreat, however, was not to last long.

Four years later, Philip arrested and tried Bernard Saisset, Bishop of Pamiers, for crimes of treason, heresy, simony, and the uttering of offensive statements. Saisset was found guilty and imprisoned by his archbishop. The royal court asked Boniface to remove Saisset from his bishopric. Boniface refused the royal request, despite the facts of the case against Saisset, and demanded that the king have Saisset immediately released. More drastically, Boniface revoked all the privileges previously granted to the king for limited influence in church affairs. Boniface acted from his firm belief that the Church and the Papacy must be completely independent of secular control or interference. This uncompromising position was, perhaps, bolstered by the fact that as an Italian, deeply involved in interclan rivalries within Italy, Boniface seems to have harbored an anti-French bias.

Philip's response to Boniface's demand and revocation of privileges was powerful and unwavering. Beginning in 1302, his administration flooded France with antipapal propaganda, and royal officers drew up a list of twenty-nine accusations against the pope, charging him with blasphemy, simony, heresy, fornication, and the murder of the recently deceased Celestine V, whom Boniface allegedly had to kill in order to prevent Celestine from testifying to the French charge that Boniface had induced him to abdicate in 1294. Philip's government insisted that a council of cardinals, archbishops, and bishops from across Europe be held to determine the propriety of Boniface's actions and his suitability for the papal throne.

Boniface convoked a council in November of 1302 and the outnumbered French clergymen who attended were unable to prevent the council from approving of Boniface's actions. At the end of the meetings, Boniface issued a papal decree—the boldest and most confident statement ever made in the history of the Church about the powers of the pope. The decree, *Unam Sanctam*, contains a series of legal arguments dredged up from the archives of the Church and the writings of several twelfth century canon lawyers. Basically, the document describes Boniface's perception of Christian society: Christendom was a society in which there were two "swords," the sword of secular monarchs and the sword of the pope. The secular monarchs used their swords to protect the Church physically, while the pope used his for spiritual defense. Boniface also argued that "every human creature must be subject to the Roman pontiff" if she or he wished to gain salvation. In the pope's mind, every human committed sins and the Church, which the pope controlled, was the institution to which humans were required to turn to seek forgiveness of their sins. Thus, *Unam Sanctam* declared that the pope was the single most powerful ruler of Christian society because he controlled all human ability to gain salvation.

King Philip fired the last shot in this ongoing conflict between the pope and a secular monarch. In June, 1303, the king assembled representatives of the clergy, nobility, and towns of France and, after much careful staging and intimidation, convinced them to pass a resolution demanding that Boniface VIII be tried by a church council on the twenty-nine accusations the French had made against him. With the delicately orchestrated show of popular resentment against Boniface, the French king felt obliged to respond to his people's demand. When Philip learned that Boniface intended to have him excommunicated, Philip sent a small band of French soldiers to the papal palace at Anagni, where Boniface VIII was captured on the night of September 7. Though the inhabitants of Anagni won the release of the pope two days later, Philip's message was clear: The pope could produce legal arguments which described and defended his supreme position in Christian Europe, but forceful military action ultimately determined who held real power in Christendom. Five weeks later, on October 12, Boniface VIII died at the palace in Rome, a broken man and a conquered pope.

Summary

Boniface VIII's pontificate marked the end of a 225-year phase of papal history, a period characterized by the Papacy's struggle to maintain itself as the premier political force in Christendom on the basis of complex legal and doctrinal arguments. Boniface, having received legal training and having worked his way through the ranks of the Church's bureaucracy, understood not only the functions and intricacies of the Church as an institution but also appreciated the political value of the claim to papal supremacy. His stubborn insistence on the complete independence of the Church from secular interference reveals his devotion to an old tradition within the Church, as well as a certain unawareness of the changing realities of early fourteenth century politics. While Europeans still piously believed in the importance of the Church in the gaining of salvation, their political support and devotion were gradually being courted and won by national monarchs who had their own ideas about power and the needs of Christian society.

Bibliography

Barraclough, Geoffrey. *The Medieval Papacy*. New York: Harcourt, Brace and World, 1968. A handsomely illustrated, readable history of the papacy as an evolving institution in Europe.

Boase, T. S. R. *Boniface VIII*. London: Constable and Co., 1933. Though somewhat dated, this is still the most useful English-language biography of Boniface VIII. Boase traces Boniface's life throughout his career, focusing especially on the factional problems of the papacy and the various clashes with Philip IV.

Tierney, Brian. *The Crisis of Church and State, 1050-1300*. Englewood Cliffs, N.J.: Prentice-Hall, 1964. A collection of primary documents in translation with introductory commentary. The book contains translations of the important papal bulls of Boniface VIII, *Clericis laicos* and *Unam Sanctam*.

Ullmann, Walter. *The Growth of Papal Government in the Middle Ages*. 3d ed. London: Methuen and Co., 1970. A book for the advanced student, which traces the development of the papacy's political concerns and arguments for papal supremacy over Christian monarchs.

_____. *A Short History of the Papacy in the Middle Ages*. London: Methuen and Co., 1972. A careful survey of papal history from its development in the late Roman imperial period to the Protestant Reformation.

Wood, Charles T., ed. *Philip the Fair and Boniface VIII: State vs. Papacy*. New York: Holt, Rinehart and Winston, 1967. Wood has collected several primary documents and historical interpretations of the struggle between Boniface and Philip, providing the reader with an overview of the papal and French perspectives of the crucial events of Boniface's pontificate.

David M. Bessen

BORIS I OF BULGARIA

Born: 830; probably Pliska, Bulgaria
Died: May 15, 907; Preslav, Bulgaria
Areas of Achievement: Government and religion
Contribution: Under Boris' rule, Bulgaria was brought into the framework of Christian Europe while preserving its political independence and cultural identity. His efforts established Bulgaria as a center of Slavonic Christian culture and laid the foundation for the first Bulgarian Empire.

Early Life

Boris' father was Svinitse, the second of three sons of Khan Omortag, who ruled between 814 and 831. The pagan Bulgars were polygamous, and the identity of his mother is unknown. She was probably the daughter of a prominent noble, or boyar, family. Few reliable reports about the details of Boris' physical appearance are available. In numerous frescoes and mosaics, almost all of them posthumous, he is portrayed as a bearded, dark-haired warrior-saint dressed in Byzantine-style robes.

The pre-Christian Bulgarian society which Boris came to rule was a rather complex affair, and understanding something of its nature is essential to appreciating Boris' subsequent policies. The original Bulgars were an Asiatic, nomadic people closely related to the Huns. In 679, a large body of them crossed the Danube River and established themselves in what is now northern Bulgaria. This region was already inhabited by numerous Slavic tribes, whom the Bulgars proceeded to subjugate. The Slavs subsequently provided most of the manpower of the Bulgarian state, while the Asiatic Bulgars constituted the military aristocracy—a relationship somewhat similar to the one later established between Normans and Saxons in England. By Boris' day, there had already been considerable blending of the two groups, but the Asiatic element was still distinct and dominant. One of Boris' major accomplishments was to promote the general Slavicization of his realm's language and culture.

Boris followed his uncle Malamir to the throne in 852. Malamir had apparently been a weak ruler, and his reign remains as a hazy episode in Bulgarian history. His wars with the Byzantines and Serbs were largely unsuccessful, and he left no son to succeed him. Young Boris was initially determined to reestablish his nation's military prestige and expand the conquests of his forebears. The campaign which he proceeded to launch against the Byzantine Empire, however, achieved little, and he was diplomatically outmaneuvered by the Empress-Regent Irene. In 853, he invaded the Carolingian part of Croatia, again without notable success; in 860, he initiated an effort to conquer the Serbs on his northwestern frontier, but this campaign ended in disastrous defeat. Boris did, however, consolidate Bulgarian control over most of Macedonia, a region that would later become the cultural watershed of the Bulgarian Empire.

Life's Work

His lack of success as a conqueror soured Boris on military adventures and influenced him to take a closer look at the internal and diplomatic state of his realm. In both areas, the matter of religion was a paramount cause for concern. Boris turned his attention to this issue and there achieved his most important and lasting impact.

The traditional faith of the Bulgars was a brand of shamanism, revolving around the worship of the sun and the moon. Animal and human sacrifice was widely practiced. The Slavs also had numerous pagan cults, the most important of which was that of the god Perun. The shamans and priests of these cults were closely linked to the boyar nobles, who provided the state with most of its military leaders and administrators. Like their counterparts in Western Europe, the boyars were generally opposed to expansion or consolidation of the monarch's power.

Christianity had already made inroads into Bulgar society. Its most active agents were the Byzantines, who exported their faith as a kind of diplomatic weapon. The Byzantine, or Orthodox, church adhered to the doctrine of caesaropapism, under which their emperor served as head of both state and church. Thus, a Bulgar who accepted the Orthodox faith was technically obligated to accept the Byzantine ruler as his rightful sovereign, a position which made his conversion tantamount to treason. As a result, the Bulgar khans had generally opposed the spread of Christianity among their subjects.

The alternative to the Orthodox church was the Roman church, headed by the Pope. Although the final split between the Eastern and Western churches was still some two centuries away (1054), these two branches of Christianity were already locked in a bitter struggle for dominance, a conflict which Boris exploited to his advantage.

Boris accepted the Orthodox faith in 865. His conversion has been variously attributed to his contemplation of a vivid painting of the Last Judgment, the influence of a Greek Christian slave, and a threat of invasion from Byzantine Emperor Michael III. The first version is almost certainly fanciful, but both of the others probably contain some core of truth. Still, his conversion was undoubtedly a deliberate and practical decision. Boris had tolerated numerous Christians, including his sister, in his court. He could also see that the pagan cults had lost their spiritual vitality as well as the allegiance of much of the population. Furthermore, by breaking the power of the cults, he could reduce the influence of the boyars. Finally, he recognized that as long as Bulgaria remained pagan it would never be accepted by the Christian powers as a legitimate state; thus, it would remain isolated from the material and cultural benefits of Christian civilization.

Boris' challenge was to bring his country into the Christian fold without surrendering its independence to either the emperor or the Pope. At his baptism in September, 865, Boris accepted Michael III as his godfather and even adopted Michael as his Christian name. Boris proceeded to demand that all of his subjects follow his example, and where there was resistance he was not adverse to using force. In 866, die-hard pagans, led by dissident boyars, rebelled, but they were quickly and ruthlessly crushed. Fifty-two leading boyars were slaughtered along with their entire families; the noble opposition was thus left without leadership.

Boris hoped that the Byzantines would accept an autonomous archbishop at the head of the Bulgarian church, thus guaranteeing it some measure of independence from imperial control. Instead, the country was flooded with Greek priests who regarded Bulgaria as a Byzantine province.

In retaliation, Boris turned to Rome, and in 866, he recognized the supremacy of the Pope. The opportunity to establish his authority directly on the Byzantines' doorstep was tempting to Pope Nicholas I. He offered Boris guidance in both religious and governmental policies and sent a mission from Rome to take over the stewardship of the Bulgarian church. The Greek priests were replaced by Latin-speaking clerics whose language and manners were completely alien to the Bulgars. Moreover, the Pope refused to grant any measure of autonomy to the Bulgarian Christians.

As a result, Boris initiated a rapprochement with the Byzantines, a move abetted by the coincidental deaths of Pope Nicholas and Emperor Michael in late 867. Two years later, the Orthodox patriarch Ignatius consecrated an autonomous archbishop for Bulgaria, the candidate hand-picked by Boris.

Bulgaria's adoption of the Orthodox rite, if not a foregone conclusion, was always the most likely outcome. Physical proximity alone assured the Byzantines a predominant influence. Boris was also attracted to the caesaro-papist doctrine of state over church, whereas Rome insisted on submission to the Pope in all affairs.

Boris, however, had no intention of turning his domain into a cultural satellite of Byzantium. In 881, he briefly played host to Methodius, one of the original Orthodox apostles to the Slavs. Four years later, Boris gave permanent refuge to Methodius' followers, who had been driven from Moravia by Latin persecution. These men brought with them the Slavic Cyrillic alphabet, which freed the Bulgars from their dependence on Greek as a written and liturgical language. As a result, Bulgaria soon became the center of a flourishing Slavonic Christian culture. Boris had succeeded in using Christianization and Slavicization as means to unify his realm. His six children (by his single Christian wife) were all given Slavic or biblical names. Boris himself largely abandoned the title Khan in favor of the Slavic Kniaz (prince) or Greek Arkhon (sovereign).

Nearly sixty years old and in declining health, Boris surrendered the throne in 889 and retired to the monastery of Saint Panteleimon at Preslav. He was succeeded by his eldest son Vladimir, who showed no intention of following in his father's footsteps. Vladimir attempted to revive the pagan cults and actively courted the support of the old boyar hierarchy. The situation grew so chaotic that in 893 the aged Boris was forced to intervene against his son; Vladimir was quickly overthrown and blinded. Boris, however, did not resume the throne, but elevated his remaining son Symeon, a monk. Boris returned to the monastery, but until his death in 907, he remained Symeon's closest adviser. Soon after his death, Boris was canonized by the Bulgarian church.

Summary

Boris I inherited an embattled pagan kingdom, ruled by tribal custom and devoid of a unified or literate culture. During his reign of almost forty years, he transformed his domain into a powerful and respected Christian state under a strong central monarchy and made it the center of a vital Slavic culture.

Like many other successful ruler-reformers, Boris was both a visionary and an opportunist. His conversion to Christianity, for example, was an act of both sincere piety and practical political necessity. He openly embraced much of the style and organization of the Byzantine Empire, yet carefully avoided becoming a mere imitator or puppet. Boris was patient, and when necessary ruthless, in the pursuit of his goals. His effort to establish an autonomous Bulgarian church took almost twenty years, and his goal was finally achieved without alienating or unduly provoking the powerful Byzantine Empire.

Boris' changes laid the foundation for the First Bulgarian Empire, which would endure for another hundred years. More important, however, Boris created the foundations of a unique Bulgarian culture and nation which would later survive centuries of foreign domination and reemerge as an independent state in the late nineteenth century.

Bibliography

Anastasoff, Christ. *The Bulgarians, from Their Arrival in the Balkans to Modern Times: Thirteen Centuries of History*. Hicksville, N.Y.: Exposition Press, 1977. A useful general survey of Bulgarian history with a good chapter on the early medieval period. Particularly useful for putting Boris' reign into perspective with later Bulgarian history.

Fine, John V. A., Jr. *The Early Medieval Balkans: A Critical Survey from the Sixth to the Late Twelfth Century*. Ann Arbor: University of Michigan Press, 1983. Contains a concise but informative discussion of Boris' reign. Overall, a good description of the character and conditions of the Balkans in this formative period.

Hussey, J. M., ed. *The Cambridge Medieval History*. Vol. 4. London: Cambridge University Press, 1966-1967. Volume 4 of this standard reference work concentrates on the Byzantine Empire, but it does contain an excellent chapter on the early Bulgarian state and Boris' reign.

Lang, David Marshall. *The Bulgarians: From Pagan Times to the Ottoman Conquest.* Boulder, Colo.: Westview Press, 1976. This readable survey of medieval Bulgarian history offers a generous treatment of Boris' period. Contains numerous illustrations, plates, maps, and an excellent bibliography.

Obolensky, Dmitri. *The Byzantine Commonwealth: Eastern Europe, 500-1453.* London: Weidenfeld and Nicolson, 1971. Chapters 2 and 3 contain an objective and informative discussion of Boris, the early Bulgarian state, and Bulgar-Byzantine relations.

Runciman, Steven. *A History of the First Bulgarian Empire.* London: G. Bell and Sons, 1930. Still probably the best work on Boris and early medieval Bulgaria. Its style and its bibliography are somewhat dated, but Runciman's critical analysis of contemporary and modern sources is excellent. Also contains several useful appendices.

Richard B. Spence

BRAHMAGUPTA

Born: c. 598; Bhillamala, India
Died: c. 660; possibly Ujjain, India
Areas of Achievement: Mathematics and astronomy
Contribution: Brahmagupta wrote the book in verse entitled *Brahma sphuṭa siddhānta*, which expounds a complex system of astronomy and contains two important chapters on arithmetic, algebra, and geometry. His work on indeterminate equations and introduction of negative numbers greatly influenced the development of science in both India and Arabia.

Early Life

The Hindu astronomer and mathematician Brahmagupta was born circa 598 to a man named Jishnugupta from the town of Bhillamala (modern Bhinnmal, near Mount Abu in Rajasthan). The suffix "-gupta" may indicate that the family belonged to the Vaisya caste (composed mostly of farmers and merchants). In contrast to his predecessor, Aryabhata I (476-c. 550), who lived in relative obscurity at Pataliputra, Brahmagupta had the opportunity to live, study, and teach in Ujjain, a town in the State of Gwalior, Central India. Ujjain was then the center of Hindu mathematics and astronomy and had the best observatory in India. At Ujjain, Brahmagupta also had access to the writings of many great scientists who came before him, including Hero of Alexandria (first century A.D.), Ptolemy (second century A.D.), Diophantus (third century A.D.), and Aryabhata. Brahmagupta later drew heavily on these sources in his own writings, often correcting their errors. For example, he corrected Aryabhata's serious botch of the formulas for the surface areas and volumes of the pyramid and cone. Brahmagupta even borrowed mathematical problems, including one calling for the calculation of the position of a break in a bamboo pole ten feet long, the tip of which reached the ground three feet from the stem. This problem had first appeared in the Chinese text *Chiu-chang shuan-shu* (c. 50 B.C.-A.D. 100; arithmetic in nine sections), the authorship and date of which are very much uncertain.

Another influence of Ujjain was on Brahmagupta's style of writing. Like other Hindu scientists, including Aryabhata before him, he wrote his mathematical texts as poetry. The Indian practice was to clothe all arithmetical problems, especially those in schoolbooks, in poetic garb, fashioning them into puzzles that served as a popular amusement. Brahmagupta wrote that his mathematical problems were undertaken only for pleasure and that a wise man could invent a thousand more, or solve those presented by others, thereby eclipsing their brilliance, just as the sun eclipses the other stars in the sky.

It was at Ujjain that Brahmagupta would complete, at the age of thirty, his masterwork, the *Brahma sphuṭa siddhānta* (c. 628; the improved astronomical system of Brahma). The date of this work has been determined by consulting both commentary from later Hindu scholars and, appropriately, astronomical data.

Life's Work

The first ten chapters of Brahmagupta's *Brahma sphuṭa siddhānta* deal with various astronomical issues, including the mean and true longitudes of the planets, diurnal motion, lunar and solar eclipses, heliacal risings and settings, the lunar crescent and "shadow," conjunctions of the planets, and their conjunctions with the stars. The following thirteen chapters take up an examination of previous work on astronomy (including Aryabhata's), additions and problems (and their solutions) supplementing six of the earlier chapters, and chapters on mathematics, the gnomon, meters, the sphere, instruments, and measurements. The work's twenty-fourth and final chapter summarizes the principles of Brahmagupta's astronomical system in a compendious treatise on astronomical spheres. (Some manuscripts include an additional chapter containing tables.) All but two of the chapters deal with astronomy, but scholars have chosen those two chapters, 12 and 18, which deal with algebra and mathematics to study most intently.

Although Brahmagupta studied mathematics only for its applicability to astronomy and considered knowledge of the rules of arithmetic a prerequisite to be a *ganaca* (a student of astronomy), most scholars in the ages since he lived have studied his mathematics more closely than his astronomy. Of particular interest is his work on indeterminate equations, building on the work of both Diophantus and Aryabhata. Brahmagupta's work, along with that of Bhāskara II (1114-c. 1185), solved the so-called Pell equation, $y^2 = ax^2 + 1$, where a is a nonsquare integer. Brahmagupta showed that from one solution where x, y, and xy do not equal zero, a general formula indicating an infinite number of solutions could be derived. Brahmagupta also stated that the equation $y^2 = ax^2 - 1$ could not be solved with integral values of x and y unless a was equal to the sum of the squares of any two integers. Brahmagupta's work on these equations, with additions by Bhāskara, is highly regarded because it was not for several centuries that another mathematician, namely Joseph-Louis Lagrange (1736-1813), could completely work out the Pell equation.

Brahmagupta also studied indeterminate equations of the first order, such as this one: Two ascetics live on top of a hill of h units of height, whose base is mh units away from a nearby town. One ascetic descends the hill and walks directly to the town. The other, being a wizard, flies straight up a certain distance, x, then proceeds in a straight line toward the town. If the distance traveled by each ascetic is the same, and h is 12 and mh is 48, find x. The solution comes from the formula $x = mh/(m + 2)$, or in this case, $x = 8$.

Brahmagupta's work on the geometry of quadrilaterals, which was probably inspired from studying Ptolemy and Hero, is also a landmark in the history of Hindu mathematics. Brahmagupta found the formulas, for the first time, for the diagonals (defined as m and n) of a quadrilateral having sides of length a, b, c, and d and opposite angles of A and B, and C and D. He calculated the diagonals thus:

$$m^2 = (ab + cd)(ac + bd)/(ad + bc) \text{ and}$$
$$n^2 = (ac + bd)(ad + bc)/(ab + cd).$$

These formulas were later studied by Bhāskara, who, failing to understand that they applied only to quadrilaterals inscribed in a circle, incorrectly pronounced them unsound. Brahmagupta also figured that, if a, b, c, A, B, and C are positive integers such that $a^2 + b^2 = c^2$ and $A^2 + B^2 = C^2$, then the cyclic quadrilateral having consecutive sides aC, cB, bC, cA (which came to be called a Brahmagupta trapezium) has rational area and diagonals, and the diagonals are perpendicular to each other. These formulas are most remarkable; nothing like them had previously appeared in Hindu geometry.

Brahmagupta borrowed from Hero of Alexandria the formula for the triangular area, but he brilliantly extended Hero's formula to work with quadrilaterals that can be inscribed within circles. This idea was later built on by the ninth century Hindu mathematician Mahavira and was much admired by later commentators. Brahmagupta's other advances in mathematics included proving the Pythagorean theory of the right triangle, deriving formulas for the areas of a square and a triangle inscribed in a circle, and showing that a rectangle whose sides were the radius and semiperimeter of a circle had the same area as that circle.

Although he is now remembered mostly for his advances in mathematics and his influence on the mathematical work of later Hindus such as Mahavira and Bhāskara, Brahmagupta considered himself primarily an astronomer. Almost every Hindu commentator on astronomy discusses his work. Indeed, some of his work in astronomy is quite admirable. He provided fairly accurate figures for the circumference of Earth and the length of the calendar year. Brahmagupta gives a figure different from Aryabhata's for the circumference of Earth: 5,000 *yojanas*. Assuming that Brahmagupta's *yojana* was a short league of about 4.5 miles, that would convert his figure to 22,500 miles, which is not too far off the mark. He also tried to correct Aryabhata's computation for the length of the year, which was 365 days, 15 *ghati*, 31 *pala*, and 15 *vipala*, or 365 days, 6 hours, 12 minutes, and 30 seconds. His own figure was slightly more accurate: 365 days, 15 *ghati*, 30 *pala*, 22 *vipala*, and 30 *pratipala* (365 days, 6 hours, 12 minutes, and 9.0 seconds).

Much of his astronomy, however, is quite erroneous. Like many Hindu scientists of the time, Brahmagupta was vehemently opposed to Aryabhata's ideas that Earth revolved around the sun and spun on its axis. Why then, Brahmagupta asked, do not the lofty bodies fall down to Earth? He also questioned Aryabhata's theory of an aerial fluid that causes Earth to rotate.

Summary

Although Brahmagupta greatly extended the work of many preceding mathematicians and presented numerous valid theories of his own, it must be acknowledged that he did make some serious scientific errors. In addition to denying the aforementioned theories of Aryabhata on the place of Earth in the solar system, he gave a faulty formula for the area of an equilateral triangle. In his studies on the circle, he alternately used 3 and $\sqrt{10}$ as values for π.

Yet Brahmagupta's importance as a scientist must have been recognized during his lifetime, because he was accused of propagating scientific falsehoods to please the priests and the ignorant commonfolk. The priests were particularly opposed to the ideas that Earth was round and that it rotated around the sun. Perhaps Brahmagupta had lied to avoid the fate of Socrates (c. 470-399 B.C.).

Despite these accusations, at least two of Brahmagupta's algebraic formulations, although originally devised for use in astronomy, became widely used by Hindu traders. Of particular practical use was his rule of three, in which the Argument, the Fruit, and the Requisition are the names of the terms. The first and last terms have to be similar. The Requisition multiplied by the Fruit and divided by the Argument yielded the Produce. Brahmagupta also introduced the use of negative numbers, which he used to unify three of Diophantus' quadratic equations under a general equation. These negative numbers were especially useful to merchants in representing debts, along with positive numbers, which represented assets. Another advance in mathematics which the merchants must have found helpful was Brahmagupta's work on interest rates. By 700, Hindu merchants had introduced Brahmagupta's mathematics to the Arabs, with whom they carried on a high volume of trade. In 772, a table of sines from Brahmagupta—which, incidentally, was probably based on work by Aryabhata—reached the 'Abbasid caliph al-Mansur, and it was ordered to be translated into Arabic. The entirety of the *Brahma sphuṭa siddhānta* was translated into Arabic by 775, around the time works by other Greek and Hindu mathematicians were being translated by Arab scholars. Together, these works would greatly influence the nascent Arabic mathematics, with Brahmagupta's greatest contributions coming in the study of negative numbers and indeterminate equations.

Bibliography

Ball, W. W. Rouse. *A Short Account of the History of Mathematics*. London: Macmillan, 1888, 4th ed. 1908. A thorough overview of the history of mathematics, with a section on Brahmagupta and his work on quadratic equations (including a version of the ascetic problem with apes substituted), right triangles, and algebra, plus scattered information on his later influence on Hindu and Arab mathematicians.

Cajori, Florian. *A History of Mathematics*. London: Macmillan, 1919, 2d ed. 1924. Gives the solution to Brahmagupta's broken bamboo problem, plus formulas for Brahmagupta's work on triangles and quadrilaterals.

Eves, Howard. *An Introduction to the History of Mathematics*. New York: Holt, Rinehart and Winston, 1964, 3d ed. 1969. Includes information on Brahmagupta's studies on indeterminate equations, the Pell equation, cyclic quadrilaterals, and the rule of three, along with a discussion of his place in the history of mathematics. Some problems (with solutions) based on his formula for the cyclic quadrilateral are included.

Hofmann, Joseph Ehrenfried. *The History of Mathematics*. Translated by Frank Gaynor and Henrietta O. Midonick. New York: Philosophical Library, 1957. Includes information on Brahmagupta's work on various indeterminate equations.

Prakash, Satya. *A Critical Study of Brahmagupta and His Works*. New Delhi, India: Indian Institute of Astronomical and Sanskrit Research, 1968. A comprehensive study of Brahmagupta, his works, his sources, and the influence of his work on later writers. Contains an extensive bibliography.

Smith, David E. *History of Mathematics*. 2 vols. New York: Dover Publications, 1958. Gives numerous formulas that Brahmagupta used in studying quadrilaterals, quadratic equations, indeterminate equations, and right triangles.

Frank Wu

BUDDHA
Siddhārtha Gautama

Born: c. 566 B.C.; Lumbinī, Nepal
Died: c. 486 B.C.; Kuśinagara, India
Areas of Achievement: Religion, philosophy, and monasticism
Contribution: By his own example and teaching, Buddha showed that all
people can attain an enlightened state of mind by cultivating a combination of compassion (loving-kindness toward all beings without exception)
and wisdom (seeing things as they really are).

Early Life

The historical Buddha—known variously as Gautama, Siddhārtha, and
Śākyamuni—was born in Lumbinī, in the Himālayan foothills of what is now
Nepal. His father, Śuddhodana, was king of nearby Kapilavastu, a town
whose archaeological remains have yet to be found. His mother, Māyā, died
seven days after giving birth to the young prince; Śuddhodana then married
her sister, who brought up the boy.

According to legend, the infant's conception and birth were accompanied
by unusual signs, and he walked and talked at birth. Legend also has it that
an ancient sage prophesied that the young prince would become either a
Buddha (an enlightened one) or a universal monarch. Śuddhodana, determined on the latter career, kept his son confined within the palace walls to
prevent him from seeing unpleasant sights that might cause him to renounce
the world and take up the religious life of a wandering mendicant.

The Buddha's given name was Siddhārtha ("he who has achieved his
goal"). Later, he was called Śākyamuni (Sage of the Śākyas), because his
family was part of the warrior (*kṣatriya*) Śākya clan, which also used the
Brahman clan name Gautama (descendant of the sage Gotama). He is
described as a handsome, black-haired boy.

The oldest Buddhist canon is in the Pali language and was transmitted
orally for several hundred years after the Buddha's death; it was then written
down on palm leaves. The Pali canon records few details about Siddhārtha's
early years, but it does mention that he spontaneously entered a state of
meditation while sitting under a tree watching his father plowing. It also recounts his becoming aware of the inevitability of old age, illness, and death,
supposedly by seeing his first old man, ill man, and corpse on clandestine
trips outside the palace gates.

When he came of age, Siddhārtha was married to Yaśodharā. They had a
son who was named Rāhula (the fetter), perhaps because Siddhārtha was
already turning away from householder life. Indeed, at the age of twenty-
nine, he left home forever to seek enlightenment, initially with two teachers,
then through extended fasting and other austerities, in which he was joined

by five other ascetics. At the age of thirty-five, having failed to attain his goal, he ate enough to regain strength and sat under a tree (later known as the Bodhi Tree) at Uruvelā, near Benares, vowing to stay there until he reached enlightenment.

The Pali canon includes several different descriptions of the enlightenment that followed, "as though one were to describe a tree from above, from below and from various sides, or a journey by land, by water and by air" (Ñāṇamoli, *Life of the Buddha According to the Pali Canon*, 1972). What these accounts have in common is Śākyamuni's claim of having attained direct knowledge of the final nature of mind itself.

Examining the mind via meditation, Śākyamuni found it empty of independent existence. In combination with compassion (an altruistic attitude toward everyone, especially one's "enemies"), this knowledge led to Buddhahood. It was this discovery that Gautama Buddha would spend the rest of his life setting forth to those who came to listen to him teach.

Life's Work

The newly enlightened Buddha's first impulse was not to disseminate the truth that he had worked so diligently to uncover. He realized that every human being had the potential to attain enlightenment, just as he himself had done, but he also knew that enlightenment could not be bestowed by anyone else; each person had to reach it himself. Thus the Buddha is said to have hesitated to propagate his Dharma ("truth" or "law"), thinking that it would be too difficult for beings still deluded by craving to understand. Only his compassion for the suffering of all beings eventually convinced him to do so.

Accordingly, the Buddha set out to find the five ascetics with whom he had practiced austerities. They were not immediately convinced of his enlightenment, so he elucidated the Middle Way of avoiding both sensual and ascetic extremes. At this point the Buddha is said to have first taught the Four Noble Truths—namely, that life inevitably involves suffering or woefulness (*dukkha*), that the cause of suffering is craving or grasping, that there is a way for craving to cease, and that the way consists of the Eightfold Path of right view, right intention, right speech, right action, right livelihood, right effort, right mindfulness, and right concentration.

During this talk, which took place four miles north of Benares, in the Deer Park at Isipatana, one of the five ascetics realized that all conditioned (interdependent) things are impermanent, and he became enlightened. The remaining four soon followed suit; other wanderers and householders from all walks of life, including Rāhula and Śākyamuni's stepmother/aunt, did the same.

The formula that distinguishes a Buddhist from a non-Buddhist evolved during this time. The Buddha taught that "oneself is one's own refuge" and that all beings are, ultimately, manifestations of Buddha nature or enlightened mind. Thus Buddhists take refuge in what is called the Three Jewels or Triple Gem: the Buddha as a representation of enlightenment; the Dharma, or teaching of how to attain enlightenment; and the Sangha, the community of fellow aspirants on the path.

The Buddha continued to teach for the next forty-five years, which he spent journeying around the central Gangetic plain, giving discourses (*sū-tras*), establishing monastic guidelines (*vinaya*) as the need arose for them, and answering any questions put to him.

Śākyamuni was not concerned with metaphysical questions about the origins of the world, explaining that a man with an arrow in his chest is more sensible to address himself to removing it than to ask how it got there. The Buddha had found a way to end man's mental and physical suffering, by developing inner clarity and peace; to him, questions of how and why were not useful in progressing toward that goal.

According to the law of Karma (the law of cause and effect), to which the Buddha subscribed, wholesome actions eventually lead to good results, while unwholesome or harmful deeds result in suffering, in this or a future life. By cultivating wholesome actions of body, speech, and mind, the Buddha maintained that anyone can experience enlightenment. To do this, the Buddha advocated dissolving the obstacles of craving, anger, and ignorance by cultivating ethical conduct, moral discipline, and wisdom.

The Buddha was not immune to death, but he remained fearless and lucid when the time came. Having become ill in his eightieth year, he told one of his foremost disciples, his cousin Ananda, that he would soon die. He then asked the assembled monks three times whether they had any doubts or questions, but they remained silent. The Buddha's last words summarized his teaching: "Conditioned things are perishable by nature. Diligently seek realization." He died in meditation.

Summary

Śākyamuni elucidated seminal ideas and methods whose effect can only be compared to the teachings of Moses, Jesus, and Muhammad. He rejected some key elements of the Hindu worldview of his era—notably the caste system, the idea of a permanent self (*ātman*), and the practice of austerities—but retained the notions of Karma and rebirth. To these he added his unique insight into what is worthwhile: an altruistic aspiration to enlightenment for the sake of all beings.

Although Buddhism declined and eventually disappeared in India (where it is experiencing a revival today), it spread to Southeast and Central Asia, China, Korea, and Japan. Today there are many different schools of Buddhism, whose styles range from the baroque iconography of Tibetan tantrism to the stark simplicity of Zen. All recognize subsequent adepts on the Buddhist path and reflect the different cultures in which they have developed. All

Buddhist traditions, however, trace their lineage and the common essence of their teaching to Śākyamuni, the man who, in recorded history, first became an enlightened one, a Buddha.

Bibliography

Anderson, Walt. *Open Secrets: A Western Guide to Tibetan Buddhism*. New York: Viking Press, 1979. A straightforward introduction to the form Buddhism took in Tibet.

Gyatso, Tenzin (the fourteenth Dalai Lama). *Kindness, Clarity, and Insight*. Edited by Jeffrey Hopkins and Elizabeth Napper. Ithaca, N.Y.: Snow Lion Publications, 1984. Twenty talks ranging from succinct discussions of the nature of Karma and the role of compassion in global politics to technical explanations of various methods for attaining enlightenment.

Ñāṇamoli, Bhikku, comp. *The Life of the Buddha According to the Pali Canon*. 2d ed. Kandy, Ceylon: Buddhist Publication Society, 1978. A biography translated from the oldest authentic records and supplemented with historical notes, by an eminent English scholar-monk.

Rahula, Walpola. *What the Buddha Taught*. 2d ed. New York: Grove Press, 1974. A reliable introduction to the complexities of Buddhism. Includes a selection of texts from the Pali canon translated by the author, who is a Buddhist monk and scholar.

Reps, Paul, and Nyogen Senzaki, comps. *Zen Flesh, Zen Bones: A Collection of Zen and Pre-Zen Writings*. Rutland, Vt.: C. E. Tuttle Co., 1957. A classic introduction to Zen, including the quintessential parable of the Ten Bulls and the koan (paradox for meditation) of the "sound of one hand."

Robinson, Richard H., and Willard L. Johnson, assisted by Kathryn Tsai and Shinzen Young. *The Buddhist Religion: A Historical Introduction*. 3d ed. Belmont, Calif.: Wadsworth Publishing Co., 1982. An overview that traces the antecedents of Buddhism, describes the Buddha's life, and explains the development of Buddhism both in India and in Southeast Asia, Tibet, East Asia, and the West. Includes a glossary of key Sanskrit terms, an essay on meditation, and a list of selected readings.

Senzaki, Nyogen, and Ruth Strout McCandless. *Buddhism and Zen*. Foreword by Robert Aitken. Reprint. San Francisco: North Point Press, 1987. A reprint of the 1953 collection of talks, notes, and translations by one of the earliest and most accomplished Zen teachers in the West.

Victoria Scott

JEAN BURIDAN

Born: c. 1295; Béthune, France
Died: c. 1358; Paris, France
Areas of Achievement: Philosophy, logic, and physics
Contribution: A distinguished natural philosopher, Buridan wrote critical commentaries on the works of Aristotle and laid the foundations of the modern science of mechanics.

Early Life

Jean Buridan was born in northern France toward the end of the thirteenth century and received his early education at church schools in the diocese of Arras. His great intellectual gifts were soon manifested, and he went, as a young cleric, to study at the University of Paris. He studied philosophy and was profoundly influenced by Ockhamism. William of Ockham, an English Franciscan, espoused nominalism, a doctrine holding that individuals are the primary reality and that universal concepts have no objective referents but are only mental descriptions for similar features among individuals. Buridan's later writings often reflect Ockham's ideas and methods.

After receiving his master of arts degree around 1320, Buridan became a lecturer in natural, metaphysical, and moral philosophy at the University of Paris. He quickly achieved recognition as a gifted philosopher, but he remained a secular cleric rather than becoming a member of a religious order, and he never sought a degree in theology. Nevertheless, he was willing to introduce theology into physical questions; for example, he argued that God could create a vacuum even though Aristotle posited the vacuum's impossibility. As a teacher and writer, Buridan was not a narrow specialist and he felt free to discuss problems as wide-ranging as the dogmas of the Christian faith and the formation of mountains.

The first documentary mention of Buridan is dated February 2, 1328, and the occasion was his appointment as university rector. The document shows that he was held in high esteem by his colleagues, and records in the Vatican indicate that benefices and honors were conferred on him several times during his successful career as a lecturer and administrator. Around 1330, he traveled south to visit the papal court at Avignon and en route he climbed Mount Ventoux to make some meteorological observations.

In 1340 he again became rector of the University of Paris, and in that capacity he signed, on December 29, 1340, a statute strongly condemning certain members of the faculty of arts for applying strict logical analysis to scriptural texts without sufficiently considering the holy authors' intentions. Many scholars think that this decree was directed against Nicholas of Autrecourt, a rival Scholastic philosopher whose skeptical views have since garnered for him the name "the medieval Hume." The mild temperament discernible in many of Buridan's writings was set aside when he attacked Nicholas' errors. These condemnations, however, were not anti-Ockhamist, since Ockham's philosophy was firmly based on the principle of natural causation, which is what was impugned by Nicholas. Throughout Buridan's career, he used Ockham's doctrines to defend both natural knowledge and real secondary causes.

Life's Work

Aristotle's fourth century B.C. writings profoundly influenced Europeans in the thirteenth and fourteenth centuries, and Buridan's extant writings consist almost entirely of detailed commentaries on Aristotelian treatises. These writings clearly derived from his lectures at the University of Paris, whose curriculum was largely based on the study of Aristotle's works. For example, Buridan wrote commentaries on *Physica* (*Physics*), *De caelo* (*On the Heavens*), *Metaphysica* (*Metaphysics*), *De anima* (*On the Soul*), *Politica* (*Politics*), *De sensu et sensibilibus* (*On Sense and Sensibles*), and *Ethica Nicomachea* (*Nichomachean Ethics*).

Although much of his work evolved from his study of Aristotle, Buridan was not merely an explicator of Aristotelian ideas. On the contrary, he leveled some devastating attacks against this great philosopher, and he used these criticisms to develop his own ideas, which were themselves important advances in scientific and philosophical thought. This approach can be seen in Buridan's works on logic, where, while commenting on Aristotle, he develops a method now known as logical analysis. He used this method to formulate philosophical problems as questions about the meaning and reference of terms and the truth condition of sentences. In his primer on logic, *Summula de dialectica* (1487), as in his other logical works (*Sophismata*, 1488, and *Consequentie*, 1493), Buridan showed himself to be a follower of *logica moderna* (the new logic), in which Aristotle's logic was reconstructed on new foundations. Buridan achieved this reconstruction through the theory of the supposition of terms. Medieval logicians used the word "term" to designate descriptive signs occupying the subject or predicate positions in propositions. Ockham defined supposition as the "standing for something else" of a term in a proposition. In his opinion, as in Buridan's, what primarily determined the supposition, or referential use, of a subject or predicate term in a proposition was the verb.

Buridan went beyond Ockham by applying the new logic to many problems never before treated by anyone. One such problem was the analysis of statements in indirect discourse. Since the terms occurring in the subordinate clauses of sentences in indirect discourse purport to designate what actually is said to be known, the question of what such terms denote boils down to the question of what kinds of entities constitute the object of knowledge. Do these terms stand for really existing individual things or Platonic essences or simply the words themselves?

Buridan's most extensive treatment of this problem is found in *Sophismata*, a work devoted to the analysis of paradoxical statements that appear to be both true and false. The famous "liar" paradox is an example: Is the statement "What I am now saying is false" true or false? According to Aristotelian logic, this statement is true if it is false and false if it is true. Buridan thought that the person who makes that statement and says nothing else really is saying something false, because this sentence has to be considered together with the circumstances of its utterance, and one of these circumstances is that sentences cannot be both true and false. Thus, in this case the sentence and its circumstances make the statement false.

In philosophy Buridan was a moderate nominalist; he supported the condemnation of both the radical Ockhamism of Nicholas and the extreme Aristotelianism of the followers of Averroës. Among his philosophical discussions, Buridan is best known for his theory of the relationship of will and reason. He proposed that a person must will what is revealed to reason as the greater good but stated that the will is free to delay choice until the reason has more extensively inquired into the values and motives involved. The classic illustration of this analysis is the parable of "Buridan's ass," a story not found in the extant writings. An ass is situated between two equidistant and equivalent bundles of hay. Since the ass has no reason to choose one bale over the other, he would remain in perpetual indecision and starve to death. The source of this story is probably Buridan's commentary on Aristotle's *On the Heavens*, in which he discusses the case of a dog starving between equally attractive portions of food. Later philosophers attacked Buridan's theory of the will. In their view, when reason can find no preference, the will is still capable of decision when it is clear that delay is pointless, stupid, or even dangerous.

Despite his perceptive logical and philosophical analyses, Buridan made his most important contributions in science. Aristotle had defined science as the knowledge of universal and necessary conclusions made by demonstration from necessary though indemonstrable premises. Buridan, on the other hand, sharply distinguished between premises determined logically, through definitions of the terms, and those determined empirically, through inductive generalization from conditional evidence. He therefore rejected the thesis, common among many Scholastic philosophers, that the principles of physics are necessary in the sense that their contradictories are logically impossible. Buridan did not require the same logical rigor from the scientist as from the mathematician. According to him, if scientific truths could be imposed under pain of contradiction, then physical science would be destroyed. Through this analysis he was able to concede the possibility of God's interference with the natural order while still excluding supernatural events as irrelevant to the scientific enterprise.

In his treatment of physics and cosmology, Buridan accepted Aristotle's ideas as a basic framework for natural philosophy, but he also entertained alternative ideas as both logically possible and empirically preferable to explain certain phenomena. His most incisive criticism was directed against Aristotle's account of motion. An obvious weakness of Aristotle's theory was its inability to explain projectile motion satisfactorily. For Aristotle, a thrown object required an external moving cause continuously in contact with it. He theorized that the air, disturbed by the violent motion of throwing the projectile, kept pushing the object forward for a time. Buridan first refuted Aristotle's theory by several empirical arguments; for example, he showed that disturbing the air was not sufficient to move the projectile. He then proposed his theory of impetus as a solution.

Impetus, to Buridan, was a motive force impressed by the thrower on the projectile. He regarded this impressed force as permanent and believed that were it not for air resistance and gravity, impetus would maintain the projectile at a uniform speed. Buridan also quantified impetus as the product of the amount of matter and the speed, the same quantities defining momentum in Sir Isaac Newton's physics, although Newton's momentum is a measure of the effect of a body's motion whereas Buridan's impetus is a cause of motion. Also significant for later physics is Buridan's statement that impetus is an "enduring reality," for it suggests Newton's law of inertia: An object, once set in motion, tends to remain in motion at a uniform speed. An important difference between Newton's inertia and Buridan's impetus is that impetus would persist indefinitely for an object moving both in a circle and in a straight line whereas Newton's momentum would persist only in a straight line and would need a force to bend it into a circle.

Buridan used impetus to explain many phenomena: the acceleration of an object falling to earth, the vibration of plucked strings, the bouncing of balls, and the everlasting rotations of heavenly bodies. This last application is the most important one, and Pierre Duhem, the great French physicist, dated the beginning of modern science to Buridan's rejection of Intelligences as movers of the heavenly bodies. Buridan believed that the heavenly bodies, having been put in motion by God, continued to move because of the impetus God impressed on them; they consequently required no everlastingly active angels to keep them moving. Buridan explained rotational motion by a rotational impetus analogous to the rectilinear impetus for projectile motion. Galileo Galilei held similar views; it was not until Newton that the movements of heavenly and earthly bodies were correctly explained.

In the light of the great changes that Nicolaus Copernicus would cause in astronomy two centuries later, it is interesting that Buridan himself investigated the question of whether Earth is at rest. He believed that the daily motion of the stellar sphere and the planets could be explained by assuming either a stationary heaven and rotating Earth or the reverse. In other words, he recognized that the problem was one of relative motion. To support the theory of a rotating Earth, Buridan stressed, in typical Ockhamist manner, the desirability of explaining the phenomena by the simplest means possible. Since it was simpler to move the smaller Earth than the much larger stellar sphere, it seemed reasonable to attribute rotation to Earth while leaving the stellar sphere at rest. Despite this and other arguments favorable to a daily terrestrial motion, Buridan finally opted for a nonrotating Earth since, in his judgment, a rotating Earth could not explain why an arrow shot vertically into the air fell back to its origin rather than far to the west.

Although Buridan believed that Earth did not rotate, he nevertheless did not believe it was perfectly stationary. Indeed, he thought that Earth experienced incessant, though slight, motions that arose from continual shifts of Earth's center of gravity, caused by the redistribution of matter on its surface. Buridan explained that streams and rivers carried material from the mountains to the sea, and in this way the elevated regions of Earth became lighter and the watery regions heavier. His explanation is similar to the modern theory of isostasy, which plays a major role in physical geology.

It is not known which work written by Buridan was his last. The final documentary mention of him is dated July 12, 1358, in a statute where his name appears as a witness to an agreement between the Picard and English students and teachers of the University of Paris. Buridan, who came from this region of northern France, represented the Picards. It is possible, though there is no real evidence to support it, that he fell victim to the Black Death, which in the late 1350's took the lives of many of those who had survived its first outbreak in 1348-1349.

Summary

To many historians of science, Jean Buridan is the key figure in the development of medieval dynamics and an important precursor of modern mechanics. He successfully challenged Aristotle's theory of motion and proposed an alternative dynamics that had potentially revolutionary implications. Unfortunately, he did not generalize impetus into a theory of universal inertial mechanics. Although he used impetus to explain both terrestrial and celestial motion, he never tried to formulate a single mechanics for the whole universe because he accepted the Aristotelian dichotomy between terrestrial and celestial bodies. Buridan's ideas on terrestrial and celestial movements were developed by Albert of Saxony and Nicole d'Oresme, and his theory of impetus came to have wide acceptance in fifteenth and sixteenth century France, England, Germany, and Italy.

Other scholars see Buridan's importance more in the questions he raised than in the answers he proposed. Even when his specific contributions to physics were forgotten, the influence of his conception of scientific evidence and method lived on. In particular, he helped eliminate explanations in terms of final causes from physics. His work marks a shift from a metaphysical to an empirical attitude toward scientific problems. He vindicated natural philosophy as a field of study in its own right, and he defined the objectives and methodology of science in a way that guaranteed its autonomy with regard to theology and philosophy. In this sense Duhem is correct in saying that Buridan's work marks the start of modern science.

Bibliography
Clagett, Marshall. *The Science of Mechanics in the Middle Ages*. Madison: University of Wisconsin Press, 1959. This volume, whose purpose is to present documentary material on which to base future studies of medieval science, contains excerpts and helpful discussions of several works by Buridan on mechanics and cosmology.
Dijksterhuis, E. J. *The Mechanization of the World Picture: Pythagoras to Newton*. Translated by C. Dikshoorn. Reprint. Princeton, N.J.: Princeton University Press, 1986. This classic work, first published by Clarendon Press in an English translation in 1961, is a detailed account of the origins and development of the physical sciences. Dijksterhuis, an expert in the history of mechanics, gives a good discussion of Buridan's work.
Duhem, Pierre. *Medieval Cosmology: Theories of Infinity, Place, Time, Void, and the Plurality of Worlds*. Edited and translated by Roger Ariew. Chicago: University of Chicago Press, 1985. Ariew has translated selections from Duhem's *Le Système du monde* (1913-1959), a classic, ten-volume history of the physical sciences. The excerpts from his discussion of Jean Buridan, Albert of Saxony, and Nicole d'Oresme demonstrate the sophistication of medieval physics and cosmology.
Grant, Edward. *A Source Book in Medieval Science*. Cambridge, Mass.: Harvard University Press, 1974. This volume is part of the Source Book series, in which classical papers that have shaped the history of various sciences are collected. Several selections have been translated into English from Buridan's works on natural philosophy and are presented with commentary and annotations.
Lindberg, David C., ed. *Science in the Middle Ages*. Chicago: University of Chicago Press, 1978. Lindberg analyzes all major aspects of the medieval scientific enterprise in some detail. He discusses Buridan's work in chapters on medieval philosophy, mechanics, and cosmology.
Moody, Ernest A. *Studies in Medieval Philosophy, Science, and Logic: Collected Papers, 1933-1969*. Berkeley: University of California Press, 1975. Moody, an eminent medieval scholar, has collected several of his influential papers on Buridan in this book, among them "John Buridan on the Habitability of the Earth" and "Buridan and a Dilemma of Nominalism."

Robert J. Paradowski

JULIUS CAESAR

Born: July 12/13, 100 B.C.; Rome
Died: March 15, 44 B.C.; Rome
Areas of Achievement: Government, warfare, and literature
Contribution: With his conquest of Gaul, Caesar expanded Roman rule into
   northern Europe. He then won a desperate civil war to establish himself as
   sole ruler of the Roman world, ending the republic and preparing the stage
   for the empire.

Early Life
   The family of Gaius Julius Caesar was of great antiquity and nobility in
Roman history; Caesar was to claim descent not only from the ancient kings
of the city but also from Aeneas, its legendary founder, and his mother, the
goddess Venus. In actual life, however, the Julian clan had more history than
money and tended to favor the cause of the common people rather than the
aristocrats. The twin pressures of finance and popular politics were the dominant forces that shaped the life and career of Julius Caesar.
   During the first century B.C., the city-state of Rome had become the dominant power in the Mediterranean world, and with this expansion had come
enormous wealth, immense military strength, and a gradual but unmistakable decline in the old republic. By the time of Caesar's birth, the political
factions in Rome had coalesced into two major camps. The *populares* were
led by Gaius Marius, who was married to Caesar's aunt Julia; this group
championed the cause of the middle and lower classes. Their opponents, the
optimates, favored the upper classes and the traditional rule of the senate;
they found their leader in Lucius Cornelius Sulla. The bloody civil war between the two sides ended with Sulla's victory and assumption of the dictatorship.
   In 84, Caesar married Cornelia, the daughter of a leading follower of
Marius. This action so angered Sulla that Caesar found it prudent to secure a
diplomatic post at the court of Nicomedes, the King of Bithynia in northeastern Asia Minor. Caesar did not return to Rome until after Sulla's death.
   Once back, he embarked upon a daring and ambitious course of bringing
charges against the leading members of the *optimates*, in the hope of winning
renown and establishing his support among the followers of Marius. Unsuccessful in these attempts, Caesar journeyed to Rhodes to study oratory—
an art essential to any successful Roman politician. On the voyage, Caesar
was captured by pirates and held for ransom. Insulted by the small amount
they demanded, Caesar had them increase it and promised that when he was
freed he would return to crucify them. He was good to his word, but according to his biographer Suetonius, Caesar mercifully cut the throats of the pirates before crucifixion.

In 70, Caesar fully entered public life with his funeral oration for his aunt Julia. It was in this speech that he traced his family ancestry to the goddess Venus; more important, he launched a searing attack on the conservative party in Rome, announcing his intent to challenge their rule. The rest of his life would be spent in making good that challenge.

According to ancient writers, Caesar was tall and fair-complexioned, with a full face and keen black eyes. He enjoyed excellent health until the last years of his life, when he was subject to fainting fits which may have been epileptic. He was bald early and quite vain about it; Suetonius says that of all the honors granted him, the one Caesar used most was the privilege of wearing a laurel wreath at all times.

In his private life, Caesar was noted for his incessant womanizing; even amid the somewhat lax morality of the late republic, his escapades were cause for widespread comment. He was also exceedingly avaricious, but this may have been less a character flaw than a political necessity.

Caesar's main characteristic was his amazing energy, both physical and mental. He endured the dangers and fatigues of military campaigns without complaint or distress, and he composed his lucid, fast-moving *De bello Gallico* (52-51 B.C.; *The Gallic Wars*) and *De bello civili* (45 B.C.; *The Civil Wars*) almost before his battles were ended. He was so brilliant, in so many areas, that his contemporaries were dazzled—and historians continue to be fascinated—by him.

Life's Work

It is impossible to tell if Caesar wished to destroy the last remnants of the old republic and replace it with a formal autocracy, or whether he merely intended to become the leading citizen—although one without rivals—in the Roman world. In the end, the result was the same, for Caesar for a brief time did become supreme ruler, and the republic was destroyed. Although it was Caesar's nephew and heir Octavian (later known as Augustus) who became the first Roman emperor, it was Caesar who made the empire possible.

Following a term as quaestor (a junior military officer) in Spain in 69, Caesar returned to Rome and allied himself with Marcus Licinius Crassus and Pompey the Great; the first was the richest man in Rome, the second its leading general. Together, these three formed the First Triumvirate, which was to become the real power in the Roman world.

In 61, Caesar was appointed governor of Farther Spain and honored with a triumph for his military campaigns there. The next year, he was elected as one of the two consuls who headed the Roman government; his term of office began in 59. The rest of Caesar's career stems, directly or indirectly, from this consulship.

As one of two consuls, Caesar had to deal with his colleague, a conservative opponent. Impatient with this and other obstructions, Caesar initiated numerous highly irregular, sometimes illegal, actions. These were designed to benefit Pompey's discharged veterans, increase the wealth of Crassus, and advance the general aims of the Triumvirate. So blatant, however, were the offenses—including violence against officials whose positions made them virtually sacred—that Caesar knew that his enemies would not rest until he had been prosecuted, convicted, and condemned.

His only recourse was to remain in office, since then he would be immune from trial. He secured the provinces of Cisalpine Gaul (now northern Italy) and Illyricum (the coast of modern Yugoslavia), and soon added Transalpine Gaul (southern France), which bordered on lands unconquered by Rome.

Caesar wasted no time in finding an excuse to wage war against the Gauls, and for the next eight years he was embroiled in the Gallic Wars, which are vividly recounted in his commentaries. During his campaigns, he crossed the Rhine to drive back the German tribes and twice launched an invasion of Britain. Although his attempts on the island were unsuccessful, his second fleet numbered eight hundred ships—the largest channel invasion armada until the Normandy invasion in World War II.

In 52, the recently subdued Gauls revolted against the Romans and, led by Vercingetorix, came close to undoing Caesar's great conquests. By brilliant generalship and extraordinary efforts, Caesar pinned the Gauls in their fortress town of Alesia (Aliese-Sainte-Reine) and destroyed their army, finally ending the Gallic Wars. According to Caesar, he had fought thirty battles, captured eight hundred towns, and defeated three million enemies, of whom almost a million had been slain, another million captured. Although these figures are surely exaggerated, they do illustrate the extent of Caesar's victory. Its long-lasting effect was the opening of northern Europe to the influence of Greek and Roman culture and the rich heritage of the Mediterranean civilization.

Caesar's Gallic victories, however, had not secured his position in Rome. The Triumvirate had drifted apart, and Pompey was now allied with the senate and the conservatives. They demanded that Caesar give up his governorship and return to Rome. Knowing that such a move would be fatal, Cacsar instead attacked his opponents. In January, 49, he led his troops across the Rubicon, the narrow stream that marked the border of his province. He took this irrevocable step with a gambler's daring, remarking, "Jacta alea est" (the die is cast).

Pompey and the senatorial forces were caught by surprise, and within three months they had been driven from Italy to Greece. Caesar turned west and seized Sicily to secure Rome's grain supply, then attacked Pompey's supporters in Spain. He trapped their army near the Ebro River at Ilerda (now Lerida), and when they surrendered, he showed considerable clemency in pardoning them, in marked contrast to his earlier harsh treatment of the Gauls.

Returning to Rome, Caesar became dictator for the first time and proceeded to deal with numerous social problems, especially that of widespread debt, caused by the breakdown of the republic. In 48, he daringly crossed the Adriatic in winter and besieged Pompey's larger forces at their base of Dyrrachium (Durazzo). Forced to retire into Thessaly, Caesar turned and defeated Pompey at the battle of Pharsalus, destroying his army. Pompey fled to Egypt, hoping to rally support, but instead was murdered; the whole Roman world was in Caesar's grasp.

Following Pompey to Egypt, Caesar intervened in a power struggle between Cleopatra and her younger brother. In this, the Alexandrine War, Caesar narrowly escaped death on several occasions, but was successful in placing Cleopatra upon the throne. There followed an intense affair between the young queen and Caesar, and the son born in September, 48, was named Caesarion.

After more campaigns against foreign states in the east and the remnants of Pompey's supporters, Caesar returned to Rome in 46 to celebrate four triumphs: over Gaul, Egypt, Pontus, and Africa. Cleopatra arrived soon after to take up residence in the city; perhaps along with her came the eminent Egyptian astronomer Sosigenes of Alexandria, who aided Caesar in his reform of the calendar. This Julian calendar is the basis of the modern system.

Caesar was active in other areas. He settled many of his veterans in colonies throughout the empire, and with them many of the poor and unemployed of Rome, thus reducing the strain on the public economy. Numerous other civic reforms were instituted, many of them laudable, but most of them giving increased power to Caesar alone. Although he publicly rejected the offer of kingship, he did accept the dictatorship for life in February, 44.

This action brought together a group of about sixty conspirators, led by Gaius Cassius Longinus and Marcus Junius Brutus. Brutus may have been Caesar's son; certainly he was an avowed, almost fanatic devotee of the republic who thought it his duty to kill Caesar.

Realizing that Caesar planned to depart on March 18 for a lengthy campaign against the Parthian Empire in the east, the conspirators decided to strike. On March 15, the ides of March, they attacked Caesar as he entered the Theater of Pompey for a meeting of the senate. As he fell, mortally wounded, his last words are reported to have been either "Et tu, Brute?" (and you too, Brutus?) or, in Greek, "And you too, my child?"

Summary

"Veni, vidi, vinci"—I came, I saw, I conquered—is one of the most famous military dispatches of all time, and totally characteristic of Julius

Caesar. He sent it to Rome after his defeat of King Pharnaces of Pontus in 47, a campaign that added greatly to Rome's eastern power, but which represented almost an interlude between Caesar's victories in Egypt and his final triumph in the civil war. The message captures the essence of Caesar, that almost superhuman mix of energy, ability, and ambition.

This mixture fascinated his contemporaries and has enthralled the world ever since. Caesar was ambitious, but so were others, Pompey among them; he was bold, but many other bold Romans had their schemes come to nothing; he was certainly able, but the Roman world was full of men of ability.

It was Caesar, however, who united all these qualities, and had them in so much fuller measure than his contemporaries that he was unique. As a writer or speaker, he could easily hold his own against acknowledged masters such as Cicero; in statesmanship and politics, he was unsurpassed; in military skill, he had no peer. When all of these qualities were brought together, they amounted to an almost transcendent genius that seemed to give Julius Caesar powers and abilities far beyond those of mortal men.

The central question, in 44 and today, is to what use—good or bad—did Caesar put those qualities and abilities? Clearly, Brutus, Cassius, and the other conspirators believed that he had perverted his qualities and subverted the state and thus must be destroyed. In later years, the term "Caesarism" has been applied to those who wished to gain supreme power for themselves, disregarding the laws and careless of the rights of others. Viewed from this perspective, Caesar destroyed the last remnants of the Roman Republic and thus stamped out what liberty and freedom remained.

From another view, he was the creator, or at least the forerunner, of a new and better system, the empire, which brought order from chaos, peace from endless civil war. The ancient republic had already disappeared in all but name, had become empty form without real substance, and it was for the general good that it finally disappeared. This is the view of Caesar as archetypal ruler and dispenser of order, the view which made his very name a title of monarchs—the Caesars of Rome, the kaisers of Germany, the czars of Russia.

In the end, a sensible view of Caesar must combine a mixture of these two perspectives, seeing both his faults and virtues. He accomplished much during his lifetime, and his achievements have endured for millennia after his assassination. Even in death, Caesar is best described in the words of Shakespeare: "He doth bestride this narrow world like a colossus."

Bibliography

Caesar, Gaius Julius. *Commentaries*. Translated by Rex Warner. New York: New American Library, 1961. Caesar's own version of his conquest of Gaul and struggle in the civil war against Pompey. One of the masterpieces of classical literature, this work gives a vivid and exciting view of truly world-changing events by the major actor of his time. Indispensable for a full understanding of the period.

Fuller, J. F. C. *Julius Caesar: Man, Soldier, and Tyrant.* London: Butler and Tanner, 1965. Written by a distinguished soldier and military theorist, this work concentrates on Caesar's achievements on the battlefield, and why he was such an outstanding and innovative commander. The study, which is generally free of technical obscurities and military jargon, helps the reader understand the difficulties of Caesar's triumphs.

Grant, Michael. *Caesar.* Chicago: Follett Publishing Co., 1975. A well-written, well-researched biography of the man and his time, careful to place Caesar within the context of the fall of the Roman Republic. Caesar's accomplishments become even more impressive when viewed as part of a larger whole, and this Grant does extremely well. The volume is well illustrated.

—————————. *The Roman Emperors: A Biographical Guide to the Rulers of Imperial Rome.* New York: Charles Scribner's Sons, 1985. A brief introductory sketch of Caesar can be found in this volume. Although relatively short, it provides all the necessary information to begin an investigation of the man's life and accomplishments.

—————————. *The Twelve Caesars.* New York: Charles Scribner's Sons, 1975. Grant is one of the outstanding modern historians of ancient Rome, and this book is both a continuation of Suetonius' classical biography and a commentary upon it. Gives the reader a thorough understanding of what Caesar accomplished and an insight into why and how those accomplishments occurred.

Suetonius. *The Lives of the Twelve Caesars.* Edited by Joseph Gavorse. New York: Modern Library, 1959. Suetonius' work is the essential starting point for any study of the early Roman emperors. His biography of Caesar may lack historical rigor and objectivity, but it is a fascinating source of anecdotes and character traits. The content and style (even in translation) makes *The Lives of the Twelve Caesars* a good starting place for the beginning student.

Michael Witkoski

CALLIMACHUS

Born: c. 305 B.C.; Cyrene, Libya
Died: c. 240 B.C.; Alexandria, Egypt
Area of Achievement: Literature
Contribution: Although most of Callimachus' work has been lost, his hymns and epigrams—incorporating drama, sophistication, and a sense of history—survive as masterpieces of their kind. He set an ideal of tone and content which has influenced poets for centuries.

Early Life

The world into which Callimachus was born was a very different one from the world of the great poets and prose writers of fifth century Greece. Alexander the Great's empire had eclipsed and absorbed the old city-states and in turn had been divided into smaller warring empires after his death. Egypt had become the center of a new Greek state ruled by the Greek Ptolemies, and Alexandria had become not only a major political and commercial center and royal capital but also the center of a new and flourishing Greek culture, as rich as the old but somewhat diffident about its ability to live up to the glories of the past. Callimachus himself came from the Greek colony of Cyrene in Libya, a somewhat uneasy vassal of the Ptolemies. Although he was of a distinguished family which claimed Cyrene's founder Battus as an ancestor, it was natural for Callimachus to be drawn to Alexandria, with its promise of literary friends and royal patronage.

Callimachus began as a teacher of grammar in the suburb of Eleusis, but at length he attracted royal notice and received an appointment in the great library, which with the museum, a sort of "university complex" with lecture halls and roofed walks, was the center for the literary and scientific life of the city. Euclid and Archimedes flourished there. Not much is known of Callimachus' duties—only that he never became chief librarian and that he regarded a big book as a big evil—but the list of his lost prose works ("Catalog of Writers Eminent in All Fields of Literature," "Local Names of Months," "Rivers of the World," and so on) suggests an industrious cataloger. Compliments scattered through his work indicate royal patronage throughout his life.

Life's Work

The scanty evidence in his poems suggests that, once secure of royal patronage, Callimachus led a long, agreeable, and productive life in Alexandria. Symposia must have been frequent, although Callimachus prided himself on being a moderate drinker. It might be noted that only one of his erotic poems was written to a woman, and he was almost certainly a bachelor. He valued the didactic poet Aratus for sharing his preference for brevity and craftsmanship. He may have been ambivalent toward Apollonius Rhodius, a former pupil, for attempting a full-scale epic on the Argonauts. He wrote a romantic poem to one Theocritus, who is believed to be the inventor of pastoral poetry.

It is said that Callimachus wrote poems in every meter and that his books amounted to eight hundred (although this sum probably means counting parts of books as individual works). Callimachus sometimes brought together his shorter works under a loose framework—hence his most notable work, the *Aetia* (causes), in which a whole series of local rituals are described and explained, somewhat in the manner of Ovid's *Metamorphoses* (c. A.D. 8), which indeed it influenced.

The *Aetia* shows Callimachus' cataloging zeal, as well as his interest in religious matters and in local affairs. The revised version begins with an apology in the manner of Alexander Pope in which Callimachus satirizes the works of his Rhodian critics, including Apollonius, who bray like donkeys while his own Muse chirps like the cicada. The *Aetia*, which must have been a lengthy collection, included stories of the Graces, Hercules, the Argonauts, Ariadne, and much else. Only two episodes survive in substantial form: the charming love story of Acontius and Cydippe and a court poem which is the remote inspiration of Pope's *The Rape of the Lock* (1712, 1714), *The Lock of Berenice* (Berenice was a real queen and a native of Cyrene).

Callimachus wrote a transitional poem to lead from the *Aetia* into his other great collection, the *Iambi*, a collection of which only tantalizing fragments exist. Written in Greek iambic—a conversational meter used not only for drama but also for fables and lampoons—Callimachus' *Iambi* sounds as much like Pope's *The Dunciad* (1728-1743) as anything else. It included an Aesopian fable about the origin of language, a quarrel between the Laurel and the Olive, a satire on a pederastic schoolmaster, a poem in honor of a victor in the jar race, a serious poem honoring a friend's daughter, and finally an answer to those who criticized Callimachus for failing to specialize. There was another invective poem, the "Ibis," possibly directed at Apollonius, but of this little remains.

The *Aetia* and the *Iambi* were Callimachus' longest poems. He was also a practitioner of the *epyllion*, or little epic, which differed from the full-scale epic not only in length but also in subject matter: The central episode might indeed be heroic, but the emphasis might be on some unheroic character. Thus, in *Hecale* the ostensible subject is Theseus' taming the bull of Marathon, but most of the poem told how Theseus sheltered in the hut of an old peasant woman, Hecale.

Of all Callimachus' works, the least frustrating are the hymns—to Zeus, Apollo, Artemis, Delos, the Bath of Pallas, and Demeter—which are nearly intact. There seems no reason to doubt that these were designed to be performed as part of religious ceremonies and that they embody genuine religious feeling, as well as a feeling for nature and Callimachus' usual curiosity about local customs and traditions. *The Bath of Pallas* and *To Delos* are particularly striking.

Callimachus' epigrams, of which a fair number have survived in anthologies and other sources, including a Roman wall, contain epitaphs, votive dedications, love lyrics, and other miscellaneous short poems. Many seem to be occasional poems written as a favor to friends or patrons and have the limited appeal of occasional poetry, such as the following lament for the poet Heraclitus.

> They told me, Heraclitus, they told me you were dead;
> They brought me bitter news to hear and bitter tears to shed.
> I wept, as I remember'd how often you and I
> Had tired the sun with talking and sent him down the sky.
> And now that thou art lying, my dear old Carian guest,
> A handful of grey ashes, long, long ago at rest,
> Still are thy pleasant voices, thy nightingales, awake,
> For Death, he taketh all away, but them he cannot take.

William Cory's translation, published in 1858, lacks the conciseness which was Callimachus' ideal but is otherwise worthy of the original. Some of the epitaphs have grace and dignity which rise above the immediate occasion:

> Shipwrecked stranger, Leóntikhos found your
> Anonymous corpse and gave you burial
> On the seabeach here. His tears, though, were for
> His own mortality. Restless sailor,
> He beats over the sea like a flashing gull.

Because most of Callimachus' work is lost, his epigrams are prized. With any other poet, these occasional poems would be treated as an appendix rather than a central portion of the lifework. Scholarly editions of Callimachus, however, include dozens of isolated quotations, often mere phrases quoted in a dictionary, for the sake of preserving a rare word from this master.

Summary

Callimachus was a far greater poet than the surviving fragments would indicate; in the Greek and Roman world, which knew his work in its entirety, his prestige was enormous. When a modern scholar pieces together what is left of Callimachus' work, he can conjure up the ghosts of the *Hecale*, the *Aetia*, and the *Iambi*. He can prove how great these poems were and even give something of their flavor, but in the end he can only point to how much of Callimachus' distinguished poetry is lost. (On the other hand, if the prose works had survived, perhaps they would have only a historical interest.)

The hymns are impressive even in translation and would have been even more impressive in their liturgical setting. The epigrams, however, seldom translate well and too often depend on some figure or allusion which must be elaborately footnoted. A reader who knows Greek literature thoroughly and who can work with the available parallel editions (original Greek and English translation on facing pages) has a better chance of enjoying Callimachus; for others, there is still hope. Every so often papyruses containing fragments of Callimachus' work are found in Egypt, and perhaps a less fragmentary manuscript of the *Hecale* or the *Aetia* will surface. If that happens, Callimachus will be read as much as his rival Apollonius.

Bibliography
Callimachus. *Aetia, Iambi, Lyric Poems, Hecale, Minor Epic and Elegiac Poems, and Other Fragments*. Translated by C. A. Trypanis. Cambridge, Mass.: Harvard University Press, 1975. Provides a Greek text, a serviceable prose translation, and excellent notes.
De Romilly, Jaqueline. *A Short History of Greek Literature*. Translated by Lillian Doherty. Chicago: University of Chicago Press, 1985. Includes excellent impressionistic accounts of Callimachus and Apollonius. De Romilly doubts that Callimachus shared the "simple faith" of the Homeric hymns.
Ferguson, John. *Callimachus*. Boston: Twayne Publishers, 1980. A general survey of Callimachus, this work is interesting and thorough. Ferguson pieces together fragments of gossip to make a coherent life of Callimachus, and he includes the fragments of the poems. Callimachus' social and cultural background is treated. Ferguson compares Callimachus with T. S. Eliot. Contains an excellent bibliography.
Fraser, P. M. *Ptolemaic Alexandria*. Oxford: Clarendon Press, 1972. Gives an especially useful account of the library and museum and of Alexandrian scholars and science generally, as well as the commercial and social life of the city. Contains a chapter on Callimachus.
Lane Fox, Robin. "Hellenistic Culture and Literature." In *The Oxford History of the Classical World*, edited by John Boardman, Jasper Griffin, and Oswyn Murray. New York: Oxford University Press, 1986. An excellent survey of the cultural background, with some interesting comments on Callimachus. Includes a good treatment of literary patronage and comparisons to other Hellenistic figures. Lane Fox compares Callimachus with the Wordsworth of the River Duddon sonnets.

John C. Sherwood

GIOVANNI DA PIAN DEL CARPINI

Born: c. 1180; Pian del Carpini (modern Piano della Magione), Umbria
Died: August 1, 1252; Italy, possibly Perugia
Areas of Achievement: Religion, historiography, and exploration
Contribution: Combining a deep commitment to the religious ideals of Francis of Assisi with language and teaching abilities, Carpini extended the work of the Franciscans to Saxony, Germany, northern Europe, Spain, and North Africa. Upon his return from the first formal Christian mission to the Mongols, he wrote an important work on the history of the peoples of Central Asia.

Early Life

Giovanni da Pian del Carpini was born around 1180 in Pian del Carpini (now Piano della Magione), northwest of the Umbrian city of Perugia, which was on the route to Cortona, Italy. In the Umbrian countryside, fields and low hills were often covered in a light haze; the blue sky was reflected in nearby Lake Trasimene. The area was dominated by the ancient city of Perugia, proud and warlike, near the Tiber River. Here passed the famous and the not-so-famous, from emperors to Provençal minstrels, on their way to Rome. Across the Tiber River lay the city of Assisi, an ancient enemy.

The rising middle class in Assisi had ended the domination of the feudal nobility and sent many aristocratic families into exile in 1198. The refuge that Perugia gave these exiles resulted in a battle fought near the Tiber River in November, 1202, in which Assisi was defeated. The contentious spirit of the times was also reflected in disputes among church officials, noblemen, and city officials over property rights and sources of income.

In this unsettled, economically depressed time, young Carpini grew up. It is possible that he took part in the battle against Assisi, or he may have been studying at Bologna. In any case, he would soon have been aware of young Francis of Assisi at Portiuncula. A band of youthful followers had gathered around Francis, attracted by his spirit of simplicity, penance, and prayer. By spring, 1209, the group, now numbering twelve, went to Rome. Pope Innocent III gave his approval to the rule establishing the Order of Friars Minor to preach penance to the people.

Amid the political turbulence of the early thirteenth century, the number of Francis' disciples grew rapidly. One, Brother Giles, was assigned to the small hermitage of San Paola di Favarone outside Perugia between 1215 and 1219. Here he developed a life combining contemplation, meditation, and action. He attended the great spring, 1217, general chapter (conference) at Portiuncula, where great crowds gathered to hear Francis and the Franciscan missions were organized.

Carpini may have become a follower of Francis at this gathering or at the one in the spring of 1219 during which, according to the chronicler Giordino di Giano, ten new members were added to Francis' order. The first extant mention of Carpini notes his 1221 appointment, because of his eloquence and proficiency in Latin, to be part of a mission to Germany under Caesar of Speyer. Carpini was about forty years of age.

Life's Work

The mission to Germany was no easy assignment, for the missionaries sent out in 1219 had been badly treated and those who had gone to Morocco had been martyred. After a rocky start, however, the 1221 mission to Germany fared better. The Franciscans' first center was established in Trent. In October, the brothers met at Augsburg. Carpini and a German friar, Barnaby, were sent as missionaries to Würzburg.

In September, 1223, when Germany was divided into four administrative units, Carpini was placed in charge of Saxony as custos (warden). According to the chronicle of the mission, his preaching was very effective. As warden of Saxony, Carpini preached Franciscan ideals in towns along the Elbe River, at the frontier of European Christianity.

At the chapter gathering on August 12, 1224, at Würzburg, he was assigned to be the provincial's envoy at Cologne. In this post, Carpini was responsible for directing Franciscan activities in Germany. It was he who reported Francis of Assisi's death at Portiuncula in 1226 to the brothers.

At the Pentecostal Chapter at Cologne in 1228, the same year that Francis was canonized by Gregory IX, Carpini was designated provincial (minister) of Germany. The chronicles describe Carpini as being very fat, so fat that he had to ride about on a donkey. This man of courage and talent defended the faith before bishops and princes with a sweet nature and carried out his leadership role in a manner which his contemporaries compared to the way a mother deals with her children or a hen her chicks. He was diligent in extending the Franciscan mission, sending brothers into areas of eastern and northern Europe and establishing a convent at Metz and others in Lorraine.

In 1230, Carpini was appointed Minister of Franciscans in Spain. In 1232, at the general chapter in Rome, he was named Minister of Saxony. In mid-May, 1235, Pope Gregory IX sent a letter to the King of Tunis designating "Giovanni" as the papal ambassador and Franciscan provincial in Barbary. The reference may have been to Carpini. The appointments to Spain and possibly Barbary enabled him to develop some knowledge of Islam and the Arab world. He returned to Germany, was removed on May 15, 1239, by a general chapter, and returned again in 1241, overseeing the province of Cologne during the Mongol invasions of Eastern Europe.

After the Western losses at the Battle of Liegnitz in Silesia near the Oder River on April 9, 1241, Pope Gregory IX preached a crusade to save Poland and end the attacks of the Mongols. Although the struggle between the Pope and rulers of the Holy Roman Empire prevented any such action, fear of the Mongols continued. Further, while the death of the Great Khan Ogadai in December, 1241, together with rivalry among Mongol princes, had the effect of reducing the pressure on Western Europe, Christian Russia became a province of the Mongols. Various plans were made in the West for defense and for establishing contact with the Mongols. In 1245, the new pope, Innocent IV, chose Giovanni da Pian del Carpini to lead a mission to the Mongols. At this time, Carpini was about sixty-five years old and had been serving as penitentiary at the Papal Court.

Carpini left Lyons on Easter Day, April 16, 1245, with Stephen of Bohemia. In their journey across Germany and Eastern Europe, they were aided by church officials and various princes. At Breslau, Benedict the Pole joined the mission. By stages, they made their way to Cracow, where they were provided with beaver skins to present as gifts to the Mongols. At Volhynia, the Russian prince provided them with envoys to conduct them across Lithuanian territory to Kiev, then under Mongol control. The friars were unable, however, to obtain from the Russian rulers promises regarding escorts for their return trip.

Battling illness, Carpini's band continued on their mission, arriving at Kiev, where they exchanged their horses for Mongol ponies. Leaving early in February, 1246, they traveled south on the Dnieper River, reaching the first Mongol outpost on February 23. Here they left the ill Stephen of Bohemia and their servants. Using the Mongol post system and Mongol escorts, they continued down the Dnieper on the ice, then headed east to the Sea of Azov and the Don River, reaching Batu's center at Sarai on the Volga River on April 4. Batu received them, read the Pope's letters (translated by a Russian in the entourage of Prince Alexander Nevsky), and arranged for them to go on to the great council in central Asia for the election and enthroning of the next supreme khan.

The Franciscans left on Easter Monday, April 8, full of uncertainty. Their legs were wrapped in puttees to protect against the friction of riding. Having fasted during Lent, they were weak and had had nothing to drink but snow melted in a kettle. They arrived at the Mongols' imperial summer station, Sira Ordu, on July 22. Since leaving Sarai, Carpini and his band had covered nearly three thousand miles in 106 days. The fact that they had survived such a journey was a marvel in itself.

At the great council, there were three thousand envoys from all the Mongol subject peoples of Russia and China. The friars had little status among the host. By the time they were finally admitted to see the Great Khan Kuyuk (sometimes spelled Guyuk), they had no gifts left to offer and were shunted off to the outskirts of the camp. Only the help of Cosmos, a Russian who was Kuyuk's favorite goldsmith, prevented them from starving. Not until November would the khan receive the friars. This delay, however, gave them the time to talk to other envoys and make the observations of the Mongols that would later be so important to the West. The khan prepared a rather belligerent answer to the Pope's letter, indicating that if the West wanted peace, the Pope, emperors, kings, and all the important men would have to come to him to learn his will.

The friars received the khan's letter on November 13 and were sent on their way four days later. They traveled all winter, often sleeping in the snow, not reaching Sarai until May 9, 1247. Batu gave them safe conduct to Mochi's camp, where they found Stephen of Bohemia and their servants safe. They reached Kiev in late spring and were received with great joy. The Russian princes Daniel and Basil received them at Vladimir and charged them with letters to the Pope acknowledging the supremacy of the Pope and the Roman church. The mission then returned to Western Europe, reaching Cologne late in September. From there they traveled to Liège and Champagne, reporting to the Pope at Lyons on November 18, 1247.

As they traveled through Western Europe, Carpini gave lectures on their experiences based on an incomplete written version of their travels, of which five early manuscripts have survived. These lectures were attended by many who were eager to hear a firsthand account of the feared Mongols. Benedict the Pole also wrote an account of the trip while they were at Cologne.

The Pope was quite pleased with the results of Carpini's mission and kept him at Lyons for about three months. Here Carpini wrote a fuller account, *Historia Mongalorum quos nos Tartaros appellamus*. This version exists in two manuscripts, one at Corpus Christi College, University of Cambridge, and the other at Leyden University Library. Carpini's accounts were the first of the Mongols available to the West.

Early in 1248, the Pope sent Carpini to Louis IX in Paris. The French king was preparing for the Seventh Crusade (1248-1252); the Pope hoped to delay the king's departure, but this mission was unsuccessful. It was probably at this time that the chronicler Vincent of Beauvais, who was frequently at the court of Louis IX, acquired Carpini's manuscript and, with abridgments, included it in the last section of his work. This ensured the survival and distribution of Carpini's work. It was also in France in the spring of 1248 that the historian Salimbene heard a reading of Carpini's work at Sens.

After the mission to France, the Pope appointed Carpini Bishop of Antivari (Bar) in Dalmatia. His jurisdiction was disputed, however, by the Archbishop of Ragusa. After Carpini was ousted, he traveled to Italy to appeal to the Roman Curia and to Innocent IV, who had gone to Perugia. It was here apparently that he died on August 1, 1252, around the age of seventy-two.

Summary

Giovanni da Pian del Carpini's history was the most widely known of the early Western accounts of the Mongols. His information was vital to the West. The short version was published by Richard Hakluyt in his 1598 compilation of travel writings, but the complete version was not published until 1839 by M. A. P. d'Avezac for the Société de Géographie of Paris. Although others such as William of Rubrouck and Marco Polo traveled to the East later in the thirteenth century, Carpini was the first to offer a new understanding of the size of Asia and accurate information on the Mongols. His journey was undertaken after he had spent twenty-five years helping to establish the Franciscan Order in Spain and northern and eastern Europe. The chroniclers refer to him as a fine preacher and a learned man, yet one of great humility. Carpini was a true practitioner of the original ideals of Saint Francis of Assisi.

Bibliography
Beazley, C. Raymond, ed. *The Texts and Versions of John de Plano Carpini and William de Rubruquis, as Printed for the First Time by Hakluyt in 1598 Together with Some Shorter Pieces*. London: Hakluyt Society, 1903. The introduction includes comments on the five existing Carpini manuscripts of the shorter version of his account of the Mongols. His work appears here in both Latin and English. A brief account of the main events in Carpini's life is included in the notes. Index.
Dawson, Christopher, ed. *The Mongol Mission: Narratives and Letters of the Franciscan Missionaries in Mongolia and China in the Thirteenth and Fourteenth Centuries*. New York: Sheed and Ward, 1955. This work, part of the Makers of Christendom series, presents a brief account of the conditions of the thirteenth century and of Western Europeans' interest in the Mongols, followed by accounts of the key Franciscan travels. Helpful bibliography and genealogy tables. Includes translations of the writings of Carpini, several papal bulls, and other letters. Index and map.
Rockhill, William Woodville, ed. and trans. *The Journey of William of Rubruck to the Eastern Parts of the World, 1253-55, with Two Accounts of the Earlier Journey of John of Pian de Carpine*. London: Hakluyt Society, 1900. Reprint. Nedeln, Liechtenstein: Kraus Reprint Limited, 1967. An introduction summarizes the history of the early thirteenth century. There is an extensive bibliography to 1900, a good index, and an excellent route map showing Carpini's and Rubrouck's travels. The translations include explanatory footnotes.
Skelton, R. A., Thomas E. Marston, and George D. Painter. *The Vinland Map and the "Tartar Relation."* New Haven, Conn.: Yale University Press, 1965. This work represents the most complete version and discussion printed to date of Carpini's travels among the Mongols. The *Tartar Relation* manuscript, another account of the history and culture of the Mongols, was apparently finished by a Franciscan friar, C. de Bridia, in 1247,

around the same time that Carpini was recording his observations. This volume contains valuable maps, analyses, notes, an extensive bibliography, and indexes.

Vernadsky, George. *The Mongols and Russia*. New Haven, Conn.: Yale University Press, 1953. This is the third volume in a series on the history of Russia by Vernadsky, who is considered the modern authority on Russia and the Mongols. Includes valuable maps, genealogy charts, a basic bibliography, and index. A report of Carpini's trip appears in the chapter on the reign of Khan Guyuk.

Mary-Emily Miller

CASIMIR THE GREAT

Born: April 30, 1310; Kujawia, Poland
Died: November 5, 1370; Kraków, Poland
Area of Achievement: Government
Contribution: Casimir inherited a reunited Poland and shaped it into a major
  Central European power, which was subsequently nurtured through a bril-
  liant golden age lasting three centuries.

Early Life

Casimir was born on April 30, 1310, the third son, sixth and youngest
child, of Queen Jadwiga and King Władysław I. Stephan, the oldest, had
died in 1306, and Władysław, the second oldest, died in 1312, leaving Casimir
heir to the throne almost from birth. He was destined to become the most
notable, but unfortunately the last, monarch of the ancient Polish royal
dynasty—the Piasts.

As a prince, Casimir received a limited education. His tutors, Archdeacon
Jarosław Bogoria (later Archbishop of Kraków) and Spytko of Melsztyn, the
Castellan of Kraków, instilled in him an appreciation of diplomacy and of the
written law. From his father he learned the military craft, sharing the responsibilities of leadership with the king on numerous campaigns.

The prince's experiential education was further deepened in 1329, when he
was sent on a diplomatic mission to the Hungarian court in search of military
aid for his father's future campaigns. Sometime later, Casimir was made
administrator of Great Poland, plus the districts of Sieradz and Kujawia, ruling through his father's royal authority. The objective here was to strengthen
the frontiers against German encroachment. It is clear that Władysław was
grooming his only surviving son for the kingship.

This practical learning took deep root, and Casimir developed into a
thoughtful long-range planner and very able ruler. Yet at the same time the
future king was a person who believed in enjoying life to the fullest. His personality is best described as jovial, energetic, and highly passionate. One
might imagine that this latter characteristic greatly concerned his mother, a
restrained, pious woman who once a year ate and slept in a nearby convent
dedicated to Saint Clare.

Władysław, hoping to sober the prince's spirits by marriage, arranged his
son's betrothal to Jutta, daughter of John of Luxembourg, in 1322. Such a
union might have reconciled the houses of Piast and Luxembourg as well as
provided Poland with an ally against the Teutonic Order. Unfortunately for
diplomacy, but happily for love, the negotiations collapsed.

Casimir's romantic interests were to be realized in Aldona, a daughter of
Gediminas, Grand Duke of Lithuania. A Polish-Lithuanian alliance was
signed in the fall of 1325 and was sealed with the engagement of Casimir to

Aldona. She was to bring as her dowry not gold or silver but Polish prisoners held in Lithuanian captivity. The future bride was also required to be baptized. (She took the Christian name Anna.) The couple married on October 16 of that year.

Casimir's new wife loved games and dances and was accompanied by handmaidens, drummers, and flutists wherever she went. She enlivened a very restrained court but was not well liked by her contemporaries. In fact, the queen mother tried to prevent Aldona's being crowned alongside Casimir. Failing in the attempt, Jadwiga eventually entered her beloved convent of Saint Clare, where she spent the rest of her life. Yet clearly Aldona had pleased her husband very much, for at her death in 1339 he went into deep mourning and despair.

The coronation took place on the Feast of Saint Mark (April 23, 1333) and was a grand affair. Casimir was royally garbed by the nation's bishops in the palace on Wawel Hill. The nearby cathedral was the scene of his consecration and coronation, along with the installation of his wife as Queen of Poland. Celebrations in the form of dances, tournaments, and general merriment continued unabated for days. At the same time, the young king was provided with an able adviser, his former tutor Spytko of Melsztyn, who served the last Piast well.

Life's Work

Casimir was a more versatile political talent than his father. The coronation set in motion a brilliant reign which prepared the way for the Jagiellons and initiated Poland's golden age. The twentieth century scholar Oskar Halecki suggests three major divisions of Casimir's reign. The first decade was devoted to resolving problems inherited from his father, which necessitated finding at least temporary solutions for the protection of Polish interests. Second, the significance of Casimir's eastward expansion, undertaken to compensate for territorial concessions in the West, was critical, for it set the state's direction for the next five centuries. The final phase of Casimir's reign dealt with economic, constitutional, social, and cultural considerations.

Throughout all of these was the issue of the succession, the importance of which increased as the king entered his later years and the possibility of an heir decreased.

Pressure from the Germans of Bohemia and Brandenburg and the Teutonic Knights of the Cross (or Teutonic Order) was Poland's major problem in the fourteenth century. The order, then at the height of its power, sought outright annexation of Polish territory. John of Luxembourg, King of Bohemia, put forth a claim to the Polish throne and continually referred to Casimir as "King of Kraków." The remaining states supported the Bohemians and the Teutonic Knights of the Cross in promoting German interests to Poland's detriment.

War had been Władysław's answer to German pressure, especially that of the Teutonic Order, but this had proved costly and of limited effect. Casimir, recognizing this, sought to normalize relations with the order. Extensions of an earlier truce gave the Poles a respite in 1334 and again in 1335.

Also in 1335, John of Luxembourg was induced to renounce his claims to Poland in exchange for 400,000 silver groats and Casimir's recognition of John's suzerainty over most of Silesia. John also agreed to act as arbitrator along with the Hungarian king in territorial disputes between Poland and the Teutonic Knights of the Cross. The price was high, but improved relations with Bohemia were worth the cost.

Meanwhile, Poland and the Teutonic Order were trying to reach some understanding concerning the disputed territories. In 1320 an ecclesiastical court convened to hear the claims of the parties, but the ruling, though in Poland's favor, was not enforced. In 1339, Pope Benedict XII appointed two French clerics along with his nuncio to review the issues once again. The court heard testimony in Warsaw from February 4 to September 15. The Teutonic Knights chose not to defend themselves against the charges but to object to the legality of the proceedings, as they had some twenty years earlier. Most of the time the order kept no representation at the hearings, while Polish representatives flooded the transcript with testimony.

More than one hundred witnesses, representing a cross section of Polish society (clergy, nobles, knights, burghers, and commons), presented testimony in response to the judges' questions. Views were expressed on Poland's right to the disputed areas, on the nature of the kingdom's frontiers, and on the destructiveness of the order's repeated invasions. The judges noted whether the witness was literate, his or her age, and other circumstances which might have influenced the person's statements. A remarkable picture of Polish national feeling emerges from these documents. The judges again found in favor of the Crown. All territory was to be returned to Poland, and the Teutonic Knights were ordered to pay a huge indemnity to compensate for their destruction of property. They were also to pay the costs incurred by the Church for the hearing.

Despite the fact that the pope himself believed that the indemnity was too harsh (about twice the annual income of the Polish state) and even though no international enforcement was available, the decision helped move the order to an agreement with Casimir. Public opinion as a result of the 1321 and 1339 decisions could have restricted the flow of western funds and manpower to the Teutonic Knights, while Poland's interests would be best served by relief from western pressure and the cost of war. The Treaty of Kalisz in 1343 was the result. The order kept Chełmno, Michalów, and Pomorze (the bulk of the disputed area), while Casimir received Kujawia and Dobrzyn and a payment of ten thousand florins as an indemnity. The needed peace was finally achieved.

These concessions to German expansion in the west, especially the loss of Pomorze and Silesia, were met with much national resistance. The king was accused by both clergy and nobles of having gone too far; the latter underscored their point with raids into the order's possessions. It was against this background that Casimir began Poland's eastward movement.

Various reasons for this initiative have been offered over the centuries. Jan Długosz, the fifteenth century historian, suggested that wars with the Lithuanians and Ruthenians convinced the king to secure his western frontiers and then to expand the state to the southeast as compensation. In other words, Ruthenia drew him away from Pomorze. Others have since argued that Casimir sought to acquire Ruthenia in order to strengthen his kingdom, planning with the added power to retake these western concessions later.

The opportunity for this eastward move came when the king's cousin, the childless Bolesław, was poisoned to death by his boyars. Bolesław was a Piast prince who through family ties inherited Ruthenia and, in turn, designated Casimir as his heir. Some of this area had been historically Polish but was now peopled by Ruthenians and contested by Lithuanians and Tatars. Casimir sought to gain popular support in this region by respecting local customs and guaranteeing the rights of the Orthodox church. A number of boyars resisted his overtures—even favoring the Tatars over the Poles—while Lubart of Lithuania sought the area for himself and occupied Volhynia. The only Polish ally in these eastern campaigns was Louis I, Casimir's nephew and the son of the deceased Hungarian king, Charles I. After years of seesaw contests with various opponents in the region, Casimir succeeded in controlling twenty-six thousand square miles of Ruthenian territory, thus irrevocably setting Poland's pattern of expansion eastward.

Internal issues occupied the king throughout his reign. One of the most important of these was his intent to create a uniform legal code for the entire country; he managed, however, only to produce separate statutes for Little Poland and Great Poland. In 1347, diets were called to develop a code for each region.

Traditional customary law served as the basis for these efforts but was significantly augmented from Bohemian, Hungarian, and Italian sources. (Naturally, Italy was the home of Roman law and medieval legal studies.) The Church also contributed the influence of canon law. The codification was inspired by a desire to protect all levels of Polish society. This code provided the basis for the evolution of Polish law.

Along with the code Casimir promoted the studies of young Poles abroad. Yet difficulties in traveling the great distances to Italian schools, plus a desire to establish higher education in his country, prompted the king to request a Polish university charter from Pope Urban V. Conditions conducive to establishing such a center in Poland were now present. Political stability and economic prosperity had been achieved, many contacts with the West had been established, and the country had built a number of lesser schools, which provided the necessary intellectual climate. The Papacy saw this foundation as a base from which Catholicism might spread eastward in the wake of Polish expansion.

May 12, 1364, is the traditional date associated with the University of Kraków's foundation. The charter provided for the establishment of one chair in liberal arts, two in medicine, three in canon law, and five in Roman law. Clearly, the king's intent was the development of legal studies as paramount, probably to train civil servants for his growing administrative needs. Funds for maintaining the institution came from the royal salt monopoly at nearby Wieliczka. Control of the school was given to the Crown Chancellor, rather than to the local bishop as was customary in many foundations. The city of Kraków granted privileges to the university's staff and their families on the same day. Unfortunately, many matters regarding the school's early years are not known. Scholars do not know its first location and know little about its faculty, its student body, and, most frustrating of all, why it apparently collapsed and had to be resurrected by the first Jagiellon ruler of Poland in 1400.

On September 9, 1370, during a hunt for stags, Casimir's horse fell, and the king suffered abrasions to his left shin. Soon he was beset with a fever, which appeared intermittently for varying periods of time. By October 30, the king appeared to be in the terminal phase of his illness. He died, probably of pneumonia, about sunrise on November 5, 1370. So ended Poland's medieval dynasty.

Summary

Poland in this period was embarking on a three-century-long odyssey, a golden age. Scholarship, art, culture, and military and economic power were all components of this creative explosion that began with the reign of Casimir the Great.

One has only to travel the modern highways and byways of Casimir's medieval kingdom to appreciate the grand scale of his construction efforts. Impregnable castles and fortified towns protected the kingdom from the Teutonic Knights in Pomorze. This line then continued along the Polish-Silesian frontier, providing the same strength to Kraków. To the southeast, three other defensive systems aimed at preventing incursions from Ruthenia and helped to anchor Polish power there. To this day, it would be unusual to pass through a community of any size in this area that does not boast a church, monastery, or municipal edifice funded by the king.

Along with encouraging the economic growth and physical expansion of the towns, Casimir involved burghers and the lower gentry in national life. His promotion of members of these social classes to important administrative posts won for him their devotion. In a successful effort to weaken regionalism, he sent gentry administrators from Great Poland to Little Poland and vice versa, thus creating new ties within various provinces.

Casimir has often been referred to as "King of the Peasants." He defended them from abuses and famine, establishing state granaries for the latter purpose. He was rewarded with their devotion. Often, country folk and the poor would clog the roadway to Wawel Hill before dawn to bring the king simple gifts, tokens of their affection. He was also viewed as a protector of the Jews who fled to Poland, especially from Germany, in large numbers during his reign. Casimir twice reconfirmed the Charter of Privileges granted Jews by Bolesław the Chaste in 1264. The Eastern Orthodox in Ruthenia were also protected, and the king sought the establishment of the first metropolitan in their major city of Halicz.

Casimir's greatest failure lay in not providing for an heir to continue the Piast Dynasty. He had several daughters and three sons from various unions, but none of the latter had legal claim to paternity. As a result, the succession to the Polish throne passed to Louis of Hungary. The choice reflected the close relationship which existed between Poles and Hungarians in this period as well as the friendship and affection of Casimir for Charles I, Louis' father. Formal agreements between the two states assured the outcome. (The last agreement was signed at Buda in 1355.) On this basis, the crown of the Piasts passed to the Hungarian royal house when Casimir died.

Casimir is the only Polish monarch to have been granted the title "The Great" by his countrymen. His calls for peace over war, diplomacy over confrontation, and stability over uncertainty justify the appellation. He was a soother of the national spirit and a builder of the national wealth. He husbanded the country's resources and nurtured the Polish intellect. Most important, he protected his people.

Bibliography

Davies, Norman. *God's Playground: A History of Poland*. Vol. 1, *The Origins to 1795*. New York: Columbia University Press, 1982. Contains an excellent chapter dealing with Władysław I and Casimir.

Halecki, Oskar. *A History of Poland*. New York: Roy Publishers, 1943. Includes a comprehensive chapter on Casimir's statecraft.

Knoll, Paul W. "Casimir the Great and the University of Cracow." *Jahrbücher für Geschichte Osteuropas*, N.s. 16 (June, 1968): 232-249. Discusses the foundation of the university and Casimir's involvement in the process.

──────────. *The Rise of the Polish Monarchy: Piast Poland in East Central Europe, 1320-1370*. Chicago: University of Chicago Press, 1972. A detailed study of the development of Poland from reunification to major power under the last Piasts.

Reddaway, W. F., et al., eds. *The Cambridge History of Poland*. Vol. 1, *From the Origins to Sobieski (to 1696)*. New York: Octagon Books, 1971. Contains a chapter which deals with Casimir's wide-ranging achievements.

Vetulani, Adam. "The Jews in Medieval Poland." *Jewish Journal of Sociology* 4 (1962): 274-294. A discussion of the Jewish medieval experience in Poland, including the period of Casimir's reign. Written by one of Poland's premier legal historians.

Richard J. Kubiak

CASSIODORUS

Born: c. 490; Scyllacium, Calabria, Italy
Died: c. 585; Vivarium, Calabria, Italy
Areas of Achievement: Government, historiography, and monasticism
Contribution: Cassiodorus lived during the transition period between the late
   Roman Empire and the early Middle Ages; he aided in the cultural synthe-
   sis of Germanic, Greco-Roman, and Christian cultures. Most important,
   he was a key conservator of ancient manuscripts for later generations.

Early Life

When the Roman Empire collapsed and fell to invading Goths, Ostrogoths, and Vandals, the Germanic tribes dealt with the Romans in contrasting ways. Vandals in North Africa treated Romans as conquered subjects
and sought to destroy their culture. The Ostrogoths in Rome were quite different: Recognizing the value of the existing Greco-Roman culture, they attempted to build on that culture and assimilate what they considered worthwhile. Many had already accepted Arian Christianity and were drawn to the
education and the arts of the classical world. To that end, they hired cultured, well-educated Romans to serve in their courts and to preserve the culture of the Roman world. One of the officials who were used in that capacity
by Theodoric the Great, King of the Ostrogoths, was Flavius Magnus Aurelius Cassiodorus.

Cassiodorus was born about 490 on a luxurious estate on the south coast of
the Ionian Sea, near the modern Gulf of Squillace. The temperate climate
produced grapes, grains, and olives. Cassiodorus' grandfather was a Roman
general and his father was a wealthy, aristocratic diplomat, esteemed by the
king, who was in charge of the imperial lands and, later, of the royal treasury.
He was also the governor of Sicily and of Calabria. His family was noted for
its honesty and integrity in public service.

Cassiodorus benefited from an excellent classical education and entered
public office in the service of the Ostrogothic rulers. He was schooled in
Latin and Greek literature and, typical for aristocratic students, in rhetoric.
This educational foundation helped to develop Cassiodorus' literary gifts; he
became one of the most distinguished writers of the period.

Cassiodorus was reared a good Catholic, and he remained orthodox all of
his life. It is most interesting that he and Theodoric were able to produce a
cultural synthesis of Roman, Greek, and Gothic elements. Indeed, one of
Cassiodorus' principal works was *History of the Goths* (519), which is no
longer extant. Theodoric's Arianism did not cause undue tension with Cassiodorus' orthodox Catholic faith. Each man respected the other and both
wished to see a coexistence between clashing cultures. Theodoric achieved a
working relationship between Romans and Goths. He emulated much of the

Roman political system, retaining the offices and titles of imperial Rome. The architecture and furnishings of his palace resembled Constantinople. The army was made up of Goths while the civil government was largely composed of Romans. Cassiodorus was a key government administrator.

Life's Work

Cassiodorus served as his father's *consiliarius*, a legal assistant, and Theodoric appointed him, at the age of twenty, a quaestor, the king's private secretary and legal adviser in the preparation of administrative law. Later, Theodoric made him a consul and in 527 a magister-officiorum, giving him responsibility for polishing the writings and speeches of the quaestors. Cassiodorus' literary ability was obvious: He worded many public documents and was a confidant of the king. King Athalaric, Theodoric's grandson, appointed Cassiodorus praetorian prefect for Italy, in effect making him prime minister of the Ostrogothic civil government from 533 to 538. Cassiodorus supervised the collection of taxes and the administration of justice. Vicars, provincial governors, proconsuls, all were subordinate to him.

He ended his public career when the Byzantine Emperor Justinian I defeated the Goths in 551 and expanded westward into Italy. After fifteen years in Constantinople, Cassiodorus returned to his family's estates overlooking the Ionian Sea; in retirement, he began a second career almost as long and productive as his civil service.

Cassiodorus was sixty-five years old when he established two monasteries on his estates at Vivarium (meaning "fish pond," named after his landscaped gardens). He was primarily interested in an intellectual, peaceful monastic life, but he also sought to refresh travelers and provide for the poor from his irrigated gardens. He channeled the river Pellena into his fish ponds and used the power of the river to turn the monasteries' mills. Fresh water was abundant in this earthly paradise within sight and sound of the Mediterranean Sea.

For nearly thirty years, Cassiodorus collected a large library, supervising the preservation and copying of invaluable ancient manuscripts. His monks copied and studied the Bible, works of the church fathers, and ancient Greek and Latin classics. Cassiodorus also prepared a guide for monastic education, which was used for many generations, sought refined learning under the authority of Scripture and church tradition, and prepared a bibliography of studies on all the sections of the Bible. In his detailed instructions for accurate transcription of texts in the scriptorium, he allowed slight stylistic emendation of texts, with the exception of the text of Scripture, where particular care was made to compare the ancient copies. Cassiodorus continued writing and working into his ninety-third year; he died, at the age of ninety-five, on the peaceful estate where he had dedicated many years to preserving ancient manuscripts and to studying and teaching theology.

Summary

Cassiodorus inspired scholarly pursuits in other monasteries as well as his own. His example helped enormously in the preservation of ancient manuscripts and in creating copies of works from the classical world and from the early Christian centuries. His own writings, too, greatly enhanced historical knowledge of his own era. For example, *Variae* (537), a work in twelve volumes collected during his years in public office, contains voluminous letters, proclamations, official appointments, edicts, records of judicial decisions, and administrative orders of the Ostrogothic kingdoms. It is an invaluable source of information concerning all aspects of life in that period of history: economic, cultural, political, and diplomatic. *History of the Goths* is adulatory and one-sided, but it, too, provides detailed information concerning the Goths and their perspective of their struggle and coexistence with the Romans.

Modern knowledge of church history would be much sparser without his twelve-volume *Historia ecclesiastica tripartita* (c. 540-559), which became the principal source used in the Middle Ages for the history it covered, while *De orthographia* (c. 583) was designed to systematize the rules for copying manuscripts. The carefulness with which the monks of the Middle Ages copied and preserved ancient manuscripts has been an indispensable link for modern knowledge of the ancient and medieval worlds.

In addition to these historical efforts, Cassiodorus designed a complete book of instruction for the Western monastaries. *Institutiones divinarum et humanarum lectionum* (562), or, simply, *Institutiones*, includes a catalog of the books contained in the library at Vivarium. His division of scholarship into categories was followed throughout the Middle Ages: grammar, rhetoric, dialectic, arithmetic, music, geometry, and astronomy. Finally, Cassiodorus' *Expositio Psalmorum* (c. 540-548; *Commentary on the Psalms*) was one of his most famous expositions of Scripture and devotional works, of which he wrote many.

Cassiodorus is only a small part of the larger story in which he was a participant, but he was particularly significant historically. He played a key role in the transition from the Roman Empire to the early Middle Ages and helped to synthesize the Gothic-Greco-Roman-Christian culture that was emerging. He was a good steward for the Gothic kings but was faithful to his culture, his church, and his God also. He helped perpetuate his love of learning and organized the European monastic educational system. He organized, sorted, and classified scholarly materials which became essential tools of medieval Scholasticism. Above all, he was an essential conservator of the literary treasures of antiquity and the early Church for future generations.

Bibliography
Burns, Thomas S. *A History of the Ostrogoths*. Bloomington: Indiana Uni-

versity Press, 1984. To understand the historical importance of Cassiodorus, one needs to have a knowledge of the Ostrogoths he served. This book portrays their culture and values as well as their history. It describes the synthesis of two cultures: Germanic and Roman.

Daniel-Rops, Henry. *The Church in the Dark Ages*. Translated by Andrey Butler. London: J. M. Dent and Sons, 1959. In the conflicts involving the Germanic tribes and the fall of the Western Roman Empire, the institution that provided stability and social cohesion was the Church. This book describes in detail that troublesome period and its meaning for later days. The involvement of the Byzantine Empire in the West and its complicated system of government are also considered. One of the most intriguing elements is the conversion of the "barbarian hordes" to Christianity.

Guatkin, H. M., and J. P. Whitney, eds. *The Cambridge Medieval History*. Vol. 1, *The Christian Roman Empire and the Foundation of the Teutonic Kingdom*. New York: Macmillan, 1911. This history is still the standard work on the period. Volume 1 gives the cultural and historical setting in exhaustive detail. Noted for its accuracy and careful attention to detail.

Latourette, Kenneth Scott. *A History of Christianity*. New York: Harper and Row, Publishers, 1953. A standard and lengthy church history which includes charts and maps and is clearly outlined. Valuable for understanding the historical setting of the world in which Cassiodorus lived. Particularly valuable for seeing the role of the Byzantine Empire in that world, and its relationship to the Western Church.

O'Donnell, James J. *Cassiodorus*. Berkeley: University of California Press, 1979. The most important recent study of Cassiodorus, it analyzes the books he wrote, his career in the service of the Ostrogoths, and his establishment of and life in the monasteries of Vivarium. An unusual feature of this book is the author's explanation of his sources and the procedures used in their critical analysis.

Sinnigen, William G., and Arthur E. R. Boak. *A History of Rome to* A.D. *565*. 6th ed. New York: Macmillan, 1977. Burns's book (above) views the cultural, military, and political conflicts surrounding Cassiodorus from the perspective of the Ostrogoths; this book does the same from the Roman standpoint, explaining how the later Roman Empire changed in system and culture and how it came to terms with the occupying Germanic peoples. An important reference work for any serious student of the period. Includes maps, charts, and illustrations.

William H. Burnside

SAINT CATHERINE OF SIENA
Caterina Benincasa

Born: March 25, 1347; Siena, Italy
Died: April 29, 1380; Rome, Italy
Areas of Achievement: Religion and politics
Contribution: This patron saint of Italy and Doctor of the Church helped to persuade the Avignon papacy to return to Rome. She is also known for her mystic writings, which advocate a combination of personal ecstatic experience with active service in the world.

Early Life

Caterina Benincasa was born in Siena, Italy, the twenty-third child of Giacomo Benincasa, a cloth dyer, and his wife, Lapa Piacenti. Lapa was more than forty years old when Catherine and her twin sister, Giovanna, were born and did not believe that she could nurse both infants. She sent Giovanna to a wet nurse and nurtured Catherine herself. In her old age, Lapa remembered Catherine as a specially favored child, nursed by her mother for a full year and brought to robust health, while her less fortunate twin died. Catherine remained attached to her family throughout her life, and images of nurturing pervade her writings.

The young Catherine was also influenced by Sienese life in the mid-fourteenth century. When she was a year old, the Black Death (bubonic plague) swept through the city, beginning a series of epidemics that brought death and panic. The Benincasa family was not prosperous enough to leave the city; Catherine lost a number of siblings and spent her early years surrounded by the fear of death and of God's punishment.

Catherine also heard of momentous happenings in the larger Christian world. The Dominican monks who preached in Siena told of the popes who lived in Avignon, France, instead of in Rome. She also heard of the Christian hope for a crusade that would once and for all free the Holy Land from the Muslims who held it. These events and expectations influenced the causes that she championed later in her life.

Catherine was drawn early to the religious life. At the age of six or seven, she had her first vision of Christ smiling at her. Between the ages of seven and twelve, she continued to grow spiritually, secretly making a vow of chastity and attempting to recapture the sweet vision that had so moved her.

When Catherine reached adolescence, her family wanted to find for her a good husband. For a while, Catherine accepted this role, but when she was fifteen, her favorite older sister died in childbirth. From that time on, Catherine actively rejected the world and began the strict self-denial that marked her life. She slept little, bound an iron chain tightly about her hips, and whipped herself daily. She consumed only bread, water, and raw vegetables, and a few years later she gave up the bread and ate almost nothing at all. She wanted to conquer all fleshly desires and leave room only for the spiritual life.

By the time she was sixteen, all these activities had persuaded her family that she was serious about her calling, and she joined the Dominican order in the congregation of the Sisters of Penance. This order of nuns did not stay in a convent, so Catherine continued to live at home with her family. From 1364 to 1367, she lived in isolation, praying and having ecstatic religious experiences in which she felt that Christ was one with her in a form of spiritual marriage. These experiences would continue throughout her life. In 1370, Catherine received the command to go into the world to do God's work.

Life's Work

Catherine began her work of serving God in Siena. She cared for the poor, giving away all of her possessions and many of her family's goods. She also patiently cared for the sick. During this time of activity, she continued to abuse her body to overcome the flesh, and these austerities took their toll on her health. She was strikingly thin and often had to take to her bed, exhausted by her fasting and the ecstatic experiences that made her seem to be in a trance.

In these early years of activity, Catherine began to acquire a following. She became the spiritual mother of a group of disciples that surrounded her until her death. At this time, she also acquired critics, who did not believe that she did not eat or that her religious trances were real. She became well-known, and her influence began to extend from caretaking to political action.

The Christian world was experiencing exciting political developments in 1370. In that year, Pope Urban V abandoned the city of Rome, to which he had returned briefly, to take the papacy back to southern France. In the following year, the new pope, Gregory XI, called a crusade. Throughout 1372, Catherine was an eager supporter of that crusade. She urged people to give money and other support to the venture. The crusade never materialized, but Catherine increased her reputation as advocate of the Church's causes.

In 1374, Catherine was summoned to Florence to testify before the Dominican order. Church officials wanted to see if this young woman who was acquiring such a reputation for sanctity was in fact a servant of God. After questioning her, the officials agreed that she was indeed holy, but to be sure that she would remain so, they assigned Raymond of Capua to be her companion and confessor. Raymond stayed with Catherine throughout her life and wrote her biography. The Dominican officials were as concerned about the correctness of Catherine's perpetual fast as some of her neighbors had been, and they ordered her to eat. To demonstrate her obedience to church authority, she obeyed the order to eat, but suffered severely from the food in her stomach until she forced herself to vomit. By her obedience in trying to eat, Catherine earned permission to continue her fasting.

In 1374, Catherine's political activity began to increase. Although she had never learned to read and write, she dictated letters to Italy's political figures, urging them not to take part in Florence's war on the papacy that had been declared in 1375. She traveled to Pisa to try to dissuade other Italian cities from joining the antipapal league. She even wrote to the famous mercenary soldier, John Hawkwood, to urge him to Christian behavior. She believed that many of these internal Italian wars were increased by the Pope's continued absence in France, and she took up the cause of persuading him to return to Rome.

These political activities did not interfere with her spiritual growth. She continued her religious trances, and in 1375, she received the stigmata, the piercing of her hands and feet as Christ had been pierced. This mark of union with Christ was a high honor, but Catherine was so modest that she asked God to keep the marks invisible. (Most who received the stigmata bled from their hands and feet.) Needless to say, there was controversy for centuries about whether Catherine had received the marks, since there was no visible evidence for it. (In 1630, Pope Urban VIII pronounced her stigmata authentic, and since then, it has been accepted by the Church as fact.)

In 1376, Catherine traveled to Avignon to talk to the Pope. She urged him to reform the Church, and as a critical part of that reform, she wanted him to return to Rome. In September, 1376, Catherine's dream was fulfilled and Pope Gregory XI left Avignon to return to Rome, where he would be plagued by political problems until his death in March, 1378. Catherine's part in influencing the Pope's return is remembered as her major political accomplishment, although historians have since downplayed her role in the papal move, emphasizing the unrest and violence in France at the time as a more prominent reason for the Pope's decision.

Catherine returned to Italy, where between 1377 and 1378 she composed her great mystical work, which she simply called "Book" but which has come to be known as *Il dialogo della Divina Provvidenza* (dialogue of Divine Providence, or *The Dialogue*). In this work, she articulated more fully the mystical theology of love and service that was evident in her many letters. Catherine must have believed that her major life's work was accomplished; she had written her mystic vision and she had brought the Pope back to his rightful home in Rome. Yet political events were once more to draw her into the secular world.

After Gregory XI's death in 1378, the papacy underwent a crisis even more serious than the Pope's residence in France. Urban VI was elected to be Gregory's successor, but in September of 1378, thirteen disaffected cardinals returned to Avignon and elected Clement VII to be pope. The Church was now split into two factions. The Great Schism would last until 1415, when the Council of Constance was able again to reunite the Catholic world under one head. Catherine rallied to the support of Urban VI, whom she considered to be the rightful pope. She dictated letters to cardinals and kings, rebuking them for their betrayal of the unity and reform she had advocated. She moved to Rome to support Urban VI with her advice and prayers. Political events, however, had gone beyond that which she could change. In January, 1380, she turned to the only thing that she could control—her body. She increased her fast by refusing to drink even water. She would be a final sacrifice to save the Church. Her last months were plagued by pain and visions of demons, and on April 29, 1380, Catherine died with a final vision of the weight of the ship of the Church (that she had worked so hard to save) descending onto her shoulders.

Summary

In 1395, Catherine's confessor, Raymond of Capua, completed his *Legenda major* (*The Life of Catherine of Siena*, 1960). He wrote the long biography based on interviews with Catherine's mother and other followers. This biography was widely read and copied. In 1477, an Italian translation was made of Raymond's Latin text, and this became one of the first printed books. Catherine's life was a model for others who wanted to serve the Church through a life of self-sacrifice and mystic longing. Her influence also extended beyond the example of her life. In 1461, she was declared a saint by Pope Pius II, and she is considered, with Saint Francis of Assisi, as a patron saint of Italy.

Catherine's influence has been recognized into the twentieth century. In 1970, Pope Paul VI declared Catherine to be a Doctor of the Church. She and Saint Teresa of Ávila are the only women who have been granted this status. By bestowing the title Doctor on Catherine, the Pope declared that Catherine's writings are worthy to be studied by all Catholics.

There were several reasons that the Pope found Catherine's writings worthwhile. The first was that her mysticism, her religious ecstasies, did not cause her to retire from the world. On the contrary, Catherine believed that her mystic connection with Christ required that she work actively to help her neighbors, her church, and her world.

A second important theme in her works was that there could be no Christian life outside the hierarchic structure of the Catholic church. She believed that the blood of Christ flowed through the Church, so no one should be separate from that structure even if they had, like she, been joined mystically to Christ. This made her work actively to support the Church and the Papacy. This effort was particularly important during the late fourteenth century, when the hierarchic church was troubled by so many tensions and political problems. Hers was a voice that reminded the Church that its task was a spiritual one and reminded believers of their intimate relationship to that church.

Finally, Pope Paul VI declared her spirit of self-sacrifice to be worthy of awe. It is perhaps for this spirit that Catherine remains best known. The pious child who starved herself and abused her body to rebel against her parents' desire that she marry and to rebel against her own desires for physical comfort later continued those sacrifices to join spiritually with Christ and to serve the Church. At the end, she starved herself in a final sacrifice, attempting to save the Church she had worked all of her short life to reform.

Bibliography

Bell, Rudolph M. *Holy Anorexia*. Chicago: University of Chicago Press, 1985. Contains a well-written chapter on Catherine, which focuses on her early life and provides a psychological analysis of her asceticism, particularly her self-starvation. The book draws parallels between these austerities and those of twentieth century anorexic women. The thesis is thought-provoking, and the insights provided on Catherine's early life are invaluable. The notes are complete and lead the reader to the primary and secondary sources (particularly the Italian ones) available on the subject.

Catherine of Siena, Saint. *The Dialogue: Catherine of Siena*. Translated by Suzanne Noffke. New York: Paulist Press, 1980. Noffke provides a much-needed English translation of Catherine's famous mystic treatise. In addition, the introduction gives a short summary of the Saint's life and thought and describes the structure of *The Dialogue*. This is not for the casual reader, but indispensable for those who seek a full understanding of Catherine's theology. Contains a complete bibliography and index.

_____. *I, Catherine: Selected Writings of St. Catherine of Siena*. Edited by K. Foster and M. J. Ronayne. London: Collins, 1980. This work presents a good, accessible translation of sixty of Catherine's letters and a portion of *The Dialogue*. The letters are grouped approximately chronologically, which is helpful in understanding her development. The introduction is useful in explaining the main elements of Catherine's thought. Contains a short index and bibliography.

_____. *Saint Catherine of Siena as Seen in Her Letters*. Edited and translated by Vida D. Scudder. New York: E. P. Dutton and Co., 1927. Presents a translation of a selection from Catherine's letters. The selection is well chosen to include samples of her correspondence to her followers, to kings and queens, and to popes. The book contains a useful introduction to Catherine's life and particularly helpful chronological tables of the main events both of Catherine's life and of contemporary public events.

Giordani, Igino. *Saint Catherine of Siena*. Translated by Thomas J. Tobin. Boston: St. Paul Editions, 1975. Preserves the structure of a biography, but is primarily interested in discussing Catherine's theology. Too often, mystic rhetoric intrudes into the text, distracting the reader from the narrative. Lacks bibliography and index, but does provide twenty-six photographs of artwork depicting Catherine and sites where she lived and worked.

Levasti, Arrigo. *My Servant Catherine*. Translated by Dorothy M. White. Westminster, Md.: Newman Press, 1954. An excellent biography that incorporates a clear description of the political events which shaped Catherine's actions. This awareness of historical setting is missing in many of the other biographies. This work contains a fine bibliography and a few illustrations of artists' portrayals of Catherine.

Perrin, Joseph Marie. *Catherine of Siena*. Translated by Paul Barrett. Westminster, Md.: Newman Press, 1965. Not a biography, but rather an exposition of Catherine's thought. It draws heavily from her writings to discuss her views on such matters as apostolic sanctity, divine love, the sacraments, defeat of the flesh, and the reform of the Church. It is useful for those interested in theology and the mystic life, but it is not for the casual reader. It provides an index, but no bibliography.

Raymond of Capua. *The Life of Catherine of Siena*. Translated by Conleth Kearns. Wilmington, Del.: Michael Glazier, 1980. Provides a translation of the *Legenda major*, which was completed in 1395 by her friend and confessor and forms the basis for all subsequent biographies. The introduction gives a good background of the life of Raymond and serves to complement the life of Catherine presented in this accessible translation. Unfortunately, this edition has no bibliography or index.

Undset, Sigrid. *Catherine of Siena*. Translated by Kate Austin-Lund. New York: Sheed and Ward, 1954. This Nobel Prize-winning novelist has written a sensitive and compassionate account of Catherine's life. The work reads like a historical novel, but it accurately follows Raymond of Capua's account. Undset is able to capture the spirituality that moved Catherine. There are no notes, bibliography, or index, so the work is not particularly useful for scholars.

Joyce E. Salisbury

CATO THE CENSOR

Born: 234 B.C.; Tusculum, Italy
Died: 149 B.C.; Rome, Italy
Area of Achievement: Government
Contribution: Through his personal example, public service, and writings, Cato advocated an ideal of a powerful, prosperous state populated with self-reliant, active citizens.

Early Life

Marcus Porcius Cato was born in Tusculum, about fifteen miles from Rome. Little is known about his family, except that his father, Marcus, and great-grandfather Cato were well-respected soldiers. The name Cato, meaning "accomplished," was given to a *novus homo* (new man) who came to public attention by his own achievements rather than by connection to a distinguished family. Young Cato spent his youth on an estate in the Sabine territory, where he learned farming, viticulture, and other agricultural skills.

When Cato was seventeen, the Carthaginian general Hannibal invaded Italy and defeated several Roman armies, inflicting huge losses (more than fifty thousand Romans died at the Battle of Cannae in 216 B.C.). Cato enlisted soon after Cannae and served with distinction for more than a decade. He fought in major battles in Sicily and Italy, including the siege of Syracuse and the defeat of Hasdrubal (Hannibal's brother) at Metaurus in 207. By the time Hannibal fled Italy and Carthage surrendered, around 201, Cato's personality and career had been shaped. He had proved heroic and fearless in combat. He carried an implacable hatred for Carthage. He displayed leadership, being elected a military tribune responsible for the soldiers' welfare in and out of battle.

Cato now entered public life and held a series of elective offices. In 204 he became quaestor, the official charged with watching over public expenditures. In this capacity he accompanied the army of Scipio Africanus in its attack on Carthaginian soil. In 199 Cato became a plebeian aedile, one who administered public buildings, streets, temples, and the marketplace. A year later, Cato was one of four praetors chosen; praetor was a more significant post that included the power to dispense justice and to command an army. Cato spent his praetorship as Governor of Sardinia, where he gained a reputation for honest and frugal administration.

Important patrons as well as ordinary voters were attracted to Cato and readily supported his advancing career. The Greek historian Plutarch described Cato at this time as a man with ruddy complexion, gray eyes, and unusual public speaking skills. Cato's quick mind—his knack for striking analogies and turns of phrase—and fearless attitude made him a successful orator, valued as an ally and feared as an opponent.

Life's Work

Cato's election as consul in 195 began a period of forty-six years during which he exerted significant influence in both domestic politics and foreign affairs. Cato's leadership coincided with a period of profound change in Roman manners at home and in Roman policies toward other world powers. By the time of Cato's death, Rome had defeated its imperial rivals, conquering Greece and Macedonia and destroying Carthage, burning the city to the ground. Military and political supremacy brought Rome economic supremacy, and great wealth poured into a country where simplicity and austerity were traditional. Wealth became the basis of a leisured culture that looked to Greece for social values—a culture more intellectual, aesthetic, and self-indulgent than the Roman heritage. None of these changes occurred quickly or without dispute. Cato participated in the major controversies of the era. Could Rome dominate other nations without exploiting them? Could Romans maintain a work ethic amid unprecedented luxury? Would Greek attitudes supplant Roman ones?

Cato served as one of the two consuls appointed annually. Consuls were the senior Roman magistrates who executed the senate's will in political and military affairs. Soon after he took office, Cato went to Spain to lead the effort to subdue several tribes in rebellion since 197. Drilling inexperienced troops rigorously, Cato prepared them so effectively that they routed a veteran Spanish force at Emporiae. Cato showed mercy to the survivors and successfully induced other rebel groups and cities to surrender. Upon his return to a triumph in Rome, Cato boasted that he had captured more towns than he had spent days in Spain. Soon afterward he married a senator's daughter, a sign that a *novus homo* was now acceptable to the aristocracy.

Four years later, Cato went to Greece as military tribune with the army advancing against Antiochus, Rome's chief threat in Greece and Hannibal's protector. The army's march was blocked at the pass of Thermopylae (where three centuries before Spartan troops had held off invading Persians) until Cato led a cohort over rocks and crags to take the enemy rearguard by surprise. Cato claimed as much credit as Glabrio, the Roman commander, for the successful campaign. For years afterward, the two were political rivals.

In 189, Cato ran for the office of censor but was defeated. A censor ranked just below consul: He oversaw public morals, carried out the census, selected new members for the senate, expelled unfit senators, and conducted religious services. Previously, Cato had involved himself in important public debates about morality and ethics, such as the controversies surrounding the Oppian Law and the Junian Law. In the first, Cato argued for continuing a ban on ostentatious displays of wealth; in the second, he opposed repealing interest-rate limits. Already he was known as a champion of austerity and self-discipline in financial matters, both for the individual and for the state.

At the next election for censor in 184, Cato triumphed. Immediately he implemented the stern, rigorous platform on which he had campaigned. Though his program involved him in lawsuits for years to come, his supporters regarded his censorship as a landmark effort to reverse a perceived laxness in public standards. Cato and his cocensor expelled seven senators for unfitness, imposed a heavy tax on luxury goods, demolished private buildings encroaching on government property, fined those who neglected farms or vineyards, and renegotiated state contracts with private suppliers to reach better deals. Though contemporaries stressed the stringency of his actions, it is important to note that he executed his duties meticulously; he was careful to respect the letter as well as the spirit of the laws. For Cato, the primary goal was to see Rome thrive and prosper. Unlike many aristocratic Romans, Cato believed that public prosperity did not result from exploiting individuals—and he also believed that individuals ought not to thrive at public expense.

Certain individuals resented Cato's stern censorship and became enemies. Before his death he fought at least forty-four indictments and suits filed against him; none is recorded as successful. Each accusation became an occasion for Cato to display his well-honed oratorical skills, thereby leaving a rich rhetorical legacy for later generations. Cato took the unusual and self-confident step of publishing his speeches.

Though never elected censor again, Cato used his position in the senate to defend high standards and accountability for public officials. He prosecuted a provincial governor in 171 for manipulating corn prices; twenty years later, while in his eighties, Cato spoke against a special envoy and another governor who used their posts for profit. In 169, Cato led the supporters of the Voconian Law to keep inheritances concentrated rather than wastefully fragmented. In the same year, he argued against a triumph for a general whose troops complained of cruel treatment. In 153, Cato supported a proposal to prevent a consul from serving a second term, lest a man find public office too profitable to do without.

Cato exercised leadership in the senate through his oratory and among the educated class through his writings. Some scholars call Cato the father of Latin prose literature because of the volume and influence of his writing. The major works, which exist only in fragments (except for the treatise on agriculture), are *Ad filium*, a compendium of precepts on practical issues written for his son; *De re militari*, a manual of military training; *De agri cultura* (*On Agriculture*, 1913), a how-to guide for managing a prosperous farm; and *Origines*, a seven-book history of Rome. They are didactic works, displaying common sense rather than imagination. They suggest, however, that Cato possessed a reflective side to complement his pragmatic side: He addressed what to do and why it was worth doing. His literary works embody the moral vision of his censorship and his oratory: Knowledgeable, self-reliant individuals best lead the austere, just state.

In foreign policy, Cato seems to have advocated the restrained display of Rome's unchallenged military power. After victory in the Third Macedonian War (168), Cato sided with those anxious to see Macedonia a free ally rather than a subjugated client state. He consistently argued that smaller competitor nations and reluctant allies be treated leniently. The one exception to Cato's usual moderation made him legendary. All of his life Cato feared the resurgence of Carthage. Leading a senatorial delegation to Africa in 152, Cato saw signs of economic and military recovery. Henceforward, Cato argued that Rome must destroy her ancient rival before it grew powerful. "Carthago delenda est" ("Carthage must be destroyed") became the injunction repeatedly brought to the senate. War broke out in 149; Carthage was razed in 146. Cato died soon after the declaration of war, relieved that this time war's devastation would occur on enemy soil.

Summary

Because Cato the Censor's insistence that Carthage be destroyed dominated his last years, it has often been seen as the climactic event of his career. Without a doubt Cato was influential in securing war, and without a doubt that war changed the course of Roman history by extending Rome's dominion into northern Africa. Remembering Cato as a spokesman of steely, merciless national self-interest was easy for subsequent generations. It was—and is—too narrow an estimate of the man.

Cato's memorable reign as censor was also easy to recall, so easy that it gave the name by which history calls him. Rome reigned supreme for nearly six hundred years after Cato's death. Its life span as a great state encompassed extensive conquest, civil war, the transition from republic to empire, the acquisition of incalculable wealth, and profound social change. In times of crisis, many citizens remembered Cato. He was an emblem of personal self-control and public austerity. He knew the difference between public good and private welfare, between national prosperity and enervating materialism, between commonsensical good and rationalized failings. In subsequent neoclassical periods—Italy in the sixteenth century, England in the late seventeenth century, France and the United States in the late eighteenth century—Cato the Censor was a model of political leadership. He represented the highest civic virtue, the leader who rallied citizens by example and by eloquence to identify the public good with wise, orderly, and restrained government.

As dramatic as Cato's censorship was in combating obvious abuses, his time in office was one brief episode in a career. One must remember his lifetime of service to a civic ideal. He was not like the Old Testament prophets, men who lived obscurely until some crisis called them from obscurity to lead their people from darkness into light. His was not a lonely voice crying in the wilderness. He provided constant leadership in articulating a vision of the good state which, for the span of his life, most Romans held in common.

Bibliography
Astin, Alan E. *Cato the Censor*. Oxford: Clarendon Press, 1978. This is the definitive study in English. It analyzes Cato as soldier, politician, orator, and writer. Astin admires his subject's rugged individualism and active public service. Astin disputes the image of Cato as a puritanical traditionalist and asserts that he is important for much more than his final act of destroying Carthage.
Cicero, Marcus Tullius. "On Old Age." In *Letters and Treatises of Cicero and Pliny*, translated by E. S. Shuckburgh. New York: P. F. Collier and Son, 1909. Part of the Harvard Classics Series. Cato at age eighty-four is the hero of this philosophic dialogue. His conversation embodies Cicero's idea that in advancing years men should turn their thoughts from physical prowess to spiritual ideals in preparation for death. Cicero's wise, patient, transcendent Cato is attractive but fictitious. Cicero's essay shows some of the values Cato embodied for subsequent generations.
Livy, Titus. *The History of Rome from Its Foundations*. Translated by Henry Betterson. New York: Penguin Books, 1976. The section of Livy's landmark history called "Rome and the Mediterranean" describes Rome's competition with Macedonia after the Second Punic War with Carthage. It covers the period from 210 to 167, during which Cato was consul, censor, and senator. Working from Cato's own writings, now lost, Livy presents vivid accounts of Cato's campaign in Spain, his support for the Oppian Law, and his term as censor.
Plutarch. *The Lives of the Noble Grecians and Romans*. Translated by John Dryden. New York: Modern Library, 1967. Writing as a moralist, rather than a biographer, Plutarch analyzes the strengths and weaknesses of Cato's character. The moralist praises Cato for old-fashioned virtues of temperance, public service, and frank speaking but faults him for avariciousness. By selling aging slaves and urging others to farm for profit, Plutarch charges, Cato dehumanized the social fabric he tried to save.
Scullard, H. H. *Roman Politics, 220-150 B.C.* Oxford: Clarendon Press, 1951. This scholarly study documents the competition for political power between the son of an aristocratic family, such as Scipio Africanus, and the *novus homo*, such as Cato. Scullard provides detailed information about Cato's duties as censor, consul, and senator. He makes clear who supported Cato's policies, who opposed them, and why contemporaries took one side or the other.
Smith, R. E. "Cato Censorius." *Greece and Rome* 9 (1940): 150-165. Smith analyzes the literary portraits of Cato offered by Cicero and Plutarch. He warns that Plutarch's account especially is an exaggerated version that pits

"antique morality" against "modern morality." Smith himself judges that Cato held typical rather than reactionary opinions on wealth and empire. He concludes that Cato shaped, not stunted, Roman expansion.

Robert M. Otten

CATULLUS

Born: c. 85 B.C.; Verona, Cisalpine Gaul
Died: c. 54 B.C.; probably Rome
Area of Achievement: Literature
Contribution: Catullus was the leader of a group of poets, the *novi poetae*, who created a more native idiom for Roman poetry. Intensely personal, epigrammatic, and more colloquial than epic or dramatic, this style of poetry prepared the way and set the standards for the literary achievements of the Augustan Age.

Early Life

Like most figures of Greek and Roman antiquity, Catullus provides little information about his early life, and the ancient sources add few additional facts. His family was prominent in Verona, which was then a part of the province of Cisalpine Gaul. They also owned a villa on the peninsula of Sirmio (modern Sermione) in the Lago di Garda, about twenty miles east of Verona. Catullus' later references to this country home reveal his deep attachment to the family seat. Suetonius' biography of Julius Caesar records that Catullus' father was prominent enough to entertain Caesar during the latter's governorship of that province in the early 50's B.C.

Although his views about family ties were firmly traditional, Catullus makes no reference to either of his parents. An emotional tribute to his brother, who died near Troy, is the only mention of a relative, but it strengthens the inference that Catullus' family was closely knit.

The usual education of a wealthy and talented provincial is likely to have included study in Athens, and although there is no record of an educational sojourn in Greece, Catullus' poetry is that of a young man thoroughly imbued with Greek poetry from Homer to Callimachus. Yet his many attachments to friends from northern Italy, including several of the *novi poetae*, suggest that unlike the Augustans Vergil and Horace, Catullus did not completely detach himself from his provincial origins to become a Hellenized Roman. The demotic, vernacular coloring of his poetry is symptomatic of a mind that resisted imitation of the accepted Greco-Roman literary canons.

Life's Work

Catullus' reputation as one of the greatest poets of all Roman literature is even more remarkable because it is based on a collection of poems smaller than a fourth of Vergil's *Aeneid* (c. 29-19 B.C.) and because this collection survived antiquity in only a single copy. The 113 poems range in length from epigrams of two lines to a miniature epic of 408 lines. The near extinction of this great poet is attributable to the audacious and racy subject matter of some of his poems, which made them unsuitable for use in the schools.

It is impossible to reconstruct a dependable chronology of Catullus' poetic career on the basis of the poems themselves, and, as previously noted, the ancient sources provide little additional information. Clearly, the shortness of his life means that his oeuvre represents the work of a young poet, but nothing in it could be described as juvenilia. The poems appear to have been selected by him for publication. Poem 1 of the collection now extant refers to a "slim volume" (*libellus*) which he is dedicating to his friend the historian Cornelius Nepos, but there is no evidence that this slim volume is the same as the extant collection. There exists a scrap of another dedication also, apparently part of another collection.

The existing collection is divided into three parts on purely formal grounds. The first group, poems 1 through 60, are in a variety of meters; hence, they are called the polymetric poems. The favorite meter of this group is the hendecasyllabic, or Phalaecian, an eleven-syllable line of Greek origin that lends itself well to the colloquial tone of his work. The second group consists of eight long poems in various meters, two of them the dactylic hexameter familiar to epic poetry. The third group is written in elegiac couplets, a meter which had become popular in Hellenistic epigrams but was on its way to becoming the medium of the Latin love elegy. Yet not all Catullus' elegiac poems are on love. He wrote a poem to his dead brother, as well as a number of purely satirical pieces. Judging from what has survived, scholars agree that the elegiac couplet was Catullus' favorite medium. Within the three sections of the now-canonical collection, there is evidence of design in the ordering of the poems. The collection is not organized chronologically or by subject matter, but it betrays a subtly designed miscellany of moods and subjects, each poem contrasting with or corresponding to its neighbors in ways that sustain the reader's interest.

Because there is no known chronology, one good way to perceive the work of Catullus is through the people about whom and to whom he wrote his poems. The social character of his poetry, much of which is addressed to somebody specific, is also well served by this approach. The most visible and intense of the poet's personal relationships is with a woman he calls Lesbia, mentioned in some twenty-five of Catullus' love poems. Lucius Apuleius wrote that her real name was Clodia, and it is generally believed that she was a married woman ten years older than the poet. If Apuleius' testimony is correct, Clodia was the sister of Cicero's enemy P. Clodius Pulcher and wife (later the widow) of Q. Metellus Celer, who governed Cisalpine Gaul between 64 and 62 B.C. For her, the affair she had with Catullus was casual, one of many. For Catullus, it was the cause of both euphoria and anguish, with little middle ground. This stormy relationship lasted about six years, from perhaps 58 or 59 (before the death of Metellus in 59) to 55 or 54. The Lesbia poems are the best known of Catullus' work.

A second episode in Catullus' life, one whose dates are known more definitely, was his year of public service on the staff of C. Memmius, the Roman governor of Bithynia. Such tours of duty were a normal part of the life of young Romans of rank, and although Catullus complains loudly in his poems about Memmius' tightfisted policies and writes eloquently of the pleasure of returning home, this year of furlough (from 57 to 56 B.C.) from the stresses of his affair with Lesbia/Clodia and the high life of Rome may have contributed much to Catullus' achievement as a poet. It is a reasonable inference that the job itself was not demanding and that in his enforced isolation on the southern shore of the Black Sea Catullus had ample opportunity to study, write, and revise.

A significant part of Catullus' poetry may be described as occasional verse, that which commemorates an event of no great objective importance in such a way as to bring out its humor, irony, or emotional significance. The Greek tradition in which he chose to write was satirical, and a large number of the poems of the collection expand on the foibles of people whom the poet wished to embarrass. Some of these were amatory rivals, some were social climbers or nuisances (such as Asinius Marrucinus, the napkin thief of poem 12). Others, including the orator Cicero, the politician Julius Caesar, and Caesar's protégé Mamurra, were public figures. In spite of attacks of varying intensity (in poems 29, 57, and 93), Caesar remained an admirer of Catullus; according to Suetonius, Catullus eventually apologized for his attacks (in one of which he accuses Caesar of sexually molesting little girls) and was invited to dine with Caesar the same day.

Traditional serious poetry also exerted its attraction for Catullus. In the course of what might be viewed as a licentious life of pleasure and scandal, Catullus composed three long wedding hymns (poems 61, 62, and 63) which show every sign of a deep belief in the institution of marriage. In addition, there is an impressive long poem about the religious frenzy of a legendary young Greek named Attis, who emasculates himself in order to serve the Asiatic goddess Cybele. Notwithstanding the emphasis of the Neoterics on short poetry in a native poetic idiom, epic remained the medium of choice for the highest achievement. Catullus' effort in this genre, the miniature epic or epyllion on the wedding of Peleus and Thetis, with its digression on Theseus' abandonment of Ariadne (poem 64), ranks with his best work. Parts of it, such as Ariadne's lament, are unsurpassed in Latin literature.

Summary

Although it remains the slimmest volume on a bookshelf of classical works, the poetry of Catullus is a unique testament to the power of a young poet working in a still-raw language. As Cicero, writing a decade later, found Latin a poor vehicle for philosophy, poets of Catullus' generation had none of the vocabulary and native traditions which Greek had developed over the course of seven centuries. Instead of borrowing Greek vocabulary, themes, and genres wholesale to produce feeble imitations, Catullus set out to create a genuinely Latin poetry. The only Roman model of significant use to him was the comedian Plautus, the Umbrian stagehand-turned-playwright, who transformed Greek comedies into lively shows for untutored audiences. Though inevitably indebted to Greek inspiration for most of what he wrote, Catullus put Latin poetry on a more independent course and set the agenda for Augustan poetry: to write what Horace was to call a *Latinum carmen*, or Latin song.

Specifically, this agenda meant adapting Greek poetic rhetoric to the more subjective taste of a Roman audience, reducing the dependence on words borrowed from the Greek, modifying the rigid syntactic structure of formal Latin to gain the flexibility which Greek had long enjoyed, and broadening the range of subjects which were acceptable for poets to essay. By succeeding as conspicuously as he did in these tasks, Catullus opened the way for Latin poetry to become a worthy successor to Greek rather than a mere imitator.

Ultimately more interesting to the average reader than his place in the history of Roman poetry is the vibrant and colorful picture Catullus gives of private life in the Rome of Cicero and Caesar. As it happens, Catullus wrote for all time, but his poetry is an intimate portrait of life in his own time, written with an art which few successors dared imitate.

Bibliography

Fordyce, C. J. *Catullus: A Commentary*. Oxford: Clarendon Press, 1961. An extensive and illuminating commentary in English on the Latin text, flawed by the author's refusal to print or discuss some thirty-two poems "which do not lend themselves to comment in English."

Quinn, Kenneth, ed. *Catullus: The Poems*. 2d ed. New York: St. Martin's Press, 1973. The most recent scholarly commentary, somewhat idiosyncratic but suitable for college-level readers and beyond. Latin text of all poems, with introduction and commentary in English. A short bibliographical guide for further study of each of the poems is included.

Small, Stuart G. P. *Catullus: A Reader's Guide to the Poems*. Lanham, Md.: University Press of America, 1983. A running narrative, not of the poet's life but of his poetic achievement. Divided by topic, with sane judgments on matters of literary and scholarly controversy. Small supplements a reading of the poems by giving topical overviews. With bibliography.

Wilder, Thornton. *The Ides of March*. New York: Harper and Row, Publishers, 1948. The classic historical novel on the Rome of Cicero, Catullus, Clodius, and his sister—and Caesar, the emperor whose life ended on the title day in 44 B.C.

Wiseman, Timothy Peter. *Catullus and His World*. Cambridge: Cambridge University Press, 1985. A highly readable reconstruction of the social and political context, informative not only about Catullus but also about late republican Rome and its personalities. Richly documented, with eight pages of bibliography.

Daniel H. Garrison

GUIDO CAVALCANTI

Born: c. 1259; Florence, Italy
Died: August 27 or 28, 1300; Florence, Italy
Area of Achievement: Poetry
Contribution: Through his unique treatment of the theme of love, Cavalcanti became one of the major poets of the so-called *dolce stil nuovo* school. He exerted a major influence on Dante and the love poets of the early Renaissance.

Early Life

Guido Cavalcanti's importance as one of the early masters of European love poetry becomes all the more remarkable in view of the paucity of information about his life. He was born in the middle of the thirteenth century, the period in which the vernacular Italian literature first arose. His family was aristocratic, proud of its status as one of the most powerful families of the Guelphs, a political faction which allied itself, generally, with the pope, as opposed to the so-called Ghibellines, who favored the cause of the emperor. Throughout the thirteenth century, factious rivalries between Guelph and Ghibelline parties often resulted in bloody feuding as well as in political chaos.

Cavalcanti himself seems to have been a proud, contentious man who was disdainful of the lower classes and often upheld his honor with his fists. Yet by contemporary accounts, he was also highly educated, introspective, scholarly, and philosophical. Giovanni Boccaccio (1313-1375), in his famous *Decameron: O, Prencipe Galeotto* (1349-1351; *The Decameron*, 1620), related a popular story about Cavalcanti, illustrative of his character and wit. A group of idle young gentlemen are riding one morning and spot Cavalcanti in a pensive mood, walking among the tombs in a graveyard. They begin teasing him about his reputation as an unbeliever, as a man of little faith who sought to prove that God did not exist. Cavalcanti looks up at them and calmly answers that they can say of him anything they wish, because men should be allowed to speak freely in their own houses. The cryptic nature of Guido's retort, by which the taunters were themselves impugned as being among the dead, their intellects entombed, as it were, by their own ignorance, is indicative of the subtlety of his thought and, ultimately, of his poetry. Cavalcanti did not deny his atheism, but by turning the tables on the young gentlemen he did not confirm it either.

Certainly the image of entombment was associated with the Cavalcanti family in a scene in Dante's *Inferno*, part of *La divina commedia* (c. 1320; *The Divine Comedy*). In this circle of Hell, the heretics are encased in their sepulchers. Among these heretics and Epicureans—those philosophers who believed, among other things, that the soul perished with the body—is

Cavalcanti's father. The father cries out, looking for his son, who, he implies, will also be damned for his philosophical pride.

Life's Work

Yet if Dante condemned Cavalcanti for his heretical views, part of which formed the basis of Cavalcanti's theory of love as mortality, he also respected the man as a poet. The two, in fact, were close friends. Dedicating his *La vita nuova* (c. 1292; *The New Life*) to Cavalcanti, whom he called his "first friend," Dante relates that he once wrote a sonnet expressing in symbolic terms his vision of love and that Guido Cavalcanti admired the poem and replied to it with a sonnet of his own. Thus from about the early 1280's, Cavalcanti and Dante were admirers of each other's work, and Dante's early poetry shows the unmistakable influence of the older man.

Yet the factiousness of Florentine politics, together with Cavalcanti's own disputatious personality, resulted in a split between the two friends. As a leader of the White Guelphs, rivals of the powerful Blacks, Cavalcanti was involved in the bloody feuds near the close of the century, and there were rumors that several attempts had been made on his life. Early in 1300, Dante, then a magistrate of Florence, found himself forced to banish Cavalcanti in the interest of peace. Guido went to Saranza, but while there he contracted malaria. He was allowed to return to his native city, and it was there that he died in August, 1300, the same year in which the narrative of *The Divine Comedy* begins.

Cavalcanti's reputation rests on a handful of poems, his total output numbering about fifty sonnets, ballades, and *canzone*. Though his most characteristic poems are fraught with delicate complexity and rigorous analysis—as if he were, in effect, a philosopher or scientist parsing a rational solution to a central enigma in man's experience—his most appealing works are those sonnets which he addressed to his love, whom he named Primavera (springtime). These are marked by a humanity, a simple honesty that enhances their lyric beauty:

> Who is she who comes, on whom all gaze,
> Who starts the air to tremble, flooded with light?

Such poems as these placed Cavalcanti at the head of a school of poets whose work Dante later characterized as the *dolce stil nuovo*, the sweet new style. The subject matter of these poems might not have been new. (Indeed, the Provençal poets and troubadours of an earlier time had sung of love and its joys.) Yet the treatment of love was new. Love, to these new poets, was an ennobling experience, sanctified, as it were, by the object of that love, a woman. She was not necessarily beautiful of face; it was her gentle heart, a sort of spiritual incandescence, that was crucial in the lover's apprehension of his love. The woman's gentle heart as both the source and repository of love was an idea that took on an almost mystical significance. The loved one became an ideal of Beauty, a representation of the Divine, and, therefore, a means of salvation.

One of the earliest Italian poets to treat love in this idealized manner was Guido Guinizelli, who died about 1275. Guinizelli first identified the noble heart, *cor gentil*, as the residence of love, and Cavalcanti seems to have adopted from this older poet the idea of love as ennobling. Greater than those of Guinizelli, Cavalcanti's poems are individualistic, personal responses to the experience of love. Like the generation of English Metaphysical poets of the early seventeenth century, Cavalcanti projects a voice, a personality of lyric subtlety and power. There is an intensity in the voice, an earnestness that evokes brilliantly the force and strength of love, as in the sonnet "Gli miei folli occhi," translated as "My Foolish, Reckless Eyes." Here the poet compares his state to that of a prisoner being hauled to court, sentenced, and punished with no hope of appeal.

A characteristic of Cavalcanti's work—that quality which sets it apart from the work of his contemporaries—is this intensity by which the best of his poems maintain a tension between the experience of love as ultimate joy and as physical torture relieved only by death. His poem "Della forza d'amore" ("On the Power of Love") clearly allies joy with despair, life with death, and concludes with the poet's cursing the hour when he first fell in love.

Cavalcanti's poems treat love not so much as an emotional but as a psychological experience, a tangle of contrary forces which, tragically, kill the very subject it seeks to redeem. In many of the poems, death and grief are central to the lover's condition; love, in Ezra Pound's phrase from one of Cavalcanti's sonnets, keeps "death-watch upon the heart." For Cavalcanti, death is a metaphor emblematic not so much of the physical destruction of the body as of the psychological disintegration of the mind. A later age would use the image of the lovesick courtier, pale and wan and pining away for his beloved, but Cavalcanti's lover is not of this kind. He is not the subject of parody, but of tragedy—a personality to whom love is not spiritually invigorating but psychically ruinous. Love alienates the soul from the rational principles upon which it functions.

A rational explanation of love, in fact, is found in what is often regarded as Cavalcanti's most famous poem. Obscure, scientifically analytic, the *canzone* "Donna me prega" ("A Lady Asks Me") was the subject of many commentaries for more than two centuries. In it, Cavalcanti dissects the subject of love: He tells where it resides, who begets it, and what its nature, power, essence, and action are. This method of analysis is more characteristic of a Scholastic philosopher, well versed in Aristotle, than of a poet. Because of its abstruseness, the poem is not among his most popular, but it is important for an understanding of Cavalcanti's theory of love.

In declaring love to have its seat in the memory, that part of the soul which was then considered material, Cavalcanti suggests that love is purely physical and thus subject to death; merely material, love is an illusion of the mind, a distraction, a madness. The poem thus uses reason to indict the irrational quality of love and is a good example of Cavalcanti's contradictory aspect—a poet who sings sweetly of love though conscious of love's destructive force.

Summary

Guido Cavalcanti's contribution to the *dolce stil nuovo* was his treatment of love as a conflict between pleasure and pain, a salvific force that should redeem and purify but which in reality more often destroys. Behind the images which have become commonplace in love poetry—the beauty of the lady's eyes, her loveliness of form, her angelic face—lies a darker meaning. Love is akin to tragedy, a contradiction that men must endure to become better creatures, though it brings but bitter consolation and an agony of spirit. There is, however, little cynicism even in the darkest of Cavalcanti's poems, for love is a sweetness, a genuine ecstasy that defies explanation. As he writes in his famous *canzone*: "No one can imagine love who has never been in love."

Bibliography

Lind, L. R., ed. *Lyric Poetry of the Italian Renaissance*. New Haven, Conn.: Yale University Press, 1954. An anthology containing several of Cavalcanti's poems, including the famous translation by Ezra Pound of the *canzone* "Donna me prega." Presents a synthesis of Cavalcanti's theory of love.

Pound, Ezra. *Make It New*. New Haven, Conn.: Yale University Press, 1935. One of the earliest modern studies of Cavalcanti is found in an appreciative essay in this book, together with Pound's translation of the *canzone*.

Rebay, Luciano, ed. *Italian Poetry: A Selection from St. Francis of Assisi to Salvatore Quasimodo*. New York: Dover Books, 1969. Besides containing several fresh translations of the poems, the book is a good brief source of background material, particularly on the *dolce stil nuovo*.

Vossler, Karl. *Mediaeval Culture: An Introduction to Dante and His Times*. Translated by William Lamton. 2 vols. New York: Frederick Ungar Publishing Co., 1929, reprint 1958. Volume 2 presents a brief account of Cavalcanti's life and work, emphasizing the combination of "reflection" and "feeling" that characterizes the poet's work.

Wilkins, Ernest H. *A History of Italian Literature*. Cambridge, Mass.: Harvard University Press, 1954. Eminently readable, easily accessible, this work is a standard assessment of Cavalcanti's achievement, discussing his poetic voice and his emphasis on the psychology of love.

Edward Fiorelli

AULUS CORNELIUS CELSUS

Born: c. 25 B.C.; possibly near Narbonne on the Mediterranean coast of
France
Died: c. A.D. 50; probably Rome
Areas of Achievement: Historiography and medicine
Contribution: Celsus wrote the first complete history of medicine and the
first comprehensive account of medical and surgical procedures.

Early Life
Aulus Cornelius Celsus probably lived during the Augustan Age and the
reign of Tiberius. He is thought to have been a member of the patrician family of Cornelius. Patricians were the ruling class of Rome, nobles of wealth
and influence, and they considered the practice of medicine beneath their
dignity. Consequently, it is highly unlikely that Celsus was a practicing physician. Still, some knowledge of medicine was customary among the educated
men of Rome. The head of the household usually practiced domestic medicine on the family, slaves, and livestock. Celsus may have followed this
custom.
He was an avid reader and certainly knew both Greek and Latin. Records
for the years A.D. 25 and 26 clearly indicate that he lived in Rome.
Quintilian, the Roman rhetorician and critic, and Gaius Pliny, or Pliny the
Elder, the Roman naturalist and writer, mention Celsus with considerable
praise.
Celsus was never referred to as a physician, only as an author or compiler.
His literary interests were apparently comprehensive in scope and resulted in
an encyclopedia called *De artibus* (A.D. 25-35). There is no clear idea of the
contents and arrangement of *De artibus*. It is certain, however, that there
were five books on agriculture and also sections of unknown length on military science, rhetoric, history, philosophy, government, and law.
The only portion of this encyclopedia to survive is *De medicina* (c. A.D. 30;
The Eight Books of Medicine, 1830; better known as *De medicina*, 1935-
1938). It was a compilation from various sources such as Hippocrates' *Corpus
Hippocraticum* (written during the fifth century B.C.) and from the lost works
of Asclepiades of Bithynia, Heracleides Ponticus, Erasistratus, and others.

Life's Work
De medicina was intended primarily for practitioners. Celsus set down a
guiding principle for physicians in any age: that an accurate diagnosis must
precede treatment. Celsus noted the errors of both Empiricists and Methodists. He rejected the inflexible doctrines of the Empiricists, who advocated
the use of drugs, and the Methodists, who stressed diet and exercise. He was
influenced by Asclepiades, who established Greek medicine in Rome, and
adopted many of the physiological concepts of the Alexandrian School.

The introduction to *De medicina* constitutes a first attempt at a history of medicine and includes references to eighty medical authors, some of whom are known only through this book. Celsus gave an account of the Alexandrian school, the part played by Hippocrates, and the contributions of Asclepiades.

The book, actually eight books in one, is divided into three parts. Section 1 contains a general introduction on the efficacy of diet and hygiene. Two main chapters consider the subject of general and local diseases governed by diet. Section 2 considers diseases treated with drugs. Discussed at length are different remedies, divided into various groups according to their effects: purgatives, diaphoretics, diuretics, emetics, and narcotics. There is also an examination of those diseases which require immediate treatment, diseases presenting acute or chronic manifestations, accidental or traumatic manifestations, and diseases with external symptoms. Section 3 is devoted to surgical diseases. One division concentrates on the organs, the other on orthopedics, or bones.

Celsus held strictly to the teachings of Hippocrates concerning pathological concepts and etiology, or the study of the causes of disease. He took into consideration the influence of the seasons, the weather, the patient's age and constitution, and any sudden weight changes, increases and decreases.

Diseases of the stomach are considered at length. Treatment generally consisted of diet, massage, and baths. Celsus believed that it was better to keep the bowels open by diet rather than by purgatives. Where diarrhea and fever existed, fast was the prescription. Celsus believed in the doctrine of critical days for diseases, that is, the disease would peak within a certain number of days and then the patient would begin to recover.

In *De medicina*, Celsus addressed pneumonia, arthritis, dysentery, tonsilitis, cancer, kidney and liver diseases, tuberculosis, hemorrhoids, and diabetes. Symptoms were accurately reported for a number of diseases, such as epilepsy, and mental illnesses, such as paranoia, a form of insanity characterized by delusions. He clearly pictured the way in which malaria attacks occurred, giving a very detailed and highly accurate account of malarial fever. According to Celsus, the fever was an effort to eliminate morbid material from the body. He was the first to name the four cardinal signs of inflammation: heat, pain, swelling, and redness.

The arguments of Celsus against taking the pulse of the patient as a criterion in the identification of disease are interesting. He regarded the pulse as an uncertain indication of the health of a person, because its frequency varied considerably with the sex, age, and constitution of the patient. The pulse also varied because of the patient's nervousness when in the presence of the doctor. For these reasons, the pulse was not to be examined on the doctor's first visit.

In Celsus' time, surgery was performed on all parts of the body: goiters, fistulas, tonsils, and gallstones. Cancerous growths of lips and breasts were removed. He described ulcers, tumors, amputation, and trepanation, or the removal of part of the skull, which he regarded as a treatment of last resort.

Celsus carefully reported on plastic surgery for the repair of the nose, lips, and ears and described some dental surgery, including the wiring of teeth. He also suggested lithotomy, an operation for crushing stones in the bladder, discussed ligature, or how to tie off an artery, and presented methods for stopping hemorrhages. He was very much aware of the dangers of gangrene.

Celsus was concerned with the treatment of wounds, necrosis (decaying tissues), fractures, and dislocations. His book contains an excellent account of the treatment of various fractures and dislocations. For fractures, he recommended wooden splints held in place by wax and advocated exercise after the fracture healed. Thus, he was a forerunner to modern rehabilitative therapy. In addition, Celsus described the widely used painkillers, such as opium, and anesthetics, such as the root of the mandragora plant. The root of the plant, which contained narcotics such as scopolamine, was soaked in wine, and the wine was given to the patient to induce a deep sleep.

Celsus paid particular attention to headaches, which he regarded as coming from various sources and approved the treatment of insomnia by oil massage, which he credited directly to Asclepiades. Celsus recommended removing snake poison from a wound by sucking and correctly claimed that the venom was lethal only when absorbed into the wound, not when swallowed.

Celsus clearly recognized the importance of anatomy in medicine. He attended autopsies, and his anatomical descriptions are brief but clear, including information which shows that he knew about sutures of the cranium. He distinguished between veins and arteries and favored dissection as a means to discovering more about internal organs.

In short, Celsus taught that diagnosis and prognosis must precede treatment. In so doing, he confirmed the sound doctrine of the Hippocratic school. Celsus also advocated different types of baths, massage, hygiene, and dietary rules. He relied somewhat on drugs for treatment but emphasized the benefits of sports, such as hunting, fishing, and sailing.

Summary

Galen, a Greek philosopher and writer, prepared a medical encyclopedia which remained the standard authority until the sixteenth century. When Pope Nicholas V discovered Aulus Cornelius Celsus' work in the Vatican Library, he arranged to have it published in 1478. Thus, *De medicina* was the first classical book on medicine to be printed. It was also the first translation of Greek medical terms into Latin. The Latin nomenclature used in the book has dominated Western medicine for two thousand years.

The book is of interest for two reasons: its literary skill and the techniques presented. From a literary point of view, his work is outstanding. Celsus ranks as Rome's most important master of the encyclopedic literary form. As the first comprehensive account of surgical procedures by a Roman writer, *De medicina* provides much useful information on medicine of the Hellenistic period and on Alexandrian surgery. It includes a careful description of more than one hundred different types of surgical instruments.

Celsus' ideas on malaria, the treatment of fractures, and plastic surgery were ahead of his time. He was a disciple of Asclepiades, but unlike Asclepiades, Celsus was a great admirer of Hippocrates and was among the first to introduce Hippocrates' teaching to the Romans. During the first century, it was typical for medicine and other sciences to draw upon many sources. Celsus followed this custom and can thus be regarded as a true eclectic.

Bibliography
Allbutt, Sir Thomas C. *Greek Medicine in Rome*. London: Macmillan, 1921. A series of lectures addressed to interested physicians and others with a good medical background. Perhaps too abstract for the general reader, this volume is a complete medical history of the period, with extensive commentary on all major figures but only one brief chapter on Celsus. Excellent illustrations, bibliography, and chronology.
Castiglioni, Arturo. *A History of Medicine*. Translated by E. B. Krumbhaar. 2d ed. New York: Alfred A. Knopf, 1947. Considered a classic reference for the period, this volume contains a full translation of Castiglioni's work. Included are numerous illustrations, a full chronology, and a bibliography for each chapter. Designed for the general reader, it contains information relating to the content of *De medicina*.
Celsus, Aulus Cornelius. *De medicina*. Translated by W. G. Spencer. 3 vols. Cambridge, Mass.: Harvard University Press, 1960. This work includes both the original Latin text and a full translation of Celsus' work. It is a major source of information about the history of medicine, as well as medical and surgical procedures for the Hellenistic period.
Gordon, Benjamin Lee. *Medicine Throughout Antiquity*. Philadelphia: F. A. Davis Co., 1949. Contains only a very brief section on Celsus, along with scattered page references. The author cites facts from widely scattered fields that are not ordinarily accessible to a busy practitioner or to lay people interested in medical history. With brief reference notes and a handful of illustrations but no chronology or bibliography.
Lipsett, W. G. "Celsus, First Medical Historian." *Science Digest* 48 (October, 1960): 83-87. Gives very complete information about the various divisions of *De medicina* but concentrates on the surgical chapters. A very brief article which is perhaps too simplistic in language and approach, it does have appeal to the general reader.

Rita E. Loos

CHARLEMAGNE

Born: 742; Gaul
Died: January 28, 814; Aix-la-Chapelle
Areas of Achievement: Government, warfare, and religion
Contribution: By 800, when he was crowned emperor by Pope Leo III, Charlemagne had revived the Roman idea of universal empire, preserved through the Carolingian Renaissance much of the written legacy of the ancient world, and established the foundation for a European civilization distinct from that of ancient Rome and from the contemporary Byzantine and Islamic empires.

Early Life

Charlemagne was born about 742 in the kingdom of the Merovingian Franks, founded on the ruins of Roman Gaul by Clovis I, whose people's nominal conversion to Roman Christianity made them the allies of the Papacy against the Arian heresy. Under Clovis' factious and often-inept successors, whose cruelty was anything but Christian, the kingdom was at times split into as many as four parts. Though it was reunited by the end of the seventh century, real power by then had passed from the Merovingians to Charlemagne's ancestors, who became hereditary holders of the office of mayor of the palace. Charlemagne's grandfather, Charles Martel, ruled over an increasingly powerful Frankish state from 714 to 741, during much of which time there was no Merovingian on the throne. On his death, power passed to his sons, Pepin the Short and Carloman, though the latter entered a monastery in 747, leaving his elder brother as mayor to Childeric III. Charlemagne was the eldest child of Pepin and Bertrada, his *Friedelehe*—more than a concubine, but not canonically a wife, so that their son was arguably illegitimate. He was called Charles—the name Charlemagne, which means "Charles the Great," is an anachronism, though its usage is so common that to avoid it is pointless.

Charles Martel and especially Pepin and Carloman brought the still nearly pagan Franks more firmly within the Christian fold through cooperation with pro-papal Anglo-Saxon missionaries, the most important of whom was Saint Boniface of Wessex. This helped facilitate good relations with Pope Zacharias, whose approval allowed Pepin in 751 to depose Childeric and take for himself the title King of the Franks without fear of the stigma of usurpation. At Pepin's coronation Pope Stephen II, who had journeyed from Rome to St. Denis, personally placed the crown on the new king's head. At that time, the Pope recognized as Pepin's joint heirs Charlemagne and his younger brother, Carloman, who was born in 751 and was unquestionably legitimate, since by then his father and Bertrada were legally married. Charlemagne accompanied Pepin on his campaigns against the Lombards in northern Italy, undertaken at the behest of the Pope. Upon Pepin's death in 768, however, the seventeen-year-old Carloman—perhaps because of the circumstances of his birth—received by his father's will the central portion of the kingdom, while the twenty-six-year-old Charlemagne was left with an unwieldy strip of land running along the Atlantic coast and turning inland beyond the Rhine River. Relations between the brothers were thereafter bitter, and in 769 Carloman refused to aid Charlemagne in putting down a rebellion in Aquitaine. Carloman died in 771, however, and his vassals paid homage to Charlemagne, thus reuniting the kingdom of the Franks.

Einhard, Charlemagne's biographer and a resident at his court for twenty-three years, provided a detailed description of the ruler in his *Vita Caroli magni* (c. 829-836; *Life of Charlemagne*, 1880), though this work—modeled on the Roman historian Suetonius' rather eulogistic lives of the Caesars—must be read critically. While admitting that Charlemagne was paunchy and had a short, thick neck and a high-pitched voice, Einhard stressed his favorable features and huge physique—the opening of his tomb in 1861 revealed that he was nearly six feet, four inches tall, so that at a time when malnutrition stunted the growth of many, he was truly a giant among men. The king was cheerful, generous, and fond of the hunt, boon companions, and especially his daughters; he was also capable of fearsome anger. Einhard, the monk Alcuin of York, and others attributed to Charlemagne virtues both Christian and Stoic—wisdom, devotion to the Church, love of learning, clemency, self-control, and temperance in eating and drinking (temperance being a relative term).

By his first marriage to the Frankish Himiltrude, probably a *Friedelehe*, Charlemagne produced a son, Pepin the Hunchback (who was later barred from the succession, revolted, and was forced into a monastery). In 770 the king's mother, Bertrada, persuaded him to put aside his first wife and marry the daughter of Desiderius, King of the Lombards, though a year later Charlemagne repudiated her as well. He then married a Swabian noblewoman, Hildegarde, who bore him four sons—Charles, Pepin, Lothar, and Louis the Pious—and three daughters—Rotrude, Bertha, and Gisela. Later he married Fastrada (the mother of Theoderada and Himiltrude), who was followed by Lintgard and a series of concubines.

Life's Work

Charlemagne was above all else a warrior, carrying out some sixty campaigns, about half of which he led personally. His only failure came in 778, when he crossed the Pyrenees to do battle with the Christian Basques in Spain, was unsuccessful in an attempt to capture Saragossa, and had to settle for establishing a Spanish march (buffer state) in Barcelona. Ironically, this is his most famous campaign, for the defeat of his rearguard at Roncevaux during the return home became the basis for the eleventh century *Chanson de*

Roland (*Song of Roland*), the greatest of the medieval French *chansons de geste*, in which Charlemagne and his soldiers appear as idealized heroes. Elsewhere the king was victorious. In 773 he invaded the Lombard kingdom of Desiderius, whose daughter Charlemagne had recently repudiated and who was harboring Gerberga, his brother Carloman's widow, and her sons, potentially rivals to the Frankish throne. After successfully besieging Pavia and seizing the Lombard crown in 774, Charlemagne visited Pope Hadrian I in Rome, strengthening his ties with the Papacy by reconfirming the Donation of Pepin, in which his father had granted to the Popes the lands in central Italy known as the Papal States.

By 772 Charlemagne had begun a long series of hard-fought wars against the Saxons to the north of Frankland, which were not complete until 804. Over and over Charlemagne's forces invaded Saxony and forced the inhabitants to accept Frankish rule and the Christian faith, only to have them renounce Christ and rebel at the first opportunity. Though Charlemagne, at the beginning of these wars, destroyed the Irminsul, a wooden pillar considered sacred in Saxony, the Saxons clung fiercely to paganism, which the Frankish king found particularly offensive. Though he broke the back of Saxon resistance in 779 with the defeat of the chieftain Widekind and began sending in Christian missionaries, the Saxons revolted again in 782, so provoking Charlemagne that he had more than forty-five hundred Saxons massacred. In the last decades of the struggle, there were further massacres, massive deportations, and virtual colonization by the Franks. Thereafter Christianity took firmer root, and by a curious twist of fate it was a Saxon ruler, Otto the Great, who in the mid-tenth century revived in Germany the claim to universal empire earlier resurrected by Charlemagne, for by 800, the latter ruler had laid the foundation for a Carolingian Empire, harking back to the days of Roman domination in the West.

Meanwhile Charlemagne put down rebellions in 776 in Lombardy and in 788 in Bavaria, where Duke Tassilo III had been causing trouble for Frankish rulers intermittently since the reign of Pepin the Short. The addition of Bavaria to Charlemagne's ever-expanding territories brought him into contact with the Avars (or "Huns" as they were sometimes called), who occupied Hungary and Austria and had wreaked havoc upon the Byzantine Empire since the days of the Emperor Justinian. In 791 Charlemagne drove the Avars back into the valley of the Danube River, and by 795 his son Pepin (the son of Hildegarde) had pushed them out of Carinthia in southern Austria, capturing in the process an immense Avar treasure accumulated in part from tribute paid by the Byzantine Empire. This treasure was so great that, according to Einhard, it required fifteen wagons pulled by four oxen apiece to carry it. In any case, it was sufficient to finance Charlemagne's patronage of scholarship, support of the Church, and building of a suitably "imperial" capital at Aix-la-Chapelle (Aachen, West Germany). Though there were additional, for the most part punitive, campaigns against Slavic peoples to the east, the victories against the Avars and the Saxons marked the extent of Charlemagne's conquests; these were essentially complete by 804, even if he later faced rebellion from Brittany and in 810 marched against the Danish king Guthrodr (or Godefrid), who was assassinated before a battle could take place.

By the turn of the century, then, Charlemagne controlled all of Western and Central Europe except for southern Italy (still controlled by the Byzantine Empire), the Spanish peninsula (most of which was held by Muslims), the British Isles (in the hands of various groups of Anglo-Saxons and Celts), and Scandinavia (from which groups of Danish, Norwegian, and Swedish Vikings were already beginning to issue). He spread his influence still further through diplomatic contacts with other rulers. Between 771 and 777, he and the Byzantine Empress Irene carried on eventually unsuccessful negotiations for the marriage of his daughter Rotrude and the young Constantine VI. After Irene deposed and blinded Constantine, Charlemagne apparently proposed marriage to her, in spite of her advanced age, but she too was deposed in 802. (These proposals have led some to flights of fancy about the union of the eastern and western claimants to the Roman imperial mantle, but in practice, the difficulties associated with such a project would have been insuperable.) Charlemagne also corresponded between 789 and 796 with the most powerful of the contemporary Anglo-Saxon kings, Offa of Mercia; exchanged envoys with the mighty Islamic Caliph of Baghdad, Harun al-Rashid; and established contacts with various other rulers. Finally, by threatening Byzantine possessions in Italy, he compelled Emperor Michael I to recognize his claim to the title of Emperor in the West in 813, thirteen years after his coronation by Pope Leo III on Christmas Day, 800.

Charlemagne's coronation, during his fourth visit to Rome (the earlier ones occurred in 774, 781, and 787), is perhaps the most controversial feature of his reign. The king had gone there to restore Leo to power after an antipapal rebellion in 799 drove him across the Alps to seek assistance. Scholars are uncertain whether it was Charlemagne's advisers or those of the Pope who first proposed the imperial coronation. The *Annales regni Francorum* (c. 788-829; *Frankish Royal Annals*, 1970) indicate that it was the Franks, but according to Einhard, the king was surprised and infuriated when the Pope placed the crown on his head just as he was about to rise from prayer. If the latter is true, Charlemagne eventually accepted the coronation, as is indicated by his insistence on Byzantine recognition. The coronation was also part of later debates about the relationship of secular and ecclesiastical authority, but there is no doubt that Charlemagne exercised enormous influence over the Church inside the Carolingian Empire, even if it did not quite approach the caesaropapism of the emperors in Constantinople. Charlemagne generally cooperated with the Papacy but yielded little power—in his cartularies he frequently made law for the Church himself.

Charlemagne's support was crucial to the success of Roman Christianity in the West, where he lent it moral, political, and financial support and spread the faith into newly conquered territories, though often by the ungentle means of baptism at the point of a sword. He also built churches, like that in his capital at Aix-la-Chapelle, and it was faith that led to his patronage of that revival of learning known as the Carolingian Renaissance. From all of Europe, Charlemagne brought scholars—men like Theodulf of Orléans, Paul the Deacon, and Einhard—to work under the leadership of Alcuin of York to preserve the written legacy, both pagan and Christian, of the ancient Roman world. It is true that these clerics were no innovators and that their work made little impression on contemporary society at large, but through their preservation of knowledge, they exerted an immeasurable influence on an emerging European civilization that outlived both Charlemagne and the Carolingian Empire.

Summary

When Charlemagne died in 814, he was by far the most powerful man in Western Europe and ruled over an empire that rivaled in size that of his Roman predecessors. Yet the Carolingian Empire barely outlived him by a generation. Indeed, the seeds of its destruction were already present at his death, for even if Charlemagne had taken—or had been given—the title of emperor, with all of its historic connotations, his realm lacked the administrative machinery which had kept the Roman Empire going for centuries, even under weak, criminal, or lunatic rulers. Charlemagne owed his success to his own personality and ability, to the dynamics of an expanding empire, and to being in the right place at the right time. All of these things were transient.

In administering his far-flung empire, Charlemagne was dependent upon the aid of semiautonomous counts ruling over vast tracts of land. By giving them enough authority to be effective, he also made them powerful enough to be potentially dangerous rebels. He supervised these unpaid, noble officials by grouping together counties outside the old Frankish kingdom under provincial governors known as dukes, margraves, or prefects, and by annually sending out officers called *missi dominici* to inquire into local administration. Yet such supervision was at best less than stringent, communication was poor, and ultimately the entire system rested upon officials' loyalty to the king's person, their fear of his wrath, and his ability to offer them the prospect of further rewards as the empire continued to grow. Moreover, rebellion was a problem in even the most dynamic period of growth, by 804 the empire had ceased to expand, and a decade later, its architect and the focus of fifty years' allegiance was gone. By 843, in the Treaty of Verdun, the sons of

Charlemagne's heir Louis the Pious—Lothar, Charles the Bald, and Louis the German—had split the Carolingian Empire into three parts. Over the next century these too would disintegrate.

Yet the legacy of Charlemagne lived on. The idea of universal empire was revived by the Holy Roman emperors and continued into the modern era to influence both Napoleon Bonaparte and Adolf Hitler. More important, it was in the age of Charlemagne that barriers among the various peoples of Western Europe were broken down and that there first came into existence a new European civilization, sharing elements with, but different from, ancient Rome, Byzantium, and Islam—a civilization which, despite the political fragmentation of the ninth and tenth centuries, would survive, with a shared heritage, a common culture, and a single faith.

Bibliography

Chamberlin, Russell. *The Emperor: Charlemagne*. New York: Franklin Watts, 1987. Though lacking systematic scholarly documentation, this popular biography is based on the essential primary and secondary sources and is well written and rich in detail. It is, therefore, a very useful introduction to the subject for the nonspecialist reader.

Einhard and Notker the Stammerer. *Two Lives of Charlemagne*. Translated by Lewis Thorpe. New York: Penguin Books, 1969. A modern English translation of Einhard's biography written between 829 and 836 at Seligenstadt, where the author retired after a life of service at the court of Charlemagne and Louis the Pious, and of *De Carolo Magno*, written by the monk of St. Gall, identified here as Notker the Stammerer, for Charles the Fat between 884 and 887. The first is an extremely valuable source; the second is largely anecdotal and must be treated with considerable caution.

Fichtenau, Heinrich. *The Carolingian Empire: The Age of Charlemagne*. Translated by Peter Munz. Oxford: Basil Blackwell, 1957. One of the best works by a German historian, this study stresses more than most works the role of religion in the emperor's career. It is structured topically rather than chronologically, examining Charlemagne as an individual, the question of the imperial title, the Carolingian Renaissance, the role of the nobility and officials, the circumstances of the poor, and the decline in the emperor's final decade. Munz's introduction contains an extensive critical essay on literature in English, French, and German.

Ganshof, F. L. *The Carolingians and the Frankish Monarchy: Studies in Carolingian History*. Translated by Janet Sondheimer. Ithaca, N.Y.: Cornell University Press, 1971. A collection of articles, many of them previously available only in French or German, by a distinguished scholar, this work contains relevant articles on Einhard, Alcuin, government and institutions, Charlemagne's use of the oath and the written word, Frankish diplomacy, Charlemagne's "failure," and the decline of the Carolingian

Empire. Includes a select bibliography of Ganshof's works.

Halphen, Louis. *Europe in the Middle Ages: Selected Studies*. Edited by Richard Vaughan. Vol. 3, *Charlemagne and the Carolingian Empire*. Translated by Giselle de Nie. New York: North-Holland Publishing Co., 1977. A very highly regarded study, considered by Vaughan Halphen's masterpiece, this work is divided into three parts, covering Charlemagne's predecessors and the establishment of the Carolingian Empire, the empire under Louis the Pious, and its disintegration following the Treaty of Verdun. It is a more thorough study than most. Contains a number of plates and several very useful maps.

Havighurst, Alfred F., ed. *The Pirenne Thesis: Analysis, Criticism, and Revision*. 4th ed. Lexington, Mass.: D. C. Heath and Co., 1976. This collection contains a series of articles by a distinguished group of medievalists examining the famous thesis of Henri Pirenne, which has as its focus the age of Charlemagne. Pirenne argued that rather than a sharp break between the ancient world and the Middle Ages, there was a gradual change, and that a new European civilization emerged only in the eighth century (a view now widely accepted), with Islam rather than Charlemagne as the principal agent of change (a view generally disregarded here).

Loyn, H. R., and John Percival, eds. *The Reign of Charlemagne: Documents on Carolingian Government and Administration*. New York: St. Martin's Press, 1976. This work contains selections from several biographies of Charlemagne, Louis the Pious, and the latter's sons; from a number of Charlemagne's capitularies; from letters of Charlemagne, Alcuin, and Pope Hadrian I; and from various charters and other documents. Useful primary material, also of interest to the nonspecialist desiring to get something of the flavor of the age.

Scholz, Bernhard W., and Barbara Rogers, trans. *Carolingian Chronicles: Frankish Royal Annals and Nithard's Histories*. Ann Arbor: University of Michigan Press, 1970. A modern English translation of the royal annals, this is one of the essential primary sources for Charlemagne's life and reign. Once erroneously attributed to Einhard, it was actually compiled by perhaps three writers between 788 and 829, the last two working at the court in Aix-la-Chapelle. It differs from Einhard on some points, such as the coronation.

William B. Robison

CHARLES D'ORLÉANS

Born: November 24, 1391; Paris, France
Died: January 4, 1465; Amboise, France
Areas of Achievement: Literature and government
Contribution: Defeated and taken prisoner while leading French troops at Agincourt, Charles spent twenty-five years in captivity in England writing lyric poetry in French and English. When released, he contributed to peace negotiations and maintained a poetry salon.

Early Life

The parents of Charles d'Orléans were Louis, Duke of Orléans and brother of King Charles VI, and Valentina, daughter of the Duke of Milan. Louis had powerful influence in French politics but was a man of dissolute habits; Valentina was a gentle, cultured lady. On June 29, 1406, at age fourteen, Charles married Isabelle, who was five years older than he, daughter of Charles VI and child-widow of England's Richard II. Isabelle died September 13, 1409, after giving birth to a daughter.

In 1407, two years before Charles lost his wife, his father was murdered by hired assassins of John the Fearless, Duke of Burgundy, whose interest was in destroying rivals for control over Charles VI, who was often mentally unstable. Charles's mother, apparently exhausted by the combination of sorrow, appeals for justice, and burdens in administering the estate, died a year later.

With support from friends of his father, Charles assumed the title Duke of Orléans himself and in 1410 married Bonne, the daughter of Bernard d'Armagnac. With this alliance, Charles tried for years to avenge Burgundy's crime, coming closest in 1415 by gaining support from the king and receiving consolation in memorial masses clearing his father's name and condemning the murder; he could not, however, punish Burgundy.

Later that same year, Charles was the most important of many French nobles captured in the astonishing defeat of the massive French army at Agincourt by the much smaller English forces led by King Henry V. He was kept prisoner in England for twenty-five years, from 1415 to 1440.

Life's Work

The English considered the Duke of Orléans their most important political prisoner because of his high rank and the antagonism between England and France in these last decades of the Hundred Years' War. Henry V insisted on strong security to prevent escape and never asked ransom for Charles's deliverance. In later years, the brother of Henry V, Humphrey, Duke of Gloucester, continued this strong opposition to Charles's release. Charles probably never was actually in what most people would consider a jail; he was, however, moved every few years from such castles as Windsor to

Pontefract in 1417, Fotheringhay in 1421, Bolingbroke in 1422, London in 1425, Canterbury in 1427, Peterborough in 1428, Amthill in 1430, Dover and London in 1433, Wingfield in 1434, Calais in 1435, and London in 1437 until 1440. These frequent movements may have been to prevent him from ingratiating himself with his primary guardians.

During most of this time he was permitted to keep servants and to receive money and household goods, including wine from France. Charles was able to send messengers to oversee affairs on his estates in France and to make political appointments. He was clearly on friendly terms with at least one of his guardians, William de la Pole, Earl of Suffolk, a minor poet in English himself. In fact, when Suffolk was later accused of treason and then assassinated in 1450, one of the charges against him was that he supported release of the Duke of Orléans for ransom.

For posterity, Charles's most important activity while in captivity was writing poetry, principally love lyrics. His most characteristic verse form in these years was the ballade (sometimes called ballad), an intricate verse form requiring at least three stanzas of equal length and a refrain at the end of each stanza. Charles used twenty-one stanzaic patterns and wrote in both eight-syllable and ten-syllable lines, preferring the eight-syllable line.

During his lifetime, Charles was respected for his poetry in French. Some of his correspondence included an occasional lyric, often with a request for a poem in response, especially in letters to the later Duke of Burgundy, Philip the Good. While in captivity, however, he seems also to have written in English. A large collection of ballades, rondels, and occasional verses (6,531 lines) survive in the manuscript Harleian 682. The speaker of these poems identifies himself as Charles, Duke of Orléans; some of them are approximate translations of his French poems, others are unique. All the poems correspond in theme and verse forms to his French poems, but like Middle English verse generally, his English poems lack the grace and precision of the French lyrics.

Both in French and English the poems written during these years in England make much use of personification and allegory, a manner of expression derived from *Le Roman de la rose* (*The Romance of the Rose*), a lengthy narrative started by Guillaume de Lorris but completed by Jean de Meung more than a century before Charles's work. Charles employed such personifications as Hope, Despair, Disdain, and Sadness to represent his inner experience in these shorter lyrics, particularly in ballades. The speaker in these poems is a man restricted in his activities, frequently feeling ignored or rejected and rarely gaining satisfaction. He often calls himself a prisoner of love.

Some commentators quarrel over whether these love lyrics have historical references or are merely conventional exercises in an outmoded tradition. Attempts to identify the lady or ladies alluded to in these poems include speculation that the Peerless Lady might be Charles's first wife, Isabelle (who died six years before his capture at Agincourt); his second wife, Bonne; and various English ladies. More than one scholar has pointed to the Earl of Arundel's second wife, Maud Lovell.

An intriguing candidate for the replacement in the poet's heart following the death of the Peerless Lady is Anne Moleyns, a woman related by marriage to the Earl of Suffolk. The first letters of one of Charles's English poems spell out ANNE MOLINS, but no other evidence besides this acrostic points to such a relationship. This beloved mistress has even been identified as a personification of France itself, indicating a reappearance of Charles's patriotism for that country after years of captivity deadened any emotional ties. Most recent scholars give up on identifying the ladies and urge the beautiful expression of complex feeling in Charles's poetry as valuable for any sensitive reader.

When released from English captivity for ransom in 1440, the Duke of Orléans sincerely attempted peace negotiations between the two great powers, but not with much success. The French themselves were less interested in peace at this time because their own military power was ascending and the might of the English was in decline. Also in 1440, Charles married Marie de Clèves, niece of Philip the Good, Duke of Burgundy. Among the children was a son, Louis, born in 1462, who later became King Louis XII. Charles tried unsuccessfully to reclaim property in Asti, Italy, that he had inherited from his mother. Again, however, the more important activity in this later phase of his life was writing poetry. Though he continued to write ballades as before, his preference now was for the rondel (some commentators call these same poems rondeaux). Charles's rondels are primarily composed of thirteen or fifteen eight-syllable lines divided in three stanzas using only two rhyme sounds. Most characteristically he communicates with irony or even bawdy humor in this later poetry, often with expression of indifference to the desires or pains of love.

In his last years, while living in Blois, Charles maintained a poetry salon in his home and invited noble guests, members of his household, and other poets, such as François Villon, to participate in poetic entertainments. The Duke of Orléans died on January 4, 1465, while on a trip to Amboise.

Summary

The status of Charles d'Orléans as a major French medieval poet seems secure and even improving; he ranks alongside François Villon and above Guillaume de Machaut and Eustache Deschamps when measured by comparable representation in selective anthologies. He does not refer to historic events or draw extensively from classical or European literature for allusions. Thus, in his poetry, he is not scholarly or intellectual by Renaissance and later standards. No one can deny, however, the elegance and concision of his best poems, especially the rondels.

The question of evaluating his English poetry remains open partly as a result of uncertainty about his authorship but also as a result of insufficient attention by Middle English specialists to fifteenth century lyrics. Charles's English poetry may in fact surpass that of any English poet of his era while still falling short of his own standard in French.

In review of his achievements as a government leader, one must credit him with good intentions, as he battled for many worthwhile causes, but he is most famous for defeat. He never truly avenged his father's murder, though John the Fearless was assassinated early in Charles's captivity; the Battle of Agincourt stands as one of the most astonishing defeats in history; his attempts to gain release from captivity meant many years of frustration; and he failed to regain his property in Italy. Nevertheless, he always earned respect from his captors and loyal followers; Joan of Arc even spoke of freeing the Duke of Orléans as one of her objectives. His enforced leisure as prisoner probably led to his finding consolation in writing poetry. He was a man who achieved much in the midst of great adversity.

Bibliography

Arn, Mary-Jo. "The Structure of the English Poems of Charles of Orléans." *Fifteenth Century Studies* 4 (1981): 17-23. Argues that Charles's English poems constitute a single work representing love as an incurable disease. The two separate ladies, one admired in conventional, courtly terms, another more petulantly, are separate stages in a lover's struggle with his addiction.

Champion, Pierre, ed. *Charles d'Orléans: Poésies*. 2 vols. Paris: Librairie Honore Champion, 1923-1927, reprint 1956, 1966. The standard edition of the French poems, including the eleven English poems in two predominantly French manuscripts. The brief biography, description of manuscripts, lists of variants, notes, indexes, and glossary are in French.

Fein, David A. *Charles d'Orléans*. Boston: Twayne Publishers, 1983. Contains a brief biography and careful analysis of the major French poems (with English translations) but omits coverage of the English poems. Fein describes the early ballades as inwardly centered with personified emotions for exploring thoughts and feelings. This pensive, melancholy outlook shifts to outward orientation and irony in the rondeaux.

Fox, John H. *The Lyric Poetry of Charles d'Orléans*. Oxford: Clarendon Press, 1969. A sophisticated study of the French poems (with English translations) reviewing literary background, style, and Charles's distinctive poetic personality. Early use of personification reflects the poet's frustration, melancholy, and boredom. The humor and irony in later rondels only partially conceal this complicated outlook.

Goodrich, Norma Lorre. *Charles Duke of Orléans: A Literary Biography*. New York: Macmillan, 1963. Pleasingly written, much like a historical novel. Goodrich embellishes historical facts about Charles with descriptions of places, analogous anecdotes, and brief biographies of major contemporaries. References to poetry are appreciative, rather than analytical. Entire book is in English, including attractive translations of occasional, illustrative lyrics.

_____ . *Charles of Orléans: A Study of Themes in His French and in His English Poetry*. Geneva, Switzerland: Librairie Droz, 1967. Like a dissertation, this book compares French and English poems to prove single authorship, based on themes such as self-analysis, hope, disdain, war, and peace, but also on craftsmanship. Goodrich believes the Peerless Lady is a memory of Isabelle.

Jacob, E. F. *The Fifteenth Century: 1399-1485*. Oxford: Clarendon Press, 1961. An admirable, authoritative study of Lancastrian England. Jacob's attention to political and economic concerns and the personalities of Henry V and Henry VI gives background for Charles's imprisonment and his difficulty in peace negotiations.

McLeod, Enid. *Charles of Orléans: Prince and Poet*. London: Chatto and Windus, 1969. An engaging biographical study with bold interpretations of persons and events alluded to in his poetry (no translations for quotations in French). McLeod believes the Peerless Lady is Bonne d'Armagnac and oversimplifies and sentimentalizes political and diplomatic conflicts.

Newman, Karen. "The Mind's Castle: Containment in the Poetry of Charles d'Orléans." *Romance Philology* 33 (1979): 317-328. Takes the image of containment in Charles's verses as implying intellectual-spiritual levels of meaning in addition to imprisonment by enemies or by love. She finds a stronger "spiritual quest" in Charles than do other critics.

Steele, Robert, and Mabel Day, eds. *The English Poems of Charles of Orléans*. Reprint. London: Oxford University Press, 1970. A scholarly edition with description of manuscripts, an argument in favor of Charles's authorship, notes, and glossary. Steele offers Charles as a respectable English poet.

Watson, Harold. "Charles d'Orléans: 1394-1465." *Romanic Review* 56 (1965): 3-11. Emphasizes *Nonchaloir* or "nonchalance" as Charles's dominant theme in his mature poetry. A loser to fortune, he defends himself "against the unwanted memory of overweening sorrows." Watson sees Charles as a "modern poet" in revealing his self-contemplation and disenchantment.

David V. Harrington

CHARLES IV

Born: May 14, 1316; Prague, Bohemia
Died: November 29, 1378; Prague, Bohemia
Area of Achievement: Government
Contribution: The greatest ruler of medieval Bohemia and the last important medieval Holy Roman emperor, Charles was an efficient and effective administrator. He stabilized German political affairs, strengthened the power of his family in Bohemia and in Europe, and influenced the culture of his time.

Early Life
Charles was the oldest son of John of Luxembourg and the grandson of Holy Roman Emperor Henry VII, who died in 1313. In the confused years following the death without direct heir of Wenceslas (Václav) III, the last Přemyslid king of Bohemia, Henry had arranged for John to succeed to the Bohemian throne in 1310 and to marry Elizabeth, Wenceslas' sister. This political marriage strengthened the Luxembourg position in Bohemia, and when Charles was born in 1316 the future of the new dynasty seemed assured.

Charles's early education was unsystematic. His mother schooled him in the traditions of government and foreign policy established by the last Přemyslids and instilled in him a love of the Bohemian land. His father, whose political and cultural tastes were oriented more toward France than toward Germany, involved him in many of his European ventures. John never felt particularly comfortable or welcome in Bohemia, and the time he spent there was chiefly for obtaining the financial resources to support his activities elsewhere. It was perhaps not surprising that he and Elizabeth should quarrel, and in 1323 he took Charles from Prague to Paris to be brought up at the court of King Charles IV of France. Periodically, John included his son on his numerous knightly campaigns. As a result, Charles rapidly learned the skills of survival in the world of political intrigue.

Charles's education was not, however, wholly practical and pragmatic. While in Paris he made contact with the eloquent and learned Abbot of Fécamp, Pierre Roger, whom he asked to become his tutor. Their friendship endured and was an important factor later, when Pierre became Pope Clement VI.

The next stage in Charles's education was in the arena of practical politics. In 1331, John took him on an expedition to Italy in support of Louis IV Wittelsbach of Bavaria, who had been Holy Roman emperor since 1314. Charles was placed in a position of authority as imperial vicar in the region of Lombardy, and for two years he gained experience with the politically unstable world of the northern Italian communes. In October, 1333, he returned with his father to Bohemia, and the next year he was named Margrave of Moravia. This position gave him royal power in the absence of the king, occasions which were frequent because of John's restless knight-errantry. For most of the period between 1334 and 1346, Charles was the de facto ruler of the kingdom of Bohemia. He governed wisely and well, restoring administrative efficiency and recovering many royal prerogatives and properties.

Life's Work

Events in 1346 changed Charles's status. Opposition to the rule of Louis IV had been growing in Germany, much of it fueled by hostility from the Papacy. When Pierre Roger became pope in 1342, he had embarked upon a program to depose Louis and replace him with Charles. On July 11, 1346, a majority of electors in Germany withdrew support from Louis and elected Charles in his place. Although the electoral decision in 1346 was challenged, Charles's position was confirmed the following year when Louis died of a stroke. While some observers, both then and in later times, charged that Charles was a mere ecclesiastical puppet (they applied to him the derogatory term *Pfaffenkönig*, or papal king), the fact was that the Luxembourg family had an independent imperial tradition and Charles was a practiced and adroit politician who had broad support in Germany. His relations with the Papacy were to be close, but he was always an autonomous and powerful figure. Indeed, after Clement VI's death in 1352, Charles was really the dominant figure in continental Europe.

Immediately after his election, Charles left to join his father in a military campaign with the French against the English as a part of the Hundred Years' War. At Crécy on August 26, John was led into battle by his retainers—he had been blind for a number of years—and in the subsequent French disaster he was killed. Charles then withdrew from the conflict so that, as a contemporary observed, Bohemia would not lose two rulers in a single day. Now both emperor and king, Charles returned to Prague and began a thirty-two-year reign of great consequence for both Germany and Bohemia.

Charles's primary concern as ruler was the dynastic aggrandizement of his family. He increased the crown lands in Bohemia and Moravia, added areas in Silesia to the family holdings, obtained the district of Eger (Cheb) on the border between Bohemia and the German lands, purchased the region of Lower Lusatia in 1367, and gained control of Brandenburg in 1373 in complicated negotiations with the Wittelsbach family and the Estates of Brandenburg. As a result, the Luxembourg family achieved a prominent position in Europe, one which may be compared with the later eminence of the Habsburg and Hohenzollern families.

Subordinate, but related, to Charles's dynastic interests was his royal policy in Bohemia. He tried to strengthen kingly power against the high

Bohemian nobility. He prepared a written law code, known as the Majestas Carolina, which was submitted to the Bohemian Estates at the diet in 1355. They recognized the degree to which it would limit their traditional role as a law-interpreting body, and they refused to accept it. In other respects, and by other means, however, Charles was able to enhance royal authority. His support of urban development and commercial activity ushered in an era of prosperity for Bohemian cities. Charles used his position as emperor to ensure that Venetian trade routes with Bruges and London were shifted eastward in order to benefit the towns and merchants of his kingdom. Nowhere is Charles's impact more clearly seen than in Prague itself, for it was transformed into an imperial capital. Charles had already arranged in 1343 with his former tutor, now Pope Clement VI, to have Prague raised to an archdiocese. Now, as king, he undertook an extensive building program and founded a new commercial and settlement district.

In the lands of the Holy Roman Empire, Charles pursued a policy which was realistic and moderate. He recognized that the centuries-long imperial tradition of trying to rule northern Italy as well as the German lands was an anachronism. He went to Italy to be crowned emperor in 1355, but he made no attempt to enforce imperial claims over the unstable and contentious communes of northern Italy. Elsewhere, he arranged to be crowned king of the old Burgundian royal domaine of Arles in 1365. Nevertheless, Charles had no illusions that this kingdom could effectively be ruled as imperial territory. He eventually bestowed an imperial vicarate upon the French dauphin for the whole kingdom except for the region of Savoy.

Charles's realism was best revealed in his issuance of the Golden Bull of 1356. This imperial constitution (named for the golden seal—*bulla*) defined an orderly procedure for electing subsequent rulers; it identified the electors (four secular rulers and three ecclesiastical dignitaries), from whom a majority vote was necessary; it established the city of Frankfurt-am-Main as the meeting place for an election; and it prescribed the ceremonial procedural to be followed. While these details codified a process which had been evolving for a century, the bull nevertheless represented a statesmanlike resolution of problems which had plagued the empire for generations. Of particular note is the fact that the Wittelsbachs of Bavaria and the Habsburgs of Austria were excluded from the electorship. Moreover, there was no mention of papal prerogatives of assent to, or participation in, the election. Of equal importance for the future of German affairs was that the bull declared the electoral territories of the secular rulers to be indivisible and strengthened these electors in their own principalities to such a degree that they became practically sovereign rulers. Since the King of Bohemia was identified as one of the electors, Charles himself was confirmed in his territorial prerogatives. This accomplished what had earlier been frustrated in the Majestas Carolina.

Charles's activities were not limited to family affairs or internal politics.

Within central Europe he was clearly the leading figure in relations with Poland, Hungary, and Austria. He tended to support France against England in the Hundred Years' War. In his dealings with the Papacy, Charles promoted the popes' return to Italy from Avignon, where they had been resident since the early fourteenth century. He was a supporter of ecclesiastical reform, both in Germany and especially in Bohemia. With the outbreak of the Great Schism (or Western Schism) in 1378, though he supported the Roman pope Urban VI, Charles tried to intervene to heal the division between the two claimants to the pontifical throne. His health failed him, however, and he died in Prague late in November, 1378.

Summary

From Charles's third marriage, to the niece of the Hungarian king, there came his son Wenceslas (also spelled Wenzel or Václav), who was born in 1361 and who succeeded Charles without incident in 1378. This easy transition revealed the degree to which Charles had been successful in stabilizing and regulating German affairs. His statesmanship had given focus and direction to a process which had proceeded haphazardly in earlier generations. The effect of the Golden Bull of 1356 was not limited to the electors alone; in all the empire's principalities and city-states the same development toward territorial control may be observed. Charles recognized that the emperor had little power without a firm territorial base. His reign established the principality as the focus of German politics for the next several centuries.

Charles was also an influential religious and cultural patron. He was involved in the planning and building of the Gothic-style St. Vitus' Cathedral in Prague, he endowed many religious establishments throughout the kingdom and the empire, and he himself wrote a biography of the patron saint of Bohemia, Saint Wenceslas (c. 907-929). He also wrote a revealing autobiography, one of the few to come from a lay person in the medieval period. At his court, Charles entertained learned intellectuals and figures involved with the early Italian Renaissance. Charles was also patriotic about his Czech heritage. He referred to Bohemia as "the sweet soil of my native land," he prided himself that he could speak the language "like any other Czech," and he encouraged and patronized historians of Bohemia.

In 1347, Charles founded a university in Prague. It was the first north of the Alps and east of the Rhine. The University of Prague, which was allowed by the Papacy to have a theological faculty, quickly established its reputation under Charles's patronage as an important center of learning. By the end of the fourteenth century, it would become the European center of religious and theological controversy.

Charles's greatness lay not in wars waged or in conquests won but rather in his statesmanship, vision, and political realism. He was regarded by later Czech generations as "the father of his country."

Bibliography

Du Boulay, F. R. *Germany in the Later Middle Ages*. New York: St. Martin's Press, 1984. Although the scope of this volume goes far beyond the figure and rule of Charles, it is a useful book for understanding the larger context of Charles's reign as well as some specific aspects of his rule in Germany. It was abreast of the most recent scholarship at the time of its publication. The treatment of towns, the Church, and the structures of society and governance is especially good. The section devoted specifically to Charles (pages 36-42) draws effectively upon the important German biography by Ferdinand Seibt.

Jarrett, Bede. *The Emperor Charles IV*. London: Eyre and Spottiswoode, 1935. This biography is largely uncritical and is based on secondary materials, with little reference to the sources. The one exception is that the author provides a partial translation of Charles's autobiography. The translation is a loose one and misses many important nuances of this effort by Charles to present some of his imperial ideals, but it does communicate some of the directness of Charles's literary style.

Krofta, Kamil. "Bohemia in the Fourteenth Century." In *The Cambridge Medieval History*. Vol. 7, *Decline of Empire and Papacy*. Cambridge: Cambridge University Press, 1932, reprint 1958. Though it deals with more than the reign of Charles, the primary focus of this chapter is upon the years from 1333 to 1378. The political narrative is detailed and reliable, and the judgment upon Charles is generally favorable. A good treatment of Charles in the context of Czech history.

Thomson, S. Harrison. "Learning at the Court of Charles IV." *Speculum* 25 (1950): 1-20. A full and scholarly treatment of the cultural aspects of Charles's reign. The author not only analyzes the formal literary and educational activities connected directly with Charles but also gives attention to the general cultural milieu, including the development of the Czech vernacular and the restructuring of the German language in the royal chancery.

Walsh, Gerald Groveland. *The Emperor Charles IV, 1316-1378: A Study in Holy Empire Imperialism*. Oxford: Basil Blackwell, 1924. Provides a short sketch of Charles's imperial ideals, but treats these in a rather old-fashioned way, reflecting many of the categories of nineteenth century German scholarship. There is very little discussion of Charles's Bohemian policy and none of his leadership in the cultural sphere, except as it might be related to his political theory.

Waugh, W. T. "Germany: Charles IV." In *The Cambridge Medieval History*. Vol. 7, *Decline of Empire and Papacy*. Cambridge: Cambridge University Press, 1932, reprint 1958. Treats the political details of Charles's German policy in depth and with accuracy. The emphasis is upon the way Charles maneuvered among the other political leaders in Europe and upon his family policy. The evaluation of his accomplishments is generally negative. This is especially true with regard to what the author considers Charles's surrender of imperial prerogatives.

Paul W. Knoll

CHARLES THE BALD

Born: June 13, 823; Frankfurt am Main
Died: October 6, 877; Avrieux or Brides-les-Bain, France
Area of Achievement: Government
Contribution: Reigning during one of the most turbulent periods in European history, Charles managed to survive and pass the crown of the West Frankish kingdom to his posterity.

Early Life

Charles the Bald was the grandson of Charlemagne and the son of the Frankish emperor Louis the Pious and his second wife, Judith. At the time of Charles's birth, the emperor already had three sons: Lothair, the eldest; Louis II the German; and Pepin. Indeed, in 817 Louis had published a decree establishing the method by which the empire would be divided among the three at his death. Lothair was to succeed as emperor and Louis the German and Pepin were to hold kingdoms under his rule. Louis the German and Pepin had already been invested with the kingdoms they were to hold.

This situation was further complicated by the fact that the new empress, Judith, was of the Welf family, a noble family prominent in that section of the empire known as Alamannia (modern Alsace). This portion of the realm had been very difficult for the Carolingian Frankish rulers to control, and Louis the Pious, in marrying a daughter of this aristocratic family, believed that he could establish closer and more friendly ties. When Judith and Louis had a son, the future of Alamannia seemed secure. The elder brothers of the new prince, however, had no intention of allowing their portions of the territory to diminish. Since Judith did not want the young heir's interests to be ignored, the situation intensified. The result was civil war when, in 829, Charles was given a portion of land taken from the portions already allotted his brothers. The warring continued intermittently until Louis the Pious died in 840.

Life's Work

Charles's half brother Pepin was already dead when their father, Louis the Pious, died. Although Pepin had a son of his own, Pepin II, Charles received title to the land previously allotted to Pepin I, reserving the rights of Pepin II in Aquitaine, which Pepin II was to hold as a subkingdom under Charles's suzerainty.

In the division of the empire among the brothers, Charles received the western portions of the empire, which conformed, loosely, to what is now the nation of France, while Louis the German received the eastern portion of the empire, conforming loosely to what is now Germany. Lothair, the eldest brother and the new emperor, obtained a long, narrow strip of territory situated between what are modern France and Germany and including the modern territories of the Low Countries, Luxembourg, Alsace, Switzerland, and Italy.

Louis the German and Charles the Bald almost immediately attacked Lothair with the intention of adding to their portions bits of land detached from his. When Lothair died in 855, he was succeeded by his sons Lothair II in Lorraine, Charles in Provence, and Louis in Italy. Lothair II died in 869, after which Charles the Bald and Louis the German partitioned his realm.

Within his own kingdom, Charles the Bald had considerable difficulties. During the whole of his reign, the kingdom of France was subjected to repeated attacks by the Vikings. The Meuse, Seine, and Loire rivers were navigable by the Viking longboats for considerable distances upstream, which meant that no region, even in the interior, was safe from their raids. The speed of the Viking attacks was such that it was not possible for Charles to organize an efficient defense; as a result, he usually had to bribe the Vikings to go away.

In addition, Charles had continuing difficulties with the subkingdom of Aquitaine, ruled by his nephew Pepin II; Pepin tended to ignore his overlord and uncle, and Charles wished to dispossess Pepin. The Aquitanian nobles generally supported Pepin but kept the controversy alive as a means to prevent any stable central government from limiting their influence. Charles tried to imprison Pepin II in 855 but had to release him when Louis the German sent his sons Louis the Younger and Charles the Fat to take advantage of the situation and seize Aquitaine for themselves. Charles the Bald did not take control of Aquitaine until 864, when he imprisoned Pepin a second time, after which Pepin disappeared. In the end, Charles was never able to rule Aquitaine.

As though these problems were not enough, Charles had great difficulty keeping his nobles loyal. The partitioning of the realm had taken place amid constant conflicts among members of the imperial family. This climate of general disorder was exacerbated by the inability of the Crown to deal adequately with the Vikings.

Despite all of these problems, Charles the Bald managed to create at his court an atmosphere of cultivation and scholarship. Several of the most distinguished scholars of the Western world—including Johannes Scotus Erigena, Lupus of Ferrières, Walafrid Strabo, and Hincmar of Reims—were active in the affairs of Charles's realm.

At the end of his life, Charles became emperor. His nephew Louis of Italy had succeeded to the imperial title in 869 when Lothair had died. Conditions in Italy were disturbed as a result of the invasion of the peninsula by Muslim armies from North Africa. When Louis died in 875, Pope John VIII called upon Charles for assistance. Charles made an expedition to Italy in 875 and was crowned emperor on December 25 of that year, the seventy-fifth anniversary of the imperial coronation of his grandfather, Charlemagne. Yet Charles was unable to stem the Muslim threat to Rome and the papacy and, discouraged, retired from Italy in 877. It was while he was on the way home from Italy, with his own kingdom under attack by the Germans, that Charles died on October 6. He was succeeded by his son Louis the Stammerer.

Summary

During his fifty-four years, Charles the Bald witnessed the destruction of the great European empire created by his grandfather and the Frankish armies. Ultimately, the empire disintegrated, because it was too unwieldy and too ethnically diverse to be integrated into a cohesive whole. The chronic wars among the descendants of Charlemagne, to which Charles the Bald was a party, were merely symptomatic of larger problems which the political and social structures of the period simply could not solve.

Nevertheless, Charles the Bald was, in certain ways, a successful ruler. He managed to preserve and support the cultural activities of the Carolingian renaissance. He was also a dutiful son of the Church, cooperating fully with his bishops and promoting the continuing Christianization of the western Frankish lands. Moreover, the seeming chaos of his reign should not obscure the fact that in surviving and keeping the Crown amid myriad difficulties he achieved as much as was humanly possible.

Bibliography
Barraclough, Geoffrey. *The Crucible of Europe: The Ninth and Tenth Centuries in European History*. Berkeley: University of California Press, 1976. A useful guide to the general context of late Carolingian affairs.
Duckett, Eleanor Shipley. *Carolingian Portraits: A Study of the Ninth Century*. Ann Arbor: University of Michigan Press, 1962. Contains studies of Lupus of Ferrières, Hincmar of Reims, and Walafrid Strabo—influential scholars of the time of Charles the Bald.
Dunbabin, Jean. *France in the Making, 843-1180*. Oxford: Oxford University Press, 1985. Chapter 1 deals with Charles the Bald.
Engreen, F. E. "Pope John VIII and the Arabs." *Speculum* 20 (1945): 318-330. One of the very few studies addressing the Arab problem in Italy during the time of Charles the Bald.
Halphen, Louis. *Charlemagne and the Carolingian Empire*. Translated by G. de Nie. Amsterdam: North Holland Publishers, 1977. Part 3 of this volume discusses the affairs of Charles the Bald and his brothers.
McKitterick, Rosamond. *The Frankish Kingdoms Under the Carolingians*. New York: Longmans, Green and Co., 1983. A useful synthesis, although it does not supersede Halphen's study. The latter portion discusses the period of Charles the Bald's life.
Poupardin, René. "The Carolingian Kingdoms, 840-877." In *Cambridge Me-*

dieval History, vol. 3, *Germany and the Western Empire*. New York: Macmillan, 1922. A detailed and invaluable account of the period of Charles the Bald's life and the complicated affairs of the divided empire.

David Harry Miller

CHARLES MARTEL

Born: c. 688; place unknown
Died: October 22, 741; Quierzy-sur-Oise
Areas of Achievement: Government and warfare
Contribution: Through hard fighting and shrewd political leadership, Charles restored the political fortunes of his family and established firm government over the united Frankish realms.

Early Life

Charles Martel was one of an unknown number of children of Pepin II of Heristal, Duke and Mayor of the Palace of the Austrasian Franks. Charles's mother was Chalpaida or Alpais, one of at least three wives or concubines of Pepin II. Nothing is known of Charles's childhood or adolescence, and he is not mentioned in any source until 714. Charles had at least two half-brothers, Drogo and Grimoald II, both sons of Pepin II's leading wife, Plectrude. Both Drogo and Grimoald predeceased Pepin II, who died in 714. Since Drogo and Grimoald both left children of their own, Plectrude attempted to secure the inheritance for her grandsons and to exclude Charles, the son of a rival. Plectrude briefly imprisoned Charles at an unknown place, from which he escaped, probably by 715.

Pepin II's family, variously called the Pippinids, Arnulfings, or Carolingians, were the leading noble dynasty of Frankish Austrasia, and since 687 had been in control of Frankish Neustria as well. Pepin II managed to rule the kingdom by controlling the reigning king of the Merovingian house and by manipulating the major ecclesiastical foundations, both monastic and episcopal.

When Pepin II died in 714, the Neustrian magnates revolted from Austrasian control and attempted to bring in allies from both Frisia and Aquitaine, areas peripheral to the Frankish kingdom which had gradually detached themselves from Frankish control. The anti-Pippinid coalition managed to expel Theodebald, Charles's nephew, from Neustria. The Neustrian magnates elected Ragenfrid mayor of the palace, with Chilperic II as his king. Plectrude could not cope with the insurgency, and the remaining grandsons of Pepin II were either minors or otherwise useless in the emergency.

Life's Work

Although the circumstances of Charles's escape from prison are not known, it is recorded that he quickly rallied the Austrasian supporters of the family and dealt with the anti-Pippinid coalition. In three battles, at Amblève in 716, Vincy in 717, and Soissons in 718 or 719, Charles defeated the Neustrian forces and their Frisian allies.

From 719, Charles's major task was to restore Pippinid control in Neustria and Burgundy, which he achieved by adapting policies of his father in respect of the Church. The major monasteries and episcopal dioceses of Neustria and Burgundy were placed under abbots and bishops who were members of either the Pippinid family or Austrasian families closely related to them. Of major assistance in this undertaking was Charles's nephew Hugo, who held several episcopal and abbatial appointments in Neustria and who loyally supported the new head of the family.

With these compliant political allies in control of the major ecclesiastical foundations of the kingdom, Charles was able to seize a substantial portion of the landed properties of the churches, which he was able to use to confer conditional grants on Frankish warriors who were his personal vassals. This practice allowed Charles to develop a large professional warrior force supplementary to the common levy of freemen and which was loyal to him personally. Charles's hold on the kingdom became secure enough that when the puppet-king Theuderic IV died in 737, Charles did not bother to replace him and ruled for the last four years of his life without a king to legitimize his authority.

Having secured control of the Frankish kingdoms, Charles turned his attention to the neighboring lands. The Frisians, Thuringians, Alemannians, Saxons, Bavarians, and Aquitanians had traditionally been clients or subjects of the Frankish kingdom. Most of these territories had been able to achieve practical independence of the Franks during the stormy period before Pepin II united the kingdoms after the battle of Tertry in 687. Thereafter, they had used the charge that the Pippinid family was usurping the legitimate power of the Merovingian kings to justify continued separation. Pepin II had been too preoccupied with internal Frankish affairs to deal with the situation, although he did retake some territory in south Frisia, where he later supported the missionary activity of the Anglo-Saxon monks working with Saint Willibrord, Bishop of Utrecht, in order to establish more firmly Frankish overlordship. Charles continued and expanded the missionary patronage of his father and took advantage in particular of the availability of the Anglo-Saxon Saint Boniface, later Archbishop of Mainz, to strengthen Frankish power in other Trans-Rhenish areas.

Charles also conducted a series of military campaigns against neighboring lands to reassert Frankish overlordship. His immediate priority in this respect was Frisia, as the Frisians had participated directly in the anti-Pippinid coalition in support of the Neustrian magnates. Several campaigns were conducted against the Frisians, but it was not until the early 730's that they were finally brought under control.

Charles was also preoccupied with Aquitaine, where Eudo, a local magnate, had gained a degree of control as duke. Aquitaine, too, had participated to some extent in the anti-Pippinid coalition, although not very effectively. Moreover, Eudo was involved in a problematic association with the Saracens, Arab and Berber Muslim invaders who had entered Spain in 711 and by 720 had conquered most of the area. The Muslim raiders had crossed the Pyrenees into southern France and had ravaged several regions. Although Eudo had defeated raiding parties on several occasions, he was also attempting to use the invaders against the Franks. Eudo was unable to manipulate the Muslims as he wished, however, and in 731, he suffered a serious defeat by a large Muslim force, following which he called upon Charles for assistance. In 732, Charles met the Muslims somewhere between the cities of Poitiers and Tours in the vicinity of the Loire, where he inflicted a major defeat. This victory did not solve the problem of Muslim incursions into Aquitaine, but it did force Eudo to renew Aquitanian submission to the Franks. Aquitaine remained a problem, however, and it was left for Charles's son, Pepin III (the Short), and his grandson, Charlemagne, finally to resolve the problem.

Charles appears to have made several punitive expeditions against the Trans-Rhenish Saxons, but did not subdue them. He was also concerned with the Bavarians and may have married, as one of an unknown number of wives, a Bavarian woman, by whom he had a son, Grifo, who later proved troublesome to his successors, Pepin III and Carloman I.

Summary

Charles Martel's primary achievement was to restore the unity of the Frankish kingdom and establish a firm government, equally firmly under the control of his family. He began, but did not finally resolve, the reconquest of the peripheral areas traditionally subject to the Frankish kingdom under the Merovingian kings. His defeat of the Muslims in 732, in particular, struck the imaginations of later observers and led to his surname, Martel, meaning "the Hammer."

An important aspect of Charles's life and rule was his relationship with the Frankish church, which he definitively subjected to the governing family. While he has been criticized on this account, it must also be noted that Charles's patronage of missionaries promoted the long-term influence of Anglo-Saxons in the Frankish church and laid the foundation for the eventual alliance of the Frankish rulers with the papacy, implemented through the Anglo-Saxon missionaries. When Pope Gregory III, under siege from the Lombards, sent to Charles in 739 the keys to the tomb of Saint Peter and a link from the fetters associated with the tomb, he was explicitly recognizing the growing importance of the Pippinid family and the Frankish church.

Bibliography

Bachrach, Bernard S. "Charles Martel, Mounted Shock Combat, the Stirrup, and Feudalism." *Studies in Medieval and Renaissance History* 7

(1970): 47-75. Convincingly disputes the notion that the Frankish army was reorganized as a cavalry force under Charles.

―――――――. *Merovingian Military Organization, 481-751*. Minneapolis: University of Minnesota Press, 1972. The only modern work on the subject in English. On Charles, there is some repetition of the material in the work cited above.

Fouracre, Paul J. "Observations on the Outgrowth of Pippinid Influence in the 'Regnum Francorum' After the Battle of Tertry (687-715)." *Medieval Prosopography* 5 (1984): 1-31. An important study of the methods used by the Pippinid family to govern the Frankish territories.

Geary, Patrick J. *Before France and Germany: The Creation and Transformation of the Merovingian World*. New York: Oxford University Press, 1988. The best work currently available in English on the Merovingian period. Chapter 6 deals with the period of Charles.

Levison, Wilhelm. *England and the Continent in the Eighth Century*. Oxford: Clarendon Press, 1946. Still the best study of missionary affairs on the European continent during the lifetime of Charles and his successors.

McKitterick, Rosamond. *The Frankish Kingdoms Under the Carolingians*. New York: Longman, 1983. A modern synthesis which deals briefly with the period of Charles in the first section.

Wallace-Hadrill, John Michael. *The Long-Haired Kings and Other Studies in Frankish History*. London: Methuen and Co., 1962. An adequate and often-consulted general study of various aspects of Merovingian history. Chapter 7 deals with affairs in the lifetime of Charles.

David Harry Miller

ALAIN CHARTIER

Born: c. 1385; Bayeux, France
Died: 1429; Avignon, France
Areas of Achievement: Literature and politics
Contribution: Chartier's skillful use of the French language and his imaginative, elegant style significantly influenced the development of French poetry in the fifteenth century. As royal secretary to Charles VII of Valois, Chartier played an active role in the complex political world during the Hundred Years' War, a world which he accurately recorded in prose works of extraordinary literary and historical importance.

Early Life

Alain Chartier, the most famous poet of early fifteenth century France, the canon of the Notre-Dame de Paris, a chronicler of his time, and the creator of the literary school known as the *Grands Rhétoriqueurs*, was born in Bayeux, France, the eldest of three sons of a prominent Norman family. One of his younger brothers, Guillaume, became Bishop of Paris, and another, Thomas, like Alain, held a post as royal secretary and notary. Such distinguished service to the kings of France by the three Chartier brothers suggests that the family enjoyed a certain social and economic prominence. The young Alain attended the University of Paris and may even have been a *maître* (lecturer-teacher) at the University of Paris for a short while.

Life's Work

Although little is known of his youthful activities, by 1417, Chartier was well established both in his profession as royal secretary and as a poet. The office of "notary and secretary of the king" was a very desirable position. In addition to guaranteeing the holder a secure place within the court, it provided a rather substantial salary. A small number of notaries were also "secretaries"; that is, as the name implies, they were empowered to sign secret letters. In his position as secretary, Chartier had almost daily contact with the king while at court and, when serving as ambassador abroad, he would have been entrusted with the most sensitive matters of state politics.

For a writer and scholar such as Chartier, the secretarial post provided intellectual benefits far beyond financial security. During untroubled times he had time to compose his lyric poetry, he had easy access to the works of earlier poets through the king's magnificent library at Paris and through the renowned papal library at Avignon, and he enjoyed the companionship, inspiration, and encouragement of other poets who resided at court.

Life at court, however, was not without difficulties for Chartier. On several occasions he vehemently criticized the self-serving interests at court. In *De vita curiali* (1489; *The Curial*, 1888), he wrote:

The court is an assembly of people who under the pretence of acting for the good of all, come together to diddle each other. . . . The abuses of the court and the habits of courtiers are such that no one lasts there without being corrupted and no one succeeds there without being corruptible.

From 1410 to 1425, Chartier moved regularly with members of the king's household as they fled before the invading English armies led by Henry V. During most of Chartier's career at court, France was ravaged by constant attacks from the English as part of the Hundred Years' War, and by a virulent civil war. Chartier was deeply immersed in the political machinations of this most complex period in French history, yet he proved to be both an able ambassador and a talented and thorough chronicler. For example, his *Epistola de Puella* (letter concerning the Maid, Joan of Arc), written in 1429, describes in accurate and lengthy detail Joan of Arc's exploits and victories, including the breaking of the siege at Orléans and the crowning of Charles VII at Reims.

The last four years of his life, Chartier served as royal ambassador on a number of important missions abroad, including one to the Holy Roman Emperor Sigismund of Luxembourg in 1425 and another to the court of James I of Scotland in 1428. These were troubled times to be serving as royal ambassador; the office called for men of great talent and even greater courage. As a direct result of the prolonged and bitter fighting between the French and English, royal ambassadors faced the constant danger of assassination or being taken hostage. Chartier often mentioned in his correspondence concern for his personal safety.

In 1428, while visiting the court of James I of Scotland, Chartier negotiated an alliance which would result in military support for France. Charles also authorized Chartier to arrange for the marriage of James's daughter, Margaret Stuart, to Charles's son, Louis XI. Chartier's association with Margaret's marriage contract led to one of the most famous, yet clearly apocryphal, anecdotes of the fifteenth century. According to this often-repeated story, the beautiful young Dauphiness secretly kissed the sleeping Chartier on the lips and offered these words in defense of her action: "I kissed not the man, but rather the precious mouth from which so much beautiful poetry and so many virtuous words have issued."

The charming story of the youthful lady embracing the aging poet quickly seduced the court of Charles VII, for Chartier's ugliness, like his lyric poetry, had become proverbial. While still in his early forties, the poet's physical appearance already betrayed the effects of the rigorous and taxing life he had led as servant to the king. According to his own writings, his body had withered, his face had wrinkled, and he had become thin and pale. Nevertheless, Margaret did not appear at the French court until 1436, six or seven years after Chartier's death, and at that time she was only twelve years old—hardly mature enough to have been overwhelmed by the poetic power of Chartier's lyrical works.

The connection between Chartier's professional life and his literary production is readily apparent. His poetry reflects the traditional medieval interest in allegory and the lofty concerns of love; it was written for a court audience which anticipated the use of conventional forms and commonplace subject matter. His prose, more measured, more engaged, was informed by his royal service and reflects many of the political and social concerns of the age. His literary production was relatively small, and his reputation rests largely on one poem, "La Belle Dame sans merci" ("The Beautiful, Pitiless Lady"), and one long prose piece, *Le Quadrilogue invectif* (1489; *The Invective Quadrilogue*, late fifteenth century).

In "La Belle Dame sans merci" (the French title is still most often used in English, probably because of the influence of John Keats's poem of the same name), a young lover engages in a debate with his pitiless lady. The young man professes a love which, if unrequited, will lead to his death. Repeatedly, the young lover's advances are repulsed by the uncompromising arguments of the lady as she defends her freedom and steadfastly resists submitting her liberty to the mastery of a man. Finally, she loses patience and summarily dismisses the lover. Devastated, he ultimately dies of a broken heart.

Reaction to Chartier's poem was swift and venomous. The professional male suitors of the court took umbrage at the disparaging portrait of the merciless lady and her lachrymose lover. They demanded a quick trial and severe punishment for the poet from the Court of Love, an actual institution which had been founded by a group of scholars and poets at the court of Charles VI on Saint Valentine's Day, 1401. The charter of the Court of Love clearly stated its purpose to "honor and praise . . . all women." According to his critics, Chartier's poem had maligned the good name of all women; as punishment, he was to be banished immediately from the court. Chartier was sufficiently troubled by the harsh reaction of the court that he penned "L'Excusation" ("The Excuse"), in which he maintained that he had simply recorded a dialogue which he had innocently witnessed while attending a party. Unappeased, the court continued to pursue the poet, adamantly calling for a public retraction and even hiring lawyers. The ultimate outcome of the matter has not been clearly determined; yet, both the reaction of the court and of the poet reveal the exceptional popularity of the poem. For two centuries it was attacked, praised, imitated, and repudiated.

Despite his profound influence on the development of French poetry, many critics maintain that Chartier's greatest contribution to French letters is his prose work, *The Invective Quadrilogue*. The word "quadrilogue" refers to the fact that four allegorical figures (France and the three "estates," or orders of French society: the knights, the clergy, and the peasantry) are involved in a heated debate (*invectif*) concerning the defeat of France at the hands of the English. Written shortly after the signing of the humiliating Treaty of Troyes, the work provides an astonishingly honest and reasoned critique of the social and political problems facing France in 1422. The plundering of the provinces by Henry V, the devastating civil conflict, the widespread starvation as a result of the war, and the dearth of leadership, which collectively had drained France of all of its former glory, set the political context for the work.

Chartier wonders whether France's ills are not the result of internal weaknesses more than foreign invasions. In the midst of his reverie, he falls asleep and has a vision of a beautiful lady, the personification of France, standing beside a dilapidated palace, its former richness now only barely evident. Kneeling before her are three troubled men, representing the knights, the clergy, and the peasantry. The lady admonishes the men for their laziness and cowardice and forthrightly blames their indolent behavior for the destruction of France. Responding to the lady's bitter attacks, the knight and the peasant accuse each other of causing France's defeat. As the dialogue becomes more quarrelsome, the clergy intervenes and demands an end to the destructive bickering, because, he observes, it is just such petty behavior which is at the very root of France's problems. For France to regain her rightful place among nations, all three estates must work together. In the end, the lady underscores the wisdom of the clergy as she reminds her people that a love of the common good will overshadow individual needs and lead France to glory. If all will work together, she counsels, then the fortunes they seek individually will accrue to them all collectively. *The Invective Quadrilogue* affected its readers powerfully in 1422 and through the centuries has been cited as one of the finest statements of patriotic "prose propaganda."

Summary

After November, 1428, no records or official documents bear the name of Alain Chartier. Most likely, he was promoted to member of the royal council as the reward for long and faithful service to the king; thereafter, he would have had his own secretary. He died at Avignon and was buried there in the Church of Saint-Antoine.

His life was one of devotion to public service and to his art. First and foremost, he was a patriot, willingly serving his country as artist and ambassador. His work revealed his love of France and her people, as well as his fervent desire to find ways to reconcile the combative elements within French society. His prose style, always controlled, often elegant, set the standard for French writers for more than two hundred years. A prominent modern critic, Gustave Lanson, calls Chartier a fifteenth century Balzac, referring to his ability to control and elevate the French language. Generations of poets have looked back on Chartier as the "Father of French Eloquence." Although modern readers may find Chartier's didactic works tiresome, his lyric works frivolous, and his use of medieval rhetorical devices pedantic, it was not so in his own time. His humanism and his erudition were greatly admired by his contemporaries, who referred to him respectfully as Master Alain.

Bibliography
Hale, J. R., J. R. L. Highfield, and B. Smalley, eds. *Europe in the Late Middle Ages*. Evanston, Ill.: Northwestern University Press, 1965. This collection of essays provides valuable background information on life in fourteenth and fifteenth century Europe. P. S. Lewis' essay on "France in the Fifteenth Century" supplies helpful information on political and social life at court and makes direct reference to Chartier's work.
Hoffman, Edward J. *Alain Chartier: His Life and Reputation*. New York: Wittes Press, 1942. One of the earliest and most complete treatments of Chartier's life and works. This volume includes a full account of Chartier's life and analyses of his major works. Portions of major works are cited in their original version. Of particular interest is Hoffman's assessment of Chartier's influence on French letters.
Laidlaw, J. C., ed. *The Poetical Works of Alain Chartier*. London: Cambridge University Press, 1974. Laidlaw's chapter on Chartier's life is the most thorough treatment available in English. A second chapter provides brief but helpful introductions to all the poems. The remainder of the volume, however, is devoted to detailed study of the 113 manuscripts which contain Chartier's poetical works.
Patterson, Warner Forrest. *Three Centuries of French Poetic Theory: A Critical History of the Chief Arts of Poetry in France, 1328-1630*. 2 vols. New York: Russell and Russell, 1966. Volume 1 contains an informative introduction to the historical and intellectual context in which Chartier and his contemporaries wrote. Patterson's entry on Chartier is highly informative. Volume 2 contains examples of Chartier's work in the original French.
Tilley, Arthur, ed. *Medieval France*. New York: Hafner Press, 1964. A standard text which provides a rapid and readable account of the history, literature, art, and architecture of medieval France. Although the entry on Chartier is brief and the evaluation of his work necessarily attenuated, Tilley's work offers a concise introduction to the principal writers of the early fifteenth century and places Chartier in this context.

William C. Griffin

CHENG HO
Ma San-po

Born: c. 1371; K'un-yang, Yunnan, China
Died: between 1433 and 1436; possibly Calicut, India
Areas of Achievement: Government and exploration
Contribution: An imperial eunuch, Cheng Ho commanded the Ming Dynasty's voyages of exploration in the early fifteenth century, sailing farther than any person in history at that time.

Early Life

Cheng Ho was born into a Muslim family surnamed Ma (a Chinese transliteration of Muhammad) at K'un-yang in Central Yunnan, a province in southwest China. Although little is known about his family, it apparently had a tradition of foreign travel and adventure, since both his father and grandfather made the traditional Muslim pilgrimage to Mecca.

Cheng Ho's Yunnan was a frontier region heavily populated by non-Chinese ethnic groups (principally Tibeto-Burman). Formerly a loose confederation of tribal states known as Nanchao, Yunnan had been conquered by the Mongols in the thirteenth century during their invasion of China. The cities of Yunnan had a thin veneer of Chinese culture, but the civilization of the countryside remained essentially non-Chinese.

At the beginning of the Ming Dynasty (from 1368 to 1644), Chinese generals campaigned in Yunnan to wrest control of the area from the Mongols. The founder of the Ming, Chu Yüan-chang, also known as Hung-wu, sent about 300,000 troops under the control of a redoubtable commander in chief named Fu Yu-te to subdue the region. In the process, Fu recruited eunuchs, castrated males, into the service of the new dynasty.

Eunuchs were employed at the Chinese court to manage internal palace affairs, particularly those of the emperor's harem. Despite the opposition of the imperial bureaucracy, eunuchs frequently exerted remarkable power in Chinese politics. Because most emperors lived in seclusion from the outside world, they relied on the eunuchs to bring them information and to advise them on matters of state. At times in Chinese history, eunuchs usurped effective control of the government from the emperor and his bureaucracy. While this was not particularly true of the emperors Cheng Ho served, his rise to power does illustrate the influence eunuchs have frequently enjoyed in Chinese history.

Cheng Ho became a eunuch in 1381, when he was about ten years old. He was assigned to the emperor's fourth son, Chu Ti, who eventually became the third Ming emperor and ruled under the reign title of Yung-lo. Cheng Ho's long service with Chu Ti earned for him access to wealth and power. A huge, commanding man (his family records claim that he was seven feet tall, with a waist five feet in circumference, glaring eyes, and a stentorian voice), he distinguished himself as a warrior in Chu Ti's armies, particularly in campaigns against the Mongols from 1393 to 1397. He played a key military role in Chu Ti's rebellion and usurpation of the throne and thus became one of the emperor's most powerful advisers.

During the climactic battle in Nanking that toppled the emperor Chien-wen and brought Chu Ti to the throne, the Ming palace area was burned and the deposed emperor apparently escaped. The fate of the deposed emperor remains a mystery, for he was never seen again. Chu Ti (by then known as Yung-lo), seeking to complete his conquest by finally eliminating Chien-wen, sent one of his trusted advisers throughout China in search of the former emperor and dispatched Cheng Ho on seven maritime expeditions to the "Western Ocean" (a term used to denote South and Southeast Asia).

Life's Work

Cheng Ho's voyages were the most spectacular maritime expeditions China ever launched. They began in 1405 and continued until 1433. During this period of twenty-eight years, Cheng Ho directed seven voyages which visited some thirty-seven countries and reached as far as Aden at the southeastern end of the Red Sea and the east coast of Africa. Cheng Ho was the driving force behind these expeditions, which ceased with his death.

Cheng Ho was promoted to the position of director of eunuch affairs and was granted the surname Cheng in 1404, just before he was appointed commander in chief of the first expedition. In comparison with the early European voyages of exploration, Cheng Ho's expeditions were gigantic. His largest ships measured 440 feet long and 186 feet wide, the medium-sized ships measured 370 by 150 feet, and the battleships, which were equipped with cannon, measured 180 by 68 feet. Some of the vessels had four decks and watertight compartments. (In contrast, Christopher Columbus' largest ship, the *Santa Maria*, was less than eighty feet long.) Each of the voyages carried more than twenty thousand men.

Chinese sources offer two reasons for the launching of these expensive expeditions. First, Yung-lo wanted to trace the whereabouts of the deposed emperor, who might have fled into Southeast Asia. While this may have been one of the reasons for the first expedition, it apparently was not primary, for Cheng Ho made few efforts to search for Chien-wen. The succeeding voyages, which ranged as far as Africa, obviously were not mounted in order to search for the former emperor. It is more likely that Yung-lo authorized the voyages in order to demonstrate China's power and prestige to the world. Unlike the later Europeans, the Chinese were not exploring the world in search of commercial gain, for they did not believe that the non-Chinese could offer them products, ideas, or institutions which could equal their own. Believing that he was the Son of Heaven in control of all people on Earth, the Ming emperor sought to gain the allegiance of as many nations as he could. Paradoxically, then, it appears that the Chinese launched Cheng Ho's voyages, one of the most costly operations in history, for nonmaterialistic reasons.

It was the case, however, that the Chinese, particularly in the southeastern part of the country, had for centuries been engaged in overseas trade. As population pressures increased, they sailed abroad with Chinese products and returned with exotic goods of various kinds. Overseas trade proved extremely profitable, and consequently many southeastern seaports flourished. The migration of Chinese merchants to various parts of Southeast Asia began long before the Ming Dynasty. Seamanship improved with each succeeding generation, so that when Yung-lo ordered the mounting of his huge expeditions, Cheng Ho could readily recruit his officers and crewmen. Moreover, the Chinese had perfected shipbuilding techniques and navigation skills to the level that they could undertake massive voyages of exploration. Their ships could travel as fast as six knots per hour, and their knowledge of the compass permitted accurate navigation. So it was that Cheng Ho could lead seven huge and highly successful expeditions which nearly led to the Chinese discovery of Europe.

Cheng Ho's first voyage left the central coast of China in the summer of 1405 with a twenty-seven-man crew and sixty-two large and 255 small vessels carrying cargoes of silk, embroideries, and other such products. The colossal fleet called at Champa (the southeast coast of contemporary Vietnam) and fought to clear the strategic Strait of Malacca of the powerful Chinese pirates who had plagued the area for decades. Cheng Ho's victory over the pirates made passage through the straits safe and enhanced Ming prestige in Southeast Asia.

The second voyage left China in the fall of 1407 and eventually reached Calicut on the southwestern coast of India. Cheng Ho extended imperial gifts and greetings to the ruler of Calicut, who had frequently sent gifts to the Chinese emperors. On the return leg of the voyage, Cheng Ho called on Siam and Java, where he intervened in Javanese politics and established a ruler friendly to the Ming.

The third voyage began in September, 1409, and lasted until June, 1411. It again visited Calicut but traveled onward to Siam, Malacca, Sumatra, and Ceylon, where Cheng Ho defeated a Ceylonese king and carried out extensive trade. The fourth voyage took 27,670 men and sixty-three large vessels far beyond India to the Maldives, Hormuz, and Aden. As a consequence of this journey, nineteen countries sent tributary missions to the Ming capital at Nanking. During the fifth voyage, from 1417 to 1419, Cheng Ho escorted the envoys of these missions home. Cheng Ho brought strange and exotic animals, such as giraffes, ostriches, zebras, and leopards, back with him to China. The sixth voyage, lasting from 1421 to 1422, also reached Aden and the east coast of Africa. Before a seventh expedition could be launched, Cheng Ho's patron, Yung-lo, died, and opponents of the voyages recommended that they be abandoned. Eventually, however, the final Cheng Ho voyage left China in late 1431 and returned in July of 1433. It once again visited the Arabian peninsula, including Mecca, and eastern Africa. It appears that Cheng Ho may have died in 1435 or 1436 at the age of sixty-five. The exact date of his demise is obscure, however, and one source maintains that he died early in 1433 at Calicut and was later buried in Nanking.

Not much is known about Cheng Ho's private life. He may have had an adopted son, and he made his permanent home in Nanking. He undoubtedly retained his Islamic faith, which facilitated his interchanges with the Muslim states of Southeast Asia, Africa, and Arabia, but he was interested in Buddhism and Chinese folk religion. He was a man of unique power and influence. To have led so many massive expeditions would have required a rare combination of navigational, managerial, and diplomatic skills.

Summary

Cheng Ho's achievements mark him as one of the great explorers of all time. His organizational and command skills were extraordinary, he established firm contacts with nearly forty countries in the "Western Ocean," and he provided China with detailed geographical information about the outside world. The commercial contacts he initiated continued even though the Ming government terminated the large-scale voyages upon his death.

The Ming did not continue the voyages for three reasons. First, the costs were extremely high and did not result in significant economic gains. Second, dangers on China's northern and western frontiers, where the Mongols and other central Asians threatened the Ming, distracted Chinese attention from overseas adventures. Third, and most important, the Chinese saw little need to explore areas outside the "Middle Kingdom." They believed China was a superior civilization which did not need to go overseas to propagate Chinese beliefs. Others could come to China to learn, but China had no desire to convince outsiders of the efficacy of its beliefs and institutions. Moreover, most Chinese believed they were economically self-sufficient and needed no foreign goods. Thus, even though Cheng Ho's voyages were spectacular, they were by no means essential to Chinese life and were discontinued as abruptly as they began.

In 1497, only sixty-four years after Cheng Ho's last expedition, Vasco da Gama reached India, thus inaugurating the era of European imperialism in Asia and reversing the direction of exploration. If the Chinese had continued Cheng Ho's efforts—establishing permanent bases, maintaining their sea power, and founding a vast empire—it is possible that the course of world history would have been altered profoundly. China might have "discovered" Europe. Instead, Europeans "discovered" China, Ming sea power declined, and Portugal created vast maritime empires. China remained landlocked, and its failure to develop seafaring capabilities eventually invited European imperialism.

Cheng Ho's expeditions were important in their own right, as they established patterns of Chinese diplomacy and trade as far as the coasts of Arabia and Africa and momentarily stimulated China's commerce. In the final analysis, however, the voyages remain a Chinese historical aberration, a trip down a blind alley, since the Chinese did not continue their explorations. Still, historians will continue to wonder how world history might have been different if Cheng Ho, the Chinese Columbus, had been succeeded by an equally adventurous voyager.

Bibliography

Chan, Albert. *The Glory and Fall of the Ming Dynasty*. Norman: University of Oklahoma Press, 1982. This volume, a reasonably comprehensive history of the Ming empire, describes the personalities, culture, politics, and economics of the era, enabling the reader to place Cheng Ho and the voyages of exploration in historical perspective.

Duyvendak, J. J. *China's Discovery of Africa*. London: Arthur Probsthain, 1949. Duyvendak is the leading Western historian of Cheng Ho's excursions, and this book summarizes his research. It is a consequence of his scholarship that the English reader knows with confidence the dates of the voyages, the dimensions of the ships, the names of Cheng Ho's subordinates, the routes each voyage took, and other details of the expeditions.

Li, Dun J. *The Ageless Chinese: A History*. New York: Charles Scribner's Sons, 1978. A general survey of Chinese history, this book provides a fine general account of Cheng Ho's expeditions and places them in the larger context of Chinese history and culture. It contains a good map summarizing the seven voyages of exploration and also reproduces a map of China made during the Ming Dynasty.

Needham, Joseph, ed. *Science and Civilization in China*. Vol. 3, *Mathematics and the Sciences of the Heavens and Earth*. London: Cambridge University Press, 1959. Needham, whose works on Chinese science are classics, examines geography and cartography in this volume. Profusely illustrated and rich with descriptions, this book describes Chinese explorations and mapmaking and assesses Cheng Ho's voyage in the light of Chinese science and technology. Needham is a good source for further bibliographic suggestions.

Stevens, Keith. "Three Chinese Deities." *Journal of Royal Asiatic Society* 12 (1972): 19-27. Stevens provides information on Cheng Ho's relationship to the Chinese sea goddess, T'ien-fu, to whom he erected a tablet of honor on the south central coast of China. Cheng Ho was not reluctant to worship the patron goddess of the sea, even though he was a Muslim.

Willets, William. "The Maritime Adventures of Grand Eunuch Ho." *Journal of South-East Asian History* 2 (1964): 25-42. Willets summarizes some of Cheng Ho's encounters with Southeast Asian monarchs and pirates, indicating the nature and extent of his interaction in the internal politics of the region.

Loren W. Crabtree

CH'IN SHIH HUANG TI
Cheng

Born: 259 B.C.; Han-tan, Chao, China
Died: 210 B.C.; Ping-tai, Sha'chin, China
Areas of Achievement: Warfare, government, and law
Contribution: Shih Huang Ti unified the warring states of the Chou Dynasty into the first centralized government in China's history, expanded the state to the south, built the Great Wall, and established the cultural system that characterized China until the twentieth century.

Early Life

Ch'in Shih Huang Ti, meaning "First Sovereign Emperor Ch'in," is the imperial title chosen in 221 B.C. by Chao Cheng, king of the state of Ch'in, after his conquest of the Six States of the Middle Kingdom, known later as China. Cheng was born in Han-tan, capital of Chao, in troubled circumstances during a turbulent era called Warring States. His mother, who was from a prominent family in Chao, was a concubine of the merchant Lü Pu-wei before becoming the wife of Tzu-ch'u, a prince of the house of Ch'in who was living in Han-tan as a hostage to guarantee a truce between Ch'in and Chao.

In 257, when Cheng was two, Ch'in broke the truce and attacked Chao. With Lü Pu-wei's money, Tzu-ch'u escaped to Ch'in forces. His wife and son were protected by her parents until 250, when the royal family was reunited in Hsien-yang, capital of Ch'in. The following year, Tzu-ch'u inherited the monarchy and rewarded his benefactor with the chancellorship. Three years later, in 246, Tzu-ch'u died, and thirteen-year-old Cheng became king.

Lü Pu-wei remained chancellor, and King Cheng conferred upon him the additional title of Second Father. Lü Pu-wei maintained an entourage of three thousand attendants, many of whom were traveling scholars who served feudal lords and kings as consultants and officials. As the king matured, he was most influenced by Taoists and the Legalist Li Ssu.

Li Ssu came from Ch'ü-fou to Ch'in because he was abandoning Confucianism and weakness to embrace Legalism and strength. A century earlier, Shang Yang and Duke Hsiao had transformed Ch'in by eliminating feudalism, unifying the culture of several groups in the Wei valley, concentrating political power in the hands of the ruler, and enforcing the new laws with harsh punishments. The reforms had been inspired by the School of Law, one of many schools of thought that flourished during the period of Warring States. Convinced that Confucianism's reverence for tradition could never control the nobles and bring peace, Li Ssu hoped that Legalist Ch'in could end the strife among the Six States. Upon arrival at Hsien-yang, Li Ssu became one of Lü Pu-wei's retainers.

Almost as soon as Cheng came of age in 238, he faced a major crisis. Lao

Ai, a provincial governor, rose in rebellion and had to be suppressed. An investigation into the circumstances of the revolt implicated Lü Pu-wei. Lao Ai and all of his relatives were executed, but the Second Father was only banished to a distant province. With the fall of Lü Pu-wei, Li Ssu became chancellor. He persuaded the king that Ch'in armies could conquer the enfeebled Six States "like sweeping the dust from the top of the kitchen stove."

Life's Work

Since 360, Ch'in had expanded at the expense of the older states in the east and the barbarian kingdoms to the south. The nobility of the Six States regarded Ch'in with disdain and fear—disdain because Ch'in's Tartar origins meant that the people of Ch'in were not true Hua people and fear because of the ferocity of Ch'in armies. Since 320, Ch'in armies had killed more than 952,000 soldiers, almost half of whom had already surrendered. Ch'in warriors were said to have the hearts of wolves and jackals, and Cheng was soon to be referred to in dread as the "Tiger of Ch'in."

At age twenty-five, Cheng began the conquest and annexation of the Middle Kingdom. When his native city Han-tan was taken, Cheng buried alive all members of the families that had harassed him and his mother in his youth. Alarmed at the success of Ch'in forces, the crown prince of Yen tried to have Cheng assassinated, but the attempt failed.

The oldest known picture of Cheng is a Han stone relief showing the king evading his attacker. The relief reveals no distinguishing features, and the following description by Cheng's adviser Wei Liao may be more reflective of attitude than observation:

> The king of Ch'in has a waspish nose, eyes like slits, a chicken breast and a voice like a jackal. He is merciless, with the heart of a tiger or wolf. . . . There is no staying long with such a man.

Wei tried to leave Ch'in but was detained by the king and given the responsibility of planning military strategy. The remaining kings struggled in vain to save themselves from the Tiger of Ch'in, but Wei's strategy and Ch'in's armies were unstoppable. Han statesman Chia I wrote of Cheng,

> Cracking his long whip, he drove the universe before him, swallowing up the eastern and western Chou and overthrowing the feudal lords. He ascended to the highest position and ruled the six directions, scourging the world with his rod, and his might shook the four seas.

In 221, Ch'i, the last of the Six States, surrendered, and Cheng began his transformation of the Middle Kingdom.

Because he intended to centralize power, Cheng regarded the traditional title Son of Heaven inadequate and the title of king too parochial to be suitable to the new role he intended to play as head of state. He chose *huang ti*, words that had both religious and political connotations and meant "sovereign emperor." He prefixed the title with *shih*, meaning "first," because he intended for his descendants to head the new system for "generations without end."

Shih Huang Ti worked closely with his chancellor Li Ssu to crush the feudal system that they blamed for causing the wars and sufferings of the last five centuries. From all over the new empire, the defeated nobles traveled to the emperor's palace and surrendered all of their weapons. The weapons were melted down and recast as bells and statues. The nobles' castles were razed, and the nobles themselves, some 120,000 families, were stripped of their ancestral lands and required to live in Hsien-yang. Shih Huang Ti continued to confer titles of nobility as rewards for meritorious service, but these titles brought to the recipient only honor, not lands and power.

Power was awarded to individuals with administrative ability. Ties to the emperor were based upon the impersonal majesty of the law, not family status or friendship. Officials functioned in districts called commanderies and prefectures and applied the new Legalist system, which drastically changed the lives of the peasants.

Called the "common people," the peasants had lived a chattel-like existence on feudal estates. Shih Huang Ti designated them "black-headed people" to signify their rise in status from contempt to favor and from servitude to freedom. Peasants then registered as their own the land they actually worked and began paying taxes. Shih Huang Ti colonized thinly populated Ch'in and newly conquered lands to the south with villagers from older, more crowded areas.

Shih Huang Ti and Li Ssu established a remarkable degree of unity in the variegated culture of the former Six States. A decree abolished the bewildering variety of logographic systems of writing and required the literati to use an ancient system reformed by Li Ssu himself. Other decrees standardized coinage, axle gauges, road widths, weights and measures, and the quality of merchandise.

When a group of scholars and officials petitioned the emperor to restore the old feudal system, Li Ssu believed that Confucian regard for custom meant that the emperor's authority had not been fully accepted. At the chancellor's suggestion, Shih Huang Ti ordered the intellectuals to burn all of their personal copies of literary and historical books within thirty days. These works would be available at the royal library, and individuals could possess practical works, books on medicine, agriculture, and magic. Offenders were to be tattooed on the face and sentenced to hard labor. Eventually, Shih Huang Ti condemned 460 recalcitrant scholars to be buried alive.

Harsh penalties were essential to the Legalist system. Some of the other penalties that greeted hapless convicts were confiscation of property, dismemberment by chariots, branding the top of the head, execution of families, exposure of corpses in the marketplace, and castration before being sent to labor on public projects.

With the passion of a megalomaniac, Shih Huang Ti launched massive construction projects. Working as convicts or corvée laborers, possibly as many as three million men—about 15 percent of the population—built a road system that connected the major cities of the empire, dug a canal seventy-seven miles long, and constructed palaces for the transplanted nobles. At least 700,000 convicts worked on Shih Huang Ti's enormous palace and his elaborate mausoleum. The most famous of his construction projects was the Great Wall, which connected several existing castles and walls and then added more wall until there was a border twenty-five feet high and fifteen hundred miles long separating the agrarian Middle Kingdom and the steppe nomads.

The First Emperor ordered the Great Wall built to keep out the Huns, because a Taoist seer warned him that Ch'in would be overthrown by "Hu." Taoist influence on the emperor revealed itself in many other ways. Taoist advisers convinced the emperor that the Chou Dynasty had been an age of fire and that Shih Huang Ti was to usher in an age of water. The severity of Legalism was necessary so that the empire could be brought swiftly into harmony with cosmic design. Black, the magical color for water, became the predominant color on Ch'in clothing and flags. Commoners were named the "black-headed people." Water's magical number, six, figured repeatedly in the uniform standards; for example, official hats were six inches high, and six feet made one pace. Shih Huang Ti renamed the mighty Yellow River "Powerful Water."

The Taoist doctrine of the True Man became a veritable obsession with Shih Huang Ti. By conforming to Taoist regimens of breathing, meditation, and sacrifice or by consuming an elixir prepared by a True Man, one could become immortal. On inspection tours, the emperor searched for True Men in the forests and on the tops of sacred mountains. He dispatched two expeditions eastward in search of three immortal islands. Neither expedition returned; both may have reached Japan. In 212, when Shih Huang Ti was forty-seven, court magicians persuaded him that by becoming more mysterious to his subjects he could accelerate his metamorphosis. Accordingly, the emperor isolated himself from all but a few assistants and changed rooms and palaces frequently.

His desire for immortality had as its twin necrophobia. As Shih Huang Ti worked on state documents—twenty-five pounds of bamboo strips a day—he kept an unsheathed sword across his knees. To discuss the subject of death was forbidden in his presence, and only on his deathbed did he designate one of his twenty sons as the crown prince.

Summary

The incompetence of Ch'in Shih Huang Ti's successors provoked the first peasant uprising in Chinese history and ended the Ch'in Dynasty in 207, only three years after the First Sovereign Emperor's death. Even though the imperial dynasty lasted less than two decades, many of Shih Huang Ti's changes endured longer than two millennia. Rulers used the title "Huang Ti" until A.D. 1911. The successor dynasty, the Han, dissolved the Legalist system immediately, but within a century the nobility became so independent and quarrelsome that the concepts of concentration of power, limitation of feudal privileges, government through commanderies, awarding public office to the capable, and application of severe punishments were restored. The road system, standardization in the marketplace, and uniform script helped to give China the longest continuous high culture in human experience. The Great Wall is virtually unchallenged in its claim to be the largest man-made structure in world history. Finally, the name Middle Kingdom became known to foreigners as "China," because people in Southeast Asia referred to the Middle Kingdom as "Ch'in-tan"—the land of Ch'in.

Bibliography

Bodde, Derk. *China's First Unifier: A Study of the Ch'in Dynasty as Seen in the Life of Li Ssu*. Leiden, Netherlands: E. J. Brill, 1938. A careful analysis of Ssu-ma Ch'ien's *Shih chi* (partially translated as *Records of the Historian*), written circa 90 B.C. Bodde concludes that the Han Confucianists resented Shih Huang Ti so much that they falsified his ancestry and magnified his cruelty to ensure a negative reputation. Li Ssu's important contributions to the establishment of a centralized government were thereby diminished.

Cotterell, Arthur. *The First Emperor of China: The Greatest Archaeological Find of Our Time*. New York: Holt, Rinehart and Winston, 1981. An examination of recent archaeological finds, especially Hsien-yang and the area surrounding Shih Huang Ti's tomb. Cotterell blends the archaeology with Ch'ien's history, Bodde's study, and other literature about the Ch'in Dynasty. Contains a very fine introduction by Yang Chen-ching, the curator of the museum housing the artifacts recovered from Shih Huang Ti's tomb complex.

Cottrell, Leonard. *The Tiger of Ch'in: The Dramatic Emergence of China as a Nation*. New York: Holt, Rinehart and Winston, 1962. A sometimes melodramatic account by a popular biographer of historical greats. Probably the most widely available of the books on Shih Huang Ti, this volume contains extensive quotations from Ch'ien's history and makes intensive use of Bodde's study.

Li, Yu-ning, ed. *The First Emperor of China: The Politics of Historiography*. White Plains, N.Y.: International Arts and Sciences Press, 1975. A collection of nineteenth and twentieth century studies that show more sympathy for the First Emperor than for the Confucianists. Communist writers try to put the Warring States and the Ch'in Dynasty in the context of the class struggle. A valuable appendix reproduces Ssu-ma Ch'ien's biography of Shih Huang Ti, Chia I's essay "The Faults of Ch'in," and Liu Tsung-yuan's "Essay on Feudalism."

Ssu-ma Ch'ien. *Records of the Historian*. Translated by Yang Hsien-yi and Gladys Yang. Hong Kong: Commercial Press, 1974. The alpha of Chinese history. This selection of Ch'ien's massive work includes the controversial biography of Lü Pu-wei. Ch'ien declares that the merchant—a class held in contempt by Confucianists—was Shih Huang Ti's father and that the First Emperor's mother was a lifelong debauchee. Bodde and others suspect that this biography represents a judgment against Shih Huang Ti rather than a faithful use of whatever material the Han scholar had at his disposal.

Waley, Arthur. *Three Ways of Thought in Ancient China*. Garden City, N.Y.: Doubleday and Co., 1956. Contains translations and explications of Legalism, Confucianism, and Taoism.

Paul E. Kuhl